American Newspaper Journalists, 1873-1900

Dictionary of Literary Biography

Dictionary of Literary Biography • Volume Twenty-three

American Newspaper Journalists, 1873-1900

Edited by
Perry J. Ashley
University of South Carolina

A Bruccoli Clark Book
Gale Research Company • Book Tower • Detroit, Michigan 48226
1983

Advisory Board for
NA ?Y OF LITERARY BIOGRAPHY

Louis S. Auchincloss
John Baker
D. Philip Baker
A. Walton Litz, Jr.
Peter S. Prescott
Lola L. Szladits
William Targ

Matthew J. Bruccoli and Richard Layman, *Editorial Directors*
C. E. Frazer Clark, Jr., *Managing Editor*

Manufactured by Edwards Brothers, Inc.
Ann Arbor, Michigan
Printed in the United States of America

Copyright © 1983
GALE RESEARCH COMPANY

Library of Congress Cataloging in Publication Data
Main entry under title:

American newspaper journalists, 1873-1900.

(Dictionary of literary biography; v. 23)
"A Bruccoli Clark book."
Includes index.
1. Journalists—United States—Biography—Handbooks,
manuals, etc. 2. Journalism—United States—History—19th
century—Handbooks, manuals, etc. I. Ashley, Perry J. II.
Series.
PN4871.A49   1983   070'.92'2 [B]   83-20582
ISBN 0-8103-1145-3

For Lita Grey

Contents

Plan of the Series

. . . Almost the most prodigious asset of a country, and perhaps its most precious possession, is its native literary product—when that product is fine and noble and enduring.

Mark Twain*

The advisory board, the editors, and the publisher of the *Dictionary of Literary Biography* are joined in endorsing Mark Twain's declaration. The literature of a nation provides an inexhaustible resource of permanent worth. It is our expectation that this endeavor will make literature and its creators better understood and more accessible to students and the literate public, while satisfying the standards of teachers and scholars.

To meet these requirements, *literary biography* has been construed in terms of the author's achievement. The most important thing about a writer is his writing. Accordingly, the entries in *DLB* are career biographies, tracing the development of the author's canon and the evolution of his reputation.

The publication plan for *DLB* resulted from two years of preparation. The project was proposed to Bruccoli Clark by Frederick G. Ruffner, president of the Gale Research Company, in November 1975. After specimen entries were prepared and typeset, an advisory board was formed to refine the entry format and develop the series rationale. In meetings held during 1976, the publisher, series editors, and advisory board approved the scheme for a comprehensive biographical dictionary of persons who contributed to North American literature. Editorial work on the first volume began in January 1977, and it was published in 1978.

In order to make *DLB* more than a reference tool and to compile volumes that individually have claim to status as literary history, it was decided to organize volumes by topic or period or genre. Each of these freestanding volumes provides a biographical-bibliographical guide and overview for a particular area of literature. We are convinced that this organization—as opposed to a single alphabet method—constitutes a valuable innovation in the presentation of reference material. The volume plan necessarily requires many decisions for the placement and treatment of authors who might properly be included in two or three volumes. In

some instances a major figure will be included in separate volumes, but with different entries emphasizing the aspect of his career appropriate to each volume. Ernest Hemingway, for example, is represented in *American Writers in Paris, 1920-1939* by an entry focusing on his expatriate apprenticeship; he is also in *American Novelists, 1910-1945* with an entry surveying his entire career. Each volume includes a cumulative index of subject authors. The final *DLB* volume will be a comprehensive index to the entire series.

With volume ten in 1982 it was decided to enlarge the scope of *DLB* beyond the literature of the United States. By the end of 1983 twelve volumes treating British literature had been published, and volumes for Commonwealth and Modern European literature were in progress. The series has been further augmented by the *DLB Yearbooks* (since 1981) which update published entries and add new entries to keep the *DLB* current with contemporary activity. There have also been occasional *DLB Documentary Series* volumes which provide biographical and critical background source materials for figures whose work is judged to have particular interest for students. One of these companion volumes is entirely devoted to Tennessee Williams.

The purpose of *DLB* is not only to provide reliable information in a convenient format but also to place the figures in the larger perspective of literary history and to offer appraisals of their accomplishments by qualified scholars.

We define literature as the *intellectual commerce of a nation*: not merely as belles lettres, but as that ample and complex process by which ideas are generated, shaped, and transmitted. *DLB* entries are not limited to "creative writers" but extend to other figures who in this time and in this way influenced the mind of a people. Thus there will be volumes for historians, journalists, publishers, and screenwriters. By this means readers of *DLB* may be aided to perceive literature not as cult scripture in the keeping of cultural high priests, but as at the center of a nation's life.

DLB includes the major writers appropriate to each volume and those standing in the ranks immediately behind them. Scholarly and critical counsel has been sought in deciding which minor figures to include and how full their entries should be. Wherever possible, useful references will be made to figures who do not warrant separate entries.

Each *DLB* volume has a volume editor responsible for planning the volume, selecting the figures

---

*From an unpublished section of Mark Twain's autobiography, copyright © by the Mark Twain Company.

for inclusion, and assigning the entries. Volume editors are also responsible for preparing, where appropriate, appendices surveying the major periodicals and literary and intellectual movements for their volumes, as well as lists of further readings. Work on the series as a whole is coordinated at the Bruccoli Clark editorial center in Columbia, South Carolina, where the editorial staff is responsible for the accuracy of the published volumes.

One feature that distinguishes *DLB* is the illustration policy—its concern with the iconography of literature. Just as an author is influenced by his surroundings, so is the reader's understanding of the author enhanced by a knowledge of his environment. Therefore *DLB* volumes include not only drawings, paintings, and photographs of authors, often depicting them at various stages in their careers, but also illustrations of their families and places where they lived. Title pages are regularly reproduced in facsimile along with dust jackets for modern authors. The dust jackets are a special feature of *DLB* because they often document better than anything else the way in which an author's work was launched in its own time. Specimens of the writers' manuscripts are included when feasible.

A supplement to *DLB*—tentatively titled *A Guide, Chronology, and Glossary for American Literature*—will outline the history of literature in North America and trace the influences that shaped it. This volume will provide a framework for the study of American literature by means of chronological tables, literary affiliation charts, glossarial entries, and concise surveys of the major movements. It has been planned to stand on its own as a vade mecum, providing a ready-reference guide to the study of American literature as well as a companion to the *DLB* volumes for American literature.

Samuel Johnson rightly decreed that "The chief glory of every people arises from its authors." The purpose of the *Dictionary of Literary Biography* is to compile literary history in the surest way available to us—by accurate and comprehensive treatment of the lives and work of those who contributed to it.

The *DLB* Advisory Board

Foreword

Newspapers have become so commonplace in the everyday lives of the American people that social observers, and particularly historians, have overlooked them as a vital institution within American society providing an indispensable service—the delivery of information and opinion. If the individuals in a democratic society are to be informed about the issues which constantly confront them, then society must devise the means for the dissemination of information. Before the 1890s and the discovery of the "mass market" of readers by the national magazines, this function was served almost solely by newspapers for the average American citizen for two centuries.

In observing the growth of the American cities and the impact it had on newspapers, sociologist Robert E. Park noted in 1925 that "if public opinion is to continue to govern in the future as it has in the past, if we propose to maintain a democracy as Jefferson conceived it, the newspaper must continue to tell us about ourselves. We must somehow learn to know our community and its affairs in the same intimate way in which we knew them in the country villages." He suggested that newspapers should continue "to be the printed diary of the home community" and that local news "is the very stuff that democracy is made of. Marriages and divorce, crime and politics, must continue to make up the main body of our news."

During the last three decades of the nineteenth century, the American newspaper was going through the final stages of its evolution from a vehicle of opinion into a medium which emphasized news, human interest, and entertainment. As a result, journalists began exercising independence from domination by political parties. As Whitelaw Reid saw it, this independence gave newspaper editors the opportunity to sever their party affiliations; more important, in his view, was the new freedom to criticize political parties from within. Frank Luther Mott says that "a chief reason for this change was the shift in emphasis from editorial comment and preoccupation with affairs of government to wider fields of news and to more intimate human interests. This change in the news concept took newspapers away from the politicians and put them in the hands of reporters." This new approach should not be interpreted to mean that the journalists were no longer interested in politics. Editors still endorsed party leaders in national, state, and local elections. Editors and publishers,

such as Murat Halstead, Whitelaw Reid, Carl Schurz, and Horace White, frequently were named as delegates to state and national conventions and usually served on critical committees, such as platform and rules.

This was, however, the age of the "New Journalism," with Joseph Pulitzer setting the pace. In his prospectus for the *New York World*, published 11 May 1883—the day after he purchased the paper—Pulitzer noted that there was room in New York City for a newspaper "that is not only cheap but bright, not only bright but large, not only large but truly democratic—dedicated to the cause of the people rather than that of purse potentates—devoted more to the news of the New than the Old World—that will expose all fraud and sham, fight all public evils and abuses—that will serve and battle for the people with earnest sincerity." Edwin and Michael Emery characterize the daily newspapers of this period as "low-priced, aggressive, and easily read" and note that the newspapers "appealed to the mass audience through improved writing, better makeup, use of headlines and illustrations, and a popularization of their contents." The average reader in the late nineteenth century bought newspapers for local news, human interest, romance, tragedy, conflict, entertainment, and, perhaps, editorial opinions. In the attempt to catch the attention of the average citizen and the barely literate immigrant, some metropolitan newspapers drifted into sensationalism, which led by the late 1890s to the era of "Yellow Journalism." It was an age in which news was "marketed," and those newspapers which were successful in meeting the needs of the public survived.

In these same three decades, the United States was rapidly moving from an agrarian to an industrial society, a movement which brought with it demands for social, political, and economic reforms. The rapid growth of the cities was far outstripping the capacity of local governments to provide critical services; someone was needed to champion the "causes" of urban working-class Americans. This work the newspaper publishers and editors did through their famous editorial campaigns and crusades aimed at making life better for all. The *New York Tribune* promoted a fresh-air fund; the *New York World* campaigned for funds to build a pedestal for the Statue of Liberty; the *Kansas City Star* promoted community improvements and helped run the gamblers out of the city; and the

Chicago Daily News advocated fresh-air sanatoriums. Wide-scale moves were also undertaken to dislodge the political party "machines" through revisions of election procedures.

At the same time, over 11,000,000 immigrants came to the "land of promise" and needed some means to help overcome what Oscar Handlin calls "the shock of alienation" in their effort to separate from an old culture and become assimilated into a new one. The census of 1900 showed that one out of seven persons living in the United States was foreign born. As the populations of individual communities swelled with the influx of new immigrants, associations or "mutual aid societies" were formed to help provide for such needs as housing, food, and work. The mutual aid societies began to publish newspapers in the immigrants' native languages, reporting activities within the community ignored by the English language press while keeping the immigrants informed about world affairs. The influx of immigrants led to an increase in the foreign language press from 315 newspapers in 1880 to 1,150 in 1900.

The special interest press continued to grow in the late nineteenth century as farmers, workers, and blacks found newspapers the best medium available to plead their causes. The last frontiers were being settled, and the migrants depended almost entirely on the little frontier newspaper for their news from the outside world—and to tell the outside world how great life was in the American West.

The major concern throughout the nation in the last third of the nineteenth century was healing the wounds of the Civil War. Newspapers served as a major forum for the discussion of reunification. Some editors, such as Henry Grady, the spokesman for the "New South," actually became identified with the issue.

Growth in the number of newspapers published and aggregate circulation were astounding during these thirty years. While the population of the country was doubling to almost 76,000,000 by 1900, the total number of daily newspapers was increasing fourfold, and the total circulation was increasing sixfold. Using census data and the few newspaper directories which are available for the period, Alfred McClung Lee has estimated that there were 574 daily newspapers with a total circulation of 2,600,000 being published in 1870, and that by 1899 the number of daily papers had grown to 2,226 with 15,000,000 circulation. At the same time the nondaily press—the weekly, biweekly, and

triweekly newspapers—were increasing from about 4,500 in 1870 to around 16,000 by the turn of the century. Discounting by as much as twenty-five percent for what Mott calls the "class newspapers"—those published for a rather small, elite readership—these were still substantial years of growth in the newspaper industry. Mechanical developments—stereotyping, the typecasting machine, the web-perfecting press, photoengraving, and color printing—made possible the great circulation wars in cities like New York.

Scores of thousands of individuals filled the ranks of newspaper publishers, editors, and writers these three decades. Many of them performed for a brief period and then retreated into oblivion without as much as a by-line to record their presence. Even with some of the major figures who are represented in this volume, little could be found about their personal or professional lives to help explain their choices of the reading materials they prepared for their readers each day. Since the large daily newspapers were the trend setters for the rest of the nation, they will seem to dominate this volume. But, in addition, there are representatives of the strong regional dailies, the frontier press, the foreign language press, and the black press. An effort has also been made to present a balance between publishers and editors, reporters and columnists, men and women.

Some of the persons in this volume have long been recognized as literary figures, political leaders, or social and political observers, yet it is often forgotten that they spent part or all of their lives associated with newspapers. For instance, some literary figures such as Samuel Clemens began their writing careers with newspapers where their characteristic philosophies and styles were first conceived and perfected. Other examples include Ambrose Bierce, Jane Cunningham Croly, Richard Harding Davis, Finley Peter Dunne, Eugene Field, Harold Frederic, Henry George, Joel Chandler Harris, George Peck, Jacob Riis, and Carl Schurz. In these instances, the attempt here is to put their journalistic activities into perspective with their other accomplishments.

This volume and others concentrating on American journalists, which will follow, are intended to present accurately the lives and careers of journalists representing the entire 280 years of American newspaper journalism from colonial times to the present. Here, then, are their stories.

—*Perry J. Ashley*

Acknowledgments

This book was produced by BC Research. Karen L. Rood is senior editor for the *Dictionary of Literary Biography* series. Philip B. Dematteis was the in-house editor.

The production manager is Lynne C. Zeigler. Art supervisor is Alice A. Parsons. The production staff included Angela D. Bardin, Mary Betts, Josie A. Bruccoli, Patricia Coate, Claudia Ericson, Lynn Felder, Joyce Fowler, Nancy H. Lindsay, Cynthia D. Lybrand, Laura Ingram, Walter W. Ross, Patricia C. Sharpe, and Joycelyn R. Smith.

Joseph Caldwell is photography editor. Jean W. Ross is permissions editor. Charles L. Wentworth did the photographic copy work.

Valuable assistance was given by the staff at the Thomas Cooper Library of the University of South Carolina: Lynn Barron, Sue Collins, Michael Freeman, Gary Geer, Alexander M. Gilchrist, Jens Holley, David Lincove, Marcia Martin, Roger Mortimer, Harriet B. Oglesbee, Jean Rhyne, Karen Rissling, Paula Swope, and Ellen Tillett.

American Newspaper Journalists, 1873-1900

Mary Clemmer Ames
(6 May 1831-18 August 1884)

Maurine H. Beasley
University of Maryland

MAJOR POSITION HELD: Washington columnist, *New York Independent* (1866-1884).

BOOKS: *Victoire* (New York: Carleton, 1864);
Eirene; or, A Woman's Right (New York: Putnam's, 1871);
A Memorial of Alice and Phoebe Cary with Some of Their Later Poems (New York: Hurd & Houghton, 1873; London: Low, 1873);
Outlines of Men, Women and Things (New York: Hurd & Houghton, 1873);
His Two Wives (New York: Hurd & Houghton, 1875);
Ten Years in Washington: Life and Scenes in the National Capital as a Woman Sees Them (Hartford, Conn.: Worthington, 1875);
Memorial Sketch of Elizabeth Emerson Atwater: Written for Her Friends (Buffalo: Courier Company, 1879);
Poems of Life & Nature (Boston: Osgood, 1883).

Mary E. Clemmer Ames Hudson was believed to be the highest paid American newspaperwoman of the post-Civil War era. Yet she always minimized her commitment to a career. According to Edmund Hudson, her second husband, she truly believed that "the best thing that can happen to any woman is to be satisfactorily loved, to be taken care of, to be made much of, and to make much of the life and the love utterly her own in her own home." Her ambivalence toward a career stemmed from her desire to preserve her image as a respectable Victorian woman at the same time as she worked doggedly to climb to the top of a competitive occupation. An examination of her life shows the inner conflicts of a woman who maintained, on the one hand, that all she wanted was to be cherished and protected, while, on the other hand, she achieved success as a political writer.

Born in Utica, New York, she took pride in her Anglo-Saxon background. She was the eldest of a large number of children, of whom seven lived to maturity. Her parents were Abraham Clemmer, of Alsatian Huguenot stock, and Margaret Clemmer, who had emigrated from the British Isle of Man. The father, handsome but impractical, failed repeatedly to earn a living as a tobacconist, grocer, or merchant. As a child, Mary attracted attention with her poetry at the Westfield, Massachusetts, school which she attended after the family moved to that area in 1847. Like many of the women journalists of her day, she began her career as a poet; while still a schoolgirl, she published verses in the *Springfield* (Massachusetts) *Republican*, edited by Samuel Bowles; Bowles later became a close friend.

The family's financial misfortunes precipitated her marriage at the age of twenty to Daniel Ames, a Methodist minister who later held Presbyterian pastorates in New York and Minnesota. Apparently the marriage proved a mistake from the start. The couple lived apart from time to time; Mrs. Ames was desperately unhappy, even to the point of considering suicide.

Her newspaper career started in 1859 when she sent reports in the form of letters from New York City, where she was living temporarily, to the *Utica Morning Herald* and the *Springfield Republican*. In New York she met the acclaimed poets and authors Alice and Phoebe Cary, who sponsored a literary salon at their home. They presented her to their circle, including Horace Greeley and other editors, who encouraged her aspirations for a career in journalism.

After a brief period as principal of a boys' school in Jersey City, New Jersey, Daniel Ames obtained a federal post in Harpers Ferry, West Virginia, during the Civil War. There Mrs. Ames was briefly taken prisoner by the Confederates, and she observed the surrender of the town to Union forces. She later described her experiences in a novel, *Eirene; or, A Woman's Right* (1871), which drew attention partly because of her graphic scenes of the war around Harpers Ferry.

During the Civil War Mrs. Ames lived in Washington as well as in Harpers Ferry. In the capital, discontinuing her efforts to write, she nursed the Union wounded in army hospitals. She also made long-lasting friendships with several notables, including Congressman Portus Baxter and Senator Justin S. Morrill of Vermont. With the end of the war and her final separation from Ames in 1865 (they were divorced in 1874), her journalistic career started in earnest.

On 4 March 1866, her first "Woman's Letter from Washington" appeared in the *Independent*, an influential New York weekly with a wide circulation and a radical Republican political orientation. Although loosely tied to the Congregational church, the *Independent* covered general news. The column was an immediate success, but Mrs. Ames used it to point out that fame did not appeal to her as a "true woman." A few weeks after it began, she contended, "That fame is a curse which soils the loveliness of the womanly name by thrusting it into the grimy highway, where it is wondered at, sneered at, lied about, by the vulgar, the worldly, and the wicked."

While Mrs. Ames frequently returned to the subject of a woman's role in her column, her subjects ranged widely over the fields of politics and personalities. Topics covered repeatedly included concern for justice toward freed slaves and a devotion to radical Republican principles, descriptions of Congress and its leading members, calls for improved morality in Washington, and commentary on women government workers. Although she was proud of not being a social reporter per se, she often mentioned social activities, if only to warn against their corrupting influence.

Mrs. Ames gained much material by observing Congress and did not hesitate to pinpoint lawmakers she thought guilty of ineptitude or undue pomp. Crusading for men of higher integrity to enter politics, she called Senator Salsbury of Delaware a drunk and attacked Senator James G. Blaine of Maine as "a beneficiary of railroad corporations for his own personal enrichment." A foe of President Andrew Johnson, she criticized his policies on the grounds that they would permit the South to oppress the newly freed slaves. Firmly convinced that the Northern victory in the Civil War had advanced human rights, she displayed hatred of political figures, like Johnson, whom she believed were plotting to betray these gains.

As a correspondent, Mrs. Ames stood in the forefront of the group of enterprising women seeking opportunities in Washington journalism after the Civil War. According to the U.S. Congressional Directory of 1879, at least 20 women, representing 12 percent of the total of 166 correspondents, were recognized representatives of newspapers. Among them were Sara J. Lippincott, who wrote as "Grace Greenwood" for the *New York Times*, and Emily Edson Briggs, who used the pen name "Olivia." Most of them focused on social affairs, but some, like Mrs. Ames, broadened their scope. Unlike her contemporaries, she signed her columns with either her own name or her initials. Considering herself above society writers, she referred to these colleagues by the derogatory nickname of "Jenkins," ridiculing in her column their descriptions of ornate wardrobes: "Dress as a fine art must ever be a delight to esthetic eyes; but to be forever shuffling the small coin of Jenkins adjectives over it . . . is fearfully small business for an immortal soul." (First given to a writer for the London *Morning Post* whose descriptions of fashionable society exhibited servility and vulgarity, the name "Jenkins" was a nineteenth-century term for journalists who wrote gossip columns for a penny a line.)

Her columns drew readers to the *Independent*. A year after she started on the "Woman's Letter," Theodore Tilton, editor, and Oliver Johnson, managing editor, praised her work. In a letter to her Johnson quoted Tilton as saying, "I find also in my travels much commendation expressed of Mrs. Ames' letters. She is your card, and she is a trump." She received letters from admiring readers, including ministers, state legislators, newspaper editors, and politicians, who praised her condemnation of political leaders for morally questionable conduct.

As a Washington correspondent for the *Independent*, she proved that a woman could become a figure of importance to politicians. Schuyler Colfax, vice-president of the United States from 1869 to 1873, unsuccessfully begged her to uphold his innocence when his name figured in the Crédit Mobilier scandal. Other politicians sought her friendship.

Mrs. Ames's keen eye on Congress never observed it from the reporters' gallery, although women correspondents of the period had access to it. She assured her readers she was too modest to venture in, asserting, "We can never write 'before folks,' nor take notes in sight of all these reporters; but we can look, listen, and remember." Her vantage point was the ladies' gallery. To her a woman correspondent had little need to pattern herself after her male colleagues. Mrs. Ames exclaimed in her column in 1870: "Because a woman is a public correspondent it does not make it at all necessary that she as an individual should be conspicuously public—that she should run about with pencils in her mouth and pens in her ears; that she should invade the Reporters' Galleries, crowded with men; that she should go anywhere as a mere reporter where she would not be received as a lady. It is a class of women who like to do these things, who wish to make themselves personally conspicuous, who choose to do all that they do in a loud, intrusive manner, who provoke antagonism and bring reproach upon an entire class." Mrs. Ames was not the only *Independent* Washington correspondent: articles written by men accompanied her column, giving a less editorialized view of the news. Trading on the Victorian mystique that a woman was different from and purer than a man, she held herself up as a woman dedicated to elevating the moral tone of Gilded Age politics. Enumerating in her column the

high standards she hoped to attain, she used the third person: "Because she is a woman, hers is a higher work. It is her work to help exalt the standards of journalism, and in the midst of an arduous profession to preserve intact the dignity and sweetness of individual womanhood."

Mrs. Ames's financial situation improved after Henry C. Bowen, publisher of the *Independent*, employed her from 1869 to 1872 to work for his *Brooklyn Daily Union* as well as the *Independent*. A facile writer, Mrs. Ames so impressed Bowen with her ability to turn out various assignments, including book reviews, columns, and even advertising copy, that he paid her $5,000 in 1872. This was believed to be the largest salary paid an American newspaperwoman up to that time.

In common with other nineteenth-century advocates of women's rights, Mrs. Ames recognized the inequalities of women's position but never foresaw women adopting the same standards as men. Instead she looked forward to a future in which men would be raised to the allegedly "pure" standards of women. Although she supported suffrage, she did not publicly work in its behalf. Urging women to back Ulysses S. Grant for president in 1872, she advised them to avoid unseemly campaigning and to stay behind the scenes, asserting that "only in this higher realm of politics can woman reign without detriment to herself or without reflex injury to man."

Yet as the scandals associated with Grant's second term multiplied, she attacked the president's "cronyism," which had led to the appointment of corrupt officials. When society writers accused her of personal pique against the administration, she denied it hotly: "The difference in this matter between my questioning sisters and myself is that: They peck away privately and personally against the faults and foibles of the presidential family, member by member; while I, having no time whatever for tattle, speak professionally, because it is my business to do so. . . ." Similarly, she defended other journalists against attacks from those exposed as being corrupt. Reporters, she held, had an obligation to the public to disclose the true state of government. Still, she remained loyal to the Republican party, believing it had preserved the nation during the Civil War.

Following her divorce, Mrs. Ames resumed her maiden name, Clemmer, and brought her aged parents to live with her in a town house she purchased on Capitol Hill.

When Rutherford B. Hayes was inaugurated as president in 1877, she greeted him as the savior of the nation. In his wife, Lucy Webb Hayes, nicknamed "Lemonade Lucy" because of her Methodist refusal to serve liquor at the White House, Clemmer saw a vision of womanly purity. She wrote copiously about Mrs. Hayes for both the *Independent* and the *Cincinnati Commercial*, for which she became a Washington correspondent during the Hayes administration. In general, her *Commercial* articles repeated material in the *Independent*.

Pressed to produce weekly columns, she ranged from the profound to the trivial, writing one week on the future of democratic institutions and the next on the Washington weather. Her writing suffered from many of the defects common to its period—excessive sentiment, piety, and verbosity. Always interested in the White House, she defended the Hayes administration from charges of parsimony in arranging for state dinners. She feared that President James A. Garfield, who succeeded Hayes, would not match up to his predecessor. When Garfield was killed by a disappointed office-seeker, she wrote, "Heaven was kind to his fame to take him when it did."

Skeptical of Chester A. Arthur, who followed Garfield, she disliked his administration's stand on the question of women in politics. Alluding to the influence of unsavory women lobbyists, she wrote: "The question is not whether women shall or shall not influence public events, but, their powers being an acknowledged fact, the question is whether that power shall be subtle, secret, unacknowledged, equivocal, or whether it shall be legal, legitimate, open, honorable as the sunlight."

In addition to her newspaper work, Clemmer wrote six books during the 1870s—*Eirene* and a second novel, *His Two Wives* (1875); two memorial books (the one to her friends the Carys drew critical acclaim); and two volumes based on her Washington columns. Her literary output declined after she suffered a skull fracture in a carriage accident in 1878, although she published a book of poems in 1883.

Of her marriage on 19 June 1883 to Edmund Hudson, a well-known Washington journalist who edited the *Army and Navy Register*, she made no mention in her column, even though she described sights seen on their European honeymoon. Columns boosting General John Logan as a presidential candidate constituted her last work in the spring of 1884. Stricken with paralysis, she died of a cerebral hemorrhage in her Washington home.

According to her obituaries, she was a slender, graceful, and dignified woman with blue eyes, light-brown hair, and high coloring traced to her Manx ancestry. Obituaries pointed out that she began writing newspaper columns for two dollars each and was earning the then impressive sum of forty dollars or more when she died. The *Independent* stressed that her letters "commanded her a position in the selectest society of Washington, and [that] she took her rank as a recognized leader in the literary circles of the day." It also praised her for being a "remarkably womanly woman [who] loved home cares, to attend to the house, to go to market, to dress with a woman's elegance, to identify herself with a woman's life and woman's duties and hopes." In a eulogy, Senator Morrill commented, "Mary Clemmer has been the trusted friend of many eminent men—of [Senator Charles] Sumner, of [John Greenleaf] Whittier and of [President] Garfield. . . . She has made herself a power believed and feared."

In spite of personal timidity, Mary Clemmer showed it was possible for a woman to function as a powerful Washington correspondent if she turned her most obvious attribute and disadvantage—her sex—into a potent weapon. By stressing the Victorian mythology that women upheld a higher moral code than men, she claimed the right to criticize public affairs in the name of morality. At the same time, she was able to present herself as a "true woman" more concerned with the spiritual and domestic spheres than the material. Writing before women were enfranchised, she took maximum advantage of her position as an "outsider" in politics, scorning the corruption that marked the seams of the male-run Gilded Age.

Other:

Letters to Senator Bainbridge Wadleigh in support of woman suffrage, in *History of Woman Suffrage*, edited by Elizabeth Cady Stanton, Susan B. Anthony, and Matilda J. Gage (Rochester, N.Y.: Susan B. Anthony, 1886), III: 111-112, 262.

Biographies:

Lilian Whiting, "Mary Clemmer," in *Our Famous Women: An Authorized Record* (Hartford, Conn.: Worthington, 1884);

Edmund Hudson, *An American Woman's Life and Work: A Memorial of Mary Clemmer* (Boston: Ticknor, 1886).

References:

J. Cutler Andrews, "Mary E. Clemmer Ames (Hudson)," in *Notable American Women, 1607-1950*, edited by Edward T. James (Cambridge, Mass.: Belknap, 1971), I: 41;

Maurine H. Beasley, "Mary E. Clemmer Ames," in *American Women Writers: From Colonial Times to the Present*, edited by Lina Mainiero (New York: Ungar, 1979), I: 44-45;

Beasley, "Mary Clemmer Ames: A Victorian Woman Journalist," *Hayes Historical Journal* (Spring 1978): 57-63;

Sarah K. Bolton, "Our Mary Clemmer," *Independent* (28 August 1884): 1;

Sherwood Bonner, "Mary Clemmer," *The Cottage Hearth* (February 1875): 29-30;

"Death of Mary Clemmer Hudson," *Washington* (D.C.) *Evening Star* (19 August 1884), p. 1;

"Mary Clemmer," *Arthur's Home Magazine* (December 1884): 670-672;

"Mary Clemmer," *Cincinnati Commercial* (11 February 1878), p. 5;

"Mary Clemmer Hudson," *Literary News* (September 1884): 263-264.

Papers:

A collection of letters written to Mary Clemmer Ames and a file of her columns are at the Rutherford B. Hayes Library, Fremont, Ohio.

James Gordon Bennett, Jr.
(10 May 1841-14 May 1918)

Steven D. Lyons
Louisiana State University

MAJOR POSITIONS HELD: Managing editor, *New York Herald* (1866-1872); publisher, proprietor, *New York Herald*, *New York Evening Telegram*, *New York Herald–European Edition* (1872-1918).

James Gordon Bennett, Jr., sometimes known as "the Younger," was born into the world of journalism. His father had built for his son a virtual empire based on the first sensational newspaper in the United States, the *New York Herald*. The Younger, raised in Europe almost entirely removed from his father, had by the time of early manhood established a reputation as a playboy. His lavish life-style and escapades have been accorded more space in the history books than his journalistic accomplishments. In contrast to his father, who wished to be a recorder of the news, James G. Bennett, Jr., had a flair for making it happen.

Because of his arrogant and domineering personality, combined with his enthusiasm for yachting, his colleagues often referred to the younger Bennett as "the mad Commodore"; it was not beneath him to use his status to motivate, intimidate, and persuade those who came into contact with him either personally or professionally. Soon after he was made managing editor of the *Herald* in 1866 at the age of twenty-five, Bennett told his staff, "I want you fellows to remember that I am the only one to be pleased. If I want the *Herald* to be turned upside

Culver Pictures

down, it must be turned upside down."

Despite Bennett's eccentricities, he assumed full responsibility for the *New York Herald* and dedicated himself to making it the best newspaper in the world. He is credited with bringing to the newspaper business much of the type of coverage that is popular today, and, between his pranks and scandals, binges and cruises, he somehow managed to supervise every detail of publication, including content. Rather than depending on surveys and polls, Bennett operated on the assumption that he could create the public's desire for information himself, and then satisfy it in full measure. One such incident, which exemplifies both his lavish spending sprees and his dominance over the paper's content, involved the use of the Atlantic cable in 1866. Although the *Herald* and the *Tribune* endeavored to be the first with a message under the sea, Bennett is usually afforded historical accreditation for the feat. Bennett wasted no time or money in monopolizing the new means of communication; and upon the signing of the peace treaty with Austria, he ordered the speech of King William of Prussia to be sent in full via cable at a cost of $7,000 in gold.

Bennett, Sr., residing quietly out of the limelight, accepted his son's extravagance on the basis that his son's love of money would be enough to keep him from losing or wasting too much of it. Besides this, the elder Bennett had confided all policy matters to his son's discretion and did not want to interfere. While Bennett, Sr., at first felt that his son regarded the paper only as a means of making money, it was later revealed that the Younger had come to share the love for the paper that his father had felt. In 1869, when a syndicate offered to buy the paper for $2.2 million, Bennett stated, "There is not money enough in the world to buy the *Herald*," but it "could be had for three cents a copy any time."

Bennett's profligacy was deep-rooted. Taken to Paris by his mother to protect him from the violence that often surrounded the Older's life, the boy acquired habits that would persist throughout his life. While growing up, Bennett received the best that money could buy; his education was practically void of peer contact, as he received private tutoring under the direction of his mother. It was perhaps this early experience of a life of luxury that made irrational and unlimited spending his major characteristic. Unlike his father's humble beginnings as a schoolteacher, proofreader, and freelance writer, the young Bennett had, at an early age, become accustomed to the finer things in life and

expected them to continue without the practice of frugality. At the time of his death it seemed as though he had almost willingly left a declining business of the *Herald*, its Paris edition, and the *Evening Telegram*.

Given his servant-sheltered upbringing, Bennett should have turned into a proper little sissy. But, through some inherent toughness, he was a scrappy youth and as willing to use his fists as his father had been. Someone, possibly a servant, had led him astray when he was very young, and he was experienced in matters of sex and alcohol soon after reaching puberty. His life in Paris had left him with a command of the French language, which, in American eyes, certified him as an awesomely cultured individual. Despite his youthful antics and the disapproval of his father, he was welcomed into New York's "fast set," a pleasure-loving group of middle-aged brokers, sportsmen, clubmen, rounders, and all-around good fellows who flourished on the postwar inflation. There were various qualifications that allowed entry into the infamous group, and Bennett lacked none of the essentials: money, social connections, trim boats, an appreciation of wine and women that approached connoisseurship, a hearty if not refined sense of humor, a contempt for those who did not belong, style, form, and dash. E. P. Mitchell, a neighborhood friend and later editor of the *New York Sun*, described the Younger as "admired reverently" as "the beau ideal of the man of the world and all-around daredevil," with his tall, erect frame and blade of a nose. It is surmised that his wealthy, European upbringing was the reason for his transformation of the *Herald* into a reflection of his own tastes and prejudices—offering more sensational news coverage as well as expertise in military, nautical, social, and European news.

Bennett's changes and additions to the *Herald*, though extravagant, were comparable to the changes his father had made in journalism during his time. As a Washington correspondent for the *New York Enquirer*, Bennett, Sr., wrote, "I changed the whole tone, temper, and style of Washington correspondence," which until then had consisted of "heavy, flat, stupid, and disagreeable" accounts of what was said on the floor of Congress. The elder Bennett began his own newspaper, the *New York Herald*, from the basement of a Wall Street building, with the first edition greeting readers on a May day in 1835. It was printed on a double sheet of four pages, 10½ inches wide and 14 inches long; the first word below the title was a typographical error, "ptblished daily by James Gordon Bennett & Co."

The elder Bennett, while establishing himself and the *Herald*, changed the whole ideology of contemporary journalism. It was the heyday of personal journalism, and the newspapers ran page after page of opinions rather than hard news. Bennett, Sr., found it much more interesting to report the activities of his competitors, or a brutal murder; to him, the things that constituted his environment were worth more than the happenings of Europe or Asia. (Later, however, his son would again turn to Europe as a source of much of the *Herald*'s news.) Up to the elder Bennett's time there were taboos against reporting bankruptcies or social affairs; he soon changed all that. The Older made use of sensational news items that shocked the reader but increased the paper's circulation. Thousands of new readers were attracted by the way Bennett handled the murder of Helen Jewett, a young prostitute whose body was found in a house of assignation on Thomas Street. According to the *Herald*, the young lady had been brutally murdered with a hatchet, and Bennett, covering the story himself, did not spare the gore which spattered the death scene. Bennett's stories helped absolve a young clerk from prosecution by pointing to a jealous woman as the slayer. The coverage of the sensational crime, coupled with rivals' charges that Bennett had taken a $13,000 bribe to establish a case for the initial suspect, increased the *Herald*'s circulation by 10,000. It was this type of circulation record breaking that built for Bennett an empire of wealth and influence.

Although the *Herald* had stated in the beginning, "We shall support no party, be the organ of no faction or coterie, and care nothing for any election or any candidate from President down to constable," it was forced to take a pro-Lincoln political stance during the Civil War. It was after the South fired on Fort Sumter that Bennett, Sr., and his *Herald* came to the side of President Lincoln in calling for a united country. Before this, the elder Bennett had editorialized, more from a business sense than proslavery sentiments, that the South should be allowed to secede from the Union. Always thinking of the business end of the news, he first felt that a war would be devastating, especially one that was to take place on home soil. But because of a drastic change in public opinion concerning the

Bennett's ocean-going yacht, the Lysistrata, *in Villefranche Harbor, near Beaulieu, France*

war, Bennett changed his mind and called for his son to return from Paris to enlist in the Union navy.

Prior to this announcement the younger Bennett had been studying at the Ecole Polytechnique. On returning to America, he was commissioned a third lieutenant on 14 May 1861. It is likely that his commission was more of a gift for his father's newly avowed support for the war effort than any evidence of the younger Bennett's valor or leadership abilities. The elder Bennett, prior to his son's arrival, had donated the family yacht *Henrietta* for use by the navy. The younger Bennett was conveniently posted to the yacht during his enlistment so that he would not have to serve on a vessel that lacked the necessary luxuries of food and wine, or as a junior officer under persons who were undoubtedly inferior to him in every way except rank. When the navy finished with the schooner and decommissioned it, the young officer resigned.

After the war Bennett, Jr., was placed in an internship for two years on the *Herald*'s staff. He had spent much of his adolescence and young manhood abroad, away from the business that would eventually be his; his internship was two years of intense training in various departments of the paper, with the intent of instilling the love and sense of responsibility his father had for the newspaper business. Although the young Bennett found himself in privileged company, he still lacked the self-confidence his father exuded. Much of his instability was undoubtedly traceable to a feeling of unworthiness when he compared himself with his father; he needed some kind of success of his own. But Bennett, although handed life on a silver platter, had backbone. The born editor had survived numerous escapades, childlike antics in high and low society, and sporting events that reeked of danger and adventure; he knew he could survive anything his peers had to offer him in terms of paying his dues. One contemporary wrote, "It is the contention of many who worked under Bennett, Jr. that if he had been born with his own way to make in life instead of having come into the world with a gold spoon in his mouth, he would have achieved real greatness."

Early in his career Bennett made the decision not to become one of those lackluster heirs who sit behind a desk and let the family business slip through their fingers. If he could not match the writing skills, the experience, and the intellect of those around him, he would outdo his contemporaries in simple hard work, enterprise, and originality. He had a nose for news and, better yet, the ability to anticipate or make it himself; a willingness to spend huge amounts of money and effort to get it; and a determination to accept responsibility for his decisions. He brought to the *Herald* a new form and style unmatched by his contemporaries. After only a few months as managing editor he proposed to start publishing an afternoon edition under the title of the *Evening Telegram*. The *Herald* was still a bright sheet in comparison to the other papers of the day, but under the aging elder Bennett it had tended to play down the crime news and theatrical scandal in favor of a more sedate and dignified approach. The Younger's idea was to make use of the juicier items now neglected by the *Herald* by splashing them all over the newspaper, which proved to be a sound idea, since the afternoon readers found gory details of murders and assaults much easier to stomach than the morning readers.

The *Evening Telegram* was printed on pink paper, ran four- to six-column pages, and sold for one cent. The paper, which was like nothing New Yorkers had ever seen, had a striking resemblance to the tabloids of today. It carried stories of murders and suicides described in loving detail, a column of cable news, and another column of telegraphic bulletins. All of these stories were topped with large black headlines. The *Evening Telegram* never really caught on as the *Herald* had, but it did lay the groundwork for Hearst, Pulitzer, and the others who refined its methods. Bennett, Sr., was surely pleased with the innovative paper, for it was the counterpart to the *Herald* he had known in his younger days. Shortly before his twenty-seventh birthday and after only a few years as a newspaper executive, Bennett, Jr., was given full proprietorship of the *Herald* and *Evening Telegram*.

Despite his personal lack of literary expertise or even knowledge, he kept the *Herald* well staffed with notable literary talents of the time. These writers contributed essays or travel pieces to the editorial pages and the Sunday sections. Bennett appreciated the circulation-pulling quality of names like Mark Twain, Walt Whitman, Charles Edward Russell, Charles Nordhoff, and Robert Hunt Lyman, all of whom were contributors or staff members at one time or another.

Much of Bennett's fame rests on the fact that he was an avid sportsman who devoted much time, effort, and money to his pastimes and encouraged others to do the same. He is credited with introducing polo to the United States and participated in the first transatlantic yacht race in 1866. Bennett also encouraged ballooning and automobile racing by offering huge trophies, large sums of money, and more than average news coverage. This thirst for adventure and general desire for publishing accomplishments instigated the greatest adventure story of his time.

On 27 October 1869 Bennett granted the interview that would ensure his place in the history of journalism. It was on that day that he handed out the most important assignment of his or Henry M. Stanley's career: Stanley was to lead an expedition through central Africa in hopes of finding the Scottish missionary-physician-explorer Dr. David Livingstone, who had been lost in the jungle and last heard of three years previously. Bennett knew that the story would sell lots of newspapers. As always with the wealthy publisher, money was no object: Stanley's orders were "to find Livingstone at all costs." Stanley wired back a series of travel stories from various countries and then went into the un-mapped interior to find the missing missionary. Livingstone was the Albert Schweitzer of his day: a poor Scottish boy who somehow managed to gain a sufficient education to become a medical mission-ary; and more than that, he was an explorer who had blazed a path through South Africa, crossed the great Kalahari Desert, explored the Zambezi and Lake Ngami, and "discovered" and named Victoria Falls. The reporter in pursuit of the famed doctor was a man who had lived through life's toughest tests as an orphan and a soldier in both the Union and Confederate armies. Stanley had managed to survive it all, and he found his place among the famous as the discoverer of Dr. Livingstone in a small Arab colony named Ujiji. The ironically low-key meeting of the two men—after the enormous hardships Stanley had endured in the search—was immortalized in Stanley's account of it and gave a new catch-phrase to the English language:

> Doffing my helmet, I bowed and said in an inquiring tone, "Dr. Livingstone, I pre-sume?"
> Smiling cordially, he lifted his cap, and answered briefly, "Yes."

Although Bennett financed several other explorations by Stanley after the Livingstone ad-venture, the friendship which had started as a bril-liant collaboration ended in a vengeful and ugly manner. The young editor who longed for notori-ety had received none of the praise for finding the missionary; thus, he grew weary and jealous of the journalist-explorer and the attention bestowed upon him. After spending a considerable amount of time in Europe recuperating and recounting the story of how he had found Livingstone, Stanley

Henry Morton Stanley in 1872, the year he found Dr. David Livingstone in Africa

received a three-word cable: "STOP TALKING. BENNETT." In a final interview of Stanley by a reporter for the *Herald* the famed explorer was asked, on Bennett's orders, if he beat his wife. Ben-nett, who had heard that the newlywed had taken to woman beating instead of brush beating, wanted nothing more than to discredit the man who had taken fame away from him. After the interview, neither party ever corresponded with the other again.

Bennett went on to sponsor other explora-tions, including the 1875 attempt by the *Pandora* to discover the Northwest Passage and the ill-fated 1879-1881 expedition by George Washington De Long to try to find the North Pole. De Long and his party died of starvation after their ship, the *Jeannette*, was crushed by ice and they tried to make their way to Siberia on foot.

Though Bennett was impulsive, erratic, prod-igal with money, egotistical, and often arrogant, he also had many good intentions. During the panic of 1873 he opened soup lines in the New York slums. Like any venture the young Bennett undertook, the project was full of flair and extravagance: to ensure that the people were getting proper food, he fed the slums with soup and sandwiches from the famed Delmonico's. He once contributed $100,000 to re-lieve distress in Ireland and organized the *Herald*'s free ice fund (ice was then a luxury) for New York's crowded tenements during the hot weather. He is also credited with building the memorial that marks the site of Fort Washington on upper Manhattan Island.

During the years that Bennett was struggling to make a name for himself in the world of journalism, the deaths of both of his parents took place. Bennett, Sr., died at his Washington Heights residence on Saturday, 1 June 1872. He had not been ill, though for five years he had been inactive and supposedly enjoyed these last few quiet years of his life. The cause of his death was a stroke of apoplexy, which had befallen the almost seventy-seven-year-old journalism tycoon a week earlier. Oddly, the *Herald* carried no biographical account of its founder in its next issue, printing only the news of his death. On Monday it did publish several biographies printed by other papers, which referred to him as "the greatest journalist the world ever produced." His death gave the younger Bennett total control of both the *Herald* and the *Evening Telegram*. His mother did not long outlive his father. She died in Sachsen, Germany, on 28 March 1873 of cancer. Like her husband, she died in the arms of hired servants; she had insisted that her son not be sent for while she was conscious. When he did arrive, two hours before she expired, she had long been in a coma. During her illness, she exemplified the same tenacity that her husband and son had possessed: she would not allow the doctor to speak of her danger, seemed unwilling to contemplate death, and met it stoically.

On Monday morning, 9 November 1874, many New Yorkers were thrown into a panic by a story that filled the entire front page of the *Herald*, detailing the escape of all the wild animals from the Central Park Zoo. The reports told in graphic detail of citizens being mauled, mutilated, and killed by lions, tigers, elephants, and snakes. At the very end of the long story was a brief disclaimer, stating that the entire article was "a pure fabrication"; the justification given for printing it was to call attention to the lack of preparation for dealing with such a catastrophe, should it in fact occur. The stunt has gone down in journalism history as "the wild animal hoax."

As Bennett aged, his interest in and desire to return to Europe grew in intensity. His childhood had apparently ingrained in the tycoon the feeling that Europe was his home, and from 1877 onward he lived mostly in Paris. He remained in complete control of his New York papers, however, cabling instructions to his editors each day; reporters could not be hired or fired without his approval. The *Herald*'s editorial committee met with an empty chair and a fresh copy of the paper at the head of the table, as if Bennett might walk in at any moment. It was not beyond Bennett to demand the presence of a New York department head in his office in Paris; once the staff member arrived, he might be sent home without even meeting with Bennett. This infuriated the New York editors, who viewed their time as very important. Bennett, however, was not to be bothered with lower-level managerial opinion concerning his orders. Once when Bennett summoned a member of the New York staff to Paris, the editor in charge demurred, cabling that the man was "indispensable." Bennett sent for a list of men who were presumed to be in this class. A dozen names were forwarded to him. He discharged all of them, stating, "I will have no indispensable men in my employ."

In spite of Bennett's absentee control and idiosyncratic ways, the *Herald* reached a circulation of 100,000 from 1873 to 1876, rising to 150,000 on occasion. Circulation increased when the price was lowered from four to three cents in 1876, surpassing Charles A. Dana's two-cent *Sun*. The *Herald* dropped to two cents to try to meet the competition

Paris office of the New York Herald—European Edition, *established in 1887*

The Herald Building in Herald Square. Based on the Palazzo del Consiglio in Verona, the building was completed in 1894.

of Joseph Pulitzer's *World* in 1883 and rose to a circulation of 190,500 in 1885; but that was its high point, and the *World* outstripped it the following year. The 1883 price cut provoked a revolt among newsdealers, who found themselves receiving only a third of a cent per copy of the *Herald*, as compared with more than half a cent for the other two-penny papers. Organized demonstrations were held against Bennett and the *Herald* (and given extensive coverage in the *World*). On cabled instructions from Bennett, 500 newsstands were set up exclusively for the *Herald*; but Bennett was finally forced to yield to the dealers' demands in the summer of 1884. Meanwhile, to make up for the cut in price, the *Herald* had raised its advertising rates. The result was that the *Herald*—which for a generation had had more advertising than any other paper in America, and possibly in the world—was surpassed in 1886 by the *World* in advertising as well as in circulation.

A more successful 1883 venture was Bennett's establishment, along with silver king John W. Mackay, of the Commercial Cable Company. Competition from this enterprise forced Jay Gould's Western Union to reduce cable tolls almost fifty percent; and the Mackay-Bennett transatlantic cable allowed the *Herald* to excel in its coverage of European news.

At the age of forty-six, Bennett decided to

spend his time and money on a new enterprise: and nothing pleased him more than spending both on a newspaper. In 1887 he decided to expand his paper overseas to Paris. The endeavor, most often referred to as the *Paris Herald*, was—according to Bennett's angry insistence—the "European edition of the *New York Herald*." Regardless of its name, it became an established media source for Americans during World War I and again in World War II, until the Germans occupied Paris and closed all the newspapers. Though the paper proved highly respectable and—eventually—profitable, Bennett had initially instituted it as a place where he could retreat from the too-familiar New York headquarters and keep himself busy; for a number of years the Paris edition lost $100,000 annually. Bennett also established a short-lived London edition in 1889-1890.

The *Herald* continued to be respected for its news coverage in the early years of the twentieth century. War correspondent Joseph L. Stickney covered Admiral Dewey in Manila Bay, Richard Harding Davis reported from the Boer side in the South African war, and Oscar King Davis and W. H. Lewis gave top coverage of the Russo-Japanese War. The paper also gave detailed reports, supplemented by photographs and artwork, of disasters such as the sinking of the excursion boat

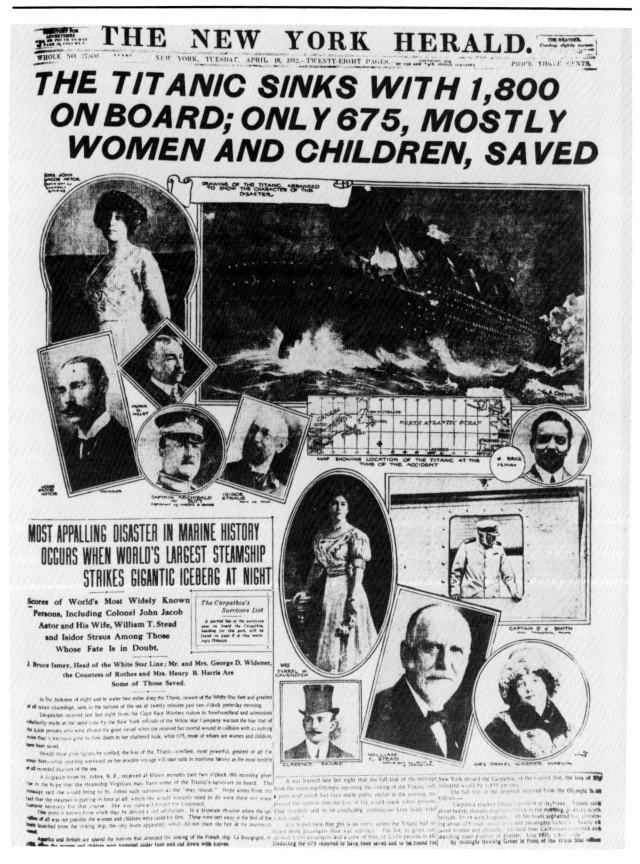

Front page of the New York Herald *for 16 April 1912, showing the paper's innovative use of illustration*

General Slocum in 1904 and the *Titanic* in 1912.

On 10 September 1914 James G. Bennett, Jr., finally settled down to a wife. The man who had found amorous affairs with chorus girls aplenty and had claimed bachelorhood for years married his longtime companion, the Baroness de Reuter, formerly Maud Potter of Philadelphia. She was the widow of Baron George de Reuter, whose family had founded the British news agency. She had married the baron in 1891 and lived with him until his death in 1909, was the mother of two grown sons, and was reputed to be one of the most beautiful middle-aged women on the Continent. She was also gentle, understanding, and tolerant. Bennett had known her for years and valued her companionship. What finally sent the publisher over the matrimonial brink was never revealed, but the marriage was said to be one of devotion and admiration. After the wedding she moved into Bennett's Paris apartment, where she remained until her death in 1946.

Early in 1918 Bennett caught a severe cold that verged on pneumonia and heavily taxed his heart and lungs. Several weeks later, when he had partially recovered, Mrs. Bennett took him to the gentler climate at Beaulieu. He failed to throw off the effects of the illness, however, and superstitiously began brooding over the approach of his seventy-seventh birthday on 10 May. His father had died of a stroke on his seventy-seventh birthday, and Bennett was sure that he would go at the same age and in the same manner. Late in April he and Mrs. Bennett attended a charity ball in Monte Carlo, at which a clairvoyant insisted on telling his fortune. According to Mrs. Bennett, the seeress told him that his two dogs would die, and that this would be followed by the death of some member of his household. When a little later the two Pekingese died, Bennett was convinced that the rest of the prophecy would also be fulfilled. He gave up all hope of fighting his illness from that moment. "It was my death she saw in the cards," he insisted. "I know that it will happen as she said. I have lived out my life."

Early in the morning of 10 May he suffered a massive brain hemorrhage. Specialists tried to revive the aged tycoon but could do nothing for him. His heart was failing, uremia developed, and, as the *Paris Herald* reported, "his breathing gradually became fainter and fainter." At 5:15 A.M. on 14 May his breathing stopped altogether, as Mrs. Bennett held the hand of the man who had thrown away more money than any other American of his time: an estimated $30,000,000 drained from the profits of his papers. The obituaries were as unsentimental and bland as the publisher would have wanted. Bennett was buried in Passy, across the street from

Bennett disembarking for one of his last visits to New York City

the house where Clemenceau lived, after brief services in Trinity Church in Paris. The only markings on his gravestone are two owls, who are there to guide and watch over the pagan. Almost immediately after Bennett's death, the *Herald*, the *Evening Telegram*, and the *Paris Herald* were sold to Frank Munsey for $4,000,000. In 1924, Munsey sold the New York and Paris editions of the *Herald* to Ogden Reid and his wife, Helen Rogers Reid, for $5,000,000; the *Herald* was then absorbed into the *Herald Tribune*.

Biographies:

Don C. Seitz, *The James Gordon Bennetts, Father and Son* (Indianapolis: Bobbs-Merrill, 1928);

Oliver Carlson, *The Man Who Made News, James Gordon Bennett* (New York: Duell, Sloan & Pearce, 1942);

Kenneth Norman Stewart and John Tebbel, *Makers of Modern Journalism* (New York: Prentice-Hall, 1952);

Harold Herd, *Seven Editors* (London: Allen & Unwin, 1955);

Richard O'Connor, *The Scandalous Mr. Bennett* (Garden City: Doubleday, 1962).

Reference:

"Anglo-American Trouble-makers: J. G. Bennett & J. T. Delane," *History Today* (February 1956): 88-95.

Ambrose Bierce
(24 June 1842-11 January 1914?)

Whitney R. Mundt
Louisiana State University

See also the Bierce entries in *DLB 11, American Humorists, 1800-1950* and *DLB 12, American Realists and Naturalists.*

MAJOR POSITIONS HELD: Editor, *San Francisco News Letter* (1868-1871); editor, *San Francisco Wasp* (1881-1886); columnist, *San Francisco Examiner* and *New York Journal* (1887-1906).

SELECTED BOOKS: *The Fiend's Delight*, as Dod Grile (London: John Camden Hotten, 1873; New York: A. L. Luyster, 1873);

Nuggets and Dust Panned Out in California, as Dod Grile (London: Chatto & Windus, 1873);

Cobwebs from an Empty Skull, as Dod Grile (London & New York: Routledge, 1874);

The Dance of Death, by Bierce and Thomas A. Harcourt, as William Herman (San Francisco: Privately printed, 1877; corrected and enlarged edition, San Francisco: Henry Keller, 1877);

Tales of Soldiers and Civilians (San Francisco: E. L. G. Steele, [1892]); published simultaneously as *In the Midst of Life* (London: Chatto & Windus, 1892; revised and enlarged edition, New York & London: Putnam's, 1898);

The Monk and the Hangman's Daughter, by Bierce and Gustav Adolph Danziger (Chicago: F. J. Schulte, 1892);

Black Beetles in Amber (San Francisco & New York: Western Authors Publishing, 1892);

Can Such Things Be? (New York: Cassell, 1893; London: Cape, 1926);

Fantastic Fables (New York & London: Putnam's, 1899);

Shapes of Clay (San Francisco: W. E. Wood, 1903);

The Cynic's Word Book (New York: Doubleday, Page, 1906); enlarged as *The Devil's Dictionary*, volume 7 of *The Collected Works of Ambrose Bierce* (New York & Washington: Neale, 1911);

A Son of the Gods and A Horseman in the Sky (San Francisco: Elder, 1907);

The Shadow on the Dial and Other Essays, edited by S. O. Howes (San Francisco: A. M. Robertson, 1909); revised and republished as *Antepenultima*, volume 11 of *The Collected Works of Ambrose Bierce* (New York & Washington: Neale, 1912);

Write It Right (New York & Washington: Neale, 1909);

The Collected Works of Ambrose Bierce, 12 volumes (New York & Washington: Neale, 1909-1912)—1) *Ashes of the Beacon, The Land Beyond*

the Blow, For the Ahkoond, John Smith, Liberator, Bits of Autobiography; 2) *In the Midst of Life*; 3) *Can Such Things Be?, The Ways of Ghosts, Soldier-Folk, Some Haunted Houses*; 4) *Shapes of Clay, Some Antemortem Epitaphs, The Scrap Heap*; 5) *Black Beetles in Amber, The Mummery, On Stone*; 6) *The Monk and the Hangman's Daughter, Fantastic Fables, Aesopus Emendatus, Old Saws with New Teeth, Fables in Rhyme*; 7) *The Devil's Dictionary*; 8) *Negligible Tales, The Parenticide Club, The Fourth Estate, The Ocean Wave, "On with the Dance!," Epigrams*; 9) *Tangential Views*; 10) *The Opinionator, The Reviewer, The Controversialist, The Timorous Reporter, The March Hare*; 11) *Antepenultimata*; 12) *In Motley, Kings of Beasts, Two Administrations, Miscellaneous*;

Battlefields and Ghosts, edited by Hartley E. Jackson and James D. Hart (Palo Alto: Harvest Press, 1931);

Selections from Prattle by Ambrose Bierce, edited by Carroll D. Hall (San Francisco: Book Club of California, 1936);

Enlarged Devil's Dictionary, edited by Ernest J. Hopkins (Garden City: Doubleday, 1967);

The Ambrose Bierce Satanic Reader, edited by Hopkins (Garden City: Doubleday, 1968).

Bitter Bierce, the caustic columnist. Thus was Ambrose Gwinnett Bierce best known, and thus is he best remembered. Yet in his lifetime he embraced several careers: soldier, expatriate litterateur, gold prospector, and newspaper writer. It is the latter career which established his reputation, but his short stories—many of them inspired by his military experience—have been anthologized frequently. His success as a literary artist could not have been predicted from his origins as a farmboy in the Appalachian foothills of southern Ohio.

Ambrose Bierce was born 24 June 1842 on a farm in Meigs County, Ohio, near the border of what was to become West Virginia. He was the tenth of thirteen children born to Marcus Aurelius and Laura Sherwood Bierce, and he was the youngest of those who survived infancy. In 1846 the Bierces moved to northern Indiana, near Warsaw. There Ambrose went to school, and, at the age of fifteen, gained his early journalistic experience as printer's devil on the *Northern Indianan*.

At seventeen he was sent for a year to the Kentucky Military Institute, where he acquired other skills which were to serve him well in the ensuing years: mapmaking, surveying, drafting, engineering, and tactics.

His training proved useful sooner than he expected, for on 12 April 1861—a year after his return to Indiana from the Kentucky Military Institute—Fort Sumter was fired upon, and on 19 April Bierce enlisted as a private with the Ninth Volunteer Infantry. During his three-month stint he acquitted himself properly in skirmishes and found his bravery noted in newspaper dispatches. Perhaps because he had gained respect in military life that had escaped him as the youngest of ten children, he reenlisted in August. Promoted to sergeant, Bierce endured the drill and the discipline with a surprising degree of adaptation, considering his later reputation for chafing under the discipline of domestic life. In April his regiment underwent its first stern test at Shiloh, and the carnage there Bierce retained in memories which were to become the stuff of his finest short stories. In December Sergeant Bierce became Second Lieutenant Bierce, and in February 1863 he was promoted to first lieutenant and assigned as topographical officer on the brigade headquarters staff of Gen. W. B. Hazen. In this capacity he surveyed the lay of the land, noting military advantages and disadvantages and

8 SAN FRANCISCO NEWS LETTER AND [Sept. 25, 1869.

Cleaning the Augean Stable.

As a type of impotence your average Government clerk is tolerably satisfactory. In the very nature of things he can be nothing more than an animated machine, and in point of fact he is seldom even animated. Confined to a routine of petty duties which neither vary with the seasons nor suffer change by the precession of the equinoxes—with no incentive to exertion, and constantly tortured with the fear of removal, he becomes essentially narrow-minded, peevish, jealous and spiritless, and acquires a habit of fawning. He has not usually a soul above figures, and is as incapable of incubating an idea as is a plucked hen of hatching a chicken on a marble slab. We have known a whole bevy of these gentlemen to be thrown into a conniption fit by having an opinion exploded suddenly in their midst. We have ourselves taken a fiendish delight in driving a score of them in consternation from their ledgers to the unspeakable derangement of the public business, by carelessly cracking a thought upon their astonished pates. We speak of the average Government clerk, for there are exceptions, and the reader who belongs to the guild will naturally consider himself a notable one. Possible he is—probably he is not. For a good many years the Branch Mint in this city has been the head-quarters of this kind of thing. Within the walls of that useful institution Imbecility seems to have set up her ancient solitary reign, and few have been the attempts to dislodge her. Occasionally some rebellious subject has struggled out of the leading strings, and signalized his secession by a feeble attempt at some stale dishonesty; but his laudable aspirations have usually been nipped in the bud, and things went on as before. The rise and fall of these rebellions have formed about the only epochs in the Mint history, and in the long dead calm which has succeeded them, time has been reckoned from the inception of the swindle or the escape of the culprit, as among Christians from the birth of Christ, or among Mahometans from the Hegira. In the blank quiet of Mint life, clerks and employees have sprouted, and vegetated, and grown lank and colorless, like the long white potato-shoots nourished in the congenial damps of a dark cellar. For their sake we are pleased to note that the new Superintendent is lopping them off and casting them upon the rich mould of an independent existence, where we pray God they may take root and bear tubers of amazing growth, and where we know they will do no such thing. They are too far gone. Still we rejoice that they are to have a chance to develop what of vitality remains in them. Viewed in this light we regard the advent of Gen. Lagrange as a positive service to humanity, and we trust the good work may go on until all but *News Letter's* particular friends (the exceptions aforesaid) are removed, and their places supplied by countless hosts of our admirers—a revised list of whom may be obtained at this office by an order from the Superintendent. So shall this refuge of hoary Incapables be converted into an asylum for unappreciated merit and neglected genius, and the slow shilling of conventional dullness be coined into the nimble sixpence of clerical efficiency.

An Ebullient Taxpayer.

At the meeting of the Board of Supervisors, last Monday evening, a communication was received from Mr. Daniel Boyle, "practical mason," protesting against the manner in which the work is doing upon the Harrison street bridge. He showed that the contract with the city is violated in every particular, and in the most open and bare-faced manner. Daniel Boyle's simple soul is very much agitated thereat, and he clamors for his rights as a taxpayer. Daniel is quite well aware of his importance as the one hundred and fifty thousandth part of a sovereign community, and means to assert his prerogative of keeping things municipally straight. Poor Daniel; practical mason but impractical reformer! Do you not know that the good Supervisors smiled intelligently into one anothers honest eyes as your visionary communication was read and quietly "referred?" Know you not that that letter has already begun to sleep the sleep that knows no breaking? Those Supervisors, Daniel, are disposed to deal gently with the erring contractor, for they are an amiable folk who believe in the good old saying "live and let live." They have provided so well for their own living, out of that ninety-eight thousand, that it is only through extreme leniency on their part that the poor contractor can hope to provide for his. If he sticks to his agreement—made before the "preliminary expenses" were settled—he loses money and disgraces his profession of contractor. But if he disregards the plans and specifications to which he prematurely appended his autograph, some howling Daniel Boyle will get after him in the public prints. Like a sensible man, however, he prefers to do the latter, and like sensible accomplices the Supervisors allow him to do it. And Daniel may thank his stars that when he bearded the lions in their den he escaped unlacerated from the claws of the plethoric and good-natured beasts. We hope it will be understood that our remarks have no personal application, for we have not the remotest suspicion of who the contractor is, nor do we know the name of a single Supervisor in the Board, much less one who voted for the Harrison street swindle. The only man we know in this business is that practical mason in a state of ebullition, Daniel Boyle; and to him our final advice is—Boyle on!

The Latest Eagan Swindle.

The case is like this—very like indeed: The St. James Church property is mortgaged to a considerable extent. There is one mortgage upon it for (say) six thousand dollars. Perhaps the mortgagees are the City Bank and the Peoples' Insurance. Possibly Messrs. Horner and Murphy will correct us if we are wrong. Bishop Kip, good soul, yielding to the pious importunities of Father Eagan, gave the latter a letter of marque, authorizing him to make unlimited reprisals upon the benevolent purses of the faithful for means to discharge the debt. This, with his accustomed alacrity when money is to be got, he did; thereby collecting (say) four thousand dollars. But with his unfortunate habit of procrastination when money is to be paid, he pocketed the same, reporting to the worthy Bishop that he had paid it upon the mortgage; yea, even unto the mortgagees aforementioned. Upon investigation this turns out to be a lie—as above intimated. Poor Eagan has told so many falsehoods lately that he has entangled himself in a very web of mendacity, and even the most credulous of the elect will no longer believe him under oath. Even Badger, and Cobb, and McDermott, turn away the head at the mention of his name. He is also Treasurer of Mrs. ——'s boarding house, which, it is said, has fallen into evil ways, and is not exactly what it "used to was." And then those twenty-three dresses which were made last year, and have never been used! Heigh-ho! fashions change and we change with them. But not Eagan. No, no, not Eagan! He is immutable as the heavens. He will remain a sinner to the last. So shall we.

A Spalpeen.

Probably very few people are aware that there exists—or rather, we should say, is allowed to exist, in this city and century a man named Michael Fennell. It is equally true, and equally to be deplored, that this Fennell is an idiot of gigantic proportions, and conducts a newspaper of even more immense imbecility than himself. In the last issue of his monstrous emptiness, this Fennell fellow makes a gross, vulgar and essentially stupid attack upon the private character of Mr. W. H. L. Barnes, a man who is accustomed to have his boots blacked each morning by Mr. Fennell's social superior, and is also in the habit, we suppose, of using one of them to admonish men of the Fennell ilk when by using the same side of the street they exhibit an unpardonable familiarity. As to the motive of the attack we know nothing, further than that Mr. Barnes has the misfortune to be a gentleman, and that Mr. Fennell has not, which, by the class to whom the latter is a disgrace, is usually considered sufficient provocation for any assault which does not involve personal danger to the ruffian making it. We have no particular interest in the affair, aside from a benevolent desire to acquaint Mr. Barnes with the fact that the mud has really been cast, and to point out the caster, that he may be stepped on at the castee's convenience. We believe there is a rank kitchen vegetable called the dog-fennel, the seeds of which are used, by persons of execrable taste, for the flavoring of pies. If the odor of the dog Fennell under discussion is allowed to permeate the under-crust of society, we trust that some method may be found to prevent the nauseous taint from rising to the top.—*News Letter, Sept. 18th.*

Some Excellent Fooling.

EDITOR NEWS LETTER:—I find the following card in all the daily papers:

Having called upon the Editor of the *News Letter* for the name of the author of a scurrilous article which appeared in the last number of that paper, wherein my name is mentioned, I was informed it was written by a man named Boyce. I have no hesitation in pronouncing this invisible fellow—to me, at least—a liar, a scoundrel and, perhaps, a coward.
MICHAEL FENNELL.

Now this must have cost Mr. Flannel six or seven dollars, which I think you ought to pay. That's my idea of justice. You ought to also to have published in the dailies—at our joint expense—an equal number of cards, denying that I am either a liar or a scoundrel. With regard to my cowardice, as Mr. Flannel seems himself to have some lingering doubts about that, it would hardly pay to go to any expense to contradict it. Besides, I am not quite sure about it myself; I wouldn't bet heavily on my courage when confronted by a big Irishman, with a meat-hound looming up in the dim distance. I can't help admiring the exquisite non-committal manner in which Mr. Flannel puts forth a modest bud of doubt in relation to my courage. Evidently he thought I might myself put forth a "tender shoot," and he did not care to rush into the presence of his maker with a lie in the Flannel mouth. He might have spared himself the uneasiness. I am not painfully brave, and wouldn't fight a girl baby—unless I could take some diabolical advantage, and put a head on her before she could get a lick in. Still, I intend, merely as a matter of duty, to chew up Mr. Flannel and spit him him against a stone wall the first time I catch him coming out of Dr. Zeile's steam bath house. You may tell him this, as I do not wish to eat a man without giving him time to collect what debts he may have outstanding. This is a courtesy that I always extend to the parties I devour, and I find it pays to be civil to a man just before serving him a scurvy trick. He never forgets it. I am glad you told Mr. Flannel my name, as I directed you to do, but you must have been awfully frightened to get it Boyce, and make him spend six or seven dollars abusing a person whom I know to be as harmless as he is distant. Boyce keeps a corner grocery in Chicago. *My* name is Boyd. I may also mention *en passant* that my foot is on my native heath. I reside at the Lick, where I shall be happy to unbend from my usual dignity and have a cheerful chat with Mr. Flannel. But I solemnly warn him that a discussion with pistols is not in my line, and I have an unconquerable aversion to his national weapon, the sanguinary shilelah. I never fight with anything more murderous than a sausage stuffer.

Since writing the above apology I observe that Mr. Flannel has spent some more dollars publishing me as Bierce. Will some one kindly tell me who I am? Also, he and two others, all armed with heavy canes, have broken my head, or Boyce's head, or Bierce's.

I like to abuse people in your paper; it makes things lively. Goose-fennell!

Very truly yours, H. E. BOYD, (or BOYCE, or BIERCE.)

As a piece of cold cheek we think the above caps anything likely to be exhibited at the Mechanics' Fair; we do, indeed. If Mr. Boyd (we are sure it's Boyce) writes us any more scurrilous articles he will hear from us. It makes things lively, as he says, but there is nothing we covet so much as dignified repose. It is our *forte*. We regard Boyce (or Boyd) as an unmitigated scoundrel—always regarded him so; and if he comes fooling about this office any more, we shall dispatch an errand boy for the last man lacerated the moment we see him emerge from the Bank Exchange. Who the devil is Boyd, (or Boyce, or Bierce)? ED. NEWS LETTER.

Cacoethes.

Among the many things animate and inanimate—and really it is difficult to determine to which class our subject belongs—which the railroad has brought us, is the Pullman Palace Car. We pray the railroad to take it away. It makes one's flesh creep to think of it, and the worst fate we can wish the gentleman who seem to have no regular occupation and devote all their leisure to dinning its praises into our ears, is that they may be compelled to ride in it from here to Omaha, without a change of clothing. For what is the nastiness of the ordinary street car or ferry-boat compared with the supernatural filth of this vehicular abomination? The perverted ingenuity of the world's spirit of invention seems to have been concentrated in the Pullman sty upon the production of cushions, and carpets, and mattresses, for the secretion of insect life and all nameless unpleasantnesses. The specimen on exhibition at the Pavilion is exceeding fair to look upon, for it is new. But let it be used a few months for the transportation of unassorted humanity, and it would be a valuable investment for the ambitious entomologist. In the Eastern States the intolerable nuisance of cushions in public conveyances is being abandoned. The clean slat seats of our own Mission street cars are worthy of imitation in this line, and we hope to see them generally adopted. People who have used the Pullman cars for long distances have confided to our unwilling ear the story of their sufferings, and we protest in the name of cleanliness against them. Happily they are too cumbersome to be used upon the heavy grades of our own roads, and the traveling public is not likely to be called upon to perform upon the Scotch fiddle. Otherwise we should pray for the advent of some California Duke of Argyle, to plant convenient posts at all way stations. The cheerful brakeman could then vary his announcements with an occasional "ten minutes for scratching."

The Old Nick.

The daily papers seem all at once—*Bulletin* a trifle ahead, as usual—to have discovered that Nicolson pavement is a failure. With that keenness of foresight so characteristic of the true journalist, we made that discovery some years ago, and proclaimed it from a house top on Clay street. As was to have been expected, Time has paid us the graceful compliment of establishing our reputation for sagacity upon a stable and enduring basis. Nicolson *is* a failure; *vide* all along Montgomery street and elsewhere. By the way, *won't* the Board have that on Montgomery all taken up and replaced by some more of the same kind? We think the Board will; its action in all similar cases warrants the hope. The Nicolson having now been indisputably proven to be utterly worthless, and being pretty generally abandoned in all other cities, nothing remains for our Municipal sages but to adopt it at once, and order it laid down upon every street, and some distance out into the sand hills. Twenty-eight cents per square foot affords a fine field for the display of legislative talent and acquisitive instinct. Keep it not from us; let us quickly have it. The Stowe, however, is good.

Still Another Attempted Swindle!

In the sale which Jas. J. Robbins made to the Nicolson Pavement Company, he transferred the patent right for this coast and all renewals thereof. On this understanding the Company relieved Robbins of a business he was unable to carry on, and from utter financial destruction. He is now endeavoring to destroy the investment made in the business by gentlemen whom he persuaded into embarking with him in the Nicolson Pavement Company, by claiming either as principal or agent to hold the renewal of the patent and to sell royalties for the use of the pavement. Rotten, very!

A Card.

The callous hide of the individual in question was not to be stung by any such trifle as being called a coward and a liar.—*Chronicle.*

Charles DeYoung, of the *Chronicle*, is "a liar, a scoundrel and, perhaps"—indeed quite probably—"a coward."

MARRIED.—In New York, Sept. 13th, by the Rev. Dr. Scott, William Henry Dutton, Jr., of California, to Miss Mary E. Talbot, daughter of William C. Talbot, Esq., of San Francisco.

—— A letter of yesterday's date, from Virginia, Nevada, states that Mr. Sutro's important tunnel enterprise will break ground at its mouth on Monday next.

Specimen of Bierce's first regularly appearing column, which he wrote from 1869 until 1871

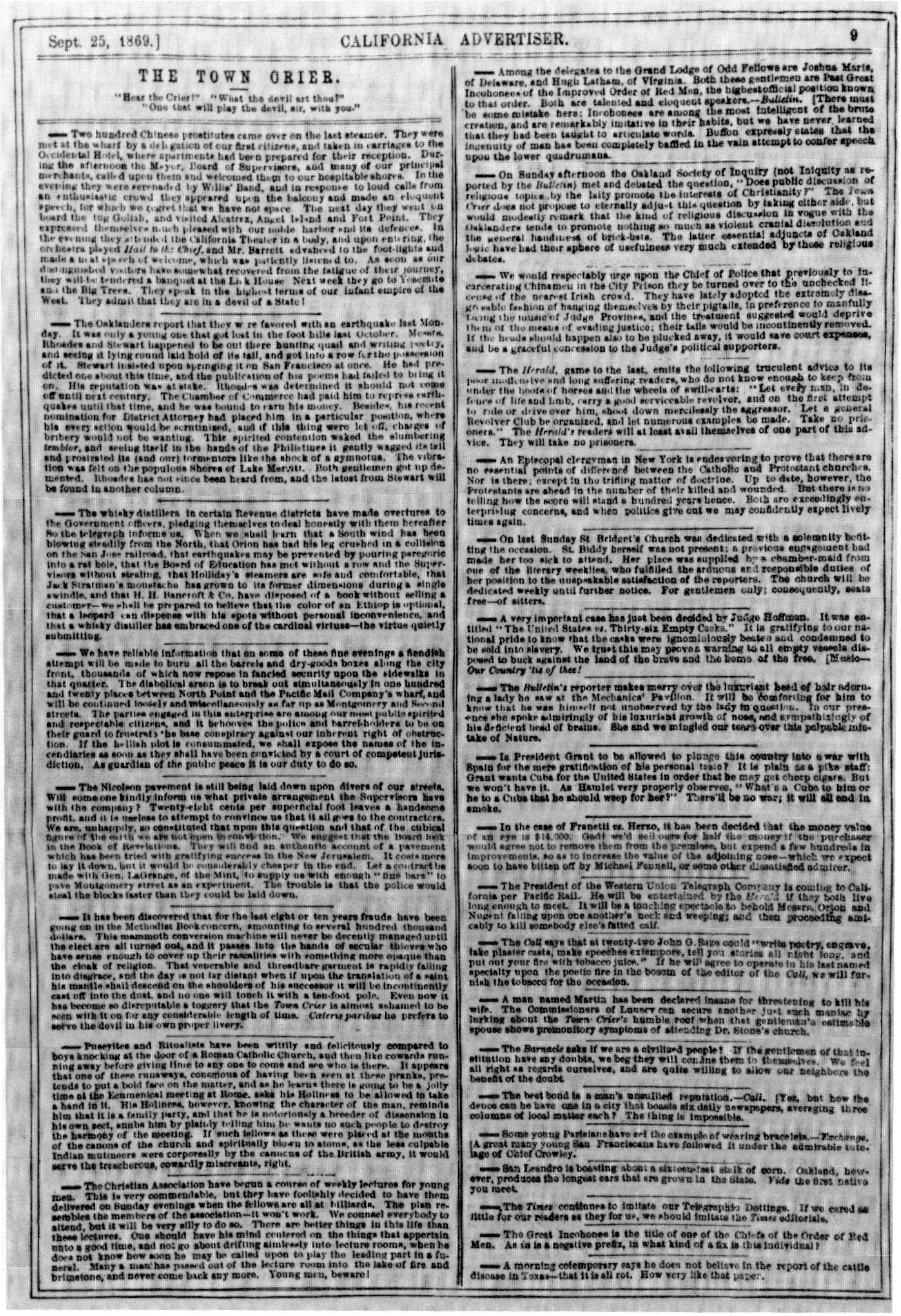

Sept. 25, 1869.] CALIFORNIA ADVERTISER. 9

THE TOWN CRIER.

"Hear the Crier!" "What the devil art thou?"
"One that will play the devil, sir, with you."

—— Two hundred Chinese prostitutes came over on the last steamer. They were met at the wharf by a delegation of our first citizens, and taken in carriages to the Occidental Hotel, where apartments had been prepared for their reception. During the afternoon the Mayor, Board of Supervisors, and many of our principal merchants, called upon them and welcomed them to our hospitable shores. In the evening they were serenaded by Willis' Band, and in response to loud calls from an enthusiastic crowd they appeared upon the balcony and made an eloquent speech, for which we regret that we have not space. The next day they went on board the tug Goliah, and visited Alcatrez, Angel Island and Fort Point. They expressed themselves much pleased with our noble harbor and its defences. In the evening they attended the California Theater in a body, and upon entering, the orchestra played *Hail to the Chief*, and Mr. Barrett advanced to the foot-lights and made a neat speech of welcome, which was patiently listened to. As soon as our distinguished visitors have somewhat recovered from the fatigue of their journey, they will be tendered a banquet at the Lick House. Next week they go to Yosemite and the Big Trees. They speak in the highest terms of our infant empire of the West. They admit that they are in a devil of a State!

—— The Oaklanders report that they were favored with an earthquake last Monday. It was only a young one that got lost in the foot hills last October. Messrs. Rhoades and Stewart happened to be out there hunting quail and writing poetry, and seeing it lying round laid hold of its tail, and got into a row for the possession of it. Stewart insisted upon springing it on San Francisco at once. He had predicted one about this time, and the publication of his poems had failed to bring it on. His reputation was at stake. Rhoades was determined it should not come off until next century. The Chamber of Commerce had paid him to repress earthquakes until that time, and he was bound to earn his money. Besides, his recent nomination for District Attorney had placed him in a particular position, where his every action would be scrutinized, and if this thing were let off, charges of bribery would not be wanting. This spirited contention waked the slumbering *temblor*, and seeing itself in the hands of the Philistines it gently wagged its tail and prostrated its (and our) tormentors like the shock of a gymnotus. The vibration was felt on the populous Shores of Lake Merritt. Both gentlemen got up demented. Rhoades has not since been heard from, and the latest from Stewart will be found in another column.

—— The whisky distillers in certain Revenue districts have made overtures to the Government officers, pledging themselves to deal honestly with them hereafter So the telegraph informs us. When we shall learn that a South wind has been blowing steadily from the North, that Orion has had his leg crushed in a collision on the San Jose railroad, that earthquakes may be prevented by pouring paregoric into a rat hole, that the Board of Education has met without a row and the Supervisors without stealing, that Holliday's steamers are safe and comfortable, that Jack Stratman's moustache has grown to its former dimensions during a single swindle, and that H. H. Bancroft & Co. have disposed of a book without selling a customer—we shall be prepared to believe that the color of an Ethiop is optional, that a leopard can dispense with his spots without personal inconvenience, and that a whisky distiller has embraced one of the cardinal virtues—the virtue quietly submitting.

—— We have reliable information that on some of these fine evenings a fiendish attempt will be made to burn all the barrels and dry-goods boxes along the city front, thousands of which now repose in fancied security upon the sidewalks in that quarter. The diabolical arson is to break out simultaneously in one hundred and twenty places between North Point and the Pacific Mail Company's wharf, and will be continued loosely and miscellaneously as far up as Montgomery and Second streets. The parties engaged in this enterprise are among our most public spirited and respectable citizens, and it behooves the police and barrel-holders to be on their guard to frustrate the base conspiracy against our inherent right of obstruction. If the hellish plot is consummated, we shall expose the names of the incendiaries as soon as they shall have been convicted by a court of competent jurisdiction. As guardian of the public peace it is our duty to do so.

—— The Nicolson pavement is still being laid down upon divers of our streets. Will some one kindly inform us what private arrangement the Supervisors have with the company? Twenty-eight cents per superficial foot leaves a handsome profit, and it is useless to attempt to convince us that it all goes to the contractors. We are, unhappily, so constituted that upon this question and that of the cubical figure of the earth we are not open to conviction. We suggest that the Board look in the Book of Revelations. They will find an authentic account of a pavement which has been tried with gratifying success in the New Jerusalem. It costs more to lay it down, but it would be considerably cheaper in the end. Let a contract be made with Gen. LaGrange, of the Mint, to supply us with enough "fine bars" to pave Montgomery street as an experiment. The trouble is that the police would steal the blocks faster than they could be laid down.

—— It has been discovered that for the last eight or ten years frauds have been going on in the Methodist Book concern, amounting to several hundred thousand dollars. This mammoth conversion machine will never be decently managed until the elect are all turned out, and it passes into the hands of secular thieves who have sense enough to cover up their rascalities with something more opaque than the cloak of religion. That venerable and threadbare garment is rapidly falling into disgrace, and the day is not far distant when if upon the translation of a saint his mantle shall descend on the shoulders of his successor it will be incontinently cast off into the dust, and no one will touch it with a ten-foot pole. Even now it has become so disreputable a toggery that the *Town Crier* is almost ashamed to be seen with it on for any considerable length of time. *Cæteris paribus* he prefers to serve the devil in his own proper livery.

—— Puseyites and Ritualists have been wittily and felicitously compared to boys knocking at the door of a Roman Catholic Church, and then like cowards running away before giving time to any one to come and see who is there. It appears that one of these runaways, conscious of having been seen at these pranks, pretends to put a bold face on the matter, and as he learns there is going to be a jolly time at the Ecumenical meeting at Rome, asks his Holiness to be allowed to take a hand in it. His Holiness, however, knowing the character of the man, reminds him that it is a family party, and that he is notoriously a breeder of dissension in his own sect, snubs him by plainly telling him he wants no such people to destroy the harmony of the meeting. If such fellows as these were placed at the mouths of the canons of the church and spiritually blown to atoms, as the less culpable Indian mutineers were corporeally by the cannons of the British army, it would serve the treacherous, cowardly miscreants, right.

—— The Christian Association have begun a course of weekly lectures for young men. This is very commendable, but they have foolishly decided to have them delivered on Sunday evenings when the fellows are all at billiards. The plan resembles the members of the association—it won't work. We counsel everybody to attend, but it will be very silly to do so. There are better things in this life than these lectures. One should have his mind centered on the things that appertain unto a good time, and not go about drifting aimlessly into lecture rooms, when he does not know how soon he may be called upon to play the leading part in a funeral. Many a man has passed out of the lecture room into the lake of fire and brimstone, and never come back any more. Young men, beware!

—— Among the delegates to the Grand Lodge of Odd Fellows are Joshua Maris, of Delaware, and Hugh Latham, of Virginia. Both these gentlemen are Past Great Incohonees of the Improved Order of Red Men, the highest official position known to that order. Both are talented and eloquent speakers.—*Bulletin*. [There must be some mistake here: Incohonees are among the most intelligent of the brute creation, and are remarkably imitative in their habits, but we have never learned that they had been taught to articulate words. Buffon expressly states that the ingenuity of man has been completely baffled in the vain attempt to confer speech upon the lower quadrumana.

—— On Sunday afternoon the Oakland Society of Inquiry (not Iniquity as reported by the *Bulletin*) met and debated the question, "Does public discussion of religious topics by the laity promote the interests of Christianity?" The *Town Crier* does not propose to eternally adjust this question by taking either side, but would modestly remark that the kind of religious discussion in vogue with the Oaklanders tends to promote nothing so much as violent cranial dissolution and the general handiness of brick-bats. The latter essential adjuncts of Oakland logic have had their sphere of usefulness very much extended by these religious debates.

—— We would respectably urge upon the Chief of Police that previously to incarcerating Chinamen in the City Prison they be turned over to the unchecked license of the nearest Irish crowd. They have lately adopted the extremely disagreeable fashion of hanging themselves by their pigtails, in preference to manfully facing the music of Judge Provines, and the treatment suggested would deprive them of the means of evading justice; their tails would be incontinently removed. If the heads should happen also to be plucked away, it would save court expenses, and be a graceful concession to the Judge's political supporters.

—— The *Herald*, game to the last, emits the following truculent advice to its poor inoffensive and long suffering readers, who do not know enough to keep from under the hoofs of horses and the wheels of swill-carts: "Let every man, in defence of life and limb, carry a good serviceable revolver, and on the first attempt to ride or drive over him, shoot down mercilessly the aggressor. Let a general Revolver Club be organized, and let numerous examples be made. Take no prisoners." The *Herald's* readers will at least avail themselves of one part of this advice. They will take no prisoners.

—— An Episcopal clergyman in New York is endeavoring to prove that there are no essential points of difference between the Catholic and Protestant churches. Nor is there; except in the trifling matter of doctrine. Up to date, however, the Protestants are ahead in the number of their killed and wounded. But there is no telling how the score will stand a hundred years hence. Both are exceedingly enterprising concerns, and when politics give out we may confidently expect lively times again.

—— On last Sunday St. Bridget's Church was dedicated with a solemnity befitting the occasion. St. Biddy herself was not present; a previous engagement had made her too sick to attend. Her place was supplied by a chamber-maid from one of the literary weeklies, who fulfilled the arduous and responsible duties of her position to the unspeakable satisfaction of the reporters. The church will be dedicated weekly until further notice. For gentlemen only; consequently, seats free—of sitters.

—— A very important case has just been decided by Judge Hoffman. It was entitled "The United States *vs.* Thirty-six Empty Casks." It is gratifying to our national pride to know that the casks were ignominiously beaten and condemned to be sold into slavery. We trust this may prove a warning to all empty vessels disposed to buck against the land of the brave and the home of the free. [Music—*Our Country 'tis of thee!*

—— The *Bulletin's* reporter makes merry over the luxuriant head of hair adorning a lady he saw at the Mechanics' Pavilion. It will be comforting for him to know that he was himself not unobserved by the lady in question. In our presence she spoke admiringly of his luxuriant growth of nose, and sympathizingly of his deficient head of brains. She and we mingled our tears over this palpable mistake of Nature.

—— Is President Grant to be allowed to plunge this country into a war with Spain for the mere gratification of his personal taste? It is plain as a pike staff: Grant wants Cuba for the United States in order that he may get cheap cigars. But we won't have it. As Hamlet very properly observes, "What's a Cuba to him or he to a Cuba that he should weep for her?" There'll be no war; it will all end in smoke.

—— In the case of Franetti *vs.* Herzo, it has been decided that the money value of an eye is $14,000. Gad! we'd sell ours for half the money if the purchaser would agree not to remove them from the premises, but expend a few hundreds in improvements, so as to increase the value of the adjoining nose—which we expect soon to have bitten off by Michael Fennell, or some other dissatisfied admirer.

—— The President of the Western Union Telegraph Company is coming to California per Pacific Rail. He will be entertained by the *Herald* if they both live long enough to meet. It will be a touching spectacle to behold Messrs. Orton and Nugent falling upon one another's neck and weeping; and then proceeding amicably to kill somebody else's fatted calf.

—— The *Call* says that at twenty-two John G. Saxe could "write poetry, engrave, take plaster casts, make speeches extempore, tell you stories all night long, and put out your fire with tobacco juice." If he will agree to operate in his last named specialty upon the poetic fire in the bosom of the editor of the *Call*, we will furnish the tobacco for the occasion.

—— A man named Martin has been declared insane for threatening to kill his wife. The Commissioners of Lunacy can secure another just such maniac by lurking about the *Town Crier's* humble roof when that gentleman's estimable spouse shows premonitory symptoms of attending Dr. Stone's church.

—— The *Barnacle* asks if we are a civilized people? If the gentlemen of that institution have any doubts, we beg they will confine them to themselves. We feel all right as regards ourselves, and are quite willing to allow our neighbors the benefit of the doubt.

—— The best bond is a man's unsullied reputation.—*Call*. [Yes, but how the deuce can he have one in a city that boasts six daily newspapers, averaging three columns of local matter each? The thing is impossible.

—— Some young Parisians have set the example of wearing bracelets.—*Exchange*. [A great many young San Franciscans have followed it under the admirable tutelage of Chief Crowley.

—— San Leandro is boasting about a sixteen-feet stalk of corn. Oakland, however, produces the longest ears that are grown in the State. *Vide* the first native you meet.

—— The *Times* continues to imitate our Telegraphic Dottings. If we cared as little for our readers as they for us, we should imitate the *Times* editorials.

—— The Great Incohonee is the title of one of the Chiefs of the Order of Red Men. As *in* is a negative prefix, in what kind of a fix is this individual?

—— A morning cotemporary says he does not believe in the report of the cattle disease in Texas—that it is all rot. How very like that paper.

recording his observations in meticulously drawn maps.

Meanwhile he had acquired a lady love, Miss Bernie Wright, whom he called Tima. But his love appeared not to be reciprocated, as he confirmed in the summer of 1864 when he returned to Warsaw to recuperate from a head wound which almost took his life—the result of a sharpshooter's bullet at Kennesaw Mountain. In September he rejoined the Union forces in time to fight for possession of Nashville. Following that campaign his unit retired to Alabama, where Bierce requested discharge. It was granted on 16 January 1865, and Bierce ended nearly four years of military service—wounded in battle, cited for bravery, and filled with images of war that were to remain with him for the rest of his life. It was an experience which matured him and inspired him to his greatest literary efforts, an experience which he would recall with pride and nostalgia. And it was an experience which he attempted to relive many years later, when his literary life was drawing to a close.

But in 1865 that life was still before him. Meanwhile he earned his living as a special agent for the Federal Treasury Department, working out of Selma, Alabama, trying to confiscate cotton which ostensibly belonged to the Confederate government but which private cotton growers were attempting to reclaim. It was a situation fraught with jeopardy, and distasteful as well to the honest Bierce, who refused to take advantage of the opportunities for personal profit.

His old unit demobilized in October 1865, and Bierce's revered former commanding officer, General Hazen, offered him a captain's rank if he would join Hazen's Western expedition as an engineering attaché. Bierce promptly accepted and joined the small detachment in July at Omaha. From then until November the group made its way across the wilds of Nebraska, through Montana, Idaho, Utah, Nevada, and into California, arriving finally in San Francisco, where Bierce found that his expected captaincy was in fact a proffered commission as a second lieutenant. He rejected the offer in disgust and left Hazen's inspection tour to remain in California.

It is not clear when he first formed the notion that he might be a writer; but shortly after he took up residence in San Francisco and began supporting himself as a watchman at the mint, he tried his hand at poems and essays which he offered to the local media. The *Californian* accepted his poem "Basilica" for its edition of 21 September 1867, and thus encouraged, he began submitting elsewhere as

well. Bierce succeeded so well as a free-lancer that by the middle of 1868 he was invited to join the staff of the *News Letter*; by December, he was its editor. As editor he began writing a column called "The Town Crier" and acquiring a reputation for epigrammatic wit. He continued to contribute to other journals, including the *Overland Monthly*, edited by Bret Harte. It was this magazine which published his first short story, "The Haunted Valley," in July 1871.

During this period of early literary and journalistic success he met Mary Ellen ("Mollie") Day, who became his wife on Christmas Day 1871. It was a match her mother apparently sought to discourage; but Capt. Holland Hines Day, a mine owner, was more receptive toward his acerbic prospective son-in-law and provided the wherewithal for a honeymoon in England.

Thus began another episode in Ambrose Bierce's life: a three-year exile as an expatriate litterateur. Some of his work had reached the shores of the mother country already, and Bierce found it not too difficult to break into print. Before long he was penning paragraphs for *Figaro* and for *Fun*, and betweentimes he was collecting and editing his older pieces for *The Fiend's Delight*, which was published in 1873 under the pseudonym of Dod Grile. The rather odd pen name apparently was constructed from the name of Douglas Jerrold (1803-1857), whose play *Ambrose Gwinett; or, A Sea-side Story* had been the source of Bierce's given name. That same year Bierce's second book, *Nuggets and Dust*, appeared under the same pseudonym, and in 1874 *Cobwebs from an Empty Skull* was published with the name of Dod Grile on the title page. Both were collections of previously published writings.

His personal life was becoming somewhat more complicated: a son, Day, was born in December 1872, and Mollie's mother arrived the following summer for an extended visit. In April 1874 another son, Leigh, was born, and shortly thereafter Mrs. Day returned to San Francisco. In just under a year Mollie followed her, taking Day and Leigh along. She was already pregnant with their third child, although Bierce had not been told. Upon learning that his family was about to be blessed with an addition, he took leave of England, though it is apparent that under different circumstances he would have remained.

Thus Ambrose Bierce found himself faced with the necessity of beginning still another career to support Mollie, Day, Leigh, and Helen, who was born in October 1875. He became associate editor of a weekly newspaper called the *Argonaut* and began a column at first entitled "Prattler," later renamed "Prattle," modeled somewhat on the old "Town Crier." Bierce also collaborated with T. A. Harcourt on an elaborate literary hoax published in book form as *The Dance of Death* (1877). Purporting to be an attack on the libidinous qualities of the waltz, it was in fact a sensuous depiction of them, as in this passage, which describes a couple "knit and growing" to one another: "He is stalwart, agile, mighty; she is tall, supple, lithe, and how beautiful in form and feature! Her head rests upon his shoulder, her face is upturned to his; her naked arm is almost around his neck; her swelling breast heaves tumultuously against his; face to face they whirl, his limbs interwoven with her limbs; with strong right arm about her yielding waist, he presses her to him till every curve in the contour of her lovely body thrills with the amorous contact. Her eyes look into his, but she sees nothing; the soft music fills the room, but she hears nothing; swiftly he whirls her from the floor or bends her frail body to and fro in his embrace, but she knows it not; his hot breath is upon her hair, his lips almost touch her forehead, yet she does not shrink; his eyes, gleaming with a fierce intolerable lust, gloat satyrlike over her, yet she does not quail; she is filled with a rapture divine in its intensity—she is in the maelstrom of burning desire—her spirit is with the gods." The book was published under the name William Herman, and Bierce elaborated on the hoax in his column by castigating the supposed author and his book, which Bierce termed a "sustained orgasm." It was a commercial success, assisted by the comments of those who found the author prudish as well as those who found his strictures morally uplifting.

But Bierce was not satisfied with his work on the *Argonaut* or with his future there, and he was already contemplating a new career: gold prospector. Bierce became general agent of the Black Hills Placer Mining Company, in charge of completing a flume which would bring water from Spring Creek to Rockerville, near Deadwood in Dakota Territory. He arrived in June 1880 to find the project in disarray, its management structure confused. Finding he could not clarify his authority, he abandoned his efforts and returned to San Francisco in January 1881.

Bierce resumed his "Prattle" column, but not for the *Argonaut*; rather he became editor of the weekly *Wasp*, and in its pages he began in earnest his "Devil's Dictionary," a series of cynical, sometimes misanthropic definitions eventually collected in *The Cynic's Word Book* (1906). Some examples:

ABSURDITY, n. A statement or belief man-

ifestly inconsistent with one's own opinion.

ALONE, adj. In bad company.

BIRTH, n. The first and direst of all disasters.

BORE, n. A person who talks when you wish him to listen.

DIPLOMACY, n. The patriotic art of lying for one's country.

FIDELITY, n. A virtue peculiar to those who are about to be betrayed.

GRAVE, n. A place in which the dead are laid to await the coming of the medical student.

IMMORAL, adj. Inexpedient.

LAWYER, n. One skilled in circumvention of the law.

LITIGATION, n. A machine which you go into as a pig and come out of as a sausage.

NOVEMBER, n. The eleventh twelfth of a weariness.

OPTIMIST, n. A proponent of the doctrine that black is white.

PEACE, n. In international affairs, a period of cheating between two periods of fighting.

PHYSICIAN, n. One upon whom we set our hopes when ill and our dogs when well.

POLITENESS, n. The most acceptable hypocrisy.

PRUDE, n. A bawd hiding behind the back of her demeanor.

RASH, adj. Insensible to the value of our advice.

REPORTER, n. A writer who guesses his way to the truth and dispels it with a tempest of words.

SAINT, n. A dead sinner revised and edited.

SUCCESS, n. The one unpardonable sin against one's fellows.

TRUTHFUL, adj. Dumb and illiterate.

ZEAL, n. A certain nervous disorder afflicting the young and inexperienced.

In 1911 Bierce revised his diabolical lexicon, added ninety-four words, and published it as volume seven of his *Collected Works* (1909-1912). In the eighty-odd years since then, Bierce's misanthropic contribution to linguistic history has achieved a separate life in a variety of popular editions and in one scholarly edition, the *Enlarged Devil's Dictionary* (1967), edited by Ernest J. Hopkins. Hopkins discovered that Bierce had omitted some 850 words from the version in *Collected Works*—some through inadvertence, some presumably because the only copies were in San Francisco newspaper files, while he was editing his manuscripts in Washington. In any event, the dictionary is the work by which Bierce is often remembered, and its cynicism is the disposition which Bierce is often perceived to exhibit. But during his editorship of the *Wasp* from 1881 to 1886, the "Devil's Dictionary" was simply a satiric tool with which to amuse his readers and discombobulate his targets. And many were stung by the satire of the man who signed himself A. G. Bierce—leading one reader to speculate that the initials stood for "Almighty God."

Abuse was not the sole note he sounded in the pages of the *Wasp*. In them he published his reminiscence of Shiloh, signaling his nostalgic interest in the Civil War—a nostalgia that lasted until his death. "And this was, O so long ago!," he wrote in "What I Saw of Shiloh": "How they come back to me—dimly and brokenly, but with what a magic spell—those years of youth when I was soldiering! Again I hear the far warble of blown bugles. Again I see the tall, blue smoke of camp-fires ascending from the dim valleys of Wonderland. There steals upon my sense the ghost of an odor from pines that canopy the ambuscade. I feel upon my cheek the morning mist that shrouds the hostile camp unaware of its doom, and my blood stirs at the ringing rifle-shot of the solitary sentinel. . . . O days when all the world was beautiful and strange; when unfamiliar constellations burned in the Southern midnights, and the mocking-bird poured out his heart in the moon-gilded magnolia; when there was something new under a new sun; will your fine, far memories ever cease to lay contrasting pictures athwart the harsher features of this later world, accentuating the ugliness of the longer and tamer life?"

The *Wasp* had provided Bierce with a vehicle to express wrath and reminiscence. But when the paper was sold in 1886, he was forced once more to enter a new phase in his career. His enforced departure from the *Wasp* turned out to be a fortuitous circumstance, however; William Randolph Hearst was then building the staff of the *San Francisco Examiner*, and he was eager to hire the man whose "Prattle" had become the talk of the town. In March 1887 Bierce began writing a column for the *Examiner*. His association with Hearst was to continue for over twenty years in a rather rocky relationship which found Bierce resigning from time to time, only to be rehired once his affronted dignity had been restored—usually by Hearst himself. The association found Bierce writing also for the *New York Journal* and, later, *Cosmopolitan* as well. His columns were of the same nature as before: censure,

Caricature of Bierce in the Wasp *in the early 1890s, when Bierce was no longer with the journal*

abuse, and satire. At the same time, he was entering a period of literary creativity during which he produced short stories of Civil War adventures almost certainly autobiographical. *Tales of Soldiers and Civilians* appeared in 1892, and it contains his best work. Among the stories published there are "A Horseman in the Sky," "An Occurrence at Owl Creek Bridge," and "Chickamauga." Many of the stories in the collection appeared first in the pages of the *Examiner*. Bierce's reputation rests more on the short stories than on the wit of his *Devil's Dictionary*, although that has achieved long-lasting fame. Three of his stories have been produced as films: "An Occurrence at Owl Creek Bridge," "Chickamauga," and "The Mocking Bird." The first of these won the Short Film Grand Prix at the Cannes Film Festival in 1962 and an Academy Award as the Best Live-Action Short Subject in 1963; the following year it was shown on CBS network television. The film was produced without dialogue and preserves the bitter irony of the short story as Bierce wrote it. It is the story of Peyton Farquhar, a well-to-do Alabama planter and slave owner about to be hanged by Federal troops from the cross timbers of the Owl Creek Bridge. As he awaits his fate—apparently sentenced to death for attempted sabotage of the recently repaired bridge—his terrified mind recalls his wife and children, and the agony of his loss distorts his sense perception so that time itself seems stopped. At that instant Farquhar falls, the rope breaks, and he plunges into pain, darkness, and water. Loosing his bonds, he swims quickly away from the troops, who are firing at will. The current swirls him downstream and onto a sandy spit of land. Rising, he begins running for the sanctuary of his home and the arms of his wife, who stands waiting with a smile of ineffable joy. Peyton Farquhar reaches out to clasp his beloved, but he is wrenched violently backward away from her as his neck is broken by the hangman's rope, and he is left dangling from Owl Creek Bridge. His escape was a fantasy that flashed through his mind as he fell through space.

Two other books appeared in 1892. *The Monk and the Hangman's Daughter* was coauthored with Dr. Gustav Adolph Danziger, who had translated it from the German for Bierce to polish into English. Danziger was to become entangled with Bierce in a kind of love-hate relationship, as they quarreled over the copyright to that book as well as over other matters. Danziger's biography of his friend Bierce, published in 1929 under the name Adolphe de Castro, remains an important source of information despite its self-centered perceptions. *Black Beetles in Amber* is a collection of satirical verse. Bierce was a failed poet, but he recognized his limitations; hence his verse sounds mightily like his prose, as in this couplet from "The New Decalogue":

> Kiss not thy neighbor's wife. Of course
> There's no objection to divorce.

Or the first stanza of "A Rational Anthem":

> My country, 'tis of thee,
> Sweet land of felony,
>   Of thee I sing—
> Land where my fathers fried
> Young witches and applied
> Whips to the Quaker's hide
>   And made him spring.

This period of increased literary activity was also for Bierce a period of personal crisis. In 1888 he left his wife, angry that she had accepted letters from a male admirer, and in 1889 his son Day was killed as the result of a gun duel over a lady whose affections both men aspired to enjoy. (Neither did, as both died in the dispute.) Day was only sixteen.

In 1893 still another collection of Bierce's short stories was published. *Can Such Things Be?* is a ghostly series which depends for its effect in part on psychology, in part on fantasy. One story, entitled

"A Resumed Identity," was suggested by Bierce's own experience in the Civil War as a member of Hazen's Brigade and by his return years later to the scene of a battle at Stone River. The stories are generally characterized by Bierce's terse prose, flair for irony, and preoccupation with the macabre.

Hearst dispatched Bierce to Washington in 1896 to fight the good fight against Collis P. Huntington, a railroad tycoon who had borrowed a great deal of money from the government and now was lobbying a bill through Congress which would forgive the debt or reduce it dramatically. Bierce labeled him a "railrogue" and much worse. He commuted between Washington and New York during the campaign, which was published in both the *Examiner* and the *Journal*, and his editorials were thought to have been instrumental in killing the bill. But while Bierce happily joined in the fight against Huntington, he was not inclined to support Hearst's "war" in Cuba, and in a series of articles in Hearst's own newspaper, he opposed United States involvement. It was an unusual relationship between Hearst and his star writer; Hearst apparently was willing to tolerate much.

Bierce's ninth book, *Fantastic Fables*, was published in 1899. It is a collection of pithy tales with morals to be inferred, as in "Deceased and Heirs":

> A Man died leaving a large estate and many sorrowful relations who claimed it. After some years, when all but one had had judgment given against them, that one was awarded the estate, which he asked his Attorney to have appraised.
> "There is nothing to appraise," said the Attorney, pocketing his last fee.
> "Then," said the Successful Claimant, "what good has all this litigation done me?"
> "You have been a good client to me," the Attorney replied, gathering up his books and papers, "but I must say you betray a surprising ignorance of the purpose of litigation."

In late 1899 Bierce moved back to Washington, partly because he wished to be closer to his son Leigh and partly to cover politics for the *New York Journal*. On 4 February 1900, the *Journal* printed a characteristic piece of his work, a quatrain of political commentary:

> The bullet that pierced Goebel's breast
> Can not be found in all the West.
> Good reason: it is speeding here
> To stretch McKinley on his bier.

The verse referred to the assassination of Governor-elect William Goebel of Kentucky and seemed to suggest that President William McKinley—archenemy of Hearst's *Journal*—should be similarly dispatched. The following year President McKinley lay dead—victim of an assassin's bullet. The verse was dredged up and used to attack Hearst himself, as if somehow it was proof of a conspiracy. But Hearst never mentioned to Bierce the trouble his wit had caused.

In the year of McKinley's death, Bierce's son Leigh also died. It was a bitter loss: his two sons dead, his marriage ended, his daughter, Helen, about to marry—Ambrose Bierce's personal life must have seemed devoid of affection. Not that he sought affection, or even deserved it; but his personal relationships seemed to mirror the tenor of his work.

His pain did not deter him from his writing, and in 1903 he brought out his tenth book, *Shapes of Clay*. It was a collection of verses, some written many years before, and it did not meet with instant critical acclaim. One couplet seemed to express his attitude toward critics of his books:

> My! how my fame rings out in ever zone—
> A thousand critics shouting:
> > "He's unknown!"

Still another poem, in a more serious vein, perhaps was written in a moment of self-pity:

> Fear not in any tongue to call
> Upon the Lord—He's skilled in all.
> But if He answereth my plea
> He speaketh one unknown to me.

Self-pity may have been a mood not uncalled-for; in 1905 Mollie finally divorced him, and several months later she died. Although they had been separated for some time, they had remained man and wife. She apparently heard that he wished to be free to remarry, and for that reason filed for divorce. She had once confessed to her daughter, Helen, that she could never love anyone but Bierce; he had once confessed to Helen that Mollie was the only woman he had ever loved; yet apparently they could not confess their mutual love to one another.

Bierce, of course, had his articles and his books to console him. And he had a new outlet for his work: *Cosmopolitan* magazine, which Hearst had recently purchased. He also was preparing for publication that collection of definitions dubbed by the publisher *The Cynic's Word Book*. Bierce much preferred his choice of title: *The Devil's Dictionary*. Not long after publication of his satiric lexicon, a friend, S. O. Howes—with Bierce's permission—began collecting a number of his essays for publication as *The Shadow on the Dial and Other Essays*; it appeared in 1909. Although greeted with hostility, the essays represent some of Bierce's most thoughtful writing, and the prose, as always, is lucid and terse.

Even as Howes was proceeding with that collection of essays, Bierce himself had begun a collection of his works to be published in twelve volumes. Once the project was under way in earnest, he resigned as columnist from *Cosmopolitan*, which had continued to pay his salary long after he had ceased to write for Hearst's newspapers. Thus he ended his association of twenty-two years with William Randolph Hearst. The first two volumes of *The Collected Works of Ambrose Bierce* appeared in 1909; other volumes appeared as they were published until in 1912 the entire set was completed. Thus was his

Bierce, age sixty-nine, with two close friends from the latter part of his life: Carrie Christiansen, his secretary and platonic companion, and Walter Neale, his publisher

opus concluded; the prolific Bierce had completed his life's work.

Once his *Collected Works* had appeared, Bierce visited his daughter, Helen, and made plans for a trip to Mexico. He seemed to have a premonition of his approaching death—or perhaps a wish for it. In a letter to his niece he wrote: "Good-bye—if you hear of my being stood up against a Mexican stone wall and shot to rags please know that I think that a pretty good way to depart this life. It beats old age, disease, or falling down the cellar stairs. To be a Gringo in Mexico—ah, that is euthanasia!"

He left Washington in October, toured the battle areas where he had fought in the Civil War, traveled through New Orleans on his way to Laredo, and crossed the Rio Grande into Mexico. There, as he well knew, the countryside was in the throes of the revolution. His last letter, dated the day after Christmas 1913, states that he expected to leave Chihuahua for Ojinaga the next day. That city, across the Rio Grande from Presidio, Texas, was captured 11 January 1914, following a siege of several days. In all likelihood, Ambrose Bierce died in that battle. He was never heard from again, and his disappearance remains a mystery, despite efforts to track his progress.

Bierce's reputation rests primarily on the coruscating wit of his *Devil's Dictionary* and on the bitter irony of a few short stories. *The Devil's Dictionary*, by which he is best known, has no rival; its multiple editions attest to its continuing life, and it remains the basis for his fame as a humorist. The short stories, especially those drawing upon his Civil War experiences, are carefully crafted tales which depend upon ironic reversal for their impact. They place Bierce in the tradition of literary naturalism, where he suffers by comparison with Stephen Crane and others. The leading Bierce scholar, M. E. Grenander, prefers to regard him as an impressionist because of his concentration on the subjective perceptions of his protagonists and his use of the "epiphany," or moment of sudden awareness, by which his characters come to understand reality.

Bierce was also a poet of some skill, as attested by two volumes of verse in his *Collected Works*. But these efforts can never form the basis for his reputation, for he was essentially just a versifier. Nor can his journalism—by nature ephemeral—justify his niche in literary history. But he was, at the peak of his career, one of the most influential journalists in the United States. His role in arousing public op-

position to and subsequently defeating a bill in Congress which would have forgiven an immense debt owed by railroad magnates to the U.S. government is perhaps the prime example of the power of his column.

Bierce's work places him securely in the traditions of American realism and humor, although clearly on the second level, beneath Mark Twain, Edgar Allan Poe, and Stephen Crane, among others. His journalistic efforts have not received the same critical attention as his short stories and epigrams, but they deserve the kind of scholarly analysis that will preserve his name in the history of American journalism.

Letters:

The Letters of Ambrose Bierce, edited by Bertha Clark Pope (San Francisco: The Book Club of California, 1922).

Bibliography:

Joseph Gaer, ed., *Ambrose Gwinett [sic] Bierce: Bibliography and Biographical Data* (New York: Franklin, 1968).

Biographies:

Adolphe de Castro, *Portrait of Ambrose Bierce* (New York: Century, 1929);

Paul Fatout, *Ambrose Bierce: The Devil's Lexicographer* (Norman: University of Oklahoma Press, 1951);

Richard O'Connor, *Ambrose Bierce: A Biography* (Boston: Little, Brown, 1967).

References:

Cathy N. Davidson, *Critical Essays on Ambrose Bierce* (Boston: Hall, 1982);

M[ary] E[lizabeth] Grenander, *Ambrose Bierce* (Boston: Twayne, 1971);

Stuart C. Woodruff, *The Short Stories of Ambrose Bierce: A Study in Polarity* (Pittsburgh: University of Pittsburgh Press, 1964).

Papers:

Ambrose Bierce's papers may be found at various libraries, including the Huntington Library, San Marino, California; the Library of Congress; Stanford University Libraries; and the American Literature Collection of the University of Southern California.

George W. Childs

(12 May 1829-3 February 1894)

Jacqueline Steck
Temple University

MAJOR POSITION HELD: Owner and publisher, *Philadelphia Public Ledger* (1864-1894).

BOOKS: *Recollections of General Grant* (Philadelphia: Collins, 1885);
Recollections (Philadelphia: Lippincott, 1890).

George William Childs rose from poverty and obscurity to a position of tremendous wealth and influence as owner of the *Philadelphia Public Ledger*. During his ownership, the *Public Ledger* was the "prestige" newspaper in Philadelphia, operating on a news and advertising policy that shunned scandal and sensation. As an employer, Childs implemented many progressive labor practices, including pensions and insurance. He also gained a national and international reputation as a collector and philanthropist.

Almost nothing is known about Childs's early years. Most biographers say he was born 12 May 1829 in Baltimore, Maryland. In his autobiography, *Recollections* (1890), Childs made no reference to his parents or the circumstances of his birth. He may have been an orphan or illegitimate; the latter theory was outlined in an anonymous, unflattering 1873 pamphlet on Childs attributed to his father-in-law and former business partner, Robert Evans Peterson.

Childs said he always had "a rather remarkable aptitude for business," beginning during his school days when he bartered "boyish treasures" with the other students. At the age of eleven, he spent the summer working as an errand boy in a Baltimore bookstore, earning $2 a week. He wrote: "And I enjoyed it. I have never been out of employment; always found something to do, and was always eager to do it, and I think I earned every cent of my first money."

At thirteen, he joined the U.S. Navy and spent fifteen months based at Norfolk, Virginia, as an apprentice on the *Pennsylvania*. He disliked navy life, however, and went back to Baltimore for a little more schooling. In 1844, he moved to Philadelphia. A child of fourteen, he arrived in the city with no friends, no family, no job, and no money. But he was smart, ambitious, full of energy, and willing to

work. He got a job as a clerk and errand boy in the bookstore of Peter Thomson at the corner of Sixth and Arch Streets, where he worked from morning to night for $3 a week. He began going to book auctions with Thomson in the evenings, learning the business and eventually buying valuable titles at cheap rates. "In this way I assisted Mr. Thomson for four years; his business kept increasing," Childs wrote. As the store owner's representative, Childs traveled to Boston and New York for book trade sales and at the ages of sixteen and seventeen got to know the leading figures in American publishing, including the Harpers and the Lippincotts.

When he was eighteen, Childs decided to go

into business for himself, and he opened a small store in the old *Public Ledger* building at Third and Chestnut Streets. Childs's autobiography does not say what kind of store it was, but it is believed he sold such items as cigars and patent medicines. The business was successful, but he aspired to greater things: his friends said he used to boast that one day he would own the *Public Ledger*. He later wrote: "If this is true, and doubtless it is, I do not seem to have over-reached myself at that early age."

In 1850, he joined the publishing firm of R. E. Peterson Company, which in 1854 changed its name to Childs and Peterson. The firm experienced considerable success, most of it attributed to Childs. Best-sellers produced by the publishing house included Dr. Austin Allibone's three-volume *Critical Dictionary of English Literature and British and American Authors* (1858), which was dedicated to Childs, and Dr. Elisha Kent Kane's *Arctic Explorations* (1856), which earned $70,000 in royalties for its author. Childs said he was the person who convinced Kane to write a popular book rather than a strict scientific account that would have less general interest. (Kane did not have much chance to enjoy his royalties: he died in 1857.)

The publisher's autobiography is silent on his personal and business dealings with Peterson. But the anonymous pamphlet attributed to Peterson contains a bitter attack on the younger man. The pamphlet suggests that Childs deceived Peterson into selling his share of the business in 1860. Peterson also grew to regret his generosity in taking Childs into his home and treating him like one of the family; the pamphlet quotes proverbs such as: "Bring not every man into thine house; for the deceitful man has many trains" and "Receive a stranger into thine house, and he will disturb thee and turn thee out of thine own." It concludes with a quote from Scots poet Robert Burns: "Lord! A louse, sir, is still a louse, / Though it crawl on the curls of a queen."

At some point during this time, Childs married Emma Bouvier Peterson, his partner's daughter and the granddaughter of Judge John Bouvier. Little is known about their relationship, except that they had no children and loved to entertain guests. Childs makes only passing reference to his wife in his *Recollections*.

Childs ran the publishing business alone until 1862, when he went into a brief partnership with J. B. Lippincott. The anonymous pamphlet suggests that Childs undercut Lippincott on a deal and this was the reason the partnership ended. Childs gives no details, but writes with genuine affection

and respect about the way Lippincott carried on after Childs left the book publishing business in 1863. That year, Childs founded the *American Publishers' Circular and Literary Gazette*, which he continued to publish until 1879. In 1864, he saw an opportunity to realize his long-standing dream of owning the great newspaper that had provided shelter for his humble business: the *Public Ledger* was in trouble, and Childs believed he could buy it.

The *Ledger* had been founded in 1836 by William M. Swain, Arunah S. Abell, and Azariah H. Simmons in the original wave of "penny papers" that spread from New York in the 1830s. In its early days, it was a cleaned-up version of the *New York Herald*—full of sensational news, but without the extreme bad taste that often characterized the *Herald*. Within two years of its founding, the *Ledger* was printing more than 20,000 copies a day, and its popularity continued to grow steadily. But by 1864, there was trouble: Simmons had died, and the Civil War paper shortage had inflated production costs. "To all appearances it was as prosperous as ever," Childs wrote, but the paper was losing about $3,000 a week, and the financial crisis was straining the partnership of Swain and Abell. Childs thought the biggest problem was that the owners were selling the paper at too low a price per issue. "They seemed to regard the past prosperity of the *Ledger* as due alone to its selling for a penny. They forgot that in 1864, the purchasing power of a penny was not what it was before the war. Cheapness, indeed, was a vital feature of the journal; but to sell the *Public Ledger* for a penny was to half give it away." Childs approached the owners to see if they were interested in selling. Abell, who was running the *Baltimore Sun*, agreed immediately; but it took a little longer to convince Swain, who had been in charge of the Philadelphia paper. On 3 December 1864 George W. Childs became proprietor of the *Public Ledger* for a purchase price of slightly more than its annual loss, then estimated at $150,000. Most of the money actually came from banker Anthony J. Drexel, Childs's closest friend, who became a silent partner in the *Ledger*. (When it became apparent that Childs would have no children, Drexel named his youngest son George W. Childs Drexel, to ensure that the publisher's name would be carried on. Ironically, that son also died without issue.)

A week after taking over the paper, Childs announced "two simple but radical changes": he doubled the price per copy and raised advertising rates to a profitable level. The paper experienced a sudden drop in both circulation and advertising, but customers were soon won back. Childs explained: "The *Ledger* was already an 'institution' of the city: for twenty years it had been the established medium of communication between employers and employed, between buyers and sellers, landlords and tenants, bereaved families and their friends. To very many people, it was a necessity."

The publisher, who was aided for the next twenty-five years by editor in chief William V. Mc-Kean, also instituted a new policy for news copy and advertising. He decided that the pages of the *Ledger* should be suitable reading for the entire family. The paper would not print scandal, sensation, or stories of vice and passion. The content of advertisements was also screened to ensure there was nothing in them that might be considered offensive; ads that did not live up to the standard set by Childs and McKean were rejected.

Childs took a very personal interest in his paper. "For several years, I seldom left the editorial rooms before midnight, averaging from 12 to 14 hours a day in the office. I strove to elevate its tone, and think I succeeded." He also elevated its circulation: in 1876, the *Ledger* was printing 90,000 copies a day, and although the new *Philadelphia Record* eventually took over as circulation leader in the morning market, the *Public Ledger* remained on top in respectability and prestige. Childs published only six days a week, resisting all suggestions that the paper could profit from a Sunday edition. He also published a popular *Public Ledger Almanac*, distributed free of charge each year to subscribers.

As soon as Childs purchased the newspaper, he began looking for a new headquarters. He found a suitable spot at Sixth and Chestnut Streets, where for a price of $500,000 he erected the new *Public Ledger* building. Again, Drexel bankrolled much of the enterprise. The building, a handsome structure that still stands, was opened 20 June 1867 with considerable fanfare. According to a commemorative book Childs published to record the event, the elite of Philadelphia turned out to tour the plant. The celebration continued with a lavish banquet for 500 guests.

McKean, who spoke at the opening, said Childs had three goals in mind in the construction of the new building: he wanted it to be an efficient printing plant, a pleasant and wholesome place to work, and an ornament to the city. The composing room, pressroom, and reporters' room were carefully warmed, ventilated, and lit. There were well-ventilated bathrooms for the workers, "who avail themselves freely of the privilege afforded them." Richard T. Ely, a Johns Hopkins professor of political economy, in an article published in *Recollections*

extolling the publisher's virtues as an employer, described the work place: "He furnishes the most cheerful, wholesome, often luxurious rooms for the entire working force of the *Ledger*, and in the printers' apartment he has not even forgotten to use those colors on the walls which are least trying to their heavily-taxed eyes."

Childs was known as a progressive employer and was popular with his employees, particularly the typographers. He paid good wages, often higher than union scales. Feminist leader Elizabeth Cady Stanton praised him for hiring women in his printing plant and paying them the same wages as men. He also instituted a pension plan, life insurance, vacations with pay, and Christmas bonuses. He hosted banquets for the ragged crew of *Public Ledger* newsboys on Christmas and Independence Day. In 1867, he was made an honorary member of the Philadelphia Typographical Society. A year later, he gave the union a large, enclosed plot of ground in Woodlands Cemetery near Philadelphia to serve as a printers' burial place. A speaker at the dedication ceremony said Childs's employment practices took care of workers during their careers, his insurance policies took care of their families after their deaths, "and even then he does not desert them—he provides this beautiful and magnificent burial-lot for the repose of their lifeless bodies."

In 1876, the International Typographical Union (ITU) lowered its rates for typesetting. A delegation of *Public Ledger* typographers went to see Childs about a possible pay cut. According to Ely, the union was willing to have its rates lowered from 45 cents per thousand ems to 40 cents, the new ITU rate. But Childs, who was making a lot of money from the newspaper, said he could see no reason why wages should be cut and continued paying his workers at the old rate, a gesture which cost the publisher several thousand dollars a year. Ten years later, in 1886, Childs and Drexel each gave the International Typographical Union $5,000, which was used to start a union fund named after them. The union's newspaper, the *Craftsman*, tried to bring Childs forward as a candidate for president of the United States in the 1888 campaign; in its 25 February 1888 issue, the paper said: "George W. Childs before the people! It is too good to be true." The idea gained some support, particularly in newspaper circles, but Childs decided not to run. Philadelphia typographers honored Childs on his fifty-ninth birthday with a testimonial banquet at Dooner's Hotel on 12 May 1888. Guests included members of Congress and representatives of the printing and publishing industries.

Physically, Childs was short—only five feet, seven inches in height—somewhat rotund, florid of face, and balding. But his features were regular, and he was not unattractive. The *American Phrenological Journal*, in an analysis of the shape of his head, pronounced him "a manly man." His biographer describes him as modest, but this is open to some question. Like many nineteenth-century newspaper owners, he engaged in a great deal of self-promotion: he printed favorable comments about himself and his newspaper in the pages of the *Public Ledger*, and he seemed to enjoy producing pamphlets or books to commemorate events in the *Ledger*'s history or in his life as a philanthropist. His autobiography could hardly be described as self-effacing: the chapters he wrote contain clear recognition of his talents, while the article about his relations with employees is almost fawning in tone.

The publisher owned a city house at Twenty-first and Walnut Streets, a "country home" named Wootton in nearby Bryn Mawr, and "a handsome cottage" on Long Island. He loved to rub shoulders with the rich and famous, and much of his autobiography is taken up by accounts of his encounters with prominent Americans and Europeans. He met General U. S. Grant in 1863, and the two men became close friends. In 1885, Childs wrote a lengthy article, "Recollections of General Grant," for a biography of the Civil War hero who became president. Two chapters of Childs's autobiography deal with Grant, "one of the truest and most congenial friends I ever had." Henry Wadsworth Longfellow and Charles Dickens were also close friends. Childs gained fame at home and abroad for the parties he gave; the guest list for a reception for Dom Pedro II, Emperor of Brazil (later deposed), had 600 names, and a note in his autobiography describes the party as "perhaps the most notable gathering of people ever assembled in any private house in America." The list of guests who visited Childs's homes through the years is indeed impressive. It includes Presidents Hayes, Arthur, and Cleveland; Generals Grant, Sherman, Meade, Sheridan, Hancock, McDowell, and Patterson; Chief Justice Waite; various Drexels, Astors, Cadwaladers, and Vanderbilts; Thomas A. Edison; Andrew Carnegie; Charlotte Cushman; the duke and duchess of Buckingham; the duke of Newcastle; the duke of Sutherland; Lords Dufferin, Rosebery, Houghton, Ilchester, Ross, Iddesleigh, Rayleigh, Herschell, Caithness, and Dunraven. Other guests ranged from Oscar Wilde to Bishop Doane, from Helena Modjeska to Henry Irving, from Herbert Spencer to Walt Whitman.

The interest in rare books and manuscripts Childs had acquired as a clerk attending book sales with Thomson continued throughout his life, and he collected a large and valuable library. His "treasures" included an eclectic assortment of manuscripts, ranging from a 17 May 1703 handwritten sermon by Cotton Mather to the seventeen-page manuscript for Edgar Allan Poe's "Murders in the Rue Morgue." The 1841 Poe manuscript had quite a history, Childs wrote: it was rescued from the rubbish heap twice and survived three fires before finding its way into the library of the publisher. Childs's collection also included two volumes from Charles Dickens's personal library and an array of poems, letters, and manuscripts by Burns, Swift, Longfellow, Bryant, Holmes, Tennyson, Pepys, Pope, Shelley, Keats, Voltaire, Irving, and Goethe. One of his favorite collections was a folio of portraits and autographs of every president of the United States from Washington to Harrison. "Eight of the letters are personal ones from the various presidents to myself," he wrote proudly. Childs gave much of his collection to the Drexel Institute (now University) when it opened in 1892; other possessions of the publisher went to the school after his death. Most of the more valuable manuscripts, including the Poe story, have since been sold; but Drexel University still has many of Childs's things, including a valuable Rittenhouse clock.

The publisher was known as a philanthropist as well as a collector. In Philadelphia, where his newspaper called for many social and civic reforms, he worked to secure Fairmount Park, now one of the city's most attractive features. He was also one of the founders of—and major contributors to—the Zoological Garden, the Pennsylvania Museum, and the School of Industrial Arts of Philadelphia. In 1887, President Cleveland appointed him a member of the board of visitors to the West Point military academy. At a board meeting that June, General Sheridan asked Childs about a portrait of General Grant the publisher had presented to the academy. "So we went down and saw the portrait, one nearly of full length," Childs wrote later. "Sheridan admired it very much; and I turned to him and said, 'Now, general, if I outlive you I will have your portrait painted to hang alongside of Grant's.' So it came about." Childs also had General Sherman painted, and the three portraits were formally presented to the United States government on 3 October 1889.

Childs donated money for several monuments in Britain, including an elaborate Shakespeare memorial fountain in Stratford-upon-Avon. The fountain, sixty feet tall and elaborately decorated, was given as "the gift of an American citizen to the town of Shakespeare in the Jubilee Year of Queen Victoria." It was dedicated 17 October 1887 in an impressive ceremony led by the actor Henry Irving. The Stratford-upon-Avon *Herald* reported: "All things combined to give *éclat* to the important event of Monday last—the inauguration of the handsome fountain given by Mr. Childs, of Philadelphia. . . . [Irving] was studiously brief, but what a large amount of feeling and meaning his few words contained! The inaugural speech over, the water was turned on, and the fountain was dedicated to the public forever. Cheers followed the announcement, and the formal ceremony soon came to an end. . . . There were mutual congratulations: common praise of Mr. Childs's magnificent gift, of the architect's skill and taste, of the builder's sound workmanship. The whole proceedings were happily conceived and successfully carried out."

Childs also gave Westminster Abbey in London a memorial window honoring the poets Herbert and Cowper in 1877. A window honoring Milton was given to St. Margaret's, Westminster, in 1888. Childs gave the Church of St. Thomas in Winchester a reredos in memory of Bishops Launcelot, Andrews, and Ken, and he was the largest contributor to a memorial window for the Irish poet Thomas Moore in the church of Bromham, England.

Despite all his other interests, he kept in close touch with the goings-on at the *Ledger*. On 18 January 1894, his private secretary heard a thud in the publisher's office. He rushed inside and found Childs lying on the floor, unconscious and partially paralyzed: he had suffered a stroke. Childs was taken to his Philadelphia home, and his wife was called back to the city from their Bryn Mawr estate.

Childs lingered, drifting in and out of consciousness, for more than two weeks, dying 3 February 1894.

Mourners streamed to the city from New York and Washington. For three days the *Public Ledger* devoted at least two and one-half pages in each edition to tributes; telegrams; messages of sympathy; statements from political, business, religious, and union leaders; and editorial comments from newspapers across the country on Childs's death. He was buried in a mausoleum in Laurel Hill Cemetery after one of the largest funerals in Philadelphia's history.

The *Ledger* went to the Drexel family; in honor of the late publisher, George W. Childs Drexel was installed as head of the enterprise. The Drexel family sold the *Ledger* a few years later.

Biography:
James Parton, *George W. Childs: A Biographical Sketch* (Philadelphia: Collins, 1870).

References:
Col. J. W. Forney, *Anecdotes of Public Men* (New York: De Capo Press, 1970);

Frederick Hudson, *Journalism in the U.S. from 1690 to 1872* (New York: Haskill House, 1968);

Memorial Service in Honor of the Late George W. Childs (Philadelphia: Goodman, 1894);

Eugene Munday, "Historical Sketch of the *Public Ledger* of Philadelphia," supplement to *Public Ledger* (July 1870);

The Printers and Mr. Childs (Philadelphia: Lippincott, 1890).

Papers:
George W. Childs's papers are at Drexel University.

Samuel Langhorne Clemens
(Mark Twain)

James Glen Stovall
University of Alabama

See also the Clemens entries in *DLB 11, American Humorists, 1800-1950* and *DLB 12, American Realists and Naturalists*.

BIRTH: Florida, Missouri, 30 November 1835, to John Marshall and Jane Lampton Clemens.

MARRIAGE: 2 February 1870 to Olivia Langdon; children: Langdon, Olivia Susan (Susy), Clara, Jane Lampton (Jean).

MAJOR POSITIONS HELD: Reporter, *Virginia City Territorial Enterprise* (1862-1864); reporter, *San Francisco Morning Call* (1864); correspondent, *Sacramento Union*, (1866); correspondent, *San Francisco Daily Morning Alta California* (1866-1869); editor, *Buffalo Express* (1869-1871).

AWARDS AND HONORS: M.A., Yale University, 1888; LL.D., University of Missouri, 1902; elected to the American Academy of Arts and Letters, 1904; Litt.D., Oxford University, 1907.

DEATH: Redding, Connecticut, 21 April 1910.

SELECTED BOOKS: *The Celebrated Jumping Frog of Calaveras County, and Other Sketches* (New York: C. H. Webb, 1867; London: Routledge, 1867);
The Innocents Abroad, or The New Pilgrims' Progress (Hartford, Conn.: American Publishing Company, 1869); republished in 2 volumes as *The Innocents Abroad* and *The New Pilgrims' Progress* (London: Hotten, 1870);
Mark Twain's (Burlesque) Autobiography and First Romance (New York: Sheldon, 1871; London: Hotten, 1871);
The Innocents at Home (London: Routledge, 1872);
Roughing It (Hartford, Conn.: American Publishing Company, 1872);
A Curious Dream; and Other Sketches (London: Routledge, 1872);
The Gilded Age: A Tale of Today, by Twain and Charles Dudley Warner (Hartford, Conn.: American Publishing Company, 1873; 3 vol-

Samuel Clemens as a young reporter in San Francisco, about 1864 (Milton Meltzer)

umes, London: Routledge, 1874);
Mark Twain's Sketches, New and Old (Hartford, Conn.: American Publishing Company, 1875);
The Adventures of Tom Sawyer (London: Chatto & Windus, 1876; Hartford, Conn.: American Publishing Company, 1876);
Old Times on the Mississippi (Toronto: Belford, 1876); republished as *The Mississippi Pilot* (London: Ward, Lock & Tyler, 1877); expanded as *Life on the Mississippi* (London: Chatto & Windus, 1883; Boston: Osgood, 1883);
An Idle Excursion (Toronto: Rose-Belford, 1878);

expanded as *Punch, Brothers, Punch! and Other Sketches* (New York: Slote, Woodman, 1878);

A Tramp Abroad (London: Chatto & Windus / Hartford, Conn.: American Publishing Company, 1880);

The Prince and the Pauper (London: Chatto & Windus, 1881; Boston: Osgood, 1882);

The Adventures of Huckleberry Finn (London: Chatto & Windus, 1884); republished as *Adventures of Huckleberry Finn* (New York: Webster, 1885);

A Connecticut Yankee in King Arthur's Court (New York: Webster, 1889); republished as *A Yankee at the Court of King Arthur* (London: Chatto & Windus, 1889);

Pudd'nhead Wilson, A Tale (London: Chatto & Windus, 1894); expanded as *The Tragedy of Pudd'nhead Wilson and the Comedy of Those Extraordinary Twins* (Hartford, Conn.: American Publishing Company, 1894);

Following the Equator (Hartford, Conn.: American Publishing Company, 1897); republished as *More Tramps Abroad* (London: Chatto & Windus, 1897);

The Man That Corrupted Hadleyburg and Other Stories and Essays (New York & London: Harper, 1900); enlarged as *The Man That Corrupted Hadleyburg and Other Stories and Sketches* (London: Chatto & Windus, 1900);

What Is Man? (New York: De Vinne Press, 1906); expanded as *What Is Man? and Other Essays* (New York & London: Harper, 1917);

Mark Twain's Speeches, edited by F. A. Nast (New York & London: Harper, 1910);

The Mysterious Stranger: A Romance, edited by Albert Bigelow Paine and Frederick A. Duneka (New York & London: Harper, 1916); expanded as *The Mysterious Stranger and Other Stories*, edited by Paine (New York & London: Harper, 1922);

The Curious Republic of Gondour and Other Whimsical Sketches (New York: Boni & Liveright, 1919);

Mark Twain's Speeches, edited by Paine (New York & London: Harper, 1923);

Europe and Elsewhere, edited by Paine (New York & London: Harper, 1923);

Mark Twain's Autobiography, edited by Paine, 2 volumes (New York & London: Harper, 1924);

Sketches of the Sixties, by Twain and Bret Harte (San Francisco: Howell, 1926);

Mark Twain's Notebook, edited by Paine (New York & London: Harper, 1935);

Letters from the Sandwich Islands Written for the Sacramento Union, edited by G. Ezra Dane (San Francisco: Grabhorn, 1937);

The Washoe Giant in San Francisco, edited by Franklin Walker (San Francisco: Fields, 1938);

Mark Twain's Travels With Mr. Brown, edited by

Mark Twain at Work, edited by Bernard De Voto (Cambridge: Harvard University Press, 1942); Harvard University Press, 1942);

Mark Twain, Business Man, edited by Samuel Charles Webster (Boston: Little, Brown, 1946);

Mark Twain of the "Enterprise," edited by Henry Nash Smith (Berkeley: University of California Press, 1957);

Traveling with the Innocents Abroad: Mark Twain's Original Reports from Europe and the Holy Land, edited by Daniel Morley McKeithan (Norman: University of Oklahoma Press, 1958);

Letters from the Earth, edited by De Voto (New York: Harper & Row, 1962);

Mark Twain's San Francisco, edited by Bernard Taper (New York: McGraw-Hill, 1963);

"What Is Man?" and Other Philosophical Writings, edited by Paul Baender (Berkeley: University of California Press, 1967);

Clemens of the "Call": Mark Twain in San Francisco, edited by Edgar M. Branch (Berkeley: University of California Press, 1969);

Mark Twain's Notebooks and Journals, volume 1, 1855-1873, edited by Frederick Anderson, Michael B. Frank, and Kenneth M. Sanderson; volume 2, 1877-1883, edited by Anderson, Lin Salamo, and Bernard L. Stein; volume 3, edited by Robert Pack Browning, Frank, and Salamo (Berkeley: University of California Press, 1975, 1979).

COLLECTIONS: *The Writings of Mark Twain*, Autograph Edition, 25 volumes (Hartford, Conn.: American Publishing Company, 1899-1907);

The Writings of Mark Twain, Hillcrest Edition, edited by Paine, 25 volumes (New York & London: Harper, 1906);

The Writings of Mark Twain, Definitive Edition, edited by Paine, 37 volumes (New York: Wells, 1922-1925).

Samuel Langhorne Clemens, known to America and the world as Mark Twain, is one of the most loved and read men of American letters. Especially noted for his novels *The Adventures of Tom Sawyer* (1876) and *The Adventures of Huckleberry Finn* (1884), which examined the innocence and adventure of growing up in America's heartland, Clemens is often presented as a kindly, white-haired man with a gentle smile behind his broad mustache and a genial, unassuming wit. That was, for a time at least, the image of Mark Twain. The Samuel Clemens of real life was a complex, guilt-ridden, and at times bitter man who scorned the pretensions of his Victorian age while trying to live up to them. He was a shameless self-promoter; he constantly worried about money and tried many nonliterary and usually unsuccessful schemes to get it; he sought the approval of America's literary elite and often did not receive it. In his final years he developed a bitterness that bordered on misanthropy. Yet his and succeeding generations remember him as the man who wrote the "growing up" stories with which Americans could identify.

Clemens started in the writing business via newspapers; he was a reporter, travel writer, and for a short time an editor. His more than twenty years of association with journalism did not make him a particularly distinguished practitioner, but by the time he left it, he was one of the most famous authors in America. The nation's editors and readers expected different things from their journalists in the nineteenth century than they do in the twentieth, and Clemens supplied many entertaining pieces which at times paid him rather handsomely. Even during his days as a journalist, Clemens never saw himself as merely a gatherer of facts but as a user of facts to make a point with his sharply honed wit. Clemens's development as a successful novelist took place against the background of the journalism of his day, and even though he eventually found writing for newspapers tedious drudgery, he owed the profession much for providing a beginning for his later successes.

Clemens was born on 30 November 1835, the fifth child of John and Jane Clemens, who had recently moved from Jamestown, Tennessee, to Florida, Missouri. Clemens's father had held several government posts in Tennessee and had acquired some 75,000 acres in and around Jamestown, but the family was not rich or even well-to-do. In fact, one business failure after another led the family in 1839 to Hannibal, a small town on the Mississippi River which Samuel Clemens eventually immortalized in his two most famous books. Clemens spent many of his boyhood summers on a farm owned by his uncle, John Quarles, and he later described it as "a heavenly place for a boy."

Clemens's carefree boyhood ended in 1847 when his father died and he was apprenticed to the local print shop owner as a printer's devil. His brother Orion (pronounced with an accent on the first syllable) soon bought the weekly *Hannibal Journal*, and young Clemens was taken into the business

Clemens as a fifteen-year-old printer's devil
(Mark Twain Estate)

at the "extravagant wage" of $3.50 a week. The wage meant little, as Clemens wrote later, because Orion "was never able to pay me a single penny as long as I was with him."

Being so close to the printed word, Clemens was soon bitten by the writing bug and sometime in 1848 or 1849 his first pieces were published. Life in the print shop was unappealing, however, and Clemens never took to it. He set type by hand and hated it—which might account in some part for his fascination years later with the Paige typesetting machine, a fascination which would drive him toward bankruptcy. As a printer's devil, Clemens "worked, not diligently, not willingly but fretfully, lazily, repiningly, complainingly, disgustedly, and always shirking the work when I was not watched."

Men who could set type by hand could find work anywhere, and many of them became wanderers. So it was with young Sam Clemens. He traveled to St. Louis in 1853 and began a brief career as a tramp printer. He worked for a short while in the composing room of the *St. Louis Evening News*, then left for New York City where he worked as a composer for a print shop. During the winter of 1853-1854, he went to Philadelphia (during a brief stint as a typesetter for the *Philadelphia Inquirer*,

Orion Clemens, owner of a series of short-lived newspapers
(Nevada State Historical Society)

Clemens wrote Orion that he was slower than the slowest man in the composing room) and then to Washington, D.C., from which he sent travel letters to his brother's new newspaper in Muscatine, Iowa. He was back in Missouri later that year, working again for the *St. Louis Evening News* and then for yet another paper owned by the luckless Orion, this one in Keokuk, Iowa. By 1856, Clemens had had about all he could stand of composing rooms, and he found his way out by proposing to travel to South America and send back travel letters to the *Keokuk Post* for five dollars a letter.

Clemens never made it past New Orleans, however. His journey down the Mississippi River convinced him that life as a riverboat pilot was the only life to lead. He persuaded his boat's captain to take him on as a cub in April 1857, and by 1859 he had earned his pilot's certificate. He gave up all thoughts of the composing room during the four years he was on the river.

The Civil War cut this idyllic career short. Clemens considered himself a Southern loyalist and feared being forced to join the Union forces as a riverboat pilot. He joined the Confederate army as a

second lieutenant and stayed for all of two weeks—a fortnight he later explained and burlesqued in "The Private History of a Campaign That Failed" (1885). He deserted and joined Orion, an abolitionist and Union loyalist who had just received a patronage appointment as secretary of the Nevada Territory. Together, with Sam paying the coach fare, they "lit out for the territory."

With Orion safely installed in office, Clemens set out to find what adventure he could; his experiences were later set down in the book *Roughing It* (1872). He went to Lake Tahoe to stake out timber claims and accidentally started a forest fire. Next he became a prospector for silver, but he had no luck at finding the elusive metal; instead, he found men and situations and rediscovered his talent for writing about them. Using the pen name "Josh," he began sending humorous sketches to the *Virginia City Territorial Enterprise*. By August 1862 he had an offer to join the staff at $25 a week, and he hiked 130 miles to accept it.

Clemens took his first journalistic training with the *Territorial Enterprise* reporting the news as it happened. The *Territorial Enterprise* was more than a paper of record, however, and it often gave free rein to its writers. Clemens took advantage of this freedom by concocting several fantastic newspaper hoaxes, some of which were believed by the paper's readers. Nor was Clemens above feuding, especially with his fellow journalists, as in this passage directed at the editor of the *Carson Independent*: "It is my unsolicited opinion that he knows very little about anything. And anybody who will read his paper calmly and dispassionately for a week will endorse that opinion. And more especially his knowing nothing about Carson, is not surprising; he seldom mentions that town in his newspaper. If the Second Advent were to occur here, you would hear of it first in some other newspaper."

In February 1863, Clemens used the pseudonym "Mark Twain" for the first time, and that name soon became as much a part of his identification as Clemens. The name is traditionally believed to have come from the Mississippi River, a leadman's term meaning two fathoms, but there is some evidence that the name originated in Nevada. Clemens's own story, that he stole it from a river pilot he once satirized, has never been confirmed. The origin of "Mark Twain" remains a minor literary mystery.

Clemens's journalistic career took him to the territorial capital, Carson City, where he supplied the *Territorial Enterprise* with reports on the legislature and the Constitutional convention. His writ-

Composing room of the Virginia City Territorial Enterprise, *the paper in which Clemens first used the pen name Mark Twain*
(Nevada State Historical Society)

ings and personality drew attention to himself, and he became a favorite among his circle of politicians and journalists. He was asked to deliver the "Governor's message" at the burlesque Third House in December 1863. It was one of the first of many humorous lectures he was to present during the next forty years.

Drinking, fighting, bawdy stories, journalistic hoaxes—they were all part of Clemens's world in Nevada. That combination got him in and out of minor scrapes, but it finally ended his stay in the territory. In May 1864, Clemens wrote that money raised by Carson City ladies for sick and wounded soldiers was really going for a "Miscegenation Society Somewhere in the East." No laughter followed this reference: the Republican party had been fighting off the rumor that it favored miscegenation, and those connected with the fund raising were deeply offended. Clemens later added that he nearly fought a duel with another editor over the story and that since dueling was illegal in Nevada, he had to leave for California. That part is doubtful; what is more probable is that he no longer could write and live with the wild abandon he had known in Nevada.

Clemens went to San Francisco, a place he had

visited some months earlier and where he had become relatively well known. There he got a job on the *Morning Call*, a paper which allowed him considerably less freedom (and probably required of him more work) than the *Territorial Enterprise*. He had to cover police court, fires, street squabbles, and a nightly round of six theaters, all of which he found to be "fearful drudgery—soulless drudgery—and almost destitute of interest. It was awful slavery for a lazy man." Clemens found refuge in a literary circle and contributed one article a week to the *Golden Era* for $50 a month. At one point he demanded better conditions from the *Morning Call*: "I told the *Call* folks to pay me $25 a week and let me work only in daylight," he wrote to his mother and sister. "So I get up at ten every morning and quit work at five or six in the afternoon. . . . I work as I always did—by fits and starts." When Bret Harte, whom he greatly admired, became editor of the *Californian* (a literary journal), Clemens began contributing to it.

Clemens could not ignore injustice, and he was particularly revolted by official corruption and the inhumane treatment of the Chinese. These subjects soon became the targets of his pen, and his attacks found their mark. He made many enemies in San Francisco and decided that his absence would cool

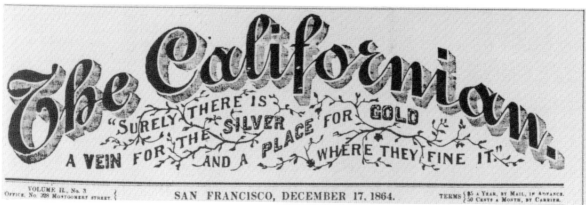

Flags of some papers in which Clemens's early work appeared. The Carpet-Bag *was a humorous weekly, published in Boston, which printed "The Dandy Frightening the Squatter" by "S. L. C." in 1852; the* Call *gave Clemens his first San Francisco job; the* Golden Era *paid him fifty dollars a month for an article a week; the* Californian *was a literary weekly edited by Bret Harte.*

off some of the sentiment building against him. He retreated to Angel's Camp in the Sacramento Valley and took up the only honorable profession there—mining. Clemens spent a dreary winter in 1864-1865 and apparently found little or no gold. He did hit on another treasure, however: he met several superb storytellers and gathered a wealth of plots, characters, and situations. One story would soon become particularly valuable to him: Ben Coon, one of Angel's Camp's best yarn spinners, told an old tale of a man who had a jumping frog and used him for betting purposes. When Clemens returned to San Francisco, a letter was waiting for him from Artemus Ward, asking for a sketch for a book Ward was planning. (He had met Ward, whose real name was Charles Farrar Brown, in Virginia City. Ward had come to town on a lecture tour, and when he encountered Clemens and his colleagues on the *Territorial Enterprise*, his visit was stretched into twelve days of "continuous celebration.") By the time he finished the sketch, Ward's book had already gone to press, but the *New York Saturday Press* picked up the story and published it as "Jim Smiley and his Jumping Frog" in November 1865. It was an immediate success and brought Clemens, under the name Mark Twain, a fame that he had hoped for but not expected. The story, later retitled "The Celebrated Jumping Frog of Calaveras County," was Clemens's literary introduction to the influential East Coast. Four years after it was published, Clemens expressed his pride in it to his fiancée Olivia Langdon, saying, "It is the best humorous sketch America has yet produced."

Back in San Francisco, Clemens wrote sketches for several West Coast papers through 1865 until fame reached him via the jumping frog story late in the year. By now he had reached the point where editors were willing to invest in his by-line rather than his subject matter. For a publication to have something by the increasingly famous Mark Twain brought a certain amount of prestige, not to say readers and revenue. Clemens had begun to live the good life of a journalist—he could travel, work when he pleased, and write about whatever he chose. By March 1866 he had been commissioned by the *Sacramento Union* to write a series of travel letters on the Sandwich Islands (Hawaii), and he left on the steamer *Ajax* for what he later called "these enchanted islands."

The commission had scheduled Clemens to stay in Hawaii for one month, but that month was stretched into five. He was thoroughly enchanted by the islands, the climate, and the natives. He examined many facets of the place in his letters to the paper, but they were sporadic because Clemens was easily distracted. At one point, six weeks lapsed between reports, and when he resumed, Clemens confessed but made no apologies: "It has been six weeks since I touched a pen. In explanation and excuse I offer the fact that I spent that time (with the exception of one week) on the island of Maui. I got back only yesterday. I never spent so pleasant a month before, or bade any place good-bye so regretfully. . . . I went to Maui for a week and remained five. I had a jolly time. I would not have fooled away any of it writing letters under any consideration whatever. It will be five or six weeks before I write again. I sail for the island of Hawaii tomorrow, and my Maui notes will not be written up until I come back." Such was Clemens's sense of deadlines. Yet this method of writing was the one he used all his life: he never wrote in a steady stream unless absolutely pressed. He saw his mind as a well which could run dry; at those times he would have to stop and let it fill up.

Clemens did engage in some solid journalism on this trip and obtained a scoop that increased his fame. The *Hornet*, a clipper ship that had achieved notoriety by beating the *Flying Cloud* in a New York-to-San Francisco race by only forty minutes, had burned in the middle of the Pacific, and fifteen seamen were cast adrift for forty-three days with only ten days' provisions. On 21 June 1866 they washed ashore on a Hawaiian beach. Clemens at the time was bedridden with boils, but he saw he had a story. He was carried on a cot to the hospital in Honolulu where the seamen had been taken, and he listened as they were questioned about their experiences. He stayed up all night writing the story of their survival and barely got it aboard a ship leaving for San Francisco the next morning. The story was a sensational one and widely reprinted. When Clemens arrived in San Francisco a short time later, he found a $300 bonus waiting for him for the scoop. The story was later published by *Harper's New Monthly Magazine* as "Forty-three Days in an Open Boat"; but much to his horror, it appeared in the magazine's annual index under the name "Mark Swain." Clemens, however, had his scoop, the kind journalists dream of and only a few are lucky enough to get. It became yet another reason for readers and editors to respect the by-line of Mark Twain.

Clemens had told his brother Orion that his two most powerful ambitions were to be a riverboat pilot or a preacher. He had to give up the first because of the Civil War and could not undertake the second because he lacked "the necessary stock in trade—i.e., religion." Now back in California, he felt the "call" to literature. He would make his living, he said, by exciting "the laughter of God's creatures." To that end, he and the *San Francisco Daily Morning Alta California*, one of the newspapers bidding for his talents, contracted for a world tour beginning in the Orient. Clemens changed his mind and decided to visit first the East Coast and his family in the Midwest, then start his world tour beginning in Europe. He left California late in 1866 full of hope for the future and good feelings about his immediate past. In San Francisco, he wrote his mother, he was leaving "more friends than any newspaperman that ever sailed out of the Golden Gate. The reason I mention this with pride is because our fraternity generally leave none but enemies here when they go."

Clemens sailed to Panama, crossed the isthmus, and sailed for New York, sending back several travel letters to the *Alta California* about his voyage. He arrived in New York on 12 January 1867, and set about to discover the city on his own terms. He reported on all he saw, including the city's most scandalous play, the high prices, and anything that put on a show. He even wrote that he had spent a night in jail—for trying to break up a fight, according to his story. The next morning he was "marched to the Police Court with a vile policeman at each elbow, just as if I had been robbing a church, or saying a complimentary word about the police, or doing some other supernaturally mean thing." The charges, he said, were dropped, and no record was made of the arrest. Consequently, the truth of the story is doubtful, but his report represents Clemens's attempts to experience and write about everything New York had to offer. One of the city's major attractions was its preachers, and the most famous of all was Henry Ward Beecher. Clemens met him, heard him preach, and was fascinated. This contact was the first of many that Clemens had with the Beecher family during his life.

Late that spring, Clemens saw the publication of his first book, a collection of short stories and sketches headed by the retitled frog story: *The Celebrated Jumping Frog of Calaveras County, and Other Sketches*. He was happy to see the book in print and looked forward to big sales (which never materialized), but he later wrote to Bret Harte that the book "is full of damnable errors and deadly inconsistencies of spellings." The book was to cause Clemens headaches later because of the casualness with which he entered into the agreement with his publisher; he had to sue to regain his copyright over the material.

Soon after this publication, Clemens delivered his most important lecture to date, his New York debut before a packed house in the Cooper Union on 6 May 1867. The lecture went well, even though Senator William Nye of Nevada, who was supposed to introduce Clemens, did not show up. Clemens introduced himself and gave a lecture which led a reviewer for the *New York Tribune* to write: "No other lecturer, of course excepting Artemus Ward, has so thoroughly succeeded in exciting the mirthful curiosity, and compelling the laughter of his hearers." Other reviews carried on in a similar vein. Clemens had established his reputation in an area other than writing—an area which would prove to be very valuable to him in the later years of his life.

Clemens's association with Henry Ward Beecher indirectly led him to his next major assignment, which helped him build the bridge from his journalistic to his literary career. Beecher's church sponsored a tour of Europe and the Holy Land to begin in the summer of 1867. Clemens persuaded the *Alta California* editors to pay his passage fee of $1,250 and contracted to send them a series of travel letters at $20 each. In addition, he agreed to supply a few travel letters to Horace Greeley's *New York Tribune*. Much of what Clemens wrote on this voyage of the *Quaker City* was a straightforward travel-book account of what he saw, but interwoven through all of his letters was an irreverence which endeared him to his readers. In August the tour sailed into Yalta, where Czar Nicholas II was summering at the imperial palace. Clemens speculated on how the grandeur of the Russian Empire could be invested in one man—who looked so human up close: "I had a sort of vague desire to examine his hands and see if they were flesh and blood, like other men's. . . . if he were grievously ill, all would know it before the sun rose again; if he dropped lifeless where he stood, his fall might shake the thrones of half the world! If I could have stolen his coat I would have done it. When I meet a man like that, I want something to remember him by."

The voyage of the *Quaker City* lasted from 8 June to 19 November. Clemens wrote fifty-three letters for the *Alta California*, six for the *Tribune*, and three for the *New York Herald*. His view of the world broadened, and he established himself as one of America's major humorous writers. Clemens for the most part enjoyed himself immensely. Even though most of the passengers were members of the clergy, Clemens sought out several with whom he could have a rollicking good time. In addition, he met two people who would exercise continuing in-

Mrs. Mary Fairbanks, correspondent for her husband's Cleveland Herald. *Mrs. Fairbanks was Clemens's editor and moral censor on the* Quaker City *voyage and his friend for the next thirty-two years (Mark Twain Estate).*

fluence on his life: Mrs. Mary Fairbanks of Cleveland, who was the editor and occasionally the moral censor of his travel letters; and Charles Langdon, who showed Clemens a portrait of his sister Olivia, the first time he saw the woman who was to become his wife.

The day after the *Quaker City* returned, an "obituary" of the voyage by Clemens appeared in the *Herald*. It was written to "make the Quakers get up and howl in the morning," and so it did. "I'm tired of hearing about the 'mixed' character of our party on the *Quaker City*. It was not mixed enough—there were not enough blackguards aboard in proportion to the saints—there was not enough genuine piety to affect the hypocrisy." That article might have begun a promising stint with the *Herald* had Clemens accepted the offer of the paper to join its staff. For some reason, however, he felt his prospects would be better if he became secretary to Senator William Stewart of Nevada in Washington.

The job offered him six dollars a day, required little of his time, and gave him some leisure to write. He had begun to receive inquiries on turning his *Quaker City* letters into a book and was beginning to consider doing so. The secretaryship did not give Clemens the anchor he expected, however; he refused to take even his meager duties seriously, and he found his employer insufferable. Clemens, too, was insufferable, reverting to the Western bohemian, carefree life-style that he had enjoyed in Nevada. In less than two months, the senator and the humorist parted company.

Clemens did not lack for opportunities while in Washington. He decided to expand his newspaper career with the thought that it would help solidify his reputation as a writer. He became the Washington correspondent for the *New York Tribune* and also contributed to the *New York Herald*; he soon expanded his work to include a variety of newspapers in the Midwest and West. Clemens collected about $800 a month from these assignments. He also signed on to write occasional articles for *Galaxy* magazine, and he turned down numerous invitations to lecture. He found hobnobbing with Washington's elite easy and the grind of daily journalism difficult to sustain. Though he was in Washington during the major political story of the decade, the impeachment and trial of President Andrew Johnson, Clemens was not much interested in this story and concentrated rather on the personalities he encountered. Many of the impressions he gathered during these days appeared five years later in his satiric novel *The Gilded Age* (1873). Because of mounting difficulties in publishing his travel book, Clemens left Washington two months before the impeachment controversy ran its course in May.

Clemens had begun negotiations for publication of *The Innocents Abroad* in December with a publisher in Hartford, Connecticut. The letters would take much rewriting and expanding if they were going to be a respectable book. That winter and spring he had planned to keep up his Washington correspondence and work on the book, which he hoped to finish in the summer. The plan might have worked had he not received bad news from the West: the editors of the *Alta California*, hearing about Clemens's book, were making plans to gather his letters together and publish a book of their own. The paper considered Clemens's work property which it had paid for, and the editors did not appreciate Clemens negotiating on his own. Clemens had no choice but to go back to California to try to come to some understanding with the editors, and he arrived there in April. To support himself while negotiating, he conducted a lecture tour which met with great success. The *Alta California* editors soon relented and gave up all plans for publication of a book. That left Clemens free to work on his book while remaining in California and lecturing. Newspaper journalism was behind him for the moment while he pursued other projects.

The manuscript for *The Innocents Abroad* was delivered to the publisher in the summer of 1868, but it remained unpublished for about a year, causing Clemens a great deal of frustration. In the meantime, he had begun serious courtship of Olivia Langdon, whom he had met during Christmas 1867. He lectured extensively and wrote occasional letters to the *Alta California*, which still accepted his material despite their dispute. He and Olivia became engaged in February 1869, after close scrutiny by her parents. Having committed himself to settling down, he looked around for a suitable source of stable income: the Langdons were wealthy coal operators and expected their daughter's husband to achieve some mercantile respectability.

Clemens's solution to the problem of the bohemian turned businessman was to find a newspaper to invest in, and there were several possibilities. The husband of Mary Fairbanks, his friend from the *Quaker City* voyage, owned the *Cleveland Herald*, and Clemens approached him about buying a part interest. This idea met with little success, so Clemens spent the spring of 1869 looking for other opportunities. The paper he wanted most was the *Hartford Courant* because of Olivia's desire to live in that city, but the owners were not anxious to have him in their business (although one of them, Charles Dudley Warner, later collaborated with him on *The Gilded Age*). Finally, Clemens's future father-in-law, Jervis Langdon, offered to lend him $25,000 to buy a third interest in the *Buffalo Express*. The deal was consummated in August 1869, and much to his surprise, Clemens found himself a propertied person—a far cry from the footloose existence he had known in Virginia City only six years before.

At first Clemens took his duties as editor and part owner of the *Express* very seriously, partly because it was expected of him and partly because he was honestly trying to reform himself to please his future in-laws. In his first editorial he somberly set forth his good intentions, and then cut through them with his bohemian humor. For example, in describing his planned work habits, he wrote: "I am simply going to do my plain, unpretending duty, when I cannot get out of it; I shall work diligently

Clemens at the time he was editor of the Buffalo Express. *This picture, with journalist George Alfred Townsend (left) and Buffalo Courier editor David Gray, was taken at the Mathew Brady studio in Washington in July 1870 (Culver Pictures).*

and honestly and faithfully, when privation and want shall compel me to do it; in writing, I shall always confine myself strictly to the truth, except when it is attended with inconvenience. . . ." Clemens in fact lived up to many of his good intentions: he took part in every phase of the paper's editorial operation and urged his reporters "to modify the adjectives, curtail thin philosophical reflections and leave out the slang"; he toned down the typography to give the *Express* a more respectable look; and he editorialized against the injustices of lynchings and discrimination.

The Innocents Abroad was finally published in July 1869, and the reviews and sales of the book went well from the very beginning. Clemens used his position with the *Express* to promote the book whenever he could. Even more important was a favorable review which appeared in the prestigious *Atlantic Monthly*, representing the Eastern literary establishment from which Clemens desperately wanted acceptance. The review was written by William Dean Howells (who later became a close friend of Clemens's) and said, "There is an amount of pure

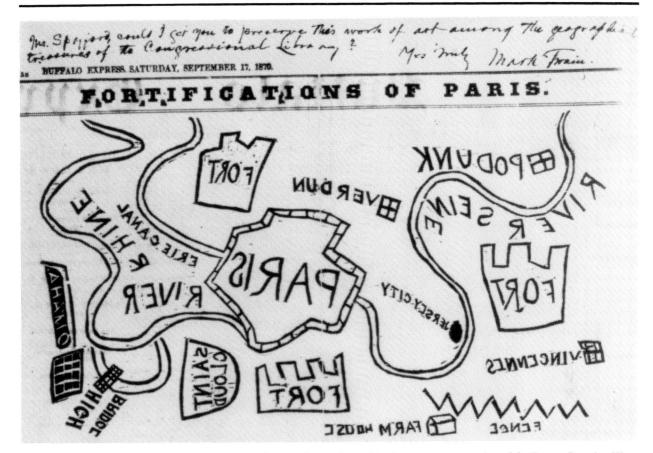

Clemens's map of Paris, purposely engraved to print backwards, a satire on big-city newspaper reporting of the Franco-Prussian War. The inscription at the top offers the map to Ainsworth Spofford, the Librarian of Congress (Library of Congress).

human nature in the book that rarely gets into literature."

Clemens and Olivia Langdon were married on 2 February 1870, and they were given a large house (cost: $43,000) in Buffalo as a wedding present by Olivia's father. Soon thereafter, Clemens resumed his contact with *Galaxy* magazine, writing weekly articles for $2,400 a year. His life was taking a direction which seemed to be clearly satisfactory, and yet the first year of marriage was disastrous. A friend visiting Olivia died in their house of typhoid fever, and a short while later Olivia's father fell ill and died. Their first child was born prematurely, and Olivia was bedridden; soon after the birth, she too contracted typhoid and came close to dying. These distractions proved to be too much for Clemens to get any real work accomplished; though he did start several major projects, he did not follow through on any of them. He found his writing for *Galaxy* increasingly burdensome, and he was spending less and less time in the *Express* office. He was also plagued with doubts as a writer; even though *The Innocents Abroad* was selling exceptionally well, he

began to wonder if he could ever again produce anything as good. Yet he wanted desperately to write another book and decided he would have to free himself from his business encumbrances to do so. In the spring of 1871 he severed his connection with *Galaxy* and sold his interest in the *Buffalo Express*, losing about $10,000 of his original investment. These moves represented the end of his career in journalism; but they did not separate him from the profession entirely, as later events would demonstrate. He also sold his house in Buffalo, a city he had come to detest, and moved to Quarry Farm near Elmira, New York. He worked through the summer on *Roughing It*, which was published early in 1872.

The move to Quarry Farm had drained Clemens financially, despite fairly brisk sales of *The Innocents Abroad*. During the winter of 1871-1872 Clemens fell back on his second means of earning money, the lecture tour. It was yet another distraction from writing but one which he could not avoid then or later. Lecturing had its good points—it made money, and it served as useful advertising for

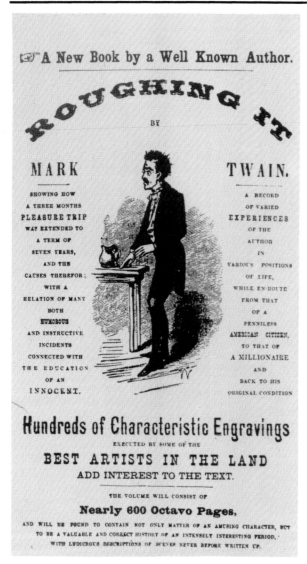

Prepublication advertising circular for Clemens's fifth book (New York Public Library)

his work. Clemens also gained personal gratification from the warm receptions which he usually received; but the cost was separation from his family, a situation he never enjoyed.

The Clemenses decided to make Hartford, Connecticut, their nonsummer home in October 1871. Hartford was chosen because of the presence of the Nook Farm community, a society of liberal intellectuals, several of whom were friends of the Langdon family. Clemens's wife had been raised in circumstances very different from his own: the Langdons were staunch abolitionists and their house had served as a station on the Underground Railroad for runaway slaves before the Civil War. Nook Farm was the kind of place Clemens had

sought for acceptance, and the community took him in as one of its own. He developed some lasting friendships there. With these people Clemens could be whatever he chose—liberal scold of society, Western humorist, rich and eccentric. The Clemenses rented a house in Hartford until 1874 when their own was completed—a rambling, elaborate twenty-eight-room structure of Gothic turrets, porches, balconies, and decks. It cost Clemens more than $120,000 to build and furnish it. His family lived there until 1891, and he sold it in 1903; today it serves as the Mark Twain Museum.

With the move to Hartford, Clemens was finally achieving some stability, if not routine, in his family life. The family's first child, Langdon, died soon after coming to Hartford, but other children populated the family—Susy, born in 1872; Clara, 1874; and Jean, 1880. The Clemenses spent the winter months in Hartford and the summers at Quarry Farm, where Sam did most of his writing. Even then Clemens was a sporadic worker, often handling several projects at one time: he would work on one until he lost interest or inspiration or was distracted by another; most of his ideas were never completed. In this way, during the next twenty years, Clemens produced most of the literature for which he is famous: *The Gilded Age*, *The Adventures of Tom Sawyer*, *A Tramp Abroad* (1880), *The Prince and the Pauper* (1881), *Life on the Mississippi* (1883), *The Adventures of Huckleberry Finn*, *A Connecticut Yankee in King Arthur's Court* (1889), and *Pudd'nhead Wilson* (1894). Clemens's life was punctuated with trips to Europe and periodic lecture tours; the most famous of the latter was a tour with fellow writer George Cable in 1884-1885. The tour was not an unmitigated success, but it did help the two authors promote their most recent books. The major nonwriting projects of Clemens's life during this time were his publishing business and the Paige typesetting machine.

Clemens's business associations almost inevitably soured into bitter vendettas against his partners. He never found a publisher with whom he was completely satisfied, and by the 1880s he was getting into the business himself. In 1884 he owned the Charles L. Webster and Company publishing house, named for his nephew, who managed it. Originally established to publish his own works, Clemens always thought the company could, with luck, make him a great deal of money. Aside from Clemens's books, the company had one major success, the publication of the *Personal Memoirs* (1885) of Ulysses S. Grant, who had gone bankrupt after his two terms as president and whose memoirs were

Clemens on the porch of his Hartford home with his wife, Olivia, and daughters Clara, Jean, and Susy
(Yale University, Morse Collection)

a deathbed attempt to pay off his mammoth debts. After much personal negotiation, Clemens won the Grant contract for his company, and the book made publishing history. Even before Grant had finished writing, the publisher's salesmen had taken orders for more than 100,000 copies. Grant died just after finishing the book, but soon afterwards, his widow received a royalty check for $200,000; eight months later a second check came for $150,000. The Grant success required a vast expansion of the publishing company, and no other books sold well enough to sustain this expansion. One book for which Clemens had high hopes was the authorized biography of Pope Leo XIII, a copy of which, he thought, could be sold to every Catholic in Christendom. The sales amounted to considerably less than that, and although the book eventually made money, it did not make enough. The firm also took on autobiographies of other Union commanders, such as McClellan, Sheridan, and Custer, and it might have become a profitable venture if Clemens had not

used its resources to feed the insatiable appetite of another of his projects—the Paige typesetter.

The Paige machine held a dual fascination for Clemens. He lived in an age of developing machinery, and he saw big money being made as these marvels were put to use; he wanted to be part of this development. In addition, Clemens had spent too many hours handsetting type to easily forget the drudgery that printers endured; if he could find something to relieve that drudgery, printers of the future would never have to suffer what he suffered. The Paige typesetter, he thought, offered him a way to satisfy both of these interests. Clemens had dabbled in inventing, having taken patents on an adjustable clothing strap, a memory game, and an improvement on scrapbooks. His fascination with machinery had led him to become the first major author to use a typewriter and to have the first telephone in Hartford installed in his house. The Paige typesetter overwhelmed him with its size and intricacy, however, and at first he attributed human

The Paige typesetting machine on which Clemens lost more than $200,000 in investments

qualities to it. His initial contact with the typesetter and its smooth-talking inventor, James Paige, came in the early 1880s. Clemens let his imagination run away with its possibilities. He began to calculate the huge profits he might reap from the machine, and his initial investment of $5,000 seemed small enough.

Clemens received soothing assurances from the inventor along with demands for more money. By 1887, he had put $80,000 into the machine; he tried to interest others in the enterprise and seemed for a time to have some investors lined up, only to be bitterly disappointed. By 1891, some $190,000 had been invested, and still no working model had been produced. (Meanwhile, the Mergenthaler machine had become operational and had begun to corner the market.) Depleted of funds, the Clemenses closed their Hartford house and left for Europe, where they could live less expensively. By 1895 Clemens had invested more than $200,000 in the machine and still had hopes for it, but he also realized that he had no way of paying his present obligations. He needed a rescuer and found one in Henry H. Rogers, a director of Standard Oil and an admirer of Clemens. Rogers, one of the most ruthless businessmen of an age known for that type, took over Clemens's finances and worked to set his house in order. He administered the proper testing for the Paige typesetter and found that it was too delicate to work well; consequently, he halted all of Clemens's investments in it. (The machine now resides in the basement of Clemens's Hartford house.) Rogers then guided the author through complicated bankruptcy proceedings, out of which Clemens emerged with debts of about $100,000. He was not legally bound to pay these debts, but the thought of bankruptcy had been so wrenching to his wife that she insisted that he retire every obligation. That he did in the next three years by writing and a world lecture tour.

In the middle of these efforts, Clemens received a severe personal blow. His oldest daughter, and his favorite, Susy, died at the age of twenty-four in 1896. She had not gone with the rest of the family to Europe, but had stayed behind in New York and was struck down by meningitis. Clemens received the news of her death just after returning to England from lecturing in South Africa. He was devastated and remained so for a long time. Nearly a decade later he wrote, "It is one of the mysteries of our nature that a man, all unprepared can receive a thunderstroke like that and live." Despite his deep sense of grief, Clemens's efforts to pay off his debts bore fruit, and by 1900 he and his wife decided it was time to return to America after an absence of more than five years. America warmly welcomed them back.

As a senior statesman of American letters, Clemens occupied a position of notoriety and some influence. Suddenly he was in great demand by journalists, and reporters found that he had opinions on just about every topic of the day. His calendar was filled with a whirlwind of banquets and luncheons. He was widely photographed and thus widely recognized; his distinctive white mane and mustache were not easy to miss in any event. To

supplement these features he began wearing a white flannel suit for almost every public appearance. When not being interviewed, Clemens was writing numerous articles for magazines and newspapers, expressing his myriad opinions and championing a variety of causes.

Clemens's wife began her last serious illness in 1902. They were advised by doctors to return to Italy, which they did the next winter. Olivia continued to decline, and she finally succumbed at their villa in Florence in 1904. Soon after that Clemens put their Hartford house up for sale and bought a house on Fifth Avenue in New York City.

Two major writing projects occupied Clemens during these last years. One was his posthumously published autobiography (1924), which consisted more of flights of fantasy than a faithful recounting of events: he was, after all, writing the life story of Mark Twain, not of Samuel Clemens. The other was his bitter denunciation of mankind, *Letters from the Earth* (1962), which also would not be published until after his death. He appointed Albert Bigelow

Clemens in 1903, looking out of his octagonal study at Quarry Farm, his summer home near Elmira, New York (Mark Twain Memorial, Hartford)

Paine as his biographer and the executor of his papers. In 1906 he testified before a congressional committee considering copyright reform, a cause he had long advocated. The next year he traveled to England one last time to receive an honorary degree from Oxford University. He met with a steady stream of famous visitors and maintained an active banquet schedule. His second daughter, Jean, died in 1909 after several years of strained relations with her father. Four months later, on 21 April 1910, Clemens died at his last home near Redding, Connecticut. He was seventy-four years old.

Clemens spent some sixty years as a writer, but he was associated with newspapers for only about a third of that time and spent fewer than ten years in full-time reporting and editing. He developed no particular fondness for newspapers in general and thought newspaper writing was on a much lower level than writing books or magazine articles. Yet his thoughts on newspapers were not totally negative: writing for them might not appeal to him, but he realized the role newspapers could play in American society. Answering Matthew Arnold's criticism concerning the "irreverence" of the American press, Clemens wrote, "Its frank and cheerful irreverence is by all odds the most valuable quality it possesses. For its mission—overlooked by Mr. Arnold—is to stand guard over a nation's liberties, not its humbugs and shams. And so it must be armed with ridicule, not reverence . . . to my mind a discriminating irreverence is the creator and protector of human liberty. . . ."

His burlesque of newspapering in "Journalism in Tennessee" (1869) reveals in a comic way the lengths to which editors may go to restructure facts to suit their own purposes. Not that Clemens had anything against that practice: much of his own journalism shows the same tendency. Clemens was a humorist first and a journalist second. Yet his purpose in his writings, as is the case with any good journalist, was to seek the truth. As George Bernard Shaw wrote to him in a tribute in 1907: "I am persuaded that the future historian of America will find your works as indispensible to him as a French historian finds the tracts of Voltaire. I tell you so because I am the author of a play in which a priest says, 'Telling the truth's the funniest joke in the world,' a piece of wisdom which you helped to teach me."

Letters:
Mark Twain's Letters, edited by Albert Bigelow Paine, 2 volumes (New York & London: Harper, 1917).

Biographies:
Albert Bigelow Paine, *Mark Twain, A Biography*, 3 volumes (New York & London: Harper, 1912);

Milton Meltzer, *Mark Twain Himself* (New York: Crowell, 1960);

Justin Kaplan, *Mr. Clemens and Mark Twain* (New York: Simon & Schuster, 1966);

Justin Kaplan, *Mark Twain and His World* (New York: Simon & Schuster, 1974).

References:
Paul Fatout, *Mark Twain in Virginia City* (Bloomington: University of Indiana Press, 1964);

William M. Gibson, *The Art of Mark Twain* (New York: Oxford University Press, 1976);

William R. Gillis, *Gold Rush Days with Mark Twain* (New York: AMS Press, 1969);

Kenneth S. Lynn, *Mark Twain and Southwestern Humor* (Boston: Little, Brown, 1959);

Effie M. Mack, *Mark Twain in Nevada* (New York: Scribners, 1947);

Henry Nash Smith, ed., *Mark Twain: A Collection of Critical Essays* (Englewood Cliffs, N.J.: Prentice-Hall, 1963);

Smith, *Mark Twain: The Development of a Writer* (Cambridge: Belknap Press, 1962).

Papers:
Mark Twain's papers are located at the University of California Library, Berkeley.

John A. Cockerill

(5 December 1845-10 April 1896)

Jo Anne Smith
University of Florida

MAJOR POSITIONS HELD: Editor, *Dayton Daily Ledger* (1868); managing editor, *Cincinnati Enquirer* (1872-1877); managing editor, *St. Louis Post-Dispatch* (1879-1883); managing editor, *New York World* (1883-1891); editor, *New York Commercial Advertiser* (1891-1894); special correspondent, *New York Herald* (1895-1896).

BOOK: *Custer Battlefield, Burlington Route* (Chicago: Poole, 1898).

John A. Cockerill, perhaps the finest editor to come out of Joseph Pulitzer's "talent hunts," teamed with Pulitzer in establishing the *St. Louis Post-Dispatch* and the *New York World* as leading nineteenth-century newspapers. With an energy and perfectionism that matched his great publisher's, Cockerill implemented Pulitzer's "new journalism" strategies, using attention-grabbing human interest stories and innovative display to win readers, and solid news coverage, lively prose, and tight editing to keep them. Extolled in a Eugene Field poem as "very smart indeed," "Johnny" Cockerill had a keen news sense and a pragmatic managerial style that won him accolades as the ideal managing editor. Yet his outstanding service was marred by a series of tragic and disillusioning events.

Born 5 December 1845 at Locust Grove, Ohio, Cockerill was christened Joseph Daniel Albert Cockerill. His parents soon dropped "Joseph" and "Daniel," his father's and grandfather's names, in favor of "John." John was the third of five children of Joseph and Ruth Eylar Cockerill and was to display throughout his life the inquisitiveness and self-reliance his parents instilled in their children. As a schoolboy, Cockerill excelled in history, spelling, and grammar. Interests in law and government were whetted by his father, who had been a teacher and lawyer prior to service in both the state legislature and the United States Congress. Coming from a home where news was much discussed, it was not surprising that the nearby newspaper office of the *West Union Scion* attracted Cockerill. After a number of visits to its windows to watch type being set, he mustered the courage to go in and ask editor Sam

Burwell to show him how it was done. The boy's pluck in trying to master the cases in a single long afternoon impressed Burwell, who gave young Cockerill a job as a printer's devil.

On occasion, Burwell allowed the youngster to compose brief items for publication. Cockerill later recalled that his "first essay for print," written for Burwell, filled him "with a pride and sense of importance that I never felt since." The single line, typical of Burwell's policy of mentioning local ads in his news columns, read: "The attention of our readers is called to the advertisement of Farm for Sale in another column." The item, "read and re-read" by its young author, was the first of many clipped and saved by his mother.

Though two years at Burwell's elbow set Cockerill firmly on the road to a career in journalism, he left the *Scion* at age fifteen to pursue more urgent business. It was 1861: Fort Sumter had been shelled in April. Cockerill's father, a colonel, and his older brother Armstead, a lieutenant, were among those mobilized. Hoping to enlist, Cockerill accompanied Armstead to Camp Chase. When he was rejected as both too small and too young, Cockerill wheedled an appointment as a drummer boy. He thus became one of the approximately 8,000 underage boys—some as young as thirteen—to serve in the Union army. At the Battle of Shiloh in 1862, he put his drum aside and shouldered a musket.

Colonel Joseph Cockerill served until 1864 and was named a brigadier general by Congress after resigning from the military. Private John Cockerill, discharged late in 1862, returned to Ohio and to journalism. With a partner, a small investment, and refreshing youthful candor ("No news of interest this week," he once announced), he published the *Democratic Union*, a competitor to Burwell's *Scion*. Two years later he became editor of the *True Telegraph*, a weekly in Hamilton, Ohio; when the paper came up for sale in October 1865, he and Armstead purchased it and remained its coproprietors until April 1867. At twenty-one, after buying out Armstead's interest, Cockerill became publisher-editor. No longer the undersized drummer boy, he had grown to be a husky six-footer who hoped one day to be a big-city journalist.

From the day he had started work at the *Scion*, Cockerill's primary interest had been news. He thought newspapers should carry more and longer news items, especially about local events, and that news stories deserved better display than they customarily received. Even as a fourteen-year-old "helper" and delivery boy, he had made his views known, urging Burwell to put news on the paper's front page instead of the features and fiction that usually appeared there. Now an editor in his own right, Cockerill could indulge these preferences. The bold play and depth of coverage he gave to local news drew attention from larger out-of-town papers. The publisher of the *Cincinnati Enquirer*, impressed by what he saw, invited Cockerill to be the *Enquirer's* Hamilton correspondent.

In 1868, Cockerill made his first major career shift, from weekly to daily journalism. His experience at the *Dayton Daily Ledger*, lasting only a few months, proved sharply disillusioning. His copublisher at Dayton was the fiery copperhead editor Clement Laird Vallandigham. Widely known first for his work as a trial lawyer and later for his flaming oratory and political ambitions, Vallandigham had served in both the Ohio legislature and Con-

Clement Laird Vallandigham, copperhead politician and Cockerill's copublisher at the Dayton Daily Ledger *(Library of Congress)*

gress. His influence had spread through militant speeches against the Union cause and through Ohio newspapers he edited, published, or otherwise influenced. He had, for instance, spurred the founding of the *True Telegraph* in 1861 to discredit the pro-Union *Telegraph* of banker-publisher John P. Peck.

Cockerill, fascinated by knowledge of Vallandigham's career as chronicled by his *True Telegraph* predecessors, was understandably intrigued by Vallandigham's June 1868 visit to the newspaper's office. After flattering Cockerill with praise for his work on the paper, Vallandigham came to his real reason for coming to see the young editor. He planned, he told Cockerill, to attend the soon-to-begin Democratic National Convention and needed a fill-in editor at the *Ledger*; the job would provide a good chance not only to learn daily newspapering but to gain a controlling interest in the *Ledger* because of the desire of co-owner J. McLain Smith to pull out. The proposition seemed to young Cockerill too good to forgo. He soon was in Dayton and almost immediately found "filling in" to be not at all what he had expected. Vallandigham was running for a congressional seat and, for the most part, left Cockerill on his own. He did, however, supply inflated reports of his speeches (given, as typically reported by him, to "the largest crowd ever seen" in that part of Ohio). These abraded the young editor's news sense. Always more interested in news than in business and pressured on this occasion by deadlines far more demanding than he had been accustomed to on weeklies, Cockerill apparently trusted too much and inquired too little. He was reluctant in later years to comment on the Dayton experience, saying only that he lost his investment as Vallandigham was losing the election. Cockerill left the *Ledger* immediately following the November vote.

Fortunately, new opportunity arose and gave Cockerill little chance to dwell on the stinging blows to pride and pocketbook. Favorably remembered at the *Enquirer*, he was hired by that paper in 1869. His rise there was swift: enterprising reporting brought him quick promotions, first to city editor and later to managing editor. He developed a signature style as a supervisor: sharp-gazed and loud, he dominated the newsroom with remarks that were sometimes withering, often profane, and invariably perceptive. Some members of his staff professed to love him and others to fear him, but there was little disagreement about his superior talents as an editor.

While abrasive to individual reporters, Cockerill championed reporters as a class, regarding them as the key to a paper's greatness. When he recognized unusual promise in a reporter, he could be uncharacteristically gentle in nurturing it. Cockerill's careful grooming of shy free-lancer Lafcadio Hearn gave the *Enquirer* a big story and Hearn, later to be well known as a novelist, a needed boost. Driven to social retreat by his gnomelike stature and extremely weak eyesight, Hearn at first would not even present his editorial contributions in person. Cockerill detected a stunning talent in Hearn's finely honed prose. Upon meeting the young writer and finding him "sensitive as a flower," Cockerill assigned Hearn to a desk in his own office rather than exposing him to the newsroom. Hearn's precise and delicate way with words allowed him to walk a narrow editorial line, handling the touchiest of subjects without arousing publishers' fears or readers' outrage. So it was to Hearn that Cockerill turned when he received a report that there had been a grisly "cremation" murder at a Cincinnati tannery. Hearn recorded every detail of the victim's final agony, as well as of the romantic entanglement that presumably led to his murder. Cockerill assigned two sketch artists to the story and gave generous front-page play to text and illustration. Regular and extra editions carrying the "Tanyard Murder" sold out. The story received national play, and the *Enquirer* enjoyed the first of many circulation boosts while under Cockerill's direction. The Cockerill-Hearn combination clicked on several more major stories before Cockerill, feeling that Hearn was growing too strident, reluctantly fired his "best writer."

Very much in charge in the newsroom, Cockerill was known there as "the Colonel." It was a title he neither approved of nor applied to himself. He often pointed out that his father had been a real colonel whereas he himself had not risen above the rank of private. Once, in an editorial, he tried to lay the title to rest. But his protestations did not succeed, and he remained "Colonel" Cockerill throughout his career.

As the *Enquirer* grew—quadrupling its circulation during Cockerill's editorship—its influence grew, too, planting political dreams in the mind of its publisher, John McLean. As he had in Dayton during the Vallandigham campaign, Cockerill once again found his paper's political coverage laboring under uncomfortable restraints. Though there is no indication that these led to any "breaking point" between McLean and Cockerill, Cockerill's biographer Homer W. King indicates that subtle seeds of discord were, by that time, being sown: McLean had begun to resent Cockerill's reputation for having "built" the *Enquirer* and sought a way to "ease out" the popular editor. A handy vehicle for doing so presented itself in 1877. Offering Cockerill a "breather" from arduous local competition, McLean sent the editor abroad to cover the Russo-Turkish War for the *Enquirer*. It was an assignment Cockerill pursued with characteristic vigor, winning acclaim for coverage of the Russian capture of

Nicopolis. But when he returned to Cincinnati, Cockerill found that McLean, without informing him, had installed himself in the managing editor's chair and had no intention of relinquishing it.

Once more a disillusioned job hunter, Cockerill's next stop was Washington. There he helped launch the *Washington Post* (later owned by McLean) in 1877 and introduced his thorough, aggressive brand of news coverage and a few newsroom innovations, including addition to the staff of a woman reporter, Calista Halsey. He had been editor of the *Baltimore Gazette*, where he had promised readers "terse and pointed English," for only a few months when he was tapped by Joseph Pulitzer to become managing editor of the *St. Louis Post-Dispatch*. Though Cockerill was "found" in one of Pulitzer's patented talent hunts, he was by no means unknown to the St. Louis publisher. The two had met in Cincinnati in 1872 at a convention of Liberal Republicans; Pulitzer, a delegate, also was covering the convention for the *St. Louis Westliche Post*. *Enquirer* reporter Cockerill had talked with him at length, and the two had discovered, on that occasion, that they shared a number of common interests and views.

In Pulitzer, Cockerill at last had found a publisher whose dedication to the news product rivaled his own; in Cockerill, Pulitzer had found a man some described as the "perfect" editor. Pulitzer biographer Don Carlos Seitz calls Cockerill a man after Pulitzer's own heart—"one who had wit, quick decision and willingness to face the music on all occasions, no matter how loudly it played." Opposite in many of their skills, talents, and personality traits, the two men had on-the-job styles that complemented one another. Pulitzer—the more artistic, intellectual, and scholarly—had vision. Cockerill—witty, earthy, street smart—could make the daily wheels turn. Pulitzer had the greater capability for reflection; Cockerill acted on impulse—at times, some thought, to the point of recklessness. Pulitzer, an easily frazzled introvert, sought quiet and solitude; Cockerill, a robust and booming extrovert, enjoyed bright lights and convivial company. As a writer, Pulitzer tended to sound pedantic and shrill, whereas Cockerill's prose flowed freely, enlivened by apt idiom and irreverent wit. Both were demanding masters and blunt critics given to profanity. Yet they inspired loyalty among their employees by recognizing, developing, and valuing talent. When Pulitzer was away from the paper, as he often was, he trusted Cockerill to "run the shop." When Pulitzer was in-house, the two collaborated well, though Cockerill once remarked that the publisher was "the best man in the world to have in a newspaper office for one hour in the morning" but a "damned nuisance" the rest of the day.

Cockerill filled his own days with the myriad details of getting out the news. Quick to react to soft paper, worn typefaces, or ink "running light," he took poor printing almost as a personal affront. Within the newsroom, he shepherded all aspects, prose and pictorial, from breaking news to letters to the editor. Buoyant in outlook, Cockerill matter-of-factly welcomed praise, especially when it came from "Mr. P.," and stood up boldly to criticism. Once, responding to a minister's shocked and scolding letter regarding an "irreligious" cartoon, Cockerill wrote: "My Dear Sir: Will you kindly go to hell?" On another occasion, when the *Post-Dispatch* was threatened with a libel suit by a young man falsely identified as the author of a mash note to a chorus girl, Cockerill ran an editorial containing a tongue-in-cheek apology. Noting that the paper had promptly corrected the mistaken identity, he called the correction "full, ample and somewhat tinctured with the oil of humiliation and sprinkled with the dust of regret." Cockerill slyly concluded that in addition, credit was due to "our little faux pas" and resultant correction for allowing "thousands of people to now know" the complainant to be "an innocent steady-going youth," whereas prior to the publication they would not "have known him from his Satanic Majesty's off ox."

Cockerill's single-minded absorption in the news product, coupled with his apparent lack of either business acumen or outside ambitions, suited Pulitzer well. It was the wary publisher's style to keep employees both competitive with one another and ignorant of the overall scope of his newspapers' operations. Years later, Cockerill, having been put over the competitive hurdles and beginning to suspect his rewards were not commensurate with his input, was to break with his longtime editorial associate; but the days at the *Post-Dispatch* were perhaps the period of closest teamwork for the two. In his early camaraderie with Cockerill, Pulitzer even became the only publisher to join the press club Cockerill founded in St. Louis. The two men collaborated in a vigorous editorial campaign urging street improvements and the building of a park system while warring against taxdodgers and the heads of gambling and prostitution rings, all of this under a platform of serving "no party but the people." While building circulation and popular support, the aggressive campaign also made some enemies. Among them was congressional candidate James O. Broadhead, a lawyer who had incurred

Alonzo W. Slayback, St. Louis lawyer whose shooting by Cockerill ended Cockerill's career at the Post-Dispatch

Cockerill's editorial wrath by dumping the city as his client in a lawsuit against a gas company and promptly agreeing to represent the gas company. Cockerill dubbed Broadhead's law firm "Grimshaw, Grabshaw and Bagshaw" and called the candidate unfit for Congress.

When friends of Cockerill learned that Broadhead's partner, Alonzo W. Slayback, had vowed to avenge Broadhead's honor, they urged Cockerill to buy a gun for protection. He carried a weapon for a few days, then pronounced himself "tired of the damned thing" and stowed it in his desk drawer. Meeting Slayback at a club both belonged to, Cockerill urged him to stop baiting the *Post-Dispatch* and reminded Slayback of the editorial consideration extended to him a year earlier. On that occasion, Pulitzer had stopped the presses and ordered an inflammatory "card" (a published accusation often preliminary to a duel) that accused Slayback of cowardice to be withheld from publication. When Slayback subsequently publicly called the *Post-Dispatch* a "blackmailing sheet," Cockerill

responded by publishing the "card." Within hours, on 13 October 1882, Slayback and another lawyer, William Clopton, arrived at Cockerill's office, where Cockerill was talking to business manager John M. McGuffin and composing room foreman Victor C. Cole. Moments later, Slayback lay dying on the office floor. The *Post-Dispatch* men testified afterward that Slayback was aiming a pistol at Cockerill when McGuffin grabbed at Slayback's weapon and Cockerill fired his. Clopton said neither he nor Slayback was armed and that Slayback had been trying to remove his coat, not reach for a weapon, when Cockerill snatched the gun from his desk drawer and fired. A gun, not Cockerill's, was recovered near Slayback's body.

The tragedy had immediate and long-range repercussions for the *Post-Dispatch*. Shortly after Cockerill had left the office to turn himself in to the police, crowds gathered and threatened to burn the building and "get" the editor. Subsequent exoneration of Cockerill by a grand jury did not solve the *Post-Dispatch*'s problems. Before the newspaper slowly righted itself, more than 2,000 readers had canceled their subscriptions. Pulitzer, who had returned to town to back his editor, felt it was obvious that Cockerill could not remain at the paper.

John M. McGuffin, Post-Dispatch *business manager who went to New York with Cockerill to help Pulitzer remake the* World

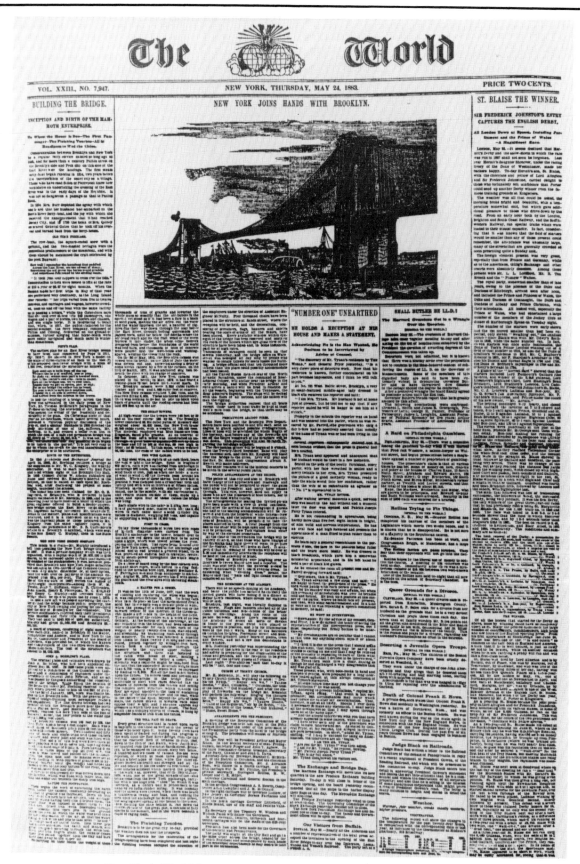

New York World *front page announcing the opening of the Brooklyn Bridge*

Morose since the shooting, which he steadfastly maintained was an act of self-defense, Cockerill found dismissal from the *Post-Dispatch* a shattering blow.

Pulitzer, too, was devastated by the post-shooting hostility in St. Louis. A number of historians share the view that the Slayback tragedy, though not his sole reason for the move, provided the final impetus behind Pulitzer's decision to attempt to realize an old dream of cracking the New York newspaper market. Soon, Pulitzer had entered into the negotiations with Jay Gould that led in May 1883 to the purchase of the *New York World*. The new owner soon was pacing the newsroom shouting, "Condense! Condense!" and demanding more spice in the *World*'s headlines. Within a few days, he had decided the *World*'s incumbent editors would not do and sent word for Cockerill and McGuffin to "come at once!" Before long, the *World*'s polished but prim style gave way to headlines that shrieked "Baptized in Blood," "Screaming for Mercy," and "A Mother's Crime." Cockerill urged reporters to write their stories "as you would tell it to a friend." What had been planned before the Pulitzer takeover as a routine announcement on the opening of the Brooklyn Bridge became in Cockerill's hands something akin to an extravaganza, and thousands turned out to witness the event.

Pulitzer and Cockerill built a base of strong local news coverage and aggressive editorials beneath the circulation-boosting human interest items. The *World* began a steady climb from a circulation of under 20,000. On 2 September 1884, *World* staffers donned celebratory top hats to cheer the 100-gun salute fired to mark a 100,000 circulation. Increasingly heavy local coverage, vigorous editorial support of Grover Cleveland's presidential candidacy, and liberal use of woodcuts, including innovative caricatures of prominent local figures, increased the *World*'s growing dominance in a market that had once "belonged" to the *Herald* and the *Sun*. Months earlier, the *Herald* had been forced to lower its price to meet the *World*'s competition; now it was even buying promotional ads in the *World*. Charles A. Dana's fading *Sun*, which had feuded bitterly with Pulitzer, now played its trump card, claiming that Cockerill had escaped indictment in the Slayback shooting only because of Pulitzer's "hold upon the district attorney." The answering editorial, probably written by Cockerill, described Cockerill as "one who was cruelly forced to defend himself against the premeditated assault of an armed man" and chided the *Sun* for behavior it

decried as "the venomous malignity of a decaying newspaper." Unlike the *Post-Dispatch*'s faltering response to criticism after the shooting, the *World* emerged from the exchange stronger than before.

New means of circulation-building were found when old ones lost steam. The *World* developed a new featured by-line, that of "Nellie Bly." "Nellie" was Elizabeth Cochrane, a Pittsburgh reporter who "camped" in the *World* office until she talked her way into a job. Accounts vary as to whose idea it was for her to feign insanity in order to do an "inside" account of conditions in a local asylum: some say Pulitzer dreamed up the assignment, others that it was Cochrane's own idea. Among those attributing it to Cockerill, one report even

"Nellie Bly" (Elizabeth Cochrane), New York World *reporter, preparing to leave on her attempt to circle the globe in less than eighty days (Library of Congress)*

described the "blue flames" that shot from his eyes when the bright idea struck. Whatever its genesis, the series was developed and played under Cockerill's hand, and he almost certainly was the source of subsequent assignments in which Nellie took on two longtime *World* targets—a crooked lobbyist and white slave "recruiters." Both reporter and editor regarded these assignments as far more significant than the stunt for which Cochrane was to be remembered—beating Jules Verne's "eighty days" on a globe-circling trip.

By the time Nellie Bly began attracting new readers to the *World*, it had topped 250,000, trumpeting that figure as the largest circulation ever achieved by an American newspaper. It was during that period that Pulitzer's weakened eyesight took a drastic turn for the worse. Though he sought specialists the world over, Pulitzer had suffered a detached retina and would spend the rest of his life in semidarkness. The mid- and late 1880s, with Pulitzer away from the paper much of the time trying to regain his health, brought trials and tribulations of other sorts to Cockerill. With growing responsibilities had come growing fatigue, and Cockerill at last admitted to Pulitzer a need of assistance. Pulitzer hired Ballard Smith of the *Herald*, presumably to fill the role of assistant managing editor. Apparently in an effort to test and spur both editors, Pulitzer blurred the lines of Smith's responsibilities. Soon Smith and Cockerill were at odds: Smith felt subjugated; Cockerill accused Smith of insubordination. Animosity between the two hurt both men's work. Eventually Smith was "farmed out" to the *World*'s Brooklyn edition. The experience seemed at least temporarily to take the edge off Cockerill's keenness and to dampen his customary joie de vivre.

Things were changing in Cockerill's personal life as well. In 1884, he met, courted, and married a young actress, Leonora Barner, who, though of limited theatrical talent, had captivated the forty-two-year-old bachelor with her beauty and vivacity. Nearly everyone but Cockerill, who was reputed to be the highest-paid editor in the nation, seemed to suspect that Leonora, half Cockerill's age, saw mainly dollar signs in the dark-haired editor. Though apparently happy at first, the relationship was from all accounts a one-sided one. Cockerill doted on his young bride, dreamed of raising a family, and drafted a will leaving everything to Leonora. She, in turn, grew bored and petulant and before long began seeing another man.

At the same time that he was undergoing personal trauma in his married life, Cockerill suffered

political miseries. Long a loyal Democrat and formerly an enthusiastic booster of President Cleveland, he felt Cleveland's "free trade" policies were a sellout of the American working man. In 1888, Cockerill transferred his allegiance to the Republican party. This placed him at cross purposes with the *World*'s editorial policy, still in lusty support of Cleveland. At least one content analysis of the *World*'s news pages from that period concluded that Cockerill did not let his deep disenchantment with the Democrats and Cleveland cause any distortion of the news; both parties alternately were angered by *World* coverage of the campaign.

Not all developments in the late 1880s were unhappy ones. It was during that period that Cockerill orchestrated some of Nellie Bly's triumphs. It was then, too, that he became deeply involved in the New York Press Club and in 1888 began the first of five terms as its president. Nevertheless, subtle changes were under way at the *World*. Pulitzer, in his near-blindness and his extreme sensitivity to noise, had become an absentee publisher. In 1890, he called upon Cockerill to help him draft a formal statement announcing to the staff his withdrawal from an active role at the paper. Again, Pulitzer delegated by fragmentation, choosing three men—Cockerill among them—to direct the *World*. Although Cockerill was named "editor in charge," Pulitzer had not made it clear exactly who directed what or who, ultimately, enjoyed the last word. Inevitably, the three squabbled. In more peaceful moments, they compared notes and discussed the *World*'s great financial successes. Cockerill, typically "slow" in business matters, began to suspect "Mr. P" had not treated him as well as his workload warranted. Surviving letters and memos do not settle precisely what occurred in 1891; some sources say Pulitzer and Cockerill had a "noisy quarrel," others that Pulitzer was enraged by an "impertinent memo" from Cockerill suggesting improvements in his contract. Whatever the cause, Pulitzer chose to oust Cockerill from the *World* and reassign him to the *Post-Dispatch*. Wanting none of such a change, Cockerill simply walked out.

For the next four years, under financing from railroad magnate Collis P. Huntington, Cockerill labored to reestablish two faltering New York papers, the *Commercial Advertiser* and the *Continent* (soon to become the *Morning Advertiser*). Cockerill managed to improve the papers' circulation, appearance, and journalistic integrity but could not dent the *World*'s dominance and never was able to turn the papers into true money-makers; in 1894, he withdrew. Meanwhile, he had become something of a "senior statesman" as a commentator on the state of newspapering, contributing to such publications as *Harper's* and *Review of Reviews*. He was a critic more of practices than of personalities, but two of his favored targets—sensationalism and absentee ownership—obviously cut close to the bone of his long association with Pulitzer.

Having left New York newspaper competition for the first time since 1883, Cockerill tried to reorder his life. He offered Leonora a generous divorce settlement, but she failed to make the requisite trip to South Dakota to finalize the matter. Cockerill, so often lax in business details, neglected to press the divorce issue or to make any change in his 1888 will leaving his estate to Leonora and naming Pulitzer, his "good friend," as executor. Soon he was caught up in new assignments. He toured the West in 1894 and wrote a series of articles about Brigham Young, the Mormons, and the future of Utah. Not long thereafter, Cockerill was en route to Japan, hired by the *New York Herald* to report for its foreign news service. There, he enjoyed a cordial reunion with Lafcadio Hearn. The ever-gregarious Cockerill soon established a multitude of news contacts and friendships in Japan, becoming, according to one contemporary source, the "most popular" foreigner in that land. At one point, Cockerill was invited to the imperial palace by the emperor of Japan, who, citing the American journalist's role as "faithful historian," conferred on him the Third Order of the Sacred Treasure. Cockerill was deeply touched; the honor had never before gone to a journalist and had been given only twice before to a recipient who was not Japanese. High Japanese esteem for Cockerill later cooled when Cockerill wrote dispatches pointing out what he believed to be serious blunders in Japan's policy toward Korea. *Herald* publisher James Gordon Bennett, Jr., at that point elected to give Cockerill a new assignment: he was to go first to Cairo to report on a British-Egyptian military expedition up the Nile, and then was to proceed to London.

On 10 April 1896, Cockerill stopped by the barbershop of his Cairo hotel to get a haircut. After exchanging pleasantries with the barber, he grew silent, then toppled heavily from the chair. He never regained consciousness, dying of apoplexy 2½ hours later. Tributes, verbal and floral, poured in from many persons in many lands, including a major share of the world's great journalists; none came from Joseph Pulitzer. Leonora, never finally divorced from Cockerill, played a prominent role in arranging the rites, five separate ceremonies in New York and St. Louis. Three weeks after Cockerill was buried in St. Louis, Leonora remarried. Though the will was contested by Cockerill's relatives, Leonora received the estate.

It would be equally unfair, as some have done, to credit Pulitzer for Cockerill's success or Cockerill for the *World's*. Pulitzer's business shrewdness and editorial vision saw the horizons of "new journalism"; Cockerill's canny sense of news and news play and splendid managerial carry-through kept Pulitzer's publications in sight of those horizons. Neither as creative nor as intellectual as his publisher, Cockerill nonetheless was a prototype managing editor, an able guide of staff and story. The phrase "one of the best" dominates both contemporary and retrospective assessments of his editorships. According to Pulitzer biographer Seitz, Cockerill rated as irreplaceable. "No one ever," Seitz wrote, "came into the editorship [of the *World*] who fitted in so well with Mr. Pulitzer and at the same time was able to rally men to himself and inspire them with his zeal and energy."

Periodical Publications:

"The Newspaper of the Future," *Lippincott's Monthly Magazine* (August 1892): 220-226;

"Some Phases of Contemporary Journalism," *Cosmopolitan* (October 1892): 695-703;

"Indictment and a Remedy: Colonel Cockerill on Newspapers," *Harper's Weekly* (5 November, 1892);

"The Trend of the Great Daily," *Review of Reviews* (November 1893): 449-451;

"Brigham Young and the Modern Utah," *Cosmopolitan* (September 1895): 501-512;

"Lafcadio Hearn: The Author of Kokoro," *Current Literature* (June 1896): 476;

"How to Conduct a Local Newspaper," *Lippincott's Magazine* (September 1896): 395-399.

Biography:

Homer W. King, *Pulitzer's Prize Editor* (Durham, N.C.: Duke University Press, 1965).

References:

Calder M. Pickett, *Voices of the Past* (Columbus, Ohio: Grid, 1977);

Julian S. Rammelkamp, *Pulitzer's Post-Dispatch 1878–1883* (Princeton, N.J.: Princeton University Press, 1967);

Don Carlos Seitz, *Joseph Pulitzer, His Life and Letters* (New York: Simon & Schuster, 1924);

W. A. Swanberg, *Pulitzer* (New York: Scribners, 1967);

Oswald Garrison Villard, *Some Newspapers and Newspapermen* (New York: Knopf, 1923).

Papers:

John A. Cockerill's papers are at Columbia University.

James Creelman

(12 November 1859-12 February 1915)

Ronald S. Marmarelli
Central Michigan University

MAJOR POSITIONS HELD: Reporter, foreign correspondent, *New York Herald* (1878-1893); war correspondent, *New York World* (1894-1896), *New York Journal* (1896-1900); special correspondent, editorial writer, *New York World* (1900-1906).

BOOKS: *On the Great Highway: The Wanderings and Adventures of a Special Correspondent* (Boston: Lothrop, 1901; London: Kelly, 1901);
Eagle Blood (Boston: Lothrop, 1902; London: Kelly, 1902);
Why We Love Lincoln (New York: Outing, 1909);
Diaz, Master of Mexico (New York: Appleton, 1912).

James Creelman was one of the more prominent figures among the cohort of journalists whose activities contributed to creating the image of the late nineteenth century as the "Golden Age of the Reporter" in American journalism. As a correspondent for Bennett, Pulitzer, and Hearst, Creelman traveled the world to interview the great men of his time and to report on the conflicts between men. He covered three wars and several other conflicts in the 1890s, and his intense drive to be on the scene of battle and in the middle of the action gained him exclusive stories and several wounds. All the while, his dispatches became notable events in themselves, as did his activities. "Journalist Famous For Exploits" was the way the *New York Times* headlined his obituary. Arthur Brisbane, Hearst's premier editor, described Creelman in 1898 as "a newspaper writer whose business and delight consist in telling about the big things that really happen in this world. The bigger the better, of course." Another Hearst man remembered Creelman as "a journalist with an exceedingly adventurous disposition—one of the sort who believes in making news when there is none."

This adventurous disposition was evident at an early age. Creelman was born in Montreal, Canada, on 12 November 1859, the son of Matthew and Martha Dunwoodie Creelman. A few years after his parents separated and his mother moved to New York City, Creelman saved a pocketful of coins and set out at the age of twelve to be with his mother. He made the trip of some 400 miles mostly on foot and arrived at his mother's rooming house with worn-out shoes and a nickel in his pocket. Creelman settled in with his mother but soon rebelled against her insistence that he attend school; instead, he got a job in the printing plant of the Protestant Episcopal church's newspaper, where he learned the printer's trade. (Again, he acted in spite of his mother's objections; she was a staunch Presbyterian.) After some brief and irregular work for the *Brooklyn Eagle*, where an editor discouraged him from writing poetry, and a course of study at Talmage's Lay Theological College, Creelman was hired as a cub reporter at the age of eighteen by the *New York Herald*.

Creelman first risked his life for a story in the winter of 1878. He was sent to interview Paul Boynton, who had invented an aquatic suit that would keep a person afloat, and Creelman was told to try out the suit. The reporter and the inventor each donned a floating suit, got into the river, and floated away. They drifted for an hour, heading toward the open sea, before being picked up by a fishing boat. The following year, Creelman was sent to Montreal to make a balloon ascension in the "Page Iron Airship." Referring to the experience years later as "Newsgathering in the Clouds," Creelman wrote: "Looking through the pages of the note-books that carry the story of my boyish days in journalism, I find a few rough scrawlings that bring to mind a bright Canadian sky, the green slopes of

Mount Royal, a chattering crowd spread out on one of the lacrosse fields of Montreal, and a great, glistening, yellow gas bag wobbling in circles above an iron cage, with huge fan wheels, in which I was to make a journey through the air for the edification of the insatiate American newspaper public." Creelman had won the right to make the ascension by a toss of a Canadian penny with another correspondent. After several hours in the air, the airship crashed to the ground and was dragged for miles over farm fields. Creelman suffered a broken right arm.

Subsequent assignments included covering the Hatfield-McCoy feud in Kentucky, where he was shot at by one of the Hatfields; traveling in the American West, where he interviewed Sitting Bull; and reporting the burial of Ulysses S. Grant in Au-

gust 1885. Recalling the interview with Sitting Bull, Creelman wrote in his memoirs that to get to his subject he "had paddled down the muddy waters of the Missouri with Paul Boynton, the adventurous traveller, who spent his time floating along the rivers of the world in an inflated rubber suit." Creelman described his meeting with Sitting Bull: "There he stood—the mightiest personality of a dying people whose campfires were burning in America before Solomon built the temple in Jerusalem—native America incarnate, with knife and tomahawk and pipe, facing a stripling writer from a New York newspaper, and telling the simple story of his retreating race. . . . The scribblings of the correspondent, which he regarded with disdain, suggested nothing to his mind of the irresistible power of publicity, that conqueror of armies and dynasties and civilizations. To him it was mere foolishness."

Not long after his Western trip, Creelman was involved in yet another "exploit" involving Paul Boynton, this time in New York City. In the spring of 1884, during an international dispute between Russia and England, a British cruiser and a Russian cruiser were anchored offshore. Boynton, an anglophobe, boasted that he could float out to the British cruiser at night and attach an imitation torpedo to the ship without being seen. Creelman represented the *Herald* among a crew of reporters who went out in a rowboat at midnight to accompany Boynton, who succeeded in attaching the mock torpedo. The party was taken into custody by British marines, however. In his account of the misadventure, Charles Edward Russell wrote that

Creelman, whose courage, presence of mind, and readiness to wit have been proved since in many trying emergencies, including those of a score of battlefields . . . now stood forward and in a manner perfectly cool but determined and aggressive said:

"This thing has gone far enough. I am an American citizen. I demand to know by what right I am seized in American waters by British sailors and brought on board a British ship. I demand the instant release of myself and my party and I can assure you that the matter will not end even at that. . . . I am an American citizen in the pursuit of my regular and lawful calling and you have not the slightest right to interfere with me."

The party was released soon after.

In 1889, Creelman was sent to Europe to become the *Herald*'s special correspondent there. He headed the short-lived London edition of the paper

Some of Creelman's interview subjects: Sitting Bull (above, left), who regarded Creelman's "scribblings . . . with disdain"; Pope Leo XIII (above, right), whom Creelman interviewed only after a long struggle with the Vatican bureaucracy; Count Leo Tolstoy (left), who considered reporters "an irreverent tribe"; King Kojong of Korea (opposite page, left), whom Creelman regarded as merely "a big piece of news"; and King George of Greece (opposite page, right), whom Creelman interviewed just prior to the Greco-Turkish war

in 1889 and 1890 and was editor of the Paris *Herald* from 1891 to 1892. During his years in Europe, Creelman interviewed Pope Leo XIII and Henry Stanley; traveled to Russia to investigate persecution of Jews and to interview Tolstoy; and achieved high esteem in journalistic circles. In *On the Great Highway* (1901), Creelman related in what he described as "pages from the experiences of a busy man" details of these assignments, and he noted:

> The author has attempted to give the original color and atmosphere of some of the great events of his own time, and leaves the duty of moralizing to his indulgent patrons. . . .
>
> The frequent introduction of the author's personality is a necessary means of reminding the reader that he is receiving the testimony of an eyewitness.

Throughout his reminiscences, Creelman commented on the nature and role of journalists and newspapers of his time and revealed much of his own style of reporting. Concerning his interview with Leo XIII in 1891, at a time when there was much interest in the pope's views on social unrest

and social justice, Creelman wrote: "It was all very well to sit at an editorial desk in Paris and plan an interview with the Pope. But I had not been a week in Rome before I began to understand the seeming hopelessness of carrying profane journalism into the presence of the white Vicar of Christ, sitting at the heart of the mysterious Vatican." He was advised to give up the idea, but "the persistent spirit developed in an American newspaper office is not easily daunted. As the difficulties gathered, my ambition to interview the Pope grew more intense. It became an absorbing passion." Upon finally being given the pope's consent, "I left the palace drunken with joy. How my old comrades in New York would stare when they learned that I had reached the unreachable! How my newspaper would herald the feat to the ends of the earth!"

Meanwhile, he was sent to Brindisi, Italy, "to meet Henry M. Stanley, the explorer, who was on his way back from Africa, after rescuing Emin Pasha from the perils of the Equatorial Province." Since Creelman was with the *Herald*, for whom Stanley had first gone into Africa years before to find the missionary David Livingstone, he got an exclusive story. Creelman was preoccupied, however, and he recalled that "as I walked along the stone quay of

Brindisi with the weatherbeaten man whose deeds had once inspired me with visions of the possibilities of my profession, and heard him talk of the riches of Africa, my mind turned always to Rome." Three days later he had his audience with the pope.

> There, behind all the pomp and ceremony, sat a gentle old man, with a sweet face and the saddest eyes that ever looked out of a human head. . . . It was a presence at once appealing and majestic.
> That moment I forgot my newspaper and the news-thirsty multitudes of New York.

In their conversation, the pope asked: "You are not of the Faithful?" Creelman replied: "I am what journalism has made of me."

Later that year, while in Russia looking into the persecution of Jews, "and trying to keep the Emperor's busy police from penetrating the secret of my mission," Creelman wrote, "a letter from James Gordon Bennett directed me to find Count Tolstoy, and learn whether his real views of modern marriage were presented in 'The Kreutzer Sonata,' the extraordinary book which was then attracting attention throughout the civilized world." Creelman spent several days and nights discussing and debating issues of marriage, theology, political philosophy, and literature with Tolstoy and observing him with his people. At one point, Tolstoy commented: "You newspaper writers are an irreverent tribe." Creelman wrote later: "The statement being true, I made no reply. Presently the Count forgot the subject."

Creelman was unhappy working for Bennett because of the publisher's policy requiring that stories be published without by-lines. Although his achievements were widely known among journalists, he wanted wider recognition and an improvement in his chances for advancement. He was by now a married man, having wed Alice Leffingwell Buell of Marietta, Ohio, on 3 December 1891. From the end of 1892, he edited Bennett's *New York Evening Telegram*, but he finally broke with Bennett in 1893 and worked briefly as associate editor of the *Illustrated American* and manager of the London edition of *Cosmopolitan* magazine.

In 1894, Creelman joined Joseph Pulitzer's *New York World*. Bennett paid tribute to his former prize reporter and to his rival by announcing Creelman's new association with the *World* on the *Herald*'s front page. A picture of Creelman was captioned "Great Reporter!" Pulitzer's picture was captioned "Great Editor!"

Pulitzer dispatched his new correspondent to Asia to cover the Sino-Japanese War, which started in August 1894, and Creelman's work soon gained him new notoriety. Creelman praised the "brave and humane" Japanese with their modern military organization and tactics and expressed disdain for the outdated and brutal practices of the Chinese in his reports on the decisive battle at Pyongyang for control of Korea. He told of Chinese fighting in the rain under colorful oilpaper umbrellas and dying in great numbers in futile cavalry charges. He worked, he wrote later, "by lantern light on the outmost ramparts to escape the terrific sounds of victory that roared between the shattered walls of the old city, while the reek of a thousand half-buried Chinese corpses rose from the darkened field over which the conquering soldiery still marched northward in pursuit of Korea's oppressors." He carried his dispatch to Chemulpo for delivery to Japan and cable to San Francisco, from where it was to be telegraphed to New York. "When I arrived in the dirty little Korean seaport, weary and sickened by the bloody field of Ping Yang [as it was then spelled], a messenger handed me a cablegram from Ohio. It contained two words—'Boy—well.' It was the announcement of the birth of my first child. Thirteen tissue paper tags, bearing the seals of thirteen different headquarters of the Japanese army, showed that the news had been carried from battlefield to battlefield to reach me. The news of a new life was brought to me from the other side of the world, just as I sent word of a thousand freshly slain."

On his way back to Pyongyang, Creelman found that the main Japanese fleet was nearby after having defeated the Chinese fleet. He received a full and exclusive briefing from the Japanese admiral and his staff and celebrated with the Japanese naval officers, who toasted his son's health with champagne.

After the Japanese victory in Korea, Creelman went to Seoul to interview the king of Korea. He later described his intentions and offered these observations on journalism: "An interview with the King would give a quaint variety to the endless descriptions of fighting. The American public must be allowed to see the inmost throne of the royal palace; American journalism must invade the presence of the hermit monarch—to touch whose person was an offense punishable by death—see his face, question him, and weave his sorrows into some up-to-date political moral. The artificial majesty of kings, after all, counts for little before the levelling processes of the modern newspaper power. It may be intrusive, it may be irreverent, it may be destructive of sentiment; but it gradually breaks down the walls of tradition and prejudice that divide the human race." Creelman faced one problem because of his dress. "My rough corduroy riding dress, spurred boots, flannel shirt, and slouch hat were all I had." Suitable clothing was soon gathered, and the journalist met the monarch. Reflecting on the majesty and mystery surrounding the royal personage, Creelman resolved the potential problem of being awed by the scene: "Yet I could see no good reason why an American newspaper correspondent should not be quite comfortable in the presence of this exalted being. He was for the moment simply 'a big piece of news.' " (Creelman apparently made more of the interview than its content merited; an American diplomat reported that the interview was sensationalized and observed that Creelman probably put words into the king's mouth.)

After Korea, Creelman next accompanied the Japanese army on its invasion of Manchuria. He was soon on the trail of forces led by the Japanese commander Field Marshal Count Oyama and traveled by pony all night to reach the headquarters before the fighting began at Kinchow, Talien-wan, and Port Arthur. "I did not dare to stop," he recalled. "An artist might tarry on the road and gather materials for his pencil," he said, referring to Frederic Villiers, who was on assignment for the *Herald* and had decided to rest, "but a correspondent, responsible for the news, must not halt. The field marshal was ahead, and with him there might be rival correspondents. Who knew what might happen that very night?" He reached his destination but was too late for the Battle of Kinchow. After witnessing the fighting around Talien-wan, Creelman rode with Japanese forces on their way to Oshozima. A nearby explosion of an artillery shell wounded his horse, and Creelman fell to the ground, suffering a broken rib and a knee injury. He returned to Kinchow.

A few days later, Creelman headed for Port Arthur for the coming battle. After witnessing the furious fighting that ended with the Chinese fleeing the city on 21 November 1894, he and other correspondents observed the entry of the victorious Japanese and the massacre of Chinese in the city. Creelman's first brief cable was not received at the *New York World* until 11 December. The fall of Port Arthur had been known for days, but the massacre was only rumored. The *World* published Creelman's signed dispatch on 12 December under the headline "A Japanese Massacre": "The Japanese troops entered Port Arthur on November 21 and massacred practically the entire population in cold blood. The defenseless and unarmed inhabitants

were butchered in their houses and their bodies were unspeakably mutilated. There was an unrestrained reign of murder which continued for three days. The whole town was plundered with appalling atrocities. It was the first stain upon Japanese civilization. The Japanese in this instance relapsed into barbarism. All pretense that circumstances justified the atrocities are false. The foreign correspondents, horrified by the spectacle, left the army in a body." The abbreviated version was followed by a longer one. The story was hotly debated for weeks; reports that the Japanese had offered Creelman a bribe not to write it and conflicting accounts of the extent of the slaughter were featured in the *New York Herald*. Public opinion turned against the Japanese. The *World* reported on 17 and 18 December that the Japanese foreign minister had verified Creelman's account.

Writing a few months later, Russian artist Valerian Gribayédoff concluded: "Abundant evidence has . . . been brought forward to show that Creelman spoke the truth. Even the *Herald*'s artist, Villiers, not to mention Mr. Cowan of the *London Times*, and many American naval officers, all present on the occasion, have since fully corroborated his story; Villiers backing up his testimony with irrefragable proof in the shape of photographs taken on the spot. For the first time in its history, the *Herald* has been outdone in the field of war correspondence. *Tempora mutantur!*" (This last fact must have given Creelman special satisfaction, apart from the satisfaction of having achieved general fame.) The Russian paid tribute to his colleague: "Creelman is made of the clay from which spring crusaders, reformers, and martyrs. His judgment may often be open to question; his good faith, sincerity, loyalty, perseverance, and manliness never. Barely thirty-four years of age [*sic*], Creelman has passed through more experiences than ninety nine hundredths of his fellow craftsmen." Upon his return to New York, the *World* honored Creelman at a testimonial dinner.

After what must have been some relatively quiet months in 1895, Creelman was sent to Cuba in February 1896 to cover the Cuban insurrection against Spain. He was a key figure in the mounting campaign against the Spanish, as, Creelman wrote in 1901, "the American newspaper correspondents, treading the secret precincts of insurgent activity, in the shadow of the royal palace, saw to it that the lamp of American sympathy was kept trimmed and burning brightly." He soon was filing stories of Spanish atrocities and was summoned to the presence of Captain-General Don Valeriano Weyler, the

Spanish commander in Cuba, whom Creelman labeled "The Butcher" and "the most sinister figure of the nineteenth century." The Spanish official railed against American newspapers and reporters ("Men like you," Weyler declared, "who excite rebellion everywhere—meddlesome scribblers") and threatened Creelman with death if he persisted.

With a page-one story of four columns in the *World* of 1 May 1896, Creelman told of investigating reports of the killing of some fifty Cuban civilians in a rural district near Havana; he provided names and dates of death of thirty-three victims. The *World* responded with an editorial calling for United States intervention. Creelman later described finding the evidence with the guidance of "two patriotic Cubans": "A few strokes of a spade uncovered the ghastly evidences of murder. The hands of the slain Cubans were tied behind their backs. The sight revealed by the flickering light of our lanterns would have moved the hardest heart. I made a vow in that moment that I would help to extinguish Spanish sovereignty in Cuba, if I had to shed my blood for it. That vow was kept." Confronting Weyler with the evidence of atrocities, Creelman was threatened with expulsion; he and W. W. Gay, also of the *World*, and Frederick W. Lawrence of the *New York Journal* were expelled from Cuba a few days later. Both newspapers carried major coverage of the expulsions. Creelman wrote in a front-page article published 17 May 1896: "The horrors of a barbarous struggle for the extermination of the native population are witnessed in all parts of the country. Blood on the roadsides, blood in the fields, blood on the doorsteps, blood, blood, blood! The old, the young, the weak, the crippled—all are butchered without mercy. There is scarcely a hamlet that has not witnessed the dreadful work. Is there no nation wise enough, brave enough to aid this blood-smitten land? Is there any barbarism known to the mind of man that will justify the intervention of a civilized power? A new Armenia lies within 80 miles of the American coast. Not a word from Washington! Not a sign from the president!"

With the Cuba story now in the hands of other correspondents, Creelman returned to more routine tasks. In the fall presidential campaign, Pulitzer assigned him to travel with William Jennings Bryan. It was Creelman's last major assignment for the *World*: in late 1896, William Randolph Hearst, stepping up his campaign to top Pulitzer, hired Creelman for his *New York Journal* and sent him to Europe. As Hearst's special commissioner to the capitals of Europe, Creelman spent weeks in

Madrid, reporting on the Spanish government's response to events in Cuba. When a crisis in Asia Minor flared between Greece and Turkey, he went to Athens and interviewed King George of Greece. The crisis erupted in April into the brief Greco-Turkish War, and Creelman was sent to cover the conflict along with six other *Journal* correspondents, including Stephen Crane and Julian Ralph. He sailed on a Greek troopship to Volo, the Greek naval base in Thessaly; traveled by train to Larissa, where he surveyed the Greek forces; and then crossed into the Turkish lines "on a half-starved pony." Creelman interviewed the Turkish commander, Memdouh Pasha, and was impressed with the Turkish military strength. But then a London correspondent arrived. "I had been the first correspondent to cross the frontier and enter the Turkish lines. That fact in itself was an important thing for newspaper headlines. But now I was face to face with a rival who would undoubtedly claim the credit unless I reached the telegraph station at Larissa before him." The two raced back to Larissa, and Creelman arrived at 1:00 A.M., "splashed with mud from head to foot," to get his dispatch out.

Back in New York in the summer of 1897, Creelman observed firsthand the activities of yellow journalism, which he defined later as "that form of American journalistic energy which is not content merely to print a daily record of history, but seeks to take part in events as an active and sometimes decisive agent." He was an eager participant. Willis Abbott recalled that Creelman's enthusiasm endeared him to Hearst: " 'The beauty about Creelman,' [Hearst] said, 'is the fact that whatever you give him to do instantly becomes in his mind the most important assignment ever given any writer. Of course, it's a form of egotism. He thinks that the very fact of the job being given him means that it's a task of surpassing importance, else it would not have been given to so great a man as he. . . . Creelman finds any assignment is dignified by being given him. That's why he's so useful.' "

Creelman later wrote often in defense of the journalism that acts, and in his memoirs he recounted numerous incidents of the feverish prewar period of 1897-1898 when the *Journal* heightened what Creelman called "that crusade of 'yellow journalism.' " His recollections of that time provided the first revelation (never corroborated) of Hearst's famous telegram to Frederic Remington in Cuba: "Please remain. You furnish the pictures, and I'll furnish the war." He described Hearst's gleeful "We've got Spain now!" upon receiving the news in August 1897 of the Spanish imprisonment of

Front page of William Randolph Hearst's New York Journal, *24 February 1898, advertising the paper's preparations for covering the Spanish-American War*

Evangelina Cisneros, who later escaped with the aid of *Journal* reporter Karl Decker. Creelman was active in the campaign to stir up worldwide sympathy for the Cuban woman. "How we worked and watched for poor Cuba in those days!" he wrote. Regarding the charge that yellow journalism created news, Creelman observed:

> There is a grain of truth in this criticism; but it must not be forgotten that the very nature of journalism enables it to act in the very heart of events at critical moments and with knowledge not possessed by the general public; that what is everybody's business and the business of nobody in particular, is the journalist's business.
>
> There are times when public emergencies call for the sudden intervention of some power outside of governmental authority. Then journalism acts.

He revealed that while he was in London in May 1898, after the war had begun and Admiral Dewey had defeated the Spanish at Manila Bay, Hearst sent him instructions to buy "some big English steamer" and have it sunk in the Suez Canal to prevent a powerful Spanish fleet from getting to the Philippines to attack Dewey. Willis Abbott wrote that Creelman told him he had secured an option on a British ship and was negotiating with a captain and officers. The action was made unnecessary when the Spanish fleet turned back to Spain.

Called back to the United States, Creelman joined Hearst's army of correspondents in Cuba in June 1898 and found perhaps his greatest moment of glory, leading the charge of American troops at El Caney on 1 July 1898. Writing about it later, Creelman asserted that "the newspaper man must be in the very foreground of battle, if he would see with his own eyes the dread scenes that make war worth describing." After a five-mile hike to join the forces under General Adna Chaffee who were pinned down at El Caney, Creelman suggested a bayonet charge against a Spanish blockhouse and offered to lead it. Accompanying troops of Company F, Twelfth Infantry, Creelman, in his characteristic khaki breeches and jacket, flat-brimmed hat, and high boots, moved into combat. "This was hardly the business of a correspondent; but whatever of patriotism or excitement was stirring others in that place of carnage had got into my blood too," he wrote three years later. "When I found myself out on the clear escarped slope, in front of the fort and its deadly trench, walking at the head of a storming party, I began to realize that I had ceased

Hearst's letter to Creelman, instructing the reporter to take an active part in the Spanish-American War

to be a journalist and was now—foolishly or wisely, recklessly, meddlesomely, or patriotically—a part of the army, a soldier without warrant to kill." After the blockhouse was taken, Creelman was wounded while talking surrender terms to a Spanish officer. "I felt a stinging pain in the upper part of the left arm, as though a blow had been struck with a shut fist. The sensation was no more and no less than that which might have come from a rough punch by some too hilarious friend. . . . A Mauser bullet, entering one of the loopholes [of the blockhouse], had smashed the arm and torn a hole in my back." He staggered into a hammock and was taken down the hill to be with the other wounded. A few months after the action, Creelman wrote: "In every battle that I go through, I somehow get a melody in my head and hum it to the end of the action. I suppose it is the result of nervous excitement. A man's nerves play him some very curious tricks. All through the battle and massacre of Port Arthur in the Japanese War, I hummed the air from Mendelssohn's 'Springtime,' and during the shell fire I found myself actually shrieking it. When I started in the charge on Fort Caney, I began to hum 'Rock of

Journal *artist Frederic Remington's depiction of Creelman leading the charge at El Caney*

Ages,' and I couldn't get rid of the tune even when I was lying among the dying of Chaffee's brigade in the hospital camp. I remember that when General Chaffee leaned over me after I had been shot and asked me how I was, I couldn't answer him until I had finished, in my mind, one phrase of 'Rock of Ages.' "

Creelman described in his memoirs how his story got out:

> Some one knelt in the grass beside me and put his hand on my fevered head. Opening my eyes, I saw Mr. Hearst, . . . a straw hat with a bright ribbon on his head, a revolver at his belt, and a pencil and note-book in his hand. . . . Slowly he took down my story of the fight. Again and again the tinging of Mauser bullets interrupted. But he seemed unmoved. The battle had to be reported somehow.
>
> "I'm sorry you're hurt, but,"—and his face was radiant with enthusiasm—"wasn't it a splendid fight? We must beat every paper in the world."

In his various accounts of the incident, Creel-

man repeatedly stressed the important place in his thoughts that the Spanish flag at the El Caney blockhouse assumed. In a November 1898 article, he wrote that, after having won the blockhouse, "Suddenly I thought of the flag. It was the thing that I had come to get. I wanted it for the *Journal*. The *Journal* had provoked the war, and it was only fair that the *Journal* should have the first flag captured in the greatest land battle of the war." He was successful. Hearst ended his story of the battle with the note "The Spanish flag captured from the Spanish stone fort I will forward to the *Journal* by mail."

Creelman's service in the Spanish-American War was ended, and he was evacuated by Hearst's chartered steamship the *Sylvia* back to the United States. His work was praised by many. The *Review of Reviews* stated that "if one were to select Mr. James Creelman as the most notable of the correspondents true and proper in the late war, there would be few objectors." Later in the year, recovered from his wound, he went to the Philippines to cover the battles of American forces and Filipino rebels and suffered two minor wounds. In 1900, Creelman rejoined the *New York World* as special correspondent

Creelman in his field clothes (Culver Pictures)

and editorial writer. He was active in William Jennings Bryan's 1900 campaign and covered the death of President McKinley in 1901. Creelman joined *Pearson's Magazine* as an associate editor in 1906 and worked there until 1910. He wrote on many subjects, including President Díaz of Mexico, whom he interviewed on several occasions, and the massacres of Christians by Moslems in Asia Minor. His dispatches on the massacres appeared in a five-part series in the *New York Times*, from July to October 1909. In 1910, he became active in Republican party politics in New York City, assisting his close friend Mayor William J. Gaynor. Gaynor ap-

pointed him to the city Board of Education in 1911, but he resigned a few weeks later because of dissatisfaction with the way the schools were being run. Gaynor than appointed him president of the Municipal Civil Service Commission, and he served a stormy eighteen months in the post before resigning to become associate editor of the *New York Evening Mail* on 1 January 1913.

By January 1915, he had signed on again with Hearst and was sent to Berlin for the *New York American* to cover the European war. Shortly after his arrival, however, Creelman died of Bright's disease on 12 February. In an editorial eulogy headed "Journalism the Poorer for His Loss," The *New York Times* wrote:

> By the death of James Creelman American journalism suffers the loss of a man not only with more than ordinary ability as an observer and writer, but of one who in a very notable degree took himself with the utmost seriousness as a responsible part of whatever happenings opportunity or duty brought to his attention. . . .
> The work of his later years took Mr. Creelman into many lands and into the centre—or as near to it as courage and skill could take him—of many exciting scenes, not a few of them dangerous. In them all he was something more than an onlooker and chronicler. He had opinions of what he saw and heard, and he considered those opinions an essential part of the news he sent to his paper. That he, a reporter, was allowed thus to encroach on the editorial domain ranked him with the small group of political and military representatives of the press that is fast disappearing because of changes in conditions under which journalistic service is rendered.

Periodical Publications:
"Battle Impressions," *Cosmopolitan* (September 1898): 558;
"My Experiences at Santiago," *Review of Reviews* (November 1898): 542-546;
"James Gordon Bennett," *Cosmopolitan* (May 1902): 44-47;
"The Real Mr. Hearst," *Pearson's Magazine* (September 1906): 412-416;
"Joseph Pulitzer—Master Journalist," *Pearson's Magazine* (March 1909): 229-247.

References:
Willis J. Abbott, *Watching the World Go By* (Boston: Little, Brown, 1933);

James W. Barrett, *Joseph Pulitzer and His World* (New York: Vanguard, 1941);

Arthur Brisbane, "The Modern Newspaper in War Time," *Cosmopolitan* (September 1898): 541-557;

Jeffrey M. Dorwart, "James Creelman, the *New York World* and the Port Arthur Massacre," *Journalism Quarterly* (Winter 1973): 697-701;

Valerian Gribayédoff, "The Modern War Correspondent," *Munsey's Magazine* (April 1895): 34-41;

"James Creelman Dies in Berlin," *New York Times* (13 February 1915), p. 9;

"Journalism the Poorer for His Loss," *New York Times* (16 February 1915), p. 8;

"The Massacre at Port Arthur," *Public Opinion* (27 December 1894): 939-940;

John McNamara, *Extra! U.S. War Correspondents in Action* (Boston: Houghton Mifflin, 1945);

"The Newspaper Correspondents in the War," *Review of Reviews* (November 1898): 538-541;

Charles Edward Russell, *These Shifting Scenes* (New York: Doran, 1914);

Don C. Seitz, *Joseph Pulitzer: His Life and Letters* (New York: Simon & Schuster, 1924).

Jane Cunningham Croly
(Jennie June)

(19 December 1829-23 December 1901)

M. Kathleen Fair
Virginia Commonwealth University

MAJOR POSITIONS HELD: Columnist, *New York Tribune* (1855), *Noah's Sunday Times* (1855); assistant to the editor, *Rockford* (Illinois) *Register* (1859-1860); associate editor, *New York Weekly Times* (1861-1866); staff member, *New York Daily Times* (1861-1866); fashion editor, *New York World* (1862-1872); fashion editor, *New York Times* (1864-1872); columnist and woman's editor, *New York Daily Graphic* (1872-1878); columnist, *Chicago Times, Richmond Whig, New Orleans Democrat, New Orleans Picayune, Baltimore American* (1872-1898).

SELECTED BOOKS: *Jennie Juneiana: Talks on Women's Topics* (Boston: Lee & Shepard, 1864);

Jennie June's American Cookery Book (New York: American News Company, 1866);

For Better or Worse: A Book for Some Men and All Women (Boston: Lee & Shepard, 1875);

Knitting and Crochet: A Guide to the Use of the Needle and the Hook (New York: Burt, 1885);

Ladies Fancy Work: A Manual of Designs and Instructions in All Kinds of Needle-Work (New York: Burt, 1886);

Sorosis: Its Origin and History (New York: Little, 1886);

Thrown on Her Own Resources; or, What Girls Can Do (New York: Crowell, 1891);

The History of the Woman's Club Movement in America (New York: Allen, 1898).

Jane Cunningham Croly ("Jennie June") was the first woman in America to write daily for a newspaper and the first person to write and syndicate features for women. A staunch advocate of "everything for the betterment of women," she was the forerunner of today's advice, etiquette, fashion, and consumer columnists.

Cunningham was born 19 December 1829 in Market Harborough, Leicestershire, England, the fourth child of the Rev. Joseph H. and Jane Cunningham. The family moved to the United States in 1841 after being persecuted for her father's efforts to hold classes for working people. They settled first in Poughkeepsie and later near Wappingers Falls, New York. Jane Cunningham began writing at age seventeen and developed her journalistic skills as a young woman in Worcester County, Massachusetts, where she worked as a housekeeper for her brother, a Unitarian pastor. She and a coworker wrote a "semi-monthly newspaper" and read its contents to audiences in church.

Jane Cunningham Croly

She got her first job in journalism in 1855 from Charles A. Dana, who was then managing editor of the *New York Tribune*. It was virgin territory: the practice was for the few female journalists of the day to work as correspondents and to get paid space rates; Cunningham was the first woman to go to the office daily and write from a desk there. She soon adopted the pen name "Jennie June" from a character in B. F. Taylor's poem "The Beautiful River." (It was common for women writers to use alliterative pen names.)

In the mid-1800s, there was no such thing as a woman's department in newspapers, primarily because women did not generally read newspapers. But Jennie June saw an opportunity to capitalize on topics that interested women—parties, clothes, and beauty—and she developed an enviable following of male and female readers. She is credited with launching a "new school of journalism," which spawned the women's pages of the twentieth century.

On 14 February 1856, a year after she moved to New York City, Cunningham married David Goodman Croly, a $14-a-week reporter for the *New York Herald*, and the couple began what was later described as a "joint career in metropolitan journalism." Jennie June's popularity spread, and soon she was writing for the *Times* and *Noah's Sunday Times*, as well as for the *Tribune*.

After Jane Croly's sister Mary was wed to William George King, owner of the *Rockford* (Illinois) *Register*, King hired David Croly to edit the paper. Jane Croly assisted her husband in the editorial management of the paper, but, according to Jane Croly's brother John, "due to Mrs. Croly's ardent desire for a larger field . . . at the end of a year [in 1860] they decided to return to New York." The move was a fortunate one, for David Croly became editor of the *New York World* when it was founded in 1860; Jennie June became the newspaper's fashion editor. In 1868 Croly founded the *Real Estate Record and Builder's Guide*, of which he was co-owner and manager (with C. W. Sweet) until 1872, when he became editor of the *New York Graphic*.

Croly's career moves helped Jennie June to establish a following in various cities. By 1872, when Croly went with the *Graphic*, Jennie June was syndicating her articles in several newspapers. Although she did not use the term *syndication*, she developed what she called a "duplicate system of correspondence," and arranged for simultaneous publication of a fashion letter for the *Chicago Times*, the *Richmond Whig*, and the *New Orleans Democrat*, as well as newspapers in New York. By the end of the Civil War, almost every major American newspaper and magazine had published her work, and Jennie June had established herself as one of New York's best reporters.

Although she wrote primarily about fashion, Jennie June, in time, dispensed advice on all manners of topics. She wrote what is believed to be the first newspaper shopper item in 1873 in the *Tribune*, when she informed readers that "an excellent glove, fine, soft, well fitting and extremely durable has been introduced by Lord and Taylor and has become a great favorite." She advised young ladies on proper behavior in numerous situations; chastised women who applied lipstick in public; advocated sex education; developed and tested recipes, including some for infants and invalids; and wrote innumerable how-to articles on knitting, crocheting, and sewing. Her stories were a history of American fashion and changes in methods of merchandising. Biographer Ishbel Ross notes that Jane Croly's 1873 article "Returning to Town" "pictured the actual transition of trade from the small shop to the department store." Later she wrote editorials, book reviews, and drama criticism, and occasionally news stories. As a staff member of the *Daily Graphic* she investigated the condition of working women and reported on female workers living in "unheated rooms without blankets or carpets."

In her columns, Jennie June was particularly scathing about women who were wont to do nothing but dress in the highest fashions and plan parties. She heartily advocated careers as a way to make women more "self-sustaining, self-reliant and re- spected," regardless of whether they became wives and mothers. She was her own best example, though she never boasted of her ability to juggle the schedules of her busy career while rearing five chil- dren and maintaining the social life appropriate for a man of her husband's stature.

Her career was as unconventional as many of the beliefs she fostered through her columns, for in that day women who worked outside the home at any task were looked at askance. Her brother de- scribed her as an "advocate of everything for the betterment of women" and as having a "deep con- viction that women were the saving salt of all life"; Ishbel Ross said she was "perhaps the most con- spicuous example of women editors who fought for sexual equality." Her fight for equality led her in 1868 to found "Sorosis," the first women's club in America, because she and other women had been barred from a banquet honoring Charles Dickens. She called the first Woman's Congress in 1856, the second in 1869. In 1889, she founded the Woman's Press Club of New York City, because of the af- fronts to women she experienced from members of the all-male Press Club.

Although details of Jennie June's education are sketchy, she was considered one of the best- educated women of the day. She was granted an honorary doctor of literature degree from Rutger's Women's College in 1892 and was appointed to a new chair in journalism and literature there, be- coming the first woman to teach journalism in a university. At the same time Jennie June was de- veloping a following in daily newspapers, she branched out into a long and successful career in magazine journalism. In 1860 she became assistant editor of Demorest's quarterly *Mirror of Fashion*, and when that periodical was merged with the *New York Weekly Illustrated News* in 1865, Jane Croly became editor of the new publication, *Demorest's Illustrated Monthly and Mme. Demorest's Mirror of Fashions*, later called *Demorest's Illustrated Monthly*. In 1887 Jane Croly bought a half-interest in and edited *Godey's Lady's Book*. She left that magazine in 1890 to edit the *Home-Maker* and subsequently founded and edited the *Cycle*, a club organ and literary review.

David Croly had retired from daily newspaper work in 1878 and died in 1889. The Crolys' son Herbert continued the family's journalistic career as editor of the *New Republic*.

In June 1898, Jane Cunningham Croly fell and fractured her hip. She never fully recovered from the injury and retired from her journalistic career, spending most of her retirement in En- gland. Prior to her death in New York in 1901, she wrote her own epitaph:

"I have never done anything that was not help- ful to women, so far as it lay in my power."

Other:

Needle Work: A Manual of Stitches and Studies in Em- broidery and Drawn Work, edited by Croly (New York: Burt, 1885);
Letters and Monograms for Marking on Silk, Linen and Other Fabrics, for Individual and Household Use, edited by Croly (New York: Burt, 1886).

References:

Frank Luther Mott, *A History of American Magazines 1865-1885* (Cambridge: Harvard University Press, 1957);
Ishbel Ross, *Crusades and Crinolines* (New York: Harper & Row, 1963);
Ross, *Ladies of the Press* (New York: Arno, 1974);
Ross, *Sons of Adam, Daughters of Eve* (New York: Harper & Row, 1969);
Woman's Press Club of New York City, *Memories of Jane Cunningham Croly, "Jennie June"* (New York & London: Putnam's, 1904).

Charles A. Dana

Terry Hynes
California State University, Fullerton

BIRTH: Hinsdale, New Hampshire, 8 August 1819, to Anderson and Ann Denison Dana.

EDUCATION: Harvard, 1839-1841.

MARRIAGE: 2 March 1846 to Eunice Macdaniel; children: Paul, Zoe, Ruth, Eunice.

MAJOR POSITIONS HELD: Managing editor, *New York Tribune* (1847-1862); editor, *New York Sun* (1868-1897).

AWARDS AND HONORS: B.A., Harvard College, 1861 (credited as member of class of 1843).

DEATH: Glen Cove, Long Island, 17 October 1897.

BOOKS: *A Lecture on Association, in Its Connection with Religion, Delivered before the New England Fourier Society in Boston, March 7th, 1844* (Boston: Greene, 1844);
The Life of Ulysses S. Grant, General of the Armies of the United States, by Dana and James H. Wilson (Springfield, Mass.: Gurdon Bill/Cincinnati: H. C. Johnson, 1868);
The Art of Newspaper Making: Three Lectures (New York: Appleton, 1895; London: Unwin, 1895);
Lincoln and His Cabinet: A Lecture Delivered on Tuesday, March 10, 1896, before the New Haven Colony Historical Society (Cleveland & New York: De Vinne, 1896);
Proudhon and His "Bank of the People," Being a Defence of the Great French Anarchist, Showing the Evils of a Specie Currency, and that Interest on Capital Can and Ought to Be Abolished by a System of Free and Mutual Banking (New York: Tucker, 1896);
Eastern Journeys: Some Notes of Travel in Russia, in the Caucasus, and to Jerusalem (New York: Appleton, 1898);
Recollections of the Civil War; with the Leaders at Washington and in the Field in the Sixties (New York: Appleton, 1898).

As editor of the *New York Sun* for almost three decades in the post-Civil War era, Charles A. Dana

built that newspaper into one of the most important of its time. He was the central figure responsible for the *Sun*'s developing a national reputation as a "newspaperman's newspaper" because he encouraged sharp and lively writing, especially in a form the *Sun* called "the human interest story." Earlier in his career, while with Horace Greeley's *New York Tribune*, Dana had been the first American journalist to hold the title of managing editor of a newspaper.

Charles Anderson Dana was born 8 August 1819 in Hinsdale, a small town in western New Hampshire, to Anderson Dana and his first wife, Ann Denison. Charles's was the seventh generation of Danas in America, his ancestry dating back to a colonial settler, Richard Dana; on his mother's side, he counted Abigail Adams among his forebears. His early years involved a series of uprootings. When his father's modest business failed a few years after Charles's birth, the family moved to the village of Gaines in western New York. When Charles was nine, his mother died, leaving three other children besides him: seven-year-old Junius; three-year-old Maria; and David, an infant. The family then moved to the Denison homestead in northeastern Vermont; Charles was sent to live on a farm with his uncle David Denison while his brothers and sister remained with their grandfather nearby. Charles worked on the farm, attended the district school, and studied Latin on his own until he was twelve, at which time he was sent to Buffalo, then a small frontier city, where he worked as a clerk in his uncle William Dana's general store.

During the six years he spent as a clerk, Dana continued his self-education in Latin, added Greek, and read generally among the masters of English literature. When the panic of 1837 forced his uncle to close the store, young Dana made plans for a more formal education in order to satisfy his thirst for knowledge. By mid-1839 he was sufficiently prepared to enter Harvard University; he took the approximately $200 he had saved and set out for Cambridge, Massachusetts, where he enrolled as a freshman in September. Dana's experience at Harvard was hardly that of a carefree undergraduate: when his meager funds ran out, he lived with relatives in New Hampshire and Vermont and finally

Charles A. Dana in 1905 (The Bettmann Archive)

was named secretary-treasurer. Dana remained with the experiment for five years, even after the association—against his and some other members' wishes—reorganized into a phalanx according to the socialistic ideals of Fourier. Dana wrote articles, editorials, reviews, and poetry for the Brook Farm organs, the *Dial* and subsequently the *Harbinger*; he also became acquainted with Nathaniel Hawthorne, Ralph Waldo Emerson, William Henry Channing, Margaret Fuller, and Horace Greeley.

The vestiges of idealism that remained in Dana in later years seem traceable to his experience with Brook Farm, which bred in him an appreciation for the inherent dignity of manual labor and for the idea of equal pay for equal work and an openness to various religious beliefs. Some writers have commented that Dana's early idealism often seems incongruous in light of his later conservatism; but at least one of his major biographers, James H. Wilson, notes that Dana never spoke unequivocally in support of Brook Farm itself, although he did support the ideals on which it was based. Wilson concludes that Dana connected himself with Brook Farm not primarily because of a commitment to its philosophy, but because it offered him a practical way of achieving his goal of a continued education even though he did not have the money for college. Whatever his motivation, Dana believed strongly enough in the experiment (possibly in its financial prospects) to purchase, at a cost of $500 each, three of the twenty-four shares in the formal association. (It is not clear whether Dana actually borrowed the $1,500 or whether this amounted to a pledge as his share of the mortgage on the property.)

Among the members of the Brook Farm cooperative were the Macdaniel family from Maryland, consisting of a widowed mother, her son, and two daughters. Dana fell in love with the youngest member of the family, Eunice, and they were married in New York on 2 March 1846. On the night of 3 March, while the newlyweds were still away from the phalanx, the almost-completed main house was destroyed by fire due to the carelessness of the carpenters. The loss of the house, which had cost approximately $10,000, was the last blow to the struggling utopian community, and the group began to disband.

The Danas retained their connection with Brook Farm for a few months after the fire, but Dana turned his major efforts to earning a living apart from the cooperative. For about two years, he had been earning $4 per week by writing for the *Boston Daily Chronotype*; after the fire he was hired as

took a teaching job in Scituate, Massachusetts, to earn money for his expenses. During the periods he was able to return to college work, he focused his study on the classics, literature, and philosophy rather than science and mathematics. But his constant reading overtaxed his eyes, and he left after completing two years of college in 1841, giving up his intention of entering the ministry and of studying in Germany. Although a series of treatments helped improve his eyesight in later years, Dana never returned to the practice of reading at night.

While attending Harvard, Dana had developed a strong admiration for the radical social aims of Rev. George Ripley and other Transcendentalists who launched the Brook Farm Institute of Agriculture and Education in 1841 as a practical testing ground for their ideas about cooperative, democratic living in an environment that fostered intellectual growth. By September 1841 Dana had been accepted by the group and was living with them in West Roxbury, Massachusetts. His initial contribution was to teach Greek and German, among other subjects, and to work on the farm. In addition, because of his experience as a clerk in his uncle's general store, he was made a trustee for the property and management of the association and a regular employee by the *Chronotype*'s owner and editor, Elizur Wright, to read the exchanges, edit the news, and do whatever odd jobs needed to be done. In Wright's absence, he was also responsible for serving as editor, without any additional remuneration. Apparently straining under the low pay and lack of opportunities for advancement in Boston, Dana decided later that year to seek his fortune in New York.

Thanks to his acquaintance with Horace Greeley, Dana obtained the job of city editor on the *New York Tribune* and began work there in February 1847. Before the end of that year, Dana, realizing his value as a talented journalist, struck for higher pay. Greeley complied by raising Dana's salary from $10 to $14 per week, $1 less than his own. When revolution broke out in France against Louis Philippe's government in 1848, Dana's earlier interest in traveling to Europe was rekindled. Greeley refused to assign him as a correspondent at his regular salary, but promised to pay $10 for each weekly letter Dana sent to the *Tribune*. Dana made similar arrangements with four other newspapers (*Philadelphia North American and United States Gazette*, *New York Commercial Advertiser*, *New York Harbinger*, *Boston Chronotype*) for a guaranteed income of $40 (later $35 when the *Chronotype* ceased publication).

Horace Greeley, who employed Dana as city editor, foreign correspondent, and managing editor of the New York Tribune

He lived on this in Europe for eight months and at the same time supported his family in New York. At the end, he said later, he was only $63 in the red.

Dana spent July through September in Paris reporting in detail the proceedings and deliberations of the Assembly while the members framed a constitution for the new republic. He traveled to Berlin and Frankfurt during October and November to assess the Prussian revolution, then returned to Paris in early December where he covered the election and inauguration of Louis Napoleon as president. Although he suspected that Louis Napoleon would have preferred the title of emperor to that of president, Dana appears to have retained some optimism about the possibility of democratic reforms being effected through the revolution. As he wrote in his last letter to the *Tribune* from Paris, published 13 February 1849, "My sympathies were with the people when they were triumphant, and when their heroism and enthusiasm commanded the admiration of the world; they have been with them in their errors and misfortunes; they are with them still in a hope which outlives defeat and forgets disaster." Although Dana believed that war was an inevitable step along the path toward social democracy, he hoped for a peaceful outcome to the revolutions which had spread from France to Germany, Austria, Hungary, and Italy.

Dana returned to the *Tribune* in March 1849 as the newspaper's managing editor, the first American to hold that title. By then the revolutions in Europe had diminished in news value and had been replaced by the newspaper's efforts to achieve a transcontinental railroad and a protective tariff as well as the growing concern about slavery; but Dana continued to be interested in radical thinkers like Pierre Proudhon and Karl Marx. He hired some liberals and socialists, including Marx, as reporters and commentators for the *Tribune*, thus continuing and expanding Greeley's tradition of providing hospitality in the newspaper for new ideas. Dana had met Marx when he was covering the European revolutions in 1848 and invited him to become one of the newspaper's London correspondents in 1851. The one or two pounds' weekly payment helped keep Marx from starving while providing him with a significant American audience for his views. Although both parties sometimes grumbled about details related to the association, Marx remained a correspondent until Dana left the paper in 1862. Of the approximately 500 articles and editorials which Marx contributed, about one-fourth were actually written by Friedrich Engels.

Karl Marx, who submitted articles to the New York Tribune
*from London while Dana was managing editor
(Radio Times Hulton Picture Library)*

It was Greeley, of course, who defined the basic policy of the *Tribune*, but Dana lent the vitality of his writing skill to persuasive editorials about each of the important issues of the 1850s. For Dana, the railroad to the Pacific was a means of binding the nation together in preparation for extending the boundaries of the United States not only from ocean to ocean, not only throughout the North American continent, but, ultimately, throughout the Western hemisphere; the protective tariff was a means to help the nation develop sufficient self-sustaining industries to achieve this manifest destiny. (Ironically, the Dana who argued so strenuously in the *Tribune* for strong railroad companies to develop the transcontinental system became the Dana who just as forcefully criticized the monopolistic railroad companies in the *Sun* for their unbri-

dled greed and corruption.)

Dana was not a militant abolitionist, because he was basically opposed to any extreme causes; further, he believed that the South, under the protections of the Constitution, was entitled to its slaves within its region. But Dana and Greeley agreed on the wickedness of slavery and both fought vigorously to prevent its spread into the Western territories, especially Kansas and Nebraska, with Dana holding the *Tribune* to an aggressive antislavery policy even when Greeley vacillated. Dana and Greeley differed fundamentally, however, about the issue of Southern secession—a difference which led to Dana's involuntary resignation from the *Tribune*: Greeley was willing to have the South secede with slavery intact within its borders if that meant peace would be maintained, while Dana refused to tolerate the idea of the destruction of the Union and preferred even war to a divided United States. Early in 1862, without any external signs from Greeley of dissatisfaction, Dana was notified by the newspaper's board of managers that his services were no longer required. The board had acted on an ultimatum from Greeley; knowing this, Dana chose to respect Greeley's prior interest in the newspaper and accepted the dismissal without resistance. In accepting Dana's resignation in late March, the newspaper's trustees promised to continue his salary (then probably $40-50 per week) for six months after he left. Thus ended Dana's nearly fifteen years of employment on the *Tribune*.

Shortly after leaving the newspaper, Dana accepted Secretary of War Edwin M. Stanton's invitation to join the War Department. In June, he was appointed a member of a commission to audit nearly $600 million in unsettled claims against the quartermaster's bureau, at a salary of $8 per day plus a mileage allowance. The commission examined and adjusted nearly 700 claims at Cairo, Illinois, before submitting its report to Stanton in early August. After the commission's work was completed, Dana returned to New York. In November Dana was offered the position of second assistant secretary of war; but after Dana made the news public and his appointment was reported in the New York papers, Stanton capriciously recalled the offer. Dana then formed a partnership with Roscoe Conkling and George W. Chadwick to purchase much-needed, scarce cotton from parts of the Mississippi Valley occupied by the Union army. After Dana went to Memphis to carry on the business, however, he became convinced that the speculative cotton trading, although profitable, was disadvantageous to the Union, and especially to the army, because it was the means by which the South strengthened its supplies of food, clothing, and ammunition. Thus, with General Grant's support, he recommended to Stanton that all such trading be prohibited and finally succeeded in convincing President Lincoln and the secretary of war that the cotton trade should be controlled and regulated by the Treasury Department.

A few weeks after Dana had again returned to New York, he was enlisted by Stanton to go back to the Mississippi region and report on Grant's handling of his army. Lincoln and Stanton had been fed conflicting accounts of Grant's competence and sought to resolve their doubts through an impartial observer. In early April 1863, Dana joined Grant at his headquarters a few miles above Vicksburg. In subsequent weeks, traveling with Grant and his army, Dana had an exceptional opportunity to see the war firsthand and acquire a better grasp of the military situation of the North than most other men, either in the field or in Washington, D.C. After the battle of Chickamauga in September 1863, Dana's recommendation was a major factor in Stanton's decision to place Grant in command of the Union military forces of the Mississippi.

Dana finally was appointed second assistant secretary of war during the Vicksburg campaign, although the Senate did not confirm his appointment until late January 1864. For the remainder of the war, when he was not at the front or discussing plans with Stanton as Grant's representative, Dana remained in Washington, performing the ordinary work of an assistant secretary of war. Part of his job was to supervise the accounts of the War Department, which made him particularly conscious of the staggering cost of the war. This experience may well have been a major source of his later pleas in the *Sun* for economy, taxation reform, and reducing the public debt, as well as of his resentment toward the South for forcing the war expense on the nation. Another of Dana's duties was to make contracts for supplies; in this capacity, he learned techniques for detecting fraud which served him well later as editor of the *Sun*, when he published exposures of fraud and graft. Dana's experiences on the *Tribune* and as assistant secretary of war during the Civil War years gave him a knowledge of and, in some cases, influence with most of the major political candidates, cabinet officers, and other government and military officials he would be writing about in the next thirty years as editor of the *Sun*.

Almost immediately after the war was over, Dana reluctantly accepted a job as editor of the *Daily Republican*, a newspaper being established in Chicago. He initially expected to become involved in politics or some business other than journalism after the war and apparently went to Chicago thinking of it as an interim step to these other goals as well as an opportunity to rid himself of debt. The newspaper's backers, however, failed to supply the full funding they had promised. Thus Dana's efforts were crippled, and within a year he began looking for an alternative career. After the *Republican*'s offices were destroyed by fire in September 1866, Dana returned with his family to New York, intending to begin his own paper. (The *Republican* recovered in later years and was the forerunner of the *Inter Ocean*.) The competition among existing newspapers in New York appears to be the chief reason for the delay Dana experienced in finding financial backing for his project. When he was finally almost ready to begin, the opportunity to purchase an existing paper, the *New York Sun*, tempted him instead to shift his own ambitions and those of his financial backers to the *Sun*.

The *Sun* had been established in 1833 and was the first successful "penny newspaper" in the United States. (Its price had been raised to two cents in August 1864 and remained there until July 1916, when Frank Munsey bought the paper and reduced its price to one cent.) Ben Day, the original owner, had sold the paper in the depression of 1837 to his brother-in-law, Moses Y. Beach; it was from Beach's son, Moses Sperry Beach, who owned it from 1852, that Dana and his backers bought the paper for $175,000. Dana's backers included William M. Evarts, a leader of the American bar; Sen. Roscoe Conkling; Thomas Hitchcock; Alonzo B. Cornell; Cyrus W. Field; Sen. Edwin D. Morgan; George Opdyke, a former mayor; David Dows; Salem H. Wales; William H. Webb; and Freeman Clarke. Nearly all the *Sun*'s backers were Republicans with strong influence in local and national politics or business.

In January 1868 Dana began his career as editor of the *Sun*, a career that was to last until his death in 1897. Almost immediately, he changed the appearance of the paper: he reduced the number of columns on each of the standard four pages from eight to seven, widening each column in the process; he made the major headlines smaller and more uniform, while increasing the number of heads at the top of the front page from two to four; he printed the editorial articles in a larger size type; he removed the eagle and the slogan "It Shines for All" from the masthead and substituted the state motto, "Excelsior," while retaining the variation of the New York State seal. Except for emergencies, Dana retained the standard four-page format of the week-day *Sun* for almost the first twenty years of his editorship. (In 1887, the format was changed to eight smaller pages, but the change did not help the paper's then-waning circulation.) Although Dana gave news content preference over advertising, he never realized his dream of an adless newspaper; instead, the popularity of the *Sun* attracted increasing amounts of advertising. It was the pressure of increased advertising (as well as the escape of William M. "Boss" Tweed from his Madison Avenue home, where he was on one of his frequent visits to his family in the company of two guards from the Ludlow Street jail) that prompted Dana to publish the first edition of the Sunday *Sun* on 5 December 1875 in an eight-page format. Although Dana apologized in print for the "different form" of the paper, he continued to publish the Sunday edition in eight pages and sold it for three cents per copy, one cent more than the cost of the weekday edition.

Not only the form but the content of the paper reflected Dana's intellectual convictions and cultural interests. The new editor's policy appeared on the *Sun*'s editorial page on 27 January 1868. After

The New York Sun *Building at Frankfort and Nassau streets in 1868, the year Dana became editor*

promising support of the Union and independence from political parties, the prospectus promised its readers varied, complete information presented inexpensively and in a condensed and vibrant style: "The *Sun* will always have all the news, foreign, domestic, political, social, literary, scientific, and commercial. It will use enterprise and money freely to make the best possible newspaper, as well as the cheapest. It will study condensation, clearness, point, and will endeavor to present its daily photograph of the whole world's doings in the most luminous and lively manner. It will not take as long to read the *Sun* as to read the London *Times* or *Webster's Dictionary*, but when you have read it, you will know about all that has happened in both hemispheres." To achieve the spirited, human-interest style of writing he wanted, Dana was always on the lookout for superior writers. He hired bright young men, many of them college graduates and a relatively high proportion of them exceptionally talented. If the *Sun*'s exchange editor showed him an unusual article that suggested the writer had promise, Dana would invite the author to come to New York and work on the *Sun*. Or if he spotted a story in the *Sun* that showed original thinking or humor or fresh use of language, Dana would sometimes seek out the writer to express his appreciation. Dana valued good work from all his staff and paid well for it, although he offered no financial bonuses for exceptional merit or accomplishment: everyone was simply expected to do his best. Some commentators remark that Dana's praise of good work was in large part responsible for the loyalty he inspired among staff members. Dana also recognized the value of literary contributions to the *Sun* and published the work of various poets, including Walt Whitman, Eugene Field, and Ella Wheeler. To satisfy what he perceived as the public's craving for fiction, he published, especially in the Sunday edition, stories by such authors as Henry James, Robert Louis Stevenson, and Bret Harte. Dana is credited with originating the first literary syndicate in the late 1870s, through which the cost of purchasing high-quality fiction was reduced because it was non-competing."

The *Sun*'s newsroom became a school for budding journalists, where Dana was the master teacher instructing new staff members in the craft and providing a chance to advance to those who earned it. Its "alumni" included managing editor (1880-1913) Chester S. Lord; night city editor (1881-1912) Selah M. "Boss" Clarke; editorial writer Francis P. Church (who wrote the famous "Is There a Santa Claus?" editorial in 1897); reporters

Arthur Brisbane, Julian Ralph, Samuel Hopkins Adams, Richard Harding Davis, and Jacob Riis; William Mackay Laffan, who started as the *Sun's* drama critic in 1877 and successively became general art critic, business adviser, publisher, general manager, and proprietor; Carr Van Anda, who went from the *Sun's* night desk to the *New York Times*; and Edward P. Mitchell, who succeeded Dana as editor. The special democratic spirit of the *Sun* became known to journalists throughout the country and merited comment as late as 1909 by Will Irwin, who had been a *Sun* reporter himself, in *American* magazine: "This organization with its peculiar democracy, its freedom, and its good will of man to man, is probably the most admirable thing about the New York *Sun*."

Dana has been criticized for his acerbic style and cynicism. Evidence usually cited includes his "endorsements" of Horace Greeley for a plethora of public offices, including secretary of state, postmaster general, minister to England, minister to China, U.S. senator from Virginia, governor of New York, city comptroller, state prison inspector, and vice-president and president of the United States. Dana's various forms of "support" were regarded as ways of ridiculing his former boss. Greeley's *Tribune* was not the only newspaper victim of the sharp-tongued Dana, however: other New York papers vilified in the *Sun's* pages include the *World* ("stupid," "dilapidated," and "tedious" under Manton Marble and later, under Pulitzer, described as in decay) and the *Herald* (described as without principle or character). Even the *New York Times* was fair game for Dana's rapier; it was characterized as "disreputable" and, when the *Times* accused the *Sun* of deliberately suppressing Grover Cleveland's letter on the civil service question in 1884, Dana responded to the accusation editorially: "This is a new conception worthy of its origin." Newspapers outside New York, including some in Philadelphia and Cincinnati, also were victims of Dana's verbal whip.

Although the *Sun*, like other penny newspapers of the nineteenth century, was politically independent, the paper contained political endorsements and commentary during Dana's reign as editor. Early in 1868, Dana criticized President Johnson for "a conspiracy against the Constitution," but the *Sun* advised against impeaching the president; after Johnson's acquittal, the newspaper continued to be concerned primarily with the effect of the trial on the Republican party, rather than with the consequences for Johnson himself. The *Sun* supported Grant in the presidential election of 1868 but turned against the administration in its early

months. In campaigning against the corruption in Grant's administrations, the paper adopted the battle cry "Turn the rascals out," one of the many clever slogans and epithets that became characteristic of the paper under Dana. The *Sun* publicized details of chaos in the South during Reconstruction and such major scandals as Crédit Mobilier, the Whiskey Ring, the salary grab of 1873, the safe burglary conspiracy, and irregularities in the Navy Department under Secretary of the Navy George M. Robeson. In the late 1870s, Dana vehemently opposed President Rutherford B. Hayes because he had been selected by an electoral commission and had not received the popular vote over Samuel J. Tilden in 1876. (Dana had sent Joseph Pulitzer, newly arrived from St. Louis, to Washington to cover the proceedings of the electoral commission for the *Sun*.) Dana's ire was reflected in the lead editorial of the *Sun*, 6 March 1877, which began, "Mr. Hayes, who has not been elected President of the United States, but who has twice taken the oath of office, as if to make up by abundant swearing his essential lack of votes, delivered an inaugural address at Washington yesterday." Subsequently, Dana persisted in referring to Hayes as a "fraudulent President" and blamed the president "who was never elected" for the hard times endured by the country during his administration.

In the 1880s, Dana opposed Grover Cleveland for both New York governor and president because of his lack of experience—and also, according to some commentators, because Dana was personally antagonistic toward him. Because of its support of Benjamin Butler, candidate of the Greenback-Labor and Anti-Monopolist parties, the *Sun* lost an estimated 69,000 in weekly circulation during the presidential campaign of 1884. Some biographers claim that Dana championed the silver standard after Cleveland's public commitment to the gold standard in 1885 chiefly in order to discredit the administration. Dana's approval of the maximum legal limit regarding the coinage of silver during this period was contrary to all he said earlier and after Cleveland left politics. Although Dana himself favored civil service reform, the *Sun* was severely criticized for suppressing Cleveland's Christmas letter of 1884 promising to support pending reform legislation. The *Sun* explained its delay in publishing the president-elect's letter by saying "The assistant editor, who had charge of it, lost the copy from his desk, either by some person taking it or by the wind blowing it away, or the office cat eating it up; and that is all there is of it." Thus was born the

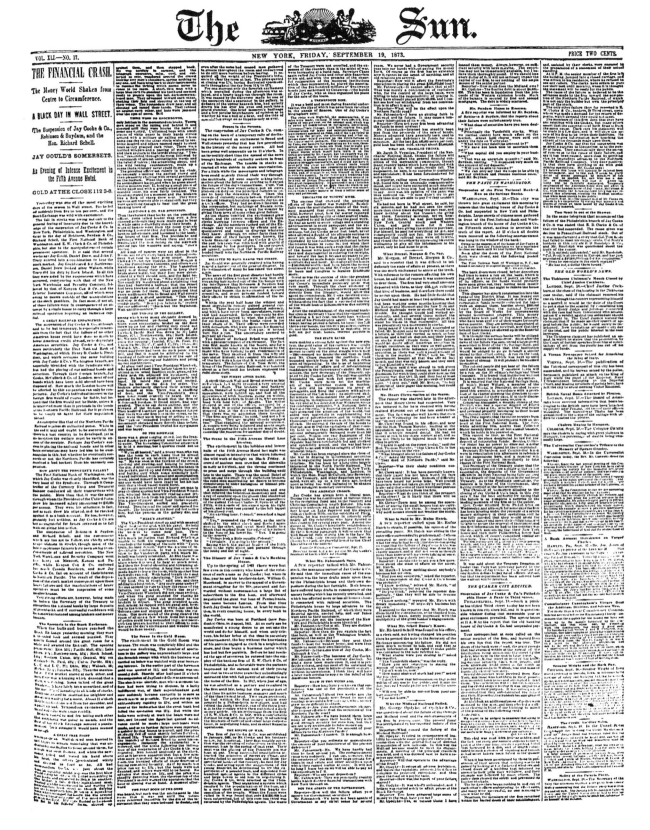

Front page of the Sun, *showing the new seven-column format introduced by Dana*

"office cat" excuse, suggested to Dana by staff member Willard Bartlett, which generated a good deal of amused comment from newspapers throughout the country. In 1888, Dana favored Cleveland's reelection to a second term because he feared the election of Gen. Benjamin Harrison would mark a return of the influences present during the Grant and Hayes administrations. Four years later, Dana opposed the third nomination of Cleveland, but when the latter was selected as the Democratic party's candidate over Dana's choice, David B. Hill, the *Sun* supported the party's nominee. Dana subsequently ridiculed Cleveland's handling of various issues, including the Hawaiian annexation question, although he did suppport some of Cleveland's policies, such as his stands against the Pullman Strike of 1894 and against England in the Venezuela boundary dispute.

In 1896, Dana opposed William Jennings Bryan and the free silver platform and supported William McKinley for president. (Dana had gradually returned to supporting the gold standard during 1895-1896.) Also in the late 1890s, Dana reiterated his long-standing support of Cuban independence from Spain. (Indeed, Dana never fully gave up his dream of annexing Cuba and Canada to the United States.) Dana opposed most internal revenues: his opposition to the income tax was one of the few constants in the *Sun*, and when the Civil War income tax was repealed in 1872, the *Sun* rejoiced. Dana believed duties on imports should be used for the support of government and to repay public debt; thus he approved of tariffs as long as they were not excessive. He also approved of real estate taxes and taxes on railroads. But he objected to using tax monies for such "expensive," "useless," "unnecessary," or "wasteful" things as City College, West Point, street cleaners, the franking privilege, or diplomatic service.

Locally, Dana exposed political corruption in the New York Democratic machine. Dana's newspaper participated in exposing Tammany in the late 1860s and early 1870s and, in the mayoral campaign of 1878, the *Sun* (that is, William O. Bartlett, who was one of the outstanding editorial writers on the paper from 1868 until his death thirteen years later) coined the phrase "No King, No Clown, / To rule this Town!" in opposing the Tammany "boss" structure. Dana also opposed New York laws permitting imprisonment for debt and, although he encouraged temperance reform for individuals and groups, he opposed New York prohibition laws as unsound and unenforceable. The ever-practical

Dana saw licensing as a preferable way of controlling the liquor traffic.

Dana's personal antipathies and animosities sometimes clouded his views of the issues and resulted in ambivalent and even contradictory editorial positions. The erratic quality of his views on policy issues of public importance made it unlikely that Dana would rank as a shaper of public opinion with major editors like Greeley, William Cullen Bryant, and Samuel Bowles. In fact, one of Dana's biographers, Candace Stone, argues that although the *Sun*'s views reached thousands of readers daily, there is little evidence to indicate that the newspaper's editorial policy ever significantly influenced the course of events. Dana's contradictoriness was evident in a number of areas. Although the *Sun* upheld workers' right to strike, when they did, the newspaper condemned them for picketing and rioting. Dana's support of feminist causes was also mixed: in the late 1860s he editorialized for higher education for women and equal pay for equal work; in the mid-1870s, he repudiated his support of coeducation and qualified his support of higher education for women by saying that college was not totally advantageous to women and should be fitted to their physical limitations. (Dana was an elitist regarding higher education even for men: he believed it should be available only to the relatively few who were able and inclined to learn. When public funds were used to support higher education, Dana thought the money should go toward training machinists, engineers, architects, inventors, and businessmen, who would be productive members of society.) Although he mildly ridiculed some of the suffragists, Dana also supported the suffragist cause generally; for example, he praised leaders of the movement in their attempt to vote in the presidential election of 1872. Yet the *Sun* opposed a woman suffrage amendment to the New York constitution in 1883 on the grounds that "nine women out of ten . . . do not care to vote." In 1885, the *Sun* insisted that women were by nature unsuited for political life.

In some respects, Dana's personal prejudices were beneficial to reporting the news. For example, his hatred for Johnson, Grant, and Hayes appears to have shaped his attitude toward the various phases of Reconstruction. In digging for reasons to condemn these three presidents, Dana contradicted himself and often changed his position on some basic issues. As a result, however, the *Sun* told the truth about the problems of Reconstruction, especially under Grant, and remained consistent in its concern for the welfare of the entire country.

The inconsistencies of Dana's views notwithstanding, a careful comparison of his early "liberalism," as evidenced in the Brook Farm years and in his coverage of the European revolutions of 1848, with his later conservatism, as reflected in his support of laissez-faire capitalism, suggests that the conservatism was there from the beginning and became more pronounced in his later years, rather than that he made a radical shift from liberalism to conservatism as time went on. As James Wilson points out, Dana's writings at the time of the Brook Farm experiment are more indicative of his hopes than of his settled convictions. Dana's youthful sympathies were theoretically on the side of democratic and even socialist principles regarding the right of the poor to share in society's wealth, but these sympathies were combined with a strong practical inclination which looked to see how the idealistic goals of the Transcendentalists, and subsequently those of the European revolutionaries of 1848, actually worked. The dominant tendency in Dana even in his youth was to measure the theories by how well they succeeded in practice. Over the years, as he saw less and less practical value in "liberal" causes, his response was more and more immediately conservative and even cynical.

When Dana and his partners bought the *Sun* in 1868, its circulation was 43,000. Within three years, it boasted an average daily circulation of almost 103,000, and by 1876, it reached a daily average of approximately 131,000. Some sources say the mid-1870s average was its highest circulation; others say the *Sun* achieved a maximum daily average of almost 150,000 in the early 1880s. By the late 1880s, its daily average had dropped to 80,000, the figure it cited for several years. On some specific occasions, the *Sun*'s circulation exceeded 200,000: for example, the Hayes-Tilden election, 8 November 1876; the Garfield-Hancock election, 3 November 1880; and Garfield's death, 20 September 1881. Politics, sports such as walking matches and prizefights, and sensational events such as hangings tended to cause the largest jumps in circulation. One of the reasons the *Sun* increased in popularity under Dana may have been its two-cent price. Until the early 1880s, most other New York newspapers charged four cents per copy. After Pulitzer bought the *World* in 1883 and lowered its price to two cents, other newspapers followed suit. The consequent decrease in the *Sun*'s circulation, combined with the further erosion of its readership as a result of Dana's support of Butler in

the presidential election of 1884, marked the end of the *Sun*'s hegemony as the leading inexpensive daily. But price alone is not a sufficient explanation of the *Sun*'s rise in popularity in the 1870s.

Dana's major contribution to journalism was to deliver on his promise to report the news in a lively, amusing style. As one of his biographers said of the paper, "No two cents provided so much amusement, malicious or good natured. . . ," and editors throughout the country expressed their admiration for the *Sun*. As the *Sun*'s ads said of the newspaper in 1870, "Its news is the freshest, most interesting and sprightliest current, and no expense is spared to make it just what the great mass of the people want." For Dana, as he expressed it in 1888, news was "everything that occurs, everything which is of human interest, and which is of sufficient interest to arrest and absorb the attention of the public or of any considerable part of it. . . . I have always felt that whatever the Divine Providence permitted to occur I was not too proud to report." Dana reiterated this idea in an 1894 lecture at Cornell University. In speaking specifically of the Sunday newspaper, Dana commented on the realistic reporting of crimes: "But is it wrong to report and to publish these things? Everybody will talk about them. The newspapers could not suppress them if they would; and if any one newspaper regularly omitted to give an account of interesting swindles, or forgeries, or murders, the people would stop reading that paper and go off and get one where they could find all the news. Besides, I have been led to conclude, in reasoning upon this subject, that if the Divine Providence permits such things to happen, we, who are merely the witnesses of its operation, may certainly stop a moment and report the facts to each other." Dana, in short, made human interest an essential feature of news writing in a more calculated way and to a greater degree than had earlier editor-publishers of penny newspapers such as Ben Day. Dana recognized the significance for the ordinary person of the texture of daily life; he understood that layers of human meaning could be reflected in the telling of a small, interesting event; and he willingly gave space to well-written stories about such events, while he denied space to events of greater consequence if they were dull in themselves or were recounted in a dull manner. As he expressed it in his 1894 lecture: "The invariable law of the newspaper is to be interesting. Suppose you tell all the truths of science in a way that bores the reader, what is the good? The truths don't stay in the mind, and nobody thinks any better of you because you have told the truth tediously. The telling must be vivid and animating."

Although the *Sun* was sometimes criticized for being sensational, it did not go to the extreme of the "yellow" journals of the 1890s. Dana, like Pulitzer in the latter's most idealistic moments, sought to integrate emotional appeal into the accuracy of the report. As Dana said in an 1893 lecture at Union College: the reporter "must learn accurately the facts, and he must state them exactly as they are; and if he can state them with a little degree of life, a little approach to eloquence, or a little humor in his style, why, his report will be perfect. It must be accurate; it must be free from affectation; it must be well set forth, so that there shall not be any doubt as to any part or detail of it; and then if it is enlivened with imagination, or with feeling, or with humor, why, you have got a literary product that no one need be ashamed of."

In addition to his achievements in government service and in the newspaper field, Dana wrote or edited a number of books during his career. In 1858, he edited an anthology, *The Household Book of Poetry*, for D. Appleton and Company of New York. (Most of his other books were also published by Appleton.) From 1858 to 1863, he and George Ripley (book review editor on the *Tribune* for nearly thirty years) served as editors for the sixteen-volume series of *The New American Cyclopaedia* (revised as the *American Cyclopaedia* in 1873-1876). In 1868, he wrote with James H. Wilson (who later became one of Dana's biographers) a campaign biography called *Life of Ulysses S. Grant*. In 1895, Appleton published three of Dana's lectures on the journalism profession under the title *The Art of Newspaper Making*. In 1896, Dana's *Lincoln and His Cabinet* appeared. In 1898, two books were published posthumously: *Eastern Journeys: Some Notes of Travel in Russia, in the Caucasus, and to Jerusalem* and *Recollections of the Civil War*, the latter with Ida Tarbell as ghost-writer.

Among the recognitions Dana received was the award of an honorary bachelor of arts degree from Harvard College in 1861; the award credited Dana as a member of the class of 1843, which would have been his graduating class had he been able to remain in school. He was president of the United Press when it collapsed and was forced into bankruptcy in 1897.

Dana's linguistic expertise was not limited to English. As a boy and at Harvard, he had mastered Latin and Greek, then added German, French, Spanish, and Italian; he also had a reading knowledge of Old Norse, Icelandic, Danish, and Por-

tuguese; and during the last years of his life he was teaching himself Russian. In his biography, Wilson noted that during the Civil War, Dana and Maj. Gen. Carl Schurz passed the time traveling from Knoxville to Chattanooga by conversing in both German and English. Also according to Wilson, Dana befriended a newly arrived captain during the siege of Vicksburg by speaking with the captain in his native tongue. The captain was a full-blooded Seneca Indian, and Dana had learned the language as a boy while working in his uncle's store at Buffalo. Dana appreciated art as well as literature: he had a small art collection and a particularly fine collection of Chinese porcelain.

In early June 1897, Dana was taken ill and, although he continued to guide the newspaper from his home until the last three weeks of his life, he never returned to the office. He died of cirrhosis of the liver on 17 October 1897 at his summer home, West Island, Dosoris, near Glen Cove, Long Island. He was survived by his wife, Eunice; their son, Paul; and their three daughters, Zoe (Mrs. William Underhill), Eunice (Mrs. J. W. Brennan), and Ruth (Mrs. William H. Draper). Paul, born 20 August 1852, had been a New York park commissioner and became associated with the *Sun* in 1880. He inherited his father's *Sun* stock when the elder Dana died and was editor of the paper from 1897 until he retired in 1903.

Newspapers throughout the country published lengthy obituaries for Charles A. Dana. But not the *Sun*. In accordance with Dana's wishes, on 18 October 1897, only two lines at the head of the editorial column noted the passing of the *Sun*'s leader:

> Charles Anderson Dana, Editor of
> The *Sun*, died yesterday afternoon.

Other:

Johann Wolfgang von Goethe, *The Auto-biography of Goethe; Truth and Poetry: From My Life*, part three, translated by Dana, edited by Parke Godwin, 2 volumes (New York: Wiley & Putnam, 1846-1847);

Johnny and Maggie, and Other Stories, edited by Dana (Boston: Crosby & Nichols, 1852);

Princess Unca, and Other Stories, translated from the German, edited by Dana (Boston: Crosby & Nichols, 1852);

Stories and Legends, translated from the German, edited by Dana (Boston: Crosby & Nichols, 1852);

Meyer's Universum; or, Views of the Most Remarkable Places and Objects of All Countries, Engraved in Steel by Distinguished Artists, with Descriptive and Historical Text, edited by Dana (New York: Meyer, 1852-1853);

Christmas Eve and Other Stories, translated from the German, edited by Dana (Boston: Crosby & Nichols, 1852);

Annie and the Elves and Other Stories, translated from the German, edited by Dana (Boston: Crosby & Nichols, 1854?);

The Scenery of the United States, edited by Dana (New York: Appleton, 1855);

The United States Illustrated, edited by Dana (New York: Meyer, 1855?);

The Household Book of Poetry, edited by Dana (New York: Appleton, 1858);

The New American Cyclopaedia: A Popular Dictionary of General Knowledge, edited by Dana and George Ripley, 16 volumes (New York & London: Appleton, 1858-1863);

Fifty Perfect Poems, selected and edited by Dana and Rossiter Johnson (New York: Appleton, 1883);

Laurence Oliphant, *Haifa; or, Life in Modern Pales-* *tine*, edited, with an introduction, by Dana (New York: Harper, 1887).

Biographies:

Edward P. Mitchell, "Mr. Dana of the *Sun*," *McClure's*, 3 (October 1894): 374-399;

James Harrison Wilson, *The Life of Charles A. Dana* (New York: Harper, 1907);

Charles J. Rosebault, *When Dana Was the "Sun"* (Freeport, N.Y.: Books for Libraries Press, 1931);

Candace Stone, *Dana and the Sun* (New York: Dodd, Mead, 1938);

Alfred H. Fenton, *Dana of the Sun* (New York: Farrar & Rinehart, 1941).

References:

Helen MacGill Hughes, *News and the Human Interest Story* (Chicago: University of Chicago Press, 1940);

Edward P. Mitchell, *Memoirs of an Editor* (New York: Scribners, 1924);

Frank M. O'Brien, *The Story of the Sun* (New York: Appleton, 1928).

Richard Harding Davis

Rosemarian V. Staudacher
Marquette University

See also the Davis entry in *DLB 12, American Realists and Naturalists*.

BIRTH: Philadelphia, Pennsylvania, 18 April 1864, to Lemuel Clarke and Rebecca Blaine Harding Davis.

EDUCATION: Lehigh University, 1882-1885; Johns Hopkins University, 1885-1886.

MARRIAGES: 4 May 1899 to Cecil Clark, divorced; 8 July 1912 to Elizabeth Genevieve McEvoy; child: Hope Harding Davis.

MAJOR POSITIONS HELD: Reporter, *Philadelphia Record* (1886), *Philadelphia Press* (1886-1889), *New York Evening Sun* (1889-1893); managing editor, *Harper's Weekly* (1890-1895); war correspon- dent, *New York Journal* (1896-1897), *New York Herald*, *Times* (London), London *Daily Mail* (1897-1900).

AWARDS AND HONORS: Campaign ribbons for service as a war correspondent.

DEATH: Mt. Kisco, New York, 11 April 1916.

BOOKS: *The Adventures of My Freshman* (Bethlehem, Pa.: Privately printed, 1884);

Stories for Boys (New York: Scribners, 1891; London: Osgood, McIlvaine, 1891);

Gallegher and Other Stories (New York: Scribners, 1891; London: Osgood, McIlvaine, 1891);

Van Bibber and Others (New York: Harper, 1892; London: Osgood, McIlvaine, 1892);

Culver Pictures

Richard Harding Davis

The West from a Car-Window (New York: Harper, 1892);

The Rulers of the Mediterranean (New York: Harper, 1894; London: Gay & Bird, 1894);

The Exiles and Other Stories (New York: Harper, 1894; London: Osgood, McIlvaine, 1894);

Our English Cousins (New York: Harper, 1894; London: Low, Marston, 1894);

About Paris (New York: Harper, 1895; London: Gay & Bird, 1896);

The Princess Aline (New York: Harper, 1895; London: Macmillan, 1895);

Cinderella and Other Stories (New York: Scribners, 1896);

Three Gringos in Venezuela and Central America (New York: Harper, 1896; London: Gay & Bird, 1896);

Soldiers of Fortune (New York: Scribners, 1897; London: Heinemann, 1897);

Dr. Jameson's Raiders vs. the Johannesburg Reformers (New York: Russell, 1897);

Cuba in War Time (New York: Russell, 1897; London: Heinemann, 1897);

A Year from a Reporter's Notebook (New York: Harper, 1897);

The King's Jackal (New York & London: Scribners, 1898);

The Cuban and Porto Rican Campaigns (New York: Scribners, 1898; London: Heinemann, 1899);

The Orator of Zepata City: A Play in One Act (New York: DeWitt, 1899);

The Lion and the Unicorn (New York: Scribners, 1899; London: Heinemann, 1899);

With Both Armies in South Africa (New York: Scribners, 1900);

In the Fog (New York: Russell, 1901);

Ranson's Folly (New York: Scribners, 1902; London: Ward, Lock, 1902);

Captain Macklin: His Memoirs (New York: Scribners, 1902; London: Heinemann, 1902);

The Bar Sinister (New York: Scribners, 1903);

"Miss Civilization": A Comedy in One Act (New York: Scribners, 1905);

Farces: The Dictator, The Galloper, "Miss Civilization" (New York: Scribners, 1906; London: Bird, 1906);

Real Soldiers of Fortune (New York: Scribners, 1906; London: Heinemann, 1907);

The Scarlet Car (New York: Scribners, 1907);

The Congo and Coasts of Africa (New York: Scribners, 1907; London: Unwin, 1908);

Vera, the Medium (New York: Scribners, 1908);

The White Mice (New York: Scribners, 1909);

Notes of a War Correspondent (New York: Scribners, 1910);

Once upon a Time (New York: Scribners, 1910; London: Duckworth, 1911);

The Consul (New York: Scribners, 1911);

The Man Who Could Not Lose (New York: Scribners, 1911; London: Duckworth, 1912);

The Red Cross Girl (New York: Scribners, 1912; London: Duckworth, 1913);

The Lost Road (New York: Scribners, 1913; London: Duckworth, 1914);

Who's Who: A Farce in Three Acts (London: Bickers, 1913);

The Boy Scout (New York: Scribners, 1914);

Peace Manoeuvres: A Play in One Act (New York & London: French, 1914);

The Zone Police: A Play in One Act (New York & London: French, 1914);

With the Allies (New York: Scribners, 1914; London: Duckworth, 1914);

"Somewhere in France" (New York: Scribners, 1915;

London: Duckworth, 1916);

The New Sing Sing (New York: National Committee on Prisons and Prison Labor, 1915);

With the French in France and Salonika (New York: Scribners, 1916; London: Duckworth, 1916);

The Boy Scout and Other Stories for Boys (New York: Scribners, 1917);

The Deserter (New York: Scribners, 1917);

Adventures and Letters of Richard Harding Davis, edited by Charles Belmont Davis (New York: Scribners, 1917).

COLLECTION: *The Novels and Stories of Richard Harding Davis*, Crossroads Edition, 12 volumes (New York: Scribners, 1916).

Richard Harding Davis was one of the most colorful, daring, and attractive figures in journalism in the late 1800s and early 1900s; he was also highly competent, honest, and dependable. Because of his dashing life-style, which seemed never to impede his ability or credibility, many of his contemporaries dubbed him the "Gibson Boy"—a suave, charming counterpart to artist Charles Dana Gibson's popular Gibson Girls. Those who disliked the image disdained and criticized the man, but seldom, with any justification, his journalistic output.

Davis was born in Philadelphia on 18 April 1864. His father was Lemuel Clarke Davis, editorial writer for the *Philadelphia Inquirer* and later editor of the *Public Ledger*. The Civil War was not going very well for the North: Grant had not yet made his thrust to Richmond nor Sherman his march to the sea; Gettysburg was just over, and many of its wounded still lay in the large base hospital in Philadelphia. There was much for Clarke Davis to write about, although, as an editorial writer, he remained more or less anonymous. Richard Harding Davis's mother, Rebecca, was a celebrity in her own right: in April 1861, she had published in the *Atlantic* magazine a rather astonishing short story, "Life in the Iron Mills"—a stark, grim tale of the sufferings of Welsh ironworkers in the mills of Wheeling (then in Virginia), the sort of thing of which young women of the day were supposedly ignorant.

Richard was the eldest of three Davis offspring; his brother was Charles Belmont and his sister, Nora. The Davises were a warm and loving family who shared educational and cultural, as well as recreational, activities. Rebecca Davis, though branded by some a feminist, did a remarkable job of blending her literary career with the mundane tasks of running a pleasant household. She gave her children a properly respectful yet intimate relationship with God; Richard retained it all his life. The Davises numbered among their friends an array of prominent personages. In the literary field there were Nathaniel Hawthorne, Ralph Waldo Emerson, Frances Hodgson Burnett, Bronson and Louisa May Alcott. Among theater people there were Mrs. John Drew and her lovely daughter, Georgie; Ethel, Lionel, and Jack Barrymore; Edwin Booth; Joseph Jefferson; Edwin Forrest; Ellen Terry; Sir Henry Irving; and scores of others. It is not surprising, then, that later in his career, Richard Harding Davis wrote some highly successful plays.

In school, young Davis was not a model scholar: he read what interested him, absorbed what seemed practical, and ignored the rest. He was a leader and did not care whom he offended when a declaration of his principles seemed necessary; he curried no one's favor. He attended Philadelphia Episcopal Academy for five years, where his averages fluctuated from good to hopeless, and withdrew two years before he was to have been graduated. He was sent to Bethlehem, Pennsylvania, to live with Rebecca's brother, Professor Hugh Wilson Harding of Lehigh University, who tutored him in Latin and mathematics. This was somewhat more satisfactory, but Davis's interests still ran to books, drama, and sports. For one year he attended Swarthmore College Preparatory School; this apparently did him no good, for he returned to live with his uncle in Bethlehem and there attended William Ulrich's preparatory school. Finally, when he did apply at Lehigh University, he passed all the entrance exams except mathematics and was admitted as a conditional student. He remained for three years and managed to avoid mathematics; to fail chemistry, French, and German; and to squeak by in Latin, physics, history, and English. He excelled in Greek history, however, and wrote for the school magazine, the yearbook, and even for outside publications. But at the end of his junior year, he was requested to withdraw. Stung to the quick, he boyishly prophesied that he would, in the end, advance further than any of his professors. After leaving Lehigh, Davis enrolled at Johns Hopkins University to study politics and labor problems, both of which he thought would be highly pertinent to a newspaper career. But once again he did not make a serious effort to master the subjects, and his career at Johns Hopkins lasted one year. If he did not glean much from his studies, Davis certainly joined the social and recreational scene with enthusiasm: he donned knickerbockers, carried a cane, wore yellow gloves, promoted the wearing of dress suits, and bought a Norfolk jacket. It is said that at Lehigh he acquired two pet snakes for which he fashioned collars and leashes; attired in a brightly colored blazer and skullcap, he could be seen escorting the reptiles on a slither about town.

When Davis reported for his first job with the *Philadelphia Record*, James S. Chambers, Jr., the city editor, was astonished to see a fashionable young dandy in a suit of English cut, carrying kid gloves and cane. Something in the young man's bearing infuriated the hard-bitten editor, who assigned Davis to seventeen or eighteen assignments each day at the grand wage of seven dollars a week. To his lot fell the unimportant obituaries, the puny fires, the negligible fights, the minor meetings—in short, any assignment that could not be decently foisted upon more experienced reporters. If Davis was daunted, he did not show it at first but went about dressed like an English gentleman, writing reams of copy about unimportant events, only to find his material ruthlessly cut to proportion by a veteran copy editor. Always interested in sports, he was caught one day by Chambers lingering over game scores at the sports desk. The editor ordered Davis to get to work at once; obligingly, Davis did so without stopping to remove his yellow kid gloves. Irritated beyond endurance, Chambers fired him for incompetency.

The shock of being fired seems to have stung Davis to serious action. He laid aside the cane and gloves and was hired by the *Philadelphia Press*. To Albert H. Hoeckley, its city editor, he admitted candidly that he had been fired by Chambers of the *Record*; he also explained about the numerous assignments of no consequence and his low pay. Apparently, Davis had learned his lesson. Hoeckley found that his new cub was a promising young writer who accepted every assignment with good grace, was quick to learn the methods of veteran reporters, and in the next two years advanced rapidly from cub to pro. He learned to be suitably aggressive, to pay attention to small details that could make a routine story colorful, and to expand or cut on demand. In his hands, routine stories became personalized and significant. Meanwhile, he was writing short stories which were published in magazines such as *St. Nicholas* and *Life*.

Working for the *Press*, Davis frequently had the satisfaction of seeing his stories on page one. The *Press* was a crusading newspaper which vigorously attacked vice of every kind. Davis participated energetically, once going so far as joining a band of thieves in order to write about their racket; afterward, he had them apprehended. Less dangerous

assignments included interviewing the poet Walt Whitman, whose lack of personal fastidiousness disturbed Davis. Nevertheless, his interview, printed and sent to Robert Louis Stevenson, earned some precious advice from the famous author: "The swiftly done work of the journalist and the cheap finish and ready-made methods to which it leads, you must try to counteract in private by writing with the most considerate slowness and on the most ambitious models. And when I say 'writing'—O, believe me, it is rewriting that I have chiefly in mind. If you will do this I hope to hear from you some day." Possibly the climax of Davis's work on the *Press* staff came with the Johnstown flood in June 1889. He did not arrive upon the scene until late, but the flood was big news for a considerable time. Davis looked for and found human interest stories others had passed over; then, after most other reporters had left, he capably covered the relief efforts. Everywhere he saw tragedy and caught it in words: he recorded the pathetic, the humorous, and the ironic, and his stories went all over the country.

After completing the Johnstown assignment, Davis returned to Philadelphia to learn that the United States was sending a cricket team, the Gentlemen from Philadelphia, to international matches in Ireland. Long an ardent admirer of the game, he was determined to cover the event but could not do so for the *Press* because that paper's highest-ranking sports editor had already been assigned. Somehow, possibly through his father's influence, Davis received an assignment from the *Philadelphia Telegraph*. Elated, he covered the cricket matches in Ireland, Scotland, and England, cabling reports of the progress of the Gentlemen of Philadelphia. He fell in love with the English countryside and people and saw endless possibilities for the stories he would some day write.

Back in New York in September 1889, Davis applied for a spot on the *New York Evening Sun* and was promptly hired by Arthur Brisbane, the managing editor. The two men were about the same age and shared interests in sports, theater, politics, and the foibles of society; Brisbane, convinced of the genius of his new reporter, gave Davis wide latitude, and from then on, Davis's star ascended rapidly. His assignments for the *Sun* included everything from the police beat to football games, festivals, horse shows, and charity events. He was drawn inevitably to the theater, where he showed an interest in the avant-garde dramas of Ibsen and Pinero.

One drawback to a career with the *Sun* was that its employees had only Sundays free, and if they wanted more time on a weekend, they had to produce additional copy. Davis racked his brains for some kind of feature which would release him after Friday's workday so that he could return to Philadelphia to see his family. In the end, it was his friend Brisbane who came up with an idea: the suave man-about-town Courtland Van Bibber was created. Resplendent in evening attire, Van Bibber took his readers to the theater and opera, dined at Delmonico's, and courted a variety of Gibson beauties. Rich, courtly, blue-blooded Van Bibber occasionally sought the company of prizefighters and servants, which made him human and endeared him to readers beyond the realm of Fifth Avenue, Murray Hill, and Washington Square. Van Bibber did, indeed, fill Davis's Saturday gap; and Davis became, for all practical purposes, Van Bibber, and Van Bibber, Davis. Davis's handsome features, debonair manner, and congenial personality made him an ideal model for the pen and brush of Charles Dana Gibson. The exciting and somewhat mysterious world of the newspaperman in which he operated gave him an added attraction. About this time, too, Davis was beginning to make his mark in the fiction world with short stories in such magazines as *Scribner's* and *Harper's*. "Gallegher, A Newspaper Story" was probably his most noted. The inspiration for the story was a copyboy named Gallagher who had worked at the *Press*.

Meanwhile, chained to the routine of the *Sun* office, Davis was restless. He refused an offer from the publisher S. S. McClure, who, having just transferred his New York man to London, wanted to put Davis in charge of his New York operation; Davis offered to serve in the London office, but McClure declined. In 1890, J. Henry Harper, Brisbane's friend, offered Davis an editorship on *Harper's Weekly*. Davis soon became managing editor and put new life into the magazine with pieces by Gertrude Atherton, Rudyard Kipling, Henry James, and a group of young reporters, including David Graham Phillips, Richard E. Burton, Andrew H. Watrous, and his brother, Charles Belmont Davis.

Knowing that he would find the managing editor's chair too confining, Davis arranged to divide his time between editing and traveling to cover stories. In January 1892, he set out by rail to do a series of articles for *Harper's Weekly*, which were published in book form as *The West from a Car-Window* (1892). In Texas, he was predictably awed by the boundless space. He left the train at Laredo to join the Third Cavalry in pursuit of a Mexican revolutionist, Caterino Garza, whom the Mexican government wished returned to that country. This

Davis in 1890, at the beginning of his career in New York

venture meant riding a horse thirty to fifty miles a day in blistering sun and endless dust in the company of veteran troopers, but Davis did it and helped capture the bandit Garza. Somewhere in the grime, dust, and heat he acquired a love for the military; this may well have been his first step on the road to becoming a war correspondent. In the course of his trip, Davis saw the Alamo, the oil fields of Oklahoma, and the mines of Colorado, and he met many Westerners who knew his writings. He saw a drunk clip Bat Masterson on the chin and live to tell the tale because he *was* drunk.

His superiors at *Harper's* valued Davis's popularity with readers but felt that an editor should spend more time in the office. In January 1893, Davis went off to Europe for several months to do a series for *Harper's Weekly* about the Mediterranean countries and Paris. The former were soon published in a book, *The Rulers of the Mediterranean* (1894). Meanwhile, *Harper's* suggested that the resumption of his editorship upon his return might best be left open. In October, the company offered him an advisory associate editorship. Little of his work appeared in *Harper's* in 1894 and early 1895, but *Scribner's* was eagerly publishing whatever he wrote. Davis relinquished the editorship at *Harper's*, thus ending a second phase in his career as a reporter. In effect, he became a free-lance journalist, which for him was highly satisfactory. He was paid well, gained in professional reputation, and was free to travel where he wished and write what he chose. William Randolph Hearst paid him $500 for a superb account of a Yale-Harvard football game in 1895. *Our English Cousins* (1894) was the result of several trips to England that Davis made about this time. In 1894, he traveled to Moscow for the coronation of Czar Nicholas II, where he was one of 300 correspondents demanding admittance to the cathedral. Davis was admitted probably because he represented a magazine, which was thought to have more lasting value and impact than a newspaper. The resulting article in *Harper's* describes the ancient pageantry in awed terms, especially the "tall Cossacks in long scarlet tunics, their breasts glittering with silver cartridge cases and their heads surmounted with huge turbans of black Astrakhan." Davis and two friends embarked on a leisurely tour of Central and South America in 1895. The adven-

ture provided material for a series of articles later collected for his book *Three Gringos in Venezuela and Central America* (1896).

During 1896-1897, Davis reported the millenium in Budapest, a Cuban insurrection, the inauguration of President McKinley, the Greco-Turkish War, and the diamond jubilee of Queen Victoria, an impressive number of important events. Some of his colleagues in New York, perhaps jealous of the success of his short stories, began accusing him of wishing to repudiate his career as a reporter: the newspaperman's world was not good enough for Davis now that he was in the magazines, they said. Davis retorted that he was still a journalist and always would be; but similar insinuations were to follow him during his entire career.

In an article about McKinley's inauguration for *Harper's*, Davis explained in detail the procedures for taking office. Then, characteristically, he added a human touch, writing that the wife of the Chinese minister "was prettily unconscious that she was the most interesting figure present." December 1896 found Davis in Cuba to get a firsthand look at the Cuban war for independence for Hearst's *Journal*. The noted artist Frederic Remington went with him to do illustrations. They were to go from Key

Davis (center) with Somers Somerset (left) and Lloyd C. Griscom: Three Gringoes in Venezuela and Central America

West, Florida, aboard Hearst's yacht, the *Vamoose*, and be guided to the headquarters of Maximo Gomez, an insurrectionist leader; from there they would send dispatches and illustrations. They were delayed when the crew of the *Vamoose*, fearful of being arrested by Spanish authorities, went on strike, and again when they ran into a raging storm. A week passed before Davis and Remington secured passage to Havana, where they were forced to accept the hospitality of the Spanish occupation forces. The next week, Remington, whom Davis found temperamental at best, gave up the venture and returned to New York. Now free to move about as he pleased, Davis went to Cienfuegos, where he attempted to establish contact with Gomez. But the *Journal* had placed him in a delicate position by announcing that he had already joined the insurgents as originally planned; consequently, the Cuban guides he tried to hire were wary of being found in his company. Davis was furious with Hearst's bungling.

Meanwhile, in New York the yellow journalists were waging all sorts of bloody battles of their own in Cuba. Havana fell several times (impossible because the insurgents lacked artillery), and unspeakable atrocities were committed by the Spaniards—all of it on paper. In Cuba, Davis tried to sort out the truth and reported that in 1897, the "war" was at a draw with all the towns and railroads in Spanish hands and the rest of the island held by the Cubans. Before leaving the United States, Davis had strongly opposed U.S. intervention in Cuba; but when he saw the wasteful pillaging of the lovely Cuban countryside, he changed his mind. Unless the United States intervened on behalf of the Cubans and declared war on Spain, he said, the conflict might go on indefinitely. The tragic plight of the innocent country people, the "pacificos," whom the Spaniards herded into towns to forestall their aiding the insurgents, moved him deeply. He described the hunger and disease among them as more terrible than the condition of the Johnstown flood survivors.

Back in New York, Hearst was still busily trying to beat out Joseph Pulitzer's *New York World*. One of Davis's dispatches mentioned the searching of three Cuban women, suspected of carrying incriminating papers, aboard an American ship in Havana harbor. He did not mention that the searches were made by a woman. Jumping to conclusions, Hearst's *Journal* charged Spanish officials with perpetrating indignities upon young women aboard the *Olivette*. Frederic Remington, who had returned to the United States weeks before and

knew nothing of the incident, was commissioned to do a half-page illustration which showed young women standing nude before several Spanish soldiers who were searching their clothing. *Journal* circulation soared and Congress demanded an explanation from Spain; war fever escalated. Furious at this example of deliberate misrepresentation, Davis struck expertly at his employer and hit a vital spot. He dispatched a letter explaining the *Olivette* search, not to Hearst but to Pulitzer: the *Journal*, not Davis, had perpetrated a lie; never again would the *Journal* be able to hire Davis. The *World* splashed the story in big headlines across its front page.

Cuba was still in trouble when Davis left in February 1897. He was in London when the news came of trouble between Greece and Turkey. The *Times* of London promptly sought his services, and he set out with Stephen Crane, who was representing the *New York Journal*. In Athens they joined John Bass, also of the *Journal*, and various other correspondents. Davis and Bass decided to stay in Velestinos, a deserted town, where they took over the mayor's house and waited for the war to develop. The next day, 4 May, it did. At dawn they heard gunfire and offered each other congratulations that they were the only correspondents to cover the second battle of Velestinos, where the Turks had been driven back a week earlier. Davis, actually under fire for the first time, sent back eyewitness accounts to the *Times*. The war lasted a month.

While at Velestinos, Davis had an attack of sciatica, which had been plaguing him off and on for some time. One leg nearly paralyzed, he was placed on a hospital ship bound for Athens, where he was bedridden for several days. Recovered from the sciatica and back in London, he visited friends and covered the queen's birthday celebration for the *Times*, which had been greatly pleased with his account of Velestinos. Meanwhile, the United States was engaged in a diplomatic struggle with Spain over Cuba. Feeling that war was inevitable, Davis hurried back to New York, where he arranged to cover the situation for the *New York Herald* and *Scribner's* as well as the *Times* of London. A short time later, he was on his way to Key West with orders that would place him aboard the flagship *New York*. He arrived on 22 April, just as war was declared and the fleet given orders to sail in two days. He could not get clearance in time to board the ship, but caught up with it later in Havana harbor. There the *New York* lay in the sunlit harbor sending relatively minor messages to one ship or another. Then the secretary of the navy ordered all correspondents except Associated Press men off the ship. Davis protested, but to no avail. Back he went to Florida to cool his heels with other newsmen for a month at the Tampa Hotel. He described this phase of the war as the "rocking-chair period" because correspondents sat daily in rocking chairs on the ample porch of the hotel, gazing across the waters to where Cuba was supposed to be. He wrote about the experience for *Scribner's*. At this point a personal problem was thrust upon Davis: President McKinley offered him a captaincy in the army. Davis wanted no one to doubt his courage or patriotism, but he felt that he had contracts to honor. Bolstered by the support of his friends, he refused the commission, but he wondered for some time afterward whether he had made the right decision.

As the days slipped by, Davis examined with interest the various military units amassed in Tampa. Teddy Roosevelt was there with his Rough Riders—dashing, well-trained cavalrymen who sat their horses with grace and pride and were the direct opposite of the uninspired regulars; the Rough Riders were real soldiers, Davis thought. The orders finally came to move out, and Davis boarded the *Segurança* with other correspondents. There he found himself in the august company of General Schafter and his staff. This proved a disadvantage, for when it came time to disembark, Schafter refused permission for all except soldiers to leave with the first landing party. Davis tried strategy but was rudely refused by Schafter. It was remarked by one of Schafter's officers that Davis never again wrote a kind word about the general; but while Davis did criticize Schafter's conduct of the entire campaign on the grounds that it was bungled, it does not seem that this was prompted by malice, because historians have agreed with Davis's assessment.

Once ashore, Davis attached himself to Roosevelt's Rough Riders, who he was sure would take the most direct route into action. Despite poor reconnaissance and poorly equipped backup troops, the Rough Riders surged ahead. "Roosevelt, mounted on horseback and charging the rifle-pits at a gallop and quite alone, made you feel you would like to cheer," Davis wrote. Roosevelt had attached a blue polka-dotted handkerchief to his sombrero, a device which the Rough Riders (and Davis) adopted. Wherever the greatest action was, there was Davis. In a discussion of American war correspondents published by *Harper's*, Davis said: "The best correspondent is probably the man who by his energy and resource sees more of the war both afloat and ashore than do his rivals, and who is able to make the public see what he saw." Throughout

the war, Davis found much wrong with its strategy and conduct, and he said so in numerous dispatches.

When at last Santiago fell and Puerto Rico was occupied by American troops after a brief skirmish, Davis was ready to go home. He had no sooner disembarked than his critics sarcastically ridiculed what he had written and suggested snidely that he was more suited to pose for Gibson. Davis knew he had written what he had seen; besides, he had the warm respect of the men with whom he had served and suffered in Cuba. It was enough.

In May 1899, Davis married Cecil Clark, a young woman he had met at least six years earlier at Marion, Massachusetts, where the Davises had a summer home. Ethel Barrymore was maid of honor, and Charles Davis was best man. Cecil was a breeder of fancy dogs which won prizes at shows. Davis, who had never had any particular interest in dogs, became fascinated, followed the shows with Cecil, and became adept at the methods of the ring.

It was the persistent barking of the dogs of war, however, that summoned Davis to his next adventure: in Africa, the Boers were revolting against England. Cecil was as fascinated as Davis by the prospects of being there, and so their honeymoon became a journey to Capetown, which was as far as the British would permit Cecil to go. She remained there with Rudyard Kipling and other of Davis's friends, while Davis went ahead to join Sir Redvers Buller's British troops. Davis's sympathies had been with the Boers from the beginning, but he joined the British because he felt he should see and report news of a distinguished modern army in action. James Gordon Bennett of the *New York Herald* and Lord Northcliffe of the London *Daily Mail*, for whom Davis was reporting the war, would have preferred the Boer angle. Davis soon regretted having requested credentials from Buller: censorship practices irked him, and British protocol for civilians accompanying troops seemed unnecessarily stuffy. Although he wore a neat uniform with the blue insignia of the Rough Riders on his hat, the old congeniality he had experienced during a summer at Oxford was gone forever: the British criticized the inept tactics of their military but were resentful of the fact that Davis agreed and said so in dispatches. He was present at the siege of Ladysmith when a relief force took over a garrison whose weary defenders were half-starved, ridden with fever, and physically debilitated. Davis described the situation movingly. The action marked a delay of several weeks in further British maneuvers; that was too long for Davis, and he decided to see the war

Davis's summer home in Marion, Massachusetts

from the Boer side. He collected Cecil at Capetown, and together they entered Boer territory by way of Lourenço Marques. Cecil's presence was unusual but the officials in Capetown approved.

The contrast between the regimented British troops and the Boer commando units was astounding. The British were precisely trained and their movements rigidly prescribed, but the Boers were an unkempt group somewhat reminiscent, Davis thought, of the motley troops that sprang up everywhere during the American Revolution. The Boers did one thing well—they handled the rifles issued them with consummate skill. Among their ranks were Danes, Italians, Germans, Swedes, Russians, and Irish-Americans, all soldiers of fortune who Davis felt were fighting to save the rights of free people. This was definitely Davis's style, and he joined their cause wholeheartedly. Cecil, always looking for adventure, wanted to experience a battle firsthand. She and Davis rode toward the front, where Boer forces were retreating from the British. At Ventersdorp they camped overnight and the next morning climbed a hill to view a British attack, nearly getting caught between the lines. When the

Boers gave up the hill, the Davises looked for another spot from which to observe the action. It was then that Davis informed Cecil that she had just been under fire for the first and last time. Undaunted, she went among the Boer troops encouraging them, but the Boers were worn out. Back in Capetown on 25 March 1900, Davis decided not to pursue the war further. Two weeks later he reversed the decision and went to Portuguese East Africa to enter the Transvaal, and he was sending dispatches from Pretoria by 18 April. After the battle of Sand River, which the Boers lost, Davis and Cecil left the area for France, where they boarded a ship to New York.

Despite his admiration for the British, which he had acquired in several visits to England, Davis felt the Boer War had been unjust and unintelligent, and he said so. His popularity among the English began to decline, and it diminished still further when he criticized in a dispatch the behavior of English officers who were prisoners of war at Pretoria. Assigned in 1902 by *Collier's* to cover the coronations of Alfonso XIII of Spain and Edward VII of England, Davis found himself being snubbed in London, and he had trouble getting tickets for the British coronation. He learned graphically that a reporter could not always write what he saw as the truth and keep his friends. It hurt, but did not deter him.

Back home in Marion and New York, Davis turned to play writing with considerable success. His dramatic output was interrupted, however, when Robert J. Collier, with whom he had been close friends for some time, asked him to cover the Japanese-Russian War for *Collier's*. Davis agreed at once, not anticipating the frustrating problems he would encounter. Accompanied by Cecil, he sailed from San Francisco in February 1904 for Japan, where war correspondents were gathering in Tokyo. Meanwhile, in New York, his new play, *The Dictator*, opened on Broadway and was an instant hit.

In Tokyo, Davis became engulfed in a situation he had not heretofore encountered anywhere, one which threatened to keep the correspondents entangled in oriental red tape indefinitely; at the same time, *Collier's* was paying him $1,000 a week, and he felt morally obligated to produce worthwhile copy. Supposedly, the Japanese were deployed in three columns, and the trick was to get assigned to one of them. Davis was assigned to the second, which did nothing; neither did the first or the third. Davis, too honest to shirk his assignment, began covering whatever features Tokyo yielded and sent them back to *Collier's*. Months passed, and the Japanese officials put off the correspondents in every way they could. Tension mounted. It would have been better had the Japanese simply said, "Go home, all of you! We do not think you are good for our war," but that was not the oriental way. At last, near the end of July, Davis climbed aboard a ship headed for Manchuria; once ashore, he could hear the heavy artillery at Port Arthur, and his spirits rose. But not for long; all correspondents were ordered north. For eleven days they rode on horseback until a severe storm forced them to take shelter in a village. Stuck there for two days, their dispatches heavily censored by the Japanese officers, the reporters climbed a hill and observed the "war" through field glasses at Anshantien. Disgusted, most of them went to bed—much to the consternation of the Japanese officers, who were insulted because nobody was looking at their "battle." Davis and some others figured that a major battle would surely take place at Liao-Yang, and they questioned the officer in charge, who positively assured them that Liao-Yang had long since been captured by the Mikado's troops. Davis and three other correspon-

dents took the road back to the coast. At Chefoo, Davis walked into the cable office to file his story and was congratulated by a smiling Chinese operator upon being the first correspondent to see the battle of Liao-Yang. When Davis said that there had been no battle, he was assured that it had been going on for six days. He had been deceived into missing the biggest action in the war thus far!

Gladly, Davis boarded the American cruiser *Cincinnati* and sailed home to New York, where he was greeted joyously by friends and besieged by young reporters. Off to Crossroads Farm he went to write articles, plays, short stories, and novels. In 1907, he made a trip to the Belgian Congo to investigate alleged atrocities for *Collier's*. It resulted in a book, *The Congo and Coasts of Africa* (1907).

Most of Davis's fictional stories ended happily, but his marriage did not: in 1910, he and Cecil were separated. Davis worked harder than ever to assuage the several sorrows that had overtaken him: besides his separation from Cecil, both his mother and father had died. It was at the theater during the performance of *Three Twins* that Davis found a new love: Bessie McCoy (in private life Elizabeth Genevieve McEvoy), an actress who wore a black Pierrot costume trimmed with huge white pompoms and who sang with sparkle and spirit an enchanting song hit about the fearsome "Yama Yama Man." At first Bessie ignored Davis, or so the story goes; gossipers and tale fabricators were hard at work the instant Davis's interest in Bessie was noted. Cecil obtained an amicable divorce in Chicago on grounds of desertion, and in 1912, Davis married the Yama Yama Girl and lived happily with her until his death.

By the time the first rumblings of World War I were heard, Davis had more or less retired from work as a war correspondent. During April-June 1914, he had reported the border troubles between the United States and Mexico, but they were hardly a war; he wrote an article for *Scribner's* about the battle of Vera Cruz entitled "When a War Is Not a War." Davis's "retirement" at Crossroads Farm was ended abruptly in 1914 when the nation's papers began screaming the news of mobilization of men and arms in Europe. The Wheeler syndicate offered Davis $600 a week plus expenses, and *Scribner's* offered him $1,000 each for four articles, to cover the action. On 4 August, one day after Germany invaded Belgium, Davis and Bessie were aboard the *Lusitania*, which less than a year later would be sunk by a German submarine. In London, Davis could not get credentials to accompany either army. Only one correspondent was assigned by the

British, and that was Frederick Palmer. Davis was not daunted: on 16 August 1914, he arrived in Brussels without credentials; Bessie remained in London. Two days later, a sad stream of refugees was flowing through the city, and word was out that Louvain had fallen to the Germans. King Albert ordered his people not to oppose the Germans, who came marching through Brussels the next day. Davis's description of this event was one of the most powerful dispatches to come out of the war: "No longer was it regiments of men marching, but something uncanny, inhuman. . . . It carried all the mystery and menace of a fog rolling towards you across the sea. The uniform aided this impression. In it each man moved under a cloak of invisibility. Only after the most numerous and severe tests at all distances, with all materials and combinations of colors that give forth no color, could this gray have been discovered. . . . It is the gray of the hour before daybreak, the gray of unpolished steel, a mist among green trees."

Still without proper credentials except for Brussels and "environs," Davis and a fellow correspondent began to follow the German army. Davis was arrested three times; the third time he was in serious danger of being shot as a British spy. In the passport picture on his identification, he was wearing a West African Field Force uniform he had adopted eight years earlier because it was exceptionally comfortable and was not like any known military uniform. Since that time, however, the English Brigade of Guards and the Territorials had adopted it; to the Germans, Davis was an English officer. His book, *With the Allies* (1914), recounts his amusing and alarming battle of wits with a young German officer who was sure he had captured a military prize; the account reads like a spy thriller. After that encounter, the Germans released Davis, only to arrest him repeatedly and release him further and further from the "environs" for which he had a pass. Finally, at Ligny, they held him in a staff room while they decided his fate. German Major Alfred Wurth recognized Davis's accent as American and was sympathetic to his plight, but he had no authority to release him. Through Wurth, Davis negotiated a daring plan. The Germans put Davis on the road to Brussels with a statement added to his pass stating that he was a "suspected spy"; if he was found off the direct road to Brussels or if he had not reported to the military governor there by midnight 26 August, he was to be shot on sight. Davis had two days to travel fifty miles on foot. Three times he bluffed his way past German guards until finally, exhausted and desperate, he flagged down a German car determined to ask that he be taken to Brussels under arrest. Davis was picked up, but not arrested, by an elderly German general whom he described as "old and kindly looking and, by the grace of Heaven, as slow-witted as he was kind."

Back in Brussels, he wasted no time getting the word "spy" removed from his credentials and a note added to the effect that he was well known to the American minister. Then he set out for the ancient city of Louvain, where he saw from a locked railroad car the burning of the city and the senseless destruction of public buildings and churches. In Sois-

The passport that almost got Davis shot as a British spy during World War I

Davis and a French officer inspect a ruined village

batteries made it impossible to avoid hitting the structure. Well aware of the positions of the French batteries and skeptical of this excuse, Davis consulted French, English, and American army experts about the margin of error that could be expected in the shelling: less than fifty to a hundred yards, he was told. Davis reported that the Germans had missed their target by one mile and had shelled the city mercilessly for four days. Another excuse was that the cathedral towers had been used for military purposes. The Abbé Chinot, curé of the cathedral chapel, assured him that this was not so.

By the end of his first tour of duty, Davis had decided that the Germans were to blame for the conflict. He did not see an imperialistic rivalry but a direct clash between good and evil. America was threatened, too, he maintained, and should not remain neutral. He took up the cause of the Allies and actively promoted it in the United States; neutrality in this conflict he saw as neglect of duty.

In August 1915, Davis spent a month in military training at Camp Plattsburg, New York, an experience that was hard on him physically. In October, he went back to the war. Although he felt that action was most likely in the Balkans, he decided that the fighting in the trenches of France had not been adequately covered. He spent time in the Artois and Champagne sectors until his departure for

sons, he saw the devastation of that city, and, he described in *With the Allies* "the utter wastefulness of war. . . . Carcasses of horses lined the road . . . motor-trucks and automobiles . . . two shattered German airships . . . they had buried their motors deep in the soft earth and their wings were twisted wrecks of silk and steel. . . . The haystacks . . . were trampled in the mud . . . smaller villages . . . empty of people . . . just as the Germans had left them. . . ." Of the dead bodies piled at abandoned aid stations, Davis wrote: "After death the human body is mercifully robbed of its human aspect. You are spared the thought that what is lying . . . in the wheatfields staring up at the sky was once a man. It appears to be only a bundle of clothes, a scarecrow that has tumbled among the grain it once protected. But it gives a terrible meaning to the word 'missing!' "

In Reims, Davis found the destruction of the magnificent cathedral a shocking desecration, the more so because he determined that it had been done purposely. The official excuse given by the German commanders for the bombardment of the cathedral was that the placement of the French

Davis (left) receiving military training at Camp Plattsburg, New York, in 1915

Salonika, Greece, at the end of November. He remained there for three weeks; then, suffering from the cold and foggy weather, which had always bothered him, he left for France. He found the people patiently and diligently trying to rebuild the country. On his way to New York, he passed through London and suggested that women might be given the suffrage because of the good work they were doing there.

The year 1915 brought Davis a great joy: his beloved daughter and only child, Hope Harding Davis, was born. In February 1916, Davis returned home for good. By this time, it was becoming evident that he was not well. Back at Crossroads Farm he suffered fainting spells but did not slacken the pace of his work. He complained of chest pains and was put to bed for three days by his doctor. On 10 April, Davis was up and about, had dinner with Bessie and, feeling nervous, had half a drink of Scotch, which brought back the chest pains. The next day he was up again reading proofs for his latest book, *With the French in France and Salonika* (1916). Having had dinner again with Bessie, he went to his study to finish up some work. He telephoned his old friend Martin Egan, a fellow journalist; the conversation ended rather abruptly, but Egan did not suspect anything wrong. When Davis did not come upstairs at midnight, Bessie called to him but received no answer. Coming downstairs to the study, she found Davis dead on the floor, the telephone dangling nearby. Swiftly the sad news spread to the literary and journalistic worlds. Davis's ashes were buried next to his mother and father in Leverington Cemetery, Philadelphia. He had died one week before his fifty-second birthday.

Besides his journalistic endeavors, Richard Harding Davis made a considerable stir in his day with his seven novels, thirteen travel books, approximately eighty short stories, and twenty-five plays. Many of the latter were produced on the New York stage and were highly successful; Ethel Barrymore starred in *"Miss Civilization."* Davis's two most famous fictional characters were Courtland Van Bibber, the man about town, and Gallegher, the newsroom copyboy. He was one of the most widely read and admired writers of his day. Critics of his work at that time seem to have been divided mainly into those who adored everything he wrote and those who from jealousy or other motives took potshots at him and his work at every opportunity. But there was a third group of more serious-minded critics who complained that his writing lacked depth, reflected an immature approach to life, and had no lasting literary merit; some claimed

he was sensational. Reviews of his plays and short stories were mixed. For some years after his death no serious critic challenged these views; then, in the 1960s and 1970s, a renewed interest in Davis sprang up, and several significant scholarly studies were done. In their annotated checklist of Davis's works, Clayton L. Eichelberger and Ann M. McDonald state: "The tendency of minor critics to be influenced by early estimates of an author, particularly if those estimates are made by generally respected spokesmen or if they appear in major literary journals, constitutes a pattern . . . [which] almost inevitably leads to critical stagnation. So it is in the case of Richard Harding Davis. . . ." John M. Solensten notes that in the 1920s H. L. Mencken put Davis through the "rigors of mortis" and, in a letter to Upton Sinclair, sarcastically classified Davis's works with other trivia he had lost in a Baltimore fire. However, discussing the letters exchanged between Davis and Theodore Roosevelt, Solensten says: "If Roosevelt who labelled the Strenuous Age, was its toothy apotheosis as president and Rough Rider, Davis, more than Jack London or Stephen Crane, was the man of the hour in journalism and fiction." Further, he affirms that social issues do underlie Davis's fiction, a fact which a number of Davis's earlier critics disputed. Again, Solensten writes: "When Richard Outcault's 'Yellow Kid' gave his name to an infamous chapter in American journalism and Randolph Hearst made Americans see red by reading yellow, Davis stood as a symbol of integrity while maintaining his rank as one of the most famous war correspondents of his day. . . . Most importantly, Davis's integrity as a journalist involved no easy reliance on objective reporting. His concept of the journalist, and to a lesser extent the short story writer, as impressionist made journalism more complex aesthetically, aligning it with important tendencies in French painting and American fiction. . . . Davis's voice becomes more significant as he is re-examined more carefully with an eye on those, including Sinclair Lewis, who followed him." Robert Waldron in the late 1960s hailed Davis as the "star reporter among the shining company of Dana and Brisbane's *New York Sun* men when he was 25. . . . Much of what he wrote did not survive his short lifetime and the first generation of legend that followed it. But the legend itself animated that enduring tradition of the newspaperman-turned-novelist, and it led the vanguard of literate young college men into city rooms, whence some would depart to write their books but where others would remain—to change the forms and substance of American journalism."

According to the late J. L. O'Sullivan of Marquette University, there are three essential elements to the practice of good journalism—truth, competence, and compassion. By these modern-day standards, Richard Harding Davis rates high; in addition, he added uniqueness, freshness, color, and excitement to his journalistic endeavor. Perhaps the hope expressed by Thomas Beer in 1924 will come true, and "Richard Harding Davis will come to a second use and fame."

Plays:

The Other Woman, New York, Theatre of Arts and Letters, 1893;

The Disreputable Mr. Reagan, Philadelphia, Broad Street Theatre, 4 March 1895;

Soldiers of Fortune, New Haven, Conn., Hyperion Theatre, 17 February 1902;

The Taming of Helen, Toronto, Princess Theatre, 5 January 1903;

Ranson's Folly, Providence, R.I., Providence Opera House, 11 January 1904;

The Dictator, New York, Criterion Theatre, 4 April 1904;

The Galloper, Baltimore, Ford's Theatre, 18 December 1905;

"Miss Civilization," New York, Broadway Theatre, 26 January 1906;

The Yankee Tourist, by Davis with lyrics by Wallace Irwin and music by Alfred G. Robyn, New York, Astor Theatre, 12 August 1907;

Vera, the Medium, Albany, N.Y., Bleecker Hall, 2 November 1908;

The Seventh Daughter, Cleveland, Colonial Theatre, 10 November 1910;

Blackmail, New York, Union Square Theatre, 17 March 1913;

Who's Who, New Haven, Conn., Hyperion Theatre, 28 August 1913;

The Trap, by Davis and Jules Eckert Goodman, Boston, Majestic Theatre, September 1914;

The Zone Police, Tunkhannock, Pa., Piatt's Opera House, 11 August 1916;

Peace Manoeuvres, Bernardsville, N.J., Somerset Hills Dramatic Association, 13 September 1917.

Bibliographies:

Henry Cole Quinby, *Richard Harding Davis: A Bibliography* (New York: Dutton, 1924);

Fanny Mae Elliott and Lucy Clark, *The Barrett Library: Richard Harding Davis, A Checklist of Printed and Manuscript Works of Richard Harding Davis in the Library of University of Virginia* (Charlottesville: University Press of Virginia, 1963);

John M. Solensten, *Richard Harding Davis (1864-1916)* (Arlington: University of Texas Press, 1970);

Clayton L. Eichelberger and Ann McDonald, *Richard Harding Davis (1864-1916): a Checklist of Secondary Comment* (Arlington: University of Texas Press, 1971).

Biographies:

Fairfax Downey, *Richard Harding Davis: His Day* (New York & London: Scribners, 1933);

Gerald Langford, *The Richard Harding Davis Years: A Biography of Mother and Son* (New York: Holt, Rinehart & Winston, 1961).

References:

"How Davis Got a Story," *Literary Digest*, 48 (23 May 1914): 1284;

"Literary Estimate," *Literary Digest*, 52 (20 April 1916): 1218-1219;

"Mr. R. H. Davis and His Comrades: Letter on Misrepresentations in the Press," *Critic*, 29 (26 September 1896): 185-186;

"Notes on Richard Harding Davis," *Bookman*, 43 (June 1916): 353-363;

Scott C. Osborn and Robert L. Phillips, Jr., *Richard Harding Davis* (Boston: Twayne, 1978);

"Portrait," *Saturday Evening Post*, 194 (17 September 1921): 10;

"Portrait," *Saturday Review of Literature*, 27 (16 December 1944): 7;

"Richard Harding Davis as Revealed by His Letters," *New Republic*, 14 (2 March 1918): 149-150;

John M. Solensten, "The Gibson Boy: A Reassessment," *American Literary Realism*, 4 (1971): 303-312;

"War Correspondent," *Collier's Weekly*, 48 (7 October 1911): 21-22.

Papers:

There are three major collections of the works of Richard Harding Davis. One, originally the property of Hope Harding Davis, is in the Richard Harding Davis Collection, Clifton Waller Barrett Library in the Alderman Library at the University of Virginia, Charlottesville. A second is on file at Charles Scribner's Sons Publishers, New York. A third is housed in the library of Lehigh University. Some other Davis items are available at the University of Pennsylvania, the University of North Carolina, and the New York Public Library.

Finley Peter Dunne

Margaret A. Blanchard
University of North Carolina

See also the Dunne entry in *DLB 11, American Humorists, 1800-1950*.

BIRTH: Chicago, 10 July 1867, to Peter and Ellen Finley Dunne.

MARRIAGE: 9 December 1902 to Margaret Abbott; children: Finley Peter, Jr., Philip, Margaret, Leonard.

MAJOR POSITIONS: City editor, *Chicago Times* (1888-1889); editor, Sunday edition, *Chicago Tribune* (1890-1891); editorial page editor, *Chicago Evening Post* (1892-1897); managing editor, *Chicago Journal* (1897-1900); editor, *New York Morning Telegraph* (1902-1904).

AWARDS AND HONORS: Member, National Institute of Arts and Letters.

DEATH: New York, 24 April 1936.

BOOKS: *Mr. Dooley in Peace and in War* (Boston: Small, Maynard, 1898; London: Richards, 1899);

Mr. Dooley in the Hearts of His Countrymen (Boston: Small, Maynard, 1899; London: Richards, 1900);

Mr. Dooley's Philosophy (New York: Russell, 1900; London: Heinemann, 1900);

Mr. Dooley's Opinions (New York: Russell, 1901);

Observations by Mr. Dooley (New York: Russell, 1902; London: Heinemann, 1903);

Dissertations by Mr. Dooley (London & New York: Harper, 1906);

Mr. Dooley Says (New York: Scribners, 1910; London: Heinemann, 1910);

Mr. Dooley on Making a Will and Other Necessary Evils (New York: Scribners, 1919; London: Heinemann, 1920);

Mr. Dooley at His Best, edited by Elmer Ellis, foreword by Franklin P. Adams (New York: Scribners, 1949);

Mr. Dooley: Now and Forever, edited by Louis Filler (Stanford, Cal.: Academic Reprints, 1954);

The World of Mr. Dooley, edited by Filler (New York: Collier Books, 1962);

Mr. Dooley on the Choice of Law, edited by Edward J. Bander (Charlottesville, Va.: Michie, 1963);

Finley Peter Dunne at the age of thirty-five (Culver Pictures)

Mr. Dooley Remembers: The Informal Memoirs of Finley Peter Dunne, edited by Philip Dunne (Boston: Little, Brown, 1963);

Mr. Dooley and the Chicago Irish, edited by Charles Fanning (New York: Arno, 1976).

Finley Peter Dunne, a newspaperman of considerable personal merit, is best remembered for the alter ego that he so carefully created and nurtured for some three decades: Martin Dooley, an Irish immigrant and saloonkeeper on Chicago's Archey Road, who dispensed wit and wisdom on the affairs of greater Chicago and the world. Through Mr. Dooley's broad Irish brogue, Finley Peter Dunne won readers and, indeed, fans on all levels of American political and economic life, as well as in Europe.

Much of Mr. Dooley's Irishness came from Dunne's own life experiences. Peter Dunne was born to Irish immigrant parents on 10 July 1867; his twin brother, John, died in infancy. Dunne, as the fifth of seven surviving children, grew up in a large Irish Catholic family. Both of his parents had emigrated from Ireland as children. The elder Peter Dunne left Queens County, Ireland, with his parents at the age of six and lived with his family in Chatham, New Brunswick, during his early years. There he learned the carpentry trade, which he later practiced in the United States. The elder Dunne's life-style was similar to that of the characters who would later populate Mr. Dooley's world: he was a Catholic, although he did not practice his faith regularly; he was a Democrat and an active political worker; and he was an Irish nationalist, although his personal memories of Ireland were quite dim. The young Dunne's mother had the greatest influence on him, as he would attest in 1886 by adding her maiden name to his own name. Ellen Finley Dunne, who came to America from Kilkenny, Ireland, shared her husband's beliefs in Catholicism, the Democratic party, and Ireland. She differed from her husband in one important aspect, however, for she loved books and, as Dunne biographer Charles Fanning puts it, "encouraged her children in reading and the life of the mind."

Dunne was a precocious child who began to talk at an early age. His mother encouraged his intellectual growth, for she was determined that her son would be more than a laborer when he grew up. Although Dunne was the only boy in the family to attend high school, his father saved him from the most popular career path for educated Irish-American youths—the priesthood—by simply declaring that no son of his would become a priest unless he personally desired that vocation. As Dunne grew up, he began to display several traits which he would use well in his journalistic career. He showed an early irreverence for the symbols of life, as evidenced by his comical descriptions of church-related events—a key to his later ability to write successful humor and satire. This ability stayed with Dunne throughout his life, although it was not fully appreciated by the gatekeepers of the media before the creation of Mr. Dooley. In fact, Dunne tried to share his humorous commentary with his West Division High School friends via the school newspaper; its editors said they appreciated his contributions, but they carried little of the material Dunne submitted, apparently afraid of offending readers. In response to this rebuff, Dunne issued a handwritten newspaper, the "Missionary," to circulate his unpublished material. Although Dunne was generally a poor student in high school, he was an excellent debater who polished his wit and ability to think fast on his feet at the expense of his opponents. He graduated last in a class of fifty, so discouraging his father that a college education for

Dunne was declared to be simply out of the question. Dunne's mother had died a year earlier after a long, debilitating bout with tuberculosis. Consequently, his father was unopposed when he declared that the younger Dunne must go to work.

Thus, in 1884, at the age of seventeen, Dunne began his newspaper career with a job on the *Chicago Telegram*, the poorest of the city's thirty dailies. The young Peter Dunne was a product of his urban environment: he knew the ways of the city and where every important office—including the police department—was; he also knew how to write. Consequently, he was well suited for his $5-a-week job as a part-time office boy and police reporter. Chicago journalism was fiercely competitive; the city's newspapers were generally good and were known for their political reporting. The leading papers were the *Daily Tribune* of Joseph Medill and the *Daily News* of Melville Stone and Victor Lawson. Dunne's job on the *Telegram* was far from such heights, but it was the start of what, without Mr. Dooley's arrival, could have been an excellent career on Chicago newspapers. During his first eight years as a journalist, Dunne held positions on six of Chicago's daily newspapers and rose from police reporter to editorial page editor. As with many other journalists, his abilities would be noticed by the editor of another newspaper, and Dunne soon would be switching jobs. He moved from the *Telegram* to the *Chicago Evening News*, where he began as a news writer with a special talent for feature stories. His writing ability and quickness of mind won the attention of Henry Ten Eyck White, the editor, who began to teach Dunne how to compose short, pithy, editorial paragraphs packed with satire and humor. Soon Dunne's writing ability and knowledge of Chicago were being displayed on the editorial page.

Opportunities to grow professionally continued to come his way. At the age of twenty, Dunne was assigned to cover the Chicago White Stockings, the city's championship baseball team. By 1887, Dunne and his colleague Charles Seymour had created the style of baseball reporting known today simply by writing news stories about baseball games rather than reciting the players' times at bat. The sports assignment took Dunne around the country, and he added experiences in Detroit, New York, Boston, Philadelphia, and Washington to his storehouse of information. By 1888, Dunne was working for the *Chicago Times* as a political writer who did both reporting and editorial writing. He soon became city editor and supervised a staff which solved a particularly messy murder case involving

Irish nationalists and criminally implicated a police officer, a scoop he always fondly remembered as one of the high points of his career.

A shake-up in the top management of the *Times* reached down to the city editor's position, and Dunne was unemployed in 1889. The day after his dismissal from the *Times*, however, Dunne went to work for the *Chicago Tribune* and immediately became one of that newspaper's top reporters. Unfortunately, he soon discovered that he did not like that role; evidencing some of the laziness that had been apparent in his high school career and that would dog his later life, Dunne found the position of a top reporter demanded more physical exertion than he was willing to expend. The job also was far too dull for his tastes; so, at the age of twenty-two, he declared that although he could do all sorts of reporting well he liked only political reporting. He displayed his dissatisfaction openly for all to see. In January 1890, Dunne was made editor of the *Tribune*'s Sunday edition; he moved to the *Chicago Herald* in 1891 as political writer. Dunne showed just how sharp his commentary could be when he covered an 1892 political meeting in which memories of the bloody shirt and the Civil War were, he believed, inappropriately raised: he concluded his story of the meeting by noting that "all of the people put on their hats and went out to see what news had come from Gettysburg, where a terrible battle is still raging." Immediately after the 1892 elections, he transferred to the *Evening Post*, which was owned by the same company. There he was put in charge of the editorial page.

During these years, Dunne still lived at home with several of his brothers and sisters; both parents now were dead. He socialized with other journalists, including writers—such as Hamlin Garland, Booth Tarkington, Theodore Dreiser, Carl Sandburg, Ben Hecht, and Sherwood Anderson—who would soon help to develop the realistic school of literature. Along with Brand Whitlock, Frederick Upham Adams, and George Ade, Dunne helped to found the Whitechapel Club, an organization steeped in secret ritual and intellectual challenge. Taking its name from the site of the Jack the Ripper crimes, the Whitechapel Club was loosely modeled on a college fraternity, complete with pranks, although on a grander scale. The members were fairly radical politically, and the club provided a safe outlet for them to express such views without endangering their jobs on Chicago's conservative newspapers; club meetings were the occasions for heated debate. Dunne blossomed in these surroundings and made many friends who would later be significant for both his social life and his professional career.

In fact, Dunne's life was beginning to change quite distinctively due to his association with the *Evening Post*, for that newspaper included coverage of art, music, the theater, and education as integral parts of its news and editorial columns. Dunne's exposure to these events was personally and professionally broadening. About this time, Mary Ives Abbott, a widow fifteen years his senior who was a successful novelist and the newspaper's principal book reviewer, assumed responsibility for his further education. As his patroness, she saw to it that Dunne met members of the social and intellectual elite of Chicago who regularly gathered at her home for conversation. Through his contacts with Mrs. Abbott and members of the Whitechapel Club, Dunne moved into increasingly exclusive Chicago social circles. His reputation among newspapermen and politicians was growing, and his position in the Irish-American community was solidified to the extent that he frequently became the official Irish representative on civic committees, including the one for the 1893 Columbian Exposition.

Dunne liked his work on the *Post* more than anything else he had done journalistically up to that point. His service as city editor of the *Times* was a close runner-up, but his current assignment allowed him to write editorials regularly, which pleased him greatly. He was encouraged to use satire and humor on the editorial page and did so in about half his commentaries. His typical editorial was short and highly sophisticated. Dunne had experimented with dialect and dialogue in his coverage of Chicago city government and his sports reporting; he tried those prose forms again in his editorials. Much of his early work in this art form was disappointingly overwritten, and the dialect spellings were badly overdone. Although his earliest dialect pieces date to 1890, Dunne initially believed that dialect was useful only when the message was humorous; even then, he considered most dialect humor in poor taste. As he said in late 1892, "There is no doubt that the dialect story is a very bad thing and abundantly deserves every uncomplimentary remark that anybody may find time to make about it," adding, "of course, it might be different if we had ever heard of anybody who had succeeded in reading one." Any lingering doubts about the value of dialect pieces, though, were discarded in the wake of the enthusiastic reception accorded the first Irish dialect pieces in the Mr. Dooley lineage, which appeared in December 1892.

The *Post* was beginning a Sunday edition, and

Dunne was asked to produce a humorous column for weekly publication. Perennially short of money, Dunne needed the extra $10 a week and accepted the assignment. The first dialect essay, "Frank's Visit to Grover," appeared on 4 December 1892 and told of an encounter between a job-seeking Chicago politician and President Cleveland. Because the tale was told by an Irishman in a bar, some scholars see this column as the first essay in the Mr. Dooley line. Dunne himself put the genesis of Mr. Dooley about a week later, citing columns based on the real-life bartender James McGarry, owner of a saloon on Dearborn Street. The first McGarry column appeared on 11 December 1892, just after the death of financier Jay Gould. The essay featured John J. McKenna, an Irishman who was an elected official even though he was a Republican. His name was actually used in the piece, although McGarry appeared in the essay as Col. Malachi McNeary, later spelled McNeery. Readers familiar with the Chicago scene, however, knew that McGarry was Dunne's model. Although the McNeery pieces were not as polished as the Dooley essays would be, they were so popular with the *Sunday Post*'s readers that when the Sunday edition ceased publication in mid-1893, Dunne was asked to continue his dialect essays in the Saturday afternoon edition. Soon, however, McNeery was sent back to Ireland: McGarry was complaining that his friends were laughing at him, and he wanted Dunne to stop using him and his saloon as models for the column.

Thus Dunne had to find a new central character for his popular essays and place that character in new but similar surroundings, for Dunne wanted to preserve the bartender-customer relationship. The result was the creation of Martin Dooley, a saloonkeeper on Archey Road in Bridgeport, a large Irish-American community in Chicago. The first article in the highly successful Dooley series appeared on 7 October 1893. In Martin Dooley, Dunne created a character with "strong personal dignity and self-command, befitting his advanced years and steady occupation, . . . known for his keenness of mind and wit." Dunne introduced Dooley as a "traveller, archaeologist, historian, social observer, saloon-keeper, economist, and philosopher, who has not been out of the ward for twenty-five years 'but twict.'" Because of the parochial nature of his experiences, most of Mr. Dooley's commentaries are introduced by the statement "I see be th' pa-apers," bringing the world to Archey Road and removing any limitation, geographic or otherwise, on the content of the essays. Mr. Dooley's commentaries are usually directed toward edifica-tion of his longtime customer and friend Hennessy, for Mr. Dooley, Dunne explained, was "opulent in good advice, as becomes a man of his station; for he has mastered most of the obstacles in a business career, and by leading a prudent and temperate life has established himself so well that he owns his own house and furniture." In addition, Dooley had "served his country with distinction" as a precinct captain from 1873 to 1875, turning in such a sterling performance that "there was some talk of nominating him for alderman. . . . But the activity of public life was unsuited to a man of Mr. Dooley's tastes; and, while he continues to view the political situation always with interest and sometimes with alarm, he has resolutely declined to leave the bar for the forum." Martin Dooley's character apparently was drawn from many influences in Dunne's life. As a bachelor, a saloonkeeper, and an Irishman, Dooley was quite similar to the departed McNeery. Dunne scholars also have found traces of Dunne's father and uncle, a contemporaneous Irish politician, and a deceased drunkard named Dooley dwelling within the Archey Road sage.

The first Dooley essays were successful, but there was no hint of the great influence they would have on Chicago and the world. These early essays, as well as all of the succeeding commentaries, were written quickly, often after deadline. Dunne was a fast writer once the inspiration for an essay hit him, but he did not usually become inspired until deadline time. Dunne soon discovered, however, that the Dooley essays were the perfect place for expanding his editorial influence and for explaining the problems of urban life at the turn of the century. Dunne would later say that he "wanted to make the world see itself through a picture of the simple life of the Irish immigrant in Chicago." Through dialect, Dunne tried "to make Dooley talk as an Irishman would talk who has lived thirty or forty years in America, and whose natural pronunciation had been more or less affected by the slang of the streets." Although there is no agreement on how dialect affected the reader's understanding of his messages, Dunne is usually congratulated for his excellent ear "for the rhythm and timing of urban Irish speech."

Philip Dunne finds the argument over his father's use of dialect distracting. "Mr. D's identity as an Irishman was the *least* important of his attributes. . . . My father's choice of an Irishman as his mouthpiece to express his own political analyses was entirely incidental. Aside from a few 'Irish' pieces, especially in the early days, he spoke always as an American, dealing with American and world issues.

The real "Archey Road": Archer Avenue in Chicago's Bridgeport district, 1885 (Chicago Historical Society)

Eliminate the brogue and the pieces stand out as what they were: pure Americana." Most Dunne scholars would at least partially disagree with Philip Dunne: to them, one of the most important contributions of the early Dooley essays was the way in which they portrayed the problems, hopes, and aspirations of the Irish immigrant during the process of assimilation into American culture. Although Dunne could have used almost any immigrant group to serve this end, he chose the Irish. With that selection, he emphasized the characteristics of one particular group to Chicago and the world. James DeMuth says that through Mr. Dooley, Dunne "confronted and diffused the prejudices of Chicagoans against the enormous foreign-born population in their city. The Irish of Chicago, particularly, had long been castigated for their sympathy with the South during the Civil War, their obstinate loyalty to the Catholic church, and their abuse of power in Chicago's influential Democratic party. Mr. Dooley, however, is a moderate, moral, and patriotic American, and—by dint of his long residence in Chicago—more native than most Chicagoans. Though he spoke with a brogue, he voiced the values Chicagoans esteemed," and he made the Irish-Americans he represented seem more like native Americans, which was, after all, the goal of the assimilation process. According to Charles Fanning, Dooley essays written between 1892 and 1900 present "a unique firsthand account of the process of assimilation into American city life of a large ethnic group," for this was the time when "the Irish were emerging as the most significant new political power on the American urban scene." The price exacted for this assimilation was "the loss of their very identity," a point Dunne has Mr. Dooley make repeatedly. "Through Martin Dooley and his friends, Peter Dunne recreates the peculiar combination of fulfillment and frustration, satisfaction and bewilderment, that went along with being Irish in America in the nineties," and he had Dooley serve as "spokesman for Bridgeport, for the point of view of an urban ethnic community whose values and attitudes were often in conflict with those held more generally in Chicago and America."

The problems immigrant groups had in accommodating their life-styles to the growing urban community of Chicago were the repeated themes of the early Dooley essays and of editorials that Dunne was writing daily as well. Usually, Dooley's comments on these problems were upbeat. Occasionally a Dooley piece would dip into pathos to discuss an alcoholic father sending his young daughter out on a winter night to buy him beer, or the heroic death of a fireman in the line of duty, or the difficulties of raising boys in Chicago. More often, however, Dunne left these problems for his regular editorials. In the first year or so of Dooley's life, Dunne had him talk about subjects other than politics about half of the time. Because he was a polished editorial writer, Dunne preferred to attack local political evils through the traditional voice of the newspaper. As

Dooley became more popular, however, Dunne allowed him to spend more of his time ruminating over local political issues. Ultimately, Elmer Ellis says, Dunne was forced to realize that Dooley "was more effective in bringing home the real corruption" than any editorial page in the city—especially when readers were already tired of the subject. In fact, Dunne's comments about reform made through Mr. Dooley enjoyed a level of acceptance unknown to Dunne the editorialist. Increasingly, Dunne found himself manipulating the dialect essays to make certain points, if only because, as Louis Filler puts it, "Dooley viewed the current scene from a fund of years and experience, which . . . Dunne himself didn't possess; he was, after all, still a young man in the middle 1890's, and had to create his own maturity out of imagination, reading, and associations." As the years passed, Dunne and Dooley were seen increasingly as a single entity, thus, as Grace Eckley points out, giving rise to the unanswered question of "whether Dunne speaks through Dooley in Dunne's own voice or whether Dooley has a voice separate from that of Dunne."

Dunne's ability to maintain such a division within himself has long been considered quite amazing. Equally impressive is the fact that as Mr. Dooley became increasingly popular, his creator was moving farther away from the point of Dooley's origins. Scholars have found, in Fanning's words, a "curious, persistent split between Dunne's life and his writing, between the successful and social young editor and his persona of an aging, worldly-wise saloonkeeper. Mr. Dooley spends a lot of time laughing at the people his creator spent a lot of time living with and emulating." This dual personality does not seem to have bothered Dunne as much as it does scholars studying his work years after his death. As his contemporary Franklin P. Adams explained it, Dunne had discovered that he could get away with far more trenchant criticism of individuals and institutions when the comments came from Martin Dooley than when those same criticisms came directly from him. Adams believed that the "social consciousness as articulated in the 'Dooley' sketches, would never have been printed unless they had been written in dialect. For editors, fearful of calling names, feel that the advertisers and the politicians and the social leaders—money, politics, and social ambition being the Achilles heels of editors and publishers—are journalism's sacred cows. But if pretense and hypocrisy are attacked by the office clown, especially in dialect, the crooks and shammers think it is All in Fun. And when the Dunnes and the Lardners die, the papers print editorials saying that there was no malice in their writing and no bitterness in their humor. Few popular writers ever wrote more maliciously and bitterly than Lardner and Dunne. They resented injustice, they loathed sham, and they hated the selfish stupidity that went with them." Dunne himself concurred as he recalled his first comprehension of this hidden strength: "While I was writing editorials for the *Post*, we became engaged in a bitter fight with the crooks in the city council. [Newspaper editor Cornelius] McAuliff and I were both hot municipal reformers but our publisher wasn't so eager. He was nervous about libel suits and loans at banks that were interested in the franchises for sale in the council. It occurred to me that while it might be dangerous to call an alderman a thief in English no one could sue if a comic Irishman denounced the statesman as a thief. So I revived Col. McNeery and used him to bludgeon the bribe-taking members of the council. I think the articles were effective. The crooks were ridiculed by their friends who delighted in reading these articles aloud in public places. . . . If I had written the same thing in English I would inevitably have been pistolled or slugged, as other critics were. But my victims did not dare to complain. They felt bound to smile and treat these highly libellous articles as mere humorous skits."

A change in ownership at the *Post* and its sister paper, the *Times-Herald*, in 1896 curbed Dunne's freedom of editorial comment. The Dooley essays were also affected because the new owner was a Republican who demanded that Dunne stop featuring the Irish Republican politician McKenna as a frequenter of Martin Dooley's saloon and primary target of Dooley's barbs. The edict ultimately benefited the Dooley essays, for it led to the inclusion of Mr. Hennessy, a typical Irish-Catholic Democrat, in the pieces; but, unable to tolerate such restrictions on his editorial freedom, Dunne soon changed jobs again. In late 1897 he joined the *Chicago Journal* as managing editor and editorial page supervisor. In 1898, Mr. Dooley began appearing in the pages of the *Journal*, but the relationship between that publication and Mr. Dooley was not totally satisfying. Dunne was thirty years old and had been writing dialect essays for five years. Now, for the first time, he made Mr. Dooley take a position completely out of his carefully honed character; then Dunne forced the Irishman into another first, that of taking a position directly opposed to one supported by the newspaper. The *Journal*, a practitioner of yellow journalism, was an unquestioning supporter of the Spanish-American War. When Mr. Dooley first began appearing in the *Jour-*

Conceptions of Mr. Dooley by various artists

nal, Dunne made him a jingoistic supporter of Manifest Destiny. After the sinking of the *Maine,* however, Dooley returned to his—and Dunne's—healthy skepticism of the military effort and began to comment satirically on American preparedness and the conduct of the war. Soon Dunne had Mr. Dooley directly contradict the editorial statements made by the *Journal* on this subject.

By 1898, Mr. Dooley was becoming nationally prominent. Seldom is it possible to state unequivocally that one particular event led to such recognition. In Mr. Dooley's case, however, an essay entitled "On His Cousin George" was directly responsible for his ascendency. The essay was written about Adm. George Dewey's defeat of the Spanish fleet in Manila Bay. Dewey's lines of communication had been cut, and the entire nation worried about his fate. The scenario provided by Dunne's Mr. Dooley appeared several days before reliable word of Dewey's victory was received, and it happened to be accurate. The combination of these factors simply catapulted Dooley into the national spotlight.

"On His Cousin George" was typical of Dunne's essays in showing the way in which Martin Dooley insinuated himself into the lives of everyone he talked about. After he explained how his subject was related to his personal well-being, Dooley then felt he could comment upon the subject in depth, as he did with Admiral Dewey:

> "Well," said Mr. Hennessy, in tones of chastened joy, "Dewey didn't do a thing to thim. I hope th' poor la-ad ain't cooped up there in Minneapolis."
>
> "Niver fear," said Mr. Dooley, calmly. "Cousin George is all r-right."
>
> "Cousin George?" Mr. Hennessy exclaimed.
>
> "Sure," said Mr. Dooley. "Dewey or Dooley, 'tis all th' same. We dhrop a letter here an' there, except th' haitches,—we niver dhrop thim,—but we're th' same breed iv fightin' men. Georgy has th' thraits iv th' fam'ly. Me uncle Mike, that was a handy man, was tol' wanst he'd be sint to hell f'r his manny sins, an' he desarved it; f'r, lavin' out th' wan sin iv runnin' away fr'm, annywan, he was booked f'r ivrything fr'm murdher to missin' mass. 'Well,' he says, 'anny place I can get into,' he says, 'I can get out iv,' he says. 'Ye bet on that,' he says.
>
> "So it is with Cousin George. He knew th' way in, an' it's th' same way out. He didn't go in be th' fam'ly inthrance, sneakin' along with th' can undher his coat. He left Ding Dong, or whativer 'tis ye call it, an' says he, 'Thank

> Gawd,' he says, 'I'm where no man can give me his idees iv how to r-run a quiltin' party, an' call it war,' he says. An' so he sint a man down in a divin' shute, an' cut th' cables, so's Mack cudden't chat with him. Thin he prances up to th' Spanish forts, an' hands thim a few oranges. Tosses thim out like a man throwin' handbills f'r a circus. 'Take that,' he says, 'an' raymimber th' Maine,' he says. An' he goes into th' harbor, where Admiral What-th'-'ell is, an', says he, 'Surrinder,' he says, 'Niver,' says th' Dago. 'Well,' says Cousin George, 'I'll just have to push ye around,' he says, An' he tosses a few slugs at th' Spanyards. . . .
>
> "Well, sir, in twenty-eight minyits be th' clock Dewey he had all th' Spanish boats sunk, an' that there harbor lookin' like a Spanish stew. Thin he r-run down th' bay, an' handed a few war-rm wans into th' town. He set it on fire, an' thin wint ashore to war-rm his poor hands an' feet. It chills th' blood not to have annything to do f'r an hour or more."

Public response to "Cousin George" was overwhelming and came at a time when Dunne was most discouraged with the ability of Chicago to correct some of the problems he had been editorializing about for several years. Despite his efforts, living and working conditions for the poor had not improved. Dunne's growing despair seeped into Mr. Dooley's consciousness as well. Fanning believes that "all through 1897 the conviction must have been mounting that his parables of suffering and injustice were falling on deaf ears: in the end, it became too painful for him to write up such stories without real hope of helping the people who served as his models. So Dunne turned his back on the Chicago Irish. Or, to put it another way, Mr. Dooley left home rather than continue to live among neighbors whose troubles he could only observe with impotent anger."

As Dunne's feeling of helplessness grew, so did Mr. Dooley's fame. Dunne had long been opposed to making his relationship with Mr. Dooley public knowledge for fear that such a revelation would adversely affect his cherished dream of building a career in newspaper management. Such an ambition was contradicted by his life-style, for Dunne was never able to save any money toward this avowed end, even though he knew that he would need quite a bit of capital if he ever wanted to publish a newspaper. Friends began urging him to publish a collection of Dooley essays about the same time that his Dooley pieces were being read and cited by an increasing number of fans—including members of President McKinley's administration who wondered, after a particularly accurate rendition of events in a cabinet meeting, just who Mr. Dooley's inside informant was. Before long newspapers around the country began to follow the pattern set by the *Boston Globe* in reprinting the Dooley essays. The essays were not copyrighted, but the newspapers republishing them did pay for using them. And even though his present employers kept most of these fees, Dunne was most thankful for every dollar he received. As usual, he was short of money.

The Spanish-American War provided the platform on which Mr. Dooley's national reputation was firmly built, with Dunne using the dialect essays to support the antiwar effort. In fact, Fanning states, "the Dooley pieces on the conduct of the war were widely appreciated, largely because so many people knew how much of the affair had been a bungled fiasco, eminently worthy of satire. Besides, we had won—easily; it was all wrapped up in four months. So the country enjoyed Mr. Dooley's fresh and funny renderings of what was at best an open secret—that there was a lot that wasn't splendid in the splendid little war." Dooley's explanation of his cousin George's activities was republished at least 100 times; his argument against American retention of the Philippines, published in January 1899, was read on the Senate floor. Such a response surprised and pleased Dunne, who was learning to enjoy the popularity accorded Mr. Dooley, could use the money available from such republications, and was an ardent anti-imperialist with an ideal forum for presenting his arguments. When friends renewed their requests that he publish a collection of Dooley columns, Dunne acquiesced. He and three close friends went through all the Dooley columns written since 1895 to select those that, with some minor editing, were published in 1898 as *Mr. Dooley in Peace and in War*. Dunne continued to refuse to use his name in connection with the Dooley essays, allowing only the use of his initials, F. P. D., at the end of the introduction. Fanning, however, says that "he must have known that this attempt at anonymity would be ineffectual.... Perhaps it was a half-serious gesture toward the separation of Finley Peter Dunne and Mr. Dooley that the world never again allowed him to make." The book was an immediate success, remaining on the best-sellers' list for more than a year. His connection with the Dooley essays became known, and Dunne was immediately flattered by reviews saying that the essays unmistakably bore "the marks of freshness, originality, and real genius."

Dunne, now thirty-one, had reached an all-time high status in life. He was the managing editor of the *Journal*, thus achieving his dream of entering newspaper management, and he was, rather unexpectedly, a "literary celebrity of some eminence," as Ellis puts it. As the Dooley essays continued to grow in popularity, this aspect of Dunne's career came to dominate all others. Flattered by the attention and always in need of the money offered by those seeking to market the wisdom which Dunne gave Mr. Dooley, Dunne began to accept some of the ways offered him to exploit Mr. Dooley's popularity. He took his first trip abroad to gather material for future essays and to meet European publishers, and he found the fans of Mr. Dooley just as ardent in Britain and France as they were in the United States. Dunne used this trip to make his only visit to Ireland, the home of his ancestors and those of the mythical Mr. Dooley. Dunne recorded his impressions of the trip for a series of columns later published under the general heading of "Mr. Dooley Abroad." The trip also offered some sobering insights into Dunne's future. When in London, for instance, Dunne had his first opportunity to write Dooley essays unencumbered by the daily newspaper routine. Unfortunately, he discovered that his difficulties in disciplining himself as a writer had followed him abroad. He also realized that mastery of a subject to the extent necessary for a Dooley essay was impossible outside of the United States. Mr. Dooley simply did not travel well, and Dunne returned him to Archey Road permanently.

By October 1899 Dunne was back at work at the *Journal*. The fame of Mr. Dooley, however, could not be ignored; it permeated all aspects of Dunne's life and assumed varying guises. Dunne, for example, agreed to write a series of articles about a young woman, Molly Donahue, for the *Ladies' Home Journal*. He soon discovered that his plan to show the strains existing between generations of Irish-Americans through the eyes of Molly, an early feminist, was unworkable, and he abandoned the project after a few essays. Likewise, he had to back out of an assignment to adapt the Dooley essays for the stage. Nor was Dunne able to write a novel with the Archey Road saloonkeeper as the central character. Martin Dooley just was not that malleable, or at least not that malleable for Dunne, his creator. Others, though, were able to depict the Dooley character in cartoons which accompanied Dunne's essays; still others were able to extol his virtues in song. Dunne's inability to transform Mr. Dooley into a character suitable for other media showed him, DeMuth says, "the narrow limits of the character he had created. To be an effective satirist, Mr. Dooley required the security of a stable home and the dignity of respected opinions. Only then could he single out the men and events that disturbed his good life and confidently satirize them." Such elements were not available outside the dialect essay.

People still were very willing to read Mr. Dooley's opinions in the dialect essays which flowed from Dunne's pen. In 1899 Dunne put together a new collection, *Mr. Dooley in the Hearts of His Countrymen*, which was also a critically praised best-seller. In fact, this second book of Dooley essays chased Dunne's first collection from the charts. By the turn of the century, the country was in the grips of "Dooley-mania." Dunne's essays were syndicated, and the sage of Archey Road was now being read coast to coast. Everywhere, Ellis says, it seemed that "Mr. Dooley was a synonym for wisdom, humor, wit, and ready sympathy for those who deserved it."

Fame, however, brought changes in the Dooley essays. No longer was Dunne able to write exclusively about Archey Road, for his new audience was more interested in national and international subjects. But the thorough understanding of the subject and insightful comment so long a trademark of Mr. Dooley remained, as did Dunne's determination to make everyone vulnerable to the sharpness of Dooley's tongue. Perhaps one of the finest examples of this universal vulnerability to Mr. Dooley's wit came with the bartender's review of Theodore Roosevelt's book *The Rough Riders* (1899), which allegedly described his regiment's adventures in Cuba during the Spanish-American War. Mr. Dooley saw Roosevelt's exploits in a slightly different vein:

> "I think Tiddy Rosenfelt is all r-right an' if he wants to blow his hor-rn lave him do it," [said Mr. Hennessy].
>
> "Thrue f'r ye," said Mr. Dooley, "an' if his valliant deeds didn't get into this book 'twud be a long time befure they appeared in Shafter's [the commanding general whom Roosevelt had publicly criticized] histhry iv th' war. No man that bears a gredge again' himsilf'll iver be governor iv a state. An' if Tiddy done it all he ought to say so an' relieve th' suspinse. But if I was him I'd call th' book 'Alone in Cubia.' "

"Alone in Cubia" brought an unexpected favorable response from Roosevelt, then governor of New York, and a request that he and Dunne meet. Dunne, afraid that contact with Roosevelt would blunt his ability to have Dooley satirize him in the future, refused the request. The meeting finally occurred as Dunne was covering his final stories as a Chicago newspaperman: the presidential nominating conventions of 1900. That brief introduction provided Dunne with one of the few scoops of his newspaper career, for Roosevelt told the journalist that after much soul-searching, he planned to accept the Republican nomination for vice-president. The meeting laid the groundwork for a long-lasting friendship between the two men without initially sacrificing one of Dunne's favorite targets for Mr. Dooley essays.

Dunne saw to it that Mr. Dooley satirized both parties during the elections of 1900. As soon as the elections were over, Dunne moved to New York. Some scholars say that Dunne left Chicago because it alone had not accorded him celebrity status after Mr. Dooley's success. Actually, Dunne no longer needed the security that a regular newspaper job provided, and he could afford to move to a more intellectually stimulating environment. Life took a brief downward swing for Dunne just after his arrival in New York, however. The third in his series of Dooley books, *Mr. Dooley's Philosophy* (1900), soon appeared on book dealers' shelves. This effort was received favorably by the critics, but they did not think it was as good as his earlier two volumes, and sales of the new book were slow. Almost as an anticlimax, Dunne contracted typhoid fever while visiting Chicago and had to stay there two months while recuperating. After his illness, Dunne revived Mr. Dooley once again, for he had not written anything since the publication of *Mr. Dooley's Philosophy*. He picked up his weekly columns for *Harper's Weekly* magazine and for his newspaper syndicate as well. In fact, some of his best work was done in the months immediately following his illness. These Mr. Dooley columns included memorable comments about President Roosevelt having Booker T. Washington come to lunch at the White House: "Well, annyhow, . . . it's going to be th' roonation iv Prisidint Tiddy's chances in th' South. Thousan's iv men who wudden't have voted f'r him undher anny circumstances has declared that undher no circumstances wud they now vote f'r him." Dunne concluded Dooley's commentary by having Dooley tell Hennessy that the Negro needed only one right in America. "What's that?" asked Hennessy. "Th' right to live," said Mr. Dooley. "If he cud start with that he might make something iv himself."

One of Mr. Dooley's most famous aphorisms came as he commented about decisions by the U.S. Supreme Court on a series of cases grouped together under the general title Insular Cases, which arose from the Spanish-American War. After explaining to Hennessy how the justices had arrived at their decisions, Mr. Dooley said, "An' there ye have th' decision, Hinnissy, that's shaken th' intellicts iv th' nation to their very foundations, or will if they thry to read it. 'Tis all r-right. Look it over some time. 'Tis fine spoort if ye don't care f'r checkers. Some say it laves th' flag up in th' air an' some say that's where it laves th' constitution. Annyhow, something's in th' air. But there's wan thing I'm sure about. . . . No matther whether th' constitution follows th' flag or not, th' supreme coort follows th' iliction returns." This and other vintage Dooley comments soon appeared in yet another collection, *Mr. Dooley's Opinions* (1901). In 1902 Dunne traveled abroad again, this time visiting London, Paris, Florence, and Rome, where he had an audience with Pope Leo XIII. The most important stop of his trip, however, was in Venice, where he visited Mary Ives Abbott, his old patroness, and her daughter Margaret, to whom he proposed. Dunne was thirty-five at the time of the marriage in 1902.

A fifth collection, *Observations by Mr. Dooley*, appeared in 1902, and critics were amazed that the dialect essay was so durable. Mr. Dooley was indeed durable, and his creator, now a family man needing additional income, began spreading his masterpiece thin, trying to service numerous additional outlets. His dialect essays appeared fairly regularly in *Harper's Weekly* and *Collier's* and less frequently in *Century*, *Cosmopolitan*, *Ladies' Home Journal*, and *Literary Digest*. Although there was a slight protest from a few Irish-Americans about the image of an Irishman being represented by Mr. Dooley, Ellis says that the Archey Road saloonkeeper generally "was recognized as the synonym for delicious humor, penetrating common sense, and a highly American, close-to-the-soil point of view." All of this did not bring Dunne peace of mind, however; soon he was restless again. In addition to his other commitments, he began writing editorials for *Collier's* in order to help his friend Robert Collier. He soon found himself writing about the same things he discussed through Mr. Dooley—sometimes in exactly the same words—and he grew tired of it.

New York journalism beckoned him in 1902, and he became editor of the *New York Morning Telegraph*, which was owned by another friend, William C. Whitney. Once again Dunne had revived his old dream of moving into newspaper management, but his practices as editor were hardly conducive to success in that field: he spent more time lunching with Whitney than he did running the newspaper.

Indeed, some cynics even suggested that Whitney had purchased the newspaper and made Dunne editor solely so Dunne could have lunch with him on a regular basis. As far as Dunne was concerned, though, he had done his job on the publication. He had helped to establish the newspaper's guiding philosophy and had hired its staff. After that, he believed that the newspaper should be able to run itself. Dunne never really had a chance to see if his approach was workable, for upon Whitney's death in February 1904, Dunne left daily newspapering for good.

Dunne entered another period of depression after he left the *Telegraph*. He was having increasing difficulty meeting deadlines and that difficulty, in turn, brought on more depression. Newspaper editors purchasing the Mr. Dooley essays from the McClure's syndicate complained loudly about the missed deadlines; the syndicate passed the complaints on to Dunne, engendering even more depression. Dunne pointed out that because his columns had to be current, broken deadlines were inevitable. He also argued that even if he had a

Dunne as editor of the American Magazine, *1912*

A syndicated 1913 Mr. Dooley article, as it appeared in the Arkansas Gazette

column ready to go, he had the right to hold it up if he believed it to be substandard. At this point in his career, he was bringing in $1,000 an essay, and his syndicate rightfully complained of spotty production from its star property. Dunne was now settling into the pattern of behavior that had afflicted him occasionally earlier in his life and that would be his constant companion throughout the remainder of his years: he would write vigorously for a while, then begin to miss a few deadlines, and ultimately stop production altogether for a while. When fall 1903 arrived, Dunne was without his annual collection of Mr. Dooley essays for publication. The Dooley essays enjoyed their greatest popularity between 1898 and about 1910, and, in the middle of those years, Dooley's creator encountered a major writer's block.

In his personal and social life, Dunne was still quite successful. He and his wife moved with great ease among New York's social and intellectual elite; the friendship with Theodore Roosevelt was blossoming; and Samuel Clemens (Mark Twain) was a regular opponent at billiards. But this meant that the creator of Mr. Dooley was moving farther away from the environment which had led to his great success.

The muckraking movement was in its fullest flower in the early twentieth century, and, although scholars have long debated whether Dunne was a muckraker, there is no doubt that he aided the cause, for the Dooley essays obviously dealt with many situations in need of reform. Dunne, however, was never comfortable with the muckrakers' major premise that all politicians were naturally corrupt. Differences aside, Dunne joined with Ida Tarbell, Ray Stannard Baker, Lincoln Steffens, John S. Phillips, and William Allen White to establish the *American Magazine*. This new experience rejuvenated him, and, once again, he began to write Mr. Dooley essays. In 1906, he published yet another collection of past columns, *Dissertations by Mr. Dooley*, and his previous books were republished and sold as a matched set. The *American Magazine* was very attractive to Dunne at this stage in his career, for it offered him an opportunity to write in a style other than dialect. Many critics, and indeed Dunne himself, saw the Dooley essays as only a way station, a temporary stopping place before he reached his full potential and enjoyed the far greater success in American letters which awaited him. A variety of circumstances conspired to keep Dunne from using the *American Magazine* to reach that potential, but he did add to his reputation as a thoughtful writer through his contributions to "In

the Interpreter's House," a regular commentary in the magazine. The editorial columns soon became as difficult for him to write as the Dooley essays, however, for here, too, he was limited by his perfectionism and "a psychosis about the deadline, which made it nearly impossible for him to write according to a schedule." He usually was able to finish a piece once he got it started; the problem was in getting it started. In these years he was producing an "Interpreter's House" and a Dooley essay each month for the *American Magazine*, as well as a weekly Dooley essay for his newspaper syndicate. Dunne remained with the *American Magazine* from 1906 through 1913, and he wrote "In the Interpreter's House" for two years after leaving the magazine. Beginning in 1911, he also wrote "From the Bleachers," a monthly column for a labor newspaper, *Metropolitan Magazine*, as well. Although Dunne described this publication as espousing right-wing socialism, the editors placed no restrictions on what he could write or on what he could advocate. Consequently, some of his critics believe that in *Metropolitan Magazine* "Dunne expressed his own beliefs . . . more clearly than anywhere else save his personal correspondence." Despite the quality of his writing, Dunne's work here attracted little attention, and he stopped writing the columns after about six months.

By 1915, Dunne was no longer writing for any magazine or for his newspaper syndicate. He had put together another collection of Dooley essays, *Mr. Dooley Says*, in 1910, and although this volume did not attract as much notice as earlier works, Dunne was beginning to realize that his reputation as a writer would rest on the reception accorded his dialect essays. He planned to publish another Dooley collection in 1911, but sales of the 1910 volume were so poor that he abandoned the idea.

He joined the staff of *Collier's* for what would be his last concentrated venture in journalism. Given a special page for his commentary, Dunne—the staunch dissident in the Spanish-American War—became an equally strong advocate of American preparedness before and during World War I. He had been producing Mr. Dooley essays on an irregular basis during the prewar years, but stopped writing dialect pieces when the fighting began, saying that the times were far too perilous to be subjected to satire. Dunne worked for *Collier's* for a number of years, taking over as editor of the financially troubled publication in the fall of 1917. When Robert Collier died shortly after that, he left Dunne a one-third interest in the magazine as a bequest, a grant which Dunne refused due to the financial straits of Collier's widow. When she sold

Dunne with his wife, Margaret, and sons Philip, Leonard, and Finley Peter, Jr., at their Southampton, Long Island, home in 1925

the publication in 1919, Dunne was again out of a job.

By this time Dunne had a growing family and was in great need of a steady income. His friends urged him to bring Mr. Dooley back, and he published yet another volume of essays, *Mr. Dooley on Making a Will and Other Necessary Evils*, in 1919. The collection featured essays written prior to 1915, and, although the critics said that the pieces were well done, they wanted commentary on current events, not on history. Dunne was most hesitant to bring the Archey Road saloonkeeper back; his need for money was stronger than his fear of deadlines, though, and Mr. Dooley reappeared briefly in the mid-1920s. Most of these essays were revised versions of older efforts, although Dunne did write a few new columns about the 1924 presidential campaign. After the election, his old problems resurfaced; deadlines were missed, and soon he stopped providing Mr. Dooley essays for syndication. His heavy drinking compounded his problems with

deadlines, but his son Philip denied that his father was "an alcoholic in the pathological sense. He was always able to swear off the stuff when he had to." Dunne drank heavily because of "a lifelong dread of failure" as a writer, Philip said—thus suggesting another reason for Dunne's problems with deadlines.

The longer Dunne lived, the more involved he became with the rich and famous. Philip Dunne admitted that his father liked extravagant living. "He had the tastes of a Morgan or a Rockefeller. In the great Dooley days the money had rolled in. He was by far the highest-paid writer of his time. He was courted and cultivated by rich men, joined their society, and quite naturally began to live as they did. . . . So my father, after he had begun to find it hard to write and had virtually retired from the editorial field, was faced with the constant problem of finding an income to fill the insatiable maw of our extravagance." When the need for money again revealed itself, Dunne wrote Mr. Dooley essays for Joseph M. Patterson's magazine, *Liberty*. He was well paid for these weekly pieces, which were illustrated with cartoons, and the essays were quite good. It was hard, however, to get Mr. Dooley back into top form, for one of the keys to his success was his knowledge of current events, and Dunne had not been keeping abreast of world happenings. Dunne's growing list of friends in high places—including writers such as Ida Tarbell, rich men such as William C. and Payne Whitney, actresses such as Ethel Barrymore, artists such as Charles Dana Gibson, and humorists such as Mark Twain—also hampered Mr. Dooley's comeback, for Dunne now compelled Mr. Dooley to defend some people whom, in other times, he would have satirized. Soon, however, Dunne's need for the money the Dooley essays brought in was ended. In 1927, Payne Whitney died and left Dunne a $500,000 bequest, thus ending his need ever to write again. Dunne made sporadic attempts to resume his writing before his death in 1936, but he was able to only partially complete work on an autobiography he was writing with his son Philip.

Evaluations of Dunne seem to bog down when discussing the relationship between Dunne and his creation, Martin Dooley. How the Dunne / Dooley personas interacted is a proper subject for psychobiographers; the work of Dunne as evidenced through Dooley is quite within reach of other analysts, however. Most scholars seem to divide their commentary between the Dooley essays written while Dunne was still in Chicago and those written after he moved to New York. The Chicago

Dunne in his later years at Southampton

essays were vital in explaining the assimilation of immigrants and in displaying the effects of the urban environment on the people who lived within it. Several Dunne scholars debate whether the Dooley essays qualify their author as a "crackerbarrel humorist" in the tradition of Artemus Ward and James Russell Lowell's Hosea Biglow. Dunne does belong in this group, for this strain of homegrown humor moved into the city with Mr. Dooley, just as large numbers of Americans moved into urban areas. Through Mr. Dooley, DeMuth says, "Dunne recovered for his urban audience the familiar values of American tradition: economic self-reliance, informal neighborliness, honest, blunt expression, simple religious faith, and firm community loyalty." In the process, he showed that the urban immigrant could make "the conscious choices of a mature adult" in order to uphold traditional American values.

Dunne scholars also debate about whether Dunne was "like Conan Doyle and many another creator, . . . trapped into competing with his own brain child." Barbara Schaaf says that Dunne had to realize that had he "offered his thoughts on his own,

in his own speech, they probably would have generated no more than a mild interest." Dooley, however, was a different matter, and his opinions commanded readers' attention across the country and around the world.

Some scholars contend that Dunne was limited by his chosen art form, arguing that a 750-word essay appearing once a week in a newspaper could not sufficiently showcase his talents. Even if Dunne was "a prisoner of his most successful and earliest creation," Schaaf says, there is "no indication that this engendered any bitterness or resentment on his part." Regardless of limits imposed by his chosen medium, Dunne was an important contributor to the realistic movement in American literature, and his contributions must be evaluated in that light.

Another element of controversy among Dunne scholars is whether Dunne was a reformer. One argues that although Dunne "was comfortable in the reform era," he did not "consider himself a card-carrying reformer." Dunne was willing to "expose the evils he saw around him and Mr. Dooley could wield a devastating weapon in reform-type battles," but he was also willing to expose the excesses of reformers "when he felt they were getting too puffed up and preoccupied with sensationalism." The list of items which Dunne had Dooley campaign against was familiar to most reformers of that era: "imperialism, militarism, smug corruption in government and business, pretentious nonsense in education or religion, the protective tariff, fake reformers, self-deified aristocrats, and dishonest journalists." Whether Dunne actually placed himself within the ranks of reformers is immaterial, for he had Mr. Dooley comment upon the same problems that occupied other reformers of the era. The main difference in their attacks was that Dunne used humor, satire, and the dialect essay to make his points, whereas the other reformers approached their writing in a more serious manner.

Biographies:

Elmer Ellis, *Mr. Dooley's America: A Life of Finley Peter Dunne* (New York: Knopf, 1941);

Charles Fanning, *Finley Peter Dunne & Mr. Dooley: The Chicago Years* (Lexington: University Press of Kentucky, 1978).

References:

James DeMuth, *Small Town Chicago: The Comic Perspective of Finley Peter Dunne, George Ade, and Ring Lardner* (Port Washington, N.Y.: Kennikat Press, 1980);

Grace Eckley, *Finley Peter Dunne* (Boston: Twayne, 1981);

William M. Gibson, *Theodore Roosevelt among the Humorists* (Knoxville: University of Tennessee Press, 1980);

John M. Harrison, "Finley Peter Dunne and the Progressive Movement," *Journalism Quarterly* (Autumn 1967): 475-481;

Barbara C. Schaaf, *Mr. Dooley's Chicago* (Garden City: Doubleday, 1977).

Papers:
Finley Peter Dunne's papers were available to Elmer Ellis when he wrote his biography of Dunne. The papers were in the possession of family members; they have since been lost.

Eugene Field
(2 September 1850-4 November 1895)

William H. Taft
University of Missouri–Columbia

MAJOR POSITIONS HELD: Reporter, *St. Louis Evening Journal* (1873-1875); city editor, *St. Joseph (Missouri) Gazette* (1875-1876); editorial writer, *St. Louis Times-Journal* (1876-1880); managing editor, *Kansas City Times* (1880-1881); managing editor, *Denver Tribune* (1881-1883); columnist, *Chicago Morning News* (1883-1895).

SELECTED BOOKS: *The Tribune Primer* (Denver: Tribune Publishing Company, 1881);

Symbol and the Saint: A Christmas Tale (Chicago, 1886);

Culture's Garland: Being Memorials of the Gradual Rise of Literature, Art, Music and Society in Chicago, and Other Western Ganglia (Boston: Ticknor, 1887);

A Little Book of Profitable Tales (Chicago: Wilson, 1889; London: Osgood, 1891);

A Little Book of Western Verse (New York: Scribners, 1889; London: Osgood, 1891);

With Trumpet and Drum (New York: Scribners, 1892);

Second Book of Verse (Chicago: Stone, 1892);

The Holy Cross, and Other Tales (Cambridge & Chicago: Stone & Kimball, 1893);

Dibdin's Ghost (New York: DeVinne, 1893);

Love Songs of Childhood (New York: Scribners, 1894);

Echoes from the Sabine Farm, by Field and Roswell Martin Field (New York: Scribners, 1895);

Little Willie (New York: Torch Press, 1895);

An Auto-Analysis (Chicago: Morris, 1896);

The Love Affairs of a Bibliomaniac (New York: Scrib-

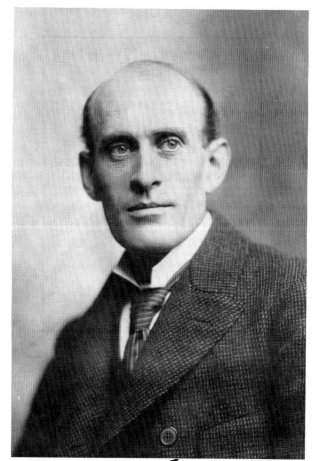

Culver Pictures

ners, 1896; London: Lane, 1896);

The House: An Episode in the Lives of Reuben Baker, Astronomer, and of His Wife Alice (New York: Scribners, 1896);

Songs, and Other Verse (New York: Scribners, 1896);

Songs of Childhood, by Field, with music by Reginald De Koven and others (New York: Scribners, 1896);

Lullaby Land: Songs of Childhood (New York: Scribners, 1896; London: Lane, 1898);

Florence Bardsley's Story: The Life and Death of a Remarkable Woman (Chicago: Way, 1897);

How One Friar Met the Devil and Two Pursued Him (Chicago: Morris, 1900);

Sharps and Flats, collated by Slason Thompson, 2 volumes (New York: Scribners, 1900);

The Temptation of Friar Goncol (New York: Cadmus, 1900);

A Little Book of Nonsense (Boston: Mutual Book Co., 1901);

A Little Book of Tribune Verse: A Number of Hitherto Uncollected Poems, Grave and Gay, edited by Joseph G. Brown (Denver: Tandy, Wheeler, 1901);

The Stars: A Slumber Story (New York: New Amsterdam Book Co., 1901);

Hoosier Lyrics (Chicago: Donohue, 1905);

In Wink-a-way Land (Chicago: Donohue, 1905);

Lover's Lane, Saint Jo (Springfield, Mass.: Cushman, 1905);

Sister's Cake, and Other Poems (New York: Hurst, 1908);

Cradle Lullabies (Chicago: Canterbury, 1909);

The Bibliomaniac's Prayer (New York: Scheuer, 1910);

Christmas Tales and Christmas Verse (New York: Scribners, 1912);

The Mouse and the Moonbeam (New York: Rudge, 1919);

Conky Stiles (Cleveland: Rowfant Club, 1925);

Wynken, Blynken and Nod, and Other Child Verses (Newark, N.J.: Graham, 1925);

Child Verses (Akron, Ohio: Saalfield, 1927);

The Sugar Plum Tree (Racine, Wis.: Whitman, 1929).

COLLECTIONS: *The Poems of Eugene Field*, Complete Edition (New York: Scribners, 1910);

The Writings in Prose and Verse of Eugene Field, 12 volumes (New York: Scribners, 1911).

Termed "the first of the columnists," Eugene Field is best known today as the poet of children. However, his poems and stories originally appeared in print in columns written for newspapers in St. Louis, St. Joseph, and Kansas City, Missouri; Denver; and Chicago. It was in the latter city that Field made "Sharps and Flats" one of the most copied columns in the nation. While Field was not the first newspaperman to write paragraphs that filled a regular column, he certainly "had a strong influence on the later development of an interesting feature of American journalism," according to the *Dictionary of American Biography*. Field's practice "differed from that of most of his predecessors; and while his audacious indulgence in personalities could not safely be followed," he did make such writing popular in America.

In some respects, Field's career reminds one of other noted literary figures, such as William Cullen Bryant and Walt Whitman. These men are remembered for their poetry; their newspaper careers have been overlooked by too many critics. Both Bryant and Whitman credited their newspaper experience with improving their poetry, much as Ernest Hemingway credited his newspaper training with improving his writing. "Field was, first of all, a journalist," according to one of his biographers, Charles H. Dennis. His column "was to be the model of many urbane and witty 'colyums,'" according to Frank Luther Mott.

Readers remember Field mostly through his widely circulated poems, such as "Little Boy Blue," "The Little Peach," "Wynken, Blynken, and Nod," "Marthy's Younket," and "Casey's Table d'Hote." His first poem, "Christmas Treasures," was widely reprinted. Such poems impressed so many Americans that many public schools have been named in his honor.

Eugene Field was born in St. Louis, probably on 2 September 1850, although there is some confusion as to the exact date. His father, Roswell M. Field, was a distinguished lawyer who was counsel to Dred Scott in his significant court case. His mother, Frances Reed Field, died in 1856, and Eugene and his older brother, Roswell, were sent to Amherst, Massachusetts, to live with a cousin, Miss Mary Field French.

Although Field attended three colleges and universities, he did not earn a degree. After preliminary studies at a private school in Monson, Massachusetts, Field spent a year (1868-1869) at Williams College, where he displayed little love for learning. After his father died in 1869, Field entered Knox College in Galesburg, Illinois, where his guardian was a professor. He was remembered at Knox as a fun-loving sophomore, although there was nothing "ill-natured or demoralizing in his fun." This characteristic continued to be a part of

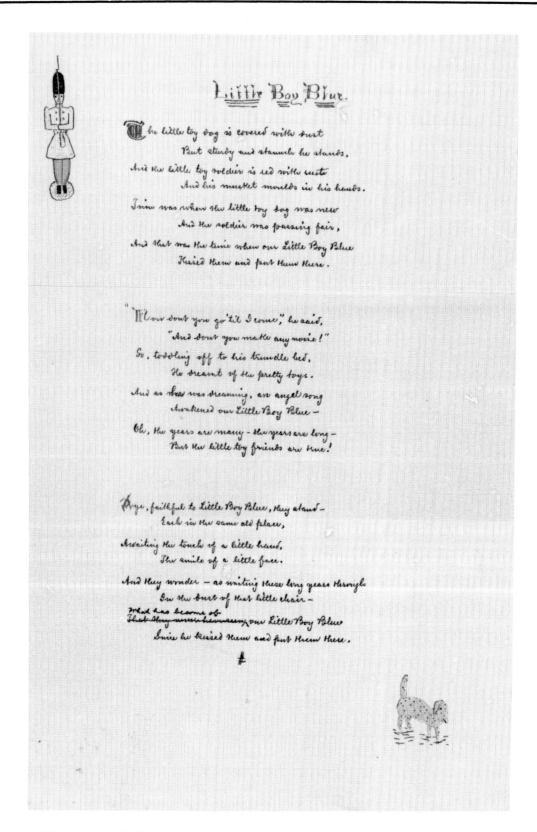

Manuscript, with illustrations by Field, for one of his most famous children's poems. The change in the last stanza was made by Slason Thompson, editor of the journal America, *where the poem first appeared (Slason Thompson,* Eugene Field: A Study in Heredity and Contradictions).

Field's personality throughout his life. The year in Galesburg may have been more significant for Field's career than he recognized at the time, for while there he contributed to the *Galesburg Register*; this was apparently his initial contact with the newspaper world.

The next year, 1870, Field joined his brother at the University of Missouri in Columbia; Roswell had entered in 1868, so both technically were juniors. Eugene has been remembered as "an inattentive, indifferent student, making poor progress in the studies of the course—a genial, sportive, fun-loving companion. Nevertheless, he was bright, sparkling, entertaining and a leader among 'the boys.' In truth he was an intellect above his fellows and a genius along his favorite lines. He was prolific with harmless pranks and his school life was a big joke." The prankster instigated many incidents, frequently involving the University of Missouri president and faculty members; the victims often refused to openly criticize Field because "he was likely to retaliate in satirical verse." In 1872, Field won the university oratory prize, a major accomplishment in those days. However, both brothers failed mathematics, a course required for graduation. Field nevertheless retained a fondness for the university. In 1884 he wrote his former landlady that "you and the other good people of Columbia should consider me one of the Columbia boys. Believe me, I always have had and always will have a large corner in my heart for the dear old town and its generous, hospitable, courtly people." A local historian wrote that Field was "hardly a model for rising generations, but he turned out all right in spite of his early shortcomings." He often referred to "poor old Mizzouri." Biographer Dennis could not decide whether Field lampooned "Missourians because of his affection for the people or because he felt cheated in some of his early endeavors." Field was not vindictive, so many believe he was honest when he voiced his love for the state.

Field collected an $8,000 advance from his father's estate and in 1872 toured Europe for six months with a college classmate, Edgar Comstock of St. Joseph. Although he was broke when he returned to St. Louis in 1873, he and Edgar's sister, Julia, were married; she was sixteen, he was twenty-three. He always considered his wife to be his greatest inspiration, and she appeared in many of his poems. They had eight children. Years later, when they were living in London, Field recalled these days in a poem titled "Lover's Lane, St. Jo.":

I would have a brown-eyed maiden

Field's wife, Julia Comstock Field

Go driving once again;
And I'd sing the song, as we snailed along,
That I sung to that maiden then.

Field's newspaper career began in 1873 with a reporter's job on the *St. Louis Evening Journal*. Within six months he became the city editor, and he often inserted humorous items along with the more serious ones, especially in writing theatrical criticisms. In 1875-1876, Field was city editor of the *St. Joseph Gazette*, but he returned to the now merged *St. Louis Times-Journal* as editorial writer in 1876. According to some accounts, "Christmas Treasures" first appeared in this paper in 1878. His first column, "Funny Fancies," appeared in the *Times-Journal*; it was widely copied by other newspapers, a practice typical of the era. "Throughout this period (in St. Louis and St. Joseph) neither as reporter nor editor did Eugene Field give evidence of special qualifications for his chosen profession. The serious business of news gathering bored him. He interlarded his interviews with extraneous flights of fancy that enlivened the copy and invited libel suits, which came to naught, because few lawyers cared to sue a joke and catch a crab." Thus did another of Field's biographers, Slason Thompson, summarize these years. Nevertheless, Field continued his newspaper career, moving to Kansas City in 1880 to become the managing editor of the *Times*. He had always loved the theater, and he became well acquainted with those who performed and toured the circuits. This love continued throughout his career; many of his poems and articles deal with theatrical personnel. Unlike many of his colleagues, Field was not a heavy drinker, but he usually occupied center stage in any such gathering with his ability to relate interesting stories. While with the *Times*, Field wrote another of his best-remembered poems, "The Little Peach." He also wrote the following lines when the *Kansas City Star* made its appearance in late 1880:

> Twinkle, twinkle, Little Star
> Bright and gossipy you are;
> We can daily hear you speak,
> For a paltry dime a week.

The poem inspired the nickname "Twilight Twinkler" for William Rockhill Nelson's successful afternoon daily.

In 1881-1883, Field served as managing editor of the *Denver Tribune*, where he was hired to make the paper "hum." The *Tribune*, owned by railroad and political leaders, dominated Colorado and Denver, and its owners were involved in many reckless activities. Field found time to contribute to a column titled "Odds and Ends." Later he collected many of his skits into his first volume, *The Tribune Primer* (1881), a ninety-eight-page, unpretentious book with a limited circulation. It is said that "a spirit of mischievous deviltry" appeared in some of Field's items. The Colorado governor sued the *Tribune* for libel, and biographer Thompson thought Field composed the primer "as a weapon of ridicule" against the official. For example, an item titled "The Wasp" offered several interpretations: "See the Wasp. He has pretty yellow Stripes around his Body, and a Darning Needle in his Tail. If you will Pat the Wasp upon the Tail, we will Give you a Nice Picture Book." Field also wrote "The Baby," which must have made many of its readers smile as they recalled incidents in their own lives: "Here we have a Baby. It is composed of a Bald Head and a Pair of Lungs. One of the Lungs takes a Rest while the Other runs the Shop. One of them is always On Deck all of the Time. The Baby is a Bigger Man than his Mother. He likes to Walk around with the Father at Night. The Father does Most of the Walking and All of the Swearing. Little Girls, you will Never know what it is to be a Father."

In Denver, Field met many famous per-

sonalities, including humorist Bill Nye and newspaper publishers Melville E. Stone of Chicago and Charles A. Dana of New York. Nye was hired to write for the *Tribune*; Stone later brought Field to Chicago, where he spent the rest of his life. Dana had made his *New York Sun* "the newspaperman's newspaper"; Field wrote a tribute to him, using some of the dialect of the day: "But Bless ye, Mr. Dana! May you live a thousan' years / To sorta keep things lively in this vale of human tears; / An' when it comes your time to go, you'll need no Latin chaff / Nor biographic data put in your epitaph; / But one straight line of English truth will let folks know / The homage 'nd the gratitude 'nd reverence they owe; / You'll need no epitaph but this: 'Here sleeps the man who run / That best 'nd brightest paper, the *Noo York Sun*.' " However, when Dana later offered Field a chance to leave Chicago and come to work in New York, the verse writer rejected the opportunity. Field believed "Chicago was as far east as he could go without sacrificing that freedom from the conventions that he believed benumbed native American literature," according to biographer Thompson.

Field's Denver column was called "Current Gossip." The best of his works there were published in *A Little Book of Western Verse* (1889). The book increased Field's fame across the country, and newspapers continued to reprint his columns. But Denver readers regarded Field merely as an eccentric newspaperman. It was not until after his death that the city erected a public memorial in his honor; it was the first community to do so.

According to some accounts Field became tired of Denver, so he accepted Stone's offer in 1883 to join the *Chicago Morning News*, launched two years previously. Dennis reports that Field put on a party to raise funds for moving to Chicago: "he played the piano, sang, recited, and gave imitations of popular actors" in an event that raised $2,000. Earlier he had written Stone asking for $100 moving expense, apologizing that "I am a deucedly poor man or I would not suggest such a thing." Field was never capable of accumulating money; but he always wanted to make more money each year, a goal he had set when he began newspapering at $10 a week. So when he and Stone discussed Field's move to Chicago, the poet prepared a memorandum listing his requirements: he agreed to work for $50 per week the first year, $50.50 the second, and $55 the third; he projected this to 1900, when he expected $100 weekly. Another requirement was possibly more meaningful: Field "shall be subordinate only to said Stone." Stone approved this; however, within a few years he sold his interest in the newspaper to Victor Lawson. When the change became known, Field immediately wrote Lawson about the "explicit understanding" he had had with Stone. Field feared he and Lawson might not work well together and offered to resign, but Lawson informed Field that he was confident the two would get along well, which they did for the next seven years. From time to time individuals who had been subjected to Field's satire would complain to Lawson, and Lawson would urge Field to be more cautious in his column. Yet on other occasions Lawson congratulated Field on columns of "the right sort." Apparently there was no actual censorship involved.

Field left reporting and editing to turn full-time to his column for the Chicago newspaper. His first column appeared on 16 August 1883, titled "Current Gossip"; on 31 August it was renamed "Sharps and Flats," a title taken from a play then appearing in the city. It was estimated that before his death twelve years later Field produced 7,000,000 words in his six-days-a-week column. Each containing 2,000 words of "leaded agate," these columns ranged "all the way from the most ephemeral paragraph on a passing event to as exquisite bits of prose and verse as ever illumined the pages of a newspaper," according to Thompson. The columns included both serious and humorous prose and verse. From his first column that noted, "Buffaloes are fleeing to the Yellowstone Park in great numbers," Field provided daily gossip about persons and events. With his freedom to write as he pleased, Field at times would be in conflict with the newspaper's editorial page. On occasion he wrote verses but attributed them to others, "a form of humor in which to the end he took a peculiar delight." To a limited degree he printed items actually written by others. Field often devoted a full column to one of his tales or short stories. A critical sports fan, he gave considerable space to baseball as well as to the coverage of sports personalities such as the prizefighter John L. Sullivan.

Historians have compared Field's writings to those of Will Rogers because of the humor, satire, and political comments of the two writers. Field wrote columns that developed into series about the political scene. For example, when President Grover Cleveland was married in the White House, Field wrote a series of ballads: "The Tying of the Tie," "The Kissing of the Bride," and "The Passing of the Compliment." He refused to approach politics seriously, as shown in this paragraph, titled "The Senator": "What is that Walking along the

Field in his library

Street? That, my Son, is a State Senator. Will you not Tell me all About it? No, my Son, you are too Young to hear Scandal." Field sought to "expose at a touch hypocrisy and pretense" he witnessed. Well-known personalities frequently became victims of his "sportive fancy." He loved to satirize Chicago's "somewhat ostentatious displays of its culture," a topic still utilized there by some columnists. His satire at times was taken literally: an imaginative yarn claimed that the noted magazine editor Edward W. Bok and the granddaughter of Mrs. Lydia Pinkham would marry; although Bok was naturally upset when this story went out on the press association wires, he later hired Field as a contributor to the *Ladies' Home Journal.*

Young writers were encouraged by Field, whose columns reflected the "perfect use of our mother tongue." For example, he offered these words of advice: "A young writer cannot be too careful in his choice of words; eternal vigilance is the price of a correct English style. . . . a writer must know his weapons before he can use them with effect. . . . to the study of synonyms the young writer should apply himself diligently. . . . our literature of the press is constantly improving and in the last ten years that improvement has been marked." Schoolchildren, too, often wrote to Field, their hero. His answers were copied and used by educators in their classrooms. In a column he once commented: "We are not going to have a fine American fiction until we have encouraged, trained, and cultivated in our children the God-gift, fancy. This gift first manifests itself in the trait which is vulgarly called lying, and all children have it to a degree. . . . the trouble with parents is that they consistently and incontinently set about killing the juvenile fancy as soon as it discovers itself. . . ."

Many other topics inspired Field to comment. Food, for example, was one of his favorite subjects, probably because of a stomach ailment. This illness prompted him to search for better health in Europe and in California, but to no avail. Nevertheless, indigestible dishes remained his passion.

Sabine Farm, Field's home in the Chicago suburbs

Field's fourteen months in England in 1889-1890 neither improved his health nor made him happy with everything he witnessed there. He was most unhappy about English cigars, which he termed the worst in the world. Americans who toured England upset him; he considered the typical tourist to be one who "swaggers and bloviates, snarls and brags." On the other side, he was upset by the "disparaging remarks passed upon the United States by foreigners." London newspaper writers also disturbed him; he objected to their indirectness of speech, such as a description of a play as "not half bad," or a humorous speech as "not unrelieved by wit."

Field returned to the United States in 1890 after the death of his son Melvin. In the fall of 1893 he went to California, but he soon complained that he "shivered" in San Diego. He returned to Chicago in early 1894 by way of New Orleans.

Few things excited Field as much as his association with books. In his leaflet *An Auto-Analysis* (1896), he said his miscellaneous collection of books numbered 3,500. He continually turned his thoughts to books, noting that "if by fire or by water my library should be destroyed this night, I should start in again tomorrow upon the collection of another library. Or if I did not do this, I should lay myself down to die, for how could I live without the companionships to which I have ever been accustomed, and which have grown as dear to me as life itself?" He had a strong interest in the works of Horace and often paraphrased from Horace's *Odes*; he named his house in suburban Buena Park "Sabine Farm" in honor of the Roman poet. He once wrote a column on "The Evil Practice of Borrowing Books," and he expressed the thought that a person should own his own books and "should have them for companions continually around him." He objected to paper-covered books because "a book that is worth reading is surely worth keeping, and is therefore entitled to a durable dress." Field considered books to be excellent Christmas gifts, but he complained about the "badly manufactured books" issued by American publishers. His last writing, the day before his death, was the final chapter of *The Love Affairs of a Bibliomaniac* (1896). In this book, he says he started out to be a philosopher, although his grandmother wanted him to be a minister; he preferred to learn more about the world and so made his European trips.

Field died in his sleep on 4 November 1895. The newspaper he wrote for reported, "All of the children of the land mourn their laureate." Slason Thompson reflected upon Field's career in these

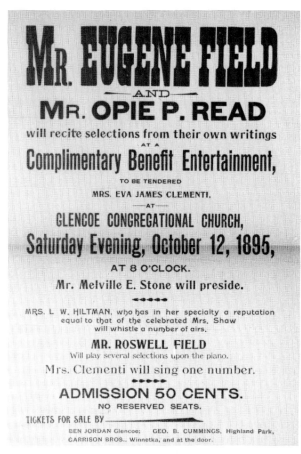

Advertising poster for Field's last public appearance. He died less than a month later.

words: "His daily column was a crystallization of the busy fancies that ran riot through his busy days and nights of light-hearted pleasure. He reflected everything he read and heard and saw, and nothing that interested humanity came amiss to his facile and felicitous pen. Out of the comedy of his nature came the sweetness of his work and out of his association with all kinds and conditions of mankind came that insight into the springs of human passion and action that shines through all he wrote. . . ."

Letters:

Some Love Letters of Eugene Field, with a foreword by Thomas B. Lockwood (Buffalo, N.Y.: Privately printed, 1927).

Biographies:

Slason Thompson, *Eugene Field: A Study in Heredity and Contradictions*, 2 volumes (New York: Scribners, 1901);

Charles H. Dennis, *Eugene Field's Creative Years* (New York: Doubleday, Page, 1924);

Thompson, *Life of Eugene Field, The Poet of Childhood* (New York: Appleton, 1927).

Reference:

Charles H. Dennis, *Victor Lawson, His Time and His Work* (Chicago: University of Chicago Press, 1935).

Thomas Fitzgerald

(22 December 1819-25 June 1891)

Jacqueline Steck
Temple University

MAJOR POSITION HELD: Founder and editor, *Philadelphia City Item* (1847-1890).

Thomas Fitzgerald's *City Item*, after a slow start, became one of the largest-circulation newspapers in Philadelphia in the 1880s and a leader in art and education matters. The newspaper was one of the earliest to provide complete baseball coverage. It also fought for many city reforms, most of which were realized during its founder's lifetime.

Little is known about Fitzgerald's early years.

He was born in New York on 22 December 1819, on the later site of the publishing house of Harper and Brothers. He exhibited his interest in newspapers at an early age: while still a teenager he went to work for the *Fredonian* of New Brunswick, New Jersey; he next became a reporter with the *New York Commercial Advertiser*. At the age of twenty, he moved to Florida, where he took an editorial job at the *Floridian* in Tallahassee, the state capital. He arrived in Philadelphia in 1844; later the same year he married Sarah Levering Riter of that city. She lived until

1876 and had several children, five of whom survived into adulthood.

In 1847, Fitzgerald realized his ambition of starting his own newspaper. With three partners, he formed a company that produced the weekly *City Item*. The first edition, seven columns wide and printed on a sheet 24½ inches by 38 inches, came off the presses on 25 September 1847. The paper was to be a lively, literary publication with enough local news to gain a large circulation in the city. The newspaper's introductory statement, composed by one of Fitzgerald's partners, John F. Carter, outlined what the paper would cover: "If a house is burnt in this city, or a store robbed, or an omnibus upset, or a fiddler hissed, or an actor applauded, or a theatre frequented, or a lecturer followed, look for it in *The City Item*. If a poor fellow goes in two with a railroad car on Market Street, or a gentleman of aldermanic rotundity falls down in his own street in a quiet, comfortable, respectable fit of apoplexy, look for it in *The City Item*. If a fair maiden is lured from the pathway of peace to the pathway of vice by a fellow with a huge pair of moustaches, look for it in *The City Item*. If an elopement takes place between one man's wife and another wife's husband, look for it in *The City Item*. You may sometimes look for it if it *don't* take place. If a pistol is discharged at Louis Philippe by an assassin, look for it in *The City Item* — particularly if the ball hits him." The original *Item* partnership did not last long: Carter withdrew weeks after the paper began, and George G. Foster's interest was bought out soon after; Robert G. L. Govett kept his share for almost two years, but eventually sold out to leave Fitzgerald sole owner.

The newspaper's style in its early days was lively and chatty, with lots of poetry and tongue-in-cheek social comment. The 4 December 1847 issue, for example, contained a story comparing the virtues of early rising and sleeping late; it concluded: "Late rising is economical in one respect — it prevents us from doing as much business as we might otherwise accomplish." Fitzgerald, however, found the going tough: he lacked both capital and business training and had difficulty obtaining advertisements and expanding circulation. But he persevered and eventually the *Item* found its niche in the crowded Philadelphia newspaper market of the last half of the nineteenth century. In 1852, the *Item* became a daily; its circulation grew until it hit its stride in the 1880s as a crusading penny paper with a pressrun that sometimes reached 200,000 copies. Fitzgerald sought to expand circulation by purchasing other publications — the *Pennsylvania Volunteer* in 1852 and *Fireside Visitor* and *Bazaar* in 1870.

He merged their subscription lists with the *Item*, but apparently made little profit from the purchases.

Fitzgerald changed the paper's title, format, and publication office several times. It was known at various times as *Fitzgerald's City Item*, the *Evening City Item*, and the *Daily Item*. From its original office at 45 South Third Street, the paper moved to 114 South Third Street, in the same building as the *Evening Bulletin*. It later moved to 28 South Seventh Street. Fitzgerald lived at 313 Spruce Street, in the Society Hill section of the city.

The editor's interests ranged from fine art to opera, from baseball to architecture, and from theater to politics. All were reflected in the pages of the *Item*. Fitzgerald used the paper as his soapbox to call for a variety of reforms in Philadelphia, and he earned a reputation as a forward-looking editor and as a leader in educational and art matters. He urged the construction of street railways and the development of a new system for numbering streets. He used the title of Colonel (although this may have been honorary) and seemed to have a love for uniforms: he advocated outfitting police officers, letter carriers, and rail conductors in them. He called for the installation of police and fire telegraph systems and thought the city should have a paid fire department, public baths, and a public morgue. He fought to demolish the old market sheds that stood in the center of Market Street, the city's major east-west thoroughfare. He lived to see virtually all of these reforms enacted.

During the Civil War, the newspaper's strong patriotic stand reflected its owner's views. While not a party organ, the *Item* leaned toward the Republicans. Fitzgerald stumped Pennsylvania twice for Lincoln, whom he considered a personal friend. Charles Sumner was impressed by Fitzgerald's speaking abilities and called him one of the best extemporaneous talkers he had ever heard. The editor was a forceful campaign orator and popular after-dinner speaker. His newspaper's creed was to be "constantly aggressive in all that relates to the equality of Man before the Law and ever striving to break down barriers of Prejudice and Caste." A frequent editorial theme was: "The worst use you can make of a man is to hang him."

Fitzgerald was an avid fan of the theater and experienced some success as a playwright. His first play, *Light at Last*, was produced at the Arch Street Theatre on 30 December 1868, starring Mrs. John Drew. Other plays included *Patrice*, produced in association with the actress Laura Keene; *Wolves at Bay*; *Tangled Threads*; *The Regent*; *Who Shall Win?*; *Perils of the Night*; and *Bound to the Rock*. For years, the *Item* paid special attention to theatrical matters and was widely cited as an authority on the stage and the careers of actors. It crusaded successfully for shutting down the rowdy "third tier" in city theaters, and it was also influential in closing the bars that once operated in theater lobbies. These measures did much to add to the respectability of the playhouse.

Music and fine arts also received considerable attention in the pages of the *City Item*. Fitzgerald organized a gallery of paintings, left in his will to the Academy of Fine Arts, and his paper was one of the earliest and most strenuous advocates of the construction of the Academy of Music. He knew the portrait artist John Naegle for many years and shortly after the artist's death wrote an article for *Lippincott's Monthly Magazine* of May 1868. In it, he wrote that he had decided to "gratify public curiosity" about Naegle by publishing a "sketch of his career, some of his opinions on art and artists, with mention of his chief works and an anecdote or two."

Early on, the paper began a campaign to improve the appearance of Philadelphia. In a number of articles, it ridiculed the red-brick monotony of the city's architecture, then mainly in the traditional Federalist style. Fitzgerald started a movement calling for the use of more modern and interesting building materials such as brownstone, marble, and granite. Within a few decades, the appearance of the city had changed markedly.

Fitzgerald was also president of a baseball club for several years and his newspaper was for some time the city's only publication to provide complete coverage of the sport. The editor lost some of his enthusiasm as baseball became more of a business; the *Item* was very critical of the new practice of paying players, describing such athletes as "hired men."

One of Fitzgerald's greatest contributions to the city was in improving its school buildings. *Item* editorials frequently called attention to the shortcomings of the schools, and Fitzgerald continued to look at the problems with a critical eye

after being appointed to the board of controllers about 1860. On his motion, the board visited other cities to look at their school systems, and the result was the construction of greatly improved school houses in various parts of the city. He was also an enthusiastic advocate of adding music to the school curriculum. Starting in 1860, he began a dogged campaign for music instruction; it took a few years, but in the end it succeeded. His pamphlet on the idea, *Music in Our Schools*, became quite popular and was reprinted in part in foreign journals.

As he aged, Fitzgerald handed over increasing responsibility for the newspaper to his sons, and in 1890, at the age of seventy-one, he retired. Riter became dramatic editor; Harrington, managing editor; and Hildebrand, business manager. Fitzgerald loved to travel and visited Europe annually, writing letters home that provided bright and lively copy for his newspaper. During a European trip in 1891 with Riter, he contracted influenza; he died at the Langham Hotel in London on 25 June. His body was returned to Philadelphia and buried next to his wife in Mount Moriah Cemetery. Fitzgerald's sons apparently lacked their father's flair for the newspaper business: the *Item* lasted until 1915, but it never regained the style and verve it had under its founder's enthusiastic hand.

Periodical Publication:
"John Naegle, the Artist," *Lippincott's Monthly Magazine* (May 1868): 477-491.

References:
Memorial History of the City of Philadelphia, edited by John Russell Young (New York: New York History Co., 1898);
Eugene H. Munday, "The Press of Philadelphia in 1870," *The Proof Sheet*, 4 (September 1870): 25-26;
John Thomas Scharf and Thompson Westcott, *History of Philadelphia* (Philadelphia: Everts, 1884).

T. Thomas Fortune
(3 October 1856-2 June 1928)

Maurine H. Beasley
University of Maryland

MAJOR POSITIONS HELD: Editor and editorial writer, *New York Globe* (1881-1884), *New York Freeman* (1884-1887), *New York Age* (1889-1907).

BOOKS: *Black and White: Land, Labor and Politics in the South* (New York: Fords, Howard & Hulbert, 1884);
The Negro In Politics (New York: Ogilvie & Rountree, 1885);
Dreams of Life: Miscellaneous Poems (New York: Fortune & Peterson, 1905).

T. Thomas Fortune was considered the most distinguished black journalist of the late nineteenth century. He wrote for both black and white newspapers but gained his prominence chiefly as editor of the *New York Age* and its forerunners, the *New York Globe* and *New York Freeman*. Under him the *Age* became the leading black newspaper in the nation. In addition, Fortune was one of the few blacks to be a frequent contributor to major white newspapers, writing for the *New York Sun* and the *Boston Transcript*. In 1887, he advocated formation of the Afro-American League, a short-lived civil rights organization that predated the establishment of the National Association for the Advancement of Colored People and the Urban League by about twenty years. During his journalistic career his political orientation changed from militant radicalism to conservatism influenced by association with Booker T. Washington, for whom Fortune acted as a ghostwriter and publicist. In his final years he was an editor of the *Negro World*, the organ of Marcus Garvey's Universal Negro Improvement Association, a back-to-Africa nationalistic movement.

Timothy Thomas Fortune was born in Marianna, Florida, one of five children of slave parents, Emanuel and Sarah Jane Fortune, who gave their family a mixed African, Irish, and American Indian heritage. His formal schooling began after the Civil War when he attended the first black school opened in the small town. Peering into the window of the print shop that produced Marianna's weekly newspaper, the *Courier*, Fortune became intrigued by the printing process. His re-

T. Thomas Fortune in 1885 (Milton Meltzer)

peated trips to the shop led to a chance to "stick type" (put letters into a small tray to form words).

When his father, a member of the Florida legislature under Reconstruction, was forced to flee Marianna due to Ku Klux Klan terrorism, the family moved to Jacksonville, losing cattle and other possessions. To help offset these losses, Fortune went to Tallahassee, the state capital, where his father got him a job as a page in the state senate. At the same time the youth continued to learn printing, spending his spare time in the shop of the local newspaper, the *Sentinel*.

In Jacksonville, where his mother died at the age of thirty-six, probably as a result of worry over

120

the earlier persecution of her husband, Fortune became an excellent student at Stanton Institute, a school established by the Freedmen's Bureau to help ex-slaves. His printing apprenticeship continued at the *Jacksonville Daily Union*, a large-circulation newspaper, and he became an expert typesetter. At the age of seventeen he received through the efforts of Congressman W. J. Purman a political appointment as a postal agent on the railroad line between Jacksonville and Chattahoochee. The following year Purman secured Fortune an appointment as a special inspector of customs in Delaware.

Encountering unexpected discrimination— being told to leave a hotel because he was "colored"—Fortune stayed with the post long enough to save money to enroll at Howard University in Washington, D.C. He arrived in the capital in 1874 with less than three years of formal schooling, although he had read widely, and was placed in the university's preparatory department.

When the bank in which he had deposited his savings failed, Fortune once again received aid from Purman, who found him a messenger's job in the Treasury Department. Fortune also worked on a new black weekly, the *People's Advocate*, while taking law classes at night. He became acquainted with Frederick Douglass, the best-known black abolitionist and political figure of the Civil War period. While he was employed on the *Advocate*, he married Carrie C. Smiley, a young woman he had known in Florida.

Fortune did not remain in Washington long, although it was there that he made a commitment to a journalistic career. The *People's Advocate* ran into financial trouble, and his wife apparently wished to go back home for the birth of their first child, a son who died. Returning to Jacksonville, Fortune taught school and resumed work as a printer on the *Daily Union*. Disturbed by the racial caste system, he decided his future lay in the less-segregated North.

In 1881 he took a job as a printer for a religious newspaper in New York City, the *Weekly Witness*, owned by a white man, John Dougall. He had been recommended by Walter Sampson, a black printer whom he had known at the *People's Advocate*. White employees struck to protest the hiring of the two blacks, but Dougall refused to give in, and Fortune stayed with the *Witness* for about a year. At the same time, Fortune and Sampson agreed to aid a black journalist, George Parker, who was struggling to publish a weekly tabloid called the *Rumor*. At Fortune's insistence, the name was changed to the *Globe*, probably in July 1881, and Fortune soon

made the paper his full-time work.

As editor Fortune developed the lucid, striking style of editorial writing which won praise from supporters and attention from opponents. A key influence was a white journalist, socialist John Swinton, who resigned as editor of the *New York Sun* in 1883 to publish *John Swinton's Paper*, promoting the views of Henry George and other reformers. Fortune commended Swinton in the *Globe* and adopted many of his economic ideas, attacking monopoly and financial capitalism, which, he said, flourished at the expense of the working classes, both black and white. These themes were restated in Fortune's book *Black and White* (1884), which denounced the racism that locked Negroes into the debt-slavery of Southern sharecropping after Reconstruction promises of land and economic assistance were not carried out. While his solution to economic exploitation called for blacks and whites to join forces, his analysis marked an outstanding document of black protest against white injustice.

By 1883 the *Globe* claimed to circulate all over the United States. Cut off from the cooperative news gathering of white publications, it carried national stories on racial matters obtained from a network of correspondents, who relayed news of political and social developments. Among them was W. E. B. Du Bois, then a schoolboy in Great Barrington, Massachusetts, who was destined to become a leading black intellectual and founder of the NAACP. Published in its own print shop under Fortune's knowledgeable eye, the paper was free of the grammatical and typographical mistakes of many black publications. It scorned "patent insides" (pages of features and filler material used by many weeklies, both white and black) in favor of outspoken editorials and columns devoted to book reviews and commentary.

At a time when state legislatures and courts were stripping blacks of the rights granted by constitutional amendment after the Civil War, Fortune proclaimed editorially, "There is no law in the United States for the Negro. The whole thing is a beggaredly [*sic*] farce." When the U.S. Supreme Court upheld a federal court action invalidating a Texas antisegregation statute, an editorial protested: "The Supreme Court now declares that railroad corporations are free to force us into smoking cars or cattle cars; that hotel keepers are free to make us walk the streets at night, that theater managers can refuse us admittance. . . . We are aliens in our own land." After a race riot in Danville, Virginia, said to have started when a black man pushed a white man off a sidewalk, a Fortune editorial stated: "If it is necessary for colored men to turn themselves into outlaws to assert their manhood and their citizenship, let them do it." When this precipitated protests in both the white and black press, Fortune replied that whites took advantage of blacks only because they considered blacks to be cowards. Fortune also drew censure when he defended the right of Frederick Douglass to marry a white woman. The editor criticized blacks who objected, writing, "It is the ceaseless but futile effort to show that the human nature of the black man and the human nature of the white man differ in some indefinable way, when we all know that, essentially, human nature is . . . the same wherever mankind is found." Concerned about the worsening situation of Southern blacks, Fortune replied to a series of articles in the *New York Sun* which referred to Negro women as "wenches and strumpets" and called the race "shiftless," "thievish," and "improvident." If blacks displayed any of these characteristics, they stemmed from white oppression, Fortune wrote. Southern laws prohibited lawful marriage between blacks and whites, and black laborers were systematically cheated, forced into improvidence, and deprived of an education, he held.

When Senator Henry W. Blair of New Hampshire asked Fortune to prepare a report on the status of Southern Negroes, Fortune proposed creation of a commission to investigate their plight and called for federal aid to education. Some editors found his ideas abhorrent, but their criticism proved he was read. When the editor of the *Macon* (Georgia) *Telegram* opposed schools for blacks on the ground that they would produce individuals like Fortune who sought "social equality," Fortune denied that blacks wished to force themselves upon whites. "What every colored man wants . . . is the concession of every right given to the white man under the laws of the United States. . . . Call this social equality if you will."

Despite the *Globe*'s influence, it stopped publication in November 1884 after Fortune refused to make it a subsidized voice of the Republican party in common with most other black newspapers of the day. In Fortune's opinion blacks owed no blind loyalty to a party that had forgotten the principles of Lincoln and Charles Sumner and refused to protect the rights of black voters in the South. He called the *Globe* an "independent" paper and urged blacks to vote for the party and candidates that would best serve their interests. In the election of 1884 he supported the Democratic candidate for president, Grover Cleveland, although others connected with the *Globe* backed the Republican James G. Blaine.

This disagreement may have been what led Fortune to discontinue the *Globe*.

Two weeks after the *Globe* folded, the first issue of Fortune's new paper, the *New York Freeman*, appeared. In it Fortune continued to be a strong voice against racism, attacking the hypocrisy of bigotry. Buttressing his editorials with statistics, journalistic reports, and a wealth of documentation, he took issue with Southern spokesmen like Henry W. Grady, who told a New York audience that Negroes shared in Georgia school funds and enjoyed the protection of the law. In a typical editorial Fortune responded: "The white men of the South—in legislatures, in courts of justice, in convict camps, in churches, in hotels and theatres, in railroad and steamboat accommodations—do not do justice to their colored fellow citizens; and when a man like Grady stands up and lies about these matters, we are here to strike the lie in the head and we shall strike it."

As part of his political independence, Fortune advocated the Prohibition party in both the *Globe* and the *Freeman*, urging blacks to "stick to lemonade and ice cream." Moreover, he wrote a pamphlet, *The Negro in Politics* (1885), documenting the Republican party's exploitation of black voters. His nonpartisanship led to a battle over the paper with Republican politicians charging that the *Freeman* did not reflect black opinion. Fortune resigned as editor in October 1887 and turned the publication over to his brother Emanuel and another journalist, Jerome Peterson, who renamed it the *New York Age*. Although officially not an editor of the *Age*, which now billed itself as a Republican paper, Fortune continued to write a column for it in which he supported President Cleveland for a second term in 1888. Some of his utterances were seen as incendiary with anarchistic overtones by contemporaries. When a black man was killed in Alabama during an attempt to aid a black woman being flogged by a white mob, Fortune warned: "It is too bad the white man of the South cannot understand the safest way to treat colored men is the just way, and that the policy of injustice and outrage will eventuate in retaliation and bitterness, which no one desires to see come to pass. Let Justice have its own."

During this period Fortune also wrote for the *New York Sun*. Like other reporters for the paper, he was paid according to the amount of copy published. Successful in a variety of assignments, he wrote for every department except the financial section. He also wrote poetry and was in great demand as a speaker for Emancipation Day celebrations, church gatherings, and other occasions. For-

*Booker T. Washington, for whom Fortune served
as a ghostwriter*

from local organizations in twenty-one states went to Chicago to hear Fortune urge creation of a nonpartisan league to direct activities for redress of racial oppression by legal and peaceful means. Fortune envisioned a national coalition of local all-black groups growing out of churches and lodges; but public support failed to materialize, and the league died. Fortune personally waged one legal battle on behalf of the New York league by bringing a successful damage suit against a Manhattan hotel saloon that refused to serve him. He was awarded $1,016.

As racial violence escalated, Fortune used the columns of the *Age* in 1898 to convene a civil rights conference at Rochester, New York, where the Afro-American Council was established. This organization faltered as factions warred over how closely it should be tied to the Republican party. Shortly before the council was scheduled to meet in Washington, Fortune made a speech accusing Republican President William McKinley of "glorifying rebellion, mobocracy, and the murder of [black] women and children." Despite these verbal fireworks, however, the council proved to be a conservative organization. It became dominated totally by the forces of Booker T. Washington, who advocated that blacks seek vocational training and acquisition of property while accommodating themselves to segregation, at least in the South.

At the close of the nineteenth century, Fortune stood out as the leading champion of black militancy, hurling defiance against disenfranchisement, lynch and mob law, unequal school funding, the chain gang, convict lease systems, and Jim Crow laws. His editorials frequently appeared in the white *Boston Transcript* as well as the *Sun*. His protests preceded those of Du Bois, who was soon to emerge as the most articulate of the anti-Washington forces.

Fortune's personal influence waned with his entry into the Washington camp. Because of his initial admiration for Washington, whose ideas on education matched his own, as well as his need for financial help, Fortune established a close connection with Washington and assisted him with writing and editing tasks, for which Fortune was not particularly well paid. While the anti-Washington black press denounced him as Washington's tool, the white press portrayed him as a militant opponent of Washington, not realizing that he was Washington's ghostwriter.

Even though Fortune's paper had an average weekly circulation of about 6,000 in the 1880s (a respectable figure in view of the 9,000 daily circulation of the *New York Times* in 1896), it never gener-

tune intended to make a full-time career of his work on the *Sun*, but the illness and death of Emanuel Fortune changed his mind.

In February 1889 Fortune took over as editor of the *Age*, returning to the Republican fold and chastising the Democrats for betraying black suffrage in the South. His militancy intensified as he published an editorial lauding the "Afro-American agitator" (a term coined by Grady, perhaps in reference to Fortune). The appearance of the "agitator," Fortune proclaimed, marked "the death knell of the shuffling, cringing creature in black who for two centuries and a half had given the right of way to white men. . . . "

Fortune's increasing distress over civil rights violations led him to issue a call in November 1889 for black organizations to send delegates to a convention in Chicago in January 1890. The move grew out of a proposal advanced in the *Freeman* in 1887 for an Afro-American League. Joining in the call were eighteen other prominent blacks, several of them editors, including W. Calvin Chase of the *Washington Bee*. According to the *Age*, 151 delegates

ated enough profit to free Fortune from financial worry. Using a small inheritance from his father, who died in 1896 after modest success in real estate in Jacksonville, Fortune moved his wife, son Fred (born 1890), and daughter Jessie (born 1883) into a small estate called Maple Hill in Red Bank, New Jersey, in 1901. A fond father, Fortune dedicated a volume of sentimental poetry published in 1905 to his children. He and his wife separated in 1906, and the estate was lost at foreclosure. Financed by white backers and Republican politicians, Washington secretly controlled most of the black press and became a silent partner in the *Age* in 1907, when Fortune sold his interest in the paper to Fred R. Moore. The sale stemmed from Fortune's alcoholism, ironic in view of his early interest in prohibition, and bouts of depression that affected his professional and family life.

Bereft of the *Age*, Fortune entered a dismal period of more than a decade struggling to find writing assignments to support himself and his family. He wrote for numerous black publications, some ephemeral, and returned to the *Age* from 1911 to 1914 as a salaried employee after having become almost a derelict, sitting in parks and begging from friends. Washington refused to lend him money to pay his rent at one point. When Washington died in 1915, Fortune wrote an article for a magazine published by the African Methodist Episcopal Church, to which he belonged. In it he divorced himself from Washington's political views but called him a great man. Fortune explained: "I helped make him leader [of the Negro people] and if I had to go over it all again I would do for him just what I did do, because I thought then, and think now, that we needed to build up the educational and business interests of the race, so that it might have some intelligence and money to back up its much-talked about justice and equality in the citizenship of the nation."

In the final years of his life Fortune recovered his mental stability. In 1919 he started writing for the *Norfolk* (Virginia) *Journal and Guide* and continued to do so until his death. Beginning in 1923 he edited Garvey's *Negro World* in New York. In this role Fortune praised the charismatic Jamaican's ability to mobilize the black masses for his program of racial separation and return to Africa. But he personally did not convert to Garvey's ideology or subscribe to his abandonment of demands for black civil rights, which brought Garvey some support from the Ku Klux Klan. Fortune wrote editorials for Garvey almost until the day of his death at the age of seventy-one.

Two years earlier he had been honored at the convention of the National Negro Press Association as the "dean of Negro journalism." In assessing his career, his biographer, Emma Lou Thornbrough, stated: "He was simply unable to adopt a patient, compromising pragmatic position on questions of human rights and human dignity. Whatever his other vagaries and inconsistencies, on this fundamental question he was consistent throughout his long career. That is the reason what he wrote and said remains relevant to a later generation, but it was also his personal curse. Unable to bend as Washington had, he was broken. But by the 1920s, after years of mental torment and degradation, he seems to have come to terms with life."

Other:

"The Editor's Mission," in *The Afro-American Press and Its Editors*, by Garland Penn (Springfield, Mass.: Wiley, 1891), pp. 481-483;

Victoria Earle Matthews, ed., *Black-Belt Diamonds: Gems from the Speeches, Addresses and Talks to Students of Booker T. Washington*, introduction by Fortune (New York: Fortune & Scott, 1898);

"The Negro's Place in American Life at the Present Day," in *The Negro Problem: A Series of Articles by Representative Negroes of Today*, edited by Booker T. Washington (New York: J. Pott, 1903), pp. 211-234.

Periodical Publications:

"Civil Rights and Social Privileges," *A. M. E. Church Review* (January 1886): 105-131;

"Why We Organized a National Afro-American League," *Afro-American Budget* (February 1890);

"The Race Problem; The Negro Will Solve It," *Belford's Magazine* (September 1890): 489-495;

"The Afro-American," *Arena* (December 1890): 115-118;

"Mob Law in the South," *Independent* (15 July 1897): 900;

"The Latest Color Line," *Liberia* (November 1897): 60-65;

"The Kind of Education the Afro-American Most Needs," *Southern Workman* (January 1898): 4-6;

"Afro-American or Negro?," *Outlook* (10 June 1899): 359;

"Good Indians and Good Niggers," *Independent* (22 June 1899);

"Politics in the Philippine Islands," *Independent* (24

September 1903): 2266-2268;

"Industrial Education: Will It Solve the Negro Problem?," *Colored American Magazine* (January 1904): 13-17;

"Haytian Revolution," *Voice of the Negro* (April 1904): 138-146;

"The Filipino," *Voice of the Negro* (May 1904): 199-202; (June 1904): 240-246;

"False Theory of Education," *Colored American Magazine* (July 1904): 473-478;

"The Voteless Citizen," *Voice of the Negro* (September 1904): 397-402;

"Who Are We? Afro-Americans, Colored People, or Negroes?," *Voice of the Negro* (March 1906): 194-198;

"Intermarriage and Natural Selection," *Colored American Magazine* (June 1909): 379-381;

"The Quick and the Dead," *A. M. E. Church Review* (April 1916): 247-252.

Biography:

Emma Lou Thornbrough, *T. Thomas Fortune: Militant Journalist* (Chicago: University of Chicago Press, 1972).

References:

Cyrus Field Adams, "Timothy Thomas Fortune: Journalist, Author, Lecturer, Agitator," *Col-*

ored American Magazine (January-February 1902): 225-227;

Michael L. Goldstein, "Preface to the Rise of Booker T. Washington: A View from New York City of the Demise of Independent Black Politicians, 1889-1902," *Journal of Negro History*, 62 (January 1977): 81-99;

Earl Ofari, "Black Activists and 19th Century Radicalism," *Black Scholar*, 5 (February 1974): 19-25;

Seth M. Scheiner, "Early Career of T. Thomas Fortune, 1879-1890," *Negro History Bulletin*, 27 (April 1964): 170-172;

C. Calloway Thomas, "T. Thomas Fortune on the 'Land of Chivalry and Deviltry,' " *Negro History Bulletin*, 42 (April-June 1979): 40-41;

Roland E. Wolseley, "T. Thomas Fortune: Dean of Black Journalists," *Crisis*, 83 (October 1976): 285-287.

Papers:

The Booker T. Washington Papers at the Library of Congress contain some Fortune correspondence. Other material may be found in a private collection in the hands of his descendants and in the Emmett J. Scott Papers at Morgan State University, Baltimore, Maryland.

Harold Frederic
(19 August 1856-19 October 1898)

William J. Thorn
Marquette University

and

Philip B. Dematteis

See also the Frederic entry in *DLB 12, American Realists and Naturalists.*

MAJOR POSITIONS HELD: Editor, *Utica Observer* (1880-1882); editor in chief, *Albany Evening Journal* (1882-1884); London correspondent, *New York Times* (1884-1898).

BOOKS: *Seth's Brother's Wife; A Study of Life in the Greater New York* (New York: Scribners, 1887; 2 volumes, London: Chatto & Windus, 1887);

In the Valley (New York: Scribners, 1890; 3 volumes,

London: Heinemann, 1890);

The Lawton Girl (London: Chatto & Windus, 1890; New York: Scribners, 1890);

The Young Emperor William II of Germany; A Study in Character Development on a Throne (London: Unwin, 1891; New York: Putnam's, 1891);

The New Exodus; A Study of Israel in Russia (London: Heinemann, 1892; New York: Putnam's, 1892);

The Return of O'Mahoney (New York: Bonner, 1892; London: Heinemann, 1893);

The Copperhead (New York: Scribners, 1893);

The Copperhead and Other Stories of the North during the
    American War (London: Heinemann, 1894);
Marsena, and Other Stories of the Wartime (New York:
    Scribners, 1894);
Marsena (London: Unwin, 1896);
Illumination (London: Heinemann, 1896); repub-
    lished as The Damnation of Theron Ware
    (Chicago: Stone & Kimball, 1896);
Mrs. Albert Grundy; Observations in Philistia (London:
    John Lane / New York: Merriam, 1896);
March Hares, as George Forth (London: John Lane,
    1896; New York: Appleton, 1896);
In the Sixties (New York: Scribners, 1897);
The Deserter and Other Stories; A Book of Two Wars
    (Boston: Lothrop, 1898);
Gloria Mundi (Chicago & New York: Stone, 1898;
    London: Heinemann, 1898);
The Market-Place (New York: Stokes, 1899; London:
    Heinemann, 1899);
Harold Frederic's Stories of York State, edited by
    Thomas F. O'Donnell (Syracuse: Syracuse
    University Press, 1966).

Perhaps the leading foreign correspondent of
his time, surely the most published, Harold Frederic provided readers of the *New York Times* with an
increasingly sophisticated understanding of the intricacies of European political, social, scientific, and
artistic life. Unflinchingly honest, keenly perceptive, well connected, and discriminating, Frederic
traversed Europe from his base in London providing the kind of cabled correspondence that distinguishes journalists from mere reporters.

Frederic left New York an awkward, uneasy,
intense—even overly serious—and energetic
young man from upstate New York who asked
editors about the social etiquette aboard steamships,
tipping, and the like. He broadened with the work
in London, dashing into the heart of a cholera
epidemic in France, covering the great and once
great in Europe, and touring Russia to investigate
the treatment of Jews. At his death, Frederic was
considered one of the best conversationalists, clubmen, and journalists in London. Along the way he
also achieved high fame as a novelist.

Frederic was born 19 August 1856 in Utica, in
New York's Mohawk Valley, to Henry and Frances
Ramsdell Frederick (he later dropped the final *k*
from his last name); he was an only child. His father,
a conductor on the New York Central, was killed in
a railroad accident when Frederic was eighteen
months old. His mother, a strong, fundamentalist
woman known as "Frank," started a vest-making
business to support herself and her son. In 1861 she
married William DeMott, who had a dairy and wood
business.

The precocious Frederic taught himself to
read by learning the letters on a soapbox in his
mother's kitchen before entering the local school;
he also developed an interest in drawing. While
attending school, he worked for his stepfather; he
later spoke to intimate friends about the hardships
of rising at 4 A.M. to milk cows and deliver to customers and the occasional embarrassment of
schoolmates' remarks about his poor and smelly
clothes. Upon graduating from the Advanced
School at age fourteen, Frederic took a series of jobs
with Utica photographers, in which he learned to
retouch photographic negatives. In 1873, he went
to Boston to study painting and writing; he lived
with a group of bohemian artists until he found a
job at the Rowell and Allen Studio as a retoucher.

He returned to Utica in the summer of 1875,
where he briefly took a retouching job with a local
photographer before joining the *Utica Morning
Herald* as a proofreader. After a few weeks with the

Herald he became a proofreader at the *Daily Observer*, where he soon rose to the status of a $9-a-week reporter and editorial writer.

As a reporter, Frederic also reviewed literature and the touring theater company performances. When Edwin Booth played Iago in Utica, Frederic wrote a lengthy analysis of both the play and the dazzling performance. He sent it to the *New York Sun*, but editor Charles A. Dana rejected it despite its high quality because New York readers well knew Booth and Shakespeare and cared little about Frederic's discovery of both.

His writing career on the *Observer* was more successful; in addition to his news stories and editorials, the paper published several of his first short stories. On 10 October 1877 he married Grace Williams, a neighbor on whom he had based the heroine of the first of these stories, "The Blakelys of Poplar Place." He also met and became a close friend of Father Edward A. Terry, a liberal Irish Catholic priest and theologian. In 1880, at the age of twenty-four, Frederic was promoted to managing editor of the *Observer*.

In August 1882, Frederic—though a staunch Democrat—accepted an offer to edit the *Albany Evening Journal*, an influential Republican paper. He left his wife and two daughters in Utica and moved in with Father Terry, who had been transferred to diocesan headquarters two years previously because his unorthodox views had antagonized other priests in the Utica area. In the 1882 gubernatorial election, Frederic and the *Journal* indirectly supported the Democratic candidate, Grover Cleveland, by opposing the Republican candidate. After Cleveland's election, he and Frederic became close friends, and the *Journal* was soon touting Cleveland for president. In March 1884, however, the paper was sold to a staunch Republican who wanted to restore its partisan character, and Frederic was out of a job.

Frederic received several offers of important editorial positions, as well as a suggestion from Cleveland that he go into politics. Frederic, who had decided to make a career in literature, declined all these offers and accepted a position as London correspondent for the *New York Times*; he planned to keep the job only for a year or two, until he could establish himself as an author. The pay was $80 a week, a figure that evidently was never increased in the fourteen remaining years of Frederic's life.

In June, he boarded the steamer *Queen* with his wife and daughters Ruth and Ruby, and sailed for London, carrying a letter of introduction from Governor Cleveland. Almost immediately after he arrived, a cholera epidemic broke out in southern Europe, killing thousands. Other correspondents were afraid to go into the region, but Frederic plunged in.

From his travels into the cholera-plagued areas of southern France, Frederic cabled America about the medical research being done on the problem, including the debate over its cause: "There is a drawn battle between the followers of Dr. Koch and the Pasteurites. Dr. Koch declares that the microbe *en virgule* (in the shape of a mark of interrogation) is the primordial cause of cholera, and that it is conveyed into the stomach by the agency of food and drink." He interviewed other researchers, reporting that they declined to give him any details of their discoveries. Frederic kept tables of cholera-related mortality, which appeared in his cables on the epidemic, linking it with filth and poor sanitation. Americans, panicky because of the steamships which had left Europe at the outset of the epidemic, learned from his cables they had little to fear and learned the precise state of medical research on cholera and its causes.

Frederic's stories on the cholera epidemic established his reputation as a correspondent, and he moved quickly to establish himself socially in London as well. His letter from Cleveland gained him entry to the exclusive Savage Club and National Liberal Club. Six feet tall, uncommonly strong, and a vigorous but dogmatic debater, Frederic was known to his clubmen to have "the heart of a babe and the hide of a rhinoceros." He formed a private club, the Ghouls, whose fifteen members included A. Conan Doyle, J. M. Barrie, W. E. Henley, and Bernard Partridge of *Punch*. He also became intimate with Irish leaders and members of Parliament such as Charles Stewart Parnell, Tim Healy, and T. P. O'Connor and adopted the cause of Irish home rule; his cables to the *Times* increasingly advocated Irish independence and influenced American opinion on the subject. He took a number of vacations in Ireland.

During his first two years in London, Frederic also completed and sold to Scribners his first novel, *Seth's Brother's Wife* (1887), a story of political corruption in Dearborn County, a fictional upstate New York district based on the Mohawk Valley; the protagonist, Seth Fairchild, grows up on a farm, becomes a newspaper proofreader, and finally rises to become an editor. Frederic went on to use the locale, some of the characters, and family names in subsequent novels and stories, much as William

Faulkner was to do with his fictional Yoknapatawpha County and its inhabitants. The novel is mainly remembered today for its bitter, depressing portrait of rural life.

Frederic returned from London in triumph in 1886, having earned a powerful reputation as a foreign correspondent able to absorb and convey the complex European political scene and particularly for his fearless coverage of the cholera epidemic. On a visit to Utica, he presented the Irish community with a scroll signed by the Irish members of Parliament and made a speech predicting that home rule would soon be won. He and Father Terry went to Washington for a White House dinner with President Cleveland. Before he returned to London, twenty-eight people threw a party for him at Delmonico's in New York, including Mayor Grace, Wayne MacVeagh, Thomas L. James, Postmaster Pearson, and *Times* publisher George Jones, who complimented him for his cholera stories. Others attending included E. Prentiss Bailey, C. R. Miller, Edward Cary, John Foord, John C. Reid, A. K. Fiske, F. D. Root, Montgomery Schuyler, Amos J. Cummings, Noah Brooks, E. A. Dithmar, and other leading journalists and intellectuals. Clearly, Frederic had come a long distance from the awkward, unsophisticated, and rustic intellectual who read Fox's *Book of Martyrs* and Hale's *History of the United States* all the way through while a youth.

Frederic returned to London and resumed his journalistic correspondence. He also completed in eight months a novel he had long planned on the American Revolution, *In the Valley* (1890). In the novel, the struggle between the colonists and the British for America is symbolically recreated in the contest between Dutch farmer Douw Mauverensen and English aristocrat Philip Cross for the hand of Daisy, an orphan girl.

As soon as he finished *In the Valley*, Frederic went to work on a sequel to *Seth's Brother's Wife. The Lawton Girl* (1890) has a double plot concerning the seduction, degradation, and rehabilitation of Jessica Lawton and an attempted takeover of a small iron works by a crooked cartel.

While waiting for his novels to appear in print, Frederic suffered a severe personal loss: his first son, Harold Frederic, Jr., whom his father had said "represents all my hopes and aspirations," died in May 1887 at the age of two. Frederic took his wife, two daughters, and infant son Hereward on a tour of Europe to try to overcome their grief. (In 1889 another son was born and also named Harold.)

Meanwhile, Frederic continued his journalism. When Emperor William I of Prussia died in

June 1888, Frederic provided an elaborate account of the funeral, reflecting his wide-ranging knowledge. In it, he sketched Bismarck, then "a feeble old gentleman," though six years younger than Gladstone. "His face is waxen and flabby, and his hands are those of a very old man, yellow."

Though his reputation as a journalist continued to grow, Frederic was not particularly happy: he had hoped to be able to get out of journalism, which he had called a "vile and hollow fool-rink" and compared to the hair shirt of an anchorite, and had sought a consular post from Cleveland, whom he visited again in 1888. But Cleveland was defeated for reelection that year, thus eliminating that escape route for the time being; the defeat of his friend and political hero was also a personal disappointment for Frederic. *In the Valley* appeared in *Scribner's Magazine* in 1889-1890 and in book form in the latter year; it received generally good reviews, even though historical novels were out of fashion at the time. The reviews of *The Lawton Girl*, which was not serialized because of its "sordid" subject matter, were mixed. But neither novel sold well enough to support Frederic's extravagant lifestyle, forcing him to continue depending on the *Times* for his main income.

In 1890, Frederic spent a month in Germany writing a series of *Times* articles on the Emperor William II; these were collected into his first nonfiction book, *The Young Emperor William II of Germany* (1891). He also made a third, and last, visit to the United States, during which he met and became friendly with the important author, editor, and critic William Dean Howells. Perhaps most significant, 1890 was the year he took as his mistress a liberated American woman, Kate Lyon.

Frederic and his shy and unsophisticated wife, Grace, had been out of intellectual harmony for some time; his relationship with Kate Lyon was emotionally fulfilling and probably stimulating to his creativity. It was also, however, an additional financial burden. His wife refused to give him a divorce, so, in 1891, Frederic undertook to support two households: his legitimate family in a house outside London and Kate in an establishment in town. The births of three children to Kate in the following three years sent Frederic ever more deeply into debt and made it impossible for him to break away from journalism.

Frederic had other problems at about this time. At his favorite London club, the Savage, he got into a dispute with an editor, Sir John Brenon. After Frederic criticized Brenon in print, Brenon sued him for libel and won. Frederic also fell out with his

Irish friends at this time by taking sides against Charles Stewart Parnell, who was involved in an adultery scandal in 1890. When Parnell died in 1891, he became a martyr, and Frederic lost favor with influential Irish politicians as well as most Irish-Americans. He also wrote some plays, but none of them was ever produced. When Cleveland returned to the presidency in 1893, Frederic tried again for a consulship, but it was not forthcoming—possibly because of his unconventional personal life.

Through it all, Frederic's journalistic output continued to be of high quality. He wrote a feature story about Jews in England, spurred by the induction of a Jewish Lord Mayor of London. After a historical review of the British treatment of Jews, Frederic concluded by observing the "high battlemented walls of caste" which separated the affluent Jews from the poor, typically immigrant Jews in London's East End.

In 1891, Frederic toured Russia to investigate anti-Semitism there and found a country of "dark and hopeless ignorance, of drunken incompetency, of frank and even smiling contempt for everything of thought and word and deed that we call honesty . . . in cottages, in fields, in churches, camps and market places—and everywhere, depressing as the picture was, it furnished the background of a whole race being hunted from its homes, despoiled of its possessions, hounded by the Cossack, and plundered by the tchinovnik, and all unpitied by anyone." After his first unflattering portrait, Frederic was virtually banned from subsequent visits to Russia. *The New Exodus* (1892), his fifth book and second nonfiction work, includes all of his cables about the life of Russian Jews.

In addition to his regular dispatches from London, which summarized the European news in politics, art, religion, and the incessant rumors of war, Frederic provided a number of special articles for extra income. These articles included interviews and sketches of Gladstone, Earl Spencer, the Danish royal family, Cecil Rhodes, Lord Russell, and Continental nobility. He also sent reviews of literature in Britain, such as Stephen Crane's *The Red Badge of Courage* (1895), Thomas Hardy's *Jude the Obscure* (1895), novels by Howells and Fuller, and the plagiarism controversy surrounding Charles Dickens and his friend Wilkie Collins.

Frederic provided *Times* readers with comparisons of British and American magazines, observing that the British believed Americans printed better magazines and books, apart from the high-priced publications from "university presses and those of Constable and other famous houses." Frederic concluded that American writers on the whole produced far superior magazine articles and short features: "The editor of Harper's or Scribner's, for example, can get from any one of a dozen well-known American writers a contribution on given lines of 6,000 words, which will be as good as anything that writer has ever done or can do. An English writer of the same rank would seize the opportunity to unload some trivial hackwork on the editor."

Frederic also compared children and child raising in Britain and America, as well as the election processes. The British, he thought, were moving toward an American system: "When all elections for a new Parliament are held on the same day throughout the three kingdoms, and no man is allowed to cast more than one vote—the points of difference between the voting systems of the two countries will be very limited indeed." He fully recognized the more substantial social and political differences which separated the two systems, even as he understood how America was providing developments which were influencing the motherland.

London's growing interest in American news intrigued him as well, as he noted in an 1896 article: "This theory that America was of no use as a news centre completely dominated London journalism when I first knew it a dozen years ago. The great provincial newspapers, like The Manchester Guardian, believed differently, and printed as much American news as came their way, but in London it remained almost an article of journalistic faith that nobody wanted to read about America." The flow of stories about American life led to comparisons between the orderly closing of London pubs and the New York crackdown on bars which ignored the closing laws. "The point is that these rules are absolutely obeyed. . . . The idea of evading [them] is never mooted."

With equal vigor, Frederic reported that London police, the "blue kings" who stunned the shah of Persia by being able to stop all vehicular traffic by merely lifting a finger, consistently perjured themselves "in the witness box against a private citizen" to support each other and blackmailed brothel owners and prostitutes. Despite the many virtues of London police, Frederic reported, these two grievances angered Londoners.

Throughout these years, Frederic continued his literary work, writing nine short stories; a comic novel, *The Return of O'Mahoney* (1892), about a deserter from the American Civil War who inherits an

Irish estate; a series of satirical sketches about a British matron, written in 1892-1893 for the *National Observer* under the title "Observations in Philistia," and collected as *Mrs. Albert Grundy* in 1896; and two novelettes about the Civil War, *The Copperhead* (1893) and *Marsena* (1894). His greatest novel, *The Damnation of Theron Ware* (1896)—an allegory of the loss of American innocence at the end of the nineteenth century—was a critical and popular success and is still read today. Theron Ware, a likable, naive young minister, is assigned to a fundamentalist Methodist parish in the Mohawk Valley. He comes under the influence of a skeptical Catholic priest, Father Forbes (modeled on Father Terry); an atheistic scientist, Dr. Ledsmar; and a beautiful, wealthy aesthete, Celia Madden. The three undermine his faith, and he loses control of his congregation until he adopts the cynical philosophy of a phony evangelist, Sister Soulsby; he then becomes a successful hypocrite. In the end, he abandons his ministry and his wife and heads west with visions of a career in politics.

The success of *The Damnation of Theron Ware* enabled Frederic to cut back on his output of articles for the *Times*; he was also accepted in British literary circles. He was now living with Kate Lyon—who called herself Kate Frederic—and their three children at Homefield, a house in Surrey. He celebrated the happiness he had found with Kate in a comic novel, *March Hares* (1896), about a despondent young man and woman who meet, fall in love, get involved in a case of mistaken identities, and finally marry.

In 1897 he met Stephen Crane, who had praised his Civil War stories and whose *Red Badge of Courage* Frederic had helped popularize; Crane and his mistress, Cora, moved into Homefield with Frederic and Kate for a time. The foursome were constant companions and took vacations in Ireland together until Crane left to cover the Spanish-American War. Frederic wrote two more novels, both set in England: *Gloria Mundi* (1898), a weak, tedious novel about a man who inherits a dukedom; and *The Market-Place* (1899), a book highly regarded by modern critics, about a ruthless speculator.

Both novels were published posthumously. Toward the end of 1897 Frederic began to feel the symptoms of heart disease, but he refused medical advice and increased his social activities, his work, and his eating, pipe and cigar smoking, and drinking. In August 1898 he suffered a stroke which partially paralyzed his right arm, making it very difficult for him to write his Saturday cables, except by sheer force of will. Before his death on 19 Oc-

tober at the age of forty-two, Frederic was attended by a horrid woman "healer," whom the coroner found to be a charlatan. His life could have been spared with proper medical attention, the inquest concluded, and only the Christian Science healer prevented it. The incident set off a wave of indignation and protest about Christian Science healing, including a series of editorials in the *New York Times*. Most found it hard to believe that a journalist so intimate with leading medical researchers of his day, including Louis Pasteur, could forsake medical attention. Kate and the healer were accused of manslaughter but were acquitted after a sensational trial when it was determined that Frederic had voluntarily rejected medical treatment. His death left both of his families heavily in debt; they were aided by contributions from friends.

As a journalist, Frederic insisted on accuracy and research, and he favored direct, plain language in grammatical structures appropriate to his age. Frederic, known for his enormous energy, at one point wrote, in addition to his *Times* correspondence, editorials and book reviews for the *Manchester Guardian*, serials, and his own novels, and edited the philatelic page for the weekly *Million*. He was also a man of contradictory traits, perhaps two separate persons: as a fellow journalist described him, "the Frederic of the books and THE TIMES letters, and the high-voiced, careless, over generous, pugnacious, gentle-hearted, hardworked, dogmatic Frederic of Fleet Street and the smoking room."

Always an ardent American, Frederic never bothered to learn a foreign language. With his rising literary fame came increased access to the political and social elite, so that by the time of his death Frederic was a major figure in London life and the dean of American correspondents in Europe. Through his eyes, Americans watched the dissolution of the German Empire and the declines of Gladstone and of the European nobility, and came to understand the intricacies of the Irish problem, which he understood better than any other American journalist. He proved able to grow with the opportunity, transmitting a wide range of observations and understanding from the Old World to the New.

Letters:

The Correspondence of Harold Frederic, edited by George Fortenberry, Stanton Garner, and Robert H. Woodward, text established by Charlyne Dodge (Fort Worth: Texas Christian University Press, 1977).

Bibliographies:

Thomas F. O'Donnell, Stanton Garner, and Robert H. Woodward, *A Bibliography of Writings by and about Harold Frederic* (Boston: G. K. Hall, 1975);

Noel Polk, *The Literary Manuscripts of Harold Frederic: A Catalogue* (New York & London: Garland, 1979).

References:

Anonymous, "Some Recollections of Harold Frederic," *Saturday Review* (London), 86 (22 October 1898): 571-572;

Gertrude Atherton, "Harold Frederic," *The Bookman* (London), 15 (November 1898): 15;

Austin Briggs, Jr., *The Novels of Harold Frederic* (Ithaca: Cornell University Press, 1969);

Everett Carter, *Howells and the Age of Realism* (Philadelphia: Lippincott, 1954), pp. 239-245;

Stanton Garner, *Harold Frederic*, University of Minnesota Pamphlets on American Writers (Minneapolis: University of Minnesota Press, 1969);

Louise Imogen Guiney, "Harold Frederic: A Half-Length Sketch from the Life," *The Book Buyer*, 17 (January 1899): 600-604;

Paul Haines, "Harold Frederic," Ph.D. dissertation, New York University, 1945;

Frank Harris, "Harold Frederic, *Ad Memoriam*," *Saturday Review* (London), 86 (22 October 1898): 526-528;

Carey McWilliams, "Harold Frederic: A Country

Boy of Genius," *University of California Chronicle*, 25 (1933): 21-34;

Thomas F. O'Donnell and Hoyt C. Franchere, *Harold Frederic* (New York: Twayne, 1961);

Arthur Hobson Quinn, *American Fiction* (New York: Appleton-Century, 1936), pp. 449-452;

Abe C. Ravitz, "Harold Frederic's Venerable Copperhead," *New York History*, 91 (January 1960): 35-48;

Arthur Warren, "Harold Frederic—The Reminiscences of a Colleague," *New York Times* (23 October 1898), p.19;

Robert H. Woodward, "Harold Frederic: A Study of His Novels, Short Stories, and Plays," Ph.D. dissertation, Indiana University, 1957;

Woodward, "Harold Frederic and New York Folklore," *New York Folklore Quarterly*, 16 (Summer 1960): 83-89.

Papers:

The Harold Frederic Papers at the Library of Congress contain manuscripts, notes, letters, diaries, and legal documents. The papers of Grover Cleveland, also at the Library of Congress, contain many letters from Frederic to Cleveland. The S. S. McClure Papers in the University of Iowa Manuscript Collection, the D. Appleton Letters in the Columbia University Library Manuscript Collection, and the Scribner Collection in the Princeton University Library all have correspondence between Frederic and his publishers regarding his books.

Legh Richmond Freeman
(4 December 1842-7 February 1915)

Thomas H. Heuterman
Washington State University

MAJOR POSITIONS HELD: Editor, *Kearney* (Nebraska) *Herald*, renamed *Frontier Index* (1865-1868); editor, *Ogden* (Utah) *Freeman* (1875-1878); *Butte* (Montana) *Frontier Index* (1878-1881); editor, *Daily Inter-Mountains* and *Inter-Mountains Freeman*, renamed *Union-Freeman*, renamed *Butte City Union* (1881-1884); editor, *Thompson Falls* (Montana) *Frontier Index* (1884); editor, *Yakima Farmer*, renamed *Freeman's Farmer*, renamed *Washington Farmer* (1884-1910).

As the young publisher of the *Frontier Index*, Legh Richmond Freeman so frequently moved the printing equipment he and his brother operated in the railroad construction towns of Nebraska and Wyoming between 1865 and 1868 that their newspaper earned the permanent sobriquet of the "Press on Wheels." The term continued to be a fitting description beyond the pioneer period up to Freeman's death in 1915 on the Pacific coast, where he published the *Washington Farmer*. Freeman's ac-

tivities have been deemed significant by journalism historians: in 1916, James Melvin Lee called the *Frontier Index* among the most interesting newspapers in the history of American journalism; in 1943, Douglas C. McMurtrie added that he had seen no more fascinating story in all the annals of American journalism.

During his years on the railroad frontier, Freeman wrote as General Horatio Vattel, "Lightning Scout of the Mountains," a nom de plume rooted in his belief in the cavalier legend of the South. He was born to Arthur Ryland Freeman and Mary Kemper Freeman at Culpeper, Virginia, on 4 December 1842. Influence of both the Old Dominion and the frontier are discernible in his youth, although he was from no Southern aristocracy. Family legend relates that Freeman's grandfather, John Hoomes Freeman, the owner of sixteen slaves in 1840, had developed a neighborly and intimate relationship with Thomas Jefferson, but he was ap-

parently merely an overseer of Jefferson's and not a private secretary, as Legh Freeman contended. Yet Legh Freeman legitimately claimed the heritage of Southern history when, in later years, he reminded his readers that he was the nephew of James Lawson Kemper, the first post-Civil War native-son governor of Virginia (1875-1879).

During the Civil War, Freeman served as a private in a Confederate Kentucky Cavalry regiment, apparently under the command of Brigadier General John Hunt Morgan. Freeman was captured in Floyd County in the Appalachian country of eastern Kentucky on 7 May 1864: a telegrapher, he was north of Pound Gap, perhaps on an intelligence mission; General Morgan moved out of Virginia through the gap on 31 May on his last Kentucky raid. Freeman was sent to the Rock Island military prison in the Mississippi River between Davenport, Iowa, and Rock Island, Illinois. He remained there until he was offered the opportunity to become a "galvanized Yankee" by volunteering for United States Army service in the western territories.

He may have agreed to support the Constitution merely to gain release, but since boyhood he had demonstrated a fascination with lore of the West. As a youth he had supposedly carved the words, "Horatio Vattel, Lightning Scout of the Mountains," in the doorpost of his father's railroad station at Gordonsville, Virginia. "That is the name I am going to take when I go out West to explore and write up the country," he is said to have explained. No doubt the story was embroidered to fit the adult life Freeman went on to achieve, but Freeman as a child had treasured a book on Indians of the West which told of explorations by early travelers and scouts. Or, as the son of a railroad man, Freeman's volunteering may have been due to a desire to be in the proximity of the fabled Pacific railroad. Whatever his motivation, Freeman did become Vattel the scout. For him, as for many other Americans born in the 1840s and 1850s who "went out West," fact caught up with fiction and even with childhood fantasy.

Freeman's regiment of Southern Yankees sighted Fort Kearny, Nebraska, on 9 April 1865, the day fellow Southerners were forfeiting their arms at Appomattox; news of the surrender reached the regiment's 800 troops that day. Soon after his arrival, Freeman became the fort telegraph operator. It is not clear whether he was initially under military command or was a civilian operator, but at one time he was paid $150 a month to attend to the Fort Kearny business of Edward Creighton's Overland

Telegraph. He was busy transmitting and decoding orders to freighters as well as attending to military dispatches.

Using his telegrapher's salary to acquire idle printing equipment at the fort, Freeman established the *Kearney Herald* in December 1865. Creighton had given him permission to use the telegraphic press dispatches free of charge. He collected pied type and whittled wooden letters with a jackknife where letters were missing from the type case. Printers were "detailed" from the ranks of the army, and the printer's devil was a drummer boy. The imposing stone was a two-inch oak plank obtained from the quartermaster's department, and the ink stone was donated by the government painter, who had used it in grinding and mixing paints.

Freeman set an annual subscription price of $6 for the four-page, semiweekly newspaper and a six-month rate of $4. He arranged the type in two columns on nine-by-fourteen-inch pages. Sharing prominent space with the newspaper's name at the top of the first page was the motto "Independence in All Things, Neutrality in Nothing." The legend was copied, perhaps, from the *Huntsman's Echo*,

which had been published in 1860 and 1861 by Joseph Ellis Johnson at Wood River Center, Nebraska Territory, a Mormon community twenty-six miles from the fort; that newspaper had carried the same words.

The fledgling editor, educated in grammar but not trained in journalism, printed many insignificant items but was able to recognize legitimate news. When Jim Bridger checked into the Overland House at nearby Kearny City, Freeman was on hand to interview the aging fellow Virginian. The mountain man was unaware that he was being labeled a "hero" and scrutinized by Freeman as the virtual prototype of Horatio Vattel. Bridger told Freeman he was en route to Washington, D.C., "to tell the authorities how to manage the Indians." Yet he admitted that an impending campaign against the Sioux by the Eighteenth United States Infantry was being "planned more sensibly than any before fitted up in this country."

The last comment proved to be of interest to General Grenville Dodge as well as to Freeman. The general urged Bridger to remain in the West, and on 26 January 1866, he was hired as chief guide for the spring campaign. He therefore led Colonel

Legh Freeman, right, and his brother, Frederick Kemper Freeman—partners in the Kearney Herald

Henry B. Carrington's Eigheenth Infantry troops when they left Fort Kearny on 19 May 1866 to open the Bozeman Trail or Powder River Road to Montana. Freeman decided to follow Bridger. He asked a brother, Frederick Kemper Freeman, to come west to take over the newspaper, although his continued proximity to the railroad and telegraph line would have ensured him a steady income as a publisher and telegrapher. But Freeman was also attracted by the Montana goldfields. And, as a young man who had grown up poring over pictures of Indians, he was drawn as well by the news that Oglala Sioux leader Red Cloud had arrived at Fort Laramie to conclude a Bozeman Trail peace treaty. Freeman covered the June treaty conferences for the newspaper, although there is some question whether he arrived before Red Cloud had departed, leaving the Bozeman Trail issue essentially unsettled.

Despite the resulting critical Indian situation, Freeman decided to move for the first time beyond the protection of the military. It was in Indian-controlled country that Horatio Vattel came alive. His mission was ostensibly to explore the Yellowstone country which he had heard described by Bridger and his partner, Lu Anderson. His activities reflected a blend of Horatio Vattel the adventurer and Freeman the profit-seeking war veteran. Some of his tales echo Bridger's yarns, but Freeman's claim of being the early reporter of Yellowstone phenomena appears verified by an account in an Omaha newspaper. It tells of "L. R. Freeman," who, in the summer of 1866, interviewed a party which was probably the first, besides early trappers, to see the geysers of the upper Yellowstone exploration; the account also tells of his subsequent report to the Union States War Department which, as the first official account, caused a sensation in the Eastern states. Freeman spent the winter of 1866-1867 on the Yellowstone, and he was camped there in April 1867 when John Bozeman and his companion Tom Coover passed him on their way to Fort C. F. Smith on the Bighorn. On 20 April, five Indians appeared at Bozeman's camp and killed him. Coover escaped and, according to Freeman's later account, made it back to Freeman's camp that night. In another incident, Freeman and his companions themselves escaped from Indians. Although Freeman did report certain activities for the newspaper, by then renamed the *Frontier Index*, his purpose in the Yellowstone country appears not to have been primarily journalistic. He wrote of the Indian attacks he survived, but he cannot realistically be included among the correspondents of the Indian campaigns who attached themselves to military units to continue war reporting techniques perfected during the Civil War. Freeman's adventures prove the inaccuracy of the portrayal in twentieth-century fiction and film of the effeminate quill pusher in Eastern clothes; Freeman's was more the swaggering, masculine writer's role exemplified by Mark Twain.

While Freeman continued alternately or concurrently as a writer, miner, land speculator, incipient stockman, and, in a sawmill venture, exploiter of the timberlands, his brother began moving the newspaper along the Union Pacific construction route. Frederick Freeman became a real estate agent as well as a town boomer. The paper was moved to North Platte and Julesburg in Nebraska Territory and to Fort Sanders and Laramie in Dakota Territory before Legh Freeman returned to the editor's chair in 1868. By then he claimed to have founded "Freemansburg" in Arizona at the head of the navigation on the Colorado River.

Readers of the *Frontier Index* looked forward to a mixture of tall tales, anecdotes, humorous essays, and travel narratives in columns adjacent to news of railroad construction and booming towns. A correspondent for the *Omaha Republican* sought out for an interview Horatio Vattel, "that great western genius whose genuine witticisms, peculiarly expressed prophesies, sensible profundities and wise sayings generally, are so extensively copied and quoted throughout this western country and California." Freeman based his tall tales upon his Yellowstone experiences, such as seeing, in a petrified tree, "a petrified bird singing a petrified song, sticking out his mouth about 10 petrified feet." (The tale is strikingly similar to one which Jim Bridger supposedly told Narcissa Whitman.) Drawing upon an incident when a band of Crows drove off his horses and supplies, leaving his party without food, Freeman wrote that he had escaped hunger when he spied a huge buck sheep: "I fired at his breast, but he being above me, the ball fell just enough to slit his belly from one end to the other, and down he tumbled, his guts rolling out, and he rolling on down into a boiling spring, the water of which was salty, and by the time we could get to him and drag him out our breakfast was all prepared. . . ." Some of his tall tales were so brief as to be slipped into the *Frontier Index* almost unnoticed among its varied paragraphs: "The Yellowstone Lake, in Wyoming Territory, is so clear and so deep, that by looking into it you can see them making tea in China."

Yet as Freeman spun his yarns, he also baited Negroes, Chinese, and Indians. The contrasting strains of Horatio Vattel's humor and hatred were not incompatible in his view. His racism stemmed partly from his Southern heritage, but in the West he was also playing to the popular sentiment about the racial groups he called "species of the animal kingdom." In a widely held Western view, Chinese coolies threatened the jobs of whites, and Indian depredations justified the red man's extinction.

Freeman's intolerance extended to politics. Under the by-line of Horatio Vattel, "General in Chief, and Editor of the official organ of the armies of Masonic Democracy," Freeman wrote, "Grant is too much nigger—too much GAR for us!" As he moved the *Frontier Index* consecutively from Laramie to Benton, Green River City, and Bear River City in Wyoming, his rhetoric warmed with the 1868 presidential campaign. Initially Freeman's criticism was relatively mild: "All that we can say of poor Grant, is that he is a *magnificent* fool. . . ." After the election, the newspaper's Democratic sentiment was even stronger: "WHAT WE EXPECT— PREPARE FOR THE WORST. Grant, the whisky bloated, squaw ravishing adulterer, monkey ridden, nigger worshipping mogul, is rejoicing over his election to the presidency . . . if Grant attempts to carry out his ambitious, nefarious plans, the streets of our eastern cities will run more blood than did the unfortunate Paris in the reign of Robesperrie

[*sic*]." Freeman did see blood run, but it was in the streets of Bear River City. Not only had he attacked the newly elected president, but as the suspected chief of Bear River City vigilantes, his columns alienated the lawless element of the community. On 13 November 1868, he reported the hanging of "three notorious robbers," ages twenty-one, twenty-two, and twenty-three, by vigilantes who had burst into the jail. On 20 November, railroad grading crews, incited by a brother of one of the victims, burst into the Bear River City jail, freed the inmates, and set fire to the building. The mob headed next for the *Frontier Index* office, ransacked the premises, destroyed all the equipment, and burned the structure. Freeman escaped on horseback to Fort Bridger, according to a witness, "so fast that you could have played checkers on his coattails," but others were not as fortunate; estimates of deaths ranged from fourteen to twenty-five. It has been generally accepted that the cause of the riot was the general lawlessness of Bear River City. In later years, Freeman said that the Union Pacific had hired the mob to end his competing real estate activity, but no evidence exists for this contention. Both explanations ignore the resentment over Freeman's editorial positions on the vigilantes and the presidential election.

After only four years on the railroad and In-

Bear River City, Wyoming, where Freeman's newspaper office was burned and he was run out of town by a mob

dian frontiers, Freeman had already verified the later assessment of his work as being "most interesting" and a "fascinating story." But forty-seven years of his publishing life remained, and he entered into this less dangerous but equally colorful era with gusto. Seven months after the Bear River City mob sent Freeman fleeing to Fort Bridger in defeat, Horatio Vattel sought his triumph in Virginia. Residents of Culpeper were handed flyers depicting a figure clad in buckskin and announcing that Freeman would lecture on "What a young man or Woman may honorably and profitably do" along the lines of the transcontinental railroads.

Freeman followed his own advice. He married Ada Virginia Miller of Strasburg, Virginia, a wartime acquaintance, and briefly returned to Rock Island, Illinois, near the prison site, to take a telegrapher's position. Then, in a speculative venture, he mined coal at Rock Springs, Wyoming, as the

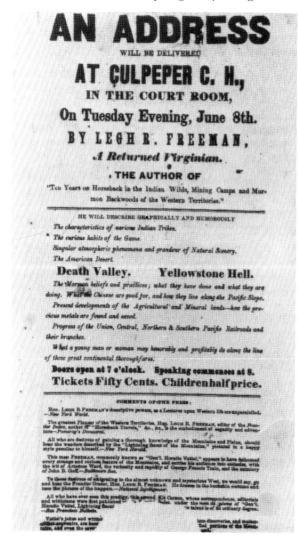

Handbill announcing one of Freeman's lectures in 1869

Union Pacific began its conversion from wood-burning engines; but the railroad monopolized the supply, so he took his family, increased by two children and the impending birth of a third, to Ogden, Utah, in 1875 to start the *Ogden Freeman*. Significantly, Freeman once again moved to a site on a transcontinental railroad, a prerequisite he set during most of his many moves.

Freeman at first offered to cooperate with the Mormons, even to the extent of defending the Mountain Meadows massacre. (A wagon train of settlers had been massacred on 11 September 1857, southwest of the present town of Enterprise, Utah. Indians and a group of Mormons were accused of the attack, and the arrest of John D. Lee in 1874 may have renewed the interest in the incident which Freeman encountered in 1875. Lee was executed on 23 March 1877.) But when he could not break into their closed economic system, he opportunistically turned on them. He sought business from the miniscule non-Mormon population in Utah and largely unsuccessfully proclaimed himself the voice of the Liberal party there. He admitted that only his horseback trips throughout the Rocky Mountains in Horatio Vattel fashion provided the subscription and advertising revenue which kept him in business in Ogden as long as four years. His Lightning Scout techniques extended to his editorial columns as well: he established a popular matrimonial bureau in his pages to unite maidens and gentile miners, and for five hours he sat in front of Brigham Young's bier in an attempt to document how little sorrow was expressed for the Mormon leader.

Freeman revived the *Frontier Index* in 1878 in Butte, Montana, where he was awaiting his wife. In bringing printing equipment from Ogden, she was fatally injured when a shotgun fell from her lurching wagon and discharged; Freeman turned to mysticism as a result of the accident. Revealing further dimensions of his opportunistic nature, the native Virginian and foe of President Grant now professed to be a "John Brown Republican." This move of expediency brought him no more success—or governmental advertising—than had his support of the Liberal party in Utah.

Freeman published newspapers under six titles during five years in Montana, a period clouded by a lengthy lawsuit. The suit was brought by publishers of the *Daily Inter Mountain* against Freeman and his *Daily Inter-Mountains* and weekly *Inter-Mountains Freeman*. Freeman successfully defended the suit, but the victory was relatively meaningless. Butte had not yet experienced its copper boom, and Freeman's ventures, including a labor newspaper

Some of the newspapers edited by Freeman in various parts of the West

partnership, were unsuccessful. In 1884, he resurrected the *Frontier Index* once again at Thompson Falls, Montana, near the Idaho border, during a gold boom which drew even Calamity Jane. By the following summer, both the gold and the prospectors had disappeared, and Freeman had to fill out his columns with extensive accounts of his philosophy of mysticism.

News that the Northern Pacific was building its line westward toward Puget Sound through the Yakima Valley of Washington Territory once again stirred Freeman. Accompanied by his three sons and the ubiquitous printing equipment, he moved to Yakima City. Eyeing the agricultural potential of the river-fed valley, he began publication of the *Washington Farmer* in partnership with the community's established editor. Freeman undoubtedly contributed an understanding of agricultural affairs from his youth in rural Virginia; he added serious reporting of agricultural news, and the result was a curious hybrid of Pacific Northwest farm journal and community weekly. But within three months his partnership arrangement was thrown into court in a dispute which Freeman linked to the issue of relocating the town to meet demands of the Northern Pacific. In addition, Freeman faced a libel suit and a third suit brought for an unpaid bill. He was largely successful in these suits and even more successful in romance: in 1886 he married Janie Nicholas Ward, a native of Georgia whom he met through a sister.

Although he and his new wife began to acquire modest parcels of property in North Yakima, Freeman was granted an even larger holding in exchange for his promise to move to Puget Sound to advertise a potential boom town. His goal was to make Fidalgo Island the western terminus of the Northern Pacific. In return, he received deeds to 367 acres offered by promoters of nearby property. He was thus assured of the publishing monopoly he had coveted but never achieved. As he moved once again in 1889, an era was drawing to a close for him. His twenty-five-year westward quest ended when he obtained the subsidy which had always previously gone to his competitors. In a way, he had personified the American westward movement, and now he felt assured that after his 3,000-mile trek, success was finally guaranteed.

In fact there was a boom on Fidalgo Island, but it occurred not at Gibraltar, where Freeman had located, but at nearby Anacortes. Freeman did not benefit directly when the first Northern Pacific train from Seattle reached the town in 1890 amid cannon salutes, festooned streets, speeches, songs, and a banquet. Belatedly Freeman sought to share in some of the profits, and he moved to Anacortes in 1892, joined by his brother Frederick, who characteristically established a real estate office. Emphasis of the *Washington Farmer* remained on the agriculture of the Pacific Northwest; however, extensive space was devoted early in 1892 to the platform of the People's party as adopted at the St. Louis convention of the Knights of Labor, Farmers' Alliances, and affiliated organizations. With the panic of 1893 compounding the financial consequences of the collapse of the Anacortes boom, Freeman, like many of his rural readers, was even more firmly attracted to the promise of populism.

In 1894, after five years on Fidalgo Island, the Freeman family returned to North Yakima. In the remaining twenty years of his life, Freeman failed to find the financial success which had been one of the forces drawing him across the North American continent. The frontier had truly turned back upon itself, and Freeman joined the Populists in seeking from political action what they could no longer find in the land. He was a delegate in 1896 to the Yakima County Populist convention; he spoke in favor of the fusion of Populists, Democrats, and Silver Republicans at a North Yakima political rally. At concurrent state conventions of the three parties, Freeman was named chairman of a conference committee which was instructed to prepare a fusion slate of state candidates. He also served as a Populist representative on a three-member Yakima County conference committee.

Freeman's political activity was insufficient to result, as he had hoped, in his nomination as a congressional candidate. Undaunted, he attempted to organize a People's party municipal ticket in North Yakima, but none of its nominees was elected. In January 1897, Freeman tried to convince state legislators to name him to the United States Senate. The *Seattle Times* reported that he had spent a week in Seattle and dutifully combed his whiskers every day in the lobby of his hotel. He established no headquarters, but distributed a circular printed in red which was headed "The Red Horse Candidate" and depicted him with "Populist whiskers," clothed in frontier garb, and mounted on a "magnificent steed." The *Yakima Herald* added that members of the legislature said that the only fault they found with the picture of the horse "was that a certain part of the animal's anatomy was astride of him."

In Freeman's remaining years, he was subjected to another series of painful, and at times humiliating, reverses. His three older sons left him in bitterness; his second wife died in 1897, leaving

Freeman as the "Red Horse Candidate" in his second unsuccessful campaign for the U.S. Senate

two young children. He was married for a third time on 11 July 1900 to Mary Rose Genevieve Whitaker of St. Paul, Minnesota. He faced a series of new lawsuits, including one involving a partnership with a son, Miller Freeman, who had established a farm publication in Seattle. He returned to his own farm publication, and lobbied in behalf of federal development of irrigation in the Yakima Valley. Although he was overshadowed by the more influential W. W. Robertson of the *Yakima Republic*, he is accorded some credit for achieving state enabling legislation in 1906 which allowed federal intervention in irrigation to ward off private wildcat schemes.

Although he did not have the support of community leaders, Freeman hoped to use his activity in behalf of federal irrigation and good roads to succeed United States Senator Samuel H. Piles, who announced that he would retire when his term

expired in 1911. The Washington legislature still named senators, but a preferential primary was scheduled for September 1910. As early as September 1909, Freeman, at age sixty-six, addressed the announcement of his Republican candidacy to the "Freemen" of Washington in a statement which read like Horatio Vattel's autobiography. As he reminded voters that he had "blazed the trail for the vanguard of civilization across the western two-thirds of America," he distributed to the press copies of the handbill announcing his 1869 lecture at Culpeper. In the election, in which 117,633 votes were cast for eight Republican candidates, Freeman polled 1,975 votes or 1.67 percent of the Republican vote cast. Still not discouraged, he announced his candidacy for the position of mayor of North Yakima shortly before his seventy-second birthday in 1914. Echoing the rhetoric of contemporary Progressives and muckrakers, he directed his campaign against the incumbent amidst charges of trusts, police protection for prostitutes and gamblers, and lack of "betterment" for the people. The incumbent mayor did lose the election in a field of four candidates, but the old Red Horse Candidate polled only 158 votes, four percent of the total.

Within eleven weeks Freeman was dead, succumbing on 7 February 1915 to Bright's disease. In delivering a eulogy, a friend of Freeman's stated that many thousands of homesteaders and their descendants owed their prosperity to Freeman's engaging and convincing depiction of the opportunities that awaited settlers in the West. Freeman did not share in his readers' prosperity. The settlers spent years developing their claims, helping to weave a deep social fabric in their communities. Freeman was unwilling or unable to share in this role, a victim of a restlessness born in the freedom which Horatio Vattel first found in Jim Bridger's country. He had sought financial security, but, unlike some frontier editors, he was temperamentally unsuited to pay the price necessary for founding a community publishing dynasty. However, although Freeman's agricultural publication in North Yakima did not result in the personal success he sought, his columns did tie together a statewide community of farmers and ranchers, affording them information about their varied interests. The eventual success of the *Washington Farmer* through successive owners attests to the need which Freeman recognized and which his publication first fulfilled.

Biographies:
Elizabeth Wright, *Independence in All Things, Neu-*

trality in Nothing (San Francisco: Miller Freeman, 1973);

Thomas H. Heuterman, *Movable Type: Biography of Legh R. Freeman* (Ames: Iowa State University Press, 1979).

Papers:

The major repository of Freeman's early newspa- pers is the Bancroft Library at the University of California, Berkeley. Family letters are in the James Lawson Kemper file of the Alderman Library Manuscripts Department at the University of Virginia, Charlottesville.

Henry George

(2 September 1839-29 October 1897)

Leonard W. Lanfranco
University of South Carolina

MAJOR POSITIONS HELD: Managing editor, *San Francisco Times* (1867); managing editor, *San Francisco Chronicle* (1868); editor, *Oakland Transcript* (1869); editor, *Sacramento Reporter* (1870); editor, *San Francisco Evening Post* (1871-1875); editor and publisher, *Standard* (1887-1891).

SELECTED BOOKS: *The Subsidy Question and the Democratic Party* (San Francisco, 1871);

Our Land and Land Policy, National and State (San Francisco: White & Bauer, 1871);

Progress and Poverty (New York: Lovell, 1879; Middleton, U.K.: J. Bagot, 1879);

Social Problems (Chicago & New York: Belford, Clarke, 1883; London: Kegan Paul, Trench, 1884);

Protection or Free Trade (New York: H. George, 1886; London: Kegan Paul, Trench, 1886);

Perplexed Philosopher (New York: Webster, 1892; London: Kegan Paul, Trench, Trübner, 1893);

Science of Political Economy (Chicago & New York: Continental, 1897; London: Kegan Paul, Trench, Trübner, 1898).

Although known principally as a political economist, Henry George began his public career as a journalist. His newspaper experience gave him the opportunity to focus his economic theories, as well as a platform by which to bring them initially to the public's attention. George, even after he had left active journalism, continued to write for newspa- pers and magazines in order to disseminate his pro- gram of social reform.

During the last years of the nineteenth century George ranked as an equal with such diverse think- ers as George Bernard Shaw, Karl Marx, Leo Tolstoy, and Sun Yat-sen. His writings were influ- ential, yet not lasting; his theories were heavily de- bated, yet not enacted; his political campaigns were strongly supported, yet he was not elected to public office. In spite of these failings, George remains an important character in American political, economic, and journalistic life.

Born in Philadelphia on 2 September 1839, George was the second child of Richard Samuel Henry and Catherine Platt Vallace George. His father was a book publisher for the Protestant Episcopal church. George grew up in a lower-middle-class, Democratic, and religiously conservative family. As a youth, he was influenced more by his grandfather, Richard George, a noted and prosperous sea captain, than by his father. George left school at thirteen in order to help his father, whose business had not prospered. After several menial jobs, George went to sea at age fifteen. Returning home fourteen months later, he began working as an apprentice typesetter for a printer. Restless and still searching for a career, he sailed as ship's storekeeper to San Francisco in 1857. For the next several years he alternated between exploring for gold and working as a typesetter in California.

In 1861, shortly after his twenty-first birthday, George joined five other young printers in buying the *San Francisco Evening Journal*. The venture proved unsuccessful, and George, who married Annie Fox in 1861, moved to Sacramento to set type for the *Union*. He returned to San Francisco in 1864 and, with a partner, repurchased the *Evening Journal*.

In 1865 the *Journal* was again unsuccessful; however, George published a fanciful article, "A Plea for the Supernatural," in the *Californian*, a weekly magazine to which Mark Twain and Bret Harte were contributors. The article did not bring him fame, but it was an early indication of his writing ability.

While working for the *Alta California* as a typesetter, George wrote an editorial for the paper regarding the assassination of Abraham Lincoln. The unsolicited article caught the editor's attention, and he asked George for additional pieces. Planning to send articles back to the paper, George joined an 1865 expedition to fight for Mexican liberation against Napoleon III and Archduke Maximilian; George was to be a lieutenant in the small company of Americans. The expedition was stopped by the United States government in San Francisco harbor.

Following the aborted expedition, George returned to a typesetting career, first for the California State Printing Office in Sacramento, and then, in September 1866, for the *San Francisco Times*. The *Times* editor, James McClatchy, who would later found a chain of California newspapers (*Sacramento Bee*, *Fresno Bee*, *Modesto Bee*), encouraged George to write editorials for the paper while continuing to work as a typesetter. Seven months later George became managing editor.

During the next year George gained experience and maturity as a writer. His editorials dealt with free trade, public franchises, women's rights, and the military. In an October 1868 *Overland Monthly* article, "What the Railroads Will Bring Us," George enunciated his developing thoughts on economics: "Those who have land, mines, established businesses, special abilities of certain kinds, will become richer for it and find increased opportunities; those who have only their own labor will become poorer, and find it harder to get ahead."

In late 1868 George joined Charles de Young's new *San Francisco Chronicle* as managing editor, but in a disagreement with de Young over policy, he left after only a few weeks. Shortly after leaving the *Chronicle* George was hired by the *San Francisco Herald* to journey to New York to seek an Associated Press franchise for the paper. The *Herald*, a newly revived Democratic newspaper, had been refused membership by the wire service because of objections by San Francisco AP members.

After failing to obtain the Associated Press service for the *Herald*, George joined his family in Philadelphia, where he began his own news service for the *Herald*. The San Francisco Associated Press members did not like George's indirect competition with their own wire service, and they were able to pressure Western Union, the only transcontinental telegraph service, to deny George use of the Philadelphia wire. George moved to New York, but Western Union raised its transmission rates to such a high level, while lowering AP's, that George and the *Herald* soon ceased the news service. George returned to San Francisco to set type and write editorials for the *San Francisco Evening Bulletin*.

George moved across the bay in 1869 to the *Oakland Transcript*, where he served as editor. George's contributions to the *Transcript* were not of great importance; however, while editor, he developed the basic thesis of his economic and tax program.

In February 1870 Governor Henry H. Haight asked George to return to the state capital to become editor of the *Sacramento Reporter*, the chief Democratic party newspaper. During the next nine months George used his position to editorialize against graft and corruption. His most regular target was the Central Pacific Railroad's request for further government subsidies. So effective were George's attacks that the railroad surreptitiously purchased the newspaper. George, rather than accept control by the Central Pacific, resigned and returned to San Francisco.

During the next several months George produced two pamphlets. The first, *The Subsidy Question and the Democratic Party*, was widely circulated and gave him name recognition throughout the state. The second pamphlet, *Our Land and Land Policy*, had a circulation of less than 1,000; however, it contained the first statement of his Single Tax theory. This theory, to which he would devote the rest of his life, dealt with the relationship between labor and land utilization.

In 1871 George joined William Hinton in founding the *San Francisco Evening Post*. This penny daily, unlike most of the other newspapers with which George had been affiliated, was not aligned with the Democratic party. The *Post* editorialized regarding a variety of causes: George advocated better working conditions for workers and reported on the success of the eight-hour law in Australia; because of his earlier ties to the sea, he strongly supported sailor's rights. Causes such as prison reform, treatment of alcoholics, women's rights, and the monopoly of the railroads were subjects for both news and editorial coverage. The *Post* began a Sunday newspaper, the *Morning Ledger*, in 1875. The *Ledger* contained news, editorials, theater and book criticisms, and was one of the first Sunday illustrated publications. In spite of this innovation, the paper was not successful financially; George lost both papers to the mortgage holder in November 1875.

During the next five years George wrote and lectured on reform topics. He was supported by a political appointment as state inspector of gas meters, which provided a modest salary and gave him the opportunity to pursue his favorite topic, tax reform. In 1879 George's keystone book, *Progress and Poverty*, was published; George had to finance the publication himself. In 1880 D. Appleton and Company agreed to republish the book from George's plates; eventually *Progress and Poverty* would sell more than 2,000,000 copies. Later that year George moved to New York in order to better advocate his social and economic theories.

For the remaining seventeen years of his life, other than one brief excursion, George did not practice journalism. He did, however, use magazines, books, and newspapers to disseminate his ideas; and he never lost his love of newspapering. In later life, according to Albert J. Nock, "facing the question whether to put his elder son into a newspaper office or send him to Harvard College, he decided against Harvard, saying that if the lad went there, he would learn a great deal that he must afterwards spend time on unlearning; whereas 'going into newspaper work, you will come in touch with the practical world, will be getting a profession and learning to make yourself useful.' "

George's move to New York marked the beginning of a more active political life. Even though he had run for the California State Assembly in 1870, he had generally been in a supportive role to other candidates. In an eleven-year period he ran three times for two major offices: mayor of New York (1886 and 1897) and secretary of New York State (1887). In none of these efforts was he successful—though in his 1886 campaign he came in second, ahead of Theodore Roosevelt.

Lecture trips to Europe occupied much of George's energies: beginning in 1881 he made six visits to spread his doctrine. While no European country adopted the Single Tax program, George was probably more respected abroad than at home. His theory, though not socialistic in nature, was seen by some as being in unity with the growing liberal trends in Europe.

George returned to newspapering on a part-time basis in 1887. He began a weekly newspaper, the *Standard*, and served as its editor and publisher until its demise in 1891. He advocated good writing and believed "that English should be written so as to be understood by even the least literate reader. . . . His rules for expression were few—'Make short sentences, avoid adjectives, use small words.' "

In addition to the *Standard*, which gave him a voice in New York, and his lecture tours, he found time to produce four more books before his death. These books expanded on the Single Tax theory which George proposed as a plan to end poverty by shifting taxes which were levied on labor and capital to the rental value of property. The theory is exemplified by such formulations as: "Taxation of land at a higher rate than the improvements thereon; full or partial exemption of improvements—the last revenue being made up by an increased levy on the land; a surtax on absentee land-ownership; in the effort to reduce speculation, a high rate of tax on the projects derived from land sales." Applications of his ideas, though not all directly attributable to George's influence, can be found today in Australia, New Zealand, Canada, South Africa, Denmark, and elsewhere.

George's death, on 29 October 1897, did not bring an end to his importance. Indeed, a major study of his theories was published in 1979. With a career that began as a typesetter and newspaperman in San Francisco and ended as an internationally known political economist, George remains an enduring part of journalistic history.

References:

Robert V. Anderson, ed., *Critics of Henry George* (Cranbury, N.J.: Fairleigh Dickinson University Press, 1979);

Steven B. Cord, *Henry George: Dreamer or Realist?* (Philadelphia: University of Pennsylvania Press, 1965);

Anna George de Mille, *Henry George: Citizen of the World* (Chapel Hill: University of North Carolina Press, 1950);

George R. Geiger, *The Philosophy of Henry George* (New York: Macmillan, 1933);

Albert J. Nock, *Henry George: An Essay* (New York: Morrow, 1939).

Papers:
Henry George's papers are at the New York Public Library.

Henry W. Grady

Ernest C. Hynds
University of Georgia

BIRTH: Athens, Georgia, 24 May 1850, to William S. and Ann Eliza Gartrell Grady.

EDUCATION: B.A., University of Georgia, 1868; University of Virginia, 1868-1869.

MARRIAGE: 5 October 1871 to Julia King; children: Henry King (changed to Henry Woodfin, Jr., after father's death), Augusta (Gussie) King.

MAJOR POSITIONS HELD: Associate editor, *Rome Courier* (1869-1870); editor, *Rome Commercial* (1870-1872); editor, *Atlanta Herald* (1873-1875); correspondent, *Augusta Constitutionalist*, *New York Herald*, *Philadelphia Times*, *Cincinnati Enquirer*, *Chicago Inter Ocean*, *Detroit Free Press*, and *Louisville Courier-Journal* (1876-1880); managing editor, *Atlanta Constitution* (1880-1889).

DEATH: Atlanta, Georgia, 23 December 1889.

BOOKS: *Anniversary Celebration of the New England Society in the City of New York, December 22, 1886* ("The New South") (New York: New England Society, 1886);

Race Problem: Address Delivered at the Annual Banquet of the Boston Merchants Association, December 12, 1889 (Boston: Boston Merchants Association, 1889);

Life and Labors of Henry W. Grady: His Speeches, Writings, etc. . . . Written and Compiled under the Immediate Supervision of the Publishers, from the Most

Culver Pictures

Reliable Sources (Atlanta: H. C. Hudgins, 1890);

The New South. By Henry W. Grady, with a Character Sketch of Henry W. Grady by Oliver Dyer (New York: Bonner, 1890);

The New South and Other Addresses, with a biography of Grady by Edna H. L. Turpin (New York:

Maynard, Merrill, 1904);
The Complete Orations and Speeches of Henry W. Grady,
     edited by Edwin Du Bois Shurter (New York:
     Hinds, Noble & Eldredge/Austin, Texas:
     South-west, 1910).

Henry W. Grady earned national acclaim for his work as a newspaperman and his tireless efforts to develop a new and better South after the Civil War. He set a model for reporters in his thorough and resourceful coverage of events such as the Hayes-Tilden election dispute in Florida in 1876 and the Charleston earthquake in 1886. He served a public need through his interpretive and insightful accounts of political and economic affairs, especially in the South. He pioneered in the development of the now-popular interview technique. Through his work as managing editor, he helped develop the *Atlanta Constitution* as the South's standard newspaper. Most important, through the columns of the *Constitution* and the lecture halls of New York and Boston, he advocated national reconciliation through the development of a New South based on industry and diversification of agriculture. Although the New South he envisioned did not come into full bloom until after World War II, Grady provided the spadework for change in the 1880s.

Henry Woodfin Grady was born 24 May 1850 in Athens, Georgia, to William S. and Ann Eliza Gartrell Grady. His father, whose Irish ancestors had come to America about 1700, was a successful businessman with a mercantile store, sawmill, and other interests. Besides material benefits, the young Grady received from him a sense of idealism, perseverance, and strong devotion to family. Grady's mother, of French Huguenot ancestry, was a happy, outgoing woman who loved people and was devoted to her family. From her, Grady received a joyous, enthusiastic outlook on life that buoyed him on many occasions. Both parents were active members of the Methodist church, and Grady was reared in that tradition.

From an early age, Grady showed an interest in communication. The family lived near his father's store, and he spent many hours there talking with all sorts of persons. His first publication came at age seven when the *Visitor*, a Methodist Sunday school magazine, published a letter he had sent in. He was educated at home by his mother until he was nine; then he entered one of the private schools that served in lieu of public education in those days. He soon became known for his intelligence, leadership, and love of reading. At the age of eleven he worked for several months in a bookstore for the privilege of reading the books when there was no work to do.

The teen years were exciting and productive for Grady, but they were not without much sadness. His father, who had organized and equipped a company to fight in the Civil War, died in 1864 of wounds received at Petersburg. A sister died in infancy, two other sisters died of scarlet fever, and a brother died of pneumonia, all in the space of only three years. Athens was not on General Sherman's path to the sea, and it escaped major devastation from the war; the people did, however, suffer privations during the war, and the college buildings were occupied for a time by federal troops. The Grady family had to sell some property to assure educations for Henry and his remaining brother and sister, but they were not financially destroyed as were many other Southern families.

In the fall of 1865, at age fifteen, Grady enrolled in a private school for boys planning to enter the University of Georgia; and while there, he made his first public speech. In January 1866, when the university reopened, he was admitted to the sophomore class. He soon joined Phi Kappa, one of the two literary societies that contributed much to a university education through their debates and discussions. In 1868 Grady was named commencement orator for Phi Kappa, and his address, "Castles in the Air," touched on his vision of the future of the South. As for his studies, he was only fair in math and science, but he excelled in history, literature, and rhetoric.

When Grady was graduated from the University of Georgia, he was only eighteen and had not decided on a career. He may have leaned toward public affairs since he had become intrigued with postwar politics in Georgia and the nation, and he determined to spend a year of postgraduate study in public speaking. Although many encouraged him to seek a master's degree at the University of Georgia, he decided instead to attend the University of Virginia, which then was considered the training ground for Southern leaders. He may also have been influenced in his choice by the fact that Charlottesville was much closer than Athens to Philadelphia, where his childhood sweetheart, Julia King, was attending a seminary.

At the University of Virginia, Grady studied modern languages, history, literature, and rhetoric and became an active member of one of the university's literary societies. He distinguished himself in debate and was deeply disappointed when not elected final orator. He learned from that experience, however, that in politics the best-qualified

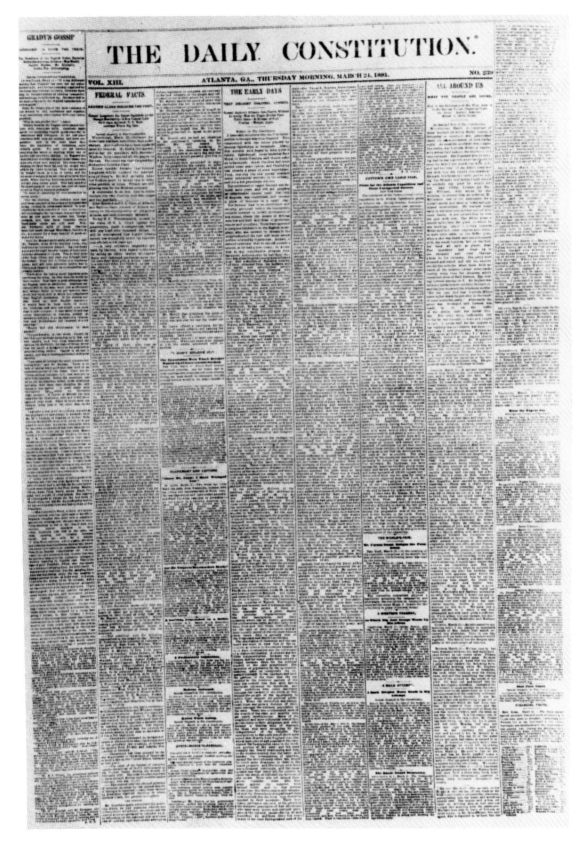

Front page of the Atlanta Constitution *before Grady reduced it from eight columns to six. An article by Grady appears in its usual place—the first column.*

person does not always get the prize. Grady's chief opponent for the honor declined his challenge to debate. A few of his rival's supporters switched their votes because of the refusal, but they were not enough to change the results. The incident did have an impact, however: the university faculty the next year abolished the election system for choosing orators. Losing the election may have been a fortunate development, for it caused Grady to turn away from politics as a possible career and left him open to the call of journalism. He had written such a humorous and descriptive letter about Virginia and Virginians to a friend at the *Atlanta Constitution* that the editor had printed it and invited him to write another. When he returned home from college, he was invited to cover events for the *Constitution*. Dr. Raymond B. Nixon suggests in his definitive biography that the two letters to the *Constitution* turned Grady's career plans to journalism.

In late August 1869 Grady was asked to represent the *Constitution* on a press excursion sponsored by the state-owned Western and Atlantic Railroad, which connected Atlanta with Chattanooga. The newsmen were accompanied on the trip by Rufus Bullock, the state's Reconstruction governor. The avowed purpose of the outing was to provide information about iron and coal deposits in northwest Georgia and to encourage the press to support action for their development. Grady described the trip for the *Constitution* in a series of semihumorous dispatches that were noteworthy for their descriptive powers. But when the newsmen adopted a resolution thanking the governor for accompanying them, Grady accused Bullock of making the trip to barter patronage for newspaper support. The governor denied the charge, but Grady stuck to his guns. The young newsman's involvement in Georgia politics had begun.

One of the stops on the Western and Atlantic trip was Rome, Georgia, where Grady's uncle, Henry Gartrell, lived. Through him Grady had met the editor of the *Rome Courier*, and while on the excursion Grady wrote a story for the *Courier*. In it he urged the people of the area to put politics aside and join in the development of natural resources, a theme he was to repeat and expand in later years. Melville Dwinell, editor of the weekly and triweekly, was so impressed by Grady that he hired him to become associate editor of the *Courier*, starting in September. In a salutatory notice, Grady wrote that he was young and without editorial judgment or experience but hoped that his enthusiasm and hard work would make up for these deficiencies. He said he entered the editorial ranks of the state with ill

feeling toward none but with kindness toward all. In that same issue, he wrote his first editorial; like others that followed, it was critical of Governor Bullock. When Grady was not writing about state politics or local matters, he occasionally expressed his views about journalism. On one occasion he praised the courage and independence of the Democratic *New York World* for exposing corruption in its own party. He attacked the whole idea of party newspapers which had been popular in the first half of the nineteenth century but had become less important with the development of the penny press and the government printing office. "No great journal can afford to be a mere party follower," he wrote. "No journal can become great, or remain great, as a party hack. The journalist has a grander function than to be merely a flag-bearer."

In late July 1870, after ten months' experience at the *Courier*, Grady decided to buy his own newspaper and purchased the *Rome Commercial*, another triweekly. Dwinell was inclined to be more cautious than Grady, and the young editor wanted the power to write as he felt called. Joel Chandler Harris, in his biography of Grady, suggests that he bought the paper within a few hours after Dwinell refused to run an editorial denouncing some type of political or financial ring in Rome. The *Courier* maintained that a meeting which had been called at the city hall was not the action of a ring or clique but a movement of Floyd County citizens who opposed the continuation of Radical rule. It appears that Grady may have wanted to take a stronger position against Governor Bullock and the Radicals than Dwinell thought proper at the time.

During his tenure as editor and proprietor of the *Commercial*, Grady demonstrated ability both as an editor and as a businessman. As an editor, he continued his attacks on Governor Bullock and his policies, and he sought to promote the development of the Rome area. Bullock eventually left the state to avoid impeachment when a Democratic legislature was elected. As a businessman, Grady showed considerable enterprise in obtaining advertising. In May 1871 he bought Rome's third newspaper, the *Rome Daily* and its *Weekly* and claimed for the *Commercial* the largest circulation of any publication in the area.

While working in Rome, Grady continued to correspond with and visit Julia King. In October 1871, the two were married at the Methodist church in Athens. Grady and Julia had been attracted to each other since childhood, and Grady once remarked that he fell out of his baby carriage trying to reach into Julia's carriage for her hand. He had first proposed marriage when he was fourteen and she was twelve, and neither had ever seriously considered anyone else. Julia was the source of great strength and comfort for Grady in the years that followed.

In the early fall of 1872 Grady and some friends tried unsuccessfully to buy a half interest in the *Atlanta Constitution*. Those negotiations served to increase his interest in the city, and in October he bought a one-third interest in the *Atlanta Herald*. He sold the *Commercial* to Dwinell, and he and Julia moved to Atlanta in November.

The *Atlanta Daily Herald* had been started in August 1872 by Alexander St. Clair-Abrams, a veteran newspaperman who had worked on several Southern papers before the war and as an editorial writer for the *New York Herald* before moving to Atlanta. The paper was sensational in approach with a considerable emphasis on crime news, perhaps to compete more favorably with the better-established *Constitution*. The paper was readable and courageous in its editorial stands, but it was unable to achieve economic stability during its more than three years of existence. Outspoken editorial policies which offended some creditors sealed the *Herald*'s fate.

During his first year with the *Herald*, Grady served primarily as business manager. Although he, St. Clair-Abrams, and Robert A. Alston, who had encouraged Grady to become involved, each owned a third interest in the paper, St. Clair-Abrams continued to dominate its editorial policies. This was frustrating for Grady, who at times was drawn into St. Clair-Abrams's disputes when he would have preferred to be aligned with a different point of view. The situation improved in November 1873 when St. Clair-Abrams withdrew from the operation to pursue other interests. Alston took over the business side of the paper, and Grady became editor, leaving him free to support candidates and issues he selected. He urged adoption of home rule legislation that would eliminate the glut of local bills in the legislature, advocated tax-supported education, and encouraged aid for the poor and destitute. He agreed that the world would be better without alcoholic beverages but questioned efforts to stop misuse of them through prohibition legislation.

As early as March 1874, Grady began to discuss his ideas about a New South based on industrial development and diversification of agriculture. He said that factories and farms were both essential to prosperity and endorsed a plan to build Atlanta's first cotton mill. He sought to encourage the immigration of good capitalists by praising Georgia's resources through special trade editions that were distributed in the Northern states. He stressed the need for diversification in agriculture because the state already had gone bankrupt once under the one-crop system. He said the New South needed men of ability and enterprise, even including those who had been associated with the carpetbag rule of the early postwar period.

Grady continually stressed the importance of a free press if the democratic system were to function properly. To help assure that freedom, he adopted a policy which forbade his employees to accept free theater tickets, railroad passes, or other gifts. "Above all human agencies, the press should be independent, fearless, truthful," Grady wrote. "It is the great director of public opinion, the guide of the people, and hence there rests upon it a fearful responsibility. It should, therefore, be above all temptation, so far, at least, as it is possible to place it on that elevated ground." He said the offer of a free ticket should be regarded by a journalist or a public official as an insult and indignity.

The *Herald*'s financial problems, engendered by the national panic of 1873, continued in 1874 and 1875. The situation was improved somewhat in April 1874 when I. W. Avery resigned as editor of the *Constitution* to become a partner in the *Herald*, but Avery remained only a year before retiring for health reasons. Alston bought his one-third interest in the paper and, with two-thirds ownership, assumed control. He became president and Grady took the title of managing editor. Despite its financial problems, the *Herald* continued to attack politicians with whom it disagreed. Unfortunately, some of these people had control of, or influence over, the credit institutions that held the newspaper's mortgages, and in an apparent reprisal, they foreclosed. Grady and Alston obtained sufficient funds to publish a few issues of an *Atlanta Courier* in February and March 1876, and Grady got backing to publish five issues of a weekly *Sunday Telegram* later that year, but both papers died for lack of money.

After the last of his three Atlanta ventures failed, Grady obtained employment as Georgia correspondent for the *New York Herald* to help support his expanding family: a son, Henry King, had been born 6 June 1873 and a daughter, Augusta King, had been born 16 August 1875. Writing for space rates did not provide enough income, however, and Grady soon sought regular employment. Evan P. Howell, who recently had bought a half interest in the *Atlanta Constitution*, hired him to write for that paper in October 1876. Grady convinced Howell that he should also employ Joel Chandler Harris, who was living in Atlanta because of a yellow fever outbreak in Savannah, and the three men together did much to advance the fortunes of the newspaper. Grady continued to serve as correspondent for the *Herald*, and in time provided similar services for other newspapers.

One of the most significant stories Grady reported for the *Constitution* and the *Herald* in the late 1870s involved vote fraud in Florida during the 1876 presidential election. The contest between Republican Rutherford B. Hayes and Democrat Samuel J. Tilden ultimately turned on the outcome of disputed votes in Louisiana, South Carolina, and Florida. Hayes needed the electoral votes in all three states to win, and—thanks to a partisan election commission—got them. Although the hearings in Florida brought out conclusive evidence of Republican fraud, the three-member canvassing board, which included two Republicans, declared Hayes the winner. Similar conclusions were reached in the other two states and by the congressional commission, which had eight Republican and seven Democratic members. The Democrats accepted the verdict, but only after Hayes pledged to remove remaining federal troops from the South and give the Southerners a chance to control their own governments. Grady reported extensively on the hearings in Florida and concluded that Tilden would have won there but for the frauds and the biased vote counters. He later got stories from persons who admitted their participation in the Florida frauds, but there was a general inclination to let the matter die because of the agreement which benefited the South. A year after Hayes's term ended, Grady recalled the incident as the ugliest chapter of American history. "It was worse than war, and more odious than treason," he wrote in the *Constitution*. "As it was the first crime of its sort in the history of the republic it will be the last. Never again will the American people be in the temper to submit to so flagrant an outrage. It was inexorably proved before the case was decided that an Alachua county politician and a negro, by stuffing one ballot box, actually stifled the voice of fifty millions of people and reversed the edicts of thirty-eight sovereign states. This juggling was afterwards confessed by the man who did it. And yet the verdict stood for four years, and the dire stress for peace enforced submission to a fraud that fixed the character of one administration."

During 1877 and 1878, Grady covered various events, including the Georgia constitutional convention of 1877, and also began his career as a lecturer. His biographer Raymond B. Nixon says

his speaking style was similar to his writing style: there was a considerable emotional quality in both. By July 1878 Grady was doing so well with his free-lance writing that he gave up his lectures and exchanged his regular job at the *Constitution* for a space-rate agreement. He did, however, with the help of Joel Chandler Harris, publish a weekly review called the *Sunday Gazette* from October 1878 until late the next year; the *Gazette* included various features, reviews, and editorials. But the freedom provided by free-lancing enabled Grady to travel and to pioneer the interview story technique. Among those he interviewed were Jefferson Davis, the former president of the Confederacy, and General William T. Sherman, the U.S. military commander who had burned Atlanta and brought victory in the South. Papers for which Grady corresponded included the *New York Herald*, *Philadelphia Times*, *Cincinnati Enquirer*, *Chicago Inter Ocean*, *Detroit Free Press*, and *Louisville Courier-Journal*. After critics questioned the use of the interview technique, Grady defended it in a front-page article in the *Constitution*. "The system of interviewing gave more dignity to a report," Grady wrote. "It brought the person interviewed and the public face to face. It enabled the correspondent to preserve the flavor of the great man's individuality, and carry his subtle characteristics into print. By leading him from the single thread of narrative into suggestive by-ways and turn-outs, all the minor lights and shades of information could be brought out."

In May 1880 Grady borrowed $20,000 from Cyrus W. Field and bought a one-fourth interest in the *Constitution*. He was named managing editor, but had responsibilities in both news and editorial areas. During the early months on the new job, he devoted much effort to the 1880 elections, in which the paper supported the national Democratic ticket. That ticket lost, in part perhaps because of prosperity in much of the country, and Grady turned his attention again to economics. He described the plight of the many Southern farmers who were perpetually in debt, and urged diversification of agriculture as one way to remedy farm problems. At the same time, he cited the area's potential for industrial development: he said it possessed cheap labor, land, water power, and fuel; had an unequaled climate; and seemed ideal for investment. To help reach Northern capitalists with his ideas of Southern development, Grady spent the winter of 1880-1881 in New York. While there he wrote several times a week for the *Constitution* and also wrote for the *New York Herald* and other papers. "Fast mails, small farms, colonies of immigrants, internal

Manuscript page of Grady's newspaper copy. His handwriting was so notoriously bad that he once received a letter addressed only to "Henry W. Crookedmark, Atlanta" (Grady Collection, Emory University).

improvements, new industries—these are the channels through which the south can command the respect and sympathy of the north—and through which she can best command her self respect," Grady wrote.

Throughout much of 1881 Grady worked on the planning and implementation of the First International Cotton Exposition, which was held in Atlanta in the fall. The exposition ran for three months, attracted 286,000 persons, and made $20,000. Its purpose was to stimulate interest in the South's industrial and agricultural resources and encourage Northern investors to help develop those resources. Grady played key roles in planning the event and in obtaining publicity for it in Northern newspapers and magazines. After the exposition, Grady renewed his attacks on the South's farm system and its absentee landlords. "Nothing can be worse for the south than the tenant system," he wrote. "Under this system the south can only grow poorer, while alien greed insists that the land shall be robbed of the last possible yield."

Beginning in 1881, Grady also introduced to the *Constitution* some of the New Journalism techniques he had observed while in New York. The number of columns on a page was reduced from eight to six, but the number of pages was increased from four to eight, and within a few years even more. The type face was changed, the contents reorganized, and coverage expanded. In time, Grady also developed a system of correspondents in Georgia counties and in key cities throughout the nation; when Congress was in session, he employed a correspondent in Washington. Grady personally wrote interpretive news articles, which frequently were printed in the upper-left-hand corner of page one, as well as some of the editorials. N. P. T. Finch and Joel Chandler Harris also wrote editorials. In addition, Grady revitalized the *Weekly Constitution*, which included not only stories from the daily but also features and special advertisements.

Although he played an active role in public affairs, including political campaigns, Grady stuck by his earlier decision to be a journalist rather than a politician. In 1882 he wrote that after thirteen years of service, he had had no cause to regret his choice. "On the contrary," he wrote, "I have seen the field of journalism so enlarged, its possibilities so widened, and its influence so extended that I have come to believe earnestly that no man—no matter what his calling, his elevation or his opportunity—can equal in dignity, honor and usefulness the journalist who comprehends his position, fairly measures his duties and gives himself entirely and unselfishly to

his work." He said that journalism was a demanding profession that required all the energies of those involved; there was no time nor was it appropriate to combine journalism with other careers. "As for me, my ambition is a simple one. I shall be satisfied with the labors of my life, if, when those labors are over my son, looking abroad upon a grander and better Georgia—a Georgia that has filled the destiny God intended for her—when her towns and cities are hives of industry, and her countrysides the exhaustless fields from which their stores are drawn—when every stream dances on its way to the music of spindles, and every forest echoes back the roar of a passing train—when her valleys smile with abundant harvests, and from her hillsides come the tinkling of bells as her herds and flocks go forth from their folds—when more than two million people proclaim her perfect independence, and bless her with their love, I shall be more than content, I say, if my son, looking upon such scenes as these can stand up and say, 'My father bore a part in this work, and his name lives in the memory of this people.' "

Beginning in 1883, Grady took an increased interest in the editorial page, although he continued to express his views in columns and signed interpretive articles and the paper had two other full-time editorial writers. He used the editorial page more often in his efforts to influence political campaigns such as the 1886 governor's race, when he helped get former senator John B. Gordon elected. He said that editorials needed to be brief and pointed to be effective, and he made use of human interest there as well as in his articles and columns. In one format or another, Grady engaged in numerous campaigns, many in some way related to his continuing interest in the development of a New South. He encouraged the establishment of a Georgia School of Technology to serve the South's new industrial development, and urged that it be located in Atlanta near the principal industries. Unlike some other Southern editors, he favored the use of some form of tariff because he thought it would be beneficial to the growth of Southern industry. He also fostered public service campaigns, such as raising funds for a new YMCA or promoting the development of boxing and baseball.

In the area of civil rights, Grady strongly advocated educational opportunities and legal rights for blacks, but not social equality. He appeared to favor the idea of separate but equal facilities. In the fall of 1883, in an editorial on the Supreme Court's rejection of the Civil Rights Act of 1875, he suggested that the line had been drawn just where it should be, where nature drew it and justice commends:

> The negro is entitled to his freedom, his franchise, to full and equal legal rights, to his share in the privileges of the government and to such share in its administration as his integrity and intelligence will justify. This he ought to have and he must have. Social equality he can never have. He does not have it in the north, or in the east, or in the west. On one pretext or another he is kept out of hotels, theaters, schools and restaurants, north as well as south.

> The truth is, the negro does not want social equality. He prefers his own hotels, his own societies, his own military companies, his own place in the theater. He is uncomfortable and ill at ease when he is forced anywhere else. Even on the railroads he prefers his own car, if he can be secure from the intrusion of disorderly persons. It is best, for his sake, as well as for general peace and harmony, that he should in all these things have separate accommodation.

Had Grady lived seventy-five or eighty years later,

he might have taken a more liberal position in regard to freedom of choice for blacks. His successors at the *Constitution*, Ralph McGill and Eugene Patterson, spoke out strongly for blacks in the 1960s. But Grady lived in the 1880s, and his call for justice and opportunity, separate but equal, may have seemed radical to many in the South who had just recently been subjects of an unjust Reconstruction.

During the middle 1880s, Grady continued his efforts to make the *Constitution* one of the nation's best newspapers. His great ability as an organizer made him an effective executive and helped the *Constitution* achieve success in all areas of newspaper work. He knew how to promote the paper and increase its advertising and circulation as well as how to provide it with good news coverage and strong editorials. At times the paper was criticized for sensationalism in its crime coverage, and it did include many details, but Grady insisted that the people wanted the information and had a right to receive it. By 1888 the weekly *Atlanta Constitution* was one of the largest such newspapers in the country.

One outstanding example of the *Constitution*'s news coverage in the 1880s was provided by Grady himself. When an earthquake in late August 1886

Grady's home at what is now 529-533 Peachtree Street, Atlanta. The house has been replaced by a commercial building.

caused havoc in Charleston, South Carolina, and surrounding areas, Grady went to that city for the story. He personally surveyed the damage and interviewed authorities and victims, then wrote a series for the *Constitution* and other newspapers on what had happened and what was being done. He said the damage was far greater than that caused by the war in Atlanta and Columbia, and called upon the nation to help provide relief for the city and its people. Thousands responded to the call. The *Constitution* asserted that it had more extensive coverage than any other newspaper, and editors of newspapers that carried Grady's reports praised him for his descriptive accounts.

The exposure and praise Grady received for the Charleston earthquake story may have been a factor in his receiving an invitation to address the New England Society of New York in December 1886. Those in charge were aware of Grady's previous exhortations about the need for national reconciliation and the redevelopment of the South and felt it an appropriate time to invite him to speak on the New South. Since he was neither a politician nor a businessman, but a journalist who was nationally known, Grady seemed an ideal person to talk of national reconciliation from the Southern point of view. Moreover, he was an eloquent speaker who could stir the emotions as well as the minds of his listeners. He wrote his speeches in advance, but did not use notes in delivering them. Although he had some tendency to rhetoric, as did many speakers of that era, he made good use of humor and anecdotes, and he had a good rhythm in his delivery.

The "New South" speech was one of Grady's best and was generally praised in the North as well as the South. It helped establish him as the spokesman of the New South and provided further opportunities for him to take his message about what the New South should be to the nation. In the speech he effectively identified himself with his audience by describing General Sherman as an able man, though careless with matches, and praising Abraham Lincoln as the typical American. He emphasized that the South desired to let the war rest and enter a new era of peace and prosperity, and he described his vision of the New South with industry, diversified agriculture, and education. He said the people wanted to resolve the Negro problem with honor and equity. Grady was careful not to dishonor the old South, which he cited for its chivalric strength and grace, but he emphasized that because of new conditions there was a need for a New South: "The old South rested everything on slavery and agriculture, unconscious that these could neither give nor maintain healthy growth. The new South presents a perfect Democracy, the oligarchs leading in the popular movement—a social system compact and closely knitted, less splendid on the surface but stronger at the core—a hundred farms for every plantation, fifty homes for every palace, and a diversified industry that meets the complex needs of this complex age."

During much of 1887 and 1888, Grady remained busy improving and expanding the *Constitution* and fostering the development of his New South ideas in Atlanta. He helped plan and carry out the Piedmont Exhibition, which included President Cleveland among its visitors, in 1887, and he helped develop a Piedmont Chautauqua, or summer university, in 1888. The *Constitution* campaigned for numerous civic improvements, including paved streets, to accommodate the rapid growth of the city during the late 1880s. Grady took pride in the opening in 1888 of Georgia Tech, which he had recommended as a vital addition to the city and state.

As a result of his "New South" speech and other activities, Grady was mentioned by persons in both North and South as a possible running mate for President Cleveland in 1888, but the candidacy never materialized. Grady's chances of being offered the role may have been hurt by his protariff views and the fact that he took the losing prohibition side in Atlanta's wet-dry dispute. It is not certain that he would have accepted the nomination even if the party had decided to go with a Southerner; the vice-presidential role has not been noted for its productivity or influence. It seems more likely that Grady would have accepted a call to run for senator, an office with a platform, had one been forthcoming. But some of the political leaders he had helped previously, perhaps because of jealousy, chose not to encourage his candidacy, and he remained a spokesman without an office. His protectionist leanings might also have discouraged some from supporting him in that race. During the campaign, Grady again became active as a speaker. He expressed concern that the Republicans might again seek to maintain power through questionable laws aimed at the South, and he urged Southerners to unite behind the Democratic party. He acknowledged the disadvantages inherent in maintaining a one-party system but expressed the view that a divided South could be even worse. Were the whites to become divided, the balance of power would fall into the hands of former slaves, who did not have the experience or knowledge to handle it well. Grady reiterated his belief that blacks should be

Julia, Henry King, Augusta, and Henry W. Grady in 1888

guaranteed their rights as citizens and should be given educational opportunities, and reminded everyone that if the South were to be elevated the Negro must be elevated with it. But he expressed fear over the possibility that the country might return to the days when Republican-controlled Negroes provided the balance of power in Southern governments.

Considering his views and influence, it is not surprising that Grady was invited to Boston in late 1889 to discuss "The Race Problem in the South." Moderate Republicans as well as Democrats were concerned that the new Republican Congress might enact legislation that would establish federal supervision over all polling places in national elections and thus damage the hopes for achieving peaceful relations among the sections. All looked to Grady as a person who both understood the South's position and wanted reconciliation. Grady became ill before making the Boston trip and was advised by his doctor to postpone the engagement, but he went anyway and spoke in Boston and several other communities before returning home a gravely ill man with only a short time to live.

In his Boston speech he called upon other Americans to have patience and confidence in the Southerners and sympathy for their difficult situation. He reiterated his thankfulness that slavery was gone forever from American soil, but he pointed out that the former slaves remained to present a problem without precedent or parallel. He said the Northerners did not understand the Southerners' attitude toward the Negroes, that they could not comprehend or measure the love Southerners had for them. He called for fairness in considering problems that arose in the South; he said the violent outbursts that occurred there were no more significant or representative than similar incidents in the North. He argued that Negroes in the South were as well-off economically, legally, and in other ways as those in the North. At a subsequent dinner meeting, Grady—by then so hoarse he could hardly talk—discussed the progress that was being made in the South. He referred to an earlier speech he had made about a funeral in Pickens County when "the South didn't furnish a thing on earth for that funeral but the corpse and the hole in the ground." He said improvements had come: there was now a marble-cutting establishment within a hundred yards of the grave and woolen mills and iron factories nearby.

Grady's visit to Boston was widely acclaimed in both North and South, and a group of Georgians was on hand to meet his train when he returned to Atlanta. But he was by then too sick to greet them, and in a few days, on 23 December, he died at the age of thirty-nine of pneumonia complicated by pleurisy. One of his last statements, made to his mother, was reprinted in the *Constitution*: "If I die, I die serving the South, the land I love so well. Father fell in battle for it. I am proud to die talking for it." His funeral, one of the largest held in Atlanta to that time, was simple but impressive. One of several presiding ministers expressed the feelings of many when he said, "The sun has gone down at noon today."

Newspapers throughout the country praised Grady for his efforts to achieve national reconciliation and foster the development of a New South. Even some who had criticized his position on the race issue were inclined to say he probably had taken as advanced a stand as he could without cutting himself off from influence over his own people. Others praised his abilities as an orator or his contribution to the development of journalism at the *Constitution*. John Temple Graves said at a memorial service that Grady had died "literally loving a nation into peace."

Henry W. Grady was the leading orator in the South and one of the nation's most respected journalists at the time of his death. He was a resourceful reporter, a vivid writer, a pioneer of the interview technique, an astute editor, and a successful salesman of his newspaper and his community. Moreover, he was recognized as the symbol of a New South based on the development of industry, diversification of agriculture, and reconciliation with the national government. Raymond B. Nixon and others are clearly justified in referring to him as "the Spokesman of the New South."

Periodical Publications:

"Cotton and Its Kingdom," *Harper's New Monthly Magazine* (October 1881): 719-734;

"In Plain Black and White," *Century* (April 1885): 909-917;

"The New South," 6 articles, *New York Ledger* (16 November - 21 December 1889).

Biographies:

Joel Chandler Harris, *Life of Henry W. Grady, Including His Writings and Speeches* (New York: Cassell, 1890);

Gentry Dugat, *Life of Henry W. Grady* (Edinburg, Texas: Valley Printery, 1927);

Raymond B. Nixon, *Henry W. Grady: Spokesman of the New South* (New York: Russell & Russell, 1943).

References:

T. R. Crawford, "Early Home of Henry W. Grady," *New England Magazine*, 2 (June 1890): 425-436;

John Temple Graves II, "Henry W. Grady," *Atlanta Historical Bulletin*, 5 (January 1940): 23-31;

Clark Howell, "Henry W. Grady," *Chautauquan*, 5 (September 1895): 703-706;

James W. Lee, "Henry W. Grady, Editor, Orator, Man," *Arena*, 2 (June 1890): 9-23;

C. F. Lindsley, "Henry Woodfin Grady, Orator," *Quarterly Journal of Speech Education*, 6 (April 1920): 28-42;

Raymond B. Nixon, "Henry W. Grady, Reporter," *Journalism Quarterly*, 12 (December 1935): 341-356;

Jack Spalding, "Henry W. Grady," *Atlanta Historical Bulletin*, 2 (September 1937): 67;

Russell F. Terrell, *A Study of the Early Journalistic Writings of Henry W. Grady*, George Peabody College Contributions to Education, No. 39 (Nashville, Tenn., 1927);

John Donald Wade, "Henry W. Grady," *Southern Review*, 3 (Winter 1938): 479-509.

Papers:

The Henry W. Grady Collection, Emory University Library, Atlanta, contains letters, scrapbooks, manuscripts, diaries, and other materials; the Henry W. Grady Collection, University of Georgia Library, Athens, contains two scrapbooks and other materials.

Murat Halstead

(2 September 1829-2 July 1908)

Joseph P. McKerns
Southern Illinois University

MAJOR POSITIONS HELD: Editor, *Cincinnati Commercial* (1865-1883); editor, *Cincinnati Commercial Gazette* (1883-1890).

BOOKS: *Caucuses of 1860* (Columbus, Ohio: Follett, Foster, 1860);

The War Claims of the South (Cincinnati: Clarke, 1876);

Historic Illustrations of the Confederacy (New York, 1890);

Life of Jay Gould, How He Made Millions, by Halstead and J. Frank Beale, Jr. (Philadelphia: Edgewood, 1892);

Life and Public Services of Hon. Benjamin Harrison, President of the U.S. (Philadelphia: Edgewood, 1892);

One Hundred Bear Stories: Historical, Romantic, Biblical, Classical (New York: Ogilvie, 1895);

The White Dollar (Philadelphia: Franklin News Co., 1895);

Life and Distinguished Services of Hon. William McKinley and the Great Issues of 1896 (Philadelphia: Edgewood, 1896);

The Story of Cuba (Chicago: Werner, 1896);

The Great Battle for Protection and Sound Money Led by Hon. Wm. McKinley, by Halstead and Melville Phillips (Philadelphia: Edgewood, 1897);

The History of American Expansion and the Story of Our New Possessions (N.p.: United Subscription Book Publishers of America, 1898);

Pictorial History of America's New Possessions, the Isthmian Canals, and the Problem of Expansion (Chicago: Dominion, 1898);

Our Country in War and Relations with All Nations (N.p.: United Subscription Book Publishers of America, 1898);

Our New Possessions (Chicago: Dominion, 1898); published simultaneously as *The Story of the Philippines* (Chicago: Our Possessions Publishing Co., 1898);

Full Official History of the War with Spain (Chicago: Beezley, 1899);

Life and Achievements of Admiral Dewey from Montpelier to Manila (Chicago: Dominion, 1899);

Triumphant America and Her New Possessions (Chi-

Murat Halstead in 1874 (Chicago Historical Society)

cago: Colonial Publishing Co., 1899);

The Politics of the Philippines: Aguinaldo a Traitor to the Filipinos and a Conspirator against the United States (Akron, Ohio: Allied Printing Trades Council, 1899);

Briton and Boer in South Africa (Philadelphia?, 1900);

Galveston: The Horrors of a Stricken City (Chicago: American Publishers' Association, 1900);

Victorious Republicanism and the Lives of the Standard-Bearers, McKinley and Roosevelt (Chicago?: Republican National Publishing Co., 1900);

Aguinaldo and His Captor (Cincinnati: Halstead, 1901);

The Illustrious Life of William McKinley, Our Martyred President (Chicago: Donohue, 1901);

Life and Reign of Queen Victoria, by Halstead and
Augustus J. Munson (Chicago: International
Publishing Society, 1901);

*The Life of Theodore Roosevelt, Twenty-fifth President of
the United States* (Akron, Ohio: Saalfield, 1902;
London: Grant Richards, 1903);

The World on Fire (N.p.: International Publishing
Society, 1902);

*Pictorial History of the Louisiana Purchase and the
World's Fair at St. Louis* (Philadelphia: National
Publishing Co., 1904);

The War between Russia and Japan (Philadelphia: National Publishing Co., 1904).

Murat Halstead had a genius for news enterprise and gained a great reputation for his independent and vigorous editorials. Under his guidance, the *Cincinnati Commercial* became one of the
most notable political and literary influences in the
United States and rivaled the *Chicago Tribune*, the
Chicago Daily News, and the *St. Louis Post-Dispatch* for
leadership among newspapers of the Middle West.
Halstead was an indefatigable worker who supposedly wrote an average of 3,000 words a day for
forty years. At first he conducted his newspaper
independent of party politics, but later he allied it
with the Republican party; Halstead was a prominent figure at Republican conventions for over fifty
years. Although he gained fame in his time as a
political reporter and a brilliant war correspondent,
he is best remembered today for his role in the
Liberal Republican movement of 1872.

Halstead was born 2 September 1829 at
Paddy's Run, Butler County, Ohio, a short distance
from Cincinnati. He was the son of Griffin and
Clarissa Willets Halstead. His grandfather, John
Halstead, had come to Ohio from Currituck
County, North Carolina, when Halstead's father
was an infant. His mother was the eldest daughter
of James Willets of York, Pennsylvania. Her family
had immigrated to the Scioto Valley, and she had
been born in Tarleton, Ohio. Murat was reared on
his family's farm, a fertile 319 acres about evenly
divided between heavily timbered hills and rich
level land. During the summer months Murat
worked on the farm, and during the winters he
attended the local Paddy's Run Academy until he
was nineteen. His mother taught him to read before
he was four years old, using the local newspaper, the
Hamilton Telegraph, as a primer. Halstead was a
rapid and eager reader as a child and soon read all
the books available at home, among them Plutarch,
Josephus, and several biographies of Andrew
Jackson. Having depleted that supply, he borrowed

books from his teachers and friends. At eighteen he
studied surveying for a while, but he had his sights
set on studying law, and one winter he enrolled in a
"select" school. He also taught for two terms at the
Colrain and Jackson schoolhouses, but in 1848 he
enrolled at Farmer's College, seven miles from Cincinnati, from which he graduated in three years.
While in college, Halstead wrote for the *Hamilton
Intelligencer* and the *Rossville Democrat*. He soon
abandoned his plans for a law career and decided to
concentrate on journalism.

After graduation he wrote for several Cincinnati newspapers—the *Atlas*, the *Enquirer*, the *Columbian*, and the *Great West*—as well as for a Sunday
newspaper he established. On 8 March 1853,
Halstead went to work for the *Cincinnati Commercial*
as a local reporter, thus beginning an association
that would last for almost fifty years. In 1854 he
purchased a one-sixteenth interest in the *Commercial*
and began to figure prominently in its future; he
soon became the news editor. Halstead reported on
the political conventions of 1856. On 2 March 1857
he married Mary Banks, a daughter of Hiram
Banks, a New Jersey merchant with business interests in Cincinnati. The couple had twelve children;
four of his seven sons entered journalism as a
career, although Halstead wished otherwise. It was
said that "the simple domestic joys he found in his
large family contributed greatly to the cheerful and
optimistic attitude he maintained toward the
world." He covered the hanging of John Brown
near Harper's Ferry, Virginia, in 1859.

Halstead's first major exposure as a political
correspondent of national repute came as a result of
his coverage of the conventions of 1860. During the
Republican convention, Halstead issued predictions up until the last few frantic days that William
Seward would be nominated. He was present when,
on 18 May 1860, Norman B. Judd of Illinois stood
on the speaker's platform in the Wigwam, a rambling frame building in Chicago, and nominated
Abraham Lincoln. In describing the tumultuous
demonstration for Lincoln that shook the building,
Halstead used these words to paint the scene for his
readers in Cincinnati: "Imagine all the hogs ever
slaughtered in Cincinnati giving their death squeals
together." (The allusion was appropriate because
Cincinnati was called "Porkopolis" and was the
center of the pork-packing industry.) He described
the celebrations for Lincoln in the towns and villages he passed through as he rode the night train
back to Cincinnati and noted that the people were
"delighted with the idea of a candidate for president
who thirty years ago split rails on the Sangamon

River—classic stream now and forevermore—and whose neighbors called him 'honest.' " Halstead's stories about the conventions, which were collected and published as a book, *Caucuses of 1860* (1860), have remained valuable as sources for Civil War historians and Lincoln scholars. Robert S. Harper says that Halstead never again rose to such literary heights, but that Halstead's five words about the Sangamon River have made him a journalistic immortal.

During the Civil War Halstead wrote political news and, according to Harper, virtually ran the *Commercial*, which strongly supported the Lincoln administration. This support did not prevent Halstead from lashing out at Lincoln; for example, in 1864, when he failed to get a postmastership for a friend, Halstead wrote: "I use the mildest phrase when I say Lincoln is a weak, a miserably weak man; the wife is a fool—the laughing stock of the town, her vulgarity only the more conspicuous in consequence of the fine carriage and horses and servants in livery, and fine dresses and her damnable airs. . . . " Halstead also represented the *Commercial* at the front during the war and established a reputation as a brilliant war correspondent. Within a year of becoming editor of the *Commercial* in 1865, Halstead became the chief stockholder and publisher, succeeding W. D. Potter, who died in 1866. Like many editors, Halstead was an autocrat on his newspaper, and there were many stockholders whose opinions he never consulted. In the Franco-Prussian War of 1870-1871, he enhanced his reputation as a war correspondent with his reports on the German armies.

Halstead's place in history was assured by his participation in the Liberal Republican movement of the early 1870s. Halstead and the *Commercial* had been staunch Republican party supporters for over a decade, but the corruption of the Grant administration and the need for reforms shook that loyalty. The *Commercial* broke with Grant and the Republican mainstream as early as 18 March 1871, when it printed that there would soon be "evidences of a widespread conviction that [Grant] is the man whose candidacy in 1872 cannot be considered endurable." Halstead and other newspaper editors who would figure prominently in the Liberal Republican movement were faithful Union Republicans who wanted the post-Civil War Republican party to be progressive and face the new issues of the period and not rest on past achievements. If the party failed to do this, then Halstead and the others were prepared to leave it for another, and that is precisely what they did in 1872. Halstead, along with Horace White of the *Chicago Tribune*, Samuel Bowles of the *Springfield Republican*, Carl Schurz of the *St. Louis Westliche Post*, and Henry Watterson of the *Louisville Courier-Journal*, called for a convention to choose a candidate to challenge Grant. The call was answered, and the Liberal Republican convention was convened in Cincinnati. Four of the editors—Halstead, White, Watterson, and Bowles—agreed to cooperate in order to defeat the candidacy of David Davis, which the four saw as a travesty of the reforms they wanted. The four dubbed themselves the "Quadrilateral" after the famous Austrian defensive position in the Alps, and although the group was divided in their support for either Charles Francis Adams or Lyman Trumbull, they agreed that a plan to defeat Davis was their priority. Before implementing the plan, the Quadrilateral agreed to limit their support to Adams, Trumbull, or Horace Greeley. None of them believed that Greeley had the slightest chance of winning the nomination.

The Quadrilateral's plan was simple. Each of the four, as well as Whitelaw Reid of the *New York Tribune*, wrote an editorial for his paper that was wired home and printed as the "leader." Each editorial pointed to a weakness in Davis's position, such as his lavish spending of money, his motley group of supporters, the taint of his overt presidential ambitions, and so on. The editorials were then reprinted in the *Cincinnati Commercial*, which was distributed to all delegates at the opening of the convention. The effect was deadly; however, neither Adams nor Trumbull won the nomination. Greeley's surprising victory left the Quadrilateral stunned and bewildered, but they felt they had no choice but to support him. They returned home and tried to present a confident attitude to their readers. Halstead was particularly disappointed by Adams's defeat, and at first he gave only qualified support to Greeley. Nevertheless, he pointed to Greeley's strong points, and soon the tenor of his support grew stronger. None of the editors could prevent the debacle of the Liberal Republican party in the November election, but the four remained close friends after the campaign and often visited each other. Halstead brought the *Commercial* back into the Republican fold after 1872. He supported Adams again in 1876 until the candidacy of Rutherford B. Hayes gained momentum. During the Hayes administration, Halstead seems to have had easy access to the president and acted as a middleman of sorts, in at least one case, between concerned Republican editors and President Hayes.

The 1880s marked the beginning of the de-

Front page of the Cincinnati Commercial *during the fourth year of Halstead's editorship*

cline of Halstead's career. Even though there were several auspicious events in the decade, including the merger of the *Commercial* and the *Cincinnati Gazette* in 1883 and Halstead's continued prominence in political affairs, his journalistic star was growing dim. When the two newspapers merged, Halstead was named editor in chief as well as president of the Commercial Gazette Company. Former president Hayes congratulated Halstead and wrote that the *Commercial Gazette* was "to be one of the greatest—perhaps the greatest—newspapers on 'the dim spot which men call earth.'" However, the paper was unable to meet the competition of the vigorous, sensational *Cincinnati Enquirer*. This failure, combined with poor financial management, resulted in the newspaper slipping from Halstead's hands. It became the *Commercial Tribune* in 1896 and was finally merged with the *Enquirer* in 1930.

Halstead remained active in Republican politics in the 1880s. In 1884 he conducted a campaign paper in New York and was optimistic about John Sherman's presidential chances. He apparently had access to President Chester A. Arthur and traveled to Washington to offer Arthur his advice. However, he was no friend of the Democratic Cleveland administration: in 1886 President Grover Cleveland fired a blast at the press—specifically directed at the *New York Sun*, the *New York World*, and the *Commercial Gazette*—for "the silly mean and cowardly lies that every day are found in the columns of certain newspapers, which violate every instinct of American manliness, and in ghoulish glee desecrate every sacred relation of private life." When the Republican Benjamin Harrison became president in 1889, Halstead returned to political favor in the White House. Harrison nominated Halstead as minister to Germany, but the Senate rejected the nomination, apparently in revenge for Halstead's sharp attacks on corrupt practices; Halstead had been particularly harsh on the Senate for its refusal to investigate the election of Senator Henry B. Payne of Ohio. Halstead considered himself complimented by the rejection. He wanted to be minister to France, but he was not nominated because he had sided with the Germans during the Franco-Prussian War, thus rendering him unacceptable to the French government.

Halstead's newspaper career ended in the early 1890s in Brooklyn, New York. When Halstead left Cincinnati in 1890 he promised to continue to contribute to the *Commercial Gazette*, but when he arrived in New York, he was offered the opportunity to edit the *Brooklyn Standard-Union*. He guided the newspaper, but did not distinguish himself, for

Halstead as editor of the Brooklyn Standard-Union
(Culver Pictures)

a few years before stepping down to concentrate on writing books. He produced a succession of quickly forgotten books, mostly biographies and contemporary histories that he wrote with paste pot and scissors and sold by subscription; the books have been described as "naive and garrulous." He also wrote regularly for *Cosmopolitan Monthly* after 1890 and visited the Philippines during the war with Spain. Eventually he returned to Cincinnati to live out the rest of his days. When he died on 2 July 1908 at his home, the headline in the *Commercial Tribune* read, "Grand Old Man of Journalism Passes Away." Among those who sent personal regrets was Halstead's old courthouse-beat reporter, William Howard Taft.

References:

William Coyle, *Ohio Authors and Their Books, 1796-1950* (Cleveland: World, 1962), pp. 267-268;

Joseph Logsdon, *Horace White, Nineteenth Century Liberal* (Westport, Conn.: Greenwood Press, 1971);

G. S. Merriam, *The Life and Times of Samuel Bowles*, 2

volumes (New York: Century, 1885);

James E. Pollard, *The Presidents and the Press* (New York: Macmillan, 1947);

Earle Dudley Ross, *The Liberal Republican Movement* (Seattle: University of Washington Press, 1970).

Papers:

Murat Halstead's manuscripts are held by the Historical and Philosophical Society of Ohio, University of Cincinnati Library.

Joel Chandler Harris

Harry W. Stonecipher
Southern Illinois University

See also the Harris entry in *DLB 11, American Humorists, 1800-1950.*

BIRTH: Eatonton, Georgia, 9 December 1848, to Mary Harris.

MARRIAGE: 21 April 1873 to Esther LaRose; children: Julian LaRose, Lucien, Evan Howell, Evelyn, Mary Esther, Lillian, Linton, Mildred, Joel Chandler, Jr.

MAJOR POSITIONS HELD: Paragrapher, columnist, associate editor, *Savannah Morning News* (1870-1876); editorial writer, columnist, associate editor, *Atlanta Constitution* (1876-1900); editor, *Uncle Remus's Magazine* (1907-1908).

AWARDS AND HONORS: Litt.D., Emory College, 1902; elected member of American Academy of Arts and Letters, 1905.

DEATH: Atlanta, Georgia, 3 July 1908.

BOOKS: *Uncle Remus: His Songs and His Sayings* (New York: Appleton, 1880;) republished as *Uncle Remus and His Legends of the Old Plantation* (London: David Bogue, 1881; revised edition, New York: Appleton, 1895; London: Osgood, 1895);

Nights with Uncle Remus: Myths and Legends of the Old Plantation (Boston: Osgood, 1883; London: Routledge, 1884);

Mingo and Other Sketches in Black and White (Boston: Osgood, 1884; Edinburgh: Douglas, 1884; London: Hamilton Adams, 1884);

Free Joe and Other Georgian Sketches (New York: Scribners, 1887; London: Routledge, 1888);

Culver Pictures

Daddy Jake the Runaway and Short Stories Told after Dark (New York: Century, 1889; London: Unwin, 1889);

Balaam and His Master and Other Sketches and Stories (Boston & New York: Houghton Mifflin, 1891; London: Osgood, McIlvaine, 1891);

A Plantation Printer: The Adventures of a Georgia Boy during the War (London: Osgood, McIlvaine, 1892); also published as *On the Plantation: A*

Story of a Georgia Boy's Adventures during the War (New York: Appleton, 1892);

Uncle Remus and His Friends (Boston & New York: Houghton, Mifflin, 1892; London: Osgood, McIlvaine, 1893);

Little Mr. Thimblefinger and His Queer Country: What the Children Saw and Heard There (Boston & New York: Houghton Mifflin, 1894; London: Osgood, McIlvaine, 1894);

Mr. Rabbit at Home: A Sequel to Little Mr. Thimblefinger and His Queer Country (Boston & New York: Houghton Mifflin, 1895; London: Osgood, 1895);

The Story of Aaron (So Named) the Son of Ben Ali (Boston & New York: Houghton Mifflin, 1896; London: Osgood, 1896);

Stories of Georgia (New York, Cincinnati & Chicago: American Book, 1896);

Sister Jane: Her Friends and Acquaintances (Boston & New York: Houghton Mifflin, 1896; London: Constable, 1897);

Aaron in the Wildwoods (Boston & New York: Houghton Mifflin, 1897; London: Harper, 1897);

Tales of the Home Folks in Peace and War (Boston & New York: Houghton Mifflin, 1898; London: Unwin, 1898);

The Chronicles of Aunt Minervy Ann (New York: Scribners, 1899; London: Dent, 1899);

Plantation Pageants (Boston & New York: Houghton Mifflin, 1899; London: Constable, 1899);

On the Wing of Occasions (New York: Doubleday, Page, 1900; London: Murray, 1900);

The Making of a Statesman and Other Stories (New York: McClure, Phillips, 1902; London: Isbister, 1902);

Gabriel Tolliver: A Story of Reconstruction (New York: McClure, Phillips, 1902);

Wally Wanderoon and His Story-Telling Machine (New York: McClure, Phillips, 1903; London: Richards, 1904);

A Little Union Scout (New York: McClure, Phillips, 1904; London: Duckworth, 1905);

The Tar-Baby and Other Rhymes of Uncle Remus (New York: Appleton, 1904);

Told by Uncle Remus: New Stories of the Old Plantation (New York: McClure, Phillips, 1905; London: Hodder & Stoughton, 1906);

Uncle Remus and Brer Rabbit (New York: Stokes, 1907);

The Bishop and the Booger-Man (New York: Doubleday, Page, 1909); republished as *The Bishop and the Boogie-Man* (London: Murray, 1909);

The Shadow between His Shoulder-Blades (Boston: Small, Maynard, 1909);

Uncle Remus and the Little Boy (Boston: Small, Maynard, 1910; London: Richards, 1912);

Uncle Remus Returns (Boston & New York: Houghton Mifflin, 1918);

The Witch Wolf: An Uncle Remus Story (Cambridge, Mass.: Bacon & Brown, 1921);

The Complete Tales of Uncle Remus, compiled by Richard Chase (Boston: Houghton Mifflin, 1955).

Joel Chandler Harris, better known today as the talented Georgian folklorist and creator of Uncle Remus who recounted numerous tales of plantation life, was first and foremost a newspaper journalist. It has not been unusual for literary figures to begin their writing careers as journalists: Mark Twain, a contemporary of Harris's, composed his first paragraphs at the typecase and served his literary apprenticeship on the *Virginia City* (Nevada) *Territorial Enterprise*; William Dean Howells, Stephen Crane, Theodore Dreiser, Ernest Hemingway, and others gained their literary apprenticeships and saw their first writing efforts published in newspapers. But for most of this group, their journalistic apprenticeships were relatively brief (although Howells served as editor of the *Atlantic Monthly* for almost fifteen years); Harris's claim to literary recognition, by contrast, flowed more directly from his efforts as a journalist. His materials were drawn from his experience while working for the *Countryman*, a weekly newspaper published on a middle Georgia plantation. His twenty-four years with the *Atlanta Constitution*, where his first Uncle Remus story was published in 1876, provided the forum for his daily writing efforts. Except for a few months in New Orleans, Harris's entire journalistic and literary career was directly tied to his native Georgia. Indeed, Harris's strength as a journalist and his lasting reputation as a folklorist and local-color writer flowed from his knowledge and understanding of plantation life—of Negro slaves, ex-slaves, poor whites, and Georgia aristocrats.

Harris was born 9 December 1848 in Eatonton, the county seat of Putnam County, Georgia, fifty miles southeast of Atlanta. His mother, Mary Harris, had eloped with a young Irish laborer, only to be deserted by him before their child was born. During his boyhood, young Harris lived in an antebellum plantation environment at Eatonton, where his mother supported herself by dressmaking, with kindly financial assistance from her neighbors. The mores of this mid-Georgian plantation culture were to become a dominant influence in the formation of Harris's character and the source of inspiration for his most enduring stories of the Southern region, both in his newspaper columns and in his many books. The knowledge of his illegitimacy may also have had a profound influence upon both his personality and his art. Harris was painfully modest and self-effacing all of his life and had a slight speech impediment that could quickly turn into a stammer when he was forced to take the verbal initiative. He adamantly refused throughout his career to read from his works or to talk informally in front of a group.

Harris's diminutive size, bright red hair, and freckled face set him apart from his classmates at Eatonton Academy for Boys, where he reportedly showed little interest in his textbooks, except for English composition. Despite his shyness, or perhaps because of it, young Harris looked outside the classroom for ways to assert himself. He is remembered by his companions as a prankster and practical joker. Throughout his life, Harris is said to

have maintained his Georgian and Irish sense of humor, privately as well as in public. As his writing reflects, he was especially fond of a well-executed practical joke.

His desire to write came early. Harris later recalled that his mother's reading of Oliver Goldsmith's *The Vicar of Wakefield* (1766) to him as a child made an impact upon him. Writing in *Lippincott's* magazine in 1886, he said: "My desire to write—to give expression to my thought—grew out of hearing my mother read *The Vicar of Wakefield*. I was too young to appreciate the story, but there was something in the humor of that remarkable little book that struck my fancy, and I straightway fell into composing little tales, in which the principal character—whether hero or heroine—silenced the other characters by crying, *Fudge!* at every possible opportunity. None of these little tales have been preserved, but I am convinced that since their keynote was *Fudge!* they must have been very close to human nature." His first exposure to the oral tradition of story telling also came from his

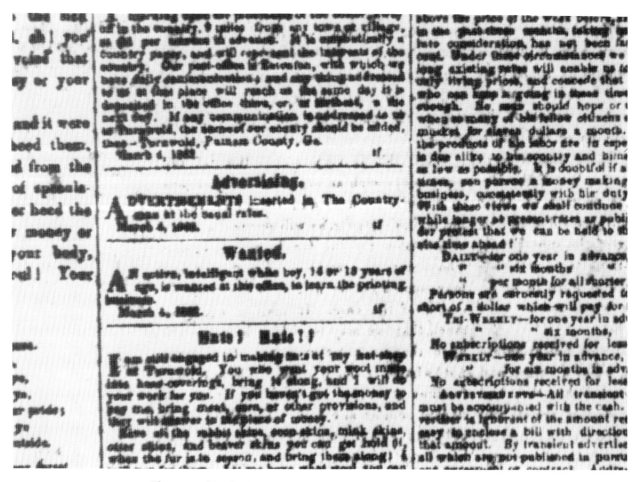

The want ad in the Countryman *that first attracted Harris to the paper*

mother, who enjoyed telling him tales.

Harris's journalistic apprenticeship, however, began at the age of fourteen after he read an advertisement in the *Countryman*, a weekly newspaper: "WANTED—An active, intelligent white boy, fourteen or fifteen years of age, is wanted at this office to learn the printing business." In March 1862 young Harris became an apprentice printer, a "printer's devil," on the *Countryman*. The newspaper had just been launched by Joseph Addison Turner, a Southern planter with a devotion to literature, on his plantation, "Turnwold," some nine miles from Harris's home. Harris lived on the plantation during four of the most eventful years in the history of the South; they were also important years in the formation of Harris's career as a journalist and writer. With time on his hands after completion of his typesetting duties, he was free to explore the Turner estate and visit the slave cabins, where he listened to the slaves' folktales. He also frequently engaged in coon hunting and in the pursuit of other fur-bearing animals. He occasionally accompanied the Turners and others on fox hunts. In his rambles over the countryside he sometimes

Printing office for the Countryman *at Turnwold Plantation, where Harris served his journalistic apprenticeship*

met with runaway slaves from other plantations.

When Harris began smuggling paragraphs of his own into the columns of the *Countryman*, Turner took him in hand, lent him books from his 6,000-volume library, and schooled him rigorously and wisely in the art of writing. Harris's appreciation and command of a clear, pure English and his often-stated conviction that a successful writer must look to life around him for his material were the result of Turner's influence.

Plantation life at Turnwold was disrupted in November 1864 when the left wing of General Sherman's army swept across Putnam County, leaving confusion and desolation in its track. The experience apparently had a disenchanting effect on Harris, who for more than two years had been setting into type Turner's brave editorials about the impregnability of the South. With the fall of the Confederacy in the spring of 1865, antebellum became postbellum, but the *Countryman* continued publication until May 1866. When Harris left Turnwold, neither he nor his defeated mentor realized that vested in the person of the *Countryman*'s apprentice printer was the most authentic vision of life on the old plantation that American literature would ever see.

Harris, then seventeen, returned to Eatonton in the spring of 1866 with little money and the prospects of employment uncertain. Even established newspapers were struggling for survival as the long Reconstruction period began, but Harris's proficiency as a typesetter soon brought him an offer of employment on the *Macon Telegraph*, owned by a former resident of Eatonton and a friend of Turner's. Harris found the offer attractive, both because the *Telegraph* was a daily newspaper and because the publisher encouraged the development of a native Southern literature; Harris saw the *Telegraph* position as giving him an opportunity for serious literary composition. He was also pleased that Macon was only forty miles from Eatonton.

In Macon, Harris began the first phase of his initiation into the more complex world outside Turner's plantation. His five or six months with the *Telegraph* were lively and interesting, but they failed to bring him the kind of professional experience he sought. He soon learned that getting out the daily *Telegraph* was more demanding than work on the weekly *Countryman*. In addition, the *Telegraph* staff engaged in drinking and general "hilarity," and the naive apprentice was often made the object of the staff's good-natured banter and jests. Harris, for example, was dubbed "Pink Top" from "Old Put."

While Harris may have been irritated to be the butt of the staffers' jokes, he found drinking the tavern brew with the staff to be relaxing and enjoyable.

In addition to his typesetting duties, Harris reviewed books and magazines and composed humorous complimentary "puffs" which thanked local merchants for gifts to the staff. He continued to write poetry, but he did not receive encouragement to publish what he considered to be his best literary effort.

One of the magazines that Harris reviewed enthusiastically for the *Telegraph* was the *Crescent Monthly*, published in New Orleans by William Evelyn, a former Confederate officer. Evelyn advertised his new magazine as being "devoted to literature, art, science, and society." The *Crescent*, Evelyn argued, was the place for the Southern writer to demonstrate his capability and to prove Southern literature worthy of a permanent place in American letters. After beating the drums for the *Crescent* in at least three reviews, Harris quit the *Telegraph* in October 1866 to become Evelyn's private secretary. As the months in New Orleans passed, however, he became discouraged in his new job. There is no evidence that the *Crescent* published any of the new secretary's offerings—at least no signed contributions are to be found. The *New Orleans Times* did publish two of Harris's poems during this period. One biographer has suggested that to a pathologically shy boy from rural Putnam County, the overwhelming size of New Orleans and its overlay of languages and cultural strains made it seem a veritable foreign country. At any rate, Harris resigned in May 1867 and went back to the familiar environment of middle Georgia.

Soon after returning to Eatonton, Harris was offered a position on the staff of the *Monroe Advertiser*, a weekly newspaper published by a former employee of the *Countryman* at Forsyth, Georgia, a small town with a population in 1860 of 608 whites and 773 Negroes. With the aid of an apprentice with whom he shared a room in the publisher's home, Harris hand set the type for the paper, prepared the forms, ran off the pages on a Washington handpress, and attended to their mailing. While the *Advertiser* carried only local news, Harris was soon composing humorous paragraphs for the paper about Georgia life and character; he also wrote a series of sketches and stories about Georgia fox hunting. These efforts gained him considerable attention from area newspapers.

The three Forsyth years were also important in that Harris learned to share something of his private self and inner anxieties with others. He developed a friendship with the publisher's sister, Mrs. Georgia Starke, who encouraged the youth to discuss his self-consciousness, and in his letters to her years after leaving Forsyth he mentioned his unfortunate past and the discomfort that his "morbidly sensitive" nature, his *absolute horror* of strangers," and his "awkwardness and clumsiness" so often caused him. Their friendship proved to be an enduring one; Harris frequently recalled Mrs. Starke's patience and "unfailing kindness," and he corresponded with her until just before his death in 1908.

Forsyth also proved to be a turning point in Harris's journalistic career. As one biographer puts it, "the youth became the man." After realistically evaluating his own abilities, Harris turned more deliberately toward a career as what he labeled a "cornfield" journalist. His humorous paragraphs in the *Advertiser* also brought an unexpected reward: in the fall of 1870 he was offered a position as associate editor of the *Savannah Morning News*, one of Georgia's most respected papers, at the then-unheard-of salary of $40 a week.

Professionally, the move to Savannah was the most advantageous one he had made since he left Turnwold Plantation in the summer of 1866. The editor of the *Morning News*, William Tappan Thompson, was the author of the "Major Jones" sketches, which were second only to A. B. Longstreet's *Georgia Scenes* (1835) in regional popularity. Harris's primary assignment on the *Morning News* was that of a paragrapher, a much practiced journalistic form during the late nineteenth and early twentieth centuries. His daily column, first called "State Affairs" and later changed to "Affairs of Georgia," consisted of humorous comments on personalities and events of current interest, which Harris garnered from the state's daily and weekly newspapers. Harris apparently enjoyed his sudden prestige and, doing his best to enter into the spirit of things, frequently joked with the staff, who nicknamed him "Red-Top," "Pink-Top," "Vermilion Pate," and "Molasses-Haired Humorist." When his paragraphs were republished in panels by newspapers around the state, they often ran under titles such as "Harris Sparks," "Harrisgraphs," "Red-Top Flashes," and "Hot Shots from Red Hair-is."

Literary critics have noted that some of Harris's paragraphs suggest the stock-in-trade jokes and one-liners of the stand-up comedian. Racial and ethnic slurs, always a part of humor, also occasionally crept into Harris's column, and in weaker moments he catered to some of the standard Southern prejudices. These random paragraphs from his "Affairs of Georgia" column indicate the tone and style of Harris's writing during this period:

> A colored couple in Putnam County whose combined age is one hundred and eighty-two years, were united in wedlock recently. They said the reason they were so precipitate about the thing, they didn't want their parents to find out.

> The colored people of Macon celebrated the birthday of Lincoln again on Wednesday. This is the third time since last October.

> A McDuffie County man broke his arm in two places and put out the eye of a grass widow recently in endeavoring to drop some molasses candy which he had picked up.

> A Lumpkin negro seriously injured his pocketknife recently by undertaking to stab a colored brother in the head.

While many of Harris's newspaper paragraphs might leave the modern reader guessing at their reference, Georgia readers in the 1870s needed no footnotes to explain the topical allusions in his writing.

Harris's talent was recognized and many tributes were paid him during the time of his employment on the *Morning News*. The editor of one Georgia paper, for example, wrote: "What shall we say of the bright, sparkling, vivacious, inimitable Harris? There is no failing in his spirit of wit and humor, playful raillery and pungent sarcasm. As a terse and an incisive paragraphist, he is unequalled in the South. One wonders at times that his fund of quips and odd fancies does not occasionally become exhausted, but the flow continues from day to day without sign of diminution or loss of volume; J. C. Harris is a genius of rare and versatile abilities." Indeed, as a humorist, Harris came upon the Southern scene at an opportune time. Georgia, as well as the rest of the South, was suffering from the sting of military defeat and facing the harsh measures of Reconstruction. Harris's humor, like that of Bret Harte, Josh Billings, Artemus Ward, and Mark Twain, had the effect of relieving the tensions of readers in those troubled times.

Despite Harris's almost immediate success on

Harris and his wife, Esther, in 1873, the year of their marriage

the *Morning News*, his innate shyness made it difficult for him to adjust immediately to his new environment in Savannah, where, as in New Orleans, he found himself among strangers. For a time he was highly sensitive about his awkwardness, particularly when he was in the presence of girls and women. His realization of the extent to which the adverse circumstances of his childhood had set him apart from the normal social pattern also troubled him. Despite his growing reputation as Georgia's most gifted young humorist, he often fell into moods of morose introspection and despair. These feelings he communicated in letters to his confidante in Forsyth, Mrs. Starke.

As the months passed, however, Harris gradually became better adapted to Savannah. He grew less sensitive about his appearance and the jests of his newspaper associates. He also became acquainted with Captain and Mrs. Pierre LaRose, a French Canadian couple who had temporarily moved to Savannah, where Captain LaRose was the owner and operator of a steamer. Early in 1872 the LaRoses' daughter, Esther, then seventeen, joined her parents, who were boarders at the Florida House in Savannah where Harris resided. Esther's youthful beauty, vivacious spirit, enjoyment of humor, and her social graces are said to have completely captivated Harris. In any case, after a courtship of a little more than a year they were married 21 April 1873. By the time of their marriage, Harris had demonstrated, even to himself, that he had the ability to succeed as a journalist. The marriage helped to provide a continuity and serenity which had been absent from his life. He continued to be shy and uncomfortable when he was among people whom he did not know, but the black moods of despair disappeared.

During Harris's six years with the *Morning News*, his "Affairs in Georgia" column grew steadily in popular favor to establish him as Georgia's foremost humorist. After his marriage, he had become content to remain indefinitely with the *Morning News*. A serious outbreak of yellow fever in Savannah during August 1876, however, caused Harris to move with his wife and their two young children to Atlanta. He intended to remain in Atlanta, where the elevation was higher and the climate less susceptible to the fever, only until the Savannah health authorities declared that it was safe to return. As it turned out, he was to spend the rest of his life there.

The *Constitution* had been founded in 1868, the same year that Atlanta was selected as the state capital, and it had become the city's leading newspaper and a major voice in the Southeast by 1876. The city, which had been reduced to rubble when Sherman's army swept through Georgia, was beginning its second decade of phenomenal growth and recovery. Between 1860 and 1870 the city's population had jumped from 9,554 to 21,789, and most of the increase had occurred following the Civil War. The pride of Atlanta and the most tangible evidence of its rebirth and vitality was the Kimball House, the hotel in which Harris and his family stayed during their first weeks there. It was during this time that Evan Howell, editor of the *Constitution*, and his new associate editor, Henry W. Grady, offered Harris a temporary position on the paper. In the issue of 21 November 1876, it was announced that arrangements had been completed for Harris to become an associate editor of the *Constitution* on a permanent basis. Although he had not directly sought the appointment, Harris had been interested in the *Constitution* since his first editorial position on the *Monroe Advertiser* almost a decade earlier.

With the acquisition of Grady and Harris as associate editors, the *Constitution* had the editorial leadership that soon brought the paper national recognition and influence. Grady, then only twenty-six, became the outspoken advocate of economic and political cooperation between the South and the North in order to create a "New South" based upon industry and business. Harris, then twenty-seven, while more temperate in his approach, was no less effective in his editorials and literary essays in demonstrating the qualities of mind and life in the agrarian Southern culture which could ease the burdens of Reconstruction and help effect a renaissance of Southern letters. The regional supremacy which the *Constitution* achieved and the national influence which it came to exert can be credited in large measure to the efforts of Grady and Harris. While both editors had a passion for a revitalized South, each was concerned about a different phase of its progress and development. Grady editorialized with an evangelistic fervor, urging industrialization as the economic salvation of the South. Harris, steeped in the cultural traditions of the old South, became a champion of the emancipation of its literature, ridding it of its ultraromantic and sectional qualities. A Southern historian has pointed out that on one side of the *Constitution*'s editorial desk Grady was exhorting the South to exploit its treasure of natural resources, while on the other side Harris was urging the South to develop its unique and original literary materials.

While Grady saw his role clearly and championed his Southern cause from the start, Harris discovered his real strength as a folklorist and writer almost accidentally. Upon joining the *Constitution* he had begun to compose a column of humorous paragraphs called "Roundabout in Georgia," much as he had done in Savannah. The resignation of Sam Small, who had contributed a series of dialect sketches featuring the observations of "Old Si" about the local scene, however, gave Harris an opportunity to try his hand with the series. Harris wrote two sketches employing the Negro dialect, both published in the *Constitution* 26 October 1876. In "Markham's Ball," following the pattern set by Small, Harris related the humorous comments of old Uncle Ben about a local political celebration. It was the other sketch, "Jeems Rober'son," which was to establish Harris as an important new voice in the tradition of American humor and story telling. The 300-word sketch, as one biographer notes, "bore the stamp of Harris's genius."

In composing "Jeems Rober'son," Harris drew upon his recollections of Negroes he had known in Putnam County and the dialect which he had heard them speak. The scene of the sketch was the Union Station opposite the Kimball House; the two characters were an old Negro, unnamed in the newspaper sketch, and a younger Negro from nearby Jonesboro who was waiting for his train to depart. Four years later Harris collected this second sketch as the first of his Uncle Remus "sayings" in *Uncle Remus: His Songs and His Sayings* (1880). The revised sketch was given the more ironic title of "Jeems Rober'son's Last Illness," and the old Negro was identified as Uncle Remus. Harris discovered in this sketch what one biographer, R. Bruce Bickley, Jr., calls the power of the vernacular, which he apparently wrote easily and instinctively. As Mark Twain advocated any good humorist should do, Harris's narrator was careful never to indicate that anything funny existed in what he was saying; he knew how to pace his story effectively; and he understood human nature.

A few days after the publication of "Jeems Rober'son," Harris wrote another sketch, "Politics and Provisions," in which two Negroes, one unnamed and the other simply called "Remus," express their disillusionment with the Republicans, who, according to rumor, had promised to give those Negroes who voted the Republican ticket all the provisions and money they needed. During November and December 1876 six other Uncle Remus stories were published. In one of them "Uncle Remus and the Savannah Darkey," Harris illustrated the difference between the speech and

Frontispiece for the first edition of Uncle Remus: His Songs and His Sayings. *Remus is depicted at the office of the* Atlanta Constitution, *where he has stopped for a chat.*

attitude of the Negroes he knew at Turnwold and those of the coastal Negroes at Savannah. In the process of developing these sketches, Harris gradually eliminated all of the fictional narrators with whom he had been experimenting except Uncle Remus.

But as literary critics have pointed out, two Uncle Remuses emerged in Harris's newspaper sketches during these early years. The first was cast as an old Atlanta Negro, formerly from the country, who liked to drop by the *Constitution*'s newsroom to talk. He was always ready to recount his troubles to reporters or to express his opinions on current politics, the activities of the Ku Klux Klan or the Union League, or any other item of current interest. Harris used the Atlanta Remus primarily to comment upon the problems facing Atlanta during Reconstruction. The other Remus was an old Negro who seemed to bear up under his troubles with a dignity which befitted his age. His wit and wisdom were portrayed as inherent qualities of his race. This latter Remus foreshadowed the emergence of

Uncle Remus, the narrator of the plantation folklore stories which were to bring their author international literary recognition. Harris the journalist apparently saw no need to reconcile the two Remus figures, but literary critics have noted that as he developed as a writer, the Atlanta Remus became more and more subordinated to the plantation narrator of antebellum folktales.

When Sam Small temporarily rejoined the *Constitution* in 1877 and resumed his Old Si sketches, Harris began writing a series of reminiscent essays and narratives about rural life for the Sunday edition. He characterized these efforts, along with later local-color stories, as ephemeral newspaper literature of the day, but they were important in Harris's literary development. They revealed that the plantation regime, as he remembered it, was looming large in his mind as a source of material upon which he might draw for his writings. This increasing interest in the antebellum South was indicated in "Uncle Remus as a Rebel," published in October 1877, Harris's first Remus sketch in nine months. Harris first explained the old man's absence from the newspaper by reporting that he had been living in the country, where he had been trying his luck as a farmer. On his first visit to the editorial rooms of the *Constitution* after his return, Uncle Remus told the reporters that nothing had turned out right for him—his crops had been a failure and thieves had stolen his chickens and pigs. "I'm a-gwine ter drap farmin' sho," he gravely declared. "I'm gwine down inter old Putmon and live alonger Mars Jeems." The story appeared in a revised version entitled "A Story of the War" in Harris's first Uncle Remus book; in it Harris told of the loyalty some of Turner's slaves had exhibited toward their master during the invasion of Turnwold by federal troops in 1864.

When Small accepted an appointment as United States commissioner to Paris in March 1878, Harris resumed his sketches of Uncle Remus in the *Constitution* with greater regularity; thirteen appeared between 10 March and 8 December. Harris continued to portray Uncle Remus as both a humorous and a serious observer of the Reconstruction years. Harris also began work on a novel, "The Romance of Rockville," which was serialized in the weekly edition of the *Constitution* between April and September 1878. As an artistic performance the novel was a failure, but the effort served to expand Harris's literary vision.

While continuing to follow his literary impulses, Harris the journalist wrote daily copy and contributed signed editorials about the problems of the day for publication in the Sunday *Constitution*. In 1878 he wrote that there "never was a time when an editor with a purpose could accomplish more for his state and his country." And, he observed, "What a legacy for one's conscience to know that one has been instrumental in mowing down the old prejudices that rattle in the wind like weeds." Biographer Bickley notes that throughout his career as a journalist, Harris worked to rid the reading public of its three "old prejudices": social and political sectionalism, literary sectionalism, and racial intolerance. Judged from the perspective of the later nineteenth century, both Harris and Grady were indeed progressive in their views concerning the social and political problems facing the South.

Harris's attitude toward social and political sectionalism often paralleled his stance opposing provincialism in literature. Harris argued, for example, that the North, more than the South, was delaying the reconciliation of the two halves of the country. If the North had sent some able, unprovincial, and humane Republican officials instead of carpetbaggers and political self-seekers to work with Southern leaders, the nation might have moved forward more peacefully. Although Southerners were by no means guiltless of the kind of provincialism so often shown by the North, Harris held that charges of political reprisals against the Negro could often be traced to the machinations of the federal agents themselves. A similar theme runs through a characteristic literary editorial of the same period: "The very spice and essence of all literature is localism. No literary artist can lack for materials in this section." Hence, "In literature, art and society, whatever is truly Southern is likewise truly American; and the same may be said of what is truly Northern." Harris viewed mere sectionalism in literature as destructive, but the "flavor of localism," he argued, graced real literary art.

Another of Harris's assignments as associate editor of the *Constitution* was the reviewing of current literary magazines and books. Not only did Harris find the task congenial, but through such reviewing he kept informed of the literary trends in American fiction. Among magazines he reviewed were *Lippincott's*, *Scribner's Monthly*, *Galaxy*, and the *Atlantic Monthly*. Of the latter, Harris wrote: "The Atlantic is the most thoughtful, the most scholarly of all our magazines, and supplies more nearly than any other all the essentials that go to fit and fill the best literary taste." In his account of how he came to write his first Uncle Remus folktale, Harris said that in reading an issue of *Lippincott's* some time in the 1870s he had come across an article dealing with

Southern Negro folklore. "This article," he said, "gave me my cue, and the legends told by Uncle Remus are the result." Harris already had produced in his Atlanta Uncle Remus an appropriate narrator for his folktales. The dialect spoken by the old-time plantation Negroes, while difficult to capture on paper, presented no real problem, for Harris had been experimenting with such dialect in the Uncle Remus sketches for three years.

Harris's first serious effort as a folklorist was "The Story of Mr. Rabbit and Mr. Fox as Told by Uncle Remus," which the *Constitution* published under the heading of "Negro Folklore" on the editorial page of its issue for 20 July 1879. Harris waited for four months for reader response before printing his second Uncle Remus folktale, this one relating the first part of the tar-baby episode. Mr. Rabbit was now called "Brer Rabbit," and to Harris's surprise, the name "Uncle Remus" was suddenly on everyone's lips. These two stories were to become a part of Harris's first Uncle Remus book. Most of the more than 180 Remus stories to be collected and published in ten books during the next twenty-seven years used the general narrative frame that Harris created in his initial Brer Rabbit sketch. In that story, Harris placed the six- or seven-year-old son of Miss Sally and Master John, owners of a large plantation in middle Georgia, at the knees of Uncle Remus, listening intently to his tale of Brer Rabbit's outwitting of Brer Fox or one of the other animals which inhabited the sketches. As the series continued, Harris worked to revise Uncle Remus's dialect, adding refining touches also to his portrait of the kindly, gentle, and wise representative of the antebellum plantation Negro. Described as venerable in features and age, Uncle Remus was accepted by readers as eminently fitted to tell the little white boy the ageless legends of his race.

Harris's narrative device of having the aged Negro relate the stories to an inquisitive white boy gave the tales an added realism. Years later Harris allowed Uncle Remus to explain: "It's mighty funny 'bout tales. . . . Tell um ez you may an' whence you may, some'll say tain't no tale, an' den ag'in some'll say dat it's a fine tale. Dey ain't no tellin'. Dat de reason I don't like ter tell no tale ter grown folks, speshually ef dey er white folks. Dey'll take it an' put it by de side er some yuther tale what dey got in der min' an' dey'll take on dat slonchidickler grin what allers say, 'Go way, man! You dunner what a tale is!' An' I don't — I'll say dat much fer ter keep some un else fum sayin' it."

The folktales, despite — or perhaps because of — Harris's painstaking care in attempting to per-

fect Uncle Remus's dialect, were immediately popular. Favorable newspaper reviews brought Harris to the attention of Joseph C. Derby, a combination manuscript scout and troubleshooter for D. Appleton and Company, a New York book publishing firm. Derby, returning from a trip to Beauvoir, Mississippi, where he had conferred with Jefferson Davis about an overdue manuscript tracing the rise and fall of the Confederate government, stopped off in Atlanta to visit with Harris. The result was *Uncle Remus: His Songs and His Sayings*, scheduled for publication in 1881. The book, which actually was released in November 1880, sold 10,000 copies within four months; it also received favorable reviews in hundreds of newspapers, making Harris, who viewed himself as a mere compiler of the tales, even more self-conscious about such instant literary acclaim. Harris's personal copy of the book indicates that he carefully revised sixty-six pages of dialect which he feared were not accurate enough.

With the publication of his first book in 1880, Harris made the transition from writing for daily newspaper consumption to the authorship of permanent literature. It would be twenty years before he would be free from the daily grind of turning out copy for the *Constitution* and could devote full time to his various literary projects, but his Uncle Remus collections and his other books, which altogether numbered more than thirty, continued to be produced throughout his journalistic career.

As Harris's literary fame increased, he discovered that he could not entirely escape the spotlight of publicity. His extreme shyness caused him embarrassment when he was interrupted in his work at the *Constitution* by curious visitors who, seeing him busy at his desk, would exclaim, "So this is the great Uncle Remus." As his reputation grew, the intrusions on his personal life increased. After 1890 he made a habit of attending the morning meeting of the editorial staff at the *Constitution*, after which he gathered up exchange papers and returned home to complete his writing assignments. The Harrises lived in West End, which at that time was an unincorporated village outside Atlanta reached by mule-drawn trolley cars. At home, Mrs. Harris protected her husband from interruptions by strangers who admired Uncle Remus and wished to meet his creator. When not busy with his writing, Harris spent his time puttering around his rose bushes and garden on his five-acre estate.

Harris's stories brought him national recognition, which meant that he could not be totally indifferent to friendly magazine editors and book pub-

Harris and his family on the steps of Snap Bean Farm, their home in suburban Atlanta

lishers who wished to honor him. After the publication of his first Uncle Remus book, he agreed to accompany Evan Howell to New York, where they were to attend a dinner at the Tile Club in honor of American authors and artists. Harris suffered through the dinner, but resisted all requests to speak or read from his stories. While in New York, Harris and Howell were also invited to be guests of honor at a dinner arranged by the editor of *Century* magazine, which had published two of Harris's plantation songs. Harris accepted the invitation, but the thought of having to sit through another dinner with celebrities at which he would be expected to speak apparently filled him with such dread that he hastily left for Atlanta.

Although Harris was extremely shy in his personal relationships except with his family or friends, he was far from being reticent in his editorials. He continued his crusade for Southern authors to tell the truth about the South, even though his previous editorial criticism of Southern writers had pro-

voked adverse reactions. Some felt that he was attempting to curry favor with Northern readers and being disloyal to his own region. In his editorial "As to Southern Literature," Harris argued that for the South to make any important contribution to world literature, it would have to get over its self-consciousness and sensitiveness so that it would be able to regard criticism "with indifference—nay, with complacence. . . ."

Among American authors who greatly admired Harris's Uncle Remus was Mark Twain. At Twain's urging, Harris went to New Orleans in the spring of 1882 to meet with him and George W. Cable, author of *Old Creole Days* (1879) and *The Grandissimes* (1880), at Cable's home. Twain, who delighted audiences with his story telling and readings, noted in *Life on the Mississippi* (1883) that Harris "deeply disappointed" a number of children in New Orleans who had flocked to meet "the illustrious sage and oracle of the nation's nurseries." They were first disappointed to discover that he was white, but they were also disappointed because he was too shy to read aloud to them the Uncle Remus tar-baby story. Twain reported that "Mr. Cable and I read from books of ours, to show him what an easy trick it was; but his immortal shyness was proof against even this sagacious strategy; so we had to read about Brer Rabbit ourselves." Though Twain failed in his efforts to get Harris to join him on the lecture circuit, he did persuade him to allow James R. Osgood of Boston to publish his next volume of folklore stories. While Twain continued to enjoy public acclaim and popularity as a literary figure and lecturer, Harris returned to Atlanta and his daily editorial tasks on the *Constitution*, where he labored for the next eighteen years while writing his magazine contributions and books in the evenings as time permitted.

Harris's second Uncle Remus book, *Nights with Uncle Remus*, was published by Osgood in 1883; some critics view this book as sufficient to secure Harris's reputation as a literary artist. It was followed by *Mingo and Other Sketches in Black and White* in 1884. But the strain of his daily editorial assignments on the *Constitution* sometimes left Harris little time to pursue his literary work. In a letter to a *Century* editor in 1886, Harris lamented delays in revising a sketch for publication. "For several months I have been suffering with fatty degeneration of the mind—and local politics," he wrote. "In other words, the newspaper grind has been harder than ever, owing to various circumstances." It was not until December 1887 that his fourth volume, *Free Joe and Other Georgian Sketches*, was published by Scribners. Between 1887 and 1900, illness as well as pressure of editorial duties on the *Constitution* prevented Harris from responding to the requests of national magazines for his sketches and stories. He produced only a few stories between 1887 and 1890, but his fifth volume, *Daddy Jake the Runaway and Short Stories Told after Dark,* was published in 1889.

The intimate relationship which had existed between Harris and Grady as associate editors of the *Constitution* since November 1876 came to an abrupt end with Grady's death at the age of thirty-nine in December 1889. Just three years before, Grady had made his triumphant address on "The New South," in which he dramatized the movement toward reconciliation of North and South, to the New England Society in New York. In the years that followed Grady had spoken frequently on the theme of the development of the South's natural resources. By contrast, Harris remained tied to his editorial desk and rarely left Atlanta. He had once accompanied Grady to Eatonton, where the latter spoke at the

Putnam County Fair; but though Harris had sat on the platform with Grady, he had declined an opportunity to address the crowd. Following Grady's death, a memorial volume compiled by the staff of the *Constitution* and edited by Harris was published. Harris wrote a biographical sketch for the book in which he pointed out the significance of Grady's contribution to Atlanta and the South through his zeal and optimism in promoting the region's material resources and advocating national unity.

Though Grady's brilliant career was cut short by his death, the decade of the 1890s proved to be highly productive for Harris. Despite his full-time duties as an editorial writer, columnist, and editor of the *Constitution* during those years, Harris found the time to write and edit fourteen books. In the introduction to *Uncle Remus and His Friends* (1892), Harris, fearing that reader interest was waning, announced that the old Negro would never again bother the public with any more of his whimsical stories. He did so reluctantly, Harris wrote, because Uncle Remus had found friends for him in all parts of the world. The creator of Uncle Remus also asserted that there was no pretense on his part that the stories were in the nature of literature or that his retelling of them touched literary art at any point. "There is nothing here," Harris wrote, "but an old Negro man, a little boy, and a dull reporter, the matter of discourse being fantasies as uncouth as the original man ever conceived of." Despite Harris's fears that public interest in regional dialect stories was diminishing, the book was well received, and Uncle Remus was later to be resurrected in other tales.

Having bade a reluctant farewell to Uncle Remus, Harris turned his efforts to six volumes of old plantation stories designed primarily for children. The favorable response to *Daddy Jake the Runaway* in 1889 probably inspired Harris to launch the series, which, one reviewer noted, resembled the adventures of Alice in Wonderland. Each book was set in the pastoral environment of the old Abercrombie plantation in middle Georgia before the Civil War. The series included *Little Mr. Thimblefinger and His Queer Country: What the Children Saw and Heard There* (1894), *Mr. Rabbit at Home* (1895), *The Story of Aaron (So Named) the Son of Ben Ali* (1896), *Aaron in the Wildwoods* (1897), *Plantation Pageants* (1899), and *Wally Wanderoon and His Story-Telling Machine* (1903).

During the 1890s Harris continued to contribute color sketches and tales focusing on Southern themes to newspapers and national magazines, making him one of the best-known regional writers in the United States. Many of the stories from *Uncle Remus and His Friends* were published in a syndicate of newspapers including the *New York Sun, Boston Globe, Philadelphia Times, Washington Evening Star, Chicago Inter Ocean, St. Louis Republic, San Francisco Examiner, Louisville Courier-Journal*, and *New Orleans Times-Democrat*. In the fall of 1893 Harris took temporary leave of his duties on the *Constitution* to cover for *Scribner's* magazine the devastation of the Sea Islands hurricanes, which had struck the islands lying off the southeast Atlantic coast.

Another noteworthy event of the 1890s was the republication of *Uncle Remus: His Songs and His Sayings* in 1895 on the fifteenth anniversary of its original publication. The text was the same, but the book was illustrated with 112 drawings by Arthur B. Frost. Harris was so pleased with Frost's insight into the character of Uncle Remus that he dedicated the anniversary edition to the artist. "The book was mine," Harris wrote, "but now you have made it

Frontispiece by Arthur B. Frost for the revised edition of Uncle Remus: His Songs and His Sayings. *Harris thought Frost had captured the true character of Uncle Remus.*

yours, both sap and pith."

Harris tried his hand at a novel for the second time in 1896 with *Sister Jane: Her Friends and Acquaintances*. Composition of *Sister Jane* was a frustrating experience for Harris, who was under no illusion concerning the artistic merits of the book. Although *Sister Jane* had a surprisingly good sale of 3,000 copies shortly after its publication, the reviews were mixed. Harris again turned his literary effort to short stories, and in 1898 *Tales of the Home Folks in Peace and War* was published. The book presented interesting sidelights on middle Georgia life during and after the Civil War, but literary critics compared it unfavorably with Harris's earlier work in *Mingo, Free Joe*, and *Balaam and His Master* (1891). Harris's next book, *The Chronicles of Aunt Minervy Ann*, which recounted Aunt Minervy's experiences during the early years of Reconstruction, was better received in 1899.

Also in 1899, Harris began to contribute to the *Saturday Evening Post* a series of stories which dealt with blockade running and spy adventures during the Civil War. All of these stories were apparently pure inventions by Harris, for there is no evidence that he did any historical research in preparing them. The series met with such popular response that the stories were published as a book in 1900 under the title of *On the Wing of Occasions*. One story in the collection singled out for praise by many critics was "The Kidnapping of President Lincoln." In it Harris created Billy Sanders, a middle-class Georgian who would enliven numerous other sketches and eventually would become Harris's narrative spokesman on current events, political issues, and politicians.

Finally, in September 1900, after a journalistic career which had spanned almost thirty years, Harris submitted his resignation to the *Constitution*. In an interview which appeared in the *Atlanta Journal* the following day, Harris emphasized that he had not resigned because of any differences between him and the *Constitution*, where he had worked for twenty-four years. His sole purpose in resigning, he said, was because he wished to devote all of his time to literature, which was more congenial and more profitable. He asked the *Journal* reporter, "Please don't make a splutter about it. Just say, in your kindly way, that an old hoss, grown tired of stopping before the same doors every day, has kicked out of the harness and proposes to keep the flies off in his own way." The *Constitution*, in its story of Harris's retirement, promised that he would continue to furnish it with contributions "whenever a subject struck his fancy."

Now that he was no longer involved in his day-to-day duties as a journalist, Harris looked forward to spending his remaining years in the quiet seclusion of his home in West End. His first project was apparently to resume work on a novel about the legendary exploits of a Negro slave named "Qua" in Georgia during the Revolutionary War. Harris's correspondence indicates that Scribners was interested in publishing the novel, but for some reason the story was never completed. The manuscript, consisting of seven completed chapters, was discovered in 1927 among the papers which Harris's family had placed at Emory University. Another novel, *Gabriel Tolliver: A Story of Reconstruction*, was published in 1902. Also published in 1902 was *The Making of a Statesman*, a collection of four stories which Harris had contributed to the *Saturday Evening Post* during 1900 and 1901.

Two years after his retirement, the *Constitution* carried a news report that Emory College would confer upon Harris an honorary degree of Doctor of Literature at its forthcoming commencement. Knowing the recipient's reputation as a shy and unassuming person, the correspondent ventured the hope that Harris would be present to receive his degree. But as biographer Paul M. Cousins notes: "It was as foreign to his modest nature to don academic regalia as it was pleasing to Mark Twain to wear the robe and insignia of his honorary Oxford University degree, and the degree was awarded in his absence."

Illness disrupted Harris's writing schedule during much of 1902 and 1903, and it was late fall of 1903 before he produced another book, *Wally Wanderoon and His Story-Telling Machine*, the last volume of the old plantation series. Harris's best literary effort during his retirement years was *A Little Union Scout* (1904), a recital of the Civil War adventures of young Harry Herndon and his Negro companion, "Whistling Jim." The novel, which had been serialized in the *Saturday Evening Post* during February and March, struck a popular response from both general readers and reviewers and sold more than 4,000 copies within a few weeks.

At the urging of the *Post*, Harris returned to his Uncle Remus stories, contributing fifteen rhymed folklore tales which were published during 1903 and 1904. These verses, plus ten of the old plantation ballads as sung by Uncle Remus in the 1880 book, were published by Appleton as *The Tar-Baby and Other Rhymes of Uncle Remus* in 1904. This was followed in 1905 by another book of tales entitled *Told by Uncle Remus: New Stories of the Old Plantation*. The little white boy of the earlier series would have been a grown man by 1905, so Harris had Uncle Remus relate the stories to Miss Sally's grandson from Atlanta, who was visiting his grandmother in the country.

Two additional Uncle Remus books completed the series. *Uncle Remus and Brer Rabbit* (1907) contained six tales and five poems and was illustrated with large, multicolored cartoons, two for each page of the text. *Uncle Remus and the Little Boy* (1910), published two years after Harris's death, contained five poems, a song, and seven stories that continued the narrative cycle in which Uncle Remus educated his young listener about animal and human behavior.

Two events climaxed Harris's long career as a journalist, humorist, and folklorist. One was the visit of President Theodore Roosevelt to Atlanta in October 1905. Mrs. Roosevelt, who insisted on meeting Harris, had caused him to be invited to a reception at the governor's mansion, and he later stood with her on the balcony to view the parade. The president singled out Harris for praise at a luncheon, noting that "Presidents may come and Presidents may go, but Uncle Remus stays put. Georgia has done a great many things for the Union, but she has never done more than when she gave Joel Chandler Harris to American literature." Commenting upon the president's visit to Atlanta, Paul M. Cousins notes: "In the presence of the most eminent group of men ever previously assembled in Atlanta, plain Joe Harris, Atlanta's most inconspicuous citizen, had at last been recognized as Joel Chandler Harris, the one man among them who had made the South favorably known to the nation as a whole, whose books had been reprinted in England and translated into many foreign languages." The *Constitution* carried Harris's picture on its front page the next morning, and the story featured the honor which President Roosevelt had accorded him. Harris was subsequently invited to dinner at the White House.

The other event was Harris's last publishing venture—as editor of *Uncle Remus's Magazine*, a monthly periodical launched by his eldest son, Julian, and a group of young Atlanta businessmen. Julian had resigned from the *Constitution* to become business manager of the magazine. In reluctantly accepting the position of editor, Harris was assured that he would be relieved of all financial responsibility and would be in complete control of the editorial content of the magazine. But from the beginning the magazine had problems. Planned for April, the first issue was finally printed in June 1907, but its faulty printing and botched illustrations greatly disturbed Harris, and thousands of copies had to be discarded. In recalling his father's dissatisfaction with this important first number, Julian wrote: "His training as a printer and pressman, combined with his artistic sensibilities, caused him to suffer something of an outrage; and he feared the result on the magazine's future."

The first issue of the magazine contained a chapter of Harris's new novel, *The Bishop and the Booger-Man*, which was published posthumously as a book in 1909. In each issue of the magazine, Harris contributed an editorial essay dealing with such subjects as "Progress in the Best and Highest Sense," "The Philosophy of Failure," "Houses and Homes," and "The Old and the New South." In each issue Harris also prepared an article dealing with a political question or happenings in the world of business. The narrator of such articles was usually Billy Sanders, the Civil War veteran from "The Kidnapping of President Lincoln," who had also been the central figure of a three-part story in the *Saturday Evening Post* in 1907 which was published as *The Shadow between His Shoulder-Blades* (1909). Harris also contributed new Uncle Remus stories from time to time. In November 1907 Harris took time off from his editorial responsibilities for his visit to Washington, D.C., and dinner at the White House. In reporting upon that visit, Harris employed the forceful vernacular language of Billy Sanders to inform readers about what impressed him most in Washington.

In May 1908, *Uncle Remus's Magazine* absorbed *The Home Magazine*, which was being published in Indianapolis by Bobbs-Merrill. In his editorial announcement of the merger, Harris stated that henceforth the magazine would be called *Uncle Remus's – The Home Magazine*. He promised to make the combined publication truly representative of all sections of the country. But Harris's health began to fail appreciably during the spring of 1908. During April and May he continued to give his attention to his editorial work, but he grew more listless and discontinued his walks among his rose gardens. On Saturday, 4 July, the *Constitution* carried the news of his death at his home in West End the preceding evening.

A boulder of Georgia granite marks Harris's grave in Westview Cemetery in Atlanta. A bronze plaque bears the words Harris had used in dedicating the fifteenth anniversary edition of *Uncle Remus: His Songs and His Sayings* to Arthur B. Frost: "I seem to see before me the smiling faces of thousands of children—some young and fresh, and some wearing the friendly marks of age, but all children at heart—and not an unfriendly face among them. And out of the confusion, and while I am trying hard to speak the right word, I seem to hear a voice lifted above the rest, saying: 'You have made some of us happy.' And so I feel my heart fluttering and my lips trembling, and I have to bow silently and turn away, and hurry back into the obscurity that fits me best." In a letter to Ambrose Bierce in 1896, Harris had written: "I am simply a cornfield 'journalist,' and have never held any higher position, even in that field, than that of writer of political editorials. For twenty years this has been my trade, and it has left me small opportunity to even attempt literary work." But as a talented columnist and the leading editorial writer for the *Constitution*, one of the most prestigious newspapers in the South, Harris clearly left his mark on the history of the Reconstruction and post-Reconstruction periods, even in his role as a journalist.

It is often the fate of writers who are widely read and highly honored in their own day to be ignored by succeeding generations. Though many of his books are out of print, the republication of *The Complete Tales of Uncle Remus* (1955) almost fifty years after the author's death attests to a lasting interest in Harris's literary narrator and the

Atlanta Constitution *cartoon on the occasion of Harris's visit with Theodore Roosevelt, 19 November 1907*

painstaking care and fidelity with which his middle Georgia speech was captured. Harris's celebrated use of reverse psychology in the tar-baby story has made "being thrown into the briar patch" an internationally recognized metaphor.

Harris's keen perception of the particulars of language and human psychology has continued to impress scholars and literary critics. R. Bruce Bickley has observed that "Harris's own supersensitive nature made him acutely aware of the subtle gestures, glances, and innuendoes that often convey enormous meanings"; Uncle Remus, Billy Sanders, Aunt Minervy Ann, and Mingo "are vital and enduring characters because they themselves are accomplished narrative artists and students of human nature who bring us easily into their world and let us walk around in it with them." Linguists and folklorists continue to be impressed by Harris's discerning ear for speech patterns and his eye for the details of folk tradition. As an early recorder of Negro dialect and folklore, Harris produced a useful anthropological and linguistic profile that would otherwise have been unobtainable.

Harris considered his Uncle Remus stories "genuine folklore tales" and viewed himself as a mere recorder of the stories. He wrote to Mark Twain in 1881 that he was "perfectly aware that my book has no basis of literary art," though he said that he appreciated the fact that "everybody has been so kind to the old man." Authorities are generally in agreement that Harris did himself an injustice in ascribing to himself the role of "transcriber." Twain, in responding to Harris's letter, noted that "Uncle Remus is most deftly drawn and is a lovable and delightful creation; he and the little boy and their relations with each other are bright, fine literature, and worthy to live." Literary critics today would seem to agree with that assessment.

The day following his death, the *Constitution* said of Harris: "From all of his studied unobtrusiveness, the man wrought himself a broad and firm place in the spiritual history and traditions of his people; and it is from things spiritual that the things of substance take their color and substance. . . . His reputation is worldwide because he was the articulate voice of that humble race, whose every mood and tense he knew with complete comprehension. His mission was—and is—broader. For his folklore and his novels, his short stories and his poems breathe consistently a distinguished philosophy. It was the creed of optimism, of mutual trust, and of tolerance of all living things, of common sense and of idealism that is worthwhile because it fits the unvarnished duty of every hour."

Other:

F. R. Goulding, *The Young Marooners*, introduction by Harris (New York: Dodd, Mead, 1887);

Irwin Russell, *Poems*, introduction by Harris (New York: Century, 1887);

Life of Henry W. Grady, edited by Harris (New York: Cassell, 1890);

F. L. Stanton, *Songs of a Day*, introduction by Harris (Atlanta: Foote & Davies, 1893);

Stanton, *Songs of the Soil*, introduction by Harris (New York: Appleton, 1894);

Jennie T. Clarke, *Songs of the South*, introduction by Harris (New York: Doubleday, Page, 1896);

Eugene Field, *The House, an Episode in the Lives of Reuben Baker, Astronomer, and of His Wife Alice*, introduction by Harris (New York: Scribners, 1896);

Howard Weeden, *Bandanna Ballads*, introduction by Harris (New York: Doubleday & McClure, 1899);

Rudolph Eickenmeyer, Jr., *Down South: Pictures*, introduction by Harris (New York: Russell, 1900);

A. B. Frost, *Drawings*, with verses by Wallace Irwin, introduction by Harris (New York: Collier, 1904).

Letters:

Mark Twain to Uncle Remus: 1881-1885, edited by Thomas H. English, Emory University Sources and Reprints, series 7, no. 3 (Atlanta: Emory University Press, 1953).

Bibliography:

William Bradley Strickland, "A Check List of the Periodical Contributions of Joel Chandler Harris (1848-1908)," *American Literary Realism*, 9 (Summer 1976): 207-229.

Biographies:

Julia Collier Harris, *The Life and Letters of Joel Chandler Harris* (Boston: Houghton Mifflin, 1918);

Robert Lemuel Wiggins, *The Life of Joel Chandler Harris, from Obscurity in Boyhood to Fame in Early Manhood* (Nashville, Tenn.: Publishing House Methodist Episcopal Church, South, 1918);

Paul M. Cousins, *Joel Chandler Harris: A Biography* (Baton Rouge: Louisiana State University Press, 1968).

References:

R. Bruce Bickley, Jr., *Joel Chandler Harris* (Boston: Twayne, 1978);

Stella Brewer Brookes, *Joel Chandler Harris—*

Folklorist (Athens: University of Georgia Press, 1950);

Alvin P. Harlow, *Joel Chandler Harris: Plantation Storyteller* (New York: Julian Messner, 1941);

Julian Collier Harris, *Joel Chandler Harris as Editor and Essayist* (Chapel Hill: University of North Carolina Press, 1931);

Sumner Ives, *The Phonology of the Uncle Remus Tales*,

Publication of the American Dialect Society no. 22 (Gainesville, Fla.: American Dialect Society, 1954).

Papers:

Manuscripts, letters, and other pertinent materials are in the Joel Chandler Harris Memorial Collection, Emory University, Atlanta, Georgia.

Evan P. Howell

(10 December 1839-6 August 1905)

Wallace B. Eberhard
University of Georgia

MAJOR POSITION HELD: Editor in chief, *Atlanta Constitution* (1876-1897).

Southerner in the late-nineteenth-century tradition and style, lawyer, politician, civic mover-and-shaker, forthright newsman, executive, and shrewd judge of talent: all of these expressions describe Evan P. Howell, the native Georgian who helped to put the young *Atlanta Constitution* on its feet, financially and editorially, and guided its progress for twenty years before editorial control passed to one of his sons.

His journalistic experience was scant when he acquired a half interest in the *Constitution* in October 1876. A native of Warsaw, Georgia, Evan Park Howell was the first of eight children born to Clark Howell and his second wife, Effiah Jane Park Howell. (Clark Howell already had one child by his first wife and would later have two more by a third.) The family moved to Atlanta when Howell was nine years old; they lived in the town for two years, then moved to a home on the bank of the Chattahoochee River, outside of Atlanta. Howell completed a two-year course at the Georgia Military Institute in Marietta and read law in the small town of Sandersville for a year before enrolling at the University of Georgia's Lumpkin Law School, from which he graduated in 1859. The Civil War broke out only a few weeks after he began the formal practice of law, however, and he enlisted in the Confederate army. At about the same time, on 6 June 1861, he married Julia Erwin of South Carolina. His war service was distinguished and active, and he rose from the enlisted ranks to become captain of an

Evan P. Howell

artillery battery which was in the thick of many battles, including Chickamauga, Lookout Mountain, and Atlanta. At the war's end he returned to the family home north of Atlanta with his wife and the first of their seven children, and cut and sold timber from his father's lands, timber much needed for the rebuilding of the city. His entry into journalism came in 1867, when he became a reporter and then city editor for the *Atlanta Intelligencer*, but he worked there only a year before resuming the practice of law full-time. He was elected solicitor general for Atlanta, and then, in 1873, to the first of three terms as a state senator.

Howell was retained as an attorney by the *Constitution*, which had been established in 1868. The newspaper had grown in status and circulation under the management of William A. Hemphill and a succession of editors. Edward Y. Clarke had purchased a half interest in the paper when he became editor in 1870, and the Clarke-Hemphill combination was successful in surpassing a half-dozen rival newspapers. But the work apparently took its toll on Clarke, who sold his share of the newspaper to Howell on 18 October 1876. At the same time, Howell succeeded Clarke as editor in chief.

Howell combined his background and talents in skillful fashion in the post. He was the son of a well-known Atlanta judge, and in his own right a war hero, a prominent attorney, and a local and state officeholder. He was acquainted with the field of journalism through his brief apprenticeship as reporter and editor on the *Intelligencer* and as counsel to the *Constitution*. He also brought a strong sense of responsibility to public service and to straightforward and aggressive news gathering and writing. And he assembled about him a group of equally talented and dedicated journalists who continued to build the *Constitution* as the "South's Standard Newspaper." On 19 October 1876—the day after he acquired his *Constitution* stock—he hired Henry Woodfin Grady, only moments before Grady was to leave Atlanta for a position in Augusta. Grady in turn urged the hiring of Joel Chandler Harris, then a writer for the *Savannah Morning News*, who had come to Atlanta to escape the yellow fever epidemic on the coast. The Howell-Grady

Political cartoon in the Macon Telegraph *showing the differing positions taken by* Atlanta Constitution *officers during the 1887 prohibition campaign: Howell (left) favored the "wets"; editor Henry W. Grady (right) supported the "drys"; Howell's partner, William A. Hemphill–like the paper–remained neutral.*

partnership fell naturally into place and had a profound influence on the state and the region. Grady's position provided a platform for his lively and aggressive brand of journalism and a public career as spokesman for the New South, but without Howell's encouragement and support, Grady might not have been as successful as he was.

Though Grady seems to overshadow Howell as a journalist, the latter brought his own special talents as reporter, writer, and editor to the job. Grady's reportage from the Charleston earthquake of 1886 is well known, but Howell was with him as part of the team from the *Constitution* that made its way into the devastated heart of the city and brought out reports which were circulated nationwide. The two seldom differed in editorial viewpoint. The notable exception to their likemindedness came in a vote on prohibition of liquor in Atlanta in 1887: Grady favored the drys and Howell the wets. The paper took no editorial stand, though both sides were vigorously covered, with the wets winning by 1,117 votes.

Howell's standards were high and strict. One reporter who broke into journalism under Howell recalled what "the Captain" told him: "Get your news straight. I want you to print it all, and print it right, . . . but don't ruin a woman's life for a newspaper story. If a man does anything, get it straight and print it, and when he comes around the office looking for a retraction, I want to be able to put my finger on it and say, 'It is true.' " The *Constitution* prospered under the Howell-Grady leadership, staying ahead of its competition in circulation, turning profits for its investors, and providing a significant voice on public issues and politics that caught the ear and respect of the rest of the nation's press.

It is next to impossible to separate Howell's journalism career from the rest of his life. He seemed to be involved in virtually every civic promotion in Atlanta from new hotels to international expositions. He encouraged the rebuilding and expansion of railroads in the region and served as a director for several of them. He was a delegate to three national Democratic conventions, each time serving on the platform committee. In 1888 he served on the commission supervising the building of a new state capitol; they turned back part of the money voted for the structure when it was completed under budget.

The death of the popular, energetic, and effective Henry Grady in 1889 was a critical point for the *Constitution*. Were the fortunes of the newspaper to be tied to Grady's personal popularity or was its

Howell (center, third step from bottom) with other members of the State Capitol Building Commission in 1888

reputation based on a foundation that went beyond that one individual? The answer, in retrospect, is obvious. The *Constitution* endured, even as the rival evening *Journal* crept ahead in circulation, but the continued success was due in large measure to Howell's ability to direct the editorial affairs of the publication, in the broadest sense, while maintaining his highly visible role as a civic leader. His son Clark had shown interest in journalism at an early age (and in fact barely survived a brush with death as a teenager when he fell down an open elevator shaft in the *Constitution* building). After the younger Howell had graduated from the University of Georgia and worked briefly on Eastern newspapers, he had returned to the *Constitution*'s newsroom and begun an editorial apprenticeship under the eyes of his father and Grady. When Grady died, Clark Howell became managing editor under his father, and the two worked in tandem until Evan Howell's retirement in 1897.

The editorial policies of the Howell-directed *Constitution* in this period were generally public-spirited and well motivated, with occasional dashes of political partisanship. The Howells supported improvements in public education, especially at Clark's alma mater; local option on the sale of alcohol; Jim Crow laws; and more effective laws to deal with the wave of lynchings that characterized the period. They opposed arbitrary rate and fare increases by the railroads (despite Evan Howell's close connections with those companies), meaningful reconciliation of the races, and the populist movement. The Sunday and weekday editions of the *Constitution* grew, and all editions continued to emphasize state and local issues, often trumpeting their own extensive efforts to gather and cover the news. Business manager William A. Hemphill invested heavily in ten new linotype machines and a new press in 1891, dropping net profits to their lowest point in four years, though they climbed slowly later. The Howells were in the thick of Democratic politics, personally and editorially. In 1892, for instance, they stumped early in Georgia for Senator David Hill of New York as the Democratic presidential nominee, but they lost the fight at the state level and joined in support of Grover Cleveland. Hoke Smith, editor of the *Journal*, taunted the Howells for having been on the wrong side. Smith, to the Howells' chagrin, wound up as secretary of the interior under Cleveland as a reward for his own early and constant support in the campaign. (Later, Cleveland offered Evan Howell a consulship in Manchester, England, but Howell declined the appointment.) The *Constitution*'s support of Cleveland after the election was off again, on again, as they pushed for tariff reform, the federal income tax, and other issues. The grim state of the economy did not spare the South in 1894, but the Howells tried to put as favorable a light on affairs as possible. They thumped the drums for the upcoming Cotton States and International Exposition, held in the fall of 1895, extending an invitation to Booker T. Washington and other blacks to appear, and leading a racially mixed delegation to Washington, D.C., in a successful effort to wheedle $600,000 in federal funds for the exposition. The exposition did, indeed, seem to perk up Atlanta's economy, and it provided the platform for Washington's famous address eschewing social equality for blacks, a message much applauded by white listeners. Both Howells were on the speaker's platform when Washington spoke, and they editorially endorsed his remarks in the *Constitution*. In another speech, Evan Howell, putting behind him his Civil War experience as a defender of Atlanta some thirty years earlier, told Union veterans attending the exposition that the city was theirs. Though the Howells by now were frequently in disagreement with President Cleveland, they put their disputes aside to welcome him to the exposition, asking readers to forget politics for the occasion. They returned to their own editorial criticism of the president once he

was safely back in Washington.

After an unsuccessful run for the Democratic nomination for United States senator in 1896, Evan Howell decided to retire. On 5 April 1897, the Constitution Publishing Company's board of directors accepted his resignation as president. His stock interest was sold to Hugh T. Inman, William Hemphill became president, and Clark Howell became the editor in chief of the newspaper. The elder Howell was out of journalism for the first time in more than twenty years.

When a special commission was formed by President McKinley to investigate the conduct of the Spanish-American War, Evan Howell was on it. He was once again elected to state office after retiring from the *Constitution*, this time to the House of Representatives. He ended his public life as mayor of Atlanta in 1903 and 1904, and he died the following year.

In a eulogy penned for the rival *Atlanta News*, Joel Chandler Harris summed up Howell's talents as editor and writer: "He made the *Constitution* the mouthpiece for or against every public measure that was proposed. He made the newspaper successful, for when he gained control, it was a sorry affair, even as newspapers went in the day. . . . His success was little short of marvelous, for he was not a professional journalist nor a trained writer in the technical sense." Harris noted that Howell surrounded himself with capable writers but also "was in the best sense of the word an editor . . . who could write pungently when the occasion arose," with a style all his own.

References:

A Georgian [Clark Howell], "Evan P. Howell," *Georgia Historical Quarterly*, 1 (March 1917): 52-57;

Ralph McGill, "The 'Constitution' Story," *Saturday Review* (8 June 1968): 66;

Raymond B. Nixon, *Henry W. Grady* (New York: Knopf, 1943);

Dennis J. Pfennig, "The Captain Retires: Clark Howell Takes the Helm," *Atlanta Historical Journal*, 25 (Summer 1980): 5-20;

Pfennig, "Evan and Clark Howell and the *Atlanta Constitution*: The Partnership (1889-1897)," Ph.D. dissertation, University of Georgia, 1975.

Papers:

Evan P. Howell's papers are at Emory University, Atlanta, Georgia.

Ansel Nash Kellogg

(20 March 1832-23 March 1886)

Ellen M. Mrja
Mankato State University

MAJOR POSITIONS HELD: Editor and publisher, *Baraboo* (Wisconsin) *Republic* (1856-1862); publisher, *Chicago Western Railroad Gazette* (1865-1870), *New York Railroad Gazette* (1870-1873); owner, A. N. Kellogg Newspaper Company (1865-1886).

BOOKS: *Kellogg's Auxiliary Hand-Book: Containing a History of the Origin of Auxiliary Printing; with Opinions of Publishers* (Chicago: Kellogg, 1878); *Empirical Formulae for Approximate Computation by the late Ansel N. Kellogg* (Springfield, Missouri: Dixon, n.d.).

Ansel Nash Kellogg, who has been called "The Father of the Newspaper Syndicate," is one of the forgotten persons in journalism history—a figure too often bypassed for the more colorful big-city editors and publishers of the 1800s. Yet throughout his career Kellogg did as much as anyone to revolutionize both the content offered and the technological processes used by the rural, weekly press in America. Because of his work, thousands of weekly newspaper publishers were able, for the first time, to offer their readers the syndicated matter previously reserved for the metropolitan dailies.

Kellogg was born in Reading, Pennsylvania. Little is known about his early years except that when he was two, the family moved to New York, where Kellogg was educated. After graduating second in his class from Columbia College in 1852, Kellogg spent one year studying in an architect's office. But being of a journalistic turn of mind, he left in 1854 for Wisconsin, where he was given the opportunity to work in Portage on the *Northern Republic*. The next year he moved to Baraboo, where he edited and published the *Baraboo Republic* in partnership with Henry A. Perkins from October 1856 through 1859, and as sole owner from 1860 until May 1862.

As editor and publisher of the *Republic*, Kellogg was part of the growing trend of publishers establishing papers independent of party control in the newly settled Midwest. Most of these papers were four-page weeklies, printed six to nine col-

Ansel Nash Kellogg

umns to the page, with circulations of less than 1,000. The content of the papers tended to be standard fare—some local news, one or two columns of political comments, some legal and patent medicine notices. That left a considerable amount of space necessarily taken up by "miscellany"—the fiction, poetry, and entertainment features the editor was forced to clip from newspaper and magazine exchanges and laboriously paste into the paper for filler. For example, the *Republic*'s front page for 23 June 1859 contained the following: one column was topped with a sentimental poem entitled "To the Betrothed"; spread over other columns was "A Thrilling Adventure," a short story about a chimney rescue, clipped from an English magazine; from the *Springfield Republican News* appeared the inspirational piece "What a Blind Man Can Accomplish"; also featured was an advice column entitled "Washington's Advice to a Young Lady on Love and

Matrimony." Readers' curiosity about the famous was quenched with "Celebrities—How They Look," which offered the information: "Longfellow like a good-natured beef eater. . . ."

The inside pages of the paper carried the hard news. Kellogg, a Republican, was delighted with the election of Abraham Lincoln. Page two of the 8 November 1860 issue proclaimed in a nineteen-deck headline: "All Hail! The Slave Oligarchy Broken Down! The People Want Honest Abe for President! The Union Safe at Last! Now and Forever Liberty and Union. . . . Truth is Mighty and Has Prevailed!" Such sentiment made it not only understandable but morally right to Kellogg when his first assistant and journeyman printer, Joseph I. Weirich, enlisted in the Wisconsin regiment in 1861 after Lincoln's call for volunteers. But Kellogg soon discovered he could not issue a full-sized paper alone. Out of necessity, in July 1861 he made arrangements with David Atwood and Horace Rublee, publishers of the *Wisconsin State Journal* in Madison, to print half-sheet supplements on both sides with war news; Kellogg then bought these and folded them inside his own half-sheets. The arrangement proved satisfactory, except that Kellogg quickly realized that the clumsiness of handling two separate pieces of paper could be eliminated, and costs reduced, if he ordered full sheets printed on one side from the *Journal*, instead of half-sheets printed on both sides. Thus, the 10 July 1861 *Baraboo Republic* appeared as a four-page paper, pages two and three consisting of war news printed by the *Journal* and pages one and four printed by Kellogg in Baraboo. This was the first use of Kellogg's "patent insides" for weekly papers. This type of syndication, also called "readyprints," was to play an important part in the expansion of the weekly press in the late 1800s.

The next issue of the *Republic* contained another element which would play a key role in the development of syndicated material—advertising. The 17 July issue contained a prospectus for the *Journal* and the 21 August issue carried the first syndicated legal notice, which advertised a sale of "forfeited lands." Four other weekly publishers, also shorthanded because of the war, followed Kellogg's lead by ordering printed sheets from the *Journal*. Advertisers were happy to buy space in the "patent insides" in order to reach the readers of all the papers in the arrangement. By 1862, the number of papers using this economical device had grown to nearly two dozen.

However, not all publishers were supportive of the innovation; many criticized it by boasting that their papers contained nothing but "all home print." The apprehension felt by many was expressed by the publisher of the *Portage State Register*, who wrote: "The plan, if universally adopted, would give almost absolute control of state affairs to the editors who should be employed to do all the thinking for the papers in the state." But others saw this fear as groundless and a hindrance to the development of solid reporting in the weeklies. As another publisher wryly commented: "It is undeniable that the papers in the arrangement are decidedly better than before, some of them by nearly the 14 columns of reading matter furnished by the *Journal*. The spare time gives the editors (most of whom probably stood at the case the greater part of the time) an opportunity to polish their editorials and pick up local news, and the result is . . . a decided improvement in both departments."

Throughout the next year, Kellogg watched the *Journal*'s syndicate grow to include some thirty papers; a competing syndicate begun in Milwaukee by the *Evening Wisconsin* boasted the same number. For Kellogg, the time was ripe for establishing a syndicated service independent of any newspaper affiliation. He sold the *Republic* in May 1862 to Charles E. Stuart and John W. Blake and, patenting his device of the readyprint "insides," moved to Chicago in 1865 to begin his new venture. In Chicago Kellogg purchased a nine-column weekly, the *Western Railroad Gazette*, in the hope that the paper would "help out some in making a living" if his planned independent syndicate did not take hold. By August, however, Kellogg had solicited eight orders for his service—from five weeklies in Illinois, two in Wisconsin, and one in Minnesota. On 19 August, Kellogg's service became the first continuous independent syndicate to print from type set exclusively for weekly papers.

Kellogg made sure from the start that the service would be convenient for the publishers. The readyprints were sent out C.O.D. each week so that the publisher who wished to use them needed only a few dollars on hand when he went to pick them up at the express office. All publishers received the same undated seven-column folio "insides" or, in some cases, "outsides." The content of these first sheets was made up primarily of features and other miscellaneous entertainment items. Soon, however, Kellogg added advertisements and news to the readyprint stock.

Kellogg realized the importance of promoting his new product, and in the autumn of 1865 he produced the first issue of the *Publishers' Auxiliary*, which contained two pages of syndicated material and two pages of trade news and ads geared for publishers. (Over 100 years later, in 1968, the *Publishers' Auxiliary* would merge with the *National Publisher* to become the official newspaper of the National Newspaper Association.) The promotion paid off. By the end of 1865, Kellogg was supplying 53 papers in four states with the sheets at a price of seventy cents per quire. The economy of the service he offered had so endeared itself to weekly publishers that even with the war's end, the popularity of the service continued to grow. During 1866, he added 20 more papers from three new states; the following year the syndicate grew by 33 papers, and by 60 more in 1868. By the end of 1869, a total of 193 papers from areas as far away as Mississippi, Pennsylvania, and Tennessee were using Kellogg's readyprints. Because the first readyprint sheets were all alike, no political news had been carried in them; but by 1867 Kellogg's syndicate had become so sophisticated that he could promise publishers any desired type of political matter. The operation had grown to such an extent that Kellogg hired a weekly publisher, J. M. Edson, as the first syndicate editor in journalism history. By 1871 Kellogg's syndicate served 240 papers; nationwide, competing syndicates were begun, and by 1872 some 1,000 papers were being supplied with syndicated material.

Kellogg's success, however, was nearly destroyed by the great fire that swept through Chicago in October 1871 and engulfed his plant. Workers saved what they could, but the building, filled with paper stock, was little more than a charred ruin when the flames died. One worker, who valiantly loaded up a cart with forms of type and then wheeled it down to Lake Michigan to save the forms in the water, recalled taking Kellogg to the lake's edge two days later to see what was left of his company: "When I took them over to the place where I had run the cart into the water, we found some one had pulled out the cart and taken away the contents. A few type were still on the ground and a man and some boys were picking them up. One of the boys looked up to Mr. Kellogg and asked: 'Do they belong to you?' Mr. Kellogg said: 'Yes, but you can have what is left.' Thus was taken away one of the last hopes of Mr. Kellogg, as most of the type in Chicago had been burnt up."

Despite the setback, Kellogg not only rebuilt the business in the ensuing years, but he pioneered technological changes that improved the syndicate and produced two decades of unabated expansion. In May 1872, Kellogg bought a St. Louis syndicate that supplied 116 papers. As his first order of busi-

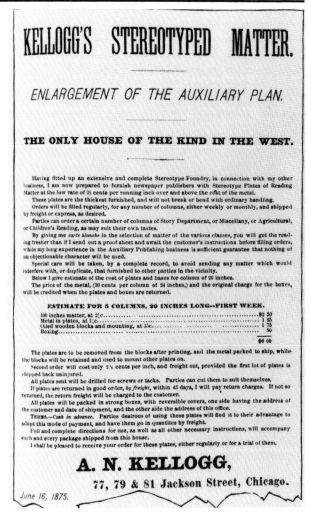

Advertisement in the American Newspaper Reporter, *1875, for Kellogg's printing plates*

ness, he set out to standardize the column width used by the papers, which most weekly publishers purposely varied in an attempt to keep their papers as individualized as possible. In the interest of economy, Kellogg convinced first the papers on the St. Louis list and then others to standardize to thirteen-em columns by exchanging their leads and rules for ones cut to the new measure. The thirteen-em remained the standard measure for decades.

Technological improvements continued in 1875 when Kellogg and his colleague James J. Schock patented a better method of making and fastening stereotyped plates. The plates were designed so that after being fastened onto a wood base, they could be cut off to any desired length at a cost of 2½ cents per inch, a process that critics derided as "editing with a saw." After printing, the plates could be removed from the base and sent back to the supply house, with Kellogg picking up the return postage. Kellogg and Schock further improved the stereotype process in 1876 and 1878 when they created the "butterfly plate," a superior method of holding the plate to the base. Kellogg later invented a lightweight celluloid plate, which further reduced transportation costs. The use of these stereotyped plates met with the same criticism from the hard-line "all home print" publishers that readyprint use had. Yet both methods saved time, labor, and expense for the weekly publisher who used them. Furthermore, readers of the papers received material which otherwise would not have appeared in the small weekly press. Despite the criticism, therefore, the use of both the stereotyped plate and readyprints continued to flourish.

Certainly one of Kellogg's highest honors was his being asked to prepare for the Centennial Exposition of 1876 in Philadelphia an exhibit of all the newspapers then served by his syndicate. The 583 papers represented twenty-five states and one Canadian province. Within four years, the Kellogg company included five branch offices that served more than 800 papers. Nationally some 3,000 weeklies—about two-fifths of all weeklies in the country—made use of readyprints.

In keeping with the monopolistic tendencies of the times, Kellogg continued to expand his holdings during the 1880s. When the A. N. Kellogg Newspaper Company was incorporated in Illinois on 5 March 1881, it showed capital stock of $200,000. In 1882 it acquired the Western Auxiliary Publishing House and its 55 papers, and the Aikens Newspaper Union with 115 more. Kellogg extended his reach into the South in 1884 with the establishment of a Memphis branch office and its list of 15 additional papers.

Kellogg went on a number of European tours before settling in New York City. In his later years, he became an invalid, but still retained the presidency of the A. N. Kellogg Newspaper Company. He died in Thomasville, Georgia, in 1886, leaving behind his wife, the former Annie E. Barnes, whom he had married in 1859 at Baraboo, and adult daughters.

At the time of Kellogg's death, his twenty years in the syndicated newspaper field had resulted in a corporation servicing nearly 1,400 papers with readyprints and thousands more with stereotyped plates. That he was a keen businessman who fulfilled an unmet need cannot be questioned; neither can his contribution to the development of the independent weekly press.

The Kellogg Company continued its expansion under Kellogg's successor as president, E. E. Pratt; although it was soon outstripped in the plate business by competitors, its readyprint business flourished until after the turn of the century. In 1906, it was purchased by its rival, the Western Newspaper Union, which had devised an "individual service" system in response to the all-home-print movement among weekly editors.

Kellogg was known by his contemporaries not only as a shrewd businessman but as a cultured "gentleman of the old school," and he was respected as a journalist who maintained high standards for his syndicated service. Some of the rules laid down by Kellogg for his editorial staff serve as evidence of his journalistic integrity:

"Spare no pain nor expense to get the best and freshest of news and literary matter."

"It is as much the mark of a good editor to know what not to print as to be able to select good and appropriate matter."

"When in doubt about the propriety of printing an article, leave it out; there is plenty of that which is unquestionably good and desirable."

"There is always room for improvement and betterment. The best is none too good for the Kellogg service."

References:

J. M. Edson, *History of the A. N. Kellogg Newspaper Company* (Chicago, 1890);

M. M. Quaife, "How A. N. Kellogg Revolutionized America's Country Press," *National Printer-Journalist* (February 1922);

Hiley H. Ward, "Ninety Years of the National Newspaper Association: The Mind and Dynamics of Grassroots Journalism in Shaping America," Ph.D. dissertation, University of Minnesota, 1977;

Elmo Scott Watson, *A History of Newspaper Syndicates in the United States: 1865-1935* (Chicago: Publishers' Auxiliary, 1936);

W.P.A. Historical Records Survey Project, *A Check List of the Kellogg Collection of "Patent Inside" Newspapers of 1876* (Chicago, 1939).

Papers:
A three-volume collection of the newspapers served by Kellogg in 1876, prepared for exhibit at the Centennial Exposition in Philadelphia, is now preserved in the library of the Chicago Historical Society.

John Armoy Knox

(March 1850-18 December 1906)

C. Richard King

MAJOR POSITIONS HELD: Editor / manager, *Texas Siftings* (1881-1892); editor / manager, *Atlanta Herald* (1892-1894).

BOOKS: *Sketches from Texas "Siftings,"* by Knox and Alexander E. Sweet (New York: Texas Siftings Publishing Co., 1882);

On a Mexican Mustang, through Texas, from the Gulf to the Rio Grande, by Knox and Sweet (Hartford, Conn.: S. S. Scranton, 1883; London: Trübner, 1883);

Texas Siftings, by Knox and Sweet (New York & Austin, Tex.: Texas Siftings Publishing Co., 1883?; London: Routledge, 1883);

Three Dozen Good Stories from Texas Siftings, by Knox and Sweet (New York & Chicago: Ogilvie, 1887);

Texas Siftings Afloat; A Devil of a Trip; or, The Log of a Three Months' Cruise of the Yacht "Champlain" through the Canadian Lakes and Rivers, down the St. Lawrence, to New York (London: Texas Siftings Publishing Co., 1888);

All about the Klondike Gold Mines (New York: Miners' News Publishing Co., 1897);

Railroad Fun, by Knox and Sweet (New York: Ogilvie, n.d.);

Texas Siftings and Texas Journalism (Austin: Department of Journalism Development Program, The University of Texas, 1977).

In Laramie, Wyoming, Bill Nye produced humorous sketches for the *Boomerang*, a publication he had founded and named in honor of his pet mule. In Little Rock, Arkansas, Opie Read penned a column of backcountry sketches, "Arkansaw Traveler," read by approximately 85,000 subscribers. In Iowa, Robert J. Burdette relied on a whimsical style and a storehouse of puns to hold the audience for his "Hawk Eye-tems" column in the *Burlington Hawkeye*. In Colorado, Eugene Field, in preparation for greater audiences, delighted readers of the *Denver Tribune* with his "Nonpareil Column" and his "Old Gossip" items. And in Austin, Texas, John Armoy Knox and his partner, Alexander Edwin Sweet (1841-1901), refined puns and sharpened their wit for *Texas Siftings*, a paper which

Austin History Center, Austin Public Library

printed some local news and conducted some crusades but appealed to its readers primarily because of its humor. Like Nye, Read, Burdette, and Field, Knox and Sweet gave readers a crackerbarrel type of writing, filled with anecdotes, homely metaphors, and proverbs; they relied on overstatement and frequently assumed the role of "wise fool." Within a decade, the partners had converted a state paper into a publication with a national following and an international edition.

Born in March 1850 in Armoy, Ireland, the son of a Belfast banker, Knox went through "uneventful" school days before going to work in a bank. After three years, in 1872, he toured the United States in search of better health; it is not known what sort of illness prompted this trip. After a year in Georgia, he visited Texas and "travelled on board of a Mexican mustang for several months." In 1872, while stationed in Austin as an agent of the Wheeler Sewing Machine Company, he became acquainted with Sweet, who had built a reputation for his humorous pieces in the *Galveston News* and *San Antonio Herald*. Knox settled in Austin and went into newspaper work also; whether Knox was writing for an Austin paper or was capital correspondent for an out-of-town publication is not certain. In any case, he and Sweet took over the office space occupied by the recently defunct *Weekly Review*, and in May 1881, with Frank P. Holland (later founder of *Texas Farm and Ranch* and *Holland's Magazine*), William O'Leary (later city editor of the *Dallas Morning News*), and W. H. Caskie (artist), they began the weekly *Texas Siftings*.

The first page of volume one, number one, on 9 May carried the traditional prospectus. Knox and Sweet, listing themselves as "proprietors, editors, and sifters," promised potential readers that the paper would not contain politics, vituperation, original poetry, a patent inside, a catalogue of crimes, coarse words or expressions, "nor anything that our wives and children should not read." The paper would include "news, humor, opinions, eight pages, live editorials, correspondence, interesting news, historical notes, short paragraphs, sense and nonsense, forty-eight columns, New York correspondence, Washington correspondence, financial and market reports, and many other features interesting to the general reader." During the first week of publication, Knox sold 112 yearly subscriptions without solicitation. He informed readers that nine traveling agents would offer subscriptions and advertising for the "state paper," which would be "for sale on the counters of every news store in the state." A single copy was priced at five cents; yearly rates were two dollars.

The first number contained a denial that Jay Gould held controlling interest in the paper. Knox and Sweet explained that the rumor was "utterly without foundation" but had been designed "to injure us in our business."

In "A Discourse on Siftings," a writer who signed himself "Fanning Mill" offered an explanation of the name as well as the intent of the *Siftings*: "If there ever was a time when a thorough-going sifter was needed that time is at hand. Our country now abounds with *threshings* that should be sifted with a very fine sieve. We need a national sieve of huge dimensions and a state sieve of no small proportions. . . . There is much truth in Texas, but it is so badly mixed with chaff that it cannot be utilized until sifted." The writer called attention to school

matters, Sunday laws, the convict system, prohibition theories, and immigration problems.

With circulation figures predicted to reach 50,000, *Texas Siftings* began its second year, and in January 1882, the proprietors promised that "during the year 1882 we shall continue to be, in politics, independent; in criticism, impartial; in the matter of publishing original poetry, abstemious; in comments, good natured; and in all things, truthful."

An early issue in the second volume contained news about plans to establish a state university in Austin, and the proprietors of the *Siftings* offered a recommendation: "Now what the editors of the Texas press expect and demand of the legislature, is that it create a department of journalism, the same to be located in Austin. The members of the faculty are to be selected from Texas editors. As is usual with such institutions the faculty will not have much to do except to exhaust the appropriation in the most agreeable manner to themselves. They are to do nothing but kill time." The *Texas Siftings* editors received praise from fellow editors and reprinted much of it in their own columns. The *New York Journal* had mentioned that Knox is "also well known both as an author and as a business man. He has written much for home and foreign magazines. His sketches published in the *Boston Post* last year were copied by the press all over the country. His style is terse, analytical, abounds in the highest class of humor and evidences a very observant mind. He carried with him into the new enterprise a knowledge of, and a capacity for business that have in all his previous undertakings commanded success." The editor of the *Weatherford* (Texas) *Daily Commercial* mentioned that the new publication was "being conducted under the able business management of J. Armoy Knox, who is widely known," and a writer for the *Grand Rapids* (Michigan) *Democrat* called Knox "not only a business man but an author of no little merit." A reporter for the *New York Elevated Railway Journal* labeled him "a journalist of vigor and ability." The office became a gathering place of Texas editors visiting the capital. William Sydney Porter (O. Henry), then a young man, often was a hunting companion and joined Knox and associates in conversation in a local beer garden.

As early as 1882, Knox and Sweet gave some thought to converting *Texas Siftings* into a national publication, and the paper began "engaging less and ever less in 'Texas sifting.'" In 1883, Knox moved to New York. Shortly after his arrival, he was reported to have fought a duel with a friend, a New York sculptor named D. B. Sheahan. The confrontation started over dinner when the artist said,

Flag of Knox's Texas Siftings

"You come from a place where justice is unknown. The administration of justice in Texas has always been a disgrace." Knox objected to this statement, and the discussion was continued in Sheahan's studio. Some sources report that in the duel that followed, Knox was wounded, "the ball passing clear through the fleshy part of the arm, below the shoulder." Other accounts indicate that "after the first fire . . . he (Knox) turned tail, but Sheahan demanded blood and Knox was forced to fire again, receiving a flesh wound."

The Associated Press reported the duel as a hoax staged for publicity purposes, and the *Austin Statesman* editorialized that whatever had happened, "Mr. Knox is just now getting any amount of gratuitous advertising. Were he to pay for it at transient rates it would take the receipts of several such papers as his to pay the bills. He is known to be an expert in the advertising business."

On 26 January 1884, Knox wrote "Dear Sweet," still in Texas: "It doesn't seem fair that while I am here shivering in what seems to be more than Arctic gelidity (gelidity is a new word, isn't it?) you should be enjoying the balmy gulf breeze down in Texas, eating dough nuts and other semi-tropical fruit fresh from the tree." After the paper's main office was transferred to the Temple Court Building in New York in February, Knox wrote his partner that "life in New York is very different from life in Texas. There is no wolf hunting, no jack rabbits coursing, no lynchings or other amusements of that class; but I am reconciled to it. . . ."

Now listed in the masthead as manager of the publication, Knox was eyeing 200,000 circulation figures, but he could not separate himself from an interest in horses and dogs. On his Texas ranch he kept more than fifty dogs, and wrote that his "favourite dissipation is hunting the jack rabbit with greyhounds, and the cayote [*sic*] with wolf hounds." He made occasional trips from New York to his ranch. When his office was in Texas, he had kept a feedbox containing oats for his horses as a part of the front-room fixtures of *Texas Siftings*; editors used the container as a footstool.

In May 1884, Knox and H. Farrar McDermott, a poet, visited Washington, the trip supplying fodder for Knox's editorial mill. He wrote in *Texas Siftings*, "I was allowed to drink lemonade out of the last glass used by Daniel Webster. Out of an ordinary glass lemonade costs fifteen cents; out of the Webster glass thirty cents is the tariff for revenue only." He visited a hatter and saw the last hat worn by Henry Clay, and a barber upon whom he called had the last razor "that brought tears to John C. Calhoun." A shave with it was one dollar. He called upon the poet Joaquin Miller, finding him in a rawhide-bottomed chair on the front porch of a log cabin, reading a book. He persuaded Miller to contribute items to *Texas Siftings*.

In June 1887, offices for *Texas Siftings* were moved to 240 Broadway, and A. Minor Griswold and Sweet were listed in the masthead as editors with Knox as manager. Three years later A. D. Berger was appointed assistant manager.

Wide acceptance of *Texas Siftings* is attested by circulation figures but also by the number of volumes reprinting popular pieces from the paper. As early as 1882, *Sketches from Texas "Siftings"* appeared, with illustrations by W. H. Caskie. Among the reprints were thirty-two pieces attributed to Knox, twenty-eight signed by Sweet, and seven co-authored. The following year, *Texas Siftings* maintained offices in New York, London, and Austin. That year, *On a Mexican Mustang, through Texas, from the Gulf to the Rio Grande* appeared. There is no preface, but Sweet and Knox had written that "prefaces are altogether superfluous." To the publisher, they wrote, "Try this book on the public without a preface. If it fails [the word *fails* has been struck] is not a success then, next time, we will buy a ready-made preface and write a book to fit it." *Three Dozen Good Stories* appeared in 1887 as an anthology of humorous pieces from *Texas Siftings*.

Knox's biggest literary success without Sweet as a coauthor was published in London in 1888. Titled *Texas Siftings Afloat; A Devil of a Trip; or, The Log of a Three Months' Cruise of the Yacht "Champlain" through the Canadian Lakes and Rivers, down the St. Lawrence, to New York*, the work was first published as weekly letters in the *Boston Herald, New York World, San Francisco Post, Chicago Herald, Toronto Mail, Milwaukee Sentinel, Philadelphia Press*, and other newspapers. An advertisement in the volume promotes the European edition of *Texas Siftings* as "the witty wonder of the age." Readers were informed that each sixteen-page issue of the paper was illustrated by eminent artists. "The best and cheapest Penny Paper in the world" was available at newsstands throughout "the United Kingdom, and in all the principal cities on the Continent of Europe, in India, and the Australian Colonies."

When he lectured on "The Humour of It" in Steinway Hall, New York, in 1888, Knox received more money from ticket sales than any other lecturer had ever received.

Knox wrote a column, "Phonographic Talks," which ran irregularly, the last one appearing 6 September 1890. Knox described, among other things, a visit to the Savoy music hall, the popularity of dyed beards, and the fuss over a streetcar conductor who had been charged with speaking rudely to his passengers.

After 1891, *Texas Siftings* began to decline in quality and circulation, and Knox disposed of his interest to Sweet, who sold the publication at a sheriff's sale to Robert Morgan in 1895. Freed from managerial responsibilities, Knox moved to Atlanta, where he became editor / manager of the *Herald*, but after two years he returned to make his home in New York. In 1900 he lost a suit against the actress Blanche Walsh (1873-1915), whom he had sought to enjoin from starring in the play *Marcell*, claiming that he had a copyrighted play of his own by the same name.

Knox averaged twenty cigars a day but was, according to the introduction to *Texas Siftings Afloat*, "abstemious in the matter of stimulants, and he claims that he 'never tells a lie'—outside of business hours." The introduction further quotes Knox as saying, "It is my habit to have business on tap during the day; at night the humorous spigot is pulled out, and some of those soul-harrowing, liver-regulating views of men and things flow out of me."

Knox spent his last years writing articles for newspapers and magazines. Afflicted with a heart disease, Knox died suddenly at his home, 203 West 108th Street, New York, on 18 December 1906.

On one occasion a *Texas Siftings* subscriber who was moving out of town called at the office to explain that he would miss the paper, but did not know what his new address would be. Knox assured him, "You can get *Texas Siftings* from any respectable newsdealer in the United States."

"But who are the respectable newsdealers?"

"You will never have any trouble finding that out," Knox assured him. "The respectable newsdealers are the ones who keep *Texas Siftings*."

Some contemporary Austin residents might have disagreed with Knox. A photograph, dated 1881, in the Travis County Collection of the Austin

An 1881 photograph of Austin's junkman in his broken-down cart, holding a copy of the Texas Siftings *logotype–evidently a satirical comment on the newspaper's content (Austin History Center, Austin Public Library)*

Public Library shows the black who served as the city's only scavenger in his "wreck of a craft with a worn out donkey," the wheels of the vehicle held together by wires and his own clothing tattered, but holding a sign reading "Texas Siftings" in the distinctive type used in the paper's masthead.

References:
Sister M. Agatha, *Texas Prose Writings* (Dallas: Upshaw, 1936), pp. 53-54;
The Handbook of Texas (Austin: Texas State Historical Association, 1953): I, 971-992;

William R. Lineman, "Colonel Bill Snort, A Texas Jack Downing," *Southwestern Historical Quarterly*, 64 (October 1960): 185-199;
C. W. Raines, *Year Book for Texas* (Austin: Gammel, 1902), pp. 399-400.

Papers:
Clipping files for John Armoy Knox are located at the Barker Texas History Center, the University of Texas, Austin, and in the Travis County Collection of the Austin Public Library.

David Ross Locke

John M. Harrison
Pennsylvania State University

See also the Locke entry in *DLB 11, American Humorists, 1800-1950.*

BIRTH: Vestal, New York, 20 September 1833, to Nathaniel and Hester Ross Locke.

MARRIAGE: 7 March 1855 to Martha Bodine; children: Robinson, Edmund, Charles.

MAJOR POSITIONS HELD: Publisher, *Plymouth (Ohio) Advertiser* (1853-1855), *Mansfield (Ohio) Herald* (1855-1856), *Bucyrus (Ohio) Journal* (1856-1861); publisher/editor, *Hancock (Ohio) Jeffersonian* (1861-1865); editor, *Toledo Blade* (1865-1888); publisher and treasurer, *New York Evening Mail* (1871-1878).

DEATH: Toledo, Ohio, 15 February 1888.

SELECTED BOOKS: *The Nasby Papers* (Indianapolis: C. O. Perrine, 1864);
Divers Views, Opinions, and Prophecies of Yoors Trooly Petroleum V. Nasby (Cincinnati: R. W. Carroll, 1866);
Swinging Round the Circle; or, Andy's Trip to the West (New York: J. C. Haney, 1866);
"Swingin Round the Cirkle." By Petroleum V. Nasby . . . His Ideas of Men, Politics, and Things (Boston: Lee & Shepard, 1867);
Ekkoes from Kentucky (Boston: Lee & Shepard, 1868);
The Struggles (Social, Financial and Political) of Petroleum V. Nasby (Boston: I. N. Richardson, 1872);
Eastern Fruit on Western Dishes (London: Routledge, 1875; Boston: Lee & Shepard / New York: Lee, Shepard & Dillingham, 1875);
The Morals of Abou Ben Adhem (Boston: Lee & Shepard, 1875);
A Paper City (Boston: Lee & Shepard / New York: Dillingham, 1879);
Hannah Jane (Boston: Lee & Shepard / New York: Dillingham, 1882);
Nasby in Exile; or, Six Months of Travel (Toledo & Boston: Locke, 1882);
Beer and the Body (New York: National Temperance Society, 1884);
Prohibition (New York: National Temperance Society, 1886);

High License Does Not Diminish the Evil (New York: National Temperance Society, 1887);
The Demagogue: A Political Novel (Boston: Lee & Shepard / New York: Dillingham, 1891);
The Nasby Letters: Being the Original Nasby Letters, as Written during His Lifetime (Toledo: Toledo Blade, 1893).

David Ross Locke, in the guise of Petroleum Vesuvius Nasby, achieved a deserved reputation as one of the most powerful of American political satirists. For more than a quarter of a century, Locke harassed those who opposed the abolition of slavery and the granting of equal rights to the freed slaves and supported a number of reform movements, including women's rights and the prohibition of liquor. A versatile writer and an innovative journalist, Locke established himself and the *Toledo Blade* as significant forces in national affairs following the Civil War.

Locke was one of that remarkable group of American journalists who learned the printing trade as apprentices and, in large numbers, went on to become owners and editors of the nation's newspapers. Born 20 September 1833 at Vestal, New York, he moved with his parents to the nearby village of Marathon, where he entered the elementary school, completing the first five grades. Then, in September 1845, an advertisement appeared in the *Cortland Democrat* for "a boy from 16 to 17 years of age . . . as an apprentice to the Printing Business," and Nathaniel Locke, who operated a tannery and shoe factory, decided the time had come for young David to go to work. Father and son walked the fourteen miles from Marathon to Cortland to apply for the job.

Although he was but twelve years old and had to stand on a box to bring his head above the frame of the printer's typecase, young Locke was hired. He began at once to demonstrate the particular talents that were to become evident in his career as an editor. The five years of apprenticeship also provided the roots of the strong libertarian strain that persisted in Locke's writings—a result of his early exposure to Jacksonian Democracy. His sympathies were with the Democratic party, and it was not until the slavery issue had produced the Republican party that he changed his political affiliation.

When his apprenticeship had been completed in two years fewer than the customary seven, Locke moved on in 1850 to Corning, New York, some fifty miles from Cortland, where he went to work on another weekly newspaper, the *Journal*. One of his fellow printers there was Marcus Mills Pomeroy, known as "Brick," who later established a Democratic newspaper at LaCrosse, Wisconsin, and became one of the most outspoken copperhead editors during the Civil War. The friendship between Locke and Mills survived their total disagreement during that later time. Another of Locke's associates on the *Journal* was a printer named A. Z. (Zack) Lombard, with whom he launched *The Fountain of Temperance*. The two young printers, whose thirst for liquor already was legendary, had little success persuading others to subscribe to their temperance journal, and *The Fountain of Temperance* soon languished.

Locke left Corning in 1851 and went to Cleveland, where he worked first on the *Herald*, then on the *Plain Dealer*. It was during his employment by the *Herald* that Locke gave early indication of the strength of his commitment to the rights of Negroes. When white printers struck against working on equal terms with John M. Langston,

then a student at Oberlin College, Locke refused to join them. Langston subsequently became United States minister to Liberia.

For the next two years, Locke traveled about the country; "tramping" was the term applied to this practice of traveling from city to city, working a few weeks or months on one newspaper before moving on to another. There is no full itinerary of Locke's tramping, but he did spend some time in the South, where he began to form unfavorable opinions concerning the treatment of Negroes, whether slaves or free men. His travels ended in Pittsburgh, where he went to work for the *Chronicle* as a compositor. He became a reporter within a few weeks, later an assistant editor, and began to contribute editorials regularly for the first time.

Promising as Locke's career appeared at this point, it was interrupted by a printer's strike that shut down the *Chronicle*. Locke and a fellow employee, James G. Robinson, now decided to go into the newspaper business for themselves. With combined cash resources of $42—most of which belonged to Robinson—they went west to Ohio in search of a newspaper for sale. On 22 October 1853, they became owners of the *Plymouth Journal*, changed its name to the *Advertiser*, and were launched on the first of a series of weekly newspaper ventures so marginal that Locke would later describe their state as a "degree of poverty from which there is no further descent."

Locke's stay in Plymouth lasted not quite two years, during which he was married on 7 March 1855 to Martha H. Bodine, daughter of one of the town's leading merchants. She stayed on in Plymouth, awaiting the birth of their first child, when Locke and Robinson moved to Mansfield in October. There they became partners with Roeliff Brinkerhoff, who had been a tutor to the Jackson family at the Hermitage, in publishing a newly established Republican party organ, the *Mansfield Herald*. Locke remained a partner for only a little more than three months. He withdrew on 30 January 1856 because, according to Brinkerhoff, he was "a little wild and rather fast, and saved nothing, and the result was, when payments on our purchase came due, Locke had no money and concluded to get out."

Six weeks later, on 15 March 1856, Martha Bodine Locke gave birth to a son, who was named Robinson after Locke's partner. On 20 March, Locke bought another weekly newspaper, the *Bucyrus Journal*. A brother, Daniel Wheeler Locke, became his partner, but he remained in the newspaper business only until July, when poor eyesight compelled his retirement. Locke then urged Robinson to rejoin him, and they became partners in publishing the *Bucyrus Journal* in April 1857. There were the usual financial problems, and in August 1860 Robinson sought to withdraw but found no takers for the offer to sell his interest. By March 1861 the financial crisis was serious, and the *Journal* appealed to subscribers for help in meeting debts which were falling due. Relief arrived in April when Robinson was appointed postmaster by the new Republican administration of Abraham Lincoln. When war broke out a month later, Locke began to make plans to join the Union forces.

Locke did not go to war, even though he raised a company of men to join the Sixty-fifth Regiment, Sherman's Brigade, in which he had been commissioned second lieutenant. He made a trip to Columbus in November to confer with Governor William Dennison, who apparently persuaded him that he could be of greater service to the Union cause as an editor than as a soldier. Returning briefly to Bucyrus, Locke wrote a touching obituary of Willie Locke Robinson, his erstwhile partner's five-year-old son, who had drowned while playing near his home.

On 13 December 1861, Locke became owner of the weekly *Hancock Jeffersonian* in Findlay, Ohio, some fifty miles northwest of Bucyrus, announcing in the issue of 27 December that he was the new editor. Again Locke provided a job for a member of his family—Otis Taft Locke, his nineteen-year-old youngest brother, who walked all the way to Findlay from the family home at Virgil, New York. In the next three years, still operating "well down to the further end of the poverty scale," he began to establish the reputation that would bring him national recognition and, more specifically, a job with the *Toledo Blade*, the newspaper through which his name was to become quite literally a household word.

As he would complain later, the name by which David Ross Locke achieved this fame was not his own. Instead it was one he had chosen as a pseudonym for a series of sketches he had begun to write—Petroleum Vesuvius Nasby. The first of these appeared on 25 April 1862 in the *Hancock Jeffersonian*. Within a year, they were being reprinted throughout the country, read with great glee by President Lincoln to the sometimes disapproving members of his cabinet, and passed along the battle lines from one Union soldier to another.

Nasby had not, of course, sprung full-panoplied from Locke's brow in the spring of 1862, but had slowly been taking shape for nine years,

during which Locke had been eking out an existence from weekly newspapers in Plymouth, Mansfield, Bucyrus, and Findlay. Notable among Locke's early adventures with humor and satire were a series of sketches signed by "J. Augustus Sniggs," which appeared over a period of about two years in the *Plymouth Advertiser*, the *Mansfield Herald*, and the *Bucyrus Journal*. Locke removed the Sniggs sketches from the files of the Mansfield newspaper because several of them had offended his wife's mother and other family members. Those which survive in the Plymouth and Bucyrus files are genuinely funny in a sense that the heavy-handed satire of the Nasby letters often is not. These tall tales of the adventures of a young man sowing his wild oats in a small town are truly hilarious. They also provide early instances of Locke's experimentation with what he insisted was "scientific spelling," as in the names of three associates of Sniggs—Jinjurheels, Brandenoaz, and Liteninfas.

Nasby begins to emerge more clearly in the Bucyrus years. "Another Paean from the Harp of a Thousand Strings" appears in the *Journal* of 27 December 1857. It begins: "My Beloved Brethering: I am an unlearnt preacher of whom you've no doubt heard before, and I now appear to expound the scriptures and pint out the narrow world leads from a vain world to the streets of Jurooslum, and my text which I shall choose for the occasion is in the leds of the Bible, somewhere between the second Chronikils and the last chapter of Timothy Titus, and when you find it you will find these words: 'And they shall gnaw a file and flee into the mountains of Hepsidam, whar the lion roareth and the wangdoodle mourneth his first born.' " Here is the "unlearnt preacher" who appears later as P. V. Nasby, pastor of the "Church of the Noo Dispensashen" at "Confedrit X Roads, Kentucky," having fled there from Wingert's Corners, Ohio. Locke also continued to experiment during the next two years with his "scientific spelling" in a series of verses entitled "Sonnits." The title of one of these is of particular interest, being addressed to "A Linkun—Ritten Wile Meditatively A Gazin at the Post Offis."

There are other, more direct links between Nasby and Locke's years at Bucyrus. Indeed, the essential content of the two sketches generally recognized as the first of the Nasby letters actually appeared in the *Journal* in 1860—almost two years before the same arguments were made by Nasby in the *Hancock Jeffersonian*. In each instance, Locke made use of reverse logic and reductio ad absurdum, weapons that were to become mainstays in his satiric arsenal. The young editor was already beginning to appreciate that satire could be effective in political argument. The outlandish dialect and the personalization of his attacks on Confederate sympathizers would be added later.

The years Locke spent at Findlay coincided almost exactly with the Civil War's duration. They were years of strife and bitterness in Hancock County—a hotbed of Southern sympathizers, including a large contingent of the Knights of the Golden Circle. Locke's editorials, supporting the Union cause and denouncing the copperheads, made him highly unpopular from the outset.

Locke had been an admirer of Abraham Lincoln since October 1858, when he had met and interviewed him after a debate with Stephen A. Douglas at Quincy, Illinois. He did not, however, hesitate to criticize the manner in which the Union military forces operated during much of 1862. His bitterest criticism was aimed at the military commanders, but his frustration with the many reverses of that first year led him to declare, on the occasion of the appointment of Edwin M. Stanton to succeed Simon Cameron as secretary of war: "We have hopes that the authorities will now quit the missionary business and begin the war. . . . We have been thus far too amiable and our course has not only emboldened the rebels but brought upon us the contempt of all nations."

Twice during the war Locke went to Washington for visits with Lincoln. The first, in 1863, was at the president's invitation. They spent an hour together, and Locke reported that Lincoln "bubbled over with good feeling" and that "he expressed a liking for my little work, which I have not the assurance to put upon paper." When Locke went to Washington a year later it was to ask Lincoln to grant a pardon to a young Ohio soldier who had returned home without leave to marry his fiancée after learning that another suitor was beginning to pay her attention. Lincoln signed the pardon without asking further questions of Locke, who observed that "no man hated blood as Lincoln did."

Lincoln's admiration of the Nasby letters was well known. Carl Sandburg reports that the president "got out of bed and paraded around the White House past midnight to find someone else awake to share his reading of Nasby." According to the diary of Gen. Isham N. Haynie, who visited Lincoln in the early afternoon of 14 April 1865, the president read four chapters of Nasby to him. Lincoln went later in the day to attend a production of *Our American Cousin* at Ford's Theatre, where he was assassinated.

Not everyone shared Lincoln's enthusiasm for Nasby; there has been a wide difference of opinion concerning what he wrote. He was one of a considerable number of American humorists and satirists who shared the use of a dialect that was supposed to represent the speech of rural or backwoods America. It was overlaid with cacography, and there was heavy reliance on the letters k, q, and z to create an outlandish appearance that was supposed to make the reader laugh. Constance Rourke has written appreciatively of these dialect humorists, suggesting that they "offered talk in a familiar tone, the next thing to conversation; and they were heard and read with an absorbed delight, as if their wide public transferred the burden of uncertain selves to these assured and unabashed provincials." Walter Blair suggests of their writing that "it may be that it was too topical since comments upon current events are less hilarious when the events are not remembered." Kenneth Lynn has dismissed them as "dull," and Mark Twain, who was a personal friend of several of them, including Locke, wrote to his copyright lawyer concerning an anthology that included works by many of them: "This book is a cemetery."

Twain's assessment would not have bothered Nasby, who had himself once declared: "Posterity may assign me a niche in the temple of massive intellex, or may not; it's all one to the subscriber. I woodn't give a ten-cent postal currency for wat the next generashen will do for me. It's this generashen I'm going for."

Within a few years after Locke's death, Nasby did not seem very funny to most readers, and many found his coarseness and the savagery of his satire offensive. That would have been all right with Nasby, who was going for the jugular; objectivity was the last thing for which he was striving. Joseph Jones has understood this in what is perhaps the most perceptive critical observation on the subject of the Nasby letters: "To his everlasting credit, Locke is unashamedly coarse; intrinsically vulgar. Most satirists and humorists of his time veered timidly away from the calculated vulgarity that properly pugnacious satire—which can have no intention of being fair-minded if it means to pack a really effective wallop—must show. The deliberately low tone, set early, is strictly maintained. The modern reader must remember this; must remind himself, at times, that for all his twentieth century freedom with four-letter words, his own taboos can render Locke (or rather Nasby) offensive to those not careful to maintain satiric perspective in addition to historical perspective on a work. The satirist . . . must be granted enough room to swing his shillelagh. Locke's was a gnarly and knotty one, particularly on the racial issue."

There are many instances of the coarseness and vulgarity to which Jones refers. Especially illustrative is what Nasby wrote of his marriage in an autobiographical sketch, which appeared in the *Weekly Blade* of 25 July 1867:

> My Dimocrisy wuzn't partikerly confirmed until I arrived at the age uv twenty-four. My father wuz intimately acquainted with me, and knowd all my carakteristics ez well ez tho he hed bin the friend uv my buzzum. One day, ez I wuz a layin on my back under a tree, contemplatin the beauties uv nacher, my parent, sez he, —
>
> "Pete" (which is short for my name), "ef yoo ever marry, marry a milliner!"
>
> "Why, father uv mine?" replied I, openin my eyes.
>
> "Becoz, my son," sed he, "she'll hev a trade wich'll support yoo, otherwise you'll die uv starvashen when I'm gone."
>
> I thot the idea wuz a good one. Thro woman a cuss come into the world, wich cuss wuz labor; and I wuz determined that ez woman hed bin the coz uv requirin somebody to sweat for the bread I eat, woman should do that sweatin for me. That nite I perposed to a milliner in the village, and she rejectid my soot. I offered myself, in rapid succeshun, to a widder, who wuz a washerwoman, and to a woman who hed boys old enuff to work, with the same result, when, feelin that suthin wuz nessary to be done to sekoor a pervision for life, I married a nigger washerwoman wich didn't feel above me. Wood you blieve it? Within an hour after the ceremony wuz pronounst, she sold her persnel property, consistin uv a wash-tub and board, and a assortment uv soap, and investin the proceeds in a red calico dress and a pair uv earrings, insisted on my going to work to support her! and the township authorities not only maintained her in her loonacy, but refused to extend releef to me, on the ground that I wuz able-bodied.
>
> Ez I left that nigger, I agin vowed to devote my life to the work of gettin uv em down to where they wood hev to support us, and that vow I hev relijusly fulfilled. I hev never felt good, ceptin when they wuz put down a peg; I hev never wept, save when they wuz bein elevated.

Nasby makes here a telling point against the unequal treatment of Negroes, though in making it he manages to offer offense to almost every imaginable sensitivity. He is coarse, he is vulgar, but these qualities make his argument the more devastating.

It was the Nasby letters which brought David Ross Locke to the attention of other editors. One of the first of these was Murat Halstead, editor of the *Cincinnati Commercial*, who offered to pay twenty dollars for each subsequent Nasby letter. "I had never hoped, even in my wildest dreams, to possess so much money," Locke later declared, "and that's the way I got my start in life as Petroleum V. Nasby." But few other editors paid Locke, though many began to use the Nasby letters with increasing frequency. Since they were not copyrighted, editors who had access to them through the system of exchange that prevailed among newspapers at the time could reprint them with no thought of paying their author. Locke did make further efforts to promote the Nasby letters as a source of income, writing to a number of editors, including Horace Greeley of the *New York Tribune*, but there were few takers.

Another admirer of the Nasby letters was Alonzo D. Pelton, publisher of the *Toledo Blade*, who found them "fresh, original and spicy," and who wrote to Locke inquiring whether he would consider going to work for the *Blade*. Negotiations went on for several months, during which Locke disposed of his interest in the *Hancock Jeffersonian*, became part owner and editor for a few weeks of the *Bellefontaine Republican*, and for several months a partner in the drug firm of Huber and Locke in Findlay. In October 1865, it was finally agreed that Locke would take charge of the local news department of the *Blade*, agreeing to furnish a Nasby letter each week, at a salary of $2,000 annually.

The *Blade* was not, when Locke went to work for it, a newspaper of particular distinction. Some twenty other newspapers were published at the time in Toledo, which had a population of just under 14,000 in the 1860 census. Founded as a weekly in 1835, the *Blade* had published its first daily edition in 1848. Even so, it offered great opportunity to a young editor known as a dedicated Republican, unequivocally opposed to slavery, firm in his belief that the newspaper represented the ideal vehicle for educating the public. Here, for the first time, David Ross Locke became part of a Republican newspaper in a city that was a metropolis when compared with Findlay or Bucyrus. Beyond this, the tenth congressional district, in which Toledo was located, was represented by James M. Ashley, one of the most outspoken of the congressional abolitionists. A particular attraction for Locke was the fact that the *Blade* published weekly and triweekly editions, which at the time were devoted primarily to county advertisements. Already he had begun to dream of editing a great weekly newspaper with a nationwide circulation, and he saw the *Weekly Blade*—insignificant as it then was—becoming that national publication.

The new man on the *Blade* began almost at once to take over the editorial page as well as the news department. Locke had great skill as an editorial writer, utilizing many of the imaginative techniques which he had developed as a weekly newspaper editor. He could write in a variety of voices, making use of reason and emotion with equal effectiveness. And, of course, he had Petroleum Vesuvius Nasby always at his side to make in a quite different manner many of the same points he espoused in his editorials.

Locke's political philosophy has been generally misrepresented and misunderstood, perhaps because he was a loyal Republican who always managed to support the candidates of his party. He was not, however, a standpat reactionary, opposed to the social and economic reforms that were being proposed during his lifetime. His opposition to slavery and his championing of the rights of the freed slaves were positions taken early and sustained with genuine fervor throughout his life. He was an early advocate of the emancipation of women and a defender of the right of laboring men to organize. Many of Locke's editorials on these issues, though written a century or more ago, are pertinent today; and they place him on the progressive side in each instance.

Almost at once after his association with the *Blade* had begun, Locke became embroiled in the bitter struggle over the Reconstruction policies of President Andrew Johnson. He did not, as some historians have represented him as doing, join forces at once with the Radical Republicans against Johnson and those more moderate Republicans who placed reconciliation above retribution. Indeed, for many months, Locke was outspokenly critical of the Radicals and a consistent supporter of the president and his policies. Both in his editorials and in the Nasby letters, Locke continued to support Johnson until April 1866. Then two events combined to convince the new editor of the *Blade* that the president was willing to sell out both party unity and the rights of the freedmen. One of these was Johnson's peace proclamation, ending military occupation of the South, restoring the right to habeas corpus and, in effect, leaving the freed slaves at the mercy of their former owners. Of this action, Locke wrote:

> The issuing of this proclamation at this time is a mistake, to use a term as mild as possible. We have advocated the receiving of the States back into full communion as soon as that could be done safely, but that time has not yet come. . . .
>
> The absolute freedom of all men, their freedom from any and all forms of slavery—their absolute equality in everything pertaining to person and property, should be placed above the caprices of the State Legislatures, and until this is done the people of the United States stand guilty before God of a breach of faith as wicked as it is cowardly.

Locke continued to express hope for a reconciliation between Johnson and the Republican (or Union) party as late as 22 June 1866. But when, on 3 July, a call was issued for a convention to be held in Philadelphia in August to launch a bipartisan campaign on behalf of congressional candidates who would support Johnson's Reconstruction program, Locke finally abandoned all hope of reconciliation. From that day on, he had no use for the president. He was irate with those moderate Republicans—"traitors," as he referred to them—who joined to help defeat the impeachment resolution brought against Johnson in the spring of 1868.

Petroleum Vesuvius Nasby was active in the fight on Reconstruction, too, recording his impressions of the president's campaign in September 1866 on behalf of candidates in the fall election who were friendly to him. These reports, published the following year in a volume entitled "*Swingin Round the Cirkle*," were illustrated by Thomas Nast, who was to become a close friend of Locke's.

Soon after the move to Toledo, Locke began to encourage Pelton to expand the role of the *Weekly Blade*. Pelton responded favorably, and within a few months its circulation had grown from about 1,000 to 12,000 readers. The content of the *Weekly Blade* now included a wide variety of material, reflecting Locke's determination to attract all members of the family. There were short stories, including several by the editor; there was poetry, advice on agricultural practices and health problems, household hints, reports on the proceedings of Congress, accounts of murders and assorted atrocities. The star attraction from the beginning was Petroleum Vesuvius Nasby. One of his letters appeared almost every week, and a continuing promotional campaign was carried on in their behalf. It was not long before the *Weekly Blade* was widely known as "Nasby's Paper," and to many readers he was a flesh-and-blood indi-

Thomas Nast illustration showing Petroleum Vesuvius Nasby preaching to his congregation at the Church of St. Vallandigum

vidual. A cartoon sketch by Thomas Nast appeared at the head of each of the Nasby letters, helping to establish the familiar image of Nasby—round, ruddy, and chin-whiskered.

Locke became part owner of A. D. Pelton and Company, publishers of the *Blade*, in 1867, along with John Paul Jones. Dr. A. P. Miller bought Pelton's controlling interest the next year, and the firm of Miller, Locke and Company was formed. As Locke's financial interest and influence in management of the firm grew, the *Weekly Blade* loomed ever larger in his plans. The editorial staff was enlarged, and the circulation continued to grow, reaching around 100,000 subscribers in 1868. Then, during the 1870s, when Locke was away from Toledo much of the time, the circulation dropped dramatically—to about 24,000 in 1875. Locke used his Toledo properties during this period as pawns in building the considerable fortune that amounted to almost a million dollars at his death. One of his

New York associates, George P. Rowell, wrote that "it used to be said that he made a good living by selling the *Blade* at one season of the year, when someone turned up who thought he could run it better than Locke did, and buying it back a few months later when the publisher found that he could not." After Locke's return to Toledo, the *Weekly Blade* began to gain circulation, reaching 117,000 in 1883 and 200,000 the following year. When he died in 1888, his weekly paper was at its peak both in numbers of readers and influence.

The 1870s found Locke engaged in a variety of activities, some of which had begun a few years earlier. His reputation as Nasby had launched him on a lecturing career in 1867, and for the next four years he traveled widely throughout the East and Midwest. Although he possessed none of the graces of the effective platform speaker, Locke was one of the most popular stars of the lecture circuit. He became a principal attraction of the Boston Lyceum Bureau when it was established in 1868 by James Clark Redpath and George L. Fall. It was in the course of this association that he became acquainted with Mark Twain, Josh Billings, and other lions of the Lyceum circuit, who gathered in Boston each December to try out their lectures before beginning their tours.

Three of Locke's lectures were published, and they are among the most powerful and effective of his writings. The best known is "Cussid Be Canaan," in which he presented many of the same arguments that characterized the Nasby letters on the subject of Negro rights. The lecture provides a devastating attack on the principal tenets of racism. The other lectures—"The Struggles of a Conservative with the Woman Question" and "In Search of the Man of Sin"—though less popular at the time, are equally effective and interesting for what they reveal of Locke's progressive views on human rights and relationships.

On a lecture tour in New England in the fall of 1868 Locke met the Reverend Francis Ellingwood Abbot, minister of the Unitarian church of Dover, New Hampshire, whose radical views had involved him in a court fight with one group of members of his congregation. At Locke's urging, the Toledo Unitarian Society invited Abbot to become its minister, and he accepted, taking over his pulpit in August 1869. Locke and Abbot at once became involved in plans for a new magazine of Free Religion, the *Index*, the first issue appearing on 1 January 1870. Locke contributed $3,000 to help maintain the new publication through each of its first two years, and during the first eighteen months, the

Index was printed on the *Blade*'s presses. Abbot moved from Toledo to Boston in August 1873, taking the *Index* with him, after protracted wrangling with some of the stockholders. The publication continued until 1880, but Locke's involvement had ended when Abbot left Toledo.

Locke's interest became more and more centered in New York after 1871, when he was named managing editor of the *New York Evening Mail*. The *Blade* was left in the hands of John Paul Jones and Frank T. Lane, on whom he had come to rely during his absence on lecture tours. Locke continued to write the Nasby letters, especially for readers of the *Weekly Blade*, and to have a hand in major decisions concerning business and editorial policies, but he spent most of his time in New York. His wife, Martha, and their three sons remained in Toledo during those years.

Locke joined the *Evening Mail* the year it was bought by Cyrus W. Field. It was also the year the *Evening Mail* moved its offices from No. 2 Park Place to 34 Park Row, where the *Tribune*, the *Herald*, and the *Sun* were among its neighbors. The *Evening Mail* had displayed no strong political convictions, though there was a slight Republican tinge to its editorials. Having played a significant part in the journalistic war on "Boss" Tweed, the *Evening Mail* remained active in "good government" efforts, supporting attempts by the Committee of Seventy to secure a reform charter for New York City in 1872.

Field had plans to move the *Evening Mail* up to a higher station among the city's newspapers, and bringing Locke in as managing editor was an important part of this effort. The number of pages in each issue had been increased from four to eight by October. Plans were announced in December to publish a new weekly edition, beginning with the new year. The *Weekly Mail* achieved a circulation of 25,000 in February 1872, but it never approached the stature of Locke's *Weekly Blade*.

During the time that Locke was managing editor of the *Evening Mail*, he conducted an advertising business nearby at 37 Park Row, as a partner in the agency of Pettengill, Bates and Company, and later in the firm of Bates and Locke. From 1873 to 1875, Locke devoted most of his time to the advertising business. He also became involved — with James H. Bates — in a venture to promote the sale of the Remington "type machine." With George Washington Napoleon Yost, who had made other unsuccessful attempts to market this early version of the Remington typewriter, they formed the firm of Locke, Yost and Bates, with offices on Broadway; Locke was in charge of the warehouse and showrooms. The Remington type machine was ahead of its time; sales languished, and Locke, Yost and Bates went out of business.

Locke's role in the *Evening Mail* now began to expand. He was named business manager at an annual salary of $7,500 by Clark Bell, who had bought the newspaper in November 1877 at a sheriff's sale to pay debts and taxes. With William Hanford White and F. B. Mitchell, Bell had formed a new company to which the property was transferred, and early in 1878, soon after Locke had been named general manager, the *Evening Mail* underwent dramatic changes. Current news, with display headlines and other innovations of the period, replaced the literary material and dispatches from resorts and watering places that had been featured on the front page. There were changes in the editorial page, too, where Locke's influence was clearly reflected in both subject matter and style. But within a few months, the *Evening Mail* was awash in controversy between Bell and White. Lawsuits followed; publication was suspended from 15 May to 3 July; finally, Clark Bell sold his interest in the newspaper to Hanford White. With Bell's departure, Locke also left the *Evening Mail*, returning soon thereafter to Toledo.

The 1870s saw Locke trying his hand at several kinds of writing, including two plays, three novels, and a number of short stories. His first play, *Inflation*, was unsuccessful and was characterized by Congressman James A. Garfield in his diary as "cheap and sensational" after a performance in 1876. The other play, *Widow Bedott*, enjoyed a considerable success in New York and throughout the country after premiering on 28 March 1879 in Providence, Rhode Island. *A Paper City*, based on a real estate boom in a midwestern town, was the novel published in 1879. *The Demagogue*, more interesting and better written, was published posthumously, appearing in 1891. Its central character is a congressman whose resemblance to James M. Ashley is so striking that Locke preferred that it not be published during his lifetime.

Many of Locke's short stories appeared in *Locke's Monthly*, one of two magazines published by the Blade Company after he had become its president late in 1876; the other was the *American Farm Journal*. The daily and triweekly editions of the *Blade* were sold in 1877, but the company bought them back a year later. Locke's other Toledo involvements during this time included the Blade

Printing and Paper Company, organized in 1873 for making books, general printing, and selling paper and stationery.

It was to the newspaper operations, however, that Locke devoted most of his attention on his return to Toledo. The *Weekly Blade* had languished in his absence and his determination that it should be a national journal of influence and reputation led him to strive for its expansion and improvement. Capitalizing on the 1880 presidential campaign, he gave enthusiastic support to the candidacy of fellow Ohioan James A. Garfield, appealing to Republicans throughout the country to subscribe to the *Weekly Blade* as a means of advancing the party's cause. Petroleum Vesuvius Nasby lent aid to these political efforts. In addition to the weekly letters, campaign booklets of Nasby's comments on issues and events were distributed widely in this and later election campaigns.

Robinson Locke was becoming increasingly active in the management of the *Blade* at this time, and his father sought to help the young man take over his various responsibilities. Locke hoped that his son would be a gentleman of culture, fluent in several languages and acquainted with European institutions and traditions. To this end, the senior Locke arranged that the two should make a tour of Europe, leaving New York in May 1881 and returning to Toledo in October. Rob Locke went back to Europe in November to pursue his studies, and his father joined him in July 1882 for a tour that included Hamburg, Cologne, Mannheim, Vienna, Florence, and Paris, staying several weeks in some places. Locke returned home in May 1883, with Rob following in July.

During the five years of life that remained to him, Locke devoted more and more time to the *Blade*—both the daily and weekly editions. The *Weekly Blade* reached its peak circulation of 200,000 in 1884. One of its most popular attractions during these five years was a series of editorials in which Locke urged his readers to "Pulverize the Rum Power!" These blistering attacks on the liquor interests played an important part in establishing Locke's national reputation, and among an entire generation of Americans growing up on the farms and in the small towns, it was with "pulverizing the rum power" that the names of Locke and Nasby became most firmly associated.

Many have found it incongruous that the author of these uncompromising attacks on liquor should have been a man who had consumed such copious quantities of it. Locke had been a heavy drinker from the time of his apprenticeship in Cortland onward. He was, beyond question, a victim of alcoholism. On the basis of what is known concerning the extent of his drinking, the wonder is that he lived so long and accomplished so much.

Some of Locke's detractors have suggested that he wrote the "Pulverize the Rum Power!" editorials for the cynical reason that he knew they were what subscribers to the *Weekly Blade* wanted to read. A favorite story is that each time he sat down to write one of these editorials, he had a waiter from his private club next door to the *Blade* building bring him a lemonade on which a generous shot of whiskey had been floated. The irony is obvious, but to accuse Locke of hypocrisy ignores his acknowledgment that he drank compulsively and had several times tried to break the habit. He was the very man who might most logically have been expected to lead this fight, having become convinced that alcohol was a crippling, debilitating force. On the basis of his own experience, Locke believed that no one can resist the urge to drink once he has acquired it. He was convinced that only by keeping liquor out of reach could a man be protected against his own weakness.

To this campaign, as to many others, Locke brought a determination to explore every aspect of the problem. The many rhetorical devices to which he resorted were used largely for variety or to emphasize factual evidence. He dug deep and ranged widely to find material supporting his position. In current editorial writing terminology, he was a good researcher. Within three months of the appearance of the first of these editorials, Locke concluded one with the admonition to "Pulverize the Rum Power!" He experimented a bit in succeeding weeks, urging readers to "Pulverize the Whiskey Power!" and to "Pulverize the Liquor Power!" His acute ear told him that his first inspiration had been the right one, and from then on, it was always the "Rum Power" he proposed to obliterate.

Locke's campaign against the liquor interests was not confined to the editorial columns. "The Confessions of a Drunkard," published serially beginning 7 January 1886, was drawn from Locke's own experiences. It provided a graphic account of the development of addictive alcoholism, beginning at the age of twelve and continuing over a forty-year period. The memoir concludes:

> I believe that Prohibition of the manufacture and sale of the great enemy of the human race is the only cure. I believe it

should be stamped out by law the same as any other aggressive evil is.

I have paid dearly for my experience with it, and I am permitted the writing of these papers in the hope that my woes might be of some use to young men who are entering upon the downward road.

I have said nothing but truth, and have tried to say what I have said in language so plain that any one may comprehend its import. I have not told all that I might have told, but I trust I have said enough to do some good.

These "Confessions" provide ample explanation of the passion and intensity Locke expended in the "Pulverize the Rum Power!" campaign. It sprang from deep personal conviction, from his own suffering and humiliation, from his realization that his successes had been diminished by his addiction.

Locke's skill and versatility as an editorial writer are demonstrated in much of what he wrote for the *Blade* in this latter period. When the banking house of C. H. Coy and Company closed its doors in May 1883, Locke launched a campaign against "busted bankers" that is a classic of the editorial techniques of which he was a master and of a style of personal journalism that was even then beginning to wane. He began by creating a cast of characters among the bank's depositors, providing specific individual victims with whose plight readers might empathize. These included a "poor woman . . . who carries newspapers"; the widowed mother and two sisters of a Captain Forsyth, shot down in "sheer wantonness" by a guard in a Confederate prison; Bentson, the blacksmith, who had lost the home and shop built on the collateral of his savings in the Coy bank. The sad plight of these and other unfortunates was contrasted with the affluence in which Cyrus H. Coy continued to live.

Satire was another weapon Locke used in the "case of the busted banker," whom he "discovered" to have existed in many other countries. He explored the various methods of dealing with them — in China, for example, where "an examination of a banker before a Mandarin of Two Tails and Three Swords was permitted." When this examination revealed that "the banker had taken money from widows and orphans, and poor laborers, and women who sold newspapers on the street of Pekin . . . he remarked that the examination need go no further." There is, Locke suggests, "something so simple, so direct, in taking a banker who has failed out into a square and chopping his head off with a very dull cleaver, that we wonder other na-

tions have not adopted it." In India, "busted bankers" are "straightway parboiled and served up to the Alligators of the Temple of Vishnu's Fortieth Incarceration." There are similar accounts of methods supposedly employed in Persia, in the Philippines, and in the Sandwich Islands, each embroidered with fanciful detail and thinly veiled references to the failure of the Coy bank and its consequences.

Locke's effectiveness as an editorial writer remains obvious today. Though there is some repetition of both subject matter and persuasive techniques, in the context of the period in which Locke wrote, they represent notable efforts to rouse the public to action — be it to prevent the use of liquor or to provide more careful regulation of banking practices. The style of the "busted banker" series is not wholly foreign to American journalism today; several of Locke's fictional characters would be at home among those who frequent the columns of Russell Baker and Art Buchwald.

It was as Petroleum Vesuvius Nasby, however, that Locke continued to be best known throughout the country. The Nasby letters appeared regularly in the *Weekly Blade*, where they had a much larger audience than was available in the daily edition, and Locke used Nasby to help carry on his various campaigns — particularly the "Pulverize the Rum Power!" effort. The methodology and the cast of characters were little changed. As always, Locke made extensive use of reverse logic and reduction to the absurd in these later Nasby letters. He put the arguments in favor of the sale and consumption of liquor into the mouths of Nasby and his particular friends, then let others — "that feend Joe Bigler, and his aider and abettor Pollock, the Illinoy storekeeper" — destroy them by applying his familiar techniques.

Locke's resentment of the fact that Nasby's nationwide reputation almost completely overshadowed his own considerable accomplishments increased in his later years. Cyril Clemens relates a tale which testifies to this resentment:

> One day he was sitting in the office of the *Toledo Blade*, busily engaged upon an editorial, when a tall, gaunt countryman appeared in the doorway and stood looking at him, saying nothing. Locke was working, without coat or vest as it was a hot, sultry August afternoon, the perspiration simply rolling down his face. Looking up he saw the man in the doorway and asked somewhat gruffly, "What do you want?" The farmer replied, "Nothing in particular, I just wanted to see Nasby."

The heat and the fact that he was greatly overworked all tended to make Locke infuriated, and he replied:

"Well, look at him. God, yes, look at him! look at him!" When the visitor had retreated with great precipitation, Locke turned to his son, Robinson, and remarked:

"I wish to God that I had never heard of that Nasby stuff. Here I am a man who has accomplished things. See the business blocks I have built. Look at the great paper I have made. See the serious books I have written. Yet on account of that damned Nasby stuff every hayseed in the country feels he has a right to step up and holler, 'Hello, Nasby.'"

Locke had indeed accomplished much that must have seemed to him more important than the Nasby letters, though he may have neglected to appreciate that, without the leg up which Nasby had provided at a critical point in his life, he would not have had the opportunities that came to him. But in his last few years, he did devote much of his time to what seems to have been a concerted effort to establish an identity of his own that would free him from the Nasby stereotype. He built a large house in a fashionable section of Toledo, became a collector of art and rare books, erected a new *Blade* building with the latest equipment, and invested extensively in both commercial and residential real estate.

Always active in politics, Locke became increasingly involved in Republican party affairs at the state and national levels. The *Weekly Blade* was a particularly useful instrument for this purpose. Locke availed himself of it in the latter months of 1887 to forestall the presidential ambitions of another Ohioan, Senator John Sherman, whom he had never forgiven for his vote against the impeachment of Andrew Johnson twenty years earlier. Locke proposed that Robert T. Lincoln, son of the martyred president, would be a better choice for the Republicans in 1888.

Newspaper editors should not seek political office, Locke insisted, and he adhered to that position with a single exception: in 1886, he accepted the Republican nomination as a candidate for alderman in Toledo's third ward. He won easily, despite strong opposition from the city's liquor dealers, and the *Blade* captioned its account of his

Parade celebrating Nasby's appointment as postmaster of Confedrit X Roads, Kentucky, as depicted by Thomas Nast

triumph "Business Beats Beer." Two months of Locke's term as alderman remained when he died on 15 February 1888.

Although he had remained active in the affairs of the *Blade* until just three months before his death, when he was confined to his home, Locke's health had been declining for at least five years. The official cause of his death was consumption—as tuberculosis was then usually known—which he had contracted in 1885. There is no doubt, however, that his health had been undermined by alcoholism, continuing over a period of many years and often manifested in the most acute forms. He had spent the winter of 1886 at Hot Springs, Arkansas, seeking relief from consumption, and the summer of 1887 at Star Island, off the coast of New Hampshire. He had tried to go back to work when he returned home, but more and more he had been confined to his home and to his bed. He had written occasional Nasby letters until 26 December, when the last one appeared in the weekly and daily editions of the *Blade*.

The death of David Ross Locke was widely mourned. Subscribers wrote to express what seemed to them an intensely personal loss. They found it hard to believe that their beloved Nasby was dead. From President Rutherford B. Hayes came the following message: "I am at this moment in receipt of the announcement of the death of D. R. Locke. I beg you to convey to his family my sincere sympathy with them in their bereavement. With his pen, Mr. Locke gained for himself a conspicuous and honorable place among those who fought the good fight in the critical years of the anti-slavery conflict before the war. During the war and after it, he was surpassed by no writer in the extent and value of his influence in the march of events until its great results were substantially secured."

George S. Boutwell, secretary of the treasury in the Grant administration, declared that "the crushing of the Rebellion can be credited to three forces: the army, the navy, and the Nasby letters." This is no doubt an overstatement of the importance of Locke's role in that conflict, but it suggests the high esteem in which the creator of Nasby was held by his contemporaries and the effectiveness of the savage satire which Locke, as Nasby, created in that crucial period. He was one of the great jour-

nalists of that or any other time.

Periodical Publication:
"Prohibition," *North American Review*, 143 (October 1888): 382-397.

Biographies:
Cyril Clemens, *Petroleum Vesuvius Nasby* (Webster Groves, Mo.: International Mark Twain Society, 1936);

John M. Harrison, *The Man Who Made Nasby, David Ross Locke* (Chapel Hill: University of North Carolina Press, 1969).

References:
James C. Austin, *Petroleum V. Nasby* (New York: Twayne, 1965);

Walter Blair, *Native American Humor (1800-1900)* (New York: American Book Co., 1939);

Roeliff Brinkerhoff, *Recollections of a Lifetime* (Cincinnati: Robert Clarke, 1900);

George Washington Cable, *Mark Twain and G. W. Cable* (East Lansing: Michigan State University Press, 1960);

Francis B. Carpenter, *Six Months in the White House* (New York: Hurd & Houghton, 1866);

Paul Fatout, *Mark Twain on the Lecture Circuit* (Bloomington: Indiana University Press, 1960);

John M. Harrison, "The Journalist as Social Critic," in *Mass Media and the National Experience*, edited by Ronald T. Farrar and John D. Stevens (New York: Harper & Row, 1971);

Joseph Jones, ed., *The Struggles of Petroleum V. Nasby* (Boston: Beacon Press, 1963);

Milton Meltzer, *Mark Twain Himself* (New York: Crowell, 1960);

Jack Clifford Ransome, "The Career of David Ross Locke and Its Significance," M.A. thesis, University of Toledo, 1947;

Constance Rourke, *American Humor* (New York: Harcourt, Brace, 1931);

William H. Taft, "The *Toledo Blade*: Its First One Hundred Years, 1835-1935," Ph.D. dissertation, Western Reserve University, 1950.

Papers:
David Ross Locke's papers are at the Rutherford B. Hayes Memorial Library, Fremont, Ohio.

Joseph B. McCullagh

(November 1842-31 December 1896)

Ellen M. Mrja
Mankato State University

MAJOR POSITIONS HELD: Reporter, *St. Louis Democrat* (1859-1860); reporter and war correspondent, *Cincinnati Gazette* (1860-1862); war correspondent and Washington correspondent, *Cincinnati Commercial* (1862-1868); managing editor, *Cincinnati Enquirer* (1868-1869), *Chicago Republican* (1869-1871), *St. Louis Democrat* (1871-1873), *St. Louis Globe* (1873-1875), *St. Louis Globe-Democrat* (1875-1896).

Joseph B. McCullagh, known as "Mack" to his contemporaries, was one of the truly great newspaper editors to dominate the Midwest during the last decades of the 1800s. As a reporter he was known for his energetic news gathering and acute writing as well as for "inventing" and perfecting the modern journalistic interview. As an editor, he was one of the founders of the New Journalism, whose influence was felt not only in the Midwest but nationally. Despite McCullagh's achievements, much of his life remains an enigma.

Joseph Burbridge McCullagh was born in 1842 in Dublin, Ireland, to John and Sarah Burbridge McCullagh. Little is known of his early years, although the *Encyclopedia of St. Louis History* reports he was one of sixteen children born to the couple.

Perhaps because of the depressed state of the Irish economy in the 1840s, the eleven-year-old McCullagh decided to leave his homeland. He found a job as a cabin boy on a ship sailing for the United States, arriving in New York in 1853. His first job in America was as an apprentice printer on a Catholic weekly, the *Freeman's Journal*. When he was sixteen, he left New York for the "Gateway to the West," St. Louis, where he became a compositor for the *Christian Advocate*, a Methodist weekly. Although McCullagh's religious affiliation is not known, it seems the religious instruction he received during these early years as well as the kindness shown him during this time by leaders in the church were influences he never forgot: despite his sometimes caustic attacks in later years on a variety of institutions, it would always be his firm policy that no religion be ridiculed. He, in fact, took pride in the *St. Louis Globe-Democrat*'s distinction as being

Joseph B. McCullagh (Missouri Historical Society)

"The Great Religious Daily," a reference to the fact that well into the 1900s the paper reported on several sermons in its Monday editions.

Encouraged by kindly mentors, young McCullagh began religious instruction; joined a literary society, where he developed the lifelong habit of voracious reading; and took a course in shorthand. Although his formal schooling had ended when he was ten, McCullagh was determined not to let this prevent him from becoming a newspaper writer. Years later he explained his philosophy to a meeting of the Missouri Press Association: "Journalism can be learned by experience reinforced by natural aptitude, but it cannot be taught by theories or courses of study."

The youth's industry did not go unnoticed. The Reverend William E. Babcock, in whose home

McCullagh boarded, urged the foreman of the backshop at the *St. Louis Democrat* to give "Joe" a job, arguing that the seventeen-year-old boy "had brains and would make his mark if given a chance." The foreman later remarked: "After he had proofread one galley, I concluded that he knew more about proofreading than I did and hired him."

McCullagh was soon given a chance to try his hand at reporting. He proved so prolific in news gathering that the first day in his new assignment he filled the column and a half reserved for local news; on the second day, two columns; and on the third day he brought in so much news that the backshop was forced to use five-point type rather than its standard size in order to fit in all his copy. McCullagh was made a permanent reporter for the *Democrat*.

Young McCullagh was not only a prolific writer; he was, more importantly, an accurate one. During the 1859-1860 session of the General Assembly in Jefferson City, McCullagh's dispatches of speeches were so accurate that he caught the attention of other papers. In 1860 he was offered the attractive salary of $100 per month to join the *Cincinnati Gazette*. McCullagh, who was earning $16 per week on the *Democrat*, accepted the offer.

In 1861 he returned to St. Louis to enlist in the Benton Cadets, a group organized to serve as a bodyguard to Union General John C. Frémont. Because of McCullagh's knowledge of shorthand, he was given the rank of second lieutenant and assigned as one of the general's stenographers. However, with Lincoln's removal of Frémont, McCullagh resigned his commission and returned to Cincinnati.

Just after he turned nineteen, McCullagh was sent into the field as a war correspondent for the *Gazette*. During the next few years, he gained a reputation as one of the war's best reporters. McCullagh more than once demonstrated courage under fire. He was one of a handful of volunteers to man the ironclad flagship *St. Louis* during the battle for Fort Donelson on 14 February 1862. The *St. Louis* sustained one and one-half hours of cannon fire during the battle. When it was over, the ship had taken fifty-seven hits and McCullagh was the only man aboard to escape the barrage unharmed. As he later remembered it: "If I had a chance to choose for a future experience between two hours on the hottest battlefield of the war and ten minutes in that pilot house, I would pick the battlefield for comfort."

In April McCullagh was with Grant's army at Pittsburg Landing in Tennessee when the Confed-erate army attacked in the Battle of Shiloh. This battle turned out to be one of the most controversial of the war and for McCullagh. According to Walter B. Stevens, one of McCullagh's protégés who later chronicled his remembrances of "Mack" in the *Missouri Historical Review*, McCullagh was shocked by the conduct of some of the Northern officers in the battle. He wrote a letter to the *Gazette* in which he complained of drunkenness and mismanagement of Union soldiers, a letter that one of his *Gazette* colleagues told him would never be printed. McCullagh answered that if the letter was not printed, he would resign. It was not, and he did.

As soon as word reached Cincinnati of McCullagh's resignation, Murat Halstead of the competing *Commercial* offered him a position as correspondent at twice the salary and a guarantee of total independence from censorship. Thus, in the spring of 1862, McCullagh joined the *Commercial*, an association that lasted six years.

McCullagh's dispatches from the field were well read, for they reflected the youth's enthusiasm and his quick thinking. His ingenuity was demonstrated in a story printed in the 16 May 1862 *Commercial*. While trying to pass through General Buell's lines in Mississippi, McCullagh was stopped by a sentry who demanded to know whether or not he was a commissioned officer. "Don't you know that none but commissioned officers are allowed to ride gray horses?" McCullagh retorted. The sentry respectfully allowed him to pass.

Part of McCullagh's success as a war correspondent was his ability to anticipate events. The *Chicago Tribune*'s George P. Upton, who reported with McCullagh during the war, later said: "Among all the war correspondents—and I know a great many of them—I never knew one who could so quickly grasp a military situation. He had the whole thing in his head all the time and could draw a diagram of the situation at any time."

During the war McCullagh, like other correspondents, developed a sense of bravery. However, as he later protested, courage was the norm and not the exception for any soldier. "The fear of battle," he wrote, "is like the fear of death, of which it is perhaps a part—it vanishes as the actual fact approaches." McCullagh had numerous opportunities to test his mettle. He and another reporter were once arrested by the Confederates for "continually publishing news that gave aid and comfort to the North"; they were released the next day. In another episode, McCullagh passed himself off in Mississippi as a Rebel soldier in order to obtain information about Confederate troop locations. He was with Grant during the siege of Vicksburg, which McCullagh said was an opportunity "of seeing the great soldier in one of the most eventful hours of his eventful life." He was also with Sherman's army on its march through Georgia.

McCullagh's dispatches were insightful, vivid, and personally involving. This sample, from the 1 June 1863 *Commercial*, is part of McCullagh's account of the battle of Champion Hill: "We (the mule and I) were traveling toward the left, in the immediate rear of Hovey's division, then fighting desperately for the ground on which it stood. Pretty soon Hovey had to fall back. I tried to indicate to my long-eared steed that I wished to do the same, but he evidenced a stubborn disposition to advance instead of retreat. I pulled one rein and then the other, but the mule wouldn't stir. I spurred the animal, but it only made him kick, and I was obliged to desist in prospect of being left on the roadside. The rebels were advancing—were already within rifle range—and the bullets were whistling in pursuit of our men, not of me, I thought, for they surely would not hit a non-combatant. And still the mule wouldn't turn back.... He then commenced an unearthly bawl, which I interpreted as my funeral dirge, which would undoubtedly have proved so had I not dismounted and led him to the rear, arriving there just in time to save myself. I have studiously avoided mules ever since...."

It is ironic that it was McCullagh's incisive reporting that eventually led to the end of his war correspondence. In the fall of 1863 he was ordered to Nashville by the Union army after he predicted—too accurately—troop movement. Undaunted, he set out for Washington, D.C., in his new assignment as capital correspondent for the *Commercial*. Although only twenty-one when he arrived in Washington, McCullagh's work there during the next four years solidified his national reputation as a journalist of merit.

McCullagh's stenographic abilities soon landed him the additional job of Senate reporter to the New York Associated Press, which made him quickly well known to members of Congress. His dispatches from the capital reflected his intuitive ability to see through to the heart of even the most complex political issues. As the *New York Times* noted in McCullagh's obituary years later, his letters "were terse, incisive and sparse of adjectives, but they revealed him as a man of ripe judgment, who could not only think quickly but soundly and grasp political situations so as to foretell their outcome." It was, however, McCullagh's relationship with Andrew Johnson that brought recognition for his work

at both the national and international levels. The two men met on the eve of Lincoln's second inaugural in 1865. When Johnson became president, he found himself mired in political controversy from which he never escaped.

As McCullagh later summarized the situation, both political parties were against Johnson: "The Democrats, though making a show of support, were secretly in league with the Republicans who were bitterly fighting him; they hated him for the past, and they were unable to use him for the present and they feared him for the future. The blood of the Republican martyr might become the seed of the Democratic church, and scatter to the winds the hopes of a whole score of Democratic candidates...." By 1867, impeachment talk filled the Capitol. In his dispatches to the *Commercial*, McCullagh followed each new development, but he tended to support the president, whom he felt was the underdog in the feud.

In July McCullagh was summoned to the White House so that Johnson could express appreciation for the reporter's defense of him. The two conversed for a half-hour, and when Johnson rose to leave, McCullagh asked permission to use the conversation as the subject of a dispatch. Johnson asked the young reporter to repeat what had been said. When McCullagh, from memory, was able to repeat all of the main points of the conversation, the president answered that if he "put it just that way ... it will be all right."

McCullagh's dispatch appeared in the 23 July 1867 *Commercial*. Five days later the White House secretary met McCullagh at the Capitol and assured him that the president thought McCullagh had "got him down to a dot" in the dispatch. Thus, McCullagh was invited back to the White House that night for a second session with Johnson. During the next nine months, Johnson held more conversations with McCullagh than with any other correspondent, a coup for the young journalist. As the relationship between the two grew closer, Johnson came to rely on McCullagh to keep him informed of Capitol developments and as someone Johnson could turn to whenever he wanted to give "these fellows (in Congress) hell."

The *Washington Post* later noted that McCullagh's interviews with the president "rocked the land" and "caused men to see red." But as historian Jim A. Hart points out, they also revolutionized reporting. Until McCullagh's dispatches appeared in the *Commercial*, interviews had been rare in any papers. Those that did appear tended to follow the question-answer format. But McCullagh was the first journalist to employ the technique now known as the modern interview. Newspapers across the country reprinted his interviews, and according to the *Post*, "all leading journals quickly conformed, and the interview became an 'institution.' " Whether or not McCullagh "invented" the interview, historians can agree that he was the first ever to interview a president. Furthermore, as biographer Charles C. Clayton points out, McCullagh was "the first newsman to establish the kind of relationship with the White House which has been capitalized on by others in recent years."

Perhaps the most famous of the Johnson-McCullagh interviews was the one that appeared in the *Commercial* on 13 February 1868, just eleven days before the House voted its resolution of impeachment on 24 February. The interview began:

> WASHINGTON, D.C., Feb. 11, 1868 — I called on the President last evening and had an interview with him of about an hour's duration. From the revival of the impeachment project and the recent correspondence between him and Gen. Grant, which I had been informed, on the authority of several eminently loyal newspapers, was literally "crushing" to A. J., I expected to find His Excellency in a prostrate and enfeebled condition, or perhaps "writhing in the agonies of despair," as Forney's two dailies would express it. But he was not prostrate, and he didn't writhe any. Quite the contrary, I never saw him more cheerful or in better health and spirits.
>
> "They're after you again, Mr. President, with an impeachment," said I. "So I hear," he said, "but I can't get at the point they're trying to make against me this time; though for that matter I haven't taken much trouble to find out."

The dispatch, which continues for two columns, is noteworthy for two reasons. First, many consider it to be the first formal newspaper interview ever reported; McCullagh himself used the word *interview* to refer to it. Second, neither in this nor in any other interview with Johnson did McCullagh take notes, but instead relied on his photographic memory to capture the quotes. McCullagh later justified the practice by saying "I am satisfied that the introduction of pen, pencil or paper would have spoiled the whole business so far as President Johnson was concerned. It would have frozen the irrascible [*sic*] current of his soul . . . to have seen a man taking it all down on cold paper."

On 2 and 3 March, the House voted eleven articles of impeachment against Johnson. Two days later the Senate was organized to hear the charges, and, largely because of his interviews with the president, McCullagh was subpoenaed as a witness for the defense. By May the trial was over, Johnson remaining in office through the grace of one vote. Perhaps no individual had been more effective in arguing Johnson's case before the public than had McCullagh.

By this time McCullagh's reputation as a top-notch journalist was firmly established. This led to his being offered his first management role, as managing editor of the *Cincinnati Enquirer*. Although a mediocre paper, the *Enquirer* did offer a new challenge to McCullagh. It is ironic that one of the bright, young reporters McCullagh hired in an attempt to improve writing was John A. Cockerill, who later would resurface as a worthy competitor on the *St. Louis Post-Dispatch*.

In 1869 McCullagh was offered managing editorship and part interest in an inconsistent Chicago paper, the *Daily Republican*. The young paper had been edited for one year by Charles A. Dana, but a disagreement between Dana and stockholders had resulted in his discharge in 1866. Since that time the paper had floundered under a number of editors. The offer to become part owner of the paper so appealed to McCullagh that he convinced a brother, John W. McCullagh, to join him in his new venture. However, the McCullagh brothers' stay in Chicago ended with the fire that destroyed much of the city in 1871. The fire not only ruined the *Republican* office, it also consumed McCullagh's invaluable library and all of his personal belongings. Although McCullagh sardonically referred to the event as "Divine dispensation," his work in Chicago was found worthy by many; Melville E. Stone of the *Chicago Tribune* later noted that "when Charles A. Dana made a failure of the paper, Mr. McCullagh was sent for, came here, and made a success of it."

That autumn McCullagh returned to the paper that had first employed him, the *St. Louis Democrat*. This time, however, he was made managing editor and given a share of the paper's ownership.

When he arrived at the *Democrat*, he found the paper riddled by internal disputes. The owners — George Fishback, William McKee, and Daniel Houser — were at odds over management of the paper. McKee, who owned one-half interest in the paper, and Houser, who owned one-sixth, believed that liberal spending for news gathering was a wise investment. Fishback, who owned one-third, disagreed. After months of bickering, Fishback demanded that his partners either buy his interest in the *Democrat* or sell theirs to him, but Houser and McKee refused to negotiate. In desperation, Fishback went to court in March and obtained an order demanding that a sale be negotiated. The sale was conducted via bidding, and when it was over, Fishback and bid $456,100 for the *Democrat*—$100 over McKee and Houser's final offer. McCullagh came away with sixteen shares in the new company.

Within weeks McKee and Houser began plans to build a competing paper and on 18 July 1872 the first issue of the *St. Louis Globe* appeared. As head of the *Democrat*, McCullagh felt duty-bound to come out swinging. He attacked the *Globe* editorially, calling it the "Robbers' Roost," implying that it stole its news from the Western Associated Press. He more than once implied that McKee was involved in graft. The editorial volleys continued for a year.

In the fall of 1873 Fishback, in an attempt to upgrade the *Democrat*, hired a college-educated journalist from the East named Newton Crane to serve as the paper's managing editor. When McCullagh was told of the impending switch, he replied, "A general doesn't take orders from a corporal." He was promptly dismissed.

Despite the hits they had taken from McCullagh, McKee and Houser immediately obtained his services as managing editor of the *Globe*. That he could make the switch so easily indicates McCullagh believed his loyalties rested with whatever newspaper he was working for.

As a new paper, the *Globe* suffered from not having a subscription to a press service; every attempt to join the Western Associated Press was vetoed by Fishback. Relief came on 6 January 1874 when the *Globe* bought—from an enterprising immigrant named Joseph Pulitzer—the *Staats-Zeitung*, a paper noteworthy only for its Associated Press franchise.

With the subscription to a news service, plus the support of publishers willing to pay for expanded news coverage, McCullagh was equipped to take on the competitive St. Louis market. Although the *Democrat* continued to receive the bulk of his attacks, he also took aim at other St. Louis papers. Of the *Republican*, which proclaimed itself the oldest paper in the city, McCullagh quipped on 3 November 1873: "The *Republican* flaunts its antiquity as proof of its sagacity, but age and experience are not always guarantees of merit." Of the *Dispatch* he commented on 5 February 1874: "The

Dispatch wants the State to build an asylum for the partially insane. We think the State has quite enough to do without taking care of the editorial staff of the *Dispatch*."

Readers enjoyed these spicy skirmishes. McCullagh's biting editorials, backed by his insistence on solid local and regional news coverage, helped the paper's circulation grow. By February 1874, McCullagh could claim that the *Globe* was printing 5,000 more copies per day than the *Democrat*. The competition for circulation was reflected in the race for advertising. By summer, Fishback was ready to sell the ailing *Democrat* back to McKee and Houser, but McCullagh advised against the sale. As he unmercifully editorialized on 8 September 1874: "We are consolidating the subscription lists of the two journals very rapidly and it is not costing us a cent beyond the making of a first class paper." McCullagh carried the feud over into 1875 by noting on 5 January that the "annual meeting of the stockholders of the *Democrat* is called for next Wednesday. Five pallbearers are to be selected." That May, McKee and Houser approached Fishback with an offer to buy the *Democrat*, perhaps because they feared that Fishback might find a tough journalist to buy the paper if they did not; it has also been suggested that by this time Fishback had learned of McKee's involvement in the Whiskey Ring fraud and threatened to expose him if McKee did not take the *Democrat* off his hands. At any rate, on 18 May Fishback sold the *Democrat* for $325,000—$131,100 less that he had paid for it three years earlier. When the first issue of the *St. Louis Globe-Democrat* appeared on 20 May, McCullagh explained to readers that the paper represented "more a marriage than a birth."

Over the next twenty-one years, McCullagh built the *Globe-Democrat* into the preeminent paper in St. Louis and one of the best in the nation. During these years McCullagh, along with contemporaries like Pulitzer, was one of the pioneers of the trend called the New Journalism. Frank Luther Mott has noted that the New Journalism had a number of characteristics, among them an aggressive coverage of news, the use of crusades and stunts, a vigorous editorial page, and promotional campaigns for the paper. Biographer Clayton maintains that McCullagh was the "architect" of the New Journalism for, with the exception of the stunts, "McCullagh was doing all the things Pulitzer used, before Pulitzer became a publisher."

McCullagh relied on outstanding news coverage to build the circulation of the *Globe-Democrat*. He

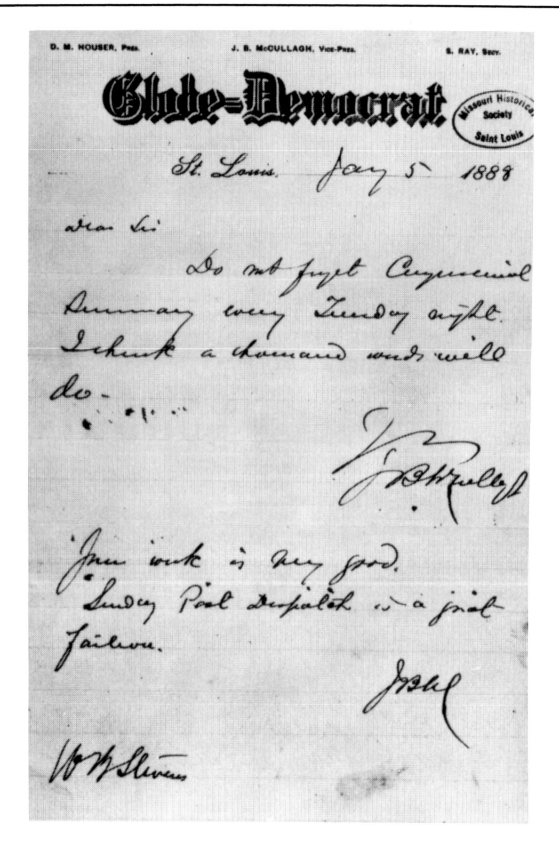

Note from McCullagh to his Washington correspondent, Walter B. Stevens, containing a dig at a rival newspaper
(Missouri Historical Society)

realized that he could not rely too heavily on the Western Associated Press if the paper was to become nationally recognized. Instead, he hired and trained hundreds of correspondents to form his own news service, which covered the territory from St. Louis to the Rockies, north to Iowa, east to Ohio, and south to Louisiana and Texas. McCullagh was fortunate to have publisher Houser's full support for the policy of paying any price for news. In the 2 May 1884 issue, McCullagh boasted: "The *Globe-Democrat* is now paying more money for the collection and transmission of telegraphic news from all parts of the world than is paid in any other newspaper in any city of the world, New York and London excepted." Theodore Dreiser, hired by the paper in 1892, reported that it was then spending $400,000 annually on telegraphed news from all parts of the world. These expenditures made it possible for the paper to keep correspondents in New York and Washington, as well as to send special correspondents to any part of the country where McCullagh found a news item he thought might interest his readers. Nor did he ignore international news: the paper received reports via the Atlantic cable from correspondents in London, Vienna, Berlin, and other European cities. Some issues of the *Globe-Democrat* carried as much as five columns of foreign news.

But McCullagh's pursuit of news involved more than reporting events once they had occurred; as an editor he again demonstrated the intuitive ability to anticipate events. As he noted in a 31 December 1883 editorial, "The great art of running a newspaper is the art of guessing where hell is likely to break loose next." It is said that McCullagh once ordered a reporter to New York via a specific train. When the reporter, in an effort to save $6, took another train, he missed the Johnstown flood. When news in the strictest sense was not forthcoming, McCullagh was not above creating items of reading interest. Early in his editorship of the *Globe-Democrat*, he stirred St. Louis for three months with the "Great Religious Controversy," a free-wheeling debate between clergy of the Catholic, Presbyterian, Methodist, Episcopalian, and Jewish faiths. Hundreds of letters from the faithful poured into the *Globe-Democrat*'s office between December 1877 and February 1878. Circulation climbed to 26,792 by the end of February.

In July 1879 McCullagh created another controversy, this time involving the state of Texas. McCullagh realized that Texas residents offered a prime opportunity for increased circulation; the seeming "lawlessness" there was a constant source of copy. Thus, he sent correspondents to every major town in the state, and dispatches began appearing in the *Globe-Democrat* that Texas newspapers called "malicious and unwarranted." McCullagh fed their ire with editorial comments like one on 16 July 1879: "If the energy that is wasted in Texas in denunciation of the *Globe-Democrat* for telling the truth about events in that state were directed to the punishment of crime and the administration of impartial justice there, the reign of lawlessness would soon be over." Texas editors finally demanded a boycott of the *Globe-Democrat*. In Marshall, an old city ordinance banning the sale of papers on Sunday was discovered and used against a newsboy selling the *Globe-Democrat* there. McCullagh reported the trial and wryly commented: "At Marshall, Texas yesterday a newsboy was tried by a jury of his peers for selling the *Globe-Democrat* on Sunday, and was fined $25 and costs. The boy sold a big bundle of *Globe-Democrats* and a single copy of the *Republican*. The specific offense being the sale of newspapers, there was no harm in selling the *Republican*, except to the misguided Texan who paid his nickel for a copy." The pettiness of the incident hastened the end of the "Texas Boycott." The *Globe-Democrat* emerged with circulation figures higher than ever.

McCullagh proved to be ingenious in finding new sources of copy. His appreciation of the interview as a news gathering device led to the first mass interview ever conducted. The poll, conducted by thirty *Globe-Democrat* reporters on 21 June 1879, was of an unsuspecting group of Ohio editors just arrived in St. Louis on excursion. Each editor was interviewed by a reporter who wore a badge declaring: "A Soft Answer Turneth Away Wrath, *Globe-Democrat* Interviewing Corps, With Malice for None and With Questions for All." After spontaneously answering questions put to them, the editors were handed a yellow card that read: "Pumped. Keep this check in your hat to avoid further disturbance." The results of the poll filled eight columns in the next day's paper and, of course, virtually every editor polled wrote about the experience when he returned to Ohio.

These "catechisms," as McCullagh referred to them, proved highly popular with the public. On one occasion he sent his team to the floor of the Merchants' Exchange to quiz the men on the Ten Commandments; members of the New York Stock Exchange were tested on their knowledge of history. But the "catechism" that gained the most notoriety was the 1891 poll of the members of the House of Representatives to test their political knowledge.

The fifteen-column story reporting the results on 8 December 1891 proclaimed in a six-deck head: "Congress Catechized, The *Globe-Democrat*'s Class in Political History Descends on the Capital, An Attempt to Ascertain What Our Statesmen Know About American History, Fourteen Simple Questions Prove Too Much for the Great Politicians, Not a Dozen Public Officers Knew How Old Washington Was When He Died...." *Globe-Democrat* readers delighted in seeing Congress humbled. McCullagh continued to use the catechism in differing forms throughout the years, and he was the first to adapt the technique to poll delegates at political conventions.

In addition to proving himself a master at news gathering, McCullagh distinguished himself as a powerful editorialist. His editorial page, according to Hart, "revolutionized the pages of St. Louis journals." McCullagh became legendary for his use of the short but penetrating editorial paragraph. Dreiser noted that with a McCullagh editorial one could expect "brilliant biting words, a luminous phraseology, sentences that cracked like a whip." The editorials were timely, always built around current national events or issues facing the city. McCullagh kept his editorials to one paragraph because, he explained, "people read the short editorials and they don't care a d--n for the long ones." The *Missouri Democrat* commented in 1896 that although McCullagh's invective was fearful, rarely did he abuse a man personally. As McCullagh once told a *Globe-Democrat* reporter: "It's no use to jump on a man just because you've got a newspaper."

Thus McCullagh did carry out editorial crusades—against gambling, the lotteries, and drinking, for example—but he usually was more of a "boomer" than a reformer. He is, in fact, credited as being the first to use the word *boom* in this sense. His most sustained crusade was the twenty-one-year effort to get St. Louis booming.

St. Louis in 1870 was the largest city in the West, with a population of over 300,000. But with its size had developed a certain complacency among its leaders. Throughout the decade, the city missed out on the prosperity being brought to other Midwestern cities by the railroads. By 1880 Chicago, the railroad hub of the West, passed St. Louis in population.

"Poor old St. Louis," McCullagh needled in an attempt to shame the citizens out of their lethargy. Because of the city's geographic location, McCullagh realized it too could become a great rail center, and he set out to convince St. Louisans of that potential. In 1882 he ordered the creation of a new

department, "The Railroads," a feature other papers scurried to imitate. Six days a week for the next ten years the paper bombarded readers with news of the railroads and the need for improved service to the city. By 1894 St. Louis had opened Union Station and was being served by twenty-four railroads, five of which were headquartered in the city. Undoubtedly much of the credit for this success can be attributed to McCullagh's foresight and relentless crusading.

In addition to business progress, McCullagh campaigned for cultural and educational progress. When citizens in 1877 failed to secure an invaluable library, McCullagh scolded: "We have nothing whatever to show in the way of art, and have spent less money in all its forms than has been devoted to furnishing a permanent home for six bears and twenty-four monkeys at the Fair Grounds." However, he did praise the city when he felt it deserved it, such as on 3 September 1884 when the city dedicated the Exposition Building. McCullagh called it "the greatest enterprise ever carried to completion by the voluntary aid of a city's own people." His efforts to "boom" St. Louis are credited as a decisive factor in the city's being chosen to host the 1904 World's Fair.

A testament to McCullagh's service to St. Louis was the fact that a group of businessmen out of appreciation once offered to raise money to buy the bachelor editor his own home. McCullagh declined the offer but added that if the men truly wanted to give him a gift, they could raise the money for the needy. Consequently $18,000 was raised and distributed to St. Louis charities. McCullagh refused the offer, he later explained, for fear "some of them might come around afterwards and want to run the paper."

This desire to remain independent of any outside influence partially explains why McCullagh's was something of an isolated life. He attended no church, although he quoted the Scriptures from memory. He once addressed a meeting of the Missouri Press Association—an address termed "an oratorical failure"—but never attended another meeting and refused to join the group. A dedicated Republican in both local and national affairs, he neither held nor sought any political appointment. As he wrote on 19 March 1883: "The editor who conducts his paper in such a way as to deserve an office is a man who cannot afford to accept it."

His lifelong interest in politics, however, was reflected in the *Globe-Democrat*'s coverage of it. McCullagh had attended his first national convention in 1864 as a *Cincinnati Commercial* reporter, and he took pride in the fact that he had personally covered all of the Democratic and Republican conventions between 1864 and 1888. Political coverage in the *Globe-Democrat* was comprehensive. When state legislatures were in session, the paper published at least one column of news per day from each of the six states in its circulation area. So thorough was his blanketing of this territory that it was not uncommon for the *Globe-Democrat* to scoop papers in their home states, events McCullagh never failed to point out to his readers. The importance McCullagh put on political news was also indicated by his establishment of a Washington bureau in 1885, a feat few other Western papers could claim. The bureau, headed until 1901 by Walter B. Stevens, produced a regular feature called "The Spoils"—one of the first investigations into federal patronage.

Although he was a partisan and often used his editorials for political bickering, he insisted that political news in the paper be as factual as any other type of news coverage. He was astute enough to realize that his responsibility as a journalist superseded his allegiance to the Republican party. He wrote on 1 January 1885: "As Gibbon says of his father's interference with one of his love affairs, 'I sighed as a lover, but obeyed as a son.' So the editor of a great newspaper, though he may often be tempted by the news of the day to suppress it as a politician, should always yield to the higher demand to print it as a journalist."

Throughout his career at the *Globe-Democrat*, the paper remained McCullagh's only involvement. The *New York Times* later described McCullagh the editor as "a journalistic recluse in his sanctum, where he worked harder than when he was a reporter." So conscientious was he in carrying out his daily duties at the paper that staffers said they could set their watches by his movements. Dreiser remembered "the Chief" as "in that small office, sitting waist-deep among his papers, his heavy head sunk on his pouter-like chest . . . his whole air one of complete mental and physical absorption in his work." McCullagh's goal, according to Dreiser, was to make the *Globe-Democrat* not only a good but a great paper. He dominated the paper totally and demanded that reporters on the *Globe-Democrat*, which he referred to as the best journalism school in the country, carry out his instructions faithfully. Correspondents had a list of forty-eight rules they were to follow, among them: "Matter sent this paper must be strictly accurate as to fact. Bogus items, manufactured sensations and highly colored articles lacking in solid basis of fact are not wanted.

Good news is often scarce. This journal desires no other. When there is nothing to send, send nothing. Never say, 'A prominent citizen says' so and so. If his name cannot be used, leave out his statement. The 'prominent citizen' never materializes when a libel suit is on trial." Some experts believe the code of ethics adopted by the American Society of Newspaper Editors in 1923 rests squarely on the principles set down by McCullagh.

The Globe-Democrat Building at Sixth and Pine Streets.
McCullagh's office was on the sixth floor
(St. Louis Globe-Democrat).

It is also noteworthy that in an era when other newspapers were taking on a yellow color, McCullagh refused to let the *Globe-Democrat* become lurid. He, like his contemporaries, did sometimes resort to the sensational as a circulation builder; he said in 1878: "If the American press were not 'sensational' in the generally accepted meaning of that word, it would not be representative." However, McCullagh insisted that the paper maintain what Dreiser described as "catholicity and solidity in editorials and news." McCullagh required that trials be covered impartially and without moralizing. He refused stories on cases of incest or seduction unless they were written with "the briefest possible mention in decent language." He once paid for, then refused to run, an expensive 6,000-word story cabled from England because he found it unfit for readers of the *Globe-Democrat*.

He demanded that writing in the paper be kept short, clear, but full. He insisted on accuracy and often called to the attention of city editors errors in statistics, names, and initials. "Always verify, always verify," he ordered. McCullagh spent the late evening hours checking the day's proofs for wordiness or inaccuracies, and as one of his reporters recalled: "Woe to the man who misquoted! McCullagh would go after him red-eyed and round shouldered!"

Despite his heavy hand, McCullagh was respected by those who worked for him as well as by those who read his paper. Dreiser writes: "Plainly he was like a god to many of them, the farmers and residents in small towns in states like Texas, Iowa, Missouri, Arkansas and Southern Illinois," for they came to the office whenever they were in the city merely to get a glimpse of him. "He was held in high esteem by his staff, and was one of the few editors of his day who really deserved to be."

As the years passed, McCullagh's health began to fail. Afflicted with both asthma and kidney problems, he became extremely obese; spending twelve-hour days in his smoke-filled office no doubt complicated matters. By 1893 he was so ill that he was forced to move into the home of his brother and sister-in-law. More and more of his editorial duties were turned over to Captain Henry King. McCullagh's brother died a short time later, and his sister-in-law married a man named Manion, who died in 1895; McCullagh continued to live with Mrs. Manion.

McCullagh did return to full-time service during the 1896 elections, when he threw himself into supporting McKinley. His success was heralded in the 4 November issue with a banner of seven strutting roosters, the *Globe-Democrat*'s symbol of victory. His work during the election, however, brought on an acute attack of asthma and, some say, nervous depression. He did not return to the *Globe-Democrat* office after 10 November.

McCullagh's death on 31 December 1896 shocked the nation. The *Post-Dispatch* broke the news in boldface headlines to St. Louis: "Killed Himself, Suicide of Editor Joseph B. McCullagh of St. Louis *Globe-Democrat*, Leaped From the Bedroom Window of His Home In the Night, His Mangled Corpse Found in the Yard by Mrs. Manion's Stable Boy, Attempted to Take Life a Few Hours Before by Turning on Gas, Had Been Ill for Many Months and Is Supposed to Have Become Deranged, Wore Out His Life at His Profession and Had Grown Weary and Despondent, Began His Career as a Printer's Apprentice and Worked His Way Up to the Highest Rank of Journalism."

Whether McCullagh purposely ended his life as his doctor declared, or whether he fell from the window during an asthmatic attack as his friends maintained, has never been answered. The *Chicago-Tribune* insisted the death was accidental, while the *New York Times* on its front page called it a suicide. Those who refused to accept suicide as the cause of death pointed to an editorial written by McCullagh on 14 August 1892 after the suicide of one of his friends. In the essay, entitled "The Philosophy of Suicide," McCullagh observed: "The true and manly course is to go on trying for success, in spite of all disappointments. That is what we are placed here for and we cannot do otherwise. The plea of despair, in short, is not a valid one."

Comments by his contemporaries served as proof of McCullagh's success. The competing *St. Louis Chronicle* called him "the greatest editor in the West . . . one of the select to which Horace Greeley, Murat Halstead and Charles Dana belong." The *Post-Dispatch* noted that "few men did more to broaden the scope of newspaper work and enterprise." Pulitzer's *New York World* called McCullagh "a political prophet," while Henry Watterson's *Louisville Courier-Journal* described him as "a thorough newspaper man from head to foot." Perhaps the most incisive comment came from another McCullagh protégé, William Marion Reedy, in his 7 January 1897 *Mirror*: "His devotion to his paper was idolatrous. No man ever loved a mistress as he loved the *Globe-Democrat*."

McCullagh's journalistic achievements cannot be overlooked. His dispatches during the Civil War still are considered to be some of the finest written in that period. As a political correspondent he broke ground in the use of the modern interview and was the first to open the doors of the White House to journalists. In St. Louis he was one of the last great personal editors of the 1800s, leaving an indelible mark on the *Globe-Democrat* and guiding its growth from a fledgling paper in a medium-sized Midwestern city to a journal with national recognition. His dedication to journalism was reflected in the careers of many students of his school, among them Stevens, Dreiser, Cockerill, Reedy, John A. Dillon, and Casper S. Yost.

McCullagh should also be noted as one of the leaders of the New Journalism. He pioneered work in new forms of gathering and writing news, and he understood the importance of presenting comprehensive, accurate, and impartial accounts to his readers. At the same time, he appreciated the power of the editorial paragraph. Although he refused to use the *Globe-Democrat* for his own interests, McCullagh became a potent force in St. Louis. As Dreiser said, "the very air of St. Louis became redolent of him."

An examination of McCullagh's career leads one to wonder why his contributions to American journalism have been so often overlooked. Part of the explanation might be that Midwestern history has, until recently, been neglected due to fascination with the Eastern seaboard. Also, McCullagh was neither a publisher nor an empire builder but remained content to stay in St. Louis in the capacity of editor for most of his life.

McCullagh can be faulted for his obsessions. His insistence on independence of thought led to a life of virtual isolation. His total absorption in his work may have sown the seeds of his own destruction. Even his death remains a mystery—the final legacy of a "public" man who, nonetheless, remained private to the end.

Biography:

Charles C. Clayton, *Little Mack: Joseph B. McCullagh of the St. Louis Globe-Democrat* (Carbondale: Southern Illinois University Press, 1969).

References:

Theodore Dreiser, *A Book About Myself* (New York: Boni & Liveright, 1922);

Jim Allee Hart, *A History of the St. Louis Globe-Democrat* (Columbia: University of Missouri Press, 1961);

Hart, "An Historical Study of the St. Louis *Globe-Democrat*, 1852-1958," Ph.D. dissertation, University of Missouri, 1959;

Hart, "The McCullagh-Johnson Interviews: A Closer Look," *Journalism Quarterly*, 45 (Spring 1968): 130-133, 138;

Walter B. Stevens, "Joseph B. McCullagh," *Missouri Historical Review*, 25-28 (October 1930-July 1934);

Stevens, "The New Journalism in Missouri," *Missouri Historical Review*, 17-19 (October 1922-July 1925);

William H. Taft, *Missouri Newspapers* (Columbia: University of Missouri Press, 1964).

Papers:

Some of McCullagh's papers, including his correspondence with Walter B. Stevens, are preserved at the Missouri Historical Society in St. Louis.

William V. McKean
(15 October 1820-29 March 1903)

Jacqueline Steck
Temple University

MAJOR POSITIONS HELD: Associate editor, *Pennsylvanian* (Philadelphia) (1850-1853); editorial writer, *Philadelphia Inquirer* (1860-1864); general manager and editor in chief, *Philadelphia Public Ledger* (1864-1891).

William V. McKean ran the *Public Ledger*, one of Philadelphia's most influential newspapers, for more than twenty-five years at the end of the nineteenth century. He used as his guiding principles a system of journalistic ethics based on fairness and accuracy in reporting and a concern for the public good. The ideas behind the maxims he penned for his editors and reporters outlasted both the *Ledger* and its editor and still apply to the news business.

William Vincent McKean was born in Philadelphia on 15 October 1820, the son of a Scots-Irish couple, William and Helen McKean. Except for a few years in Washington, Philadelphia was his lifelong home. He had little formal education: his mother taught him to read, and he had periods of study at local private schools until he was thirteen; after that, he went to work and attended night school. In 1836, he was apprenticed to the firm of Robb and Ecklin, typefounders. Beginning with hand-mold casting, he worked his way up through the business to the accounting department. His first brush with the *Public Ledger* occurred during this time. When the *Ledger*'s founders set up the newspaper in the 1830s, they ordered some ornamental type from Robb and Ecklin; young McKean was sent out to look up their references. In 1839, McKean joined the Union Library Company, a popular literary society, and became one of its most active debaters. According to contemporary historians, "it was progressive, became aggressive in its discussions, and very prominent." The lively exchange of opinions at the society helped shape McKean's later political and social ideas.

McKean was married 1 February 1841 to Hannah Rudolph, the daughter of Joseph and Susan Pastorius Tull Rudolph. In 1846 he changed careers, beginning the study of law in the office of James C. Van Dyke. He also received a government

William V. McKean

appointment, which he held for about four years; meanwhile he began writing articles on a volunteer basis for Col. John W. Forney's *Pennsylvanian*. He apparently found this last activity most appealing, for in 1850 he joined the *Pennsylvanian* as associate editor. He spent the next three years learning the newspaper business firsthand.

Forney was appointed clerk of the U.S. House of Representatives in 1853 and asked McKean to go to Washington with him. For three years, McKean worked as Forney's chief clerk, in charge of distributing public money appropriated by the House. President Pierce appointed McKean to the patent office as an examiner after the young editor left his clerk position in February 1856. He held the patent examiner position for only a few months, however, resigning to take a far more exciting job as private secretary to presidential candidate James Buchanan. Buchanan, who was to win the election that fall and serve as president from 1857 to 1861, was a fellow Pennsylvanian who had strong ties to the Southern states.

McKean quickly found himself in difficulty in his new position: his old friend Forney wanted to become editor of the *Washington Union* and public printer, a plum job at the time, but many of Buchanan's Southern supporters disliked Forney and objected. McKean was caught in the middle. His obituary in the *Public Ledger* describes his position as "an embarrassing one": "To be loyal to Mr. Buchanan and to be cognizant of the designs against his old and confidential friend, Colonel Forney, and yet to have to conceal from the latter the proceedings of his enemies, was impossible, and Mr. McKean soon resigned, greatly to Mr. Buchanan's surprise and regret."

McKean returned to Philadelphia, where he held two city jobs over the next four years. In 1860, he went back to his favorite kind of work, journalism, joining the *Philadelphia Inquirer* as an editorial writer. McKean, a longtime Democrat, had a political change of heart that year. Concerned about where the intense stresses between the Northern and Southern states might lead, he visited Washington to find out for himself just what the Southern leaders wanted. After meetings with Vice-President John Breckenridge and several senators who were personal friends, he became convinced that war was inevitable and said so in a letter to Pennsylvania Governor William Packer. From then on, he voted independently of party and, when at the *Public Ledger*, urged his readers to do the same.

He stayed with the *Inquirer* through 1864 but also did some editorial work for publisher George W. Childs. When Childs bought the financially troubled *Public Ledger* from its founders in December 1864, he asked McKean to come along as general manager and editor in chief. McKean, then forty-four years old, stayed at the newspaper until his retirement in September 1891.

In the early days of his association with the *Public Ledger*, McKean worked closely with Childs to implement the changes the publisher wanted to make. Both single-issue prices and advertising rates were raised, resulting in a temporary circulation drop. One of the publisher's priorities was finding new headquarters for the newspaper, and Childs

immediately began putting together a parcel of land at Sixth and Chestnut Streets. The new *Public Ledger* building opened 20 June 1867; it still stands.

A commemorative book published by Childs after the event says the elite of Philadelphia turned out for the opening festivities to pay "willing homage to the power of the press." McKean, speaking on behalf of Childs, told the crowd gathered in the new composing room for the opening ceremony that Childs had three objectives in mind for the building: he wanted to make it as convenient as a printing office could be; he wanted the building to be an ornament to the city; and he wanted the plant to be "a comfortable, cheerful and wholesome place for workmen to do their work in —a very important desideratum." He joked about the cost of the building: "There is a great deal else that might be said, but I will only detain you now to say this: that you, gentlemen, who are here and have seen this beautiful building and heard something of what it has cost, must not go away with the impression that the million or more dollars that are invested in the business have been the profits of the *Ledger* within a year or so. (Laughter). I feel bound to warn you not to go setting up newspapers with any idea of acquiring such an income as that of the business. (Renewed Laughter)." The festivities continued that evening with a lavish banquet for 500 invited guests. There, McKean paid tribute to Anthony J. Drexel, who had helped finance the *Public Ledger*.

McKean and Childs wanted the *Public Ledger* to be the kind of newspaper that could be read by the entire family. In his autobiography, Childs proudly quoted a local religious leader, who said the news columns of the *Public Ledger* excluded "all details of disgusting crime; all reports of such vice as may not be with propriety read aloud in the family, (and) . . . all scandal and slang." This principle applied to advertising, too: ads that did not meet the moral standards of the *Public Ledger*'s management were rejected.

A contemporary historian described McKean as "a thoroughly cultivated gentleman of sound judgment and keen sagacity, and a racy, vigorous and judicious writer." During McKean's tenure at the newspaper, the *Public Ledger* was an influential and respected force in Philadelphia, although a newcomer in the market, the *Record*, surpassed it in circulation in the early 1880s. The *Public Ledger* fought for local reforms, both social and political, and McKean was very much involved. Contemporary writers said: "In nearly all the movements in Philadelphia during this time to promote the welfare of the people, to advance their interests and to improve the efficiency of their city government, Mr. McKean has had large part as adviser and counsel,—much larger part in these capacities than even in his abundant work as an editorial writer." They added that his influence, both public and private, "has taken effect in the enactment of wholesome laws, in the choice of better officials, in the adoption of sound policy by public men, in keeping families from breaking up, and in saving men from their own ruinous appetites."

He was involved in many projects and organizations, including a commission to provide relief for the families of soldiers in the war, the Philadelphia Sanitary Fair, and incipient movements for a Centennial Exposition. He belonged to philosophical and literary societies as well as to the Philadelphia Board of Trade and the Pennsylvania Historical Society. The project which gave him the most pleasure, however, was the Children's Free Excursion program, which he organized in 1872. This involved transporting mothers and children from the tough streets and mean alleys of the city to Fairmount Park for a day of healthful food and wholesome amusements. During the six years the program lasted, some 60,000 adults and children were involved.

McKean firmly believed that there is a good side in almost every person, if people would only look for it. His faith in mankind and concern for the public good are shown clearly in some of the maxims he penned. He wrote:

> Numerous as bad men may be, remember they are but few compared with the millions of the people.

> ★★★
> The public welfare has higher claims than any party cry.

One historian described McKean's maxims as the constitution of his newspaper. They provided succinct and valuable instructions for reporters and editors on how to gather and present the news. His major concerns were for fairness, accuracy, and presentation of information in ways people could understand. He wrote:

> Grace and purity of style are always desirable, but never allow rhetoric to displace clear, direct, forcible expression.

> ★★★
> Plain words are essential for unlearned people, and these are just as plain to the most accomplished.

> ★★★
> Before making up judgment take care to understand both sides, and remember there are at least two sides. If you attempt to decide, you are bound to know both.

> ★★★
> Do not say you know when you have only heard.

> ★★★
> Take care to be right. Better be right than quickest with "the news" which is often false. It is bad to be late, but worse to be wrong.

> ★★★
> Go to first hands and original sources for information: if you cannot, then get as near as you can.

> ★★★
> It is the reporter's office to chronicle events, to collect facts: comments on the facts are reserved for the editor.

> ★★★
> Never add fuel to the fire of popular excitement.

He also had strong beliefs in justice and the rule of law. He urged reporters to "deal gently with weak and helpless offenders." He thought society's problems rarely resulted from a lack of laws, but rather from problems with enforcement. He wrote:

> Uphold the authorities in maintaining public order, rectify wrongs through the law. If the law is defective, better mend it than break it.

> ★★★
> There is no need, and therefore no excuse, for mob law in American communities.

> ★★★
> There is nothing more demoralizing in public affairs than habitual disregard of the law.

> ★★★
> There is a wide gap between accusation of crime and actual guilt.

McKean, who had no children, liked to refer to the *Public Ledger* staff as a family. He apparently was well liked by the employees. At a picnic for newsboys shortly after the new *Public Ledger* building opened, his efforts to give a short speech were drowned out by cheers. Harry Whitcraft, a *Public Ledger* staffer, described McKean as "a most lovable man"; he wrote that to join the staff of the *Public Ledger* was "to be received into the elite of Philadelphia journalism" and that having McKean in charge "alone was a guarantee of the high character and literary merit of the *Ledger* editorials and the honesty of the paper's news policy."

As his twenty-fifth anniversary with the newspaper approached, a group of employees drafted a letter to McKean proposing a large celebration to mark the occasion. Childs and Drexel supported the idea. McKean replied: "No festival celebration can add to the sterling value of that letter and I therefore respectfully ask you to forego your generous purpose as to the proposed reunion." The employees were persistent, however, and McKean eventually agreed to a public reception at the Academy of Fine Arts, followed by a private dinner.

More than 2,000 people attended the reception on 7 December 1889. The building was decked with flowers and plants, and the Germania Orchestra played waltzes and opera selections. McKean was presented with a large, intricately decorated silver vase with a gold lining. The gift of Drexel and Childs, the vase bore an inscription saying that the editor "has done his important and responsible work for the public and for the newspaper 'with conscience and common sense, honest purpose and clean hands.' " These were McKean's ideals. According to the *New York Times*, "Mr. McKean received the token in silence, but the welling up of his eyes spoke more eloquently than words of his happy appreciation of the gift."

After the reception, McKean gave a short speech to *Public Ledger* staffers in which he outlined his idea of what a newspaper should be: "The business of a newspaper is to publish information of general interest—information proper to be placed before the public—proper to go into the house and home—and to discuss it fairly when the information is important enough—to explain it—to cast light upon it—to make suggestions—to give advice—in a word, to impart useful knowledge." He said discussion of an issue "should be dispassionate, for otherwise the reader is getting hot blood, not cool reason—it should be free from undue bias, whether social, political, factional or denominational, for otherwise the reader is getting distempered prejudice instead of clear true light—it should be fair, frank and true, for otherwise you are not dealing honestly with the public."

The anniversary was noted by other newspapers. Childs collected some of the glowing editorial comments and included them in a commemorative

book he had printed privately. The *Record* of 8 December said: "We trust that when another quarter-Century shall have elapsed, these strong, earnest and high-souled men may still be found swaying the impulses and moulding the purposes of the great journal which, under their skillful and intelligent guidance, has developed so high a degree of usefulness to this community and to the general public." The *Daily News* of 9 December said: "Purity and sincerity of tone have been noticeable in every line of the paper since it came under its present ownership. As a newspaper the *Ledger* is outranked by none. And as an advertising medium its fame is as wide as civilization, and its solid prosperity increases with every successive year. Remarkable harmony has always existed in its office and to this its editor largely ascribes its prosperity. Somehow or other all Philadelphia newspaper men have a pride in the success of the *Public Ledger*."

Two years later McKean, then approaching his seventy-first birthday, retired from the *Public Ledger*. He was kept on the payroll at full salary, writing occasional editorials, but L. Clarke Davis took over as general manager while Childs became editor in chief. The *New York Times*, in a Philadelphia dispatch, said McKean's retirement was "the most important newspaper change announced in this city for some time." The article said McKean "was incessant in his labors and rarely took a vacation." As he got older, he was urged to take an extended trip to Europe and rest, but he did not want to go.

McKean seems to have lived a quieter life after his retirement. He was not well: he suffered for a number of years from Bright's disease, a kidney ailment. He died 29 March 1903 at the age of eighty-two and was buried following a funeral at his home at 200 West Logan Square. He was survived by his wife.

References:

George W. Childs, *Recollections* (Philadelphia: Lippincott, 1890);

Commemoration by the Public Ledger Family: The 25th Anniversary of George W. Childs' Ownership and William V. McKean's Direction of the Public Ledger (Philadelphia: Childs, 1890);

Benson Lossing, *The American Centenary 1876* (Philadelphia: Porter, 1876);

George H. Payne, *History of Journalism in the United States* (Westport, Conn.: Greenwood Press, 1920);

The Public Ledger Building, Philadelphia: With an Account of the Proceedings Connected with Its Open-

ing June 20, 1867 (Philadelphia: Childs, 1868);
Elwyn B. Robinson, "The Public Ledger: An Independent Newspaper," *Pennsylvania Magazine of History and Biography*, 64 (1940);
John Thomas Scharf and Thompson Westcott,

History of Philadelphia (Philadelphia: Everts, 1884);
Harry R. Whitcraft, "Fifty Years of Journalism in Philadelphia," *The Beehive*, 25 (June 1934).

John R. McLean
(17 September 1848-9 June 1916)

Mark Lipper
Shippensburg University

MAJOR POSITIONS HELD: Owner and editor in chief, *Cincinnati Enquirer* (1881-1916), *Washington Post* (1905-1916).

John R. McLean was prominent for many years as a newspaper publisher, politician, and multimillionaire. He learned journalism working from the bottom up at the *Cincinnati Enquirer*, of which his father was part owner, and of which he acquired ownership. For years he gave much financial support to the Democratic party in Ohio and used his newspaper to influence his party and his state, though he was unsuccessful in seeking public office. After failing with a newspaper in New York, McLean moved to Washington, D.C., where he became a civic leader, continued to amass a fortune in real estate and business, and purchased the *Washington Post*. Under his ownership, the paper suffered loss of prestige and revenue, but it managed to survive. After McLean's death in 1916, the *Post* fared even worse during its sixteen years under the ownership of McLean's son; it was sold in 1933. A personal friend of Joseph Pulitzer, William Randolph Hearst, and many other contemporary journalists, McLean won recognition for his business management but not for any editorial skill.

John Roll McLean (his middle name is incorrectly given as "Ray" in some sources) was born 17 September 1848 in Cincinnati, the only son of Washington McLean. "Wash" McLean, of rugged Scotch ancestry, had worked as a boilermaker and risen to manufacturing steamboats. In 1852 he bought the *Cincinnati Enquirer* in partnership with James J. Faran, a former congressman and mayor of the city. During the twenty-five years Washington McLean managed the *Enquirer*, he became a power in Ohio politics and was known as the

John R. McLean

"Warwick of the Democratic Party," in comparison to the earl who was a kingmaker in fifteenth-century England. While he often shaped policy and selected the Democratic party candidates, McLean never accepted a political office.

With their political connections, McLean and Faran built the biggest printing business in the world; but their newspaper was not as successful. It had a circulation of 16,000 in a city of 200,000 people, even though its editorial staff was headed by

Joseph B. McCullagh, who would later be recognized as one of the outstanding American journalists of the nineteenth century.

John McLean was drawn to athletics during his school days in Cincinnati. He was good enough to play with the Red Stockings, one of the best of the early baseball teams. He wanted to be a professional baseball player, but his father wanted him to become prepared to take over management of the *Enquirer*. He paid John a sizable bonus to go to college and forget the idea of a baseball career. (One biographer suggests that this was probably the first bonus ever paid for a player *not* to sign a contract.)

McLean attended Harvard for one year. One account is that he was expelled for fighting; another, that he left after being injured playing baseball. His father sent him to Heidelberg for a year where, John McLean's daughter-in-law Evalyn later concluded, he became "infected with the harsh, ruthless philosophy of Kant and Nietzsche."

McLean returned to Cincinnati and went to work at the *Enquirer* as an office boy. Later he became one of the best police reporters in the city; he was so popular that both the police and fire departments made him an honorary member of their associations. During this time, McLean struck up a friendship with another young reporter, John A. Cockerill.

Cockerill had been hired by Washington McLean early in 1869. The young journalist had been part owner of two Ohio newspapers and realized that he was better suited to editorial tasks than to proprietorships. At the *Enquirer* he soon found himself promoted to city editor; some say that his rapid promotion came because of his friendship with John McLean, while others maintain that he was promoted because of "his enterprise in getting news and his bright, snappy way of writing it up. . . ."

McLean's first step in becoming owner of the *Enquirer* came on his own initiative. He had heard that a block of the newspaper's stock was for sale in Tennessee, so he went there to buy it. He surprised his father by appearing at the next stockholder's meeting, flashing his stock certificates as credentials for his admission. In 1872 his father helped him to acquire the majority of the *Enquirer*'s stock.

McCullagh left the paper in 1869 to take a job in Chicago, leaving Faran in nominal charge of the news and editorial departments. Because he felt Faran was too involved in politics and business to do a good job as editorial head, young McLean moved his friend Cockerill into Faran's office without warning and proclaimed him new editorial head of

the paper. Faran left the *Enquirer* and never returned.

Cockerill was regarded by some of his contemporaries as a "born journalist"; he later became Joseph Pulitzer's prized editor both in St. Louis and in New York City. In Cincinnati he experimented with many aspects of what was to become the "New Journalism." He knew his community and its people, made good news judgments, wrote forceful editorials, and was skilled as a paragrapher. The most noted feature of Cockerill's editorship was the publishing of a daily stenographic record of the sensational trial in 1875 of the distinguished American clergyman Henry Ward Beecher on charges of adultery. At that time, it was considered "a most remarkable journalistic effort." Under Cockerill's leadership, the newspaper was well on its way from the 16,000 circulation it had when Cockerill was hired to the more than 90,000 circulation it would reach by 1892.

While Cockerill transformed the *Enquirer* into one of the most prosperous publishing houses of the West, he and McLean remained close friends. The editor and the businessman made a good team. One wedge that came between them, however, was McLean's political ambition: he used the columns of his paper in his attempts to achieve at least as much political prestige as his father. In *The Serene Cincinnatians*, Alvin F. Harlow wrote that "for forty years the Enquirer was the voice of John McLean the politician yearning for office . . . governor, senator, anything, which he never won."

As a Democratic leader, McLean formed an unholy alliance with the rising Republican boss, Thomas C. Campbell. Campbell's poor reputation as a criminal lawyer did not hinder the McLean-Campbell coalition, which pretended to offer a reform movement to relieve the city of the disgraceful administration of Mayor G. W. C. Johnston. The antidote was worse than the poison. Graft and lawlessness abounded in the administration of Mayor Robert M. Moore, who was owned by McLean and Campbell. Cockerill had to suffer humiliation as he read the exposés of prostitution and police payoffs in the rival *Gazette*; he could not report such matters because of his boss's political ties. These restraints were lifted when a new political group, headed by young Republican saloonkeeper George B. Cox, became the dominant power in Cincinnati and McLean lost interest in city government.

Probably the journalistic incident involving McLean that was most talked about and best remembered was the cunning way in which he deposed his chief editor and took his place. McLean's gratitude for Cockerill's profitable regeneration of the paper was overshadowed by envy for his accomplishment and longing for his status. Cockerill made the job look so easy that McLean was convinced that he could do it just as effectively. He knew, however, that getting rid of Cockerill would not be easy. The solution came in the form of an *Enquirer* headline on the Russo-Turkish War in 1877. Cockerill was first reminded that he was working too hard and should take a holiday. Then McLean cited the headline story and told his editor, "We would like you to go to Europe for a few months to report the war. Your job will be waiting for you when you return." Cockerill spent six months on his first assignment as a war correspondent. He reported the war not only for the *Enquirer* but also for the *New York Herald*, probably because the *Herald* gave McLean a reduced toll rate on its extensive cable and telegraphy service. Cockerill's reputation was greatly enhanced by his graphic war dispatches.

There are two versions of what happened next. One is that someone at the *Enquirer* instructed Cockerill to return to the United States; when the editor arrived in New York, he learned indirectly—probably through a trade journal—that his old job was not awaiting him and that McLean had moved into the managing editor's chair. The other version is that McLean had bought Cockerill only a one-way ticket to Europe in the first place; then, when Cockerill arrived in Constantinople, an awaiting telegram informed him: "Your services are dispensed with." Evans Peck says Cockerill "got back somehow, but he never loved McLean much after that."

When the first issue of the *Washington Post* appeared on 6 December 1877, Cockerill, then thirty-two years old, was its managing editor. He is credited with suggesting the newspaper's name and hiring its first woman reporter. But he stayed with the *Post* only a year and a half, then moved to the *Baltimore Gazette*. He did not know, of course, that his old boss would one day own the *Washington Post*.

McLean continued many of the practices of his deposed editor, and the *Cincinnati Enquirer* continued to prosper. In 1881 he was able to purchase full ownership.

After he had installed himself in the editor's chair, McLean plunged into politics again. Through his efforts, Bill Allen, whom he had helped to make the first Democratic governor in twenty years, was elected senator; McLean was also largely responsible for the election of Ohio governors Bishop, Hoadley, and Campbell. McLean was elected delegate at large to the Democratic convention in 1884 and held that office until he died. He was the Democratic nominee for the Senate against Sherman in 1885 and the Democratic nominee for governor of Ohio in 1889, without success in either contest. At the 1896 convention that nominated William Jennings Bryan, McLean was not only a delegate but also Ohio's favorite-son candidate, and he led the roll call for vice-president on the fourth ballot before he withdrew in the midst of a party fight. A major event of his political career in Ohio was his fight with the state's distinguished U.S. senator and influential presidential adviser Mark Hanna. The Hanna organization was said to have suffered severe damage in the encounter.

In 1881, Washington McLean turned over his interest in the *Enquirer* to his son and he retired to the nation's capital. Four years later John McLean went to Washington to marry Emily Beale, daughter of General and Mrs. Edward F. Beale. Dissatisfied with the limited influence he had in Ohio, McLean decided to establish his home in Washington in 1886, but he kept his legal and political base in Cincinnati. From that year until his death, he supervised the *Enquirer* from Washington.

McLean soon became involved in the economic and civic affairs of the nation's capital. Both his town house on I Street and his seventy-acre country estate at Friendship in the southwestern suburbs of Washington were among the showplaces of the area. From 1892 to 1911 he was president of the Washington Gas Light Company. He was a large stockholder in the Capital Traction Company, cofounder of the Washington and Old Dominion Railway in 1911, director and large stockholder in both the American Security and Trust Company and Riggs National Bank, and the owner of one of the largest hotels in the city. Soon after he had moved to Washington, word got around that he was "one of the few men who had ever made a fortune out of a graveyard": he had purchased the old Holmead Cemetery at a low price, remodeled it, divided it into building lots, and sold it at a considerable profit.

McLean did not do as well in his purchase of the *New York Morning Journal*. The *Washington Post* of 9 May 1895 announced that McLean, "one of Washington's most generous and public-spirited citizens," had acquired the *Journal*. The editorial followed with an unfortunate prediction: "That he will be successful in his undertaking, there is not the least room for doubt."

The *Journal* had been founded in 1882 by Albert Pulitzer, younger brother of Joseph, with an investment of $25,000; its sensationalism gained it a reputation as "the chambermaid's delight." McLean wanted to enter the New York newspaper market for political reasons, and he paid Pulitzer $1,000,000 for his paper. As its publisher, he increased the Democratic emphasis of the *Journal*, removed some of the entertaining content, and increased the price from one cent to two cents. Consequently, he lost his chambermaid readers and gained few others. With no outstanding editor like Cockerill, the *Journal* lagged far behind its competitors such as the *World*, the *Sun*, the *Tribune*, the *Herald*, and the *New York Times*. The *Sun* declared that the *Journal* "was published by fools for fools." While its deficits mounted, the *Journal*'s circulation fell to 77,000 and its advertising revenue dropped significantly. McLean found himself diverting *Enquirer* profits to cover *Journal* losses. So it was with some relief that he learned of William Randolph Hearst's interest in buying a New York newspaper.

With the experience he had gained as publisher of the *San Francisco Examiner*, Hearst was ready to enter the big league of New York journalism. Other newspapers were for sale in August 1895, but the *Journal* had the lowest price tag. Yet it was not the price that led Hearst to purchase the *Journal* as much as the challenge of "breathing life into the paper with the faintest pulse," according to his biographer W. A. Swanberg. McLean asked for $360,000 for half interest in the paper. Hearst offered half that amount for total ownership, and the offer was accepted so rapidly that he realized he might have purchased it for even less. When Hearst learned that the price also included the German-language edition of the paper, *Das Morgen Journal*, he remarked, "So I bought a frankfurter, too."

The *New York Times* of 3 October 1905 reported that "John R. McLean has bought from the sons of the late Beriah Wilkins an amount of the capital stock of the *Washington Post*, which, taken with other holdings, gives him a half interest in the newspaper." Asked about the purchase, McLean said: "So they're saying that about me, are they? That's about the only thing they haven't said, except that I've sold the dear old *Cincinnati Enquirer*. No, I don't care to say anything about the *Washington Post* matter at all."

McLean had shown an interest in the *Post* in 1896, when he had made a loan to the widow of Frank Hatton Wilkins's partner. The loan was secured by an option to purchase her stock in the newspaper, but McLean was never able to exercise that option. After he gained control of the *Post* from Wilkins's heirs in 1905, he spent the first two years

McLean at about the time he acquired the Washington Post *in 1905*

recreating it, using the *Cincinnati Enquirer* as his model. He attempted to appeal to all classes with political sports, theater, and society news. His introduction of bigger headlines, free classified ads, a flashy feature section, a four-page color comic section, and a sports section printed on pink paper were touches he had learned from his friend Hearst. Also, soon after he took control of the *Post*, McLean started contests to hold and win circulation in the competition with the *Star*, *Herald*, and *Times*. Much space was devoted to self-serving stories as the contests grew larger, and many observers felt this was demeaning to the formerly respectable paper.

McLean considered himself editor in chief of both the *Post* and the *Enquirer*. For a few years, using a home on H street as his office, he received callers on nonnewspaper business in the mornings; he spent the evenings at the *Post* building on E Street conducting his newspaper business. Eventually, however, his multiple interests in business, politics, and affairs of the *Enquirer* caused his attention to

Front page of the Washington Post *during the period McLean owned the paper*

the *Post* to suffer, and the newspaper gradually began to deteriorate. McLean seemed interested only in the business side of the paper, except when his friends needed his help in the news or editorial columns. Local by-lined stories became scarce except on features and in the sports and society sections. Stories from the wire service or bought from New York papers filled more of the daily's pages, few major out-of-town stories were covered by *Post* reporters, and political coverage became inconsistent. Slowly the average daily circulation of 30,000 started to diminish.

Another detriment to the health of the *Post* was McLean's personal philosophy about local news. The *Post* was a civic booster, always accenting the positive about the community. In a letter to William F. Wiles, who was in charge of the *Enquirer*'s editorial side, McLean wrote on 20 July 1914: "I would try my best to print always the good about the city—both in the news and editorial departments—for the people don't want to hear or read unpleasant news, no matter how true." This philosophy caused the paper to lose the stimulating and distinctive personality it had enjoyed under McLean's predecessors.

Two major events reported by the *Post* during McLean's eleven years at the helm were the Roosevelt-Taft split in the Republican party that led to Wilson's election and domestic reforms, and the outbreak of World War I that thrust America into a new role in international relations. In the presidential campaign of 1916, the *Post* supported former New York governor and Supreme Court justice Charles Evans Hughes, but McLean, who had had a keen interest in politics all his life, did not live to learn the outcome of the Wilson-Hughes contest. He died of cancer at Friendship on 9 June 1916 at the age of sixty-seven.

The *New York Times* of 10 June 1916 devoted a full column to McLean's obituary. The *Cincinnati Enquirer* on that day ran a column-long review of McLean's career and devoted its lead editorial to the death of its publisher. But the *Washington Post* ran only one sentence on the death of the man who had controlled it for more than a decade. At the head of its column of editorials it stated: "The *Washington Post* announces with profound sorrow the death of its editor-in-chief, Mr. John R. McLean." It carried no obituary or funeral story or settlement-of-estate story in the days that followed.

The *Post*'s lack of attention to McLean's death may have been viewed as evidence that the paper had lost respect for its owner. In his history of the first 100 years of the *Post*, Chalmers M. Roberts

states that McLean turned the *Post* into a second-rate newspaper. "His own impulses centered on the acquisition of wealth, not on creative journalism. He allowed the paper to slip into sensationalism, aping his friend Hearst. . . ." It is more likely, however, that the lack of attention to McLean's death in his own newspaper was in compliance with his expressed desire. Unlike Hearst, McLean shunned publicity about himself or his family. Neither his name nor those of his editors ever appeared in the masthead of the paper. Although his family was socially active, their activities were seldom mentioned in the ever-expanding society columns of the paper. Even when McLean's son Ned married the only daughter of Thomas F. Walsh, whose Colorado mines had made him a multimillionaire, the *Post* used no pictures and held the story down to six paragraphs on page seven.

Ned McLean succeeded his father as the owner of the *Post*. He had been pampered as a child, and early in his adulthood he had earned a reputation as a playboy with a fondness for racehorses, dogs, and fast automobiles. His years at the helm of the *Post* were painful for him and disastrous for the

McLean's son, Edward B. (Ned) McLean, who drove the Post *into bankruptcy in 1933*

paper. An alcoholic, he ended up in an asylum. His newspaper went on the auction block on 1 June 1933 and was sold for $825,000 to Eugene Meyer, whose family resurrected it and made it one of the nation's great newspapers again.

John Roll McLean was a paradox. He liked to tell how he charged his own father for a subscription to the *Enquirer*. Yet he was known to stand in front of the *Enquirer* building handing out coins to passersby, with greater amounts going to those who looked needy. Evans Peck wrote about "The Many-Sided McLean" in the February 1911 issue of *Cosmopolitan* magazine. "Out in Cincinnati," he reported, "ice is distributed to the needy in the hot months. John R. McLean pays for it. Coal is distributed in the winter time. John R. McLean settles the bills. Many of those who accept and use this summer ice and winter coal do not know that it is paid for by John R. McLean. He doesn't brass-band his philanthropies. He just likes to do these things."

About McLean's generosity in Washington, Peck wrote: "He loves to have guests and to make the guests gasp. Fussy foreign noblemen of all sorts and conditions have enjoyed handouts at the Mc-Lean Handoutery. . . ." Peck summed it up: "McLean is a character. He is, in several and numerous and various ways, a wonder. He is lovable and the unthinkable in one, the cruel and the merciful, the sage and the savage." Twenty years after his death, his daughter-in-law remembered McLean as "the oddest hybrid of gentle friend and fierce monster that I have ever known."

References:

Allen Churchill, *Park Row* (New York: Rinehart, 1958);

Alvin F. Harlow, *The Serene Cincinnatians* (New York: Dutton, 1950);

Homer W. King, *Pulitzer's Prize Editor: A Biography of John A. Cockerill* (Durham, N.C.: Duke University Press, 1965);

Evans Peck, "The Many-Sided McLean," *Cosmopolitan*, 50 (February 1911): 405-407;

Chalmers M. Roberts, *The Washington Post: The First 100 Years* (Boston: Houghton Mifflin, 1977);

W. A. Swanberg, *Citizen Hearst* (New York: Scribners, 1961).

William Rockhill Nelson

M. A. Kautsch
University of Kansas

BIRTH: Fort Wayne, Indiana, 7 March 1841, to Isaac De Groff and Elizabeth Rockhill Nelson.

MARRIAGE: 29 November 1881 to Ida Houston; child: Laura.

MAJOR POSITIONS HELD: Founder, owner, and editor, *Kansas City Star* (1880-1915).

AWARDS AND HONORS: LL.D., University of Notre Dame, 1911.

DEATH: Kansas City, Missouri, 13 April 1915.

William Rockhill Nelson distinguished himself as one of America's most powerful, crusading, and exemplary journalists by devoting his newspaper single-mindedly to the betterment of a city and its people. Nelson came to Kansas City, Missouri, where he founded the *Evening Star* in 1880, with long-established penchants for contrariness in school, business, and politics, and for making enemies. Yet he also tended toward building, leading, and fostering progress. The *Evening Star*, eventually renamed simply the *Star*, reflected Nelson's early work experience and his personality traits in a dynamic way. He directed the *Star* relentlessly in campaigns for vast civic improvements, including parks and boulevards. He crusaded ceaselessly against municipal vice and corruption. Wherever Nelson perceived threats to the progress of the city and the welfare of Kansas Citians, he flooded the community with news and editorial comment to expose the danger. By the end of his thirty-five years as owner and editor of the *Star*, Nelson had countless enemies who saw him as bul-

William Rockhill Nelson

and progress in America's history. Indeed, Nelson's vigorous life as an effective, crusading editor seems to have been foreshadowed by the accomplishments of his forebears. They included founders of cities, Revolutionary War heroes, and respected politicians. In Fort Wayne, Nelson's father was not only a newspaperman but also a court clerk, civic leader, farmer, and active Episcopal churchman. Nelson's mother was the daughter of a farmer who had helped develop Indiana as a state and who served as a representative to Congress. In later years, Nelson was proud to recall that his grandfather was possibly the first man in the world to plant one thousand acres of corn.

When Nelson was born, the nation was in a period of political turmoil, technological change, and economic uncertainty associated with rapid expansion. It was a time well suited for an ambitious individualist such as Nelson was destined to become. Advancements in communications and transportation during the period were marked by experiments with the pony express, by steamship and railroad development, and by the invention of the telegraph. In the year of Nelson's birth, America's westward push was highlighted by the departure from Independence, Missouri, of the first emigrant wagon train bound for California.

Near the turn of the century, the site of the city where Nelson's destiny was to lie amounted to little more than a rock ledge. West of Independence, it formed a natural levee near the confluence of the Kansas and Missouri rivers. It hardly had been noticed as explorers traversed the western part of the continent in the early 1800s. However, the site began to attract attention as fur trappers, traders, scouts, adventurers, and farmers began to congregate near the junction of the rivers. By 1834, it was being used as a steamboat landing for a small trading center called Westport, not far from the river junction. In 1838, traders acquired title to the rock ledge site and soon founded there what became Kansas City. The future of the town was assured in 1846 when war broke out between Mexico and the United States. The rock landing area attracted U.S. military men as a convenient unloading point as they prepared to advance on Mexico. Steamboats supplying men and guns ended up bypassing Independence on the way west and led travelers to see the future Kansas City as the gateway to the prairies beyond the Missouri River.

Nelson's youth was spent on an Indiana farm that his father bought when Nelson was one year old. Four miles east of Fort Wayne, it covered 200 acres and was known as Elm Park. Nelson read

lying and selfish; but he undeniably shaped the city's destiny in a positive way and enjoyed remarkable loyalty from *Star* readers and from the reporters and editors who had flourished under him. Commentators acclaimed Nelson—both before and after his death—as one of America's greatest editors and the *Star*, under Nelson, as one of the best newspapers in the nation, if not the world. He was acknowledged as a model of the rugged individualist, a source of vision and inspiration to all journalists who worked for him and an aggressive reformer who contributed significantly to the liberal, progressive movement that arose in the Midwest during the *Star*'s heyday.

On 7 March 1841, Nelson, the second son of Isaac De Groff Nelson, was born in Fort Wayne, Indiana. Nelson's father was the owner of the *Fort Wayne Sentinel*, a weekly newspaper. The boy's mother, of Quaker stock, was Elizabeth Rockhill Nelson. Both parents had distinguished ancestries traceable through momentous episodes of growth

Nelson at age six

widely as a youngster in books from the family library. He became accustomed to a rather privileged social standing and economic status. He also was rebellious and difficult for his parents to handle. At age ten, Nelson arranged with some friends to try to drive a political speaker out of town. From behind trees, the boys hurled eggs at the politician during an outdoor speech. A reward for the arrest and conviction of the culprits was posted. Frightened, young Nelson decided to run away from home. His brother, De Groff, turned informer, however, and Nelson's father pulled his errant son from a train. The elder Nelson called upon him to tell the truth about his attempt to run away, and the boy made a clean breast of the egg-throwing incident. Years later, Nelson recalled his confession, saying, "I shall never forget the note of satisfaction in his voice when he said: 'Well, thank God, you are not a liar, anyway.' He told me to come to him always when I was in trouble and he would see me through. I

realized then what a good father mine was."

Nelson conceded that although he never lacked affection for his father, he "resented parental restraint" and he "never enjoyed being bossed." His recollection was that "my chief end in life . . . was to break up whatever school I was attending." After repeated episodes of rebellion, the elder Nelson sent his fifteen-year-old son to the University of Notre Dame at South Bend, Indiana. At that time, Notre Dame included students of high school age in its program and was known for its strict discipline. To Nelson, it was a "Botany Bay for bad boys." Years later, when Nelson received an honorary degree from Notre Dame, he recalled that while there, "I suppose there was never an opportunity for a rebellion that I did not take advantage of." Shortly after arriving at Notre Dame, Nelson and two other boys disobediently left school to attend a circus. An instructor later sought to discipline Nelson by ordering him to memorize a lengthy poetry selection—a task that normally might have taken days. However, the boy, being blessed with an "unusually alert memory," surprised the instructor. As Nelson recalled it, "I was ready for him in a short time. When he saw how light the penalty was, he assigned several more yards of the poem for me to commit. Whereupon I refused and said I had done my task and proposed to do no more. So I found a nail and drove it through the book and clinched it on the other side." In 1858, at the end of his second year, Nelson left Notre Dame without completing his course of study. School officials wrote a letter telling his father that young Nelson should not return to the institution.

Left with the task of helping his son complete his education on his own, the elder Nelson assigned the boy, a stout youth who looked older than his seventeen years, to manage the family farm. Then, while serving as circuit court clerk, the father appointed Nelson as his deputy, and the boy began to study law.

As Nelson undertook his preparations for manhood, the nation was bitterly dividing into the two forces that ultimately would engage each other in mortal combat. The Civil War hatreds first raged out of control in the frontier territory where Nelson was to carry out the bulk of his future life's work. A pivotal event, the Kansas-Nebraska Act of 1854, drew the growing conflict between proslavery and abolitionist interests to the threshold of Kansas City. The act nullified the Missouri Compromise, which had declared free any state made from territory to the north and west of Missouri. It declared that the Nebraska territory would be divided into two potential states and that there would be self-determination on the slavery question. Proslavery forces in Missouri looked at the prospective state next door as an opportunity for expansion, but many opponents of slavery sought to head off such a development by migrating to the area that was to be Kansas. Amid the sharpening hostilities, commerce and population growth accelerated in Kansas City. Young, ambitious civic leaders saw the anticipated development of the area west of the Missouri River as foreshadowing the construction of a transcontinental railroad and began working aggressively to gather political and financial support for making Kansas City a terminal point for the railroad. They succeeded in maintaining a kind of neutrality between pro- and antislavery interests, garnering support from each side in Kansas City. Ultimately, the promoters' single-mindedness enabled them to get their way, making the city a booming railway center after the Civil War.

In Indiana, a group of Fort Wayne businessmen met on 11 December 1860 and pledged themselves "to stand by the Union of the States and proclaim to this Nation that Indiana is for the Union first, last, and forever." The younger Nelson was appointed secretary for the meeting. However, the Nelsons' pro-Union position did not mean that they favored war, and they did not support Abraham Lincoln in 1860 when he won the presidency as the Republican party's standard-bearer. As Democrats, the Nelsons were in line with the stance taken by a Lincoln opponent, Stephen A. Douglas, who advocated allowing the people of a territory to decide the slavery question for themselves. Nelson did not join the Union army, consistent with his father's wishes and with the Democratic views that dominated the Fort Wayne area at the time.

In 1862, Nelson was admitted to the bar and began practicing law and dealing in real estate. On 1 January 1863, Lincoln issued the Emancipation Proclamation; in Northern areas like Fort Wayne, critics opposed the proclamation as giving the Civil War an antislavery cast rather than a pro-Union purpose. Nelson, although he never admitted it, was accused by political foes in later years of having been a member of a secret states' rights society while in Indiana.

At the end of the war, Nelson saw a chance to become an entrepreneur in the South. The region was struggling to recover from the devastation wrought by the war and trying to cope with the fearsome tangle of hate and political shortsightedness that characterized the Reconstruction era. Nelson and a partner spent a few thousand dollars each to buy a large plantation near Savannah, Georgia, and open a general store in the town. However, falling prices for the sea island cotton they planned to harvest on the plantation ruined their hopes for big gains. Nelson left his partner to try to save the Savannah store and returned to Fort Wayne, where he bent his energies toward becoming a contractor. He built roads, bridges, and buildings in Indiana, as well as part of the southern Illinois penitentiary. His interest and expertise in construction later were reflected in his editorial crusades for civic improvements in Kansas City.

Nelson's venture into the South as a businessman and into contracting in his home state came during a volatile and corrupt period in which Republicans remained at center stage. When Nelson's interest in national politics showed itself, it was consistent with the Democratic opposition and contained elements of his future political outlook as an editor. Nelson supported the Democrats' 1876 presidential nominee, Samuel J. Tilden, against Republican Rutherford B. Hayes. Nelson served as Tilden's Indiana campaign manager after Tilden wryly told him, "As you are the only Democrat in Indiana who is not a candidate for the Presidency, I would like you to manage my campaign." Later, Nelson was said to have been particularly impressed when Tilden remarked, during a day they were together in New York, "While it is a great thing to lead armies, it is a greater thing to lead the minds of men." In a move that may have reflected Nelson's nascent interest in influencing minds, he invested in the *Fort Wayne Sentinel*, the paper his father had owned from 1840 to 1842, as a campaign tool.

Behind Tilden, the Democrats strongly aimed at a return to power that had been denied them since the war. The Democrats had been badly divided in 1864, when the party included members patriotically loyal to Lincoln but also antiwar and anti-Lincoln factions, including the copperheads with their outright Southern sympathies; Indiana was one of the copperhead strongholds. The Democrats suffered after the war at the hands of Republican radicals who aggressively consolidated their power in Congress. The Republicans feared that agrarian interests associated with the Democrats might rise again from the South and would strongly reassert decades-old resistance to tariffs and other economic policies that had enhanced the prosperity of Northern industrialists and that had, in part, led to the war.

A Republican president, U. S. Grant, oversaw such a corrupt administration, however, that it gave rise to a wave of reform by 1872. Tilden came to public attention about that time as an alternative to corruption. As a New York attorney, he headed the prosecution of the notorious Tweed Ring, which thrived in New York City on graft, bribery, and fraudulent elections. Tilden then ran for president in 1876, and his image as a reformer won him the popular vote. However, he ultimately lost after balloting irregularities threw the decision to an electoral commission controlled by Republicans.

By the time he was thirty-five and active in the Tilden campaign, Nelson had accumulated a fortune of some $200,000 through his contracting business. However, he lost it all when the store he and his partner had founded in Savannah failed; Nelson had underwritten the store's debts. Nelson appeared undaunted, saying, "Lack of self-confidence was never one of my failings. I never lost a minute's sleep over the affair. I'll win in the end." The only asset he salvaged from the financial ruin was his interest in the *Fort Wayne Sentinel*. Nelson, at thirty-seven, and a partner—Samuel E. Morss— became full owners of the *Sentinel* on 16 February 1879.

Nelson managed the Fort Wayne paper long enough to realize that his calling was to influence the times not through party politics but through journalism. As an editor, he worked under the shadow of his father, who had said, "A newspaper conducted on moral principles is better calculated to instruct a family than a poor school teacher. . . . One thing is certain and that is, that in proportion as a community increases in knowledge and general information, newspapers will increase and flourish in the same ratio." The statement had its echo in Nelson's later editorial creed in Kansas City.

The *Sentinel*, Nelson announced, would "occupy the position of an independent Democratic newspaper." He launched a lusty campaign for a waterworks for Fort Wayne; he also criticized special interests to the point that they, according to a *Sentinel* editorial, began to "fume, and rave and threaten and tear their hair and breathe forth dire predictions as to the *Sentinel*." Eventually, Nelson and Morss decided to seek a larger challenge. After considering a number of cities, they sold the *Sentinel* on 2 August 1880, and headed for Kansas City, Missouri.

The city was ripe for a man of Nelson's energies, visions, and talents. It had momentum as a commercial center and was in desperate need of leadership that could guide the city in building on past success. A hallmark of that past was the building of a bridge across the Missouri River in 1869 that secured the city's future as a railroad center.

Young civic leaders had won status for the city as a terminal railway point despite stiff competition from other cities and despite the hardships of the Civil War. After 1870, the city grew fast and wildly, trying to throw off its frontier past but having only a vague notion of its urban future.

Kansas City in 1880 consisted of a sprawl of wooden buildings, through which cut muddy or dusty streets, depending on the weather. Rats and flies, ravines, timber, cattle, stockyards, and railroad and steamboat whistles made up the city's environment. The 55,000 population included cowboys, drifters, gamblers, hustlers, streetwalkers, businessmen, families, and would-be aristocrats. Real estate speculation was rampant; yet much of the population was transient and therefore not interested in improving the quality of life in the city. One account of city life at that time depicted two men on a board sidewalk on Main Street: one said to the other, "You've got the worst muddle of a town I ever saw. Why don't you pave your street?" "Me pave it?" came the reply. "I don't care if they never pave it. I live in Louisville."

A resident of the city remembered that grading contractors who cut new streets flourished at considerable expense to taxpayers. He said that as of the early 1870s, he walked "in the middle of the road in mud shoe-top deep in bad weather." He further recalled, "Street channels had first to be cut through the hills and sidewalks came later. There was no sewerage, no water and the negro with his old mule and water barrel on a two-wheeled cart, and he astride the barrel, comprised our water works" during a drought. It was into this sprawling, aspiring metropolis that Nelson came, with his ambitions as a builder, reformer, and leader of public opinion.

Nelson's associate, Morss, stayed in Kansas City only about a year, but he gave Nelson important assistance during that time. Together, they founded the *Star* in the face of competition from three Kansas City papers: the *Times*, a Democratic party organ; the *Journal*, a Republican publication; and the *Evening Mail*, an afternoon paper aligned with the Democrats. Nelson and Morss started the *Star* with $3,000 they had earned from the sale of the *Sentinel* and with funds borrowed from friends and relatives, and tried to set the *Star* apart in the eyes of the Kansas City public. They began by deciding to undersell the competition, mimicking successful penny press ventures in the East and in Chicago. They chose to offer the *Star* six days a week for two cents an issue, as opposed to the competitors' five-cent price; a weekly subscription was

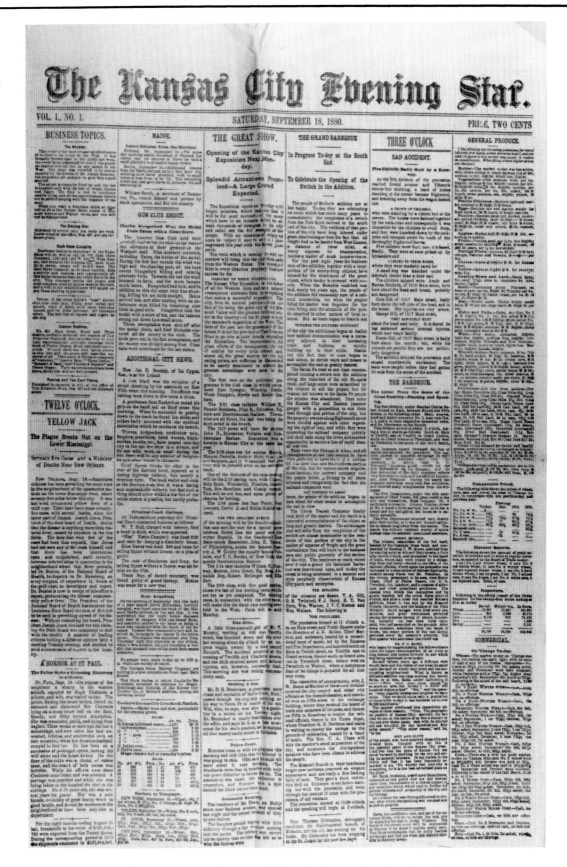

Front page of the first issue of Nelson's Kansas City Evening Star

ten cents. Nelson and Morss had a supply of pennies shipped in so newsboys could easily make change. Also, the partners arranged for the selling of advance subscriptions, which totaled three thousand before they went to press with their first edition.

On 18 September 1880, a Saturday, the fledgling newspaper organization's first issue appeared, coinciding with a town celebration of the opening of a new railroad switch. The *Star*'s publishers said they had concluded that Kansas City's growth made a "first-class, cheap afternoon newspaper an absolute necessity." They promised the *Star* would be "absolutely independent in politics, aiming to deal by all men and all parties with impartiality and fairness, expressing its views at all times with entire freedom and fearlessness." The new newspaper was to be accurate, truthful, and "strictly first-class, every issue containing one or more short stories, together with poetry, selected miscellany, etc.," and news gathered by a "large and efficient corps of reporters." (The *Star* began with seven reporters, a large number for a new paper at that time.)

The conservatively made-up front page included news of a pending Kansas City Exposition, proclaimed to be "the father of all the Western fairs," and of an accident in which a team of runaway horses injured five children downtown. It was reported that the horses also knocked a small dog under a sidewalk, leaving him "deader than a doornail." On an inside page, a man who had helped canvass the city for advance subscriptions wrote of his experiences in a column titled "A Solicitor's Sorrows." The tongue-in-cheek account marveled at how, in Kansas City, the "first noticeable phenomenon was that the lay of the land was all uphill." The writer also said he and others were frustrated by encounters with transients who had no interest in a subscription. There also were Germans and Swedes who, after hearing a long sales pitch, turned down a *Star* subscription by saying, "Na readee Inglis!" According to the writer, one solicitor who received no answer at the front door of a house proceeded to the back door, which was ajar, and surprised the lady of the house taking a bath. "The Evening Star isn't delivered at that house," the writer conceded. Bulldogs were a discouraging influence, he wrote, and managed to dissuade solicitors with methods that were "at once forcible and convincing." The writer concluded that Kansas City "has more pretty girls, more business, more ignorant servant girls, more cynical and stoical bull dogs, more big and utterly useless hills, more muddy water, and a better demand for a good cheap evening paper than any other city in the country."

The *Star*'s competitors greeted the new rival with derisive tolerance. The *Times* carried these lines by its managing editor, Eugene Field: "Twinkle, twinkle little Star / Bright and gossipy you are; / We can daily hear you speak / For a paltry dime a week." The other morning paper, the *Journal*, pinned the label "Tea Time Twinkler" on the new afternoon paper. However, the competition could not afford to take the *Star* lightly for long. By the end of four months, circulation had grown to 4,000 and by the end of the first year to 8,000. The *Star* had five reputable advertisers examine its books to verify the rising circulation claims. It got contracts with department stores so they would purchase at least some advertising every day. Revenue grew, as did circulation, which reached 10,000 in 1883, 25,000 in 1886, and 31,000 in 1889. By 1913, the *Star* sold more newspapers daily than Kansas City had houses, according to one estimate, and circulation reached 200,000 in the spring of 1915.

The strategy of developing a strong retail ad base saved the *Star* from encountering the kind of losses that weakened its competitors. Most of them depended heavily on real estate investments as a source of revenue in the 1880s; a crash in the real estate market then threw them into a financial spin from which recovery was difficult. The *Star* did not follow the same course, concentrating on its retail ad sales instead. Whether the strategy resulted from shrewd thinking or from a lack of funds to invest in real estate is not known, but it was an early example of how the *Star* always seemed to get the edge on its rivals.

The *Star*'s growth was such that the newspaper periodically had to move to more spacious quarters. On 12 March 1881, the *Star* vacated its original rented space in favor of a larger building. Other moves were made in 1882, 1889, and 1894. In 1911, the *Star* made its final move, this time into a grandly planned modern plant.

Nelson's offerings to his readers grew steadily as well. He acquired his afternoon rival, the *Evening Mail*, on 9 January 1882, and thereby got a needed Associated Press franchise. On 6 March 1890, he produced the *Weekly Kansas City Star*. An eight-page paper for farmers, it sold for twenty-five cents a year; its circulation reached 350,000 by 1915. On 29 April 1894, Nelson brought out the first issue of the *Sunday Star*. In 1901, he acquired the *Kansas City Times* and its Associated Press franchise; it became the morning edition of the *Star*. The expansions were accomplished without raising the weekly subscription price of ten cents.

Despite the journalistic juggernaut which was the *Star*, the man behind it was a relatively obscure figure. Nelson was active in the Associated Press, serving one year as vice-president and nine years as a director, but he generally remained out of public view. He seldom wrote for the *Star* and shied from speaking engagements. So far as is known, the only public post he held during his nearly thirty-five years in Kansas City was as a representative in 1912 for the Progressive party in Missouri. He made a speech to University of Missouri journalism students in 1914, but by long-distance telephone from Kansas City rather than in person. In declining an invitation to speak publicly in person, Nelson once wrote in a letter: "I am greatly flattered by your suggestion that I break the rule of a lifetime and appear in public and on stage. . . . But I discovered at a very early day that I was not cut out for a public speaker, having some regard for my reputation, I have always tried to confine myself to what I can do with at least a degree of respect." On another occasion, Nelson said, "So long as I don't show myself, I may keep the illusion for the public that I am a dashing young blade."

The fact was that Nelson had reason to be self-conscious, for he hardly cut a fashionable figure. A famous Nelson protégé, William Allen White, described the *Star* editor as "fat, bandy-legged, and pigeon-toed," a man who wobbled rather than walked. Another writer saw Nelson this way: "From the bulbous torso, with its fawn-colored vest, black coat and short thick arms, a collar suddenly expanded. It was like no other collar ever made; it widened from the neckband to take in a steadily heavier neck, an almost triple chin, and folds which rolled down at the base of his skull. His face was square, his mouth a wide, firm indenture; his chin overcame those folds beneath and jutted like Vermont granite. His nose began abruptly and ended the same way. Shaggy penthouses ruled over eyes which were really threatened by blindness, but which seemed to possess second-sight. His white hair was always rumpled, as if by pawing slaps from his fat hands. He had trouble getting into a chair and out of it. He would ask for something only once. Then he bellowed."

Yet Nelson was approachable, enjoyed socializing in small groups, and doted on his family. Nelson was married to Ida Houston, daughter of Robert Houston of Champaign, Illinois, on 29 November 1881. Laura, their only child, was born on 14 February 1883. Upon marrying, Nelson moved from a hotel to an apartment in a fashion-able area of Kansas City. In 1887, he began building a home on Oak Street south of Kansas City's downtown. The home, called Oak Hall, was made of oak and native limestone and was repeatedly expanded in subsequent years. It was exquisitely furnished and decorated, and Nelson entertained dignitaries and friends there, personally planning the menus for formal dinners. He sent his daughter to study in Paris and at fashionable women's colleges in the East. He was so possessive of her that he at first opposed and then only reluctantly accepted her marriage on 15 November 1910 to a Baltimore man, Irwin R. Kirkwood.

Nelson's broad interests got their fullest expression through his editorship of the *Star*. As the years passed, his exercise was increasingly mental rather than physical, and he sat for hours at his desk at the *Star* planning its crusades. He often outlined articles for his writers, telling them what they should say and how. Because of his notoriously weak eyesight, Nelson had his writers read their articles aloud to him; he could then edit them orally. The punchy language he liked thus found its way into the articles, allowing Nelson, in a real sense, to speak directly and personally to his public. He was a font of ideas for editorials, news articles, and cartoons, spouting them from the moment he entered the *Star* in the morning until he hoisted his bulk from his chair to go home at day's end, usually around 6:00 P.M. He had a vision for the city, and his plans for making it reality could not wait.

The *Star* crusaded for a vast array of improvements that included better roads, parks, and boulevards; lower natural gas prices; elimination of lottery and election frauds; an end to city franchise grants; improvement of the Missouri River waterway; a commission form of city government; a municipal auditorium; a new railway station; closing of saloons on Sunday; safe and decent housing and public buildings; and more culture for all Kansas Citians. Nelson also wanted free public baths, pest control, stone or concrete bridges, abolishment of the general property tax, free justice, workmen's compensation, an end to tariffs, and discouragement of medical quacks and fortune-tellers. The list of editorial goals at the *Star* was endless. Nelson once said, "I am no merchant in newspapers. I want to use the *Star* for advancing the interests of Kansas City." To Nelson, journalism was a way to "get things done."

Almost nothing escaped Nelson as a possible improvement in Kansas City, and he had no compunction about trying to see that it was accomplished. In the process, some Kansas Citians

Oak Hall, Nelson's home, which earned him the sobriquet "Baron of Brush Creek"

became resentful of Nelson, if not his outright enemies. A *Star* staffer once wrote an illustration of how a typical critic might complain: "Under the malign direction of Nelson The Star has kept things constantly stirred up. It has made tenants dissatisfied. They never used to complain about light and air. Now they won't look at a house unless every window opens on a flower garden with a humming bird in it. The Star won't let anybody alone. It insists on regulating the minutest detail of people's lives. . . . Its preaching . . . pretty nearly ruined the town."

Nelson, however, thrived on hostility. He once recalled how an editor from the *Boston Globe* had remarked, "Nelson, I don't think I have an enemy in the city of Boston." Nelson replied that if he didn't have an enemy in his town, he would move out. He prized the enmity of anyone he considered a bad man, taking it as a sign of his own rectitude, and said, "You'll always find the most clubs under the tree that has the best apples." A reader who wanted Nelson to take a more charitable view suggested, "Now, Colonel, wouldn't you feel better if you went to bed tonight knowing that you did not have one single enemy in the entire town?" Nelson replied, "No, no, no, by God! If I thought that I wouldn't sleep a wink." (The sobriquet "Colonel" seemed appropriate for Nelson, especially among those who served in the ranks of the militant crusader's newspaper army. William Allen White said, "Not that he was ever a colonel of anything: He was just

coloneliferous." Nelson was also known, derisively to his foes, as the "Baron of Brush Creek," an allusion to the fact that his Oak Hall estate overlooked a boggy channel known as Brush Creek.) When he was urged to forgive his enemies, he replied, "Humph! *You* can forgive my enemies; I'll forgive yours."

Star crusades always had the Nelson stamp. They were carried on for years if necessary, reflecting the Colonel's belief that the public could not be expected to act on a problem without being thoroughly and artfully educated. He said the public did not want to be taught as much as entertained, so the proper course was to "sneak up behind a man when he isn't looking and instruct him." Nelson plunged into the crusades himself, ordering studies, gathering data personally, building things to demonstrate how they should be done, publishing and distributing instructional pamphlets on pet subjects, and, generally, overwhelming the public with facts and figures until its consciousness was raised to a level where action would be taken. One historian wrote, "No other American newspaper ever rendered so continuous and efficient a service to its community as did the *Star*."

In its first crusade of consequence, which came during the *Star*'s first year, Nelson demanded better safety in the opera house owned by one of Kansas City's leading citizens. The *Star* lambasted the building as a "death trap." The owner, Kersey Coates, countered by calling the *Star* a "vampire" and "loathsome vermin" and by condemning the criticism as a transparent attempt to blackmail him into buying advertising in the paper. Coates vowed never to advertise in "so foul a sheet," but eventually he made improvements in the opera house and even became a friend of Nelson's. Through the opera house episode, Nelson made it clear that the *Star* would take strong stands on issues and that Kansas Citians, including advertisers, had to decide whether they were with him or against him.

Also within its first year, the *Star* embarked on another important crusade, one that led to the most visible enhancements of Kansas City: parks and boulevards. The opening salvo in Nelson's battle for beautification came on 19 May 1881 in an editorial that said: "The officials may dodge the issue and seek to excuse themselves by saying the new city charter prohibits the expenditure of money for any such purpose. This, however, will not strictly satisfy the people nor condone official negligence in this matter, as special legislation could easily be had, provided there was an earnest movement for the purpose." Marshalling facts and figures on behalf

of the campaign, Nelson commissioned studies of park and boulevard systems, devised prospective ordinances under which his ideas could be accomplished, and assigned reporters to write extensive coverage of the issue. Nelson gathered information on where to develop parks and which trees, grasses, flowers, and shrubs would be best. He planted trees experimentally and even imported squirrels from neighboring states to populate the parks.

Opposition to the *Star* came from leading citizens who doubted the wisdom and feasibility of a comprehensive park and boulevard plan. However, Nelson railed endlessly against the opposition through cartoons, news stories, and editorials. He also tried to woo those who could help, including Col. Thomas H. Swope, a seventy-year-old wealthy landholder. Nelson featured him as an outstanding citizen after Swope agreed to donate more than 1,000 acres for parklands. Yet within a year, Nelson had Swope under attack because of an unfinished, unsightly building project on land owned by Swope near the *Star* offices. An editorial cartoon on the

One of the model homes Nelson built as part of his drive to beautify Kansas City

matter so maddened Swope that he stalked into the *Star* building and grabbed one of Nelson's employees, saying, "Young man, you tell your boss that if my name *ever* appears in the *Star* again, I will kill him." Afterward, Nelson remarked, "By golly, I think he means it." The crusade for parks and boulevards continued for years. By 1900, much of the ugly muddiness of Kansas City was gone: the city had nearly twelve miles of boulevards and nearly 1,700 acres of parks. Nelson built model homes as showcases along the boulevards and encouraged residents to plant flowers and trees.

In addition to parks and boulevards, the *Star* campaigned incessantly for related types of improvements: streets, sidewalks, more and better fire and police protection, and street lights. To the former contractor, better roads were especially vital. The *Star* sought to reason with its readers about the need for roadway improvements, saying: "The City is its streets; the country is its roads; the Nation is its highways of rail and water. Civilization follows no dim forest trail; that is always the savage's route. Civilization treads established thoroughfares." But Kansas City lacked people with a strong commitment to the future. The *Star* complained: "The pinching economy, the picayunish policy, the miserable parsimony, which characterize our city government must now be abandoned or the city's growth will be most seriously retarded and her best interests greatly crippled." The *Star* sponsored tours of good roads, promoted cross-country motor races (which it then covered in a way that showed the need for better roads), and published free pamphlets on the subject. Readers were inundated with detailed information on paving, guttering, curbing, sidewalks, maintenance, bridge and viaduct construction, and traffic control.

City payments for public services also concerned Nelson. One day he asked a young reporter, "Do you know anything about the gas and gas rates in the city?" After the reporter said no, Nelson explained, "All right, you have an open mind. Go out and study the gas problem in Kansas City. Take your time. Take a month or two before you write a line, longer if you want to. But tell me when you are ready, what you think about dollar gas for Kansas City." The reporter was William Allen White, who was destined to become a famous Kansas editor. White's research resulted in findings that threatened the gas company's lucrative franchise with Kansas City, which was paying $1.60 for 1,000 cubic feet. Other cities were getting the same amount for a dollar. The gas company and its friends then prepared to rush through City Council

a grant for gas at $1.40 for thirty years. The *Star* launched a full-scale attack on the plan, denouncing the city as a partner in a get-rich-quick scheme. The plan was scrapped and dollar gas resulted. Later, the *Star* campaigned to force the gas company to comply with the terms of a supply contract. The company's lawyer protested to Nelson, "But surely, Colonel, you want to be fair to the company." Nelson, outraged, said, "By gad, that's just what I don't want to be. When has the company been fair to the city?"

Opposing public utility franchise grabs was a virtual obsession with Nelson. He contended that the city paid more than it should to companies that won the privilege of providing a service. Nelson objected that the privilege was acquired too often through corrupt political relations and stifled competition. In one such case, the question was whether a street-railway horse-car monopoly, headed by one Thomas Corrigan, should continue. Corrigan's company provided only minimal service, but it was politically powerful enough to keep the city from granting operating privileges to the competition. The *Star* said it had to "insist that competition is necessary for the protection of the public." The newspaper fought year in and year out against franchising until 1914, and the battles were heated. One Corrigan ally, enraged over the *Star*'s criticism, struck Nelson in the face—with a buggy whip, by one account. On another occasion, eight aldermen who lined up with Corrigan on the franchise issue found themselves branded the "Shameless Eight" by the *Star*. The newspaper accused them of having "sold themselves body and soul to Boss Corrigan." About 1,200 citizens gathered to vent their rage against the council; there was talk of horsewhipping and lynching until the aldermen capitulated and reversed themselves.

Once, when the council held meetings on new franchise requests, Nelson sent a reporter who knew shorthand to cover them. The *Star* published the reporter's notes in full and then hired a firm of skilled stenographers to take notes at all subsequent hearings. The *Star* printed the notes as verbatim transcripts, filling page upon page with the record of the meetings. The *Star* lost an estimated 10,000 subscribers because of the overwhelmingly tedious coverage of a single subject, but there also were signs that readers generally took the avalanche of words as evidence of the newspaper's good faith in its belief that the issue was serious.

Among the most vigorous of *Star* campaigns was one against gambling. Nelson railed against various lottery frauds, including one that only pretended to pay prize money to winners. Another evil staunchly opposed by Nelson was drinking. At the time of his death, it was noted that he "thought that whiskey was a curse, that eventually its sale would be prohibited by national law." As early as 10 September 1881, the *Star* proclaimed the merits of Sunday saloon closings. Nelson said he would drop his opposition to liquor if saloon interests could show him just one person who benefited from whiskey. "Some of the dearest friends I ever had were ruined and done to death by whiskey," he said. Nelson became especially antagonistic toward the liquor interests in 1905 after they helped defeat a city charter that the *Star* supported. He was further provoked when he observed two beer trucks harassing a Women's Christian Temperance Union parade. The upshot was that Nelson forbade beer and hard liquor advertising in the *Star*. Of the loss of the ads, Nelson said, "I guess we're making enough money without them."

Among the most visible of Kansas City's accomplishments under Nelson's guiding hand was the $6,000,000 Union Station that replaced an aging, inadequate railway depot. Also, a five-year *Star* campaign led to the building of a municipal auditorium, Convention Hall. It burned within a year of its opening in 1899, and the *Star* weighed in with another building campaign. The hall was reconstructed in three months, in time for the Democratic party convention in 1900. Kansas City was also introduced to free public baths after Nelson orchestrated a fund-raising campaign for them. He said each Kansas Citian should have an opportunity to "swim and scrub and enjoy himself without cost."

Nelson and the *Star* were in their element, however, not so much in promoting baths and buildings as in getting into political fights. Electoral fraud and political corruption flourished in Kansas City in the late 1800s, and Nelson led the *Star* aggressively against the miscreants who dominated government. By 1892, the *Star* was in full swing against political corruption, editorializing: "The fact that local politics in large cities is generally corrupt is no reason why Kansas City should consider gang rule an essential part of its metropolitan equipment." The *Star* brought about prosecutions of election crooks following poll fraud in 1894. Thereafter, Nelson unceasingly played watchdog on politicians and campaigned effectively for what he considered a vital means to good government—a nonpartisan, commission form of city government.

One politician who came to be prey for the *Star* in its political prowls, Joseph J. Davenport, showed how rough Kansas City politics could be. The *Star*

enraged Davenport, a former mayor seeking a comeback in 1894, by vigorously calling on the voters to bar the door to government office for him. Davenport finally had had all he could take; confronting Nelson at the *Star* offices, he struck the editor in the jaw and chest. The crash of Nelson's three hundred pound frame on the floor brought *Star* staffers on the run. They threw Davenport down a flight of stairs, whereupon he pulled a revolver from under his coat and aimed it at his adversaries. An editor stood above him, preparing to heave a cuspidor at Davenport. A reporter, meanwhile, sighted down the barrel of his own gun at the seething former mayor. Davenport then withdrew without a shot being fired, and Nelson went on with his attacks on politicians he disfavored. By one account, Nelson later "roared with laughter" about the incident and said he found Davenport "peculiarly lacking in virility and charm."

There were times when Nelson and the *Star* could strike an accommodation with a politician, at least if he could assist with one of Nelson's pet improvement projects. The *Star*, for example, was allied with Jim Pendergast, a Kansas City political boss, on those occasions when the Pendergast machine supported Nelson's favored reform measures, such as a bond issue for a municipal water plant and improved garbage collection. In 1895, a Pendergast lieutenant cautioned Nelson that if he wanted support for a city charter amendment to authorize park development, it would take "a little money for the workers." Nelson readily conceded later that he "made the necessary arrangements" to get his amendment through, although he did not say how much they cost.

However, for the most part, Nelson and the *Star* were notoriously at loggerheads with politicians. James A. Reed, who became mayor in 1900 and later was a U.S. senator from Missouri, was one who engaged in spectacular fights with the *Star*. He once said of Nelson, "God created the heavens and the earth, and from the ooze of the earth He created the slimy reptiles that crawl the face of the earth, and from the *residue* thereof He created Old Bill Nelson." On one occasion, a politician came to the *Star* offices to bribe one of Nelson's editors. The attempt ended in a public display of *Star* integrity: the editor flipped the roll of proffered greenbacks out a window, leaving bills to flutter like green manna to astonished passersby below. The gasping politician ran to fight with the crowd to recover his money.

Lawyers and judges also were favorite targets of Nelson's. He argued that justice should be free,

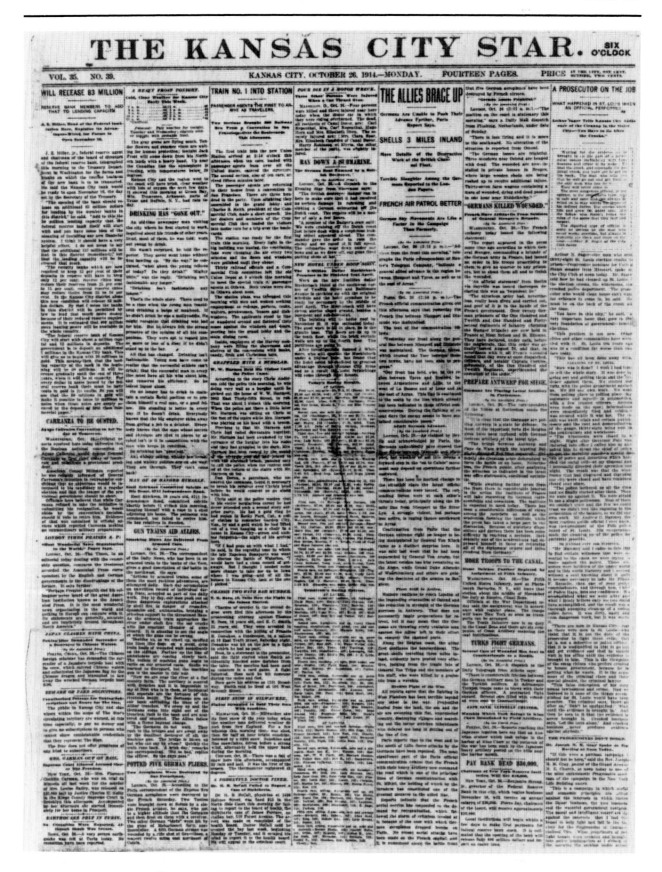

Front page of the Kansas City Star *during Nelson's last year as publisher*

with lawyers working as government-paid officers of the court. When a Pendergast machine judge accused the *Star* of being in contempt of court in 1913 because of the way a reporter wrote about a court proceeding, Nelson faced the prospect of being jailed. However, with characteristic disdain for the bench, he told his lawyers, "Give 'em hell . . . I don't care what happens. . . . If they put me in jail I'll stay there till the ants carry me out through the keyhole." A series of legal maneuvers saved Nelson from such a fate.

In national politics, Nelson held up Samuel J. Tilden as a symbol of reform and honest government. Also, Nelson emerged as a die-hard opponent of the kind of protectionism that tariffs represented and that the Democrats, in Tilden's day, had stood strongly against. When the Democratic party failed to renominate Tilden in 1880, Nelson was provoked to break from the organization and become an independent; but he was supportive of leaders in whom he saw the kind of moral courage and reformist commitment he had once perceived in Tilden. Grover Cleveland, whom the Democrats nominated for president in 1884 over strenuous opposition from machine politicians in New York, was such a candidate. The *Star* praised Cleveland as a great reformer with "nerve and backbone" and commended the "ordinarily cowardly Democrats" for not being intimidated by powerful Tammanyites who fought the nomination. Cleveland's opposition to high tariffs was one quality that especially endeared him to Nelson, although it gave Republicans an issue around which to rally. Cleveland lost the next election to Republican Benjamin Harrison, but his comeback victory in 1892 gave Nelson occasion to cheer again. The *Star*'s support appeared to help Cleveland win a surprisingly heavy vote among the newspaper's readers. Despite his support, Nelson sought no appointment in the Cleveland administration, although his original partner at the *Star*, Morss, became ambassador to Paris in Cleveland's second term. At the time, Morss was publisher of the *Indianapolis Sentinel*.

Nelson's next national political hero was a Republican who bore the all-important traits of courage, reform-mindedness, and a cool view of tariffs: Theodore Roosevelt. Nelson and Roosevelt became close friends when Roosevelt was William McKinley's vice-presidential candidate in 1900. Nelson had no criticism of Roosevelt, saying, "When you've got a big, courageous man going your way don't be critical. When I'm for a man I'm *fur* him." Nelson remained close to Roosevelt throughout his years in the presidency and played a leading role in the

unsuccessful attempt to get Roosevelt elected to the presidency again in 1912. With Nelson's support, that effort was launched through the Bull Moose party, organized by progressives when the Republicans declined to nominate Roosevelt. Nelson was visited by Eastern reporters because of his prominent role in the Bull Moose campaign—which took its name from Roosevelt's claim that he was "stronger than a bull moose." One reporter said of Nelson: "When the big-bodied, big-headed, deep-throated Missourian says 'I'm a Bull Mooser,' it is like the crashing reverberation of thunder in the mountains, tangled up with a Kansas cyclone and the booming of the northeast surf. He leaves no doubt upon the point. One will never question that he is a Bull Mooser after he has said it."

Nelson's ideals in politics were consistent. The *Star* backed candidates, regardless of party label, who he thought would help common people preserve equality of opportunity for themselves through democratic government. Nelson identified in principle with the notion that rewards should not be distributed through privilege, class, or corruption, but on the basis of service to the common good. When Nelson found national political figures who he believed stood for his ideals, he remembered them. Portraits of Tilden, Cleveland, and Roosevelt hung above his desk at the *Star*. Nelson also supported Woodrow Wilson.

Nelson died 13 April 1915 from nephritis, a liver ailment that led to uremic poisoning. He protested against efforts to keep him alive after a lengthy struggle with the illness. To his doctor, he said, "You are keeping me alive to no purpose. I thought you were my friend. You aren't acting like one. I am not afraid to die. The next time let me go. It is no kindness to keep me alive." At that, an intravenous treatment was disconnected and Nelson was allowed to die.

To some extent, the way Nelson lived his life did not square with his image as a liberal progressive seeking greater opportunities for the common man. He himself simply was not common, and he often appeared self-indulgent to the great inconvenience of others. The *Star*'s crushing success gave Nelson a virtual newspaper monopoly and a kind of dictatorial power over what Kansas Citians could read and learn. His use of that power was autocratic and, at times, even belligerent.

Also, he fairly conspicuously lived the aristocrat's life, a plane of existence well beyond the reach of most he would deign to help through his newspaper. Flanked occasionally by a bodyguard, he traveled to and from the newspaper in a carriage.

Sni-a-Bar Farm, Nelson's country retreat

Then, having the means to assure his comfort away from the *Star*, he built an elegant summer home in Magnolia, Massachusetts, and had a yacht, the *Hoosier*, custom built. He took trips abroad, returning with tapestries and paintings to grace the walls of Oak Hall, which resembled an English manor. He developed a spacious retreat known as the Sni-A-Bar farm; he built a paper mill especially for the *Star*; he developed real estate near Oak Hall and rented houses to his employees, all of which made him look much like the Brush Creek baron his critics said he was.

Even his relationships with his employees, his "*Star* family," were not those of a liberal progressive, at least by ordinary measures. He called them "helpers," not "associates" or "colleagues," and paid them niggardly wages—ninety dollars a month for a reporter and five thousand dollars a year for a top executive. He said, "Any man worth more than five thousand dollars a year would be in business for himself." Also, according to Nelson, "The surest way to ruin a good newspaperman is to put some money in his pocket." True to that kind of thinking, upon Nelson's death, his will contained no provision for his employees to continue with the paper. Indeed, the *Star*'s business manager believed Nelson wanted, in his final days, to find a way to have *Star* publication ceased for good upon his death. It was as if he could not bear the thought that the institution he had called "my life" would survive him.

Nelson had a way of making even his grandest designs seem utterly selfish. Recalling his first encounter with the corner of civilization where he had made his mark, he once said, "Kansas City was incredibly commonplace and ugly. I decided that if I were to live here the town must be made over."

Yet the behavior that opened Nelson to criticism as a self-indulgent, ruthless man cannot be isolated from deeds that clearly served others. His estate, with a value estimated between $5,000,000 and $10,000,000 at his death, was left first to provide for his wife and daughter. Upon their deaths, the *Star* was to be sold and the proceeds used to acquire artworks for the city. The William Rockhill Nelson Gallery of Art eventually was built to house the acquisitions. As Nelson intended, they served as a source of lasting education and enrichment for the people of Kansas City. His huge Sni-A-Bar farm, which originally was devoted to establishing an improved cattle breed, was to be sold for the benefit of the gallery as well under the terms of the will.

When he died, the *Star* was filled for days with remembrances of his good works, which had included spontaneous individual gifts to employees and others who found themselves in need. In addition, although not by Nelson's direct design, his long-standing loyal employees were allowed to have futures with the *Star* after all. Through the efforts of Nelson's son-in-law, an opportunity was

The William Rockhill Nelson Gallery of Art, Nelson's bequest to Kansas City

fashioned for the employees to buy it, and they did.

In a sense, Nelson offered his life as evidence that the enterprise, wit, and self-reliance of the rugged individualist could yield great fruits for the common good. The *Star* itself was one of Nelson's lasting contributions, but just as important, perhaps, were the lessons he provided in how to achieve good journalism. Historians have had no doubts about the *Star*'s quality under Nelson, granting it accolades such as "one of America's four greatest evening papers," "one of the ten best newspapers in the world," and "the best newspaper in America." The nation's liberal and progressive movement, one writer said, "centered largely around the Kansas City *Star*" and Nelson gave related forces of public opinion a "vehicle for expression which was essential to their existence."

Nelson's success depended in part on his determination to "get things done" coupled with a social, economic, and political climate that suited him. He proclaimed himself on the side of good and right at a time when Kansas Citians needed a moral, visionary leader. Moreover, Nelson pursued his

course with a persistence and adversariness that made both advertisers and readers consider an accommodation with him easier than a fight. Also, he offered the kind of newspaper that appealed to a growing middle class. At the lowest possible price, it offered cultural enrichment through literary reprints; its typography was clean, its layout simple; its content was tasteful to a fault, its news well written and intensely local.

Most important, perhaps, was Nelson's consistently proclaimed—and observed—dedication to public service. It won him not only loyal readers but also a talented, inspired staff, without which the *Star* would have accomplished little. On the surface not much appeared attractive. At what sometimes was jokingly called the "Daily William Rockhill Nelson" rather than the *Star*, reporters got low wages and no by-lines. For a time Nelson would not even let them have typewriters for fear the machines would interrupt their creative thinking. However, he worked closely with them, gave them a sense of freedom, supported them if they were sued for libel, and above all, imbued them with a sense of public spirit.

One *Star* man recalled how the association with Nelson meant showing up for work "whenever necessary, without extra pay. After all, what was money? Something transitory. But the fame of being a *Star* man would last forever. And we believed it."

Biographies:

Members of the Staff of the Kansas City Star, *William Rockhill Nelson: The Story of a Man, a Newspaper and a City* (Cambridge, Mass.: Riverside Press, 1915);

Icie F. Johnson, *William Rockhill Nelson and the Kansas City Star* (Kansas City, Mo.: Burton, 1925).

References:

William Jackson Bell, "A Historical Study of the *Kansas City Star* since the Death of William Rockhill Nelson, 1915-1949," Ph.D. dissertation, University of Missouri, 1949;

Willard Grosvenor Bleyer, *Main Currents in the History of American Journalism* (Cambridge, Mass.: Houghton Mifflin, 1927);

Courtney Ryley Cooper, "Star Man," *Saturday Evening Post* (19 December 1936): 23;

Roy Ellis, *A Civic History of Kansas City, Missouri*

(Springfield, Mo.: Elkins-Swyers, 1930);

Darrell Garwood, *Crossroads of America: The Story of Kansas City* (New York: Norton, 1948);

Charles H. Grasty, "The Best Newspaper in America," *World's Work,* 18 (June 1909): 11726-11730;

Kansas City Star Co., "The Kansas City Star: The First 100 Years—A Man, a Newspaper and a City," special centennial section, 18 September 1980;

Charles Elkins Rogers, "William Rockhill Nelson and His Editors of the Star," *Journalism Quarterly,* 26 (March 1949): 15;

Rogers, "William Rockhill Nelson: Independent Editor and Crusading Liberal," Ph.D. dissertation, University of Minnesota, 1948;

William Allen White, "The Man Who Made the *Star*," *Collier's* (26 June 1915): 12.

Papers:

Correspondence with Nelson is contained in the papers of Theodore Roosevelt, William Howard Taft, Henry Watterson, William Allen White, and Woodrow Wilson at the Library of Congress.

Crosby S. Noyes

(16 February 1825-21 February 1908)

Charles A. Fair
Virginia Commonwealth University

MAJOR POSITION HELD: Editor in chief, *Washington Evening Star* (1867-1908).

Crosby S. Noyes's contributions to newspaper journalism were his use of the editorial pages of Washington's leading newspaper to improve and develop the nation's capital and his steadfast commitment to objective reporting in a period of "yellow" journalism. This objective approach was used by his sons, who followed him at the *Star*. One of those sons, Frank, used this same edict for the modern Associated Press when he became its first president.

Using all of the influence of the *Evening Star*, Crosby Noyes faced off against Congress and several federal administrations for projects ranging from creation of Washington's park system to completion of the Washington Monument. Moreover, he used his editorial leadership to urge the federal government to take responsibility for its share of the cost of operating the District of Columbia, and he led the campaign for the establishment of a Library of Congress.

The trail to becoming a major force in the nation's capital began in a remote part of New England. Crosby Stuart Noyes was born in Androscoggin County, Maine, in the small town of Minot. His ancestors had come to Maine and Massachusetts in 1633, and his family tree included many doctors, scientists, ministers, publishers, and musicians. Not naturally robust, young Noyes could not cope with the work on his father's farm, nor with Maine's

Crosby S. Noyes (Culver Pictures)

bleak winters with heavy snows and cruel winds. His early jobs were in a harness shop and then a Lewiston cotton mill; money from the latter job and from teaching school helped pay for his education. He did not have the opportunity to go to college, but he "buried himself in books," a son later wrote. As a youth Noyes often walked ten miles to use a library in a friend's home.

The urge to be a writer came early, and a month before his fifteenth birthday, he produced his first newspaper, the "Minot Notion," a small handwritten paper of four pages. The first issue announced: "This paper is published weekly for the promotion of science, literature and the fine arts, believing as we do that these are the cornerstones of liberty. We shall not meddle with the politics, mathematics and metaphysics, but leave such subjects to older heads. Our paper will be filled with useful and entertaining matter and a few riddles and enigmas. We shall be happy to receive communications." Grandson Newbold Noyes, in a short biography, notes that while the "Minot Notion" soon suspended publication, the declaration of policy stated in that first issue remained the philosophy of Crosby S. Noyes to the end of his life.

Noyes wrote items for various New England

publications, but could not endure the harsh winters, and so, with the pledge of several newspapers to accept his letters for publication, he ventured to Washington to launch his journalistic career. Washington was a "struggling country village, with zig-zag grades, no sewerage, no water supply except from pumps and springs; unimproved reservations, second-rate dwellings and streets of mud and mire" when he arrived on New Year's Eve, 1847, on a farm wagon loaded with produce and with $1.61 in his pocket.

His promised pay for serving as the Washington correspondent for one Philadelphia and several New England newspapers was only $1 per letter, so he sought additional work. He toiled in a bookshop by day, ushered in a theater at night, and served as a route agent for the *Baltimore Sun*.

Before 1848 was over, he began reporting for a weekly journal, the *Washington News*. He stayed with the *News* and continued stringing for the out-of-town newspapers for six years, covering Congress, the executive and judicial branches, and local news. His reputation as a Congressional reporter was established, but in 1855 he took a year off to walk throughout Europe and send back articles to the *Portland* (Maine) *Transcript*.

Back in Washington, Noyes went to work for the *Evening Star*, a small, four-page paper that was "struggling for circulation and advertising patronage." The *Star* had been started 16 December 1852 as a penny daily by Captain Joseph Borrows Tate, who sold it one year later to W. D. Wallach. As a reporter for Wallach, Noyes covered nearly every topic in Washington, ranging from sports to church affairs, debates in Congress to political meetings. Within a year, his salary was $12 per week, and he was confident enough about his future to marry his childhood sweetheart from Maine, Elizabeth Williams.

As the saber rattling that preceded the Civil War grew louder, Noyes's responsibilities at the *Star* increased, and he was promoted to assistant editor. He was also elected alderman, representing the seventh ward (South Washington) in 1863, and served for two years.

Noyes's close working relationships with ranking government officials paid off as the *Star* got exclusive or first access to news. Secretary of War Edwin M. Stanton was willing to talk with few newsmen, and Noyes was one of that small number. President Lincoln handed the text of his second inaugural address to Noyes as he stepped from the podium; the *Star* published the speech the same day.

While the nation's capital had been a boom town in the years before and during the Civil War, many people departed the city after the war. In 1867 publisher Wallach, fearing an economic panic, decided to end his twenty-nine-year journalism career and gave Noyes forty-eight hours to raise $100,000 to buy the *Star*. The price was considered extravagant at the time, but Noyes was able to find the necessary partners to buy the paper: Samuel H. Kauffmann, an Ohio newspaper publisher who was then working for the U.S. Treasury Department; George W. Adams, correspondent for the *New York World* and many other out-of-town papers; Alexander R. Shepherd, former president of the Washington Common Council, who later became territorial governor of Washington and is credited with the development of modern Washington; and Clarence B. Baker. Kauffmann was named president of the new firm, *The Evening Star* Newspaper Company, and Noyes was named editor in chief, a title he retained until his death forty-one years later. Within a few years, Noyes, Kauffmann, and Adams each gained one-third control of the newspaper.

Noyes's intentions for the *Star* were to make it first and foremost a local newspaper, the voice of the people of Washington, who he believed had been neglected by the national government. His statement of purpose, published 31 October 1867, said, "We mean that it [the *Star*] shall be independent, outspoken, honest, expressing itself freely upon all questions of public interest, but always, we trust, with fairness and good temper.... As a newspaper we mean that *The Star* shall occupy the first rank."

Noyes's term as an alderman had taught him much about this city that was struggling to support the seat of the national government without financial assistance. He wrote often and strongly about the need for adoption by Congress of the Organic Act of 1878, which would require the federal government to pay half the cost of operating the city, and as vice-chairman of the Committee of 100, he lobbied in Congress for passage of the measure. He led successful campaigns to prevent the use of parklands as sites for additional federal office buildings and for reclamation of the flats of the Potomac River.

Noyes was primarily interested in the improvement of the city as a community. The *Star* led fights for clean streets and an end to dumping of garbage in the Potomac River; started a Santa Claus Club to help the needy; campaigned for the construction of bridges; and called for the establishment of a juvenile court, public playgrounds, a tuberculosis hospital, a workhouse reformatory, and a rehabilitation center for alcoholics. This latter project came from Noyes's conviction that alcoholism was an illness, not a crime. While some of his campaigns brought quick results, others did not. The alcoholism rehabilitation center was not established in Washington until 1947, thirty-nine years after his death. In the year he died he began a campaign to construct a Lincoln monument. That effort, and many others, were continued by his son Theodore, who succeeded him as editor in chief.

Some of Noyes's causes were unpopular. He backed his former partner, Shepherd, when the governor called for the rebuilding of the city. Although ugly charges were hurled at Shepherd and the *Star*, the campaign succeeded. Noyes also locked horns with powerful political interests, including three railroads which had laid tracks throughout the city on public property. By publishing running totals of deaths at railroad crossings and reports of total time daily that traffic was delayed by trains, and by circulating petitions to Congress to get the railroads off public property, Noyes led the effort to get the rail lines moved and the trains all directed to a central Union Station. Parkland was a major interest to him, and his sustained efforts to make Rock Creek Park a reality resulted in the signing by President Harrison of the necessary legislation in less than two years. His campaign for Potomac Park, which includes the Tidal Basin with its famed cherry blossoms, took twenty-seven years, but eventually a disease-ridden marsh was replaced by a park that is one of the most famous in the nation.

Noyes kept the *Star* from being labeled a political organ by backing issues and not parties. His grandson wrote that Noyes's dominating principle as editor was

that it is better to praise than to blame, better to find the good than the bad, better to build than to destroy, and such were the instructions to all of his staff.

Conservatism was his watchword—not the conservatism of cowardice, but the conservatism of reserve. He preferred to withhold the full power of his denunciation for objects worthy of his force, and the result was that whenever he entered the lists as defender of a faith or antagonist of an evil, his activity was more effective than it would have been if he had been constantly embroiled in quarrels or engaged in personal abuse.... He wished his paper to represent the best thought, the best works, the highest ideals and the purest morals.

Front page of the Washington Evening Star *in the thirty-ninth year of Noyes's editorship*

Henry Watterson, a famed journalist who worked for Noyes at the *Star*, said in a eulogy: "He had his opinions and he stood to them, but he was a tolerant man, and as he advanced in years, he gained in that dignity and weight which are the emanations only of assured position and the consciousness of duty done."

While Crosby Noyes was quick to face off against Congress on an issue involving his beloved city, he was modest about public appearances in general. An exception was his presentation of a paper at the World's Press Parliament in St. Louis in 1904, in which he traced the development of the American press and lashed out at the sensationalism of the "yellow" press. He repeatedly scored "the penny dreadful . . . packed with horrors" and "calculated to impress upon the reader the belief that there is an universal, worldwide carnival of crime going on all the time." He would not tolerate sensationalism in his newspaper, which was sometimes described as dull but thorough. His philosophy was: "When in doubt, stick to the facts, and nothing but the facts."

In the 100th anniversary edition of the *Evening Star* (16 December 1952), editor B. M. McKelway wrote of the *Star*'s approach to reporting:

> An almost imperceptible growth of a new concept of the function of news reporting is becoming more established every year as a distinguishing characteristic of American journalism.
>
> Under that concept, the news of what happens belongs to the people—in a sense, it is public property. And this being so, it is beyond the just powers of any individual— publisher, editor, reporter, rewrite man—to tamper with that news by coloring it with bias, diluting it with fancy, or diminishing it with suppression. . . .
>
> . . . That concept, in the Star's belief, justifies the principle of freedom of the press. Its general application will do more to preserve that freedom than any of the other journalistic achievements of the past century.

Crosby Noyes drilled this philosophy into his sons, Theodore and Frank, who had joined him at the *Star*. Frank, who served as the *Star*'s president for many years, took his father's nothing-but-the-facts attitude with him when he became the first president of the modern Associated Press in 1900 and maintained that approach in the thirty-eight years that he served as head of the news service. Writing about the AP in 1913, Frank Noyes said: "Its func-

tion is simply to furnish its members with a truthful, clean, comprehensive, nonpartisan . . . report of the news of the world. . . . Our function is to supply our [AP] members with news, not views. . . ." The antisensationalism philosophy of the elder Noyes, as carried on by his son at the AP, may have had considerable impact upon modern American journalism.

Another of Noyes's rare appearances as a public speaker was on 13 June 1907 at the Jamestown Tercentennial Exposition, where he gave a speech on "Journalism since Jamestown." The speech was a rambling overview of the growth of the American press, especially during his lifetime.

Noyes traveled extensively during the last thirty years of his life, both within the United States and abroad. He was especially attracted to the Orient, visiting Japan several times; he donated his collection of Japanese art to the Library of Congress in 1905. His travel letters appeared as unsigned "editorial correspondence" in the *Star* between 1872 and 1891.

Throughout his life, Crosby Noyes remained, at heart, a reporter. Indeed, he had covered some of the big stories of his era—the trial and execution of John Brown, the assassination of President Lincoln and the subsequent trial and executions of the conspirators, the impeachment proceedings against President Andrew Johnson, and the bimetalism campaign. He had a major hand in the development of the capital from a town of 37,000 to a city of more than 300,000 people. At his death in 1908, the *Star* dominated Washington journalism and was one of the most prosperous papers in the nation. President Theodore Roosevelt called Crosby Noyes "one of the two or three leading citizens and most distinguished men of Washington." Noyes's funeral was attended by the vice-president, secretary of state, speaker of the House of Representatives, and the chief justice of the U.S. Supreme Court, as well as by ambassadors of two foreign nations.

Biography:

Newbold Noyes, "Crosby Stuart Noyes: His Life and Times," *Records of the Columbia Historical Society of Washington, D.C.*, 40-41 (1940): 197-225.

References:

Samuel H. Kauffmann, *The Evening Star (1852-1952): A Century at the Nation's Capital* (Washington, D.C.: Newcomen Society, 1952);

Frank B. Noyes, *The Associated Press* (Washington, D.C.: U.S. Government Printing Office, 1913);

James Atkins Noyes, *Noyes Pedigree* (Boston: Clapp, 1899);

Kenneth Stewart and John Tebbell, *Makers of*

Modern Journalism (Englewood Cliffs, N.J.: Prentice-Hall, 1952), pp. 455-457;

Oswald Garrison Villard, *Some Newspapers and Newspaper-men* (New York: Knopf, 1923), pp. 170-192.

Edgar Wilson (Bill) Nye
(25 August 1850-22 February 1896)

Charles C. Russell
University of South Carolina

and

Philip B. Dematteis

See also the Nye entry in *DLB 11, American Humorists, 1800-1950.*

MAJOR POSITIONS HELD: Associate editor, *Laramie City Sentinel* (1876-1877); correspondent, *Denver Tribune* and *Cheyenne Sun* (1876-1877); cofounder and first editor, *Laramie Boomerang* (1881-1883); columnist, *New York World* (1887-1896).

SELECTED BOOKS: *Bill Nye and Boomerang; or, The Tale of a Meek-Eyed Mule, and Some Other Literary Gems* (Chicago: Belford, Clarke, 1881);

Forty Liars, and Other Lies (Chicago: Belford, Clarke, 1882);

Boomerang Shots (London & New York: Ward, Lock, 1884);

Hits and Skits (London & New York: Ward, Lock, 1884);

Baled Hay: A Drier Book Than Walt Whitman's "Leaves o' Grass" (Chicago & New York: Belford, Clarke, 1884);

Bill Nye's Cordwood (Chicago: Rhodes & McClure, 1887);

Remarks (Chicago: A. E. Davis, 1887);

Nye and Riley's Railway Guide, by Nye and James Whitcomb Riley (Chicago: Dearborn, 1888); republished as *Nye and Riley's Wit and Humor* (New York: Neely, 1896); published again as *On the "Shoe-String" Limited* (Chicago: Thompson & Thomas, 1905);

Bill Nye's Chestnuts Old and New. Latest Gathering (Chicago & New York: Belford, Clarke, 1888);

Bill Nye's Thinks (Chicago: Dearborn, 1888);

An Aristocrat in America: Extracts from the Diary of the

Right Honorable Lord William Henry Cavendish-Bentinck-Pelham-Clinton-St. Maur-Beauchamp-De Vere, K. G. (By one of Them) (New York: Ivers, 1888);

An Almanac for 1891 (New York: Privately printed, 1890);

Bill Nye's Red Book (Chicago: Thompson & Thomas, 1891);

Sparks from the Pen of Bill Nye (Chicago & New York: Neely, 1891);

Bill Nye's History of the United States (Philadelphia: Lippincott, 1894; London: Chatto & Windus, 1894);

Bill Nye's History of England from the Druids to the Reign of Henry VIII (Philadelphia: Lippincott, 1896);

A Guest at the Ludlow and Other Stories (Indianapolis & Kansas City: Bowen-Merrill, 1897);

Bill Nye, His Book (Chicago: Smith, 1900);

Bill Nye's Western Humor, edited by T. A. Larson (Lincoln: University of Nebraska Press, 1968);

Bill Nye's Grim Jokes (Chicago: Conkey, n.d.).

Edgar Wilson (Bill) Nye treated a generation of newspaper readers to two decades (1876-1896) of humor, written simply and naturally. He used words as symbols of things familiar to his readers, whether he was writing about characters of the Old West, describing the sights of the World Exposition in Paris in 1889, or telling his *New York World* readers about such celebrities as Boss Tweed, Horace Greeley, Frederic Remington, Robert Ingersoll, the Astors, the Goulds, or the Vanderbilts. He fitted his language to his audience, garnishing to suit an occasion or a personality. Will M. Clemens, in his book

Culver Pictures

Famous Funny Fellows, recorded that during 1880-1882 Bill Nye "wrote a larger quantity and a better quality of first-class, genuine humor, than any other funny man in America."

Nye was given his pen name because readers of the *Laramie City* (Wyoming Territory) *Sentinel* in 1876 were familiar with the Bill Nye in Bret Harte's poem "Plain Language from Truthful James." Thus, Edgar Wilson Nye became forever Bill Nye. He earned his fame as a humorist by comparing the mundane things of everyday life with one another and noticing wherein they agreed or differed. He brought to newspaper writing a comic imagination and a philosophy that humor, like good coffee, depends on the quality of the raw material and the care devoted to its preparation.

Nye was born to Franklin and Elizabeth Mitchell Loring Nye on 25 August 1850 in Shirley, a village in Maine that consisted of "a cluster of houses and a red sawmill." The sawmill was important: at the first sign of winter, Franklin Nye would

say goodbye to his family and disappear into the woods. There he would practice his skill as a lumberman until the thaw.

The two years Nye lived in Shirley were hardly vivid in his memory, yet his own children recalled with delight their father's version of the family's departure from Maine. Nye's son Frank Wilson Nye quotes his father in *Bill Nye: His Own Life Story* (1926): "he took his parents by the hand and, telling them that Piscataquis County, was no place for them," he led them by rail to Buffalo, by boat through the Great Lakes to Milwaukee, again by rail to Madison, and by wagon to Hudson, Wisconsin, in the Kinnic Kinnic Valley of St. Croix County. This valley provided Nye with his formal and informal education. The formal was sparse: sixteen weeks at the local academy and two terms at a military school in River Falls. Informally, his education was enhanced while he worked as a farmer, miller, teacher, and eventually as a law clerk in an office in Chippewa Falls. In 1876, at the age of twenty-five—dissatisfied with working as a correspondent for two small local papers, the *Hudson Star* and the *Chippewa Falls Weekly Herald*, and disappointed by his inability to find employment with Minneapolis and St. Paul newspapers—Nye decided to find out more about the country in which he lived.

It was in Cheyenne, Territory of Wyoming, that Nye's funds ran out. Former Wisconsin resident John J. Jenkins, United States attorney for the Territory of Wyoming, arranged with J. H. Hayford, editor of the *Sentinel* in nearby Laramie City, for Nye to fill a vacant reporting slot. After joining the *Sentinel* in May 1876, Nye rose within a few months to the position of associate editor at a salary of $12 a month plus room and board. As a straight reporter, Nye was less than satisfactory: he tended to omit pertinent details from his stories, such as the amount of property loss in a fire. But from the beginning, he introduced humor into his items.

Aristotle was an astronomer without a telescope, a biologist without a microscope, a chemist without a laboratory; Nye had been a humorist without a showcase. At the *Sentinel* he found it. He carefully avoided portmanteau words—those loaded with a whole suitcase full of meanings. He expressed himself by using particular rather than general, concrete rather than abstract words. He used a discreet economy of words in displaying an abundance of prejudices. Indians and Mormons were frequent targets in his columns, essays, and editorials. For example: "The Indians are not treacherous and bloodthirsty as some would suppose. Only the live ones are that way. Wooden Indians are also to be relied upon."

The Indian bias is again displayed in the *Sentinel* essay: "An Indian is not always dead when he has that appearance. . . . When some avenging fate overtakes a Ute and knocks him into pi, and this makes a Piute out of him, and flattens him out like a postage stamp, and pulverizes him, and runs him over the amalgamator, and assays him so that he lies in a retort like a seidlitz powder, then I feel I can trust him." In an essay called "The Fragrant Mormon," Nye wrote:

> When I was a boy I had two terrible obstacles to overcome, and I have dreaded them all my life until very recently. One was to eat a chunk of Limberger [*sic*] cheese, and the other was to look at a Mormon emigrant train.
>
> After I visited the train I thought I might as well go and tackle the Limberger cheese, and be out of my misery. I did so, and the cheese actually tasted like a California pear, and smelled like the atter [*sic*] of roses. It seemed to take the taste of the Mormons out of my mouth.

In *Bill Nye's Western Humor* (1968), T. A. Larson says: "Nye frequently drew upon his day-to-day experiences, and in so doing recorded accurate details of frontier life. In his attitudes he usually reflected popular Western viewpoints. Indians, braggarts from the East, carpetbagger officials, hypocrites, and frauds of all kinds he despised. . . . Of course he laughed at himself more than he did at anyone else."

Nye's seven years in Laramie were extremely busy. On 7 November 1876, he was elected justice of the peace, a post to which he was reelected four years later. He also became a correspondent for the *Denver Tribune* and the *Cheyenne Sun*. He passed the bar examination—which he had not been able to do in Wisconsin—and began to practice law. He also did some speculating on silver claims in the Laramie area.

During his first week on the *Sentinel*, Nye had written a tribute to spring:

> That choice season of the year has come when the venerable overshoe and the vacant castor-oil bottle are called upon to resign their respective positions in the backyard, and the house goes into a Committee of the Whole and investigates the cellar and the woodshed.
>
> It is now time to dig pie plant and shake

Nye and Clara Frances ("Catalpa") Smith at the time of their marriage

the luscious fruit from the asparagus tree.

The young man with the sorrel side whiskers and the mild skim-milk eye will proceed to coo the old, old story into the cleanest ear of his soul's idol.

The front gate will make ready for the spring campaign and prepare to support the united weight of two hearts that beat as one.

In March 1877, Nye launched his own spring campaign and married Clara Frances (Fanny) Smith, whom he dubbed "Catalpa." Around the same time, he was appointed notary public. In September, he ran unsuccessfully for the territorial legislature. In October, Nye resigned from the *Sentinel* and tried to build his law practice. Clients were not numerous, but his experience provided him with material for the humorous sketches he continued to write for the *Cheyenne Sun* and the *Denver Tribune*. He also began contributing articles to *Texas Siftings*, *Peck's Sun*, *Puck*, and the *Detroit Free Press*. At some point between 1877 and 1880 he was appointed United States land commissioner.

Nye returned to full-time journalism in early 1881 when he and other Republicans started the *Laramie Boomerang* to counter the Democratic *Laramie Times*, which had been established in 1879. Nye was made editor, and he named the paper for his "meek-eyed" mule. "Catalpa" Nye described the arrival of the stray mule: "This funny little creature appeared on the streets of Laramie from no one knew where. It ambled up to Edgar and rubbing its nose against his sleeve, brayed earnestly in his ear. From that time on, the arrival was known as Bill Nye's mule, Boomerang." Bill Nye described the arrival of the newspaper *Boomerang*: "A company incorporated itself and started a paper of which I took charge. The paper was published in the loft of a livery stable. That is the reason they called it a stock company. You could come up the stairs into the office or you could twist the tail of the iron gray mule and take the elevator." According to David B. Kesterson, "Nye's most important role on the *Boomerang*, as far as literary posterity is concerned, was, of course, as columnist. He wrote a daily humorous column and then collected his best efforts for a whole page in the weekly issue which soon grew out of the daily. It was these columns that made and sustained the *Boomerang*.... National circulation, especially of the weekly edition, grew substantially during the second year of publication. Not only did subscriptions come in from all states and several foreign countries, but leading newspapers throughout the Western World set up ex-

The office of the Laramie *(Wyoming)* Boomerang
(University of Wyoming)

changes." Charles A. Dana of the *New York Sun* was one of the subscribers.

Nye played with words much as a cat plays with a mouse—catching them, then permitting them to slip away to see what the results would be. While editing the *Boomerang* Nye was asked to introduce a visiting lecturer, Eli Perkins, to a Laramie audience. The lecture was to be on lying, so Nye introduced his as Eliar Perkins. Then in his column following the Perkins lecture, Nye wrote:

When Eli Perkins was passing through Laramie, he said he was traveling for his wife's pleasure.

"Then your wife is with you?" suggested our reporter.

"No, no," said Eli: "she is in New York."

As Nye's humor brought him fame, the famous were often the butt of his humor. Nye said his first meeting with General William Tecumseh Sherman was in one of the eating houses along the Union Pacific Railway lines. Nye's recollection was that Sherman sat at one end of the table, "throwing a life-preserver to a fly in the milk pitcher."

Nye's first book, *Bill Nye and Boomerang; or, The Tale of a Meek-Eyed Mule*, appeared in 1881; it is a collection of his columns in the *Sentinel* and the *Boomerang*, some of them rewritten, along with a few original pieces. In October 1882, Nye received an appointment as postmaster in Laramie to add to his offices of justice of the peace, land commissioner,

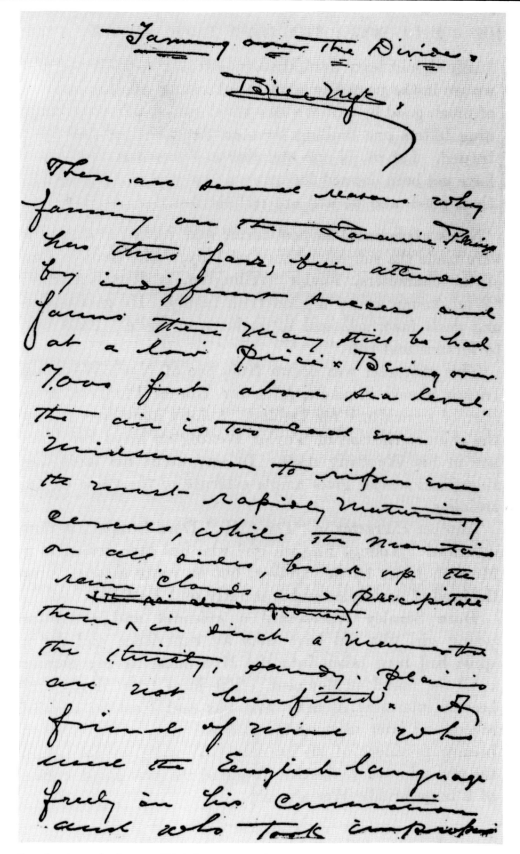

Page from the manuscript for one of Nye's humorous articles (Frank Wilson Nye, Bill Nye: His Own Life Story)

and notary public. The same year, his second book, *Forty Liars, and Other Lies* (named for the Forty Liars Club over which Nye presided in Laramie), was published; it was so popular that a second, expanded edition was brought out the same year.

In those early Laramie years Nye developed a regional humor in his columns that had a universal appeal. Had he not been stricken by cerebrospinal meningitis in November 1882, he probably would have spent the remainder of his professional life in Laramie; but doctors advised him to leave the 7,200-foot altitude and seek elevations more conducive to his health. After spending the winter and spring convalescing in Greeley, Colorado, Nye returned to Laramie to resign from the *Boomerang* and settle his numerous other affairs. He resigned his postmastership in a letter to the president of the United States, in which he advised that "the safe combination is set on the numbers 33, 66 and 99, though I do not remember at this moment which comes first, or how many times you revolve the knob, or which direction you should turn it at first in order to make it operate." He concluded the letter: "Mr. President, as an official of this Government I now retire. My term of office would not expire until 1886. I must, therefore, beg pardon for my eccentricity in resigning. It will be best, perhaps, to keep the heart-breaking news from the ears of European powers until the dangers of a financial panic are fully past. Then hurl it broadcast with a sickening thud."

The national reputation Nye had won for himself in Laramie survived while he spent three rather happy years recovering near his boyhood home in Hudson, Wisconsin. His writing took on a more leisurely pace, yet he continued to draw on themes centered around his Wyoming days. These were good enough for the *Boston Globe*, which began taking a weekly letter from him. Two collections of his newspaper pieces, *Boomerang Shots* and *Hits and Skits*, were published in London in 1884; Nye's own third book, *Baled Hay: A Drier Book Than Walt Whitman's "Leaves o' Grass,"* appeared the same year.

In 1885, Nye made his debut on the lecture circuit, beginning a career that would last until his death—and probably even hasten that death by the toll that it took on his fragile health. Nye was extremely popular as a lecturer: the combination of the outrageous things he said with his deadpan expression and the wild gesticulations of his long, thin arms struck his audiences as hilariously funny.

On the platform Nye could speak out strongly for causes he felt were important, yet he realized that a comic phrase often made the opinions more

acceptable. He strongly advocated the establishment of professional schools of journalism, and in an address to the Wisconsin State Press Association at Whitewater on 11 August 1885, he set forth his ideas about what should be taught in journalism schools once they were established:

> If I were to suggest a curriculum for the young man who wished to take a regular course in a school of journalism, preferring that to the actual experience, I would say to him, devote the first two years to meditation and prayer . . . devote five years to the peculiar orthography of the English language . . . three years with the dumb bells, sand bags, slung [*sic*] shots and tomahawk. . . .
>
> . . . ten years should be given to learning the typographical art . . . five years to the art of proof-reading . . . fifteen years should then be devoted to the study of American politics . . . then take a medical and surgical course . . . then ten years should be given to the study of law.
>
> The student will, by this time, begin to see what is required of him and enter with great zeal upon the further study of his profession . . . a theological course of ten years . . . and the final ten years may be profitably devoted to the acquisition of a practical knowledge of cutting cordwood, baking beans, making shirts, lecturing, grinding scissors, etc. . . .
>
> With the course of study that I have mapped out, the young student would emerge from the college of journalism at the age of 95 or 96, ready to take off his coat and write an article on almost any subject.

Finding during his first season on the circuit that the burden of carrying an entire evening's performance alone was too great, Nye formed a lecturing team with the Indiana poet James Whitcomb Riley in 1886. Their popularity on the lecture circuit was said to rival the appeal of Mark Twain and Josh Billings. The two men also combined their talents in a book, *Nye and Riley's Railway Guide* (1888), which was a best-seller and was republished under other titles over the next seventeen years.

Nye also wrote two plays during his Wisconsin years. Little information is available about "Gas Fixtures" (1886). The autobiographical "The Village Postmaster" (1886) was rewritten as *The Cadi* in 1891 and achieved success on Broadway and on tour.

It was a letter to the *New York World* in 1886, following a record-breaking snowstorm in Ashe-

Nye with fellow lecturers Eugene Field (left) and James Whitcomb Riley in Indianapolis, 1886

ville, North Carolina, where Nye had moved to continue his recovery, that won him a spot on that newspaper. Nye sent his description of what it was like "In My Sunny Southern Home" during a blizzard of such magnitude to John A. Cockerill, managing editor of the *World*. Cockerill showed the letter to publisher Joseph Pulitzer, who decided that "a man who could produce such humor as this while convalescing should be in the exclusive employ of the newspaper with the biggest circulation of the day."

Nye had misgivings about the *World* offer and was not sure his humor would please metropolitan tastes. But as his health improved in the French Broad Valley of western North Carolina, he gave the offer more careful thought. However, it was to his journalist friends in the West that Bill Nye turned for advice as to the wisdom of the change. He had a number of friends on the *Chicago Daily News*, including Eugene Field, Will Vischer, Opie Read, Finley Peter Dunne, and the editor, Melville E. Stone. Of this group, Nye's most staunch supporter was Stone, who advised Nye to accept what he regarded as an offer no Western newspaper could duplicate.

In the spring of 1887, Nye arrived in New York to assume his role as columnist for the *World* at a salary of $150 a week. Walt McDougall, an artist assigned to illustrate the Nye stories, developed a caricature of Nye showing a billiard-ball head on a pipe-stem body. This portrait became so well known that McDougall once drew it on an envelope and added "New York"; this was sufficient identification for the letter to reach Nye the next day. Nye's comment on the caricature is typical of his brand of humor: "Everywhere I go I find people who seem pleased with the manner in which I have succeeded in resembling the graphic pictures made to represent me in the 'World.' I can truly say that I am not a vain man, but it is certainly pleasing and gratifying to be greeted by a glance of recognition and a yell of genuine delight from total strangers." McDougall and Nye formed a partnership in producing the weekly letter for the *World*; the partnership developed into a close friendship. McDougall later wrote of Nye: "Of the many men with whom I have been intimate there is not one who has worn so well, for whom an honest admiration has increased

One of the famous caricatures of Nye by New York World *cartoonist Walt McDougall*

rather than lessened with intimacy."

Nye's peers felt he could draw a smile from anyone, except probably the Shinnecock Indians, whose sense of humor, according to Nye, had been removed by a surgical operation. Many of his *World* columns dealt with New York scenes, institutions, and personalities; he concocted a fictional friendship between himself and Jay Gould which was the subject of a series of articles. He also dealt satirically, but perceptively, with art and literature. He widened his perspective in June 1889 with a trip to Paris to cover the international exposition for the *World*; on the way back, he visited London, where he met Bret Harte and claimed to have chided Harte for using his name in "Plain Language from Truthful James" (in actuality, of course, Nye's pen name had derived from the poem). In January 1890 James Whitcomb Riley, suffering from ill health and alcoholism, retired from the lecture circuit; Nye finished the season teamed with a musical group. Several more of Nye's books were published during his New York years: *Bill Nye's Chestnuts Old and New. Latest Gathering* (1888) and *Bill Nye's Thinks* (1888), collections of older pieces from his newspaper columns and earlier books; *An Almanac for 1891* (1890), a calendar listing both real and comical events as having occurred on each date; and *His Fleeting Ideal: A Romance of Baffled Hypnotism* (1890), a composite novel written in conjunction with P. T. Barnum, John L. Sullivan, and others (Nye wrote the final chapter).

A tragic event of 1890 was the death of Nye's young son Ned on 1 July; Nye attributed this to the unhealthy northern climate. In addition, he had had his fill of the big city (even though he had been living in the village of Tompkinsville on rural Staten Island). Therefore, he arranged with Pulitzer to have his Sunday column continued in the *World* and syndicated to other papers, and in March 1891 he moved his family back to the Asheville, North Carolina area. When Cockerill resigned as editor of the *World* in a dispute with Pulitzer later in the spring, Nye, out of loyalty to Cockerill, withdrew his column from the *World* and placed it in the papers purchased by his friend. The following January, however, Nye allowed his syndicate, the American Press Humor Association, to place his column in the *World* again. Ultimately, some seventy papers were buying his writings on a regular basis from the syndicate.

In September 1891, Nye's old play "The Village Postmaster"—rewritten and retitled *The Cadi*—opened at the Union Square Theatre on Broadway and ran for three months before going on the road. The play's success with audiences (it was not as successful with critics) seems to have been due to the fact that the central character was based on the popular and familiar Nye himself. Nye also continued lecturing, teaming with Alfred P. Burbank, who performed interpretive readings of literary works (and who, coincidentally, looked so much like Nye that audiences sometimes mistook him for the more famous humorist).

In 1892, Nye finished building his country retreat at Arden, North Carolina, and moved his family into it. Named Buck Shoals, his new home was adjacent to the vast Biltmore estate; Nye wrote some wry columns about his "farmer" neighbor, George W. Vanderbilt II, similar to his earlier depiction of his "friendship" with Jay Gould.

Nye did some traveling in 1893 in addition to his lecture tour: in the summer, he attended and wrote about the World's Fair in Chicago; and in September, he made a second trip to London, where he was a guest at a dinner given in honor of Emile Zola. The following January, he teamed up with a new lecturing partner, William Hawley Smith, because Burbank had become terminally ill. Nye then skipped the winter 1894-1895 lecture season in order to spend a few months in Washington, D.C., to gather material for columns about politics. His partly serious, partly comical *Bill Nye's History of the United States* was published in 1894.

Nye went on a voyage to the Bahamas in January 1895, but the trip ended badly and almost tragically: the ship, the *Cienfuegas*, wrecked near Nassau and sank. Nye and the rest of the passengers and crew were rescued, but the manuscript of Nye's only attempt at writing a novel—titled "Thelma"—went down with the vessel. Nye never tried to rewrite the novel. He did, however, write one more play, *The Stag Party*. Coauthored with Paul Meredith Potter, it was panned by the critics and ran for only twelve performances on Broadway in December 1895. Ironically, the play's failure may have been at least partly due to Nye's conscious decision to keep his own personality out of it and instead try to develop a variety of characters; but it was the well-known Nye persona that had contributed largely to the success of *The Cadi*.

Meanwhile, Nye had begun his last lecture season in the fall with yet another new partner, *Boston Herald* cartoonist Bert Poole. Poole's part was to rapidly draw cartoons to illustrate Nye's lectures; but Nye's health, which had been precarious ever since he was stricken with cerebrospinal meningitis in 1882, was failing rapidly, and he was unable to carry the speaking burden alone. The season was a

Nye's home at Buck Shoals, North Carolina

disaster, and many spectators believed Nye was coming on stage drunk. He returned to Buck Shoals, where he died after a stroke on 22 February 1896. Two more books on which he had worked were published posthumously: *Bill Nye's History of England From the Druids to the Reign of Henry VIII* (1896), which he had intended to bring up to his own time, but was cut off by his illness and death; and *A Guest at the Ludlow and Other Stories* (1897), another collection of short pieces.

At his peak, Bill Nye was one of the most popular humorists of his day, along with Mark Twain, Finley Peter Dunne, David Ross Locke (Petroleum V. Nasby), and Ambrose Bierce. Today, he is virtually forgotten. The reasons for this are unclear, for while he was certainly not as great an artist as Mark Twain, many of his columns are still hilariously funny. Furthermore, like Twain and Bierce and unlike Dunne and Locke, Nye avoided the dialect form, which was considered amusing at the time but has lost favor today. Also—again like Twain and Bierce and unlike Dunne and Locke—many of his pieces are on universal themes and can be appreciated apart from the context in which they were written, rather than being restricted to political events and personalities which are now only of historical interest. As David B. Kesterson points out, modern appreciation of Nye might be inhibited by the brief nature of most of his works, which were designed as newspaper columns or lectures; when

one tries to read through a collection of these, they begin to appear repetitious. But, Kesterson concludes, "Despite the drawbacks, there is still enjoyment in him. . . . Nye's ability to see irony in almost everything and his sardonic tone of voice are certainly in vogue in the late twentieth century. . . . Nye at his best is indeed still funny."

Plays:

The Cadi, New York, Union Square Theatre, 21 September 1891;

The Stag Party, by Nye and Paul M. Potter, New York, Garden Theatre, 17 December 1895.

Other:

His Fleeting Ideal: A Romance of Baffled Hypnotism, a composite novel with chapter 12 by Nye (New York: J. S. Ogilvie, 1890).

Letters:

"Letters of Riley and Bill Nye," edited by Edmund H. Eitel, *Harper's*, 138 (March 1919): 474-484;

Letters of Edgar Wilson Nye Now in the University of Wyoming Library, edited by Nixon Orwin Rush (Laramie: University of Wyoming Library, 1951).

Biography:

Frank Wilson Nye, *Bill Nye: His Own Life Story* (New York: Century, 1926).

References:

Paul L. Armstrong, "History of the Post Office at Laramie, Wyoming," *Annals of Wyoming*, 11 (January 1939): 52-60;

Walter Blair, "The Background of Bill Nye in American Humor," Ph.D. dissertation, University of Chicago, 1931;

W. E. Chaplin, "Bill Nye," *The Frontier*, 11 (March 1931): 223-226;

Chaplin, "Bill Nye in Laramie," *Second Biennial Report, State Historian of Wyoming* (Sheridan, Wyo.: Mills, 1921-1923), pp. 142-158;

Chaplin, "Some of the Early Newspapers of Wyoming," *Wyoming Historical Society Miscellanies 1919* (Laramie: Laramie Republican Co., 1919), pp. 7-24;

Will M. Clemens, *Famous Funny Fellows: Brief Biographical Sketches of American Humorists* (Cleveland: W. W. Williams, 1882);

Levette J. Davidson, "Bill Nye and the Denver Tribune," *Colorado Magazine*, 4 (January 1927): 13-18;

E. J. Edwards, "Nye, the Humorist," *Colorado Springs Daily Gazette*, 17 January 1892, p. 8;

Diane Elissa Heestand, "The Writing of Bill Nye in Laramie," M.A. thesis, University of Wyoming, 1968;

David B. Kesterson, *Bill Nye (Edgar Wilson Nye)* (Boston: Twayne, 1981);

Kesterson, *Bill Nye: The Western Writings* (Boise: Boise State University, 1976);

Walter McDougall, "Bill Nye as Seen by Walt McDougall," *Book Lovers Magazine*, 1 (June 1903): 604-605.

Papers:

Many letters, documents, and works by and about Nye are located in the Bill Nye Collection of the American Heritage Center at the University of Wyoming library.

Oswald Ottendorfer
(26 January 1826-15 December 1900)

Barbara Creswell
University of Alabama

MAJOR POSITION HELD: Proprietor, *New Yorker Staats-Zeitung* (1859-1900).

Oswald Ottendorfer, a revolutionist refugee, was the most distinguished editor of the *New Yorker Staats-Zeitung*, the foremost of American German-language newspapers. He found employment on the *Staats-Zeitung* in 1850 and later married the widow of the founder. Ottendorfer's influential paper became a strong supporter of the Union cause during the Civil War.

Ottendorfer was born on 26 January 1826 in Zwittau, Moravia, then a province of Austria-Hungary, now in Czechoslovakia. He was the youngest of six children of Vincenz Ottendorfer, a clothmaker in fair circumstances, and Catharine Neumeister Ottendorfer. While Ottendorfer was still young, his parents moved to Galicia, and he was sent to live with a married sister at Brünn. He attended the school of his native town and the gymnasia of Leitomischl and Brünn. At the age of twenty he left to enter the University of Vienna, where he studied mainly philosophy. He transferred to the University at Prague to learn the Czech language and law.

In 1848 he returned to Vienna with plans of finishing his course at Padua, which belonged to Austria, but liberal uprisings in various sections of the German-speaking countries interrupted his education. The revolution was about to break out; it had already broken out in Paris, where Louis Philippe had fallen. Young Ottendorfer was enthusiastic for the overthrow of the reactionary regimes in Austria and Germany, and he took an active part in the revolt against the Metternich government in Vienna. At the outbreak of the Schleswig-Holstein War, he volunteered to fight against Denmark.

When he returned to Vienna, where the people had taken control, he was made lieutenant under Robert Blum in the mobile guard. He fought on the barricades in Dresden and participated in the

Oswald Ottendorfer

renewed attempt at revolution in Prague. In October the revolutionists were beaten; many were killed, but Ottendorfer escaped. He was concealed by a porter in a bookstore for several days until the excitement had passed, then he fled across the Bohemian frontier to Saxony.

The following year he was back in Prague, involved with the students in the struggle between the imperial armies and the Hungarians and Bohemians. When the students were defeated and his companions fled for their lives, he was again protected and eventually escaped dressed as a woman. He was at Baden during the revolution there and escaped to Switzerland, where he stayed for several months. At this point he had decided to return to Vienna and turn himself in to the government, thinking he would be let off with a brief sentence; but on his arrival he learned through a friend that he would without doubt lose his life if he remained, so he left for New York. He arrived penniless, without friends, and unable to speak the language: he knew Latin, Greek, French, Hebrew, and a few Slavic languages, but not English. The first employment he found was too hard for him and

made him ill. When he recovered, he was hired to work in a soda-water factory. Finally, he was offered a subordinate position in the counting room of the *Staats-Zeitung*, owned by Jakob Uhl and his wife Anna. The daughter of a Wurzburg merchant, Anna Behr lived in an age when higher education for women was frowned upon, and she had received only a common-school training. However, she had displayed an early aptitude for learning. In 1836 or 1837 she left Germany with a relative for the United States, determined to make her own way. The first year she lived with a brother in Niagara County, New York. In 1838 she became acquainted with and later married a young printer, Jakob Uhl. When they purchased the *Staats-Zeitung*, she did her full share as compositor, secretary, and general manager. The paper developed from a triweekly to a daily publication. Uhl devoted more space to foreign and domestic news and less to political polemic than did the other German-language papers of the time. In 1852 Uhl died and his widow continued to attend the growing business, in addition to raising their six children. Ottendorfer became assistant to Mrs. Uhl and an important factor in the publication of the *Staats-Zeitung*.

The period from 1850 to 1870 is characterized as the golden age of the German-language press in the United States. In 1856 the daily circulation of the *Staats-Zeitung* was 15,300; the other two German papers in New York had a combined daily circulation of 5,700, and four German weeklies reported 16,200 readers. The level of German-American journalism rose sharply after 1848 because of the contributions of highly educated refugees and the high caliber of the German immigration as a whole.

Ottendorfer was greatly interested in activities of the German Society of New York, an immigrant aid society. Its interests included furnishing medical and nursing services for newly arrived immigrants and Germans who had been in the United States less than five years and could not speak English. However, the society received only lukewarm support from the *Staats-Zeitung*.

Germans were as intolerant in the contest between Continentalism and Puritanism as their American critics, and the radicals, in particular, made derogatory references to "American Barbarians and Methodists." Ottendorfer played a prominent role in demonstrations against Sunday laws. Germans and other immigrant groups defended their right to observe the Sabbath in the European manner. For them, Sunday was a time for dances, parades, card clubs, and visits to beer gardens. When July fourth fell on a Sunday, and Americans suggested postponing the celebration until the following day, it became a matter of principle for German radicals to insist that the day be observed appropriately on the Sabbath.

There were approximately 1,000 beer cellars in New York in the 1850s, and the annual consumption of beer by the Germans of the city amounted to a million dollars. A mass meeting of Germans was called to protest against temperance legislation. The *Staats-Zeitung* fought for "unrestricted personal liberty" as vigorously as any radical paper and reported, without comment or criticism, an attack on a German-Methodist minister in Watertown, Wisconsin, who had preached against liquor in a German community.

In 1856 Ottendorfer was among the few immigrant radicals campaigning for the Democratic party. Even though he did not condone slavery, he supported Stephen A. Douglas. The party split between Douglas and Jefferson Davis factions in the convention proved especially embarrassing to him both as publisher of the *Staats-Zeitung* and as a friend of Douglas.

Ottendorfer was made editor in 1858; the following year, on 23 July, he married Mrs. Uhl, who had refused several tempting offers of purchase for the paper during the period from 1852 to 1859 when she served as sole manager. After her marriage to Ottendorfer, she remained involved in managerial duties and received visitors, many of whom were soliciting her philanthropic assistance, in her private office.

In 1859 Ottendorfer visited Europe, traveling through Germany, France, and Italy. He avoided Austria, even though he had been given permission to go there.

The *Staats-Zeitung* had one of its most successful periods, both financially and as a journal of genuine influence, during the regime of Ottendorfer. The paper developed along sound lines under his direction, circulation increased, and the latest mechanical improvements were installed. Ottendorfer had excellent business skills and was eager to adopt the methods of the best American dailies. The *Staats-Zeitung* developed from an insignificant foreign newspaper into an influential, widely read metropolitan organ.

By 1869 the *Staats-Zeitung* was an eight-page paper. Telegraphic news and reports from correspondents in Europe made up the first page. Pages two and three were devoted to advertising, and page four carried a lead article normally written by Ottendorfer himself. Page six carried a serial novel, and pages seven and eight covered local news. The

modern appearance and makeup of the *Staats-Zeitung* approached the style of a typical American daily. The press turned out papers at the rate of 8,000 an hour.

In 1865 Ottendorfer went to Europe again and asked for permission to visit Austria, but it was denied. In 1869 he did visit the country and later concluded that the Austro-Prussian War of 1866 and the Austrian defeat at Koniggratz had done Austria much good by accomplishing for the country what defeat at Sedan in the war of 1870 did for France.

Ottendorfer employed many immigrant radicals on his staff, although the *Staats-Zeitung* had always been a conservative paper. Dr. Julius Wurzburger, who had been expelled from Munich in 1849, was an associate editor. Hans Rittis, who had served a jail sentence in Prague, edited the Sunday edition. Emil P. Anneke was a reporter for the *Staats-Zeitung* before he joined the *Detroit Volksblatt*.

The long survival of the *Staats-Zeitung* resulted from the significance placed on advertising, local news, and circulation-building devices. It was operated for a profit and not for propaganda. Circulation reached 55,000, and the owners claimed the largest circulation of any German paper in the world. By 1872 a rotary press capable of turning out 12,000 sheets per hour was acquired. The next year the business erected its own building.

After the Civil War, Ottendorfer favored reconciliation; he opposed the administration's Reconstruction policy. He fought Tammany Hall and the corruption of the Tweed Ring. He was elected on the New York City Liberal Republican ticket as alderman in 1872. In 1874 he was an unsuccessful candidate for mayor of New York.

Festivals commemorating the birthday of the German inspector general of Washington's army during the American Revolution were popular in the Eastern states and were planned as patriotic counterdemonstrations against nativist attacks on foreigners. Ottendorfer was among those who usually provided oratory for these events. He also was selected to address the group at the dedication exercises of the Free German School of the New York City school system, where children would not be exposed to theology or sectarianism.

He gained a reputation as an independent, civic-minded American and had much interest in public affairs and charities. He and his wife, who died in 1884, were extremely generous in supporting philanthropic deeds. The Ottendorfer Branch of the New York Public Library exists in a small red building on Second Avenue; at the time of its establishment in 1884, the library was in a fashionable neighborhood. It served thousands of refugees from Hitler's Europe, in whose Americanization the Ottendorfer Library and the *Staats-Zeitung* played a vital part. Located in a Jewish-Polish section of the city, it has been deserted by its once opulent clientele.

By 1884, the four presses at the *Staats-Zeitung* had a capacity of 48,000 copies per hour of an eight-page paper. It was rumored in 1890 that Ottendorfer had disposed of the *Staats-Zeitung* for the large sum of $4,000,000, but the rumor was denied by Ottendorfer, who had only made a change in the management of the paper because of his advancing age and the condition of his health. He had, along with members of his family owning the 500 shares comprising the stock of the paper, given fifty of these shares to Herman Ridder, a businessman of experience and courage. Technically, editorial control remained under Ottendorfer until the end of the century, although he virtually retired from an active role in the business in 1887. Under the adminstration of Ottendorfer and Ridder, the *Staats-Zeitung* reached its greatest influence and prosperity. In 1888 the paper was enlarged to twelve pages. In 1890, Ottendorfer did retire from the business and spent the rest of his life in Europe; Ridder became manager. An evening edition, the *Abendblatt*, was added, mainly to meet the competition of the *New York Herald*.

The German-language press was devoted to sound-money principles until the end of the century, when inflation dropped out of politics as a partisan issue. In numerous excellent lead articles the *Staats-Zeitung* consistently favored sound money and publicized the evils of irredeemable paper and the perils of depreciated silver dollars. After his retirement Ottendorfer was made honorary president of the Deutsch-Amerikanische Gut-Gild Liga, and his speeches for the gold standard were circulated throughout the country by the Republican National Committee.

He donated $400,000 to build and endow an educational institution (die Ottendorfer'sche Freie Volksbibliothek) in Zwittau, Moravia, and founded a home for aged and indigent men on Long Island, New York. In his will he bequeathed $100,000 to the Isabella Hermath Home for Aged Women, named in memory of a deceased daughter of his wife, supplementing a gift he made of the same amount a few days before his death; $20,000 each to the New York Free Circulating Library, the Charity Organization Society, the Cooper Union, and the German hospital and dispensary; $25,000 to the American Museum of Natural History; and $10,000 each to the Society for Ethical Culture and the German Ladies' Society for the Relief of Destitute Widows and Orphans. Each employee of the *Staats-Zeitung* received a share in proportion to his salary in a total bequest of $450,000. Ottendorfer died in New York City, 15 December 1900.

He was universally respected as a man of high character, steadfast liberalism, and great social-mindedness. The Ottendorfer Memorial Fellowship, awarded each year to an American student of German language and literature for study abroad, was established in his memory. *Harper's Weekly* said at the time of his death: "In politics, benevolence, business and social life, he was active and distinguished. Ottendorfer was a democrat, and when there was a choice among Democrats, he chose wisely. His career has been highly honorable and useful."

References:

E. S. Martin, "This Busy World," *Harper's Weekly* (December 1900): 29;

Carl Wittke, *The German-Language Press in America* (Lexington: University of Kentucky Press, 1957);

Wittke, *Refugees of Revolution* (Philadelphia: University of Pennsylvania Press, 1952);

A. E. Zucker, *The Forty-Eighters* (New York: Russell & Russell, 1950).

George W. Peck

(28 September 1840-16 April 1916)

Charles C. Self
University of Alabama

MAJOR POSITIONS HELD: Editor / publisher, *Jefferson County* (Wisconsin) *Republican* (1860-1863), *Ripon* (Wisconsin) *Representative* (1866-1868); columnist, *New York Democrat* (1868-1871); editor / publisher, *La Crosse* (Wisconsin) *Democrat* (1871-1874), *La Crosse Sun* (1874-1878), *Peck's Sun* (Milwaukee) (1878-1890).

BOOKS: *Adventures of One Terence McGrant. A Brevet Irish Cousin of President Ulysses S. Grant* (New York: Lambert, 1871);
Peck's Fun: Being Extracts from the "La Crosse Sun" and "Peck's Sun," Milwaukee, compiled by V. W. Richardson (Milwaukee: Symes, Swain, 1879);
Peck's Sunshine: Being a Collection of Articles Written for Peck's Sun, Milwaukee, Wis., Generally Calculated to Throw Sunshine instead of Clouds on the Faces of Those Who Read Them (Chicago & St. Louis: Belford, Clarke, 1882);
Peck's Bad Boy and His Pa (Chicago: Belford, Clarke, 1883; London: Routledge, 1887);
Peck's Bad Boy, No. 2: The Grocery Man and Peck's Bad Boy (Chicago & New York: Belford, Clarke, 1883);
Mirth for the Million: Peck's Compendium of Fun, edited by "Elmo" (Thomas W. Handford) (Chicago: Belford, Clarke, 1883);
Peck's Boss Book (Chicago & New York: Belford, Clarke, 1884);
Will He Marry Her? A Domestic Drama for Home Reading (Chicago: Rhodes & McClure, 1885);
How Private Geo. W. Peck Put Down the Rebellion; or, The Funny Experiences of a Raw Recruit (Chicago & New York: Belford, Clarke, 1887);
Peck's Irish Friend, Phelan Geoheagan (New York: Lovell, 1887);
The Prohibition Question: A Study of Its Results in Kentucky, Tennessee, Georgia, Oklahoma, Alabama, Louisiana, Texas, North Dakota and Maine (Milwaukee: Allied Printing, 1890);
Peck's Uncle Ike and the Red Headed Boy (Chicago: Belford, 1899);
Sunbeams: Humor, Sarcasm and Sense (New York: Hurst, 1900);
Peck's Red-Headed Boy (New York: Hurst, 1901);

George W. Peck

Peck's Bad Boy Abroad (Chicago: Stanton, 1904);
Peck's Bad Boy with the Circus (Philadelphia: McKay, 1906);
Peck's Bad Boy with the Cowboys (Chicago: Stanton & Van Vliet, 1907);
Peck's Bad Boy in an Airship (Philadelphia: McKay, 1908).

George W. Peck was a talented writer and editor who built a political career in part by satirizing authority in one of the great best-sellers of the late nineteenth century and a series of accompanying volumes. He is probably better remembered today for his incisive satire than for his prominence as mayor of Milwaukee and governor of Wisconsin, even though he was one of only three Democrats to have been governor from the time Wisconsin achieved statehood in 1848 until his death in 1916. His fame stems chiefly from the humorous accounts of the mischief of a young prankster in the late 1800s who was especially fond of playing tricks on his father and on local church authorities. *Peck's Bad Boy and His Pa* (1883) became the prototype for a generation of young prankster stories and books that followed in the early twentieth century. It was a best-seller in its time and made Peck's newspaper, *Peck's Sun*, famous not only in Milwaukee but nationwide. It also made George Peck's name a household word to a generation of Americans.

George Wilbur Peck was born in Henderson, New York, in 1840 to David B. and Alzina Peck. He was the oldest of three children. His parents took him to live on a farm at Cold Spring, Jefferson County, Wisconsin, in 1843. They later moved to Whitewater, where Peck was educated in the common or public schools until 1855. He learned the printer's trade and became a printer's devil on the weekly *Register* in Whitewater before he was fifteen. In the early days he worked as a journeyman printer for several newspapers in Whitewater. In 1860, he married Francena Rowley of Delavan, Wisconsin, and shortly thereafter purchased a half-interest in the weekly *Jefferson County Republican*. He and his wife had two sons, George W. Peck, Jr., and Roy W. Peck. He continued as a publisher and editor of the *Republican* until 1863, when he enlisted as a private in the Fourth Wisconsin Cavalry. He was soon promoted to sergeant and was commissioned a second lieutenant in 1864. He served with the cavalry until he was mustered out and the unit disbanded in 1866.

Following the war, Peck returned to Ripon, Wisconsin, and in 1866 he began a newspaper called the *Representative*, to which he contributed his first humorous articles. One skit, in Irish dialect, was published in 1868 and signed "Terence McGrant"; it satirized the nepotism rampant at the start of Grant's first term as president. The article caught the attention of Marcus M. "Brick" Pomeroy, a well-known Wisconsin publisher and humorist who was starting a New York City newspaper, the *Democrat*, with the blessing of Tammany Hall. Pomeroy offered Peck a place writing "Terence McGrant" letters, and Peck moved to New York. The columns proved so popular that they were brought out with illustrations in a book called *Adventures of One Terence McGrant* in 1871. Thus began Peck's prolific career as an author of books of humor.

That same year, 1871, Peck returned to La Crosse, Wisconsin, and became a partner in Pomeroy's nationally recognized newspaper, the *La Crosse Democrat*, which had peaked in circulation in 1868 at 100,000. Using the *Democrat* as a forum, Peck supported Horace Greeley for president in 1872. In 1874, he withdrew from the *Democrat* and began a newspaper of his own called the *Sun*. But the newspaper struggled for four years without much success, and in 1878 Peck moved it to Milwaukee and named it *Peck's Sun*. He adopted the famous slogan used several years earlier by Benjamin H. Day for the *New York Sun*, "It Shines for All."

The move proved to be an immediate success. As one *New York Times* writer later put it, "he finally took it to Milwaukee for a wider field, and it eventually proved a gold mine for its owner." It was brought out weekly more as a collection of editorial humor than as a newspaper in the modern sense. Peck began writing the "Bad Boy" stories for the *Sun*, and they soon became immensely popular. The first of the nasty tricks of Hennery, the Bad Boy, appeared in 1882. The Bad Boy is merciless in the practical jokes he plays on his drunken father. But he is no respecter of persons, and his jokes are played on everyone from his mother and ex-girl friend to the church deacon and the grocer.

The Bad Boy's tricks usually center on mischief. For example, one morning when the boy's father is trying to reform his life and become a Christian, Hennery puts ice in each of his father's boots. Another time the boy perfumes his father's handkerchief with "Jamaica Rum," wraps the handkerchief around a stack of playing cards, and slips them into his father's pocket just before he goes to church for a prayer meeting. Of course, the boy's father goes up to testify at the prayer meeting and starts to cry as he repents his sins. He reaches for the handkerchief, pulls it out, and out come all the cards, scattering on the congregation. The smell of rum fills the air. "Well, if he had shuffled them, and Ma had cut them, and he had dealt six hands, they couldn't have been dealt any better," the boy explains. "They flew into everybody's lap. The deakin that was with Ma got the jack of spades and three aces and a deuce, and Ma got some nine spots and a king of hearts, and Ma nearly fainted, cause she didn't get a better hand, I spose."

In another story, the Bad Boy refuses to obey his father and bring in kindling wood. The father tells him to bring it in by the time he returns home that night or he will take a strap to him. The Bad Boy places a large tomcat in his bed and when the father grabs in the dark what he thinks is the boy, the cat scratches and bites the father badly.

Of course, as with most humor, it is Peck's style of telling that creates the humor. Abstracting the stories makes them distinctly unfunny. Also, E. F. Bleiler, editor of the 1958 edition of *Peck's Bad Boy and His Pa*, has pointed out that Peck's book was written in a style that appealed to people of his generation. "According to modern standards," Bleiler wrote, "*Peck's Bad Boy and His Pa* is a cruel book, for there is a strong element of pain in its situations. But it must be urged in the book's defence [*sic*] that it is not cruel because G. W. Peck was a cruel man, but because he lived in an era when practical jokes were almost a cult. It was written for a generation that liked its humor strong, imaginative, and painful—for the other person."

It was these stories that drove Peck's circulation up until the newspaper was selling more than 80,000 copies of each issue. The newspaper established Peck's national reputation and made him a well-known figure around Milwaukee.

In 1883, *Peck's Bad Boy and His Pa*, which was basically a collection of the newspaper stories, was published by Belford, Clarke and Company. Later that year, a second book, *Peck's Bad Boy, No. 2: The Grocery Man and Peck's Bad Boy*, appeared. Both books were to remain in print for almost forty-five years, until 1925. Other books followed, notably *How Private Geo. W. Peck Put Down the Rebellion* (1887), a hilarious account of his Civil War experiences.

Peck's political career mirrored the development of his journalism career. Some authors have argued that it was the Bad Boy who carried Peck to the state house, an 1890 organization formed to promote Peck's campaign even called itself "Peck's Bad Boys." However, Peck had held several political offices over the years: shortly after he left the army, he became city treasurer of Ripon in 1867 while still with the *Representative*; he served as chief of police in La Crosse in 1873 during his tenure as publisher of the *La Crosse Democrat*; in 1873-1874 he was chief clerk of the lower house of the Wisconsin state legislature. However, he left politics for a time as his writing career picked up: "Then for a number of years, while the dollars rolled in, he eschewed politics as one does the plague," the *New York Times* wrote in a sketch published at the height of his political career in 1894. Following the publication of his books, his widespread reputation and name recognition opened up new opportunities for him: by the end of the 1880s, Peck was one of the best-known men in Wisconsin.

In 1889, the city of Milwaukee was anxious to host the annual encampment of the Grand Army of the Republic, a veteran's group that produced many tourist dollars. Peck took on the task of winning the event for the city and was largely instrumental in getting it. He also was credited with contributing to the success of the encampment, which included a staged nighttime naval battle on Lake Michigan. Peck's popularity and political influence accelerated rapidly following that success.

About the same time, the Wisconsin legislature, controlled by the Republicans, passed the so-called Bennett Bill, which was to produce one of the hottest campaign debates seen in Wisconsin to that time. The bill was aimed at requiring attendance in the public schools, but its controversial definition of *school* offended many of the state's minority citizens. Under the law, a school had to teach reading, writing, arithmetic, and United States history "in the English language." Many members of minority groups felt the law was aimed at Roman Catholics, who taught Latin in their schools, and especially at Lutherans, whose parochial schools gave all instruction in German. German Protestants and Irish Catholics were joined by the Polish minority in outrage against what was taken as an affront to pride in European heritage and the mother tongue, and a threat to the freedom of the parochial schools. The Democrats took up the issue, and Peck quipped for tolerance and against the bill in the *Sun*. In the spring of 1890, Peck was elected mayor of Milwaukee as a Democrat by the widest margin in the city's history. During the summer, both the Democrats and the Republicans debated how to handle what the Milwaukee mayoral elections had proved was an extremely emotional issue. The Republicans decided to stand by the law, campaigning on the slogan "The Little Schoolhouse—Stand By It." The Democrats nominated Peck for governor and, after some equivocation, came out firmly against the bill, vowing to repeal it if they were elected. The Catholic and Lutheran vote was well organized; the Lutherans were said to have marched to the polls in squads to vote for Peck. He was elected governor in November 1890 by 28,000 votes, the largest margin in Wisconsin history to that time. A Democratic majority that rode into the legislature with him repealed the hated Bennett Law in 1891 and substituted a milder form of attendance law.

When Peck became governor, his eldest son, George W. Peck, Jr., continued publishing the *Sun*. But without the elder Peck's incisive wit, the newspaper lacked its former luster, and circulation declined. It was merged with another weekly in 1894.

Peck was a genial and competent governor, and his humorous speeches were popular with voters. He was reelected in 1892, defeating former United States Senator John C. Spooner in a close race. Peck's administration has been called one of the most partisan in Wisconsin history, at least until that time; however, it is chiefly known for two things: the treasury suits and gerrymandering. Previously, it had been common practice in Wisconsin for state treasurers to lend unneeded state funds to banks around the state. With the interest collected, the treasurers pocketed $25,000 to $30,000 in additional salary for themselves and deposited large sums of money into party coffers. Peck's administration brought suit against two former treasurers and their bondsmen, claiming that the interest was public money. The administration won judgments of $725,000 and collected $373,000 of the money before it was voted out of office, and the Republican legislature released the remaining suits in 1895. The Democratic legislature during Peck's administration also redrew the legislative boundaries twice; both attempts to gerrymander to perpetuate Democratic rule were set aside by the Wisconsin Supreme Court as unconstitutional.

Peck was nominated for governor again in 1894, although he had not sought the nomination. His equivocation on the nomination seemed to portend the defeat he suffered in this try for a third term. Historians have attributed his loss to a variety of causes, including the 1893 depression, the general decline of Democratic party popularity throughout the country, the gerrymandering by the Democratic legislature, and the McKinley Tariff. Following Peck's loss, he stayed out of politics until 1904, when he made one more run at the governorship but was handily defeated by Robert M. La Follette. He then retired permanently from political office. However, several authors have pointed out that he continued to "hold court in the lobbies of the Plankinton and Pfister hotels in Milwaukee" and, together with Mayor David Rose, was considered to largely control the Democratic party in the early 1900s.

He continued to write books of humor, although none achieved the phenomenal success of the original *Peck's Bad Boy and His Pa*. That book later provided the material for the Atkinson Comedy Company's play *Peck's Bad Boy*, which toured the country for several years. Charles George wrote a version that was sold for amateur productions in 1938. Probably the most famous portrayal of the Bad Boy was by the renowned entertainer George M. Cohan, who played the character while touring as a young man with his father, mother, and sister. The paperback versions of Peck's books appeared

for years on newsstands and were popular in train stations for light reading.

Peck remained a familiar figure in Milwaukee with his gray moustache and goatee, eyeglasses, and a perennial red carnation boutonniere on his lapel. He occasionally lectured after his retirement from politics. He died 16 April 1916, after a short illness.

For a man of such notoriety in his time, Peck has been largely ignored by historians. And yet, his influence in both politics and literature is undisputed. In politics, it can be argued that Peck and the Democrats in 1890 broke the grip of the Wisconsin Republican party and dealt it a blow from which it did not fully recover for many years. While many might argue that Peck's writing is crude and that his humor is slapstick and even cruel, there can be no doubt that his following was broad or that his impact has been lasting. His writing was part of a time when, as one Wisconsin WPA writer put it, "local color became fashionable all over the country. . . . By using dialect, bad spelling and other devices, they stripped off the traditional elegance of book-characters bringing them down to homely levels." Peck was one of the best of these authors. His Bad Boy became the definitive measure of the practical joker and influenced many later writers. Peck's work is often overlooked today, but his influence remains.

Other:

Wisconsin: Comprising Sketches of Counties, Towns, Events, Institutions, and Persons, Arranged in Cyclopedic Form, edited by Peck (Madison, Wis.: Western Historical Association, 1906).

References:
H. Russell Austin, *The Wisconsin Story* (Milwaukee, Wis.: Journal Company, 1948);
Richard Nelson Current, *Wisconsin, A Bicentennial History* (New York: Norton, 1977);
J. E. and J. S. Kallenbach, eds., *American State Governors, 1776-1976*, volume 3 (New York: Oceana, 1982);
Edward S. Kerstein, *Milwaukee's All-American Mayor: Portrait of Daniel Webster Hoan* (Englewood Cliffs, N.J.: Prentice-Hall, 1966);
Allen Fraser Lovejoy, *La Follette and the Establishment of the Direct Primary in Wisconsin, 1890-1904* (Madison: Historical Society of Wisconsin, 1959);
William Francis Raney, *Wisconsin, A Story of Progress* (New York: Prentice-Hall, 1940);
Bayrd Still, *Milwaukee: The History of a City* (Madison:

State Historical Society of Wisconsin, 1948);
Ellis Baker Usher, "New England in Wisconsin," *New England Magazine*, 22 (June 1900): 458;
"The Wisconsin Election," *Harper's Weekly* (15 November 1890): 899;
Workers of the Writer's Program of WPA in Wisconsin, *Wisconsin* (New York: Duell, Sloan & Pearce, 1941).

Benjamin Perley Poore
(2 November 1820-29 May 1887)

Joseph P. McKerns
Southern Illinois University

MAJOR POSITION HELD: Washington correspondent, *Boston Journal* (1854-1883).

BOOKS: *The Rise and Fall of Louis Philippe, Ex-King of the French; Giving a History of the French Revolution, from Its Commencement in 1789* (Boston: Ticknor, 1848);
Life of Gen. Zachary Taylor, the Whig Candidate for the Presidency (Boston: Stacy, Richardson, 1848);
The Early Life and First Campaigns of Napoleon Bonaparte; with a History of the Bonaparte Family and a Review of French Politics to the Year 1796 (Boston: Ticknor, Reed & Fields, 1851);
The Marmaluke; or, The Sign of the Mystic Tie: A Tale of the Camp and Court of Bonaparte (Boston: Gleason, 1852);
The Russian Guardsman: A Tale of the Seas and Shores of the East (New York: French, 1852);
Historical Materials for the Biography of W. T. G. Morton, M.D., Discoverer of Etherization (Washington, D.C.: Gideon, 1856);
The Scout; or, Sharpshooters of the Revolution (Boston: Office of the Flag of Our Union, the Welcome Guest & Ballou's Dollar Monthly, 1860);
The West Point Cadet; or, The Turns of Fortune's Wheel (Boston: Elliott, Thomas & Talbot, 1863);
Trial of Andrew Johnson, President of the United States, before the Senate of the United States, on Impeachment by the House of Representatives for High Crimes and Misdemeanors (Washington, D.C.: Government Printing Office, 1868);
The Life and Public Services of John Sherman (Cincinnati: Sherman Club, 1880);
The Life and Public Services of Ambrose E. Burnside, Soldier,–Citizen,–Statesman (Providence, R.I.: Reid, 1882);
Life of U. S. Grant, by Poore and O. H. Tiffany (Philadelphia & New York: Hubbard, 1885);

Benjamin Perley Poore

Perley's Reminiscences of Sixty Years in the National Metropolis, 2 volumes (Philadelphia: Hubbard / New York: Houghton, 1886).

Benjamin Perley Poore was one of the first nationally known Washington correspondents after 1850, and his articles on political, military, and social affairs at the capital were published in newspapers and magazines throughout the United States. In addition to his Washington reporting,

Poore wrote numerous articles on subjects as diverse as agriculture and autograph collecting. He published several novels as well as biographies of famous men of his time, but unlike these works, which generally were forgotten after being widely read in his time, his work as a federal government researcher, compiler, and editor of government publications, indexes, and directories has withstood time and remains valuable and useful today.

His nearly sixty-seven years of life were filled with activity, including several brief stints in the military and the diplomatic corps. He also served as clerk of several important congressional committees between the 1850s and the end of his life; was considered something of an expert on agriculture; and had a good reputation as an antiquarian, amateur architect, and printer. Poore was a fixture in Washington society after 1850, and it was said that "he knew more American public men than probably any other living man." Because of this he was considered a "rich reservoir of reminiscences" and was a popular orator and after-dinner speaker.

He may have been a "jack of all trades," but the basis for his reputation and success was his role as a Washington correspondent whose influence others—including politicians—sought, respected, and envied. During the last half of the nineteenth century, when the groundwork for the present relationship between the press and the federal government was being laid, Poore was among the most important and respected of the correspondents. He was intimate with Washington's leading statesmen, most notably Senator Charles Sumner, and it was said that he never betrayed a trust, nor was he accused of a conflict of interest even though he was an employee of the government he reported on for nearly thirty years. The course of his professional career is, in many ways, the story of the development of the Washington press corps before the turn of the century. At the time of his death, his pen name, "Perley," was recognized by thousands of newspaper and magazine readers.

Poore, the oldest of four children, was born 2 November 1820 at Indian Hill, his family's 400-acre farm near Newburyport, a Massachusetts town thirty-six miles northeast of Boston. The Poore family, like other families in the region, was land-wealthy and proud of its Anglo-American heritage. At the time of Poore's birth Indian Hill had been in the family's possession for six generations, dating back to the middle of the seventeenth century. As the family's historian, Poore traced its roots to Normandy before 1066 and numbered among its lineage several prominent English bishops and gov-

ernment ministers. Poore's father, Benjamin, was a successful dry-goods merchant in Newburyport whose business interests extended into the Deep South and who frequently visited Washington, D.C., the city that would become his son's second home in later years. Young Benjamin's mother, Mary Perley Dodge, was a native of Georgetown, D.C., but her family had come originally from Hamilton, Massachusetts.

Because of the elder Poore's business, the family temporarily moved to New York City in 1822, where young Benjamin attended city schools after 1827. However, Poore's formal education was interrupted several times for extensive travel with his family. In 1831, when he was eleven, Poore's father took him to Europe, where he introduced the boy to the Marquis de Lafayette, Sir Walter Scott, and Thomas Moore. On another trip with his father in 1836, young Poore was introduced to Andrew Jackson at the Hermitage, where he obtained the aging president's autograph. Between trips Poore continued to attend day schools in New York and then was enrolled in Dummer Academy in South Byfield, Massachusetts. His father wanted his son to attend West Point and embark on a military career, but the youth had his own plans and ran away from home for two years to learn the printer's trade in a shop in Worcester. By 1836 he and his father had reconciled, apparently on the condition that a military career not be in his future. In 1838 Poore is supposed to have written his first newsletter from Washington, D.C., although it is uncertain what its contents were or to whom it was sent.

Poore's formal entry into journalism came in January 1839, when, at eighteen, he became editor of the *Southern Whig* in Athens, Georgia, a newspaper his father had purchased with the intention of making it the voice of the Whig party in the South. The *Whig* under Poore's editorship has been described as a creditable newspaper that printed clear and accurate editorials expressing conservative Whig ideas. On the whole, it was a bright and vigorous publication, but it was no match for Athens's other newspaper, the *Southern Banner*, edited by Albon Chase. Chase's paper was the strongest Democratic journal in northeast Georgia. The editorial battles between Poore and Chase were usually started by Poore but were won by Chase, who assumed a patient, patronizing tone toward the New Englander. By January 1841, Poore's stay in Athens had begun to sour. Not only was the paper losing money, but by the end of that month Poore became involved in a scandal of sorts. On the night of 30 January 1841 he held at his home in Athens a party that was to become known as the "Mulatto Ball." The party resulted in the indictment of Poore and his male friends for "dancing, carousing, hugging and embracing Negro slave women." In the ensuing trial Poore was found not guilty, but for decades afterward the rumor persisted that he was found guilty and fined $400. On 12 February Poore announced in the *Whig* that he was ceasing his duties with the paper, and his name was dropped from the masthead. However, this may only have been a ploy to remove himself from the public eye for a time, because on 13 April his name reappeared on the masthead, and he openly resumed his duties. Nevertheless, his problems continued when on 21 May the Athens newspapers reported that a friend of Poore's had confessed to helping a slave escape to the North. Poore began to receive anonymous letters, and on 18 June he announced that he would leave Athens. The issue of 13 August was the last to bear his name, and on 11 October 1841 control of the paper passed to J. W. Jones.

After leaving Athens, Poore went to Europe, where until 1844 he served as an attaché to the American legation in Brussels. He traveled to Greece, Turkey, Egypt, and North Africa as well as throughout central and southern Europe, all the while sending home letters describing what he saw. These letters were published in the *Boston Atlas* and the *Hartford Courant* and were signed "Perley." Although Poore had been paid for his articles in the *Atlas* and received commissions for his work as an authorized agent of the Massachusetts legislature to collect documents in the French archives pertaining to American colonial history, he was apparently short of money when he returned to the United States in late 1847, because he reluctantly set aside plans to attend law school to become the Washington correspondent for the *Atlas*. His stint with the paper was brief because in 1848 he took leave to write, at the request of Thurlow Weed, the campaign biography of General Zachary Taylor.

After the election he returned to Boston and assumed editorial management of the *Boston Daily Bee* on 2 December 1848. In his first month as editor he made plans to start a Sunday newspaper, *Perley's Sunday Picnic*, which appeared in January 1849 but soon failed. He also began to find his duties with the *Bee* irksome, and he relinquished control when the paper was merged with the *Atlas*. Once again he served a brief stint as the Washington correspondent for the *Atlas*. While he was in Washington, he married his cousin, Virginia Dodge of Georgetown, on 12 June 1849. By 29 December he was back in Boston to found the *Sunday Sentinel*, also known as

the *American Sentinel*, which he used to "ventilate his passion for Native Americanism." The Poores' first daughter, Emily, was born on 19 March 1850. Poore sold the *Sentinel* on 3 May 1851, when it was merged with another Know-Nothing paper, the *Yankee Nation*.

Poore spent the period between 1851 and 1854 writing to support himself and his family. In those years he wrote a biography of Napoleon Bonaparte; several short novels that were serialized in *Gleason's Pictorial Drawing-Room Companion*, a Boston weekly; and numerous articles for magazines, including a fifteen-part series on autographs and how they indicated mental character. It is not clear when Poore left Massachusetts to go to Washington as the correspondent for the *Boston Journal*, the leading Republican newspaper in the city in its time. From letters written to his wife after December 1852, it is evident that he was living in Washington and earning a steady income, but whether that income came from the *Journal* is not certain. Nevertheless, it was in 1854 that the soon-to-be famous pen name "Perley" appeared for the first time in the *Journal*. Also in 1854, Poore's second daughter, Alice, was born on 27 August. (Both of Poore's children died before their twenty-ninth birthdays.)

Poore kept the *Journal*, which was published daily except for Sundays and holidays, well supplied with Washington news. When Congress was in session he sent condensed versions of the daily proceedings of both houses, probably by mail; daily dispatches by telegraph; and his letters, also by mail, which were printed as a standing column called "Waifs from Washington." Poore averaged between one and three "Waifs" columns a week for the next twenty-nine years. The letters, which were published two or three days after they were dated in Washington, were unlike the letters of correspondents who wrote before the advent of the telegraph. They were not the primary news channel from Washington; instead they were closer in style and content to the writings of Washington columnists in the twentieth century in that they offered background, comment, and reflection on important news as well as personal items, social notices, and some gossip.

Poore, like the other early "regular" Washington correspondents, was a generalist in that he covered the House and Senate and their committees, the White House and its departments, and Washington society. Each day he made his rounds, usually beginning at breakfast with some politician, then to the Capitol for the day's business, followed by visits to the White House, the executive departments, dinner with another politician, and probably a social gathering in the evening. Washington reporting during most of Poore's career was not a year-round job, because when Congress was not in session, the correspondents, like the congressmen, abandoned the city for home. The city's society and the federal government, like the journalists who covered them, keyed their activity to Congress. This pattern would not change until the Reconstruction period when Washington correspondence would become a year-round job for the first time. This would be followed, at about the time of Poore's death in 1887, by the beginning of specialization in correspondence.

Poore was already familiar to Washington society before he began writing for the *Journal*, so he was quickly able to establish a reputation as a correspondent who had an intimate understanding of "men and measures." Poore was both an influential observer of government and an influential participant in government. He personally knew each of the presidents of his time and seemed to be particularly friendly with Abraham Lincoln and U. S. Grant. He was on intimate terms with powerful politicians such as Charles Sumner, Henry Anthony, Ambrose E. Burnside, Samuel Hooper, and Henry Wilson. Poore took advantage of these friendships, as well as his talent for research, to obtain appointments as clerk of several important congressional committees during his career, including the Foreign Relations Committees of both the House and the Senate and the Senate Committee on Printing and Records. He served as clerk of the latter for nearly two decades, and in that capacity he was the first editor and compiler of the *Congressional Directory*. Other correspondents received similar appointments, but Poore's were the most notable. The issue of conflict of interest was never raised because, in Poore's words, correspondents were "neither eavesdroppers nor interviewers, but gentlemen, who had a recognized position in society which they never abused."

Poore maintained his allegiance to the Know-Nothings until after the 1856 presidential campaign, in which he supported Millard Fillmore. He then broke with the party because of its bigotry and hostility to Roman Catholicism. Fillmore lost the election, but Poore became a celebrity because of a wager he made with Col. Robert I. Burbank that Fillmore would receive more votes in Massachusetts than John C. Frémont. The loser of the wager would push a wheelbarrow of apples from his home to the winner's. When Fillmore lost, Burbank of-

fered to release Poore from his debt, but Poore insisted on honoring the wager. It took Poore three days to wheel the apples the thirty-six miles from Newburyport to Boston. Crowds lined the route and cheered the jovial Poore onward. When he arrived in Boston he was escorted up State Street by the Boston Fusileers.

In the spring of 1852, Poore had organized the First Battalion of Rifles in Newburyport. The battalion, also known as Ben Poore's Savages, was the first corps to volunteer when the Civil War began. It became companies A, B, and C of the Nineteenth Massachusetts Regiment. Within weeks after the attack on Fort Sumter, Poore was commissioned a major in the Eighth Massachusetts Regiment under the command of General Benjamin F. Butler and stationed at Annapolis. However, after three months of drilling raw recruits, Poore was back in Washington as a civilian. Nevertheless, for the remainder of his life he was addressed as "Major Poore." He reported on the political and military aspects of the war from Washington, while the *Journal*'s great war correspondent, Charles Carleton Coffin, covered the conflict from the battlefield. Poore, like many other correspondents, agreed with the principle of censorship during war, but he hated its practice. He was one of the correspondents' leading spokesmen in the ongoing protest against the capriciousness of the censorship. He led a delegation of journalists to the home of Secretary of State William Seward to protest the closing of the telegraph offices early in the war, and he became particularly incensed when one of his dispatches was blocked because he had mentioned that it was snowing in the city. Like many Civil War correspondents, Poore saw the building of civilian and military morale as an essential part of his work. Governor John A. Andrew of Massachusetts said that Poore's services at Washington "in creating correct and loyal sentiment throughout the Union, were as important as those of a regiment on the battlefield."

After the war, Poore's duties were expanded to include coverage of the political nominating conventions; he was present at each party's gatherings until the 1880s, when his health began to fail and extensive travel became difficult. The *Boston Journal* supported Radical Republicanism and its leader, Senator Charles Sumner. However, Poore's more moderate Republicanism and his friendship with Grant began to strain his relationships with both Sumner and the *Journal*. Poore and the *Journal* supported Grant's reelection in 1872, but while he publicly expressed confidence in Grant's ability to defeat Horace Greeley, Poore privately expressed reservations in a letter to his editor, William Warland Clapp: "The danger lies in a 'Tippecanoe' White Hat fever and a general cussedness which may run Greeley in, but I can hardly imagine such a madness." Poore was not uncritical of Grant, and he blamed him for hurting the Republican party at a crucial time: "Grant's administration was not an unalloyed success. The strength of the Republican party, which might, with a careful, economical, and strictly honest admiration, have been maintained for a generation, was frittered away and its voters alienated."

Poore was a very popular man-about-town during his career in Washington. He was a storehouse of anecdotes about the famous statesmen, politicians, and military leaders of his time, many of whom he knew personally. Because of his jovial spirit and ready wit, he was among the city's most popular after-dinner speakers.

Poore has a reputation as an antiquarian primarily because of the numerous artifacts from American history that he collected and displayed at Indian Hill, where he lived when Congress was not in session. Poore also had a large collection of autographs, about 15,000, of famous people like Washington, Jackson, and Lafayette. Many of these he collected personally. (These autographs are in the Benjamin Perley Poore collection in Haverhill. Early in the 1900s, Indian Hill was heavily damaged by fire; however, part of it was restored, and Poore's descendants still live there. Many of Poore's artifacts were lost in the fire, however.) Poore was also an amateur architect and was considered something of an expert on agriculture.

With the end of Reconstruction, Poore's career began to wane. In 1880, Poore, the oldest and most distinguished member of the press corps, was sixty years old. As a young man he had been at the forefront of changes in Washington reporting, but, in the 1880s, when many of his colleagues were as much as thirty-five years younger, he found it increasingly difficult to keep pace. Also, it must be noted, many times he simply was unwilling to keep pace. For example, in 1886, when the interview story using direct and indirect quotation was standard practice, Poore called it "a pernicious habit" and a "dangerous method of communication between our public men and the people." Poore, who stuck to the routine of coverage he had used since the 1850s, began to lose his edge on the correspondents from competing Boston newspapers who were paid to stay in the city and report on the government on a year-round basis. Also, as the reports of the Associated Press became more thorough, Poore often found that he was unable to send items faster, or that what he sent duplicated the wire service's reports. Almost in a tone of despair Poore wrote to Clapp in December 1881: "I should feel easier if I could send what I believe to be true, and know that it can be edited in Boston, so as not to conflict with anything the paper may have said. . . . Between the apprehension that some one else has had my news, so that it has got to Boston ahead of me, or that I am saying the wrong thing about someone, I am more cramped that [sic] I should be."

Poore's comment about "conflict with anything the paper may have said" would not have been written a decade earlier, when the paper's political stance was clear. However, by 1881 the *Journal* had lost ground to its Boston competition following the demise of Radical Republicanism and the death of Charles Sumner in 1874. The *Journal* failed to adjust to changes in the Republican party, and Poore was unable to find any consistency in its position on the issues of the day. The strained relationship between the paper and its prized correspondent reached the breaking point in 1883, when, because of a combination of illness and the *Journal*'s refusal to give him more financial security by guaranteeing him a year-round salary, Poore resigned in April.

His resignation did not mean the end of his career, because Poore had always maintained a breadth of activity and had well-established contacts beyond the *Journal*. For example, throughout the 1860s and 1870s he had supplemented his income from the *Journal* by corresponding for the *New Orleans Daily Times*, the *Selma Morning Times*, the *Salem Evening Gazette*, the *Boston Commonwealth*, and the *Chicago Tribune*, and for magazines such as *Harper's Weekly* and the *Atlantic*. He also had an extensive involvement in producing government publications, among them *The Federal and State Constitutions, Colonial Charters, and Other Organic Laws of the United States*, which he compiled in 1877; the *Congressional Record*, which he edited in the 1870s; *The Political Register and Congressional Directory*, published in 1878; and the *Descriptive Catalogue of Government Publications of the United States, September 5, 1774-March 4, 1881*, which was published in 1885.

During the last four years of his life, Poore held on to his seat in the press galleries of Congress by representing the *Boston Budget*, the *Albany Evening Journal*, and the *Omaha Republican*; however, it is likely that because of declining health, Poore wrote only weekly letters to those papers. In the spring of 1884, his doctors told him he had Bright's disease, a kidney ailment, and he also suffered from uremia and drowsiness. Furthermore, he became overweight. He was a tall man, well over six feet, and had always tended to be portly, but in his last years his difficulty in discharging fluids caused his weight to balloon to 330 pounds.

Among the last things he wrote, besides a quickly forgotten, albeit popular, biography of U. S. Grant published in 1885, was his two-volume *Perley's Reminiscences of Sixty Years in the National Metropolis* (1886). It was called a "priceless eye-witness story of the formative period in our national life," and even though the title is somewhat misleading—Poore was actually an eyewitness for only about forty of the years he covered—it has withstood the test of time and is still widely used for information about Washington society and politics in the nineteenth century.

Poore remained active to the very end. On 17 May 1887 he delivered a manuscript on the history of the Ancient and Honorable Artillery Company of Boston, an honorary group which he had commanded, to a Washington printer. Later that day he collapsed at the Capitol and was taken to his suite at the Ebbitt House. At first the diagnosis was heat prostration, but then the doctors changed it to a heart attack. His condition was front-page news nearly every day in the *Washington Star*, and bulletins were published in newspapers in other cities. His condition began to improve, but on 24 May he took a turn for the worse, and on 28 May he had a severe seizure. He was pronounced dead at 12:30 A.M. on 29 May.

The major newspapers of the country, from St. Louis to Boston and Chicago to New Orleans, noted his passing. He was eulogized in the press as "the most prolific writer for the press of his age," and it was said that "few men . . . have accomplished so great an aggregate of work well performed." Many newspapers recognized him as the dean of correspondents in Washington. Poore had seen, and was involved in, changes in his profession that had become standard practices by the time of his death. In his last years he had difficulty keeping pace with change and was a kind of anachronism, yet to the very end he commanded the highest respect of his fellow journalists—for example, he was elected the first president of the Gridiron Club in 1885. When he died, his kind of journalism seemed to die with him.

Other:

The Federal and State Constitutions, Colonial Charters, and Other Organic Laws of the United States, compiled by Poore (Washington, D.C.: Government Printing Office, 1877);

The Political Register and Congressional Directory, edited by Poore (Washington, D.C.: Government Printing Office, 1878);

A Descriptive Catalogue of Government Publications of the United States, September 5, 1774-March 4, 1881, compiled by Poore (Washington, D.C.: Government Printing Office, 1885);

"Recollections of Abraham Lincoln," in *Some Noted Princes, Authors, and Statesmen of Our Time*, edited by James Parton (New York: Crowell, 1885);

"Chapter XI," in *Reminiscences of Abraham Lincoln by Distinguished Men of His Time*, Fifth edition, edited by Allen Thorndike Rice (New York: North American Review, 1888).

Periodical Publications:

"Washington News," *Harper's New Monthly Magazine*, 48 (January 1874): 225-236;

"The Place of Charles Sumner in History," *International Review*, 5 (January 1878): 64-74;

"Chester Alan Arthur," *Bay State Monthly*, 1 (May 1884): 265-277.

References:

Josephine P. Driver, "Ben: Perley Poore of Indian Hill," *Essex Institute Historical Collections*, 89 (January 1953): 1-18;

Joseph Patrick McKerns, "Benjamin Perley Poore of the Boston Journal: His Life and Times as a Washington Correspondent, 1850-1887," Ph.D. dissertation, University of Minnesota, 1979;

McKerns, "Ben: Perley Poore's Reminiscences: A Reliable Source for Research?," *Journalism History*, 2 (Winter 1975-1976): 125-127;

John E. Talmadge, "Ben: Perley Poore's Stay in Athens," *Georgia Historical Quarterly*, 41 (September 1957): 247-254.

Papers:

Benjamin Perley Poore's papers are located in the Benjamin Perley Poore Collection, Haverhill, Massachusetts, Public Library; the Benjamin Perley Poore Papers, Library of Congress; and the William Warland Clapp Collection, Library of Congress.

Joseph Pulitzer

Terry Hynes
California State University, Fullerton

BIRTH: Mako, Hungary, 10 April 1847, to Philip and Louise Berger Politzer.

MARRIAGE: 19 June 1878 to Kate Davis; children: Ralph, Lucille, Katherine, Joseph Jr., Edith, Constance, Herbert.

MAJOR POSITIONS HELD: Reporter, *St. Louis Westliche Post* (1868-1872); correspondent, *New York Sun* (1876-1878); publisher, *St. Louis Post-Dispatch* (1878-1911), *New York World* (1883-1911).

DEATH: On his yacht off the coast of Charleston, South Carolina, 29 October 1911.

One of the most powerful and respected newspaper publishers in American journalism history, Joseph Pulitzer built his empire with two major newspapers in the post-Civil War era. His somewhat paradoxical achievements as a "New Journalist" and "yellow journalist" of the 1880s and 1890s reflect his efforts to combine editorial crusading on behalf of the middle class (in St. Louis) and the poor (in New York) with a highly competitive and financially profitable business enterprise. His legacy to the journalism profession includes his endowment of the Columbia University School of Journalism (opened in 1912) and establishment of the Pulitzer Prizes, awarded annually since 1917.

Born in Mako, Hungary, about 135 miles southeast of Budapest, on 10 April 1847, Pulitzer was the son of a Magyar-Jewish father, Philip, and a Christian, Austro-German mother, Louise Berger. He was the second of four children: Louis was the oldest; Albert was third; and Irma was the youngest and the only girl. Both Louis and Irma died young. Philip Politzer (as the family spelled the name in Hungary) was a partner in a prosperous grain business in Mako from about 1840 until 1853, when the firm was dissolved and he moved to Budapest, where he retired and lived comfortably with his family until he died of heart disease. Louis and Joseph went to private school and had a special tutor until their father's death, when the family's financial circumstances became strained. After a

Joseph Pulitzer (Brown Brothers)

few years, Louise Politzer married a merchant, Max Blau.

Seeking a military career, in 1864 Pulitzer attempted to enlist in the Austrian army, the French Foreign Legion, and the British armed forces. All rejected him because of his weak eyes and frail physique. A recruiter for the Union army, however, accepted him and shipped him to the United States. Pulitzer collected his own enlistment bounty by jumping ship in Boston and going to New York, where he enlisted on 30 September 1864 in a cavalry regiment organized by Carl Schurz, with whom he would later be associated in St. Louis. Pulitzer saw little fighting and was released from the army in early July 1865. Later that same year, still unable to speak much English, Pulitzer left New York for St. Louis in search of work. He held a series of odd jobs, including working for several lawyers; he studied the books in one lawyer's library and was admitted to the bar. On 6 March 1867 he became a naturalized American citizen. During this period Pulitzer became friends with "Professor" Thomas Davidson, an instructor at St. Louis High School, who generously shared his wealth of knowledge and thus helped Pulitzer satisfy some of his thirst for education. The two remained close friends until Davidson's death in 1900. During these years, too, Pulitzer's circle of friends expanded to include some of the most important local German immigrants, including Schurz and Joseph Keppler, founder of the comic weekly *Puck*.

When an opening occurred on Schurz's German-language daily, the *Westliche Post*, in 1868, Pulitzer was hired as a reporter. Although he had no background in journalism, Pulitzer demonstrated an electrical energy and an exceptional capacity for work and excelled quickly in reporting and interpreting local politics and public affairs. In December 1869, he was elected as a Republican to the Missouri legislature, despite being underage at the time of the election; he served his term simultaneously as a representative of the people and as correspondent for the *Westliche Post*.

In 1872 Pulitzer was actively involved in the Liberal Republican movement, which nominated Horace Greeley for president. After the defeat of this effort to reform the Republican party, Pulitzer became a Democrat. (With a few exceptions, including opposition to William Jennings Bryan in several presidential campaigns and endorsement of Republican Charles Evans Hughes against William Randolph Hearst in the New York gubernatorial campaign of 1906, Pulitzer supported Democratic candidates for the rest of his life.) More importantly for his role in journalism history, some of the proprietors of the *Westliche Post*, who feared the paper was ruined by the Greeley campaign, sold Pulitzer a proprietary interest in the paper on what he considered liberal terms. Within a few months, apparently bored in the dull aftermath of the 1872 campaign, Pulitzer sold his interest in the paper to Schurz and Dr. Emil Preetorious. Using some of the profits from the sale, he returned to Europe to tour the continent and visit his relatives in Hungary.

Shortly after his return from Europe early in 1874, Pulitzer bought a bankrupt St. Louis German daily, the *Staats-Zeitung*, chiefly for its Associated Press franchise. He ran the paper for one day and then sold the franchise for $20,000 to the struggling

St. Louis Globe, edited by J. B. McCullagh. In 1876, the *Globe* was consolidated with another major St. Louis daily to form the *Globe-Democrat*.

Pulitzer continued to be active in local politics and even traversed the state speaking out against Grant's administration and the carpetbaggers. In late 1875, he was elected a delegate to the Missouri constitutional convention, where he argued for a moderate position between the extremes of state's rights and nationalism, supported the right of Missouri citizens to amend their constitution by convention every ten years, fought for state support of public schools, and helped secure an amendment giving St. Louis the right to a new charter. He campaigned actively for Samuel J. Tilden and the Democratic platform during the presidential campaign of 1876.

On a trip to New York in mid-1875, Pulitzer attempted unsuccessfully to buy a German weekly, the *Belletristische Journal*, conducted by Rudolph Lexow. This appears to have been Pulitzer's first serious effort to break into New York journalism. Evidence indicates also that as early as 1876, he discussed, at least casually, with editor Manton

Pulitzer at age twenty-one, about the time he began his journalism career as a reporter on Carl Schurz's St. Louis Westliche Post

Marble the possibility of buying into the *New York World*. Later the same year, after the presidential campaign had ended, Pulitzer went to New York and suggested to Charles A. Dana the initiation of a German edition of the *New York Sun*, which Pulitzer would conduct. Although Dana expressed some interest, his publisher, Isaac W. England, opposed the idea. Probably as a result of this encounter, however, Pulitzer was assigned to the Washington staff of the *Sun* as a political correspondent. His signed dispatches and editorial-page contributions appeared in the *Sun* until Tilden accepted the decision of the electoral commission giving the presidential victory to Rutherford B. Hayes; then Pulitzer traveled again to Europe. In the fall of 1877 he returned to Washington, where he completed the requirements for admission to the bar in the District of Columbia and was thus qualified to practice law in the nation's capital.

The year 1878 was particularly significant both personally and professionally for Pulitzer. He was married on 19 June to Kate Davis at the Episcopal Church of the Epiphany in Washington. Kate has generally been described by Pulitzer's biog-

Kate Davis, whom Pulitzer married in 1878
(Mrs. William C. Weir)

raphers as beautiful, charming, accomplished, and socially well connected. She was the daughter of William Worthington Davis of Georgetown, a distant cousin of Jefferson Davis, and Catherine Louise Worthington of the Maryland Worthingtons (Kate's parents were cousins). The couple honeymooned in Europe, and during their stay Pulitzer contributed a number of letters to the *Sun* concerning conditions in England and on the Continent.

Professionally, 1878 was the year in which Pulitzer purchased one St. Louis newspaper and consolidated it with another to form the *Post-Dispatch*. When he returned from Europe in late fall of that year, Pulitzer went to St. Louis, apparently intending to establish a law practice. He was attracted by a possible bargain in another realm when, on 9 December, the sheriff offered for sale on the courthouse steps a bankrupt newspaper, the *Dispatch*. The *Dispatch* had been founded in 1862 as a morning daily, the *Union*, by a group including journalist Frank P. Blair, who wanted to give President Lincoln strong editorial support. By 1878 its name had been changed; it had become an evening paper; and its ownership, in whole or in part, had changed eight times. By late 1878 its plant was a wreck, its type was worn out, and its credibility in St. Louis was virtually, if not literally, zero. It had at least one plus, however: like the *Staats-Zeitung*, which Pulitzer had bought in 1874, the *Dispatch* had an AP franchise. Pulitzer figured he could offer $2,500 for it and still have $2,700 left to run it for at least a few months. The *Dispatch*'s creditors claimed it was worth $40,000, but they accepted the $2,500 offered by Pulitzer's agent. Thus Pulitzer acquired the paper and its belongings, subject to a $30,000 lien.

The next day, a column headed "What Will He Do With It?" appeared in the rival evening paper, the *Post*. John A. Dillon, a former member of the *Globe-Democrat* staff, had founded the *Post* in January 1875. On the evening of 10 December 1878 Dillon, possibly anxious about what Pulitzer might do with that AP franchise, proposed to Pulitzer a consolidation of the two papers on equal terms. Pulitzer agreed and, on the afternoon of 12 December, the paper was issued as the *Post and Dispatch*, a title shortened two weeks later to *Post-Dispatch*.

The prospectus for the new paper embodied Pulitzer's philosophy as a "people's champion." The ideas expressed there contain the roots of a social-responsibility notion of the press and suggest why Pulitzer is often regarded as one of the "New Jour-

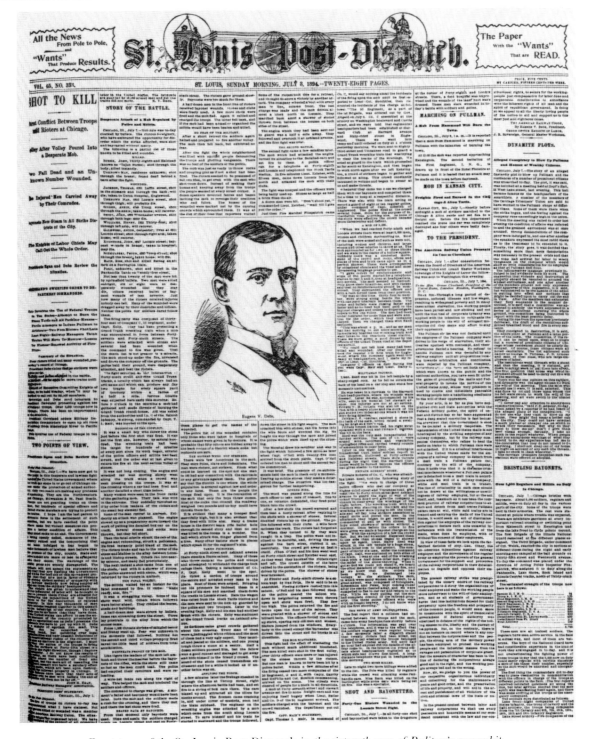

Front page of the St. Louis Post-Dispatch *in the sixteenth year of Pulitzer's ownership*

nalists" of the post-Civil War era who realized that access to the free marketplace of ideas was not automatic in an industrialized economy in which even newspapers had become "big business." The owners promised high ideals: "The *Post and Dispatch* will serve no party but the people; will be no organ of Republicanism, but the organ of truth; will follow no causes but its conclusions; will not support the 'Administration,' but criticize it; will oppose all frauds and shams wherever and whatever they are; will advocate principles and ideas rather than prejudices and partisanship. . . ."

Pulitzer crusaded against systematic tax dodging by the wealthy. He embarrassed the latter by printing in parallel columns the local tax returns from rich and poor to indicate the disproportionate amount being paid by those who could least afford it. He exposed corrupt gambling practices and supported a permanent exposition building, cleaning and repairing of streets, and the beginning of the city park system. Challenged by some of his creditors concerning his right to hold an AP franchise which had been granted to previous owners, Pulitzer took the case to the United States Supreme Court, which confirmed his possession of the franchise.

The Pulitzer-Dillon partnership lasted approximately one year, until Pulitzer bought out Dillon's interest and became sole owner. Pulitzer gathered about him talented journalists to carry out the assertive philosophy he had set for the paper. The one among these journalists most responsible for the success of the *Post-Dispatch* was John A. Cockerill, already a widely experienced newspaperman when he joined Pulitzer's staff in 1879.

Born in Ohio, 5 December 1845, "Colonel" Cockerill had been a drummer boy and bugler in the Civil War. He later said, "I saw all that I cared to of war and prefer reading about it to being in it." After an apprenticeship on various Ohio newspapers, Cockerill joined the *Cincinnati Enquirer* when J. B. McCullagh was chief of its staff. By 1872 Cockerill had become managing editor, and in 1877 he gave up the desk to become the paper's correspondent in the Russo-Turkish War. He retired from the paper on his return and served on the *Washington Post* and the *Baltimore Gazette* before joining Pulitzer in 1879.

Pulitzer continued to be actively involved in Democratic politics after the formation of the *Post-Dispatch*. In 1880 he was elected a delegate to the national Democratic convention at Cincinnati and served on the convention's platform committee. In September of that year he was a candidate for Congress in the Democratic primary, but he lost the nomination to Thomas Allen, president of the Iron Mountain Railroad. After this defeat Pulitzer gave his full attention for a while to the *Post-Dispatch*.

By 1881 the newspaper was prosperous enough to be moved to new headquarters on Market Street, where two Hoe presses were installed to meet its increasing needs. The profits by then were estimated at between $40,000 and $85,000 per year. But the growth had come at some cost to Pulitzer's health, and in early 1882, he cut back the time he was devoting to the paper and left more responsibility in Cockerill's hands.

In October 1882 the fortunes of the paper were shadowed by an event involving Cockerill. During the congressional elections of that year, Cockerill opposed editorially the candidacy of a local lawyer who was a member of a large law firm. Cockerill's strong attacks impugned not only the candidate but the entire firm, and later that month, another member of the firm, Col. Alonzo W. Slayback, went to Cockerill's office, determined to achieve satisfaction for the insults. In the course of the verbal altercation which resulted, Cockerill took a revolver from his desk and killed Slayback. Cockerill was never formally prosecuted, but the incident resulted in much negative publicity; the *Post-Dispatch* lost circulation in the highly charged critical climate, in which its policy of personal attacks was denounced. Although Pulitzer remained loyal to Cockerill throughout the episode, he also induced his former partner, Dillon, to take over the general management of the paper in an effort to restore its credibility in the community.

In subsequent years, Pulitzer continued to feel unwelcome in St. Louis (after 1889 he did not even visit the city), and the immediate effect of the excitement and anxiety resulting from the events of the Cockerill-Slayback affair was Pulitzer's further physical debilitation. Early in May 1883 Pulitzer set out for Europe, where he intended to follow his physician's advice for a long and complete rest. Instead, the European trip was aborted in New York, where Pulitzer found an opportunity from which he was to refuse ever to rest completely during the remaining years of his life.

Pulitzer's younger brother, Albert, who had come to the United States after the Civil War, was already the publisher of a moderately successful New York newspaper, the *Morning Journal*, which he had started in November 1882. (Some sources claim Pulitzer made a small contribution to the $25,000 capital investment Albert needed to start the paper, although he had little faith that Albert would succeed. The brothers were, in fact, bitter rivals, and after he bought the *World*, Pulitzer raided his brother's *Journal* for some of his best staff. Albert sold his paper early in 1895 to John R. McLean, publisher of the sensational *Cincinnati Enquirer*, who sold it later the same year to William Randolph Hearst. Albert committed suicide in Vienna in October 1909.) In 1883, also, New York had no strong Democratic voice among the city's newspapers. As Joseph Pulitzer surveyed the scene on Newspaper Row in early May, he discovered that financier Jay Gould had decided to wind up his newspaper affairs and was willing to consider the sale of his morning paper, the *New York World*.

The *World* had been established in June 1860 by Alexander Cummings, a Philadelphia journalist, as a one-cent daily with a religious orientation. In late November 1860 its price was doubled and, although Cummings sought to strengthen the paper by absorbing the *Courier and Enquirer* in July 1861 (thus gaining an AP franchise), he was forced to sell because of heavy losses. Subsequently the paper was held by a group of Democratic financiers and politicians who appointed Manton Marble managing editor. Under Marble's leadership the *World* prospered briefly as a Democratic organ in the mid- and late 1860s. Marble gained control of the paper in December 1869, but it went into decline, and he sold it in late 1876 to a syndicate headed by Thomas Scott, head of the Pennsylvania Railroad. Even under the able editorship of William Henry Hurlbert, who had been an editorial writer on the *World* for some years and foreign editor of the *Times* in the late 1850s, the paper continued to lose circulation, and in 1879, Scott sold it to Jay Gould. Gould was not particularly interested in the *World* and indeed claimed that he got the paper largely by accident. Although Gould moved the paper to a new building in 1881 and installed Hoe presses and made other improvements to modernize the plant, the *World* continued to decline. By 1883, its daily and Sunday circulations were approximately 11,000 and 15,000 respectively, and the paper was costing Gould $40,000 a year.

Thus, although the *World*, like the two other papers Pulitzer had bought, did have an AP franchise, Pulitzer was faced again with a paper that was ill regarded, low circulating, and a financial loser. Nonetheless, Pulitzer saw opportunity and challenge and opened negotiations. By 8 May, the deal was made, and Pulitzer paid Gould the first installment of the agreed-upon (and, according to most authorities, exorbitant) price of $346,000 before taking over as publisher on 10 May.

Pulitzer's prospectus for the *World*, which appeared in the paper the morning of 11 May, reflected a crusading spirit similar to that expressed in the *Post-Dispatch* in 1878. Pulitzer claimed to make no promises, but his statement in the *World* contained some general, idealistic goals and read in part: "There is room in this great and growing city for a journal that is not only cheap but bright, not only bright but large, not only large but truly democratic—dedicated to the cause of the people rather than that of purse potentates—devoted more to the news of the New than the Old World—that will expose all fraud and sham, fight all public evils and abuses—that will serve and battle for the people with earnest sincerity. In that cause and for that end solely the new *World* is hereby enlisted and committed to the attention of the intelligent public."

However idealistically inflated, the *World*'s prospectus reflects some of Pulitzer's fundamental beliefs about the purpose of his newspapers. First, it indicates his desire to appeal to a mass audience. His promise to offer in the *World* a journal "not only bright but large, not only large but truly democratic" obviously means a newspaper covering a broad scope of interests and events. But the broad range was intended to attract a large audience, one composed of readers with diverse needs for newspaper content. Pulitzer was once quoted in E. L. Godkin's *New York Evening Post* as saying, "I want to talk to a nation, not to a select committee." The desire for a mass audience was practical as well as philosophical: Pulitzer needed a large circulation for financial stability and profit. As he commented shortly before his death to Alleyne Ireland, one of his secretaries: "If a newspaper is to be of real service to the public, it must have a big circulation, first because its news and its comments must reach the largest possible number of people, second, because circulation means advertising, and advertising means money, and money means independence." The pragmatic Pulitzer was always conscious of his newspapers' ledgers, and in later years, although he would sometimes forgo information about the *World*'s content and rarely cared about the content of the *Post-Dispatch*, he always insisted on having full knowledge of the balance sheets for both newspapers.

The prospectus shows another of Pulitzer's basic concerns: his aim to crusade for the causes he championed as part of his perceived responsibility to serve the public. Principally, Pulitzer sought to achieve this through the editorial page. As many commentators have noted, he had a special affection and respect for the editorial page of his newspapers, the one page designed for readers' enlightenment and education. One biographer even claims that for Pulitzer the editorial page *was* the paper.

The result of these interests was a somewhat curious mix in his papers of flashy sex (within the Victorian framework) and crime stories and other sensational reporting on the news pages with a vital but more sober appeal in the arguments on the editorial pages. It should be noted, however, that the sensational reporting itself was at least occasionally used not only to increase circulation but also to agitate for reform: in 1884-1885, for example, the *World* published a series of articles regarding police brutality against innocent victims; finally, in the spring of 1885, the paper contained an editorial against the abuses. Later in the decade other reports, like Nellie Bly's sensational investigative articles on life in a madhouse and the working conditions of shop girls, were also accompanied or followed by editorial appeals.

Within a week after assuming ownership of the *World*, Pulitzer brought Cockerill and John B. McGuffin to New York from the *Post-Dispatch*. Cockerill was placed in charge of the editorial side; McGuffin was made head of the business department, a position which he held until his death a few years later.

As a two-cent morning daily, the *World* undercut its competition. In the resulting circulation war, the *Times* and the *Herald* reduced their prices by the end of September from four and three cents, respectively, to two cents per copy; and the *Tribune* reduced its price from four to three cents. Pulitzer viewed these changes as victories for the *World*. According to some sources, circulation of the *World* jumped from approximately 28,000 in May to 39,000 by mid-August 1883. Then Dana made the unpopular choice of supporting Benjamin F. Butler in the presidential campaign of 1884, and the *Sun*'s circulation began to shrink. In contrast, Pulitzer's editorial endorsement of Grover Cleveland helped the *World* to increase its circulation further.

As in St. Louis, in New York Pulitzer continued to be actively involved in politics, not only through the editorial pages of the *World* but also by agreeing to run for the House of Representatives. He was elected from the Ninth District of New York to serve in the forty-ninth Congress, which began in December 1885; but he was so distracted from his responsibilities as a representative by his desire to be involved in the daily activities of the *World* that he resigned from Congress, effective 10 April 1886. Pulitzer's political sympathies were fundamentally democratic, and his allegiance to the Democratic party after 1872 was solid, but he wanted to maintain political independence in order to be free to carry on his crusades for social reforms.

As a manager, Pulitzer, like Hearst, had a knack for choosing the fittest, most talented persons to be on the staffs of his papers; Cockerill was one of the best of these. But Pulitzer's management style also reflected his theory that two persons performing the same functions were each compelled to do their competitive best. Although Pulitzer may have intended the competition to be focused on doing

the most for the papers, it sometimes was directed to the antagonists' undoing of each other. Thus, for example, Ballard Smith was brought to the *World* in March 1885 from the *New York Herald* to perform duties very similar to Cockerill's. George W. Turner, who came to the *World* as business manager two years later, was placed in competition with both Cockerill and Smith. To placate Cockerill, in 1890 Pulitzer exiled Smith to the Brooklyn office of the *World*. The next year, rather than submit to their demands for stock interest in the newspaper, Pulitzer discharged Turner and assigned Cockerill to St. Louis to resume management of the *Post-Dispatch*. Cockerill refused, and he resigned to become editor of the *New York Commercial Advertiser*. This explosive end to their long association was the direct result of Pulitzer's management policy of fostering antagonisms, a policy which, although at times exhilarating, also bred tension, distrust, and resentment among many staff members. Even some of Pulitzer's most loyal staffers considered the policy mean or, at best, unproductive.

Pulitzer wanted the finest journalists for the *World*, and he was willing to pay to get them. At a time when the average reporter's salary was $20-25 per week, some staff reporters earned as high as $50-80 per week; and free-lancers often found the *World* their highest bidder. The *World* did not, in the early years at least, have a standard price per column for a story, but would pay according to how newsworthy it judged the story to be.

Yet for all the vitality infused into the staff in those early years, the makeup and typography of the *World* remained relatively unchanged for some time after Pulitzer took over. It continued generally as an eight-page daily, with each page divided into seven columns (as opposed to six columns before Pulitzer's time). Headlines continued to cover one column only, although the number of subheads in a major story increased. It was probably not until 1889 that the first two-column head appeared in the *World*. The Sunday edition ordinarily had more pages (usually twenty) after Pulitzer bought the paper and expanded its content, but the layout was as subdued as in the daily editions.

Pulitzer did introduce some minor but relatively significant changes in the appearance of the paper. He changed the flag by restoring from the 1860 editions the simple two-word title and, between the words *The* and *World*, the vignette of two globes surrounding the figure of Liberty, from which streamed rays of light. A Pulitzer typographical innovation which appeared in the paper as early as June 1883 and which was widely imitated by

The gold-domed Pulitzer Building on Park Row, which at 309 feet was the tallest structure in New York City when it opened in December 1890 (Brown Brothers)

techniques Pulitzer adopted to attract readers was the use of illustrations. He began rather timidly to illustrate the news in late May 1883 and claimed at the outset that the *World* would make no attempt to compete with the *Graphic* in this field. In subsequent months, however, the *World* printed an increasing number of cuts. Pulitzer commissioned the Russian artist Valerian Gribayédoff to produce illustrations that were often printed on page one above the fold, visible on the newsstand to those who walked by. In 1884, Walt McDougall was hired to do political cartoons. Pulitzer apparently had some misgivings about the illustrations and in about 1885 ordered them removed; but when circulation of the *World* declined in their absence, illustrations were restored to the newspaper.

During the 1880s, Pulitzer's editorial campaigns included pleas to the public for money to complete the pedestal for Bartholdi's Statue of Liberty, an exposé of political corruption involving the awarding of a streetcar franchise in the city (the "Broadway Boodlers" case), as well as crusades against the New York Central, the Standard Oil Company, the Bell telephone monopoly, the Pacific Railroad lobbyists of 1887, the Louisiana lottery, and police corruption and inefficiency.

By the end of 1888, Pulitzer's ever-frail nerves were shattered and his weak eyesight had become increasingly troublesome. After a series of trips to California and Europe, with no improvement in his health and further deterioration of his eyesight, Pulitzer finally accepted his doctors' advice that, if he was to regain his health, he must remove himself from the stress of active involvement in the daily affairs of the *World*. In October 1890 he placed control of the *World* in an executive board of its principal editors, who were to carry out his policies in his absence. Thus began Pulitzer's self-imposed exile from the offices of the newspaper—an exile which lasted until his death in 1911. Yet, although Pulitzer was physically absent during the last twenty-one years of his life, he maintained almost daily contact with the paper and exerted his influence through a barrage of cables and other messages which served as a clear reminder (if any were needed) to all his staff of his control over the content and operation of the paper.

After Turner was fired in 1891, John A. Dillon was brought to New York from the *Post-Dispatch* to serve as business manager. He was ineffective in this position and was transferred to the editorial page in the latter part of 1892. He was succeeded for a while by Frederick Driscoll, who was followed by John Norris of the *Philadelphia Record*. Norris was sent to

other newspapers was the introduction of "ears" in the empty spaces of the flag on either side of the title. At first circles, then squares or rectangles, the ears were used to advertise the newspaper's price, circulation, and other advantages, or to capsule the weather report and other similar announcements that might attract readers. Among slogans which appeared as self-advertisements in the *World*'s ears were "Bright, Newsy, and Entertaining" and "Good Stories, Bright Sketches, Fresh Gossip." By 1885, even small cartoons were placed in the ears to tout the *World*'s rising circulation or advertising achievements.

Beginning as early as May 1885, Pulitzer also experimented with the placement of the lead story on the front page. The custom at the time was to place the lead in the extreme left column of the page, the logic being that people read from left to right. Pulitzer reversed the practice by sometimes placing the lead in the far-right column and putting the second lead in the left column. Another of the

Front page of the New York World, *showing several of the alterations Pulitzer made in the paper: the flag with its double-globe logo; the "ears" on each side of the flag; the one-cent price; the placement of the lead story in the right-hand column; and the large, attention-getting illustration*

the *Post-Dispatch* in 1894.

After the breach with Cockerill in 1891, Pulitzer approved a series of editors to take his place, but none fitted the position quite so well as Cockerill. Ballard Smith was recalled from exile in Brooklyn to serve as editor in chief for a time. Pulitzer found him unsatisfactory, and in 1892, replaced him with S. S. Carvalho, who had been serving as managing editor. Carvalho's title was assistant vice-president and later publisher, rather than editor in chief, and he was given absolute authority over expenses under strict orders to reduce them. In mid-1892, Pulitzer upset the managerial structure again by putting Col. Charles H. Jones in complete charge of the editorial side of the paper, thus placing his authority in conflict with Carvalho's. The arrangement proved highly unsatisfactory, and to resolve conflicts at the *World* as well as to improve the deteriorating operations at the *Post-Dispatch*, Pulitzer appealed to Col. Jones to go to St. Louis. In February 1895, Jones became president, editor, and manager of the *Post-Dispatch* and owner of a one-sixth interest in the paper. (Jones sold his interest back to Pulitzer and left the paper in June 1897.)

The major competitive battle of Pulitzer's career began shortly after Jones's departure. The announcement in the *New York Journal* on 7 November 1895 of William Randolph Hearst's purchase of the newspaper initiated one of the most well-known newspaper wars in journalism history. By then the *World*, in its morning, evening (begun in 1887), and Sunday editions, had become one of the most successful of the New York newspapers. Particularly through his expansion of the mechanical facilities and his application of new techniques to

the content and, by the 1890s, the layout of stories in the *Sunday World*, Pulitzer was the first to demonstrate the profitability of a Sunday newspaper. Thus Hearst, who had already succeeded with the *Examiner* in San Francisco, set himself ultimately in direct competition with Pulitzer.

Hearst's assault on the *World* was both internal and external. Armed with the personal wealth accrued by his father, Hearst bought the staff of the *Sunday World*, beginning with Morrill Goddard, its editor, in January 1896. When Goddard accepted Hearst's offer to join the *Journal*, the rest of his *Sunday World* staff, including Richard Outcault, creator of the "Yellow Kid" ("Hogan's Alley") comic, went with him. Pulitzer's counteroffer to the staff resulted in their return, but only for the twenty-four hours it took for Hearst to outbid Pulitzer again. Thus began "the most extraordinary

THE OPEN-AIR SCHOOL IN HOGAN'S ALLEY.

"Hogan's Alley" comic strip drawn for the World *by George B. Luks after William Randolph Hearst hired the strip's creator, Richard Outcault, away from Pulitzer. The inscription on the "Yellow Kid's" nightshirt refers to the feud between the two publishers.*

The Pulitzer mansion on Seventy-third Street, New York City. The Pulitzers moved into the house in 1904 (Brown Brothers).

curate and unfair to claim that New York's yellow journals alone caused the conflict by fanning war fever through their hyperbolic reporting, it is clear that they capitalized on the situation in Cuba and sensationalized their reporting of the war in the screaming typography which the printing technology of the late 1890s permitted. The sensational reporting of the Cubans' struggles against their Spanish rulers began to escalate in early 1896 when Gen. Valeriano "the Butcher" Weyler was appointed captain-general of the Spanish forces in Cuba. Atrocity stories and emotionally charged descriptions of the Cubans' sufferings as well as lurid pictures of mutilation, imprisonment, and executions appeared in both the *World* and the *Journal*, although the latter is generally credited with more extreme efforts to arouse public feelings. When the United States battleship *Maine* was blown up in Havana harbor in February 1898, both papers published frenzied accounts of the event and of public reaction to it and urged the president and Congress to declare war. Throughout the six months of the war and afterwards the papers continued to report events using such yellow journalism techniques as large, boldface "scare" headlines, lavish pictures, and misrepresentation of facts.

Pulitzer's attitude toward the war seems to have been ambivalent: he reportedly liked the idea of a war, but he seems to have tired of this one shortly after it started. Always conscious of the profit margin of his newspapers, Pulitzer found the expenses of covering the fighting excessively out of proportion to the increased circulation. During this period, for the first time since he had bought the *World*, he was forced to use his own resources for working capital. Pulitzer also was stunned and disturbed by the severe criticism the *World* received for its sensational war coverage and later looked back on this period with regret.

Always one of Pulitzer's major concerns, the *World*'s editorial page declined in quality under the direction of William H. Merrill. By 1904, Merrill, then in his sixties, had been editor of the page for eighteen years. Pulitzer chafed increasingly at Merrill's lack of both initiative and editorial forcefulness and sent one of his staff on a talent search to several major cities. As a result, Frank I. Cobb, then thirty-five, who for four years had been chief editorial writer for the *Detroit Free Press*, was soon added to the staff of the *World*'s editorial page, which also included Pulitzer's oldest son, Ralph. Although Pulitzer sometimes objected to Cobb's opinions and writing style, he valued the vigor and decisiveness of both his thinking and his writing and the dynamism

dollar-matching contest in the history of American journalism." In late March 1896, Carvalho went over to Hearst's shop; and in September 1897, Arthur Brisbane, who had succeeded Goddard as editor of the *Sunday World*, also joined Hearst.

In mid-February 1896, Pulitzer reduced the price of the morning *World* to one cent (the same price as the *Journal*) in a frontal assault aimed at stopping the *Journal*'s expansion. Instead, this move crushed some of the weaker morning newspapers and gave Hearst increased credibility by serving as a clear acknowledgment of his impact on the *World*. (Pulitzer is said to have mused in later years on the irony of his reacting to the Hearst invasion in precisely the way others had reacted to him when he took over the *World* in 1883: Pulitzer reduced the price of his newspaper and raised advertising rates in 1896 just as Bennett and others had done on Pulitzer's arrival in 1883, and the advantage both times went to the newcomer.)

The most notorious episode in the circulation battle between Pulitzer and Hearst was the Spanish-American War of 1898. Although it is inac-

which Cobb consequently restored to the editorial page.

In the first decade of the twentieth century, Pulitzer urged the *World* to continue the kind of exposé reporting and editorial writing that had marked its earlier years. Prominent among the *World*'s campaigns of the early 1900s were one undertaken in 1905, at the height of the muckraking era, against corruption in the insurance industry and one in 1908-1909 aimed at uncovering the political payoffs involved in the building of the Panama Canal. The latter resulted in a fierce effort by President Theodore Roosevelt to have Pulitzer and his company, among others, indicted in federal court for criminal libel. A federal judge in New York quashed the indictment in January 1910, and a year later the United States Supreme Court upheld Pulitzer and the *World* in a unanimous decision.

During the early 1900s, too, Pulitzer developed plans for a professional course of study for journalists, a program finally established at Columbia University. As early as 1892 Pulitzer had discussed embryonic versions of such a course with Seth Low, then president of Columbia. But it was not until the cutthroat competition with Hearst had subsided in the years following the Spanish-American War that Pulitzer created the detailed plans that were to generate both the School of Journalism at Columbia and the Pulitzer Prizes.

In August 1902 he dictated a "rough memorandum" which was far more complete than the "germ of an idea" he claimed it to be. In this memorandum Pulitzer called for the establishment of a school or department of journalism, rather than simply a lectureship as he had done earlier, and compared the preparation of journalists to that of lawyers and doctors. Although Pulitzer himself had always been concerned with the business operations of his newspapers, he called in his memo for a course of study that would distinguish, as its "fundamental object," between journalism as an "intellectual profession and as a business." Pulitzer's preference for the site of this school was Columbia University (Yale was his second choice). He recommended that in addition to such practical aspects of journalism as news gathering, news writing, and editing, the curriculum include, among other things, "the history and the power of public opinion and public service, illustrated by concrete examples, showing the mission, duty and opportunity of the Press as a moral teacher." It took several years for all the details of the school's structure and curriculum to be worked out, but the School of Journalism at

Columbia, developed with a $2,000,000 endowment from Pulitzer, accepted its first class in September 1912.

The 1902 memorandum contained also Pulitzer's stipulation that Columbia allot a portion of the endowment for "annual prizes to particular journalists or writers for various accomplishments, achievements and forms of excellence. . . . Above all, there should be a prize for the greatest accuracy and reliability." Here was an early rough outline for the Pulitzer Prizes. From the beginning, the prizes were a secondary consideration for Pulitzer. They were to receive only $500,000 of the $2,000,000 endowment given to the school; they were to begin only after the journalism school had been operating for three years; and they were under the jurisdiction of the school's advisory board, which Pulitzer invested with much more than simply advisory power. Almost from the time the Pulitzer Prizes were first awarded in 1917, they have been controversial. The prizes in letters have received especially strong criticism over the years by those who per-

Portrait of Pulitzer by John Singer Sargent, painted in London in 1905. Pulitzer biographer W. A. Swanberg calls it "a remarkable portrait of duality, showing the character, intellect and intensity blended subtly with a touch of the Mephistophelian" (International Portrait Gallery).

Pulitzer's yacht Liberty, *aboard which he died off the coast of Charleston, South Carolina, in 1911 (Brown Brothers)*

ceived the advisory board as lacking the insight and expertise to recognize the quality of selections recommended by the juries, especially in the category of best novel. Generally, when the advisory board has been criticized, it has been for its tendency to reject juries' recommendations in various areas, including specific journalism categories.

Pulitzer did not live to see either of these dreams come true. He died aboard his four-year-old yacht, *Liberty*, off the coast of Charleston, South Carolina, 29 October 1911, probably of a heart attack. He was survived by his wife, Kate, sons Ralph (born 11 June 1879), Joseph, Jr. (born 21 March 1885), and Herbert (born 20 November 1895); and daughters Edith (born 19 June 1886) and Constance (born 13 December 1888). Two other daughters had died earlier: Lucille (30 September 1880-31 December 1897) and Katherine (30 June 1882-9 May 1884). His total estate, when probated, was valued at more than $18.6 million, excluding Chatwold, his home at Bar Harbor, Maine, and his cottages at Jekyll Island, Georgia.

Pulitzer never visited St. Louis after 1889, and during the last eighteen years of his life, he visited the *World* offices only three times. Nonetheless, he maintained close contact with all the operations of the *World* through mail and cable. Telegraph wires sizzled with sharp journalistic criticism when Pulitzer was displeased with the way the paper handled a particular story, but he was also quick to praise when he was satisfied and willing to reverse a negative assessment of a reporter or editorial writer

if later work met his standards for excellence. Even in the last year of his life, Pulitzer's memos to Cobb and Charles M. Lincoln, then managing editor of the *World*, contained variations of well-worn Pulitzer themes regarding quality journalism: "Accuracy, accuracy, accuracy. Also terseness, intelligent, not stupid, condensation." "Generally speaking my sympathies are with the people. . . ." "In using the word masses I do not exclude anybody. I should make a paper that the judges of the Supreme Court of the United States would read with enjoyment, everybody, but I would not make a paper that only the judges of the Supreme Court and their class would read."

Periodical Publication:

"The School of Journalism in Columbia University," *North American Review*, 178 (May 1904): 641-680.

Biographies:

Alleyne Ireland, *Joseph Pulitzer: Reminiscences of a Secretary* (New York: Kennerley, 1914); enlarged as *An Adventure with a Genius* (New York: Dutton, 1920);

Don C. Seitz, *Joseph Pulitzer: His Life & Letters* (New York: Simon & Schuster, 1924);

James Wyman Barrett, *Joseph Pulitzer and His World* (New York: Vanguard Press, 1941);

George Juergens, *Joseph Pulitzer and the New York World* (Princeton, N.J.: Princeton University Press, 1966);

Julian S. Rammelkamp, *Pulitzer's Post-Dispatch, 1878-1883* (Princeton, N.J.: Princeton University Press, 1967);

W. A. Swanberg, *Pulitzer* (New York: Scribners, 1967).

References:

Richard T. Baker, *A History of The Graduate School of Journalism, Columbia University* (New York: Columbia University Press, 1954);

James Creelman, "Joseph Pulitzer—Master Journalist," *Pearson's Magazine*, 21 (March 1909): 229-256;

John L. Heaton, *The Story of a Page* (New York: Harper, 1913);

William Inglis, "An Intimate View of Joseph Pulitzer," *Harper's Weekly*, 55 (11 November 1911): 7.

Papers:

Joseph Pulitzer's papers are collected at the Columbia University libraries and the Library of Congress.

Julian Ralph
(27 May 1853-20 January 1903)

Ronald S. Marmarelli
Central Michigan University

MAJOR POSITIONS HELD: Reporter and special correspondent, *New York Sun* (1875-1895), *New York Journal* (1895-1898).

BOOKS: *The Sun's German Barber near the Cooper Institute and the Monkey Barber by the Next Chair* (New York: New York News Company, 1883);

Along the Bowstring; or, South Shore of Lake Superior (New York: American Bank Note Company, 1891);

On Canada's Frontier: Sketches of History, Sport, and Adventure and of the Indians, Missionaries, Fur-Traders and Newer Settlers of Western Canada (New York: Harper, 1892; London: Osgood, 1892);

Our Great West: A Study of the Present Conditions and Future Possibilities of the New Commonwealth and Capitals of the United States (New York: Harper, 1893);

Harper's Chicago and the World's Fair (New York: Harper, 1893);

Dixie; or, Southern Scenes and Sketches (New York: Harper, 1895);

People We Pass: Stories of Life among the Masses of New York City (New York: Harper, 1896);

Alone in China and Other Stories (New York: Harper, 1897; London: Osgood, 1897);

An Angel in a Web (New York & London: Harper, 1899);

A Prince of Georgia and Other Tales (New York &

Julian Ralph

London: Harper, 1899);

Towards Pretoria: A Record of the War between Briton and Boer, to the Relief of Kimberly (New York: Stokes, 1900; London: Pearson, 1900);

At Pretoria· The Capture of the Boer Capitals and the Hoisting of the Flag at Pretoria (London: Pearson, 1901); republished as *An American with Lord Roberts* (New York: Stokes, 1901);

War's Brighter Side. The Story of "The Friend" Newspaper Edited by the Correspondents with Lord Roberts's Forces, March-April, 1900 (New York: Appleton, 1901; London: Pearson, 1901);

The Millionairess (Boston: Lothrop, 1902; London: Methuen, 1902);

The Making of a Journalist (New York & London: Harper, 1903).

To Julian Ralph there was no question but that success as a newspaperman depended upon one's being born to it, upon one's having a natural gift or fitness for the work. Of his own calling he had no doubt, as he indicated in recounting an anecdote from his days as a reporter for the *New York Sun*. Sent to a suburb of New York City to find a person, he sought help from a German cobbler at work in his shop:

"I beg your pardon, but I am a reporter of the *Sun*—"

"Well, well," the cobbler replied in a soothing way, "you cannot help dot."

Ralph recalled that the comment astonished him. "I could not help being a reporter, and I knew it. I had always believed I was born to be one, but who could have supposed a cobbler could have discovered all that by merely glancing at me?" Colleagues who had more than a glance of him at work as a reporter in the last quarter of the nineteenth century, whether they thought him born to be a reporter or not, often spoke of him in superlatives. He was, said fellow *Sun* reporter David S. Barry, "the greatest newspaper reporter who ever lived." It was high praise, especially since for most of his newspaper career Ralph worked on the *Sun* of Charles A. Dana, where reporting skill, stylish writing, and human interest techniques were emphasized and where the development of great reporters became commonplace. As the greatest reporter on "the newspaperman's newspaper," Ralph rose to the top in the esteem of his peers.

Ralph was born in New York City on 27 May 1853, the son of Joseph Edward and Selina Mahoney Ralph. His father was a physician, and both parents were natives of London, England, who had come to the United States as children. They enrolled their son in private schools, but at fifteen, Ralph left school to become an apprentice in the office of the *Red Bank* (New Jersey) *Standard*, where he learned the printing and newspaper business. He soon was local editor and writer. "I became a newspaper writer in a day by describing the antics of a mad bull in the streets of a village," he wrote later. Before he was twenty, Ralph had founded a competing newspaper in Red Bank, the *Leader*, which soon failed; had served briefly as local editor of the weekly *Tom's River* (New Jersey) *Courier*; and had been an editor at the *Webster* (Massachusetts) *Times*. By 1873 he was back in New York City as a reporter for the *New York Daily Graphic* in its first year of existence.

His first assignment for the *Graphic* in May 1873 was to cover the scheduled public whipping in New Castle, Delaware, of a woman for the killing of her seven-month-old son. The whipping did not take place, and Ralph later claimed he and six other New York reporters prevented it. In the first half of 1875, Ralph wrote daily stories on the adultery trial of Henry Ward Beecher. His work attracted the attention of Charles A. Dana, and Ralph soon began his twenty-year association with the *Sun*. In the following year, he married Isabella Mount of Chapel Hill, New Jersey. They had three sons, Lester, Willard, and Allan, and two daughters, Edith and Alice.

As a member of the notable staff of the *Sun*, which was guided by Dana's maxim that an "invariable law of the newspaper is to be interesting," Ralph ranged widely throughout the city and the nation, first as a general reporter, then as a special correspondent. He quickly established his reputation as a hardworking, untiring, persistent journalist with a commitment to accuracy and honesty and a devotion to serving the readers. Frank M. O'Brien, in his history of the *New York Sun*, noted that it had been said of Ralph that he "could write five thousand words about a cobblestone." O'Brien commented: "If he had done that, it would have been an interesting cobblestone. He had a passion for detail, but it was not the lifeless and worrisome detail of the realistic novelist. When he wrote a column about a horse eating a woman's hat, the reader became well acquainted with the horse, the woman, and the crowd that looked on." Ralph loved his work, saying that it wasn't until he became a reporter, after having tried his hand at being a small-town editor, that he began to enjoy life. His career as a *Sun* reporter and correspondent involved him in covering stories of all sizes and characters, from the end of the Molly Maguires in the Pennsylvania coalfields to the inauguration of presidents in the nation's capital, from the burial of an unidentified foundling to the funeral of a national hero.

In late 1876, Ralph produced a series of stories on theater safety in New York City, in the wake of the Brooklyn Theatre fire of 5 December 1876, which had claimed some 300 lives. Ralph later cited this work as exemplifying his success in getting a story despite obstacles. He first tried to check the safety of the theaters by asking to be let in to do so. He was refused. "In spite of this, the work had to be done; therefore, I went to an official of the Fire Department and induced him to obtain for me a suit of fireman's clothing and to constitute me an extra watchman at the theatres, with leave to watch in any and all of them." Thus, he was able to act in an official capacity and get the story. Another of his noted exploits occurred in the late 1870s when managing editor Ballard Smith, on a slow news day, gave him the assignment of writing a long feature on the treatment of foundlings, using as a news peg the finding of a well-dressed baby girl in a vacant lot in Harlem. The story told of the handling of foundlings from their discovery to the fate some of them faced, burial in a pauper's grave. "This was legitimate, dignified, and true journalism—the only kind that was practiced upon that newspaper," Ralph wrote later.

The decade of the 1880s found Ralph covering state and national politics, legislative and congressional affairs, and major events. He also began writing for the *Sun* a long-running series of anonymous sketches about a German barber. The sketches, begun in 1882, featured witty commentary in dialect on topics of current interest, in a manner similar to that of Finley Peter Dunne's "Mr. Dooley." Ralph said he was proudest, out of all his work, of his coverage of the New York state legislature in 1885-1886, "during two corrupt sessions." He and a few other correspondents were given credit for saving the people millions of dollars by exposing corruption and were praised for refusing to let themselves be bought off by tempting bribes. Ralph wrote that "though I earned only seventy-five dollars a week and the excitement of exposing and angering the thieves, I never regretted the course I adopted." He recalled that Dana had been urged to take Ralph off the story because he was mistaken and was harming the *Sun*. Dana replied: "Yes, yes. I suppose he does make mistakes, but we will keep him where he is because he is honest."

Ralph's coverage of the funeral of Ulysses S. Grant in August 1885 showed him at his best in doing the kind of epic reporting effort that was one of his hallmarks. As he noted in *The Making of a Journalist* (1903): "If I have done anything uncommon in newspaper work, it has been in the way of reporting the mainstream of important events completely, and at great lengths, unaided and alone. It is said that in New York, at least, I have been peculiar in possessing the—physique is perhaps the greatest requisite—to carry out tasks of the sort necessitating the nearest approach to an imitation of ubiquitousness, and resulting in from seven to ten columns of solid writing for the next day's paper." On Grant's funeral, Ralph wrote, in about seven hours, some 11,000 words, a full page of type, with a pencil. The story began: "There have not often been gathered in one place so many men whose names have been household words, and whose lives have been inwoven with the history of a grave crisis in a great nation's life, as met yesterday in this city. . . . Among them, like children amid gray-heads, or shadows beside monuments, were other men more newly famous, and famous only for deeds of peace in times of quiet and plenty. . . . And all were paying homage to the greatest figure of their time, whose mortal remains they pressed around with bared, bowed heads."

When New York was stunned by the blizzard of March 1888, Ralph was assigned the task of writing the main story for the *Sun*. The lead read: "It was as if New York had been a burning candle upon which nature had clapped a snuffer, leaving nothing of the city's activities but a struggling ember." Another of his legendary stories of the 1880s was one on a Yale-Princeton football game. It ran to five columns of type and was admired in proofs by all who read it in the *Sun* office. After the first edition was printed, it was discovered that the score of the game was missing. Ralph had forgotten to put it in, and all the deskmen and editors had been so absorbed in the article that they had not caught the omission.

Ralph continued into the 1890s as the *Sun*'s special correspondent charged with writing the big stories about the major events of the time. In an August 1893 article for *Scribner's*, Ralph described his methods for doing the big stories. For the story of the inauguration of Grover Cleveland earlier that year, for example, he said, he had begun at 5:00 A.M. with a cab tour of the city ("to catch the capital robing like a bride for her wedding"); toured the city again after breakfast; visited the White House, the Capitol, and the principal hotels; talked with the old and the new presidents; watched the inaugural ceremonies and the parade; and visited with the new First Family at the White House. Then, after "a hearty luncheon," he had "sat down at half-past one o'clock to write steadily for 12 hours, with plenty of pencils and pads and messenger-boys at hand, and with my notebook supplemented by clippings from all the afternoon papers (covering details to which I might or might not wish to refer)." Covering a national political convention, Ralph wrote, was even harder work: "There is nothing in all the business that compares with a national convention for trying the body and mind of a man who essays to master and report it; that is, if he works for a newspaper which wants the truth, regardless of its predictions or policy." The most trying task was covering a night session of balloting, Ralph wrote, describing the nearly frenetic effort of the reporter of the main story as he writes in short takes of ten to twenty words that are grabbed away by a stream of telegraph-boys. "The fevered pencil flies, every nerve is strained, every brain-cell is clear. Comment, description, reminiscence, dialogue, and explanation flow upon the impatient sheets in short paragraphs, like slivers of crystal. There is no turning back, no chance for correction or rearrangement, no possibility of changing a word that has been written. Yet there must be no mistakes, no confusion or complexity. For two or three hours, perhaps even longer, this race is kept up." Ralph relished this "hardest" yet "most intoxicating" task of the special correspondent. "Whoever does it is glad that he has lived to drink so deep a draught of that matchless elixir which keeps us all young till we die—excitement."

In 1893, Ralph also covered the trial of Lizzie Borden in New Bedford, Massachusetts. His story of 21 June 1893 tells of her reaction to the jury's verdict in her trial on charges of brutally murdering her mother and father: "Every juryman stood at right-about-face, staring at the woman. There was such a gentle, kindly light beaming in every eye that no one questioned the verdict that was to be uttered. But God save every woman from the feelings that Lizzie Borden showed in the return look she cast upon that jury! It was what is pictured as the rolling gaze of a dying person. She seemed not to have the power to move her eyes directly where she was told to, and they swung all around in her head. They looked at the ceiling; they looked at everything, but they saw nothing. It was horrible, a pitiful sight, to see her then." When the not-guilty verdict was uttered, the woman fell. "Her forehead crashed against the heavy walnut rail so as to shake the reporter of the *Sun* who sat next to her, twelve feet away, leaning on the rail. It seemed that she must be stunned, but she was not. Quickly, with an unconscious movement, she flung up both arms, threw them over the rail, and pressed them under her face so that it rested on them."

By 1894, Ralph was at the height of his reputation among journalists, "regarded by most of his profession," Frederic Remington asserted, "as the first reporter of the town." Albert F. Matthews wrote that Ralph "by general consent has become known as the foremost reporter in the United States." But it was not until Ralph began writing regularly for *Harper's Monthly* and *Harper's Weekly*, as well as other magazines, starting in 1890, that his name became known to the wider public. The *Sun* did not give its writers by-lines; the magazines did, and Ralph's prolific output of articles for the magazines, which consisted mostly of travel pieces, was also quickly collected in volumes published regularly throughout the 1890s. His success in magazine work was slow in coming, Ralph noted in urging prospective writers not to be discouraged. "I wrote occasionally for the magazines for thirteen years before I had an article accepted by one," he wrote. His own venture into periodical publishing was short-lived in 1890: his weekly *Chatter*, a literary publication printed on yellow paper, failed after six months because of financial problems.

For *Harper's Monthly* and *Harper's Weekly*, while still associated with the *New York Sun*, Ralph traveled some 25,000 miles in the United States and Canada in 1891-1892 and 30,000 in 1893. In 1894, he went on a trip of some 20,000 miles to Asia. Published collections of his pieces included *On Canada's Frontier* (1892), *Our Great West* (1893), and *Dixie; or, Southern Scenes and Sketches* (1895). Ralph also wrote several volumes of fiction, including *Alone in China and Other Stories* (1897) and *A Prince of Georgia and Other Tales* (1899), both collections of short stories, and two novels, *An Angel in a Web* (1899)—which was serialized in *Harper's* before appearing in book form—and *The Millionairess* (1902). He continued writing regularly for the magazines until his death.

During his Asian trip for *Harper's*—which commenced after the start of the Sino-Japanese War, although it had been planned previously—Ralph's reporting spurred a Senate investigation of United States policy in China. He wrote in December 1894 of an incident in which several Japanese students had been arrested as spies in Shanghai, taken to Nanking, tortured for seven days, and beheaded. American officials had promised to protect Japanese in China; the secretary of state challenged Ralph's report, and Chinese representatives in Washington denied the incident had occurred. Ralph wrote later: "Let no journalist ever forget the moral of what happened. Simply because I had never abused my opportunities by writing mere sensationalism, or untruths of any sort, the Senate took up the matter . . . purely and solely upon my written word."

Ralph's association with the *Sun* ended in late 1895 when he, along with other *Sun* reporters, was hired by William Randolph Hearst to work for Hearst's new *Journal*. The first edition of the *Journal* on 7 November 1895 featured Ralph's detailed description of the wedding of Consuelo Vanderbilt and the duke of Marlborough, beginning on the front page and continuing inside for three more pages. In early 1896 Ralph went to London as the *Journal*'s European editor. He covered the coronation in St. Petersburg of Czar Nicholas II in May of that year. In April 1897, Ralph joined six other correspondents in covering the brief Greco-Turkish War for the *Journal*, and in July he covered Queen Victoria's Diamond Jubilee. He left the *Journal* in 1898 but remained in London as a correspondent for the *New York Herald* and the *Brooklyn Eagle* and continued to write regularly for *Harper's*.

During August and September 1899, Ralph was in Rennes, France, to cover the Dreyfus court-martial. He later cited one of his experiences there to illustrate what he meant by "the sixth sense of a newspaper man," which he described as "a strange gift" and "a most mysterious quality of instinct" that irresistibly leads the reporter to news. "It frequently impels him to act against his judgment and to do things which he feels to be absurd, and yet is obliged to persist in until the reward comes with a shock like lightning from a cloudless sky." Ralph recalled that for some unknown reason he had been unable to sleep on the morning of 14 August 1899. On the way to that day's proceedings, he stopped to wire his newspaper that he expected exciting news that day. A few hours later Fernand Labori, Dreyfus's counsel, was wounded in an attack.

Late in 1899, Ralph went to South Africa to cover the Boer War for the *London Daily Mail* and *Collier's* magazine and remained there through mid-1900 accompanying the British forces under Field Marshal Earl Roberts in major campaigns. His son Lester, a magazine writer and illustrator in his own right, was with him. In March and April 1900, while with the British at Bloemfontein, Ralph and other correspondents edited a daily newspaper, the *Friend*, to entertain and inform the army in the field. Contributors included Rudyard Kipling and Arthur Conan Doyle. "Despite its whimsicalities," Ralph wrote later, "*The Friend* was a dignified newspaper and very nearly a complete one." During the

Editors of the Friend *in their office at Bloemfontein: (from left) H. A. Gwynne, Ralph, Perceval Landon, Rudyard Kipling*

campaigns, Ralph's health suffered, as he was wounded, thrown from his horse, and stricken with enteric fever. By mid-April, Ralph recalled, "We were all tiring fast. I was lame with an injury that kept laying me up, and otherwise my condition was such that for weeks I had not been able to partake of any food except milk and soda water." He went back to London and then returned to the United States in March 1902. He was appointed Eastern representative for the St. Louis World's Fair and contributed correspondence to the *New York Times*. After a prolonged illness of varying severity, Ralph died at the age of forty-nine on 20 January 1903 at his home at 118 West Seventy-sixth Street, New York City.

After his death, Ralph was remembered by one writer in the *New York Times Book Review* as "a man of prodigious energy, unquestionable desire and relish for adventure, the indomitable industry that he found necessary for success, and the good nature that is as indispensable to the journalist in China as it is at home. This irrepressible spirit of good-fellowship was perhaps his most prominent characteristic." In noting his passing, *Outlook* carried this comment: "Personally, Mr. Ralph was a very interesting talker; fresh, frank, original, full of special knowledge of remote localities and peoples, with an immense interest in life. His enthusiasm was the joy of his friends." Ralph himself stressed the importance of "good nature" in his work, classing it as "among the absolute essentials to success as a newspaper correspondent or reporter," along with an aptitude for the work, persistence, and honesty.

Ralph seemed at his most enthusiastic when writing about his work. He recognized the negative elements; but if journalism is in your blood, he wrote, "facts and figures may go hang themselves, and hardship, exposure, danger, will only serve to push you further in. The prospect of a lifetime's incessant strain and toil will prove but as the sauce to the dish." Ralph wrote that all journalists have a life that is "hard as nails," and special correspondents have it even harder, "yet neither one knows it, nor asks for sympathy. . . . These men see their strained, exciting, never-halting toil through glasses colored by sentiment or through the heat-waves of excitement. They are forever stimulated by competition and freshened by constant novelty."

Periodical Publications:
"Sixth Sense of a Newspaper Man," *Harper's Weekly* (10 June 1893): 546;
"The Newspaper Correspondent," *Scribner's* (August 1893): 150-166;
"Election Night in a Newspaper Office," *Scribner's* (November 1894): 531-544;
"The War Correspondent of To-Day," *Harper's Weekly* (8 September 1900): 854-855;
"A Yankee Correspondent in South Africa," *Century* (November 1900): 67-73.

References:
David S. Barry, *Forty Years in Washington* (Boston: Little, Brown, 1924);
Charles A. Dana, *The Art of Newspaper Making* (New York: Appleton, 1895);
Helen MacGill Hughes, *News and the Human Interest Story* (Chicago: University of Chicago Press, 1940);
"Julian Ralph," *Outlook* (31 January 1903): 240;
Albert F. Matthews, "The Metropolitan Newspaper Reporter," *Chautauquan* (November 1893): 164-168;
"Newspaper Men. Julian Ralph's Posthumous Book of Journalistic Studies," *New York Times Book Review* (5 December 1903): 909;
Frank M. O'Brien, *The Story of the "Sun"* (New York: Doran, 1918);
Frederic Remington, "Julian Ralph," *Harper's Weekly* (24 February 1894): 179.

Opie Read
(22 December 1852-2 November 1939)

Shirley M. Mundt
Louisiana State University

MAJOR POSITIONS HELD: Editor, *Arkansas Gazette* (1878-1882), *Arkansaw Traveler* (1882-1891).

BOOKS: *Up Terrapin River* (Chicago & New York: Rand McNally, 1888);
Mrs. Annie Green: A Romance (Chicago & New York: Rand McNally, 1889);
Len Gansett (Boston: Ticknor, 1889);
A Kentucky Colonel (Chicago: Schulte, 1890; London: Black, 1896);
Emmett Bonlore (Chicago: Schulte, 1891; London: Low, 1891);
Opie Read in Arkansas and What He Saw There; Comprising Popular Stories by this Famous Author (New York: Ogilvie, 1891);
A Kentucky Editor (New York: Ogilvie, 1891);
Ten Funny Stories (New York: Ogilvie, 1891);
Twenty Good Stories (New York: Ogilvie, 1891);
A Tennessee Judge (Chicago: Laird & Lee, 1893);
The Colossus (Chicago: Schulte, 1893);
The Wives of the Prophet (Chicago: Laird & Lee, 1894);
The Tear in the Cup (Chicago: Laird & Lee, 1894);
On the Suwanee River: A Romance (Chicago: Laird & Lee, 1895);
My Young Master: A Novel (Chicago: Laird & Lee, 1896);
An Arkansas Planter (Chicago & New York: Rand McNally, 1896);
The Captain's Romance (New York: F. T. Neely, 1896);
The Jucklins: A Novel (Chicago: Laird & Lee, 1896;

Opie Read

London: Black, 1897);

Bolanyo (Chicago: Way & Williams, 1897);

Old Ebenezer (Chicago: Laird & Lee, 1897);

Odd Folks (Chicago: Neely, 1897);

The Waters of Caney Fork: A Romance of Tennessee (Chicago & New York: Rand McNally, 1898; London: Unwin, 1898);

The Carpetbagger: A Novel, by Read and Frank Pixley (Chicago: Laird & Lee, 1899);

Judge Elbridge (Chicago & New York: Rand McNally, 1899; London: Unwin, 1899);

A Yankee from the West (Chicago & New York: Rand McNally, 1899);

In the Alamo (Chicago & New York: Rand McNally, 1900);

Glimpses and Epigrams of Opie Read (Chicago: Hill, 1902);

Our Josephine and Other Tales (New York & London: Street & Smith, 1902);

The Starbucks (Chicago: Laird & Lee, 1902; London: Ward, Lock, 1902);

The American Cavalier (Chicago: Thompson & Thomas, 1903);

The Club Woman and the Hero: A Comedietta (Chicago: Dennison, 1903);

The Fiddle and the Fawn and Other Stories (Chicago: Rand McNally, 1903);

The Harkriders: A Novel (Chicago: Laird & Lee, 1903);

Confessions of Marguerite: The Story of a Girl's Heart (Chicago: Rand McNally, 1904);

Adventures of a Vice-President: A Fable of Our Times (Chicago: Devereaux, 1904);

Turk: A Novel (Chicago: Laird & Lee, 1904); republished as *"Turkey-Egg" Griffin* (Chicago: Laird & Lee, 1905);

An American in New York: A Novel of Today (Chicago: Thompson & Thomas, 1905); republished as *The Colonel and the Widow, a Romance of an American in New York* (Chicago: Thompson & Thomas, 1905);

Old Lim Jucklins: The Opinions of an Open-Air Philosopher (New York & London: Doubleday, Page, 1905);

Plantation Yarns and Bayou Stories (Chicago: Donohue, 1905);

The Son of the Swordmaker: A Romance (Chicago: Laird & Lee, 1905);

Tales of the South (Chicago: Donohue, 1905);

By the Eternal: A Novel (Chicago: Laird & Lee, 1906);

My Friends in Arkansas (Chicago: Donohue, 1906);

The Mystery of Margaret (Chicago: Wessel's, 1907);

The Bandit's Sweetheart and Other Stories (Chicago: Thompson, 1907);

The Queen's Robe: A Dramatic Story (Chicago: Dramatic Publishing Co., 1908);

Our Josephine and Other Tales (Chicago: Thompson, 1909);

Kentucky Yarns (Chicago: Donohue, 1909);

Tom and the Squatter's Son: A Stirring Tale of Adventure in the Pioneer Days for Boys from 7 to 60 (Chicago: Laird & Lee, 1910);

The New Mr. Howerson (Chicago: Reilly & Britton, 1914);

"Come on Buck" (Chicago: Blackhawk Press, 1926);

The Gold Gauze Veil (Chicago: Canterbury Press, 1927);

I Remember (New York: R. R. Smith, 1930);

Mark Twain and I (Chicago: Reilly & Lee, 1940).

A vivid imagination, a knack for depicting characters he met during his travels, and the proverbial gift of gab—these were the talents that made Opie Read widely known at the turn of the century, but his popularity was too ephemeral to last even to the end of his own life. When he died in 1939, few remembered that he had been a pioneer in the newspaper business, had established the *Arkansaw*

Traveler, had traveled coast to coast entertaining audiences with his droll anecdotes and character sketches, and had authored over fifty books.

If ever a writer was influenced by his native territory, Opie Read was, for the hillbilly sketches, jokes, and stories in the *Arkansaw Traveler*; the humor in his lectures; and the characters and plots in his novels were lifted, with few exceptions, straight from his Southern background. Opie Pope Read was born 22 December 1852 in Nashville, Tennessee, the youngest of eleven children born to Guilford and Elizabeth Wallace Read. His boyhood years were spent in Gallatin, Tennessee, where his parents moved when he was barely a month old. As a preschooler Read was frequently entertained by a black shoemaker who told him stories of Brer Fox and Brer Rabbit long before Joel Chandler Harris put the tales into print. This early closeness to Negro speech made it possible for him to write dialect easily when, years later, he turned out sketches of uneducated farm people and made them characters in his novels. As Read grew older he became a storyteller himself, entertaining the neighborhood youngsters with his ghost stories, often invented on the spot. His first experience with serialized invention came when for two years he improvised sensational, romanticized stories about "Robert, the Good Shooter" to please his nephews. Read wrote of those childhood stories in *I Remember*, his autobiography published in 1930: "I associated with the unreal until the real became the unreal." Read's practical and religious parents did not view their son's inability to separate the "real" from the "unreal" as a talent; to them his inventions were lies, and they feared that he would come to no good.

Since public schools were regarded at that time as schools for poor whites, Read's parents arranged for private education for their youngest son. His first teacher was a widow who held classes in her home. Later a neighborhood school was established by a pedant who often walked in the woods with Read, talking of the Greek philosophers, although he was known to lash other students until they bled. The schoolmaster encouraged young Read's interest in literature, and the boy stole every possible moment from work on his father's farm to read. Read later wrote that his style of writing and his love for literature were influenced by his study of William Holmes McGuffey's *Readers* during those early years, but it was Benjamin Franklin's *Autobiography* that had the greatest impact on Read's choice of profession. Read wrote in his autobiography that Franklin told him what to do: "learn the printer's craft." In his late teens, Read entered Neophogen

College (now defunct) in Gallatin. Although he says little about the classes he attended during the two years he was there, he does note that the college had "an extensive library and among its books I gorged of Saturday afternoons and Sundays." At Neophogen Read met Mark Twain, who had come there to give a lecture, and Twain's remark that "real knowledge lies in the close attention we pay to little things" was an unforgettable lesson for Read. Read's observation of "little things" would later make him a favorite of millions.

Read's career as a journalist began before he left Gallatin. He sent his first sketch, signed "Crawfish," to the *Franklin* (Kentucky) *Patriot*; in it he described Bob Gardner, a man from the Gallatin community. When the paper containing the sketch arrived at the local post office, the postmaster read Read's sketch aloud to a group of men sitting around the office. One of the men was the real Bob Gardner, and as the postmaster read, the men began to look at Gardner and laugh. When the postmaster finished, Gardner stalked from the room saying, "If I ever meet that liar, I'll beat him within an inch of his life." Read was present and heard this reaction to his first published work. It amused him at the time, but it was the foreshadowing of a view that was to become common among his country readers.

Read's first job came when he was nineteen, as a result of his friendship with Andrew Kelley, a typesetter who became editor of the *Franklin Patriot* not long after Read met him. Through Kelley, Read was able to realize the dream Ben Franklin's *Autobiography* had inspired: Kelley promised to teach Read the printer's trade and give him board plus fifty cents a week. Read's work consisted largely of menial chores, but he did learn to set type, a skill which helped him to make a living of sorts until he was able to depend upon his writing for an income.

Read had worked for Kelley only a few months when he decided (with Kelley's approval) to take a job as typesetter for the *Pen*, Neophogen College's magazine. The job gave him an opportunity to improve upon his skill, and it also paid for his room and board. Read continued his friendship with Kelley, and when he left Neophogen he returned to the *Patriot* as a reporter. But soon the friendship with Kelley proved to be detrimental to Read's career at the *Patriot*. The owner of the paper grew tired of Kelley's drinking and disapproved of the influence Kelley had on Read. When Read refused to break his ties with Kelley, the owner of the *Patriot* let him go.

With experience as a typesetter and news

gatherer behind him, it was easy for Read to find work—though not always easy for him to keep working. On the day he was fired from the *Patriot* he was offered half interest in the *Scottsville* (Kentucky) *Argus*. The owner, Harry Warner, had gone into debt to buy type and a handpress and needed an editor. So Read left Franklin that day to join Warner as editor and part owner of the *Argus*. Of the first edition Read wrote that it "was so well printed that one might almost read it." Read suspected right away that there was no hope for this pioneering effort, for soon he was spending his own money for ink. He was right; a few months later, he and his partner were evicted from their leaky office in the loft of an old building because they were unable to pay their debts. Experiences he had on the *Argus* must have inspired the sketch "How T. Minus Wiggs Ran the Hawksville 'Palladium' on Business Principles." The sketch contains a humorous discussion between the editor and the typesetter and concludes with the following account:

> We rented our office from Major Blogett, a man of blustering destruction in the village. He was a lank fellow, with a heavy growth of fiery, red hair, of which he was exceedingly vain. He was a bachelor and slept in a room immediately below the office. . . .
>
> One night, while Minus and I were preparing a solution of concentrated lye, with which to wash the ink off the "forms," we heard the Major go into his room; and, by his movements, we could tell that he was drunker than usual.
>
> "I hope he won't come up after his rent while he is in that condition," said Minus. "Look here," he added, "this lye won't do. It's too strong. It takes the dots off the i's and splits the diphthongs. I'll put the jar over here till morning. Then we'll tone it down with water. There isn't a drop up here, and I don't suppose you want to go after any tonight."
>
> I said I did not, whereupon he remarked: "All right. We'll go to bed."
>
> I had just dozed off to sleep when Minus awoke me by getting up.
>
> "What's the matter?" I asked.
>
> "An infernal cat has come in here to eat up the paste, and I'm going to kill her. It's a good thing we sleep in the office. If we didn't we'd lose everything we've got."
>
> He slammed around, scared the cat nearly to death, and turned over the jar of lye.
>
> The next morning, just as we had dressed ourselves, we heard some one coming rapidly up the stairs, and the next moment Major Blogett rushed into the room.

His hair was falling off in patches. He looked at us a moment, and, seemingly with an effort to control himself, said:

> "I could stand for you fellows to beat me out of my rent—I could stand a good many things—but when I awake at morning, and find some sort of infernal juice dripping down and taking all the hair off my head, why—" He stopped for a moment, and then, taking out his watch, added:
>
> "The coach leaves here at eight o'clock. It's now one minute to eight."
>
> Minus and I were among the passengers that left on the coach that morning.

Read decided to try his luck in the larger cities, and after a short visit with his family, he headed for Nashville. He found part-time work as a typesetter and worked for a time with the Methodist Book Concern, sharing quarters with four other tramp printers. Read liked Nashville because of its historical background, but his editorials, which bore the stamp of his classical education at Neophogen, were not much in demand, and his sketches brought him no income. He soon tired of Nashville and left for Memphis with one of his roommates.

En route to Memphis, Read took odd jobs, working for a time setting type for a book on St. Paul. In Bolivar, Tennessee, he took a job on the weekly *Bulletin*, whose editor was G. H. Armstead, later editor of the *Nashville American*. But Read was eager to be on the move, and when Warner, his old friend from Scottsville, wrote that there was work in Carlisle, Arkansas, Read left the *Bulletin*.

In Carlisle, Read and Warner started anew. When Read arrived, Warner had already set up their office and residence in an empty boxcar sitting on the tracks, surrounded by weeds. Soon they had their first edition of the *Prairie Flower* ready for press. They lay back in their boxcar office-residence to rest, only to be awakened by the clink of a coupling pin. Their screams for help went unanswered, and when the train stopped, the *Prairie Flower* office was at Duvall's Bluff, twenty miles from Carlisle. Shamefaced, they hired a wagon to haul them back home. This paper, too, was doomed from the outset because of debts Warner incurred. Soon a deputy sheriff came and padlocked the press. Read quipped, "The first frost had killed the *Prairie Flower*."

But failure did not dampen Read's enthusiasm for newspaper work. After a brief stay in Little Rock, where for the first time he was able to get into the printers' union, and a visit to his parents' home in Gallatin, Read took the editorship of the *Bowling*

Green (Kentucky) *Pantagraph*, working for Elvis Porter. Read described his job as one of producing "only ten columns of matter a week, through the quick channels of lying or the slow channels of news." When Porter felt that he could no longer afford the luxury of an editor, he recommended that Read try the *Louisville Courier-Journal*.

In Louisville, Read went to Henry Watterson, whom he had met earlier in Frankfort. Watterson offered him part-time work on the *Courier-Journal*, sometimes sending him into the country to cover political disturbances. On one occasion, Watterson warned Read, "You must be very careful." "Careful to tell the truth, sir?," Read asked. "Lord, no," Watterson replied. "That would ruin us. I want you to write something that everybody will read and that nobody can remember." The statement was so close to Read's own attitude about news coverage that it is surprising that Read did not stay with Watterson longer. But he obviously had a traveling yen to satisfy, and, too, he missed his friends in Arkansas.

Back in Little Rock, Read was hired as city editor of the *Evening Democrat*. Col. J. N. Smithee, owner of the newspaper, laid down the law: "What I want is news . . . and no sketches, you understand." But when Smithee was shot in a gunfight with Maj. John D. Adams, owner of the *Daily Arkansas Gazette*, and Read covered the fight as straight news, Smithee was offended. Smithee wanted sympathetic treatment in the newspaper; Read was unwilling to yield. When Smithee recovered, he fired Read on the pretext that Read had written an untrue sketch about a Negro drayman and a little boy.

The day the *Democrat* let him go, the *New York Herald* hired him to cover the yellow fever epidemic in Memphis. It was Read's first big news assignment and an opportunity to complete the trip he had begun many months before. He was paid $30 a week for his day-to-day coverage of the epidemic. He went with a party of nurses and doctors and moved among the sick and dying, reporting names of the stricken and writing sketches of persons he met there. It was not a long assignment, but it did more to establish Read's reputation as a newsman than anything he had done up to that point.

Returning to Little Rock in 1878, Read found the *Gazette* under new management and discovered that the new owner, Maj. Hunley Sevier, was eager to hire him. As editor he would be able to write the sketches he loved to write and would be able to interview important figures who came into the area. He became friends with Gen. Thomas J. Churchill, governor of Arkansas; discussed religion and politics with Carl Schurz; met and talked with Mark Twain again while covering a cotton exposition in New Orleans; and, through an ingenious lie, was able to interview Gen. Ulysses S. Grant at a time when Grant was adamant about not seeing newsmen.

In Little Rock, Read became close friends with P. D. Benham, a sharp young businessman, and Benham's sister Ada, who on 10 June 1881 became Read's bride. Although still employed by the *Gazette*, Read was contributing more and more sketches to newspapers in the North. Believing he was underpaid at the *Gazette*, he accepted an offer in 1881 to work for the *Cleveland Leader*. His job on the *Leader* was mere hackwork, though, so when the *Gazette* requested that he return to Little Rock at a higher salary, he immediately accepted.

Back in Little Rock, however, Read was again dissatisfied with the routine work at the *Gazette*. He wanted more time to write fiction and more freedom than the *Gazette* offered. When his brother-in-law suggested that they start a weekly newspaper of their own, Read was delighted. Benham would be the business manager; Read would be the journalist. Their paper would be a humorous and literary publication called the *Arkansaw Traveler*.

Recalling his earlier failures with Warner, Read was anxious to get financial matters under control before they began publication, but he had nothing to fear with Benham managing the business end. Benham was an enthusiastic fund raiser and was soon selling subscriptions in advance at $2 per year. When they had enough money to cover equipment and publication of the first three issues, they began publication on 4 June 1882. The *Traveler*, Read said, "made a fearless first appearance." Within four months they had a circulation of 10,000 and by the end of the third year, 85,000. Read's experience as typesetter, reporter, and editor had prepared him well for his new position of writing and editing. The *Arkansaw Traveler* was a success.

It was published in a six-column format at first and usually consisted of eight pages. Its flag pictured on one side the Arkansas traveler on horseback questioning the Arkansas farmer—or squatter, as he was called—and, on the other side, the fiddler playing while the squatter danced. The pages carried Read's sketches or stories, often written in dialect; clippings from other newspapers; articles on art; notices of activities taking place locally; and sometimes poems. The paper was supported through subscriptions and through advertising promoting railway travel and sales of alcoholic beverages, patent medicines, farm animals, and other wares.

For a time the paper was favored in the Little Rock area, and its fame spread throughout the Midwest. Rural readers in Arkansas soon began to feel that Read's purpose, particularly in the sketches, was to make fun of them; politicians quickly caught the drift of rural opinion, and the *Traveler* became a target for their criticism. Out-of-state subscriptions increased, however, and Little Rock post office facilities became inadequate to handle circulation. After considerable debate about the most appropriate home for the *Traveler*, Benham and Read decided on Chicago. The move was made in 1887.

The change in location did not affect overall circulation, but it did hurt advertising. Benham and Read thought it best to form a stock company, of which Read was made president. The stock company idea appeared to stimulate advertising. The protests from Arkansas continued; one politician wrote: "Cowards, afraid longer to remain in the state, you have taken refuge among the Yankees to make fun of us." The ire expressed in Arkansas seems to have influenced the content of the paper. Soon after the move, the *Traveler* began something of a campaign to attract tourists to Arkansas. There were articles praising Arkansas's natural beauty, weather, and resources. These kinds of articles later came to include other states as well, promoting travel throughout the Midwest.

In February 1888, the six-column format was changed to three wide columns, and Read began to run more pictures. He also initiated a new attraction: installments from his own novels. Read had begun his first novels while still in Little Rock. With this interest increasing, he found in the *Traveler* the perfect outlet. *Mrs. Annie Green*, his first serialized novel, was so successful that he began another, *Len Gansett*, and followed that with *A Kentucky Colonel*. All were later published in book form. Certainly Read's exposure in the newspaper did much to boost his popularity as a novelist.

Chicago offered Read many other interests. He and Benham joined the Chicago Press Club, founded in 1879 and highly promoted by Mark Twain; Read later joined the Whitechapel Club. Both clubs offered opportunities for long conversations, poker games, and drinking bouts with leading newspapermen, writers, and politicians. Read was thrilled by the contacts he made—Robert Ingersoll, Joseph Medill, W. L. Visscher, John T.

McCutcheon, Edwin Markham, Finley Peter Dunne, Eugene Field, Grover Cleveland, and many other famous personalities—and took every opportunity to become better acquainted with such people.

In addition to his writing and club activities, Read took up golf, sometimes playing five days a week. One wonders if he had any time for family life. He and Ada Benham Read had eight children, and although Read said that after the move to Chicago they "missed the vine beneath which the children were wont to play," he rarely mentions his home life in his autobiography. Read's biographers note that Ada was very supportive of her husband, arranging her household to meet his needs, encouraging his association with those who might help him in his career as a writer, and inspiring him to think more highly of himself and his talents.

With new interests in writing fiction, golfing, and spending time at the clubs, Read began to grow weary of having to turn out sketches for the *Traveler* each week. Other contributors filled in the gaps as Read's own sketches became less frequent. By January 1892 Read had given up his position on the paper, but Benham continued as business manager for a few months. When Benham married and moved to St. Louis to publish a religious magazine, publication of the *Arkansaw Traveler* was taken over by the Review Printing Company.

To the end, the *Traveler* had its critics. One wrote: "You may think that the Lord will let up on you because you are now . . . publishing the doings of preachers but this won't offset the damned lies you've printed. . . ." But, upon Read's death years later, the *New York Times* noted: "Opie Read made a country humor sheet into a national institution, and, when it ceased publication, he continued as a national institution himself. . . . The Traveler became not so much a newspaper as a man—and when the Traveler wound up its incredible career, the man became virtually a legend."

Read occasionally worked for other newspapers after leaving the *Traveler*. He wrote a few pieces for the *New York World*, mostly interviews with such notable figures as John D. Rockefeller and William Dean Howells.

Although Read continued to think of himself as a journalist and continued to contribute sketches to various newspapers, he spent most of his time after 1891 writing fiction. When under pressure, he could turn out 10,000 words in a day. From 1891 to 1906 he averaged about two books a year, most of them novels, romances with rather thin plots car-

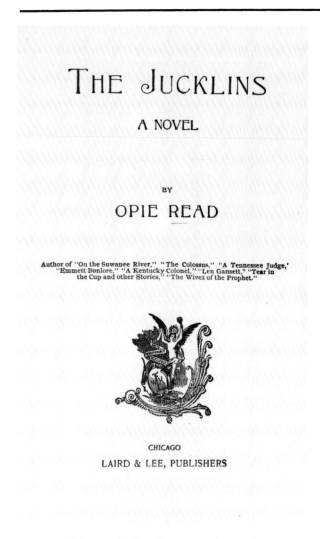

THE JUCKLINS

A NOVEL

BY

OPIE READ

Author of "On the Suwanee River," "The Colossus," "A Tennessee Judge,"
"Emmett Bonlore," "A Kentucky Colonel," "Len Gansett," "Tear in
the Cup and other Stories," "The Wives of the Prophet."

CHICAGO
LAIRD & LEE, PUBLISHERS

Title page for Read's most popular novel

ried out by the kinds of characters Read had put into his sketches over the years: sharecroppers, hillbillies, country lawyers, teachers, struggling young newspapermen. In the novels, as in the newspaper sketches, Read captured the dialect and mannerisms of the people he knew so well. The stories were set mostly in Southern areas where Read had lived, but a few reflected his life in New York and Chicago.

The Jucklins (1896), set in North Carolina, was probably Read's most popular book. It was translated into German and French and is said to have sold over a million copies. It is the story of Bill Hawes and the Jucklin family: Lim, an aging farmer who fights gamecocks for pleasure; Susan, Lim's wife, a Christian "from the stock that stood at the stake"; Guinea, the Jucklins' daughter, a "little spring branch nymph," who has been educated away from the farm; and Alf, their son, who is

hardworking and honest but easily angered. Bill takes charge of the local school, boarding at the Jucklins' house. He immediately falls in love with Guinea but learns that she is betrothed to the son of an old general, who has been a generous friend to the family. Alf is in love with Millie, the general's daughter, but she is being courted by Dan Stuart. After Alf has had a heated encounter with Stuart and Stuart's body is found in the road, Alf is arrested and charged with murder. The general, fearing a black mark against his family name, breaks the engagement of his son to Guinea. In disgrace, Lim Jucklin sells part of his farm to a neighbor and part to Bill Hawes. After Lim leaves with his wife and daughter, Bill Hawes discovers mica on the farm and is able to sell the mine to Northern capitalists for a fortune. He also uncovers new evidence that clears Alf of the murder charge. Lim, Susan, and Guinea return, and Bill is finally welcomed into the arms of Guinea. Millie in the meantime has decided that Alf is the man she truly wants to marry. Bill promises to return the farm to Lim Jucklin, to buy another farm for Alf and Millie, and to build a dream home on the bluffs of Michigan Lake for his "branch nymph." The characters are typical of the romantic novels of Read's time, and many of them strongly resemble people whom Read knew. Hawes—tall, good-looking, and eloquent—seems much like the young Read that Maurice Elfer describes in his biography. Mrs. Jucklin closely resembles Read's mother, and Guinea is in many ways like the beautiful and wise Ada Benham Read.

Several of Read's novels—*The Jucklins, A Kentucky Colonel* (1890), *The Carpetbagger* (1899), *The Starbucks* (1902), and *The Harkriders* (1903)—were dramatized. In 1912 a film was made of *The Starbucks*.

Read's novels met a need of his time. Long trips on the newly constructed transcontinental railroad meant hours of boredom for travelers. Paperbound copies of Read's novels were just the thing to relieve that boredom: they were entertaining, easy to carry, and inexpensive. The moral stamina of his heroes and heroines was appreciated by the straitlaced Victorians; the hillbilly characters and the tall tales were enjoyed by admirers of local color; and his ability to spin a yarn appealed to nearly all readers of that period.

In some ways his works were like those of Mark Twain, Bret Harte, and Charles Egbert Craddock—all popular humorists of his time. But much of his work was turned out hurriedly and carelessly under pressure of a deadline. Burton Rascoe wrote in the *Saturday Review* shortly after

Read's death that "Opie Read wrote pages and pages of pure Hemingway twenty years before Hemingway was born," but Read "sometimes left the impression that he was only two sticks behind the printer. Pages of sheer genius in dialogue, in narrative, and in invention are followed by pages so carelessly written that you can explain them only on the same grounds you explain certain passages in Dickens—that he was often behind in his copy on a story already partly on the press."

In all, Read authored thirty-five to forty novels; some were published under two different titles, and several are considered by some critics to be long stories rather than novels. At least ten of his books are collections of his short stories. His reminiscences of his meetings with Mark Twain and of the memorable stories he heard Twain tell are collected in *Mark Twain and I*, published posthumously in 1940.

Read's writing tapered off after 1914. By this time he had become famous in still another area: entertaining the public through the Chautauqua lecture system. Between 1912 and the late 1920s Read traveled all over the country, mounting podiums set up in parks, tents, or other gathering places in towns and cities of all sizes. Maurice Elfer, who knew Read well and completed his biography a few weeks before Read died, described him at the time of his Chautauqua lectures: "Tall, well-built, . . . with a countenance indicative of considerable intellect and aplomb, the dean of American fiction is, in appearance, invariably distinctive, effective. His personality and his individuality . . . and unique humor have caused him to be called 'the world's greatest platform entertainer.' His six feet and three inches of vigorous manhood . . . and his dynamic expressions have on countless occasions fired enthusiasm in the minds of dullards."

Read had been telling stories all his life, so he was at ease with his audiences. He discussed human nature, religion, and politics; spun yarns; told jokes; recounted anecdotes from his personal experiences; even offered condensed oral versions of his novels. Audiences in the small towns and rural areas were charmed by his down-to-earth philosophy, his nostalgia for the simple life of the past, and his honest approach to a life familiar to them. He was one of them, yet he had achieved fame as a newspaperman, as a novelist, and as a traveling entertainer. At the height of his lecturing career, Read made from 200 to 300 appearances a year, sometimes appearing with such celebrities as William Jennings Bryan and Governor Bob Taylor of Tennessee. Philo and Leslie Read wrote of their father

in the foreword to *Mark Twain and I*: "There is perhaps not a county in any state in the Union in which Opie Read did not lecture or tell stories. In the parlance of today, he 'got around some.' He knew, and made it a point to know, most of the prominent persons of his day. . . . While Opie Read lived for more than fifty years in the North, he was always the Arkansas Traveler, or the Kentucky Colonel to most people."

By the end of World War I Read had enjoyed four separate careers: wandering newspaperman, establishing or contributing to small newspapers in a variety of small towns; successful owner and editor of the *Arkansaw Traveler*, one of the most widely read humor sheets in the country; novelist and short story writer, appreciated by millions; and lecturer, favored by audiences all over the country. But the invention of the radio and the changes in attitudes after World War I dealt a blow to Read. There was no longer a need for the lecture series of the Chautauqua type. Read's brand of humor and his romantic fiction were suddenly out of style. He briefly tried writing syndicated features, but readers had developed new interests in social reform and realism. In 1930, when his autobiography was published, containing hundreds of anecdotes and sketches about his early career, it was hardly noticed except by old friends from the Chicago Press Club and a few elderly fans.

After the death of his wife in 1928, Read moved into an apartment owned by Mrs. Ben King at 5000 Harper Avenue, Chicago. He continued to be healthy and good-humored, enjoying his books and occasional meetings with old friends until a few months before his death. One of his sons once remarked, "Barring accidents my father will live to be a hundred years." But an accident occurred four months before Read's eighty-seventh birthday: Read fell in his apartment in August 1939 and suffered a brain concussion. Mrs. King cared for him as he lay ill during a late summer heat wave. He alternated between consciousness and unconsciousness, occasionally sitting up to talk with visitors, but lapsed into a coma near the end of October. He died shortly before noon, 2 November 1939.

After Read's death, Burton Rascoe assessed his contribution: "Read was an articulator of the robust spirit of democratic individualism which permeated the people who settled and built the river towns of the Mississippi Valley: he expressed their mores, their idiom, their lusty appetites, their quick tempers, their code of behavior, their disposition toward homely philosophy, their delight in extravagance, expansiveness and humorous exaggeration, and, above all, their essential recklessness, impatience with restraint and open defiance of the Eastern seaboard's notions of culture and polish." Read was an institution in his time, who "nourished the spirit and the dreams of men."

Those dreams were the dreams of a particular place in a particular era. In Read's heyday, "lies" and "sketches" were as good as news in newspapers; virtuous women and adventuresome men were the order of the day in novels; a lecture full of funny stories and advice was better than an evening at home with no entertainment at all. Read met a need of his own time, but not of all time. He followed Henry Watterson's advice—too well: he wrote something that everybody read but nobody remembers.

Biographies:
Maurice Elfer, *Opie Read* (Detroit, Mich.: Boyten-Miller, 1940);

Robert L. Morris, *Opie Read American Humorist* (New York: Helois Books, 1965).

References:
Fred W. Allsopp, *History of the Arkansas Press for a Hundred Years and More* (Little Rock, Ark.: Parke-Harper, 1922);

Willie Edna Durrett, "The Life and Works of Opie Read," M.A. thesis, Louisiana State University, 1951;

Burton Rascoe, "Opie Read and Zane Grey," *Saturday Review of Literature* (11 November 1939): 8;

Vincent Starrett, "Opie Read and the Great Novel," *Buried Caesars* (Freeport, N.Y.: Books for Libraries Press, 1968);

Laurence S. Thompson, "Opie Percival [*sic*] Read," *Southern Writers: A Biographical Dictionary*, edited by Robert Bain, Joseph M. Flora, and Louis D. Rubin, Jr. (Baton Rouge: Louisiana State University Press, 1979).

Whitelaw Reid

Hazel Dicken-Garcia
University of Minnesota

BIRTH: Xenia, Ohio, 27 October 1837, to Robert Charlton and Marian Whitelaw Ronalds Reid.

EDUCATION: B.A. with honors, Miami University, Oxford, Ohio, 1856.

MARRIAGE: 26 April 1881, to Elizabeth Mills; children: Ogden, Jean.

MAJOR POSITIONS HELD: Editor, *Xenia News* (1858-1860); war correspondent and Washington correspondent, *Cincinnati Gazette* (1861-1865, 1867-1868); owner, *New York Tribune* (1872-1912).

AWARDS AND HONORS: M.A., New York University, 1872; M.A., Dartmouth, 1873; LL.D., Miami University, 1890; LL.D., Princeton University, 1899; LL.D., Yale University, 1901; LL.D., Cambridge University, 1902; LL.D., St. Andrews University, 1905; D.C.L., Oxford University, 1907.

DEATH: London, England, 15 December 1912.

BOOKS: *After the War: A Southern Tour. May 1, 1865, to May 1, 1866* (New York: Moore, Wilstach & Baldwin, 1866);

Ohio in the War: Her Statesmen, Her Generals, and Soldiers, 2 volumes (New York: Moore, Wilstach & Baldwin, 1868);

Some Newspaper Tendencies: An Address Delivered before the Editorial Associations of New York and Ohio (New York: Holt, 1879);

The Cipher Dispatches (New York: *New York Tribune*, 1879);

Horace Greeley (New York: Scribners, 1879);

Town Hall Suggestions: An Address at the Opening of a New City Hall, Xenia, Ohio, February 16, 1881 (New York: Holt, 1881);

Two Speeches at the Queen's Jubilee, London, 1897 (New York: DeVinne, 1897);

Great Britain and the United States: Speech at the Dinner of the British Schools and Universities Club, New York, on the Queen's Birthday, May 24, 1898 (New York: DeVinne, 1898);

Some Consequences of the Last Treaty of Paris (London

Culver Pictures

& New York: Lane, 1899);

Our New Duties: A Commencement Address at the Seventy-fifth Anniversary of Miami University, Thursday, June 15, 1899 (New York: Miami University, 1899);

Later Aspects of Our New Duties: An Address at Princeton University on Commemoration Day, October 21, 1899 (New York: Hall, 1899);

The Treaty of Paris: Some Speeches on Its Policy and Scope (New York: Hall, 1899);

A Continental Union, Civil Service for the Islands: An Address at the Massachusetts Club, Boston, March 3, 1900 (New York: Hall, 1900);

Our New Interests: An Address at the University of California, on Charter Day, March 23, 1900 (Berkeley: University of California, 1900);

Problems of Expansion, as Considered in Papers and Addresses (New York: Century, 1900);

University Tendencies in America: An Address Delivered at Leland Stanford, Jr., University, April 19, 1901 (New York: Leland Stanford, Jr., University, 1901);

Careers for the Coming Men (New York: *Tribune* Association, 1902);

A Commencement Address before the ΦBK Society of Vassar College, June 8, 1903: The Thing to Do (New York: De Vinne, 1903);

A Commencement Address at the Law School, Yale University, June 23, 1903: The Monroe Doctrine, the Polk Doctrine and the Doctrine of Anarchism (New York: De Vinne, 1903);

Annual Address at the 42nd University Convocation of the State of New York, June 27, 1904 (Albany, N.Y., 1904);

How the United States Faced Its Educational Problem (London: Harrison, 1906);

University College, Colston Society Address, Bristol, March 30th, 1906: Scientific and Technological Education in the United States (London: Harrison, 1906);

The Rise of the United States (London: Harrison, 1906);

The Greatest Fact in Modern History: The Rise and Development of the United States (New York: Crowell, 1907);

John Bright Memorial School, Llandudno, North Wales, Opening Address, September 25th, 1907: The "Practical Side" of American Education. John Bright and the Civil War (London: Harrison, 1907);

Nottingham Chamber of Commerce. Address at Annual Dinner, November 7th, 1907: Great Britain and the United States Need Each Other (London: Harrison, 1907);

Thackeray in America (London, 1907);

Education in England: Address by Whitelaw Reid before the Associated Academic Principals of New York and the New York State Teachers Association, at Syracuse, New York, December 26, 1907 (Albany: New York State Education Department, 1908);

Luton Chamber of Commerce. Annual Dinner, April 10th, 1908: The Story of San Francisco for English Ears (London: Harrison, 1908);

"Our Foremost Friend in Great Britain": An Address by Whitelaw Reid at the Unveiling of a Tablet in Memory of Edmund Burke, Placed on His Old Residence at Bath by the Municipality, October 22nd, 1908 (London: Harrison, 1908);

London Commemorations. Winter of 1908-9. Remarks by the American Ambassador at the Poe Centenary, Authors' Club, March 1st (for Jan. 19th), 1909. The Bacon Tercentenary, Gray's Inn, Oct. 17th, 1908. The Milton Tercentenary, Mansion House, Dec. 9th, 1908. The Washington Anniversary, London Section, U.S. Navy League, Feb. 22nd,

1909 (London: Harrison, 1909);

Colossal Philanthropy: An Address by Whitelaw Reid, in Opening a Public Library at Luton. Saturday, October 1st, 1910 (London: Harrison, 1910);

Byron: Address at University College, Nottingham, on Speech Day, 29th November, 1910, for the Byron Chair of English Literature (London: Harrison, 1910);

University of Birmingham. "Makers of History in the Nineteenth Century." Closing Address, December 7th, 1910: Abraham Lincoln (London: Harrison, 1910);

Addresses 1900-1911 (London: Harrison, 1910);

One Welshman: A Glance at a Great Career. Inaugural Address, Autumn Session, University College of Wales, Aberystwyth, October 31st, 1912 (London: Harrison, 1912);

Addresses (London: Harrison, 1912);

The Scot in America and the Ulster Scot (London: Macmillan, 1912);

American and English Studies, 2 volumes (New York: Scribners, 1913; London: Smith, Elder, 1914);

Making Peace with Spain: The Diary of Whitelaw Reid, September-December, 1898, edited by Wayne H. Morgan (Austin: University of Texas Press, 1965);

A Radical View: The "Agate" Dispatches of Whitelaw Reid, 1861-1865, edited by James G. Smart (Memphis, Tenn.: Memphis State University Press, 1976).

Whitelaw Reid was a journalist who achieved fame in Civil War battle reports—some of which stand as classics—and who wielded power and influence as editor of the *New York Tribune* for more than thirty years. He was a politician who was active in directing the course of the Republican party during the last quarter of the nineteenth century, using his wit, talent, and influence to effect presidential appointments and pursuing the office of vice-president of the United States after his nomination in the 1892 election campaign. He was a diplomat who served as minister to France, as ambassador to Great Britain, and as a member of the commission sent to negotiate peace with Spain in 1898. While his role as a politician elicited deference in his lifetime and his career as a diplomat has been viewed as distinguished, it was in his work and thought as a journalist that his brilliance was most clearly revealed. In that profession, his greatest achievements were his Civil War reporting and his guidance of the *Tribune* from the era of personal journalism to the era of corporate journalism, from the stewardship of Horace Greeley through the

fierce circulation competition generated by William Randolph Hearst and Joseph Pulitzer. Reid achieved wealth and stature rivaling those of any of his contemporaries in his profession. But his rise to prominence was more steady, deliberate, and calculated—less conspicuous and dazzling—than that of any of those contemporaries. He seems never to have gone to some of the extremes to get news, or to manipulate it, that became common in the late nineteenth century. This is not to say that he did not aggressively pursue what he believed to be news or that he did not occasionally "manage" news—especially when it was politically expedient or when certain press reports could have impaired America's international relationships while he was a diplomat; but he never engaged in the kind of sensationalism prevalent in other newspapers. Though he had deep, carefully thought out concerns about Cuba, he opposed war with Spain and never used the *Tribune* to call for war; but he loyally supported President William McKinley as events moved toward war and after war was declared. Reid was very much a self-made success—a man who relied on native acumen, caution, and methodical study of circumstances in conjunction with virtually his every decision.

Whitelaw Reid grew up, the second child of Reformed Presbyterian parents, in modest circumstances on an Ohio farm. He completed grammar school at Xenia Academy, where his uncle Hugh MacMillan, the principal and teacher of classical studies, influenced his academic interests. At age fifteen, Reid entered Miami University in Oxford, Ohio, at the level of a second-year student and, after three years, graduated as the most outstanding scholar in his class.

Biographer Bingham Duncan notes that Reid was indecisive about his future after college graduation and knew only that he did not want to farm, become a minister, or be a merchant—the chief pursuits followed by members of his family. After a brief, unsatisfying effort as principal of a South Charleston, Ohio, elementary school, Reid decided to try journalism and prevailed upon his brother Gavin, nine years older than he, to join him in purchasing and editing the *Xenia News*.

Reid's interest in journalism was not new; he had grown up reading the local newspapers and the *New York Tribune*. When he was sixteen, he sent an article on the Miami University commencement to the *Tribune*. The publication of the article whetted his appetite for more by-lines. Before he was seventeen, he contributed articles to three local newspapers—the *Xenia News*, the *Oxford Citizen*, and the *Hamilton Intelligencer*. The articles generally dealt with local interests, but Reid also commented on European historical events, while another one of his articles was called "Resolutions on the Funeral of Logic." After debate began on opening the Kansas Territory to slavery, Reid sent three antislavery articles to a Kansas newspaper.

When Reid embarked on editorship of the *Xenia News*, he was not yet twenty-one. Although he was still too young to vote, his newspaper work initiated him into politics. He announced that the paper would be independent but not neutral, that it would support the Republican party but not be a "party slave" or "blindly" follow partisan leaders. Reid wrote in opposition to slavery, and on local, state, and national politics. He supported Lincoln and, with his modest newspaper, was part of a new wave that would defeat the Democratic party in Ohio in the next presidential election. When Lincoln came to Ohio on a campaign tour, Reid met and introduced him.

But the *Xenia News* was not to be a lasting effort. Only four years old when Reid acquired it, the paper had already had several owners who tried to make it financially sound. Reid had no better luck and, after two years, gave up the paper.

While editing the *News*, Reid had lost weight, and his family, concerned about his health, sent him on a vacation in the summer of 1860. While traveling nearly 3,000 miles via train, riverboat, stagecoach, and horseback into Minnesota, to the headwaters of the Mississippi and St. Louis rivers, Reid wrote articles about his experiences and observations for the *Cincinnati Gazette*, having made arrangements to do so before his departure. Perhaps because of the visibility those articles gave his name, he was asked the following spring to report on the Ohio legislature for the *Cincinnati Times*.

Reid was to write an article a day for the *Times*, but soon after he arrived in Columbus, he was asked to provide reports for the *Cleveland Herald* and the *Cincinnati Gazette*. Writing three articles daily, he earned $38 per week from the three newspapers. As his signature for the *Gazette* articles, he adopted the pen name "Agate"—a name which would soon become widely known.

During Reid's first month in Columbus, fighting began at Fort Sumter. In the ensuing legislative debate on the issues which that outbreak brought to the fore, Reid focused on the House of Representatives, where Democratic strength lay. The *Gazette* owners, pleased with his reporting, offered him a job as city editor, and Reid moved to Cincinnati in May. The same month, Ohio troops

Reid as a young man (Ohio Historical Society)

were dispatched to join federal forces stationed at Grafton, Virginia, to protect the strategic Baltimore and Ohio Railroad stretching from Washington, D.C., to Parkersburg, Virginia. The *Gazette* sent Reid, who was given the rank of captain, with the troops as an aide-de-camp. Military units in the region—known as the Rich Mountain area—were under the command of Gen. George B. McClellan of Ohio.

Seeing no military action at first, Reid sent articles to the *Gazette* describing camp life, emphasizing the troops' good spirits and criticizing the inadequacy of their uniforms. In late June, when a battle was expected near Philippi, Virginia, Reid, who was free to go with any general as circumstances offered, accompanied Gen. Thomas A. Morris. The first battle Reid witnessed occurred at Carrick's Ford on 13 July. Witnessing violent death and the agony of wounded, dying, and escaping Confederate soldiers affected him and perhaps distorted his overall view of the battle. His reports of this action were neither the best published nor the best examples of Reid's war reporting. He wrote vividly of troop actions and the suffering he saw but slighted the Union's successes in this confrontation. He wrote of the death of Confederate Gen. Robert Seldon Garnett, shot while he stood exposed signaling to his men: "In an instant, Sergeant Burlingame 'drew a bead' on him and fired. He fell instantly, and when Major Gordon reached him but a moment later, his muscles were just giving their last convulsive twist. The Major stooped down by his side, tenderly closed his eyes, bound up his face, and left a guard to protect his body."

Reid wrote of the aftermath of carnage: "Returning from the bank where Garnett lay, I went up to the bluff on which the enemy had been posted. The first object that caught the eye was a large iron rifled cannon (a six pounder) which they had left in their precipitate flight. Around was a sickening sight. Along the brink of that bluff lay ten bodies, stiffening in their own gore, in every contortion which their death anguish had produced. Others were gasping in the last agonies, and still others were writhing with horrible but not mortal wounds, surrounded by the soldiers whom they really believed to be about to plunge the bayonet to their hearts. Never before, had I so ghastly a realization of the horrid nature of this fraternal struggle. These men were all Americans—men whom we had once been proud to claim as countrymen—some of them relatives of our own Northern states."

After the battle, Reid, without a horse and anxious to file his story, sought transportation to the nearest telegraph office thirty miles away in Rowlesburg, Virginia. Learning that the body of General Garnett was to be sent via Rowlesburg to Washington, D.C., Reid and another reporter gained permission to be part of the escort. The party did not depart until noon the day after the battle and then was slowed by rugged terrain, roadblocks, and other impediments. At one point, Reid himself drove when the wagoner was too frightened to negotiate the narrow road along a Cheat River bluff. In the dark, the travelers were susceptible to fire from both sides, and Reid was forced to hide from Union snipers until the next morning. The delay caused him to miss deadlines necessary to insure that his story would have made the next day's edition.

When the story did reach the press, it was critical of the Union army and especially of General McClellan. Reid "blamed McClellan for failure to capture or destroy the enemy," sarcastically noting that the general did not live up to advance publicity about his abilities. Although the battle had resulted in Garnett's death and the demoralization of his troops, Reid blamed McClellan for the escape of most of Garnett's troops. "And this," Reid wrote pointedly, "is the culmination of the brilliant Generalship which the journals of the sensational persuasion have been besmearing with such nauseous flattery." So critical was Reid's report, in fact, that he did not mention that the mission had succeeded in gaining Union dominance over the railroad and western routes to the Shenandoah Valley.

After a month in Cincinnati following the Rich Mountain campaign, Reid was sent to cover Gen. William S. Rosecrans's headquarters at Clarksburg, Virginia. For the rest of the year, he alternated between following the army and making brief sojourns in Cincinnati. He continued to criticize the army, noting that supply costs were exorbitant; that headquarters offices were wasteful and inefficient; and that officers were poorly trained, irresponsible, and unworthy of those in their command. Finally, in February 1862, he was forced to return to Cincinnati after his complaints about defective ammunition and inadequate medical care resulted in his being denied further access to Camp Nevin, where he was stationed.

Not barred from other headquarters, he was soon on the road again. He joined Gen. Ulysses Grant's troops in Tennessee and spent six weeks in perhaps the most comfortable sojourn in the Civil War. This unit, larger than any Reid had seen, experienced better conditions and had more comfortable accommodations; and Reid, with some leisure to roam, spent a relatively relaxed period being treated almost as a guest rather than as a participant. The unit impressed Reid, especially in its capture of Fort Henry and Fort Donelson.

But on 6 April 1862, Gen. Albert Sidney Johnston's Confederates caught the bivouacked Union troops by surprise in a dawn attack at Pittsburg Landing, Tennessee. At first firing, Reid sought the best means of transportation and information and was soon on Gen. Lew Wallace's steamboat at Crump's Landing. Grant arrived shortly afterward, and while he conferred with Wallace, Reid quietly boarded Grant's boat, the *Tigress*, and accompanied the general to the battle site. The battle lasted through two days of chaos and contradictory reports. Reid, however, in his prior six weeks, had learned the territory, troop locations, regimental compositions, and commanders. He could move easily, gauge troop strength and morale, and quickly grasp the turns of events. This was the worst battle he had seen, and he pursued the story with care befitting its historical significance. It was Reid's finest hour as a reporter.

When the Confederate army withdrew, Reid accompanied the wounded soldiers aboard a steamboat to Cairo, Illinois. There, and on the train to Cincinnati, he wrote a 19,000-word story which filled thirteen columns in the *Cincinnati Gazette* and was widely reprinted in Ohio papers, in St. Louis, in Chicago, and in the *New York Tribune*. The story of the battle of Shiloh, as it came to be called, made the twenty-five-year-old Reid famous almost overnight; the report became a classic.

"Some, particularly among our officers, were not yet out of bed" when the attack came, Reid reported:

> Others were dressing, others washing, others cooking, a few eating their breakfasts. Many guns were unloaded, ammunition was ill-supplied—in short, the camps were virtually surprised—disgracefully, it might be added, unless some one can hereafter give some yet undiscovered reason to the contrary—and were taken at almost every possible disadvantage.
>
> The first wild cries from the pickets rushing in, and the few scattering shots that preceded their arrival, aroused the regiments to a sense of their peril; an instant afterward, shells were hurtling through the tents, while, before there was time for thought of preparation, there came rushing through the woods, with lines of battle sweeping the whole flank, the fine, dashing compact columns of the enemy.
>
> Into the just-aroused camps thronged the rebel regiments, firing sharp volleys as they came, and springing toward our laggards with the bayonet. Some were shot down as they were running, without weapons, hatless, coatless, toward the river. The searching bullets found other poor unfortunates in their tents, and there all unheeding now, they still slumbered, while the unseen foe rushed on. Others fell, as they were disentangling themselves from the flaps that formed the doors to their tents; others as they were buckling on their accoutrements; a few, it was even said, as they were vainly trying to impress on the cruelly-exultant enemy their readiness to surrender. . . .

As Duncan summarizes, the story told of gloom, of an army surprised, of a general caught off guard, of the ensuing confusion, heroism, the near disaster. And its criticism—overt and implied—brought upon Reid the wrath of generals. Within two weeks, Gen. Henry Wager Halleck opened war on the press with Field Order No. 54, saying that Secretary of War Edwin M. Stanton's authority over war reporting would not be recognized and that "unauthorized hangers-on" among the press would be excluded from access to military lines. A "com-mittee" of correspondents elected Reid as chairman, and at a meeting of the committee with Halleck, Reid pointed out the pitfalls of such a vague phrase as "unauthorized hangers-on." He argued that, inevitably, trying to apply the phrase would mean that unauthorized journalists would find ways to remain and report on war activity while authorized journalists would be excluded. The correspondents left the meeting believing that no self-respecting reporter would remain under the conditions imposed by Halleck, and all but three correspondents subsequently voluntarily withdrew from the lines. Reid, who was among those leaving, was ripe for a career change anyway.

The generals' wrath had only strengthened Reid's already soaring reputation, for the public agreed with his assessments of army deficiencies. His war correspondence, all signed "Agate," had made him respected by the public and editors throughout the country. As the *Gazette*'s star reporter, Reid now seemed the perfect person to cover the national news center, Washington, D.C.

Washington in the 1860s was at a zenith of political and intellectual dominance not reached again until the early twentieth century; it was a good place for a reporter to be. But Reid's reporting perspective necessarily changed during his three years in Washington. As a war correspondent, he had become a skilled military analyst on the basis of his own news gathering and observations; in Washington, however, he wrote articles from information others provided. His remaining work as a war correspondent, covering the Battle of Gettysburg and the fall of Richmond, and his coverage of the funeral of Abraham Lincoln, were virtually the only exceptions to this situation. These accounts represented outstanding reporting, but none equaled his work on the story of Shiloh. Nevertheless, few journalists attracted more attention during the Civil War than "Agate."

Washington was rife with opportunities for the less scrupulous newsmen, and congressional leaders often appointed "friendly" reporters to clerkships and committees. While there seems to be no evidence that Reid was the unscrupulous sort, he was made librarian of the House of Representatives throughout the war years, and in the third session of the Thirty-seventh Congress he was clerk of the House Committee on Military Affairs. Such positions opened doors and provided access to sources useful to a journalist. During those years, Reid became well acquainted with such notables as Salmon P. Chase, Charles Sumner, Henry Winter Davis, James A. Garfield, John Hay, and Horace Greeley.

Reid's fame brought an offer from the *St. Louis Democrat* to be leading editor at a salary of $1,300 a year; he was also asked to become editor of the *Nation* when plans for it were being formulated. The *Cincinnati Gazette*, unable to match the financial level of these offers, offered Reid a chance to buy a share in the newspaper. To do so, according to Duncan, he borrowed a sum greater than the total he had earned in his life's work.

Although he invested in the newspaper, he turned from journalism for two years. After Andrew Johnson was inaugurated as president, Reid was invited to accompany Chief Justice Chase on an inspection tour of Southern cities; on that trip, Reid resolved to become a Southern planter. The trip also gave Reid his first opportunity to visit a foreign country: he spent two days in Havana and formulated concerns about Cuba which would affect his position on the Spanish-American War in 1898. After a second Southern trip, Reid returned to Washington in December 1865 long enough to report the organization of the Thirty-ninth Congress. Then he returned to the South and bought land in partnership with Francis Jay Herron, also twenty-nine years old and a lawyer from Iowa. On their two large farms in Louisiana, they cultivated 2,000 acres of cotton and employed nearly 200 blacks. After barely clearing enough to support another such effort, Reid made a second attempt as a planter—without Herron—in Alabama in 1867. Losing the profits he had gained in Louisiana, he decided to return to journalism.

While in the South, he completed one book and began work on another. The former, *After the War* (1866), was a collection of his observations during the trip with Chief Justice Chase in 1865, and it remains a valuable source for students of the era. The second book, a two-volume tome called *Ohio in the War* (1868), impressive because of Reid's analysis and interpretation, deals with more than 100 Ohio generals who served in the Union army. Reid's assessment of their strengths and weaknesses has been supported by later studies of their military careers.

Reid went back to the *Cincinnati Gazette* at the end of 1867 and was sent to Washington in early 1868 to cover the impeachment proceedings against Andrew Johnson. Then he accepted a long-standing offer from Horace Greeley to join the staff of the *New York Tribune*.

The *Tribune* in 1868 was a $1,000,000-a-year enterprise; with more than 300,000 subscribers, its advertising, circulation, and business departments had a staff of more than thirty and took in nearly $100,000 per month. Reid, employed to work directly under the supervision of Greeley or his twenty-seven-year-old managing editor, John Russell Young, advanced in less than eight months to the latter's position after Young was forced to resign for sending Associated Press items to a nonparticipating Philadelphia newspaper in which he held an interest. By 1872, Reid owned 10 of the 100 *Tribune* shares, valued at $10,000 each.

After Greeley's ill-fated campaign for president—with an at-first-reluctant Reid as manager—and death in 1872, Reid prepared to resign. Business manager Samuel Sinclair and Western Union President William Orton were planning to buy controlling shares in the newspaper and were seeking Schuyler Colfax as Greeley's successor. However, Orton's and Sinclair's plans collapsed at the last minute, and Reid quickly took advantage of the chance to buy a controlling interest. To do so, he borrowed an undisclosed amount from financier Jay Gould, who was happy at the prospect of acquiring the friendship of a newspaper at a time when he was generating ire in many quarters. Although Reid had no intention of tailoring editorial content to Gould's liking, others suspected that this was inevitable. Reid, fearing a financial emergency of his own might open the way for Gould to buy control, was nagged by the uneasy alliance until after his marriage in 1881, when his wife's family bought the Gould shares.

As soon as he gained control, Reid ceased paying shareholders and put all profits into building and expansion. Six months later, he moved the paper to temporary quarters while he had the old building razed and began constructing on the original site "the best newspaper office in the country." In April 1875, the Tall Tower was complete, and the first *Tribune* from the new presses appeared on 10 April. By 1879, the new building was earning $85,000 in profit; still, it was another year before Reid resumed dividend payments—the first paid since Greeley's death.

The new owner found displeasing results of poor editorial and business management on the paper. Among many efficiency moves, he contracted with Western Union Telegraph—in addition to long-standing *Tribune* participation in the Associated Press—and gained for the newspaper up to 60,000 words per month at one-sixth of the regular rate. In 1875, he installed the first of Richard Hoe's web presses, and he resumed indexing of the *Tribune*—a practice which had lapsed while Young was managing editor.

Reid also attended to the paper's content,

gearing it to readers whom he thought were more intelligent and better readers than subscribers to most newspapers. He deplored sensationalism and news gimmicks, telling New York editors in an 1879 meeting that "There is not an Editor in New York who does not know the fortune that awaits the man there who is willing to make a daily as disreputable and vile as a hundred and fifty thousand readers would be willing to buy." He told the group that news gathering costs had surpassed paper as the greatest news publishing expense and that he looked to the day when the greatest expense would be for brains and literary skill.

In upgrading content, Reid dismissed some staff members and hired others; most notable among the latter were John Hay, former press secretary to Abraham Lincoln, and William Dean Howells, who was hired to write book reviews and literary columns. Upgrading the national and international correspondence, Reid hired Henry James to write on artistic and intellectual subjects from Paris.

Reid's economizing efforts ran afoul of the unions. In his first four years in control, he cut printers' wages twice, and in 1877, when he discussed a third cut, a clash with Typographical Union Number Six ensued. Reid hired as foreman outspoken antiunionist William P. Thompson, who worked out an offer the printers were likely to reject. At the same time, Reid lined up a new labor force and was ready when, after the printers did reject the offer, eighty employees went on strike. *Tribune* operations were barely interrupted, and Reid estimated that the employee changeover (with new workers at lower or unchanged salary levels) saved the *Tribune* $30,000 a year.

Reid was equally hardline and antilabor with construction workers on his new building, choosing to bargain on salaries rather than sign contracts. In May 1874, when workers balked at the salary, Reid replaced them with Italian workers at the old rates. Despite a strike by bricklayers in June, Reid estimated wage savings for the year at $75 per day as compared with prevailing rates when construction began. The actions led to friction between Reid and labor that would plague him for twenty years, especially when his proffered support for political hopefuls raised serious questions about his effect on the labor vote.

Having attended to internal affairs, Reid turned to establishing the paper's political power. In December 1877, he announced it would be a Republican newspaper and sent notices to postmasters throughout the country urging them to help expand *Tribune* circulation for the sake of strengthening the party. With the notice, he sent supporting letters bearing the signatures of appropriate local Republican chairmen. In 1878, he met with Thomas C. Platt, chief aide to Sen. Roscoe Conkling, head of the New York Republican organization, and planned a campaign to strengthen the political power of Platt, the Republican party, and the *Tribune*. Platt traveled to a half-dozen states securing party leaders as agents in pushing the *Weekly Tribune*'s circulation; in doing so, they were free to use party funds to subsidize payment for bulk subscriptions.

Reid's greatest challenge remained: before he could establish his position as an editor to be reckoned with, he had to become successfully entrenched in the upper echelons of New York political power. Reid's Washington experience had taught him much about national politics, but he had little knowledge of New York. He had few New York friends, and he knew no state political leaders who both agreed with his views and had popular standing. Reid was somewhat alienated from the party until Ohioan Rutherford B. Hayes was nominated for president in 1876. Waiting a decent interval after the nomination, Reid conveyed through a third party his assurances of *Tribune* support for Hayes. He followed that message a short time later with a personal letter expressing hearty approval for Hayes's published views. Then, shortly before Hayes's inauguration, Reid wrote the president-elect suggesting several people for cabinet posts — discreetly reminding Hayes that his advice and counsel had not been sought. That Reid's overtures were ignored indicated that he did not yet have the close position to the powerful he craved. But some luck and Reid's readiness to take advantage of it soon changed that.

The revelations of the "Cipher Dispatches," published in the *Tribune* in October 1878, put Reid within that inner circle of power, making him a recognized Republican party "dean" to be feared and respected by the Democrats and one to be consulted and listened to by incumbents and aspirants to office. The "Dispatches" also brought him his first offer of a diplomatic post. Ironically, the "Dispatches" developed out of Democratic charges of Republican corruption which led, after the 1876 election, to House and Senate committee investigations of the returns. The investigations unearthed no evidence of Republican fraud, but messages found and decoded by *Detroit Press* reporters pointed to Democratic fraud: a Democratic agent in Oregon had offered $10,000 for an elector's vote.

Perhaps because the deal never went through, Democratic congressmen saw no threat and appointed a special investigating committee, chaired by New York Representative Clarkson N. Potter, to keep alive the issue of Republican fraud.

As the committee worked, some Republicans found a batch of previously subpoenaed telegrams, in code, in a committee-room closet. (The telegrams, collected during the investigation more than a year earlier, were to have been sent back to Western Union for destruction.) After a brief perusal of the telegrams, the Republicans decided to use them to draw attention away from the Republican-corruption issue. They planted a few for Potter committee member Benjamin F. Butler to find. (Butler had boasted that he could break any code.) They sent seventeen others to Reid, suggesting publication of some with a demand for Democrats to translate them—if they had nothing to hide. Soon hundreds of coded telegrams came to Reid and the investigating committee. Decoders were put to work by Reid.

Meanwhile, Reid, in the *Tribune*, needled Democrats into more and more charges of fraud against Republicans and stronger claims of their own party's innocence of any wrongdoing. On 3 October, Reid, noting the October Democratic convention resolution that Republican fraud had abolished choice in the 1876 election, promised to expose Democratic corruption and published a few telegrams in translation. For four days, he allowed suspense to build before unfolding the story, beginning on 7 October.

The telegrams revealed that Col. W. T. Pelton, nephew of high-ranking Democrat Samuel J. Tilden, had received offers from John C. Coyle, C.W. Wooley, Manton Marble, and others regarding vote buying and had, in fact, been involved in paying large sums for votes. The telegrams had been sent to Tilden's address, where his nephew lived. Thus, even if Tilden knew nothing of the vote buying, he could not escape suspicion. The disclosures ended Tilden's political career and left the Democratic party in shambles.

Reid's position in New York and national politics was established. Hayes offered him a diplomatic post in Germany; but Reid, seeing the appointment as leading to a dead end just when he was relishing a rise in influence, declined. He wrote to John Hay on 20 March 1879 that "I declined it because it seemed a needless abandonment of a position in wh . . . my chances are at least good as ever; and in wh my independence is greater than ever. If I had gone, the paper wld. hv. slipped away from me,

inevitably;—or, if it did not, the profession wld. At the end of two years, I shld hv. had as much political preferment as the public wld. think I deserved & that career wld be ended. Without a miracle, I cldn't resume my professional career at anything like the same height. In a word, at 43 I shld. hv. reached a climax. Whatever followed wld be inferior. . . ."

Feeling thus secure, Reid bought a Lexington Avenue home in keeping with his stature. Later he would acquire Wild Air, a camp he developed from an Adirondacks cabin he bought in 1882; Orphir Farm (renamed Orphir Hall in 1902), a 700-acre estate bought in 1886 in Westchester County, three miles east of White Plains, New York; and a town house at 451 Madison Avenue, where he moved his young family in 1886. But for the moment, the brownstone at 271 Lexington Avenue suited the needs of the enterprising Reid. Using the home as a base from which to cultivate the prominent and keep close to *Tribune* management, he grew—in wealth, prominence, and influence.

Reid fence-sat, except for his long-standing opposition to Grant, during the early part of the next presidential election, but he was elated when another Ohioan, James A. Garfield, was nominated. He inundated the nominee with letters of advice. The two, who had been friends for some time, were viewed as so close during the campaign that a cartoon depicted Garfield as bride, Uncle Sam as groom, and Reid as bridesmaid.

As inauguration day approached, however, Reid was less and less in touch with Garfield, for his attention was consumed with courting twenty-three-year-old Elizabeth Mills—much against her parents' wishes. The wealthy Ogden Mills must have had misgivings about his daughter's interest in a man nearly twice her age; but he was won over, and the couple were married in April 1881.

While the newlyweds were on an extended European honeymoon, President Garfield died of an assassin's bullet. Chester A. Arthur, upon succeeding to the presidency, replaced virtually the entire cabinet. Reid found himself shut out of the inner circle. Reid and James G. Blaine, another old friend whose appointment as secretary of state Reid had heartily endorsed, commiserated by mail before Reid's return in the late fall. Reid advised Blaine to resign and prepare to run for president in 1884, and Blaine did.

The *Tribune* attacked Arthur throughout his administration and paved the way for Blaine's nomination in 1884. After that nomination, Reid, certain he would soon again be in the inner circle of power, was so visible that cartoons mocked the

Blaine-Reid "union." Bernard Gillam's cartoon in *Puck* on 4 June 1884 depicted Reid as a slave dealer removing Blaine's cloak to show him naked—except for tattoos reading "Corruption," "Anti-labor," "Northern Pacific Bonds." Reid was shown telling the gathered Republicans inspecting prospective nominees, "Now Gentlemen, don't make any mistake in your decision! Here's Purity and Magnetism for you—can't be beat!" A *New York World* cartoon by Walt McDougall, "Belshazzer Maine and the Money Kings," depicted Reid at Blaine's shoulder in the center of a dinner of wealthy Republicans. (The press had tagged the dinner attended by 200 prominent, wealthy Republicans honoring Blaine "the millionaire's dinner.")

Cleveland's victory was unexpected by the Republicans, and it cost Reid the chance to gain position and power that would perhaps have been second only to Blaine's. Although the *Tribune* supported Cleveland's chief policies, Reid subsequently attacked Cleveland and his administration while waiting for the next election. Luck favored him again when another Ohioan (and Miami University alumnus), Benjamin Harrison, was elected. Reid quickly sent advice on appointments and other matters to the president-elect. Fully expecting a

cabinet post for himself, Reid was disappointed to be offered the ambassadorship to France. Forced to accept it to prevent appearances of disharmony between the *Tribune* and the White House, Reid was confirmed as Envoy Extraordinary and Minister Plenipotentiary to the Republic of France on 28 March 1889. He and his family sailed for France on 4 May, after Reid had put Donald Nicholson in charge of the *Tribune*. Reid would not again be as active in *Tribune* affairs as he had, though he did not relinquish editorship officially until 1905. While in France, he directed Nicholson, sent materials to be published to effect ends he sought in his role as ambassador, and prohibited publication of any matter critical of France.

Leaving the ambassadorship before his term expired, Reid arrived in New York in the spring of 1892 ready to run for vice-president. He received the nomination, with Harrison as nominee for president. After being defeated in the election, Reid withdrew from public life for four years. He spent much time traveling, and while he was thus removed from *Tribune* operations, his *Tribune* associate, John E. Milholland, settled the twenty-year-old dispute with Typographical Union Number Six with an agreement that the *Tribune* would hire only union members, or give thirty days'

Cartoon by Bernard Gillam in Puck *depicting Reid as a slave dealer exhibiting James G. Blaine to Republicans in 1884*

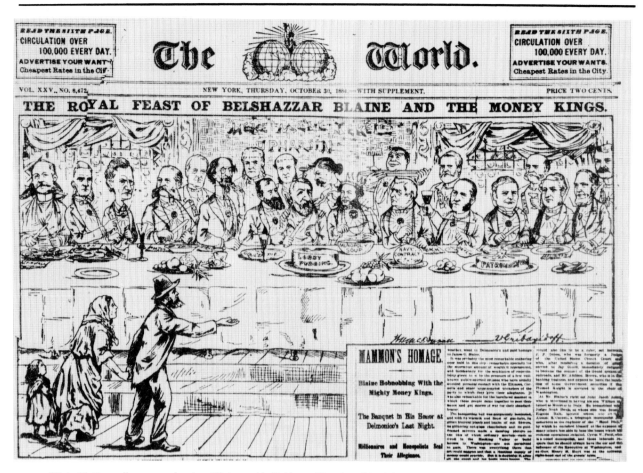

Walt McDougall cartoon showing Blaine—with Reid speaking into his right ear—at dinner with wealthy Republicans

written notice to the union of any consideration of nonmembers for employment. The *Tribune* also agreed to pay union scale wages and not to fire union members without giving written notice to the union. The union agreed to provide thirty days' written notice of any contemplated strike and pledged $5,000 as security against breaking the contract.

As the 1896 nominating committee convention approached and it appeared certain that yet another Ohioan, William McKinley, would be elected president, Reid emerged from "retirement" to bolster *Tribune* support for him. Again acting in the role of kingmaker, Reid anticipated appointment after McKinley's election. He especially wanted to be named secretary of state or, if that were not possible, ambassador to Great Britain. When neither post was offered, Reid became bitter, especially when his longtime close friend John Hay was appointed ambassador to England. Reid wrote the *Tribune* editor that because people would think he had nominated Hay, the newspaper must give

some attention to the announcement; but after that, "no more gush," Reid instructed.

Perhaps because McKinley knew of Reid's disappointment—and because of some State Department fumbles—Reid was chosen as one of the American representatives at the sixtieth anniversary of Queen Victoria's accession in the summer of 1897. Later he was chosen as a member of the commission to negotiate peace with Spain. Reid's importance to the commission was probably being exaggerated at the time, although he may have averted a break-off in talks at one point. But he was perceived as influential, especially by the Spaniards, perhaps because he was the only commission member who had an international reputation and, since he could speak French to French-speaking Spaniards, the only member who could communicate directly with both delegations. But his appointment probably stemmed from his published views on Spain and the Caribbean. Those views had changed since the early 1870s, when he had said that Spain should leave Cuba and the United States should dominate, but not acquire territory, in the Caribbean. By 1896, he privately believed the United States would eventually have to take Cuba and should hold it as a colony. But he opposed war with Spain until a few days before war was declared, and he did not openly advocate acquisition of territory until after the war began. His published argument just prior to the establishment of the peace commission was that the United States "was faced with an inevitable duty and that to remain in the islands was the only practical solution to a situation this country had neither sought nor desired."

At a point in McKinley's administration when the London embassy post was vacant, Reid told the president how much he desired the ambassadorship and how much he believed he deserved it. But such an appointment did not come from McKinley.

Thereafter, Reid was cool to McKinley, and he took no part in political machinations surrounding succeeding elections. Although he had disliked Theodore Roosevelt at first, Reid cultivated his friendship for some time and was gratified when President Roosevelt sent him in 1902 as a special ambassador to the coronation of King Edward VII. He was even more gratified when Roosevelt appointed him ambassador to Great Britain in 1905, and he served in that capacity with enthusiasm for

Caricature of Reid in Life, *3 February 1898*

The American Peace Commission, in Paris to negotiate an end to the Spanish-American War: (from left) Reid, George Gray, John Bassett Moore, William Rufus Day, William P. Frye, Cushman Kellogg Davis

the last seven years of his life.

Reid remained interested in the *Tribune* until his death, but he retired from editorial duties before sailing for England. His roles as editor and publisher were transferred to Hart Lyman, and James Martin was named managing editor. Reid, who had always assumed his son, Ogden Mills Reid, would one day take over the *Tribune*, was delighted in 1908 when he learned that Ogden had joined the staff and was doing well.

No major crises emerged to truly test Reid in his role as diplomat. His diplomatic career was thus uneventful, and most demands on him were routine, all of which he met with skill and aplomb. He continued public speaking, which he had begun at least as early as 1858, when, at the age of twenty-one, he was invited to speak during the Miami University commencement exercises. In New York, he had grown used to public speaking during his fourteen-year presidency of the Lotus Club; during the 1892 campaign, he had gained experience in making political speeches. In addition, he had spoken frequently at national holiday commemorations, medal presentations, unveilings, commencements, and on other occasions. While he was in London, his speeches drew more attention than did his other efforts as ambassador. He wanted his speeches printed and often suggested that explanatory comments preface the published speeches. Many addresses were published as books; the Library of Congress lists forty titles under his authorship. At least eight honorary degrees, some from the most distinguished universities in the world, were conferred upon him in his later years. He was a trustee of Stanford University, a member of the New York Board of Regents, and chancellor of the University of New York. Highly regarded and respected, he lived a life of distinction until his death in London on 15 December 1912. Reid, whose career had been characterized by eighteen-hour workdays, was fully active until the last week of his life. Having been plagued by asthma periodically for years, he died of pulmonary edema after a week's illness.

Ogden Reid became editor of the *Tribune* after Reid's death. The paper was merged with the *Herald* in 1924 and continued as the *New York Herald Tribune*. When Ogden died in 1947, his wife and his sons, Whitelaw and Ogden R., continued the newspaper until it was sold to John Hay Whitney in 1958. Hurt by a 1963 strike, the paper lost money through the early 1960s, and the last edition of the *Herald Tribune* appeared on 24 April 1966. A *World Journal Tribune*, a by-product of a planned merger between

Whitney, the Hearst group, and Scripps-Howard, appeared evenings and Sundays from September 1966 to May 1967.

Whitelaw Reid was the leader among Republican editors of his era. Much of his influence resulted from his perceptions of trends and his concern with progress. Though conservative in style and detached and reserved in appearance, Reid was, nevertheless, the first to innovate. He particularly kept abreast of the latest developments in printing technology and was the first to install the Mergenthaler linotype, encouraging its preliminary development in his own composing rooms. He was one of seven owners of the New York Associated Press; and in this, as in the Merganthaler Linotype Company, he made his direction felt through crucial years of growth and development. He was always concerned with the gathering, as well as the handling, of news.

A better businessman, better thinker, and more accomplished scholar than Greeley, Reid gave the *Tribune* new life, vigor, and durability at a time when it might well have floundered with so many other newspapers that did not adapt to the revolutionary changes following the Civil War. While Reid never left quite the stamp of editorial personality of Greeley or others of his era, he kept *Tribune* content at a high level—giving coverage unsurpassed in comprehensiveness to such events as the Whiskey Ring scandal, overthrow of the Canal Ring, the Pacific Mail investigation, exposure of corruption in the Grant administration, follies of the third-term movement, and the Beecher-Tilton adultery trial. Reid's *Tribune* had a more vital, more scholarly editorial page than had Greeley's. Indeed, part of Reid's legacy was in his maintenance of an influential newspaper based on talent and ability at a time when others of his profession relied on sensationalism. When others, even Joseph Pulitzer, believed the latter necessary for survival, Reid proved it was not.

When Reid took over the *Tribune* in the early 1870s, his competitors were four conservative newspapers that appealed to the middle and upper classes: the *Sun, Times, Herald,* and *World.* Of these, the *Sun* had begun the kind of journalism that foreshadowed the Hearst-Pulitzer era, and Reid predicted that one could make a fortune by making a paper so "disreputable and vile" that hundreds of thousands would buy it. But he refused to adopt such practices then or later, when Joseph Pulitzer and William Randolph Hearst built circulation, advertising, and revenues with such journalism. Regarding Republicans as representing culture and respectability, "the party of the gentry," Reid edited the *Tribune* for Republican, conservative, middle- and upper-class readers. Biographer Duncan notes that Reid regarded the *Tribune* as the keeper of the Republican conscience. While Pulitzer and Hearst, in the 1890s, appealed to the working classes who wanted public ownership of utilities and heavier taxes for the rich and the big corporations, Reid believed that for him to pursue such journalism would be to attack his own interests and those of his readers. To Reid, his readers' attitudes toward his newspaper were more important than the money to be made from large circulations based on the Pulitzer-Hearst kind of journalism. The *Tribune* suffered financially during the late 1890s and early twentieth century, although it is not clear that the Hearst-Pulitzer circulation wars were a cause. However, Reid refused offers to buy the paper and did not waver in his conservative view of journalism, except to adopt certain typographical and design methods introduced during the era.

In short, Reid's *Tribune* was perhaps not totally incorruptible, given his use of it for party ends and his censorship while in France; but it was well-written and distinguished by a critical staff, especially during the 1890s when the other large New York City newspapers could claim no such record of solid, steady professional consistency.

Other:
William Henry Smith, *A Political History of Slavery: Being an Account of the Slavery Controversy from the Earliest Agitations in the Eighteenth Century to the Close of the Reconstruction Period in America*, introduction by Reid (New York & London: Putnam's, 1903).

Biographies:
Royal Cortissoz, *The Life of Whitelaw Reid*, 2 volumes

(New York: Scribners, 1921);
Bingham Duncan, *Whitelaw Reid, Journalist, Politician, Diplomat* (Athens: University of Georgia Press, 1975).

References:
James G. Blaine, "The Presidential Election of 1892," *North American Review*, 155 (1892): 513-525;
Thomas Campbell-Copeland, *Harrison and Reid: Their Lives and Record*, 3 volumes (New York: Webster, 1892);
Donald M. Dozer, "Benjamin Harrison and the Presidential Campaign of 1892," *American Historical Review*, 54 (1948): 49-77;
Robert H. Jones, "Whitelaw Reid," in *For the Union: Ohio Leaders in the Civil War*, edited by Kenneth W. Wheeler (Columbus: Ohio State University Press, 1968);
Thomas W. Knox, *The Republican Party and Its Leaders . . . Lives of Harrison and Reid* (New York: Collier, 1892);
Henry Davenport Northrop, *The Life and Public Services of Benjamin Harrison, The Greatest American Statesman, to which is added The Life and Public Service of Hon. Whitelaw Reid* (Cleveland: N. G. Hamilton, 1892);
James G. Smart, "Whitelaw Reid; A Biographical Study," Ph.D. dissertation, University of Maryland, 1964;
Smart, "Whitelaw Reid and the Nomination of Horace Greeley," *Mid-America*, 49 (1967): 227-243.

Papers:
Whitelaw Reid's private papers are in the Library of Congress.

Jacob Riis

(3 May 1849-26 May 1914)

George Everett
University of Tennessee

MAJOR POSITIONS HELD: Owner/editor, *South Brooklyn News* (1874-1876); police reporter, *New York Tribune* (1878-1890), *New York Evening Sun* (1890-1899).

BOOKS: *How the Other Half Lives* (New York: Scribners, 1890; London: Low, 1891);
The Children of the Poor (New York: Scribners, 1892; London: Low, 1892);
Nisby's Christmas (New York: Scribners, 1893);
My Brother and I; Selected Papers on Social Topics (New York: Hunt & Eaton / Cincinnati: Cranston & Curts, 1895);
Out of Mulberry Street (New York: Century, 1898);
A Ten Years' War (Boston: Houghton Mifflin, 1900);
The Making of an American (New York: Macmillan, 1901);
The Battle with the Slum (New York & London: Macmillan, 1902);
Children of the Tenements (New York: Macmillan, 1903);
The Peril and the Preservation of the Home: Being the William L. Bull Lectures for the Year 1903 (Philadelphia: Jacobs, 1903);
Theodore Roosevelt, the Citizen (New York: Macmillan, 1904); republished as *Theodore Roosevelt: The Man and the Citizen* (London: Hodder & Stoughton, 1904);
Is There a Santa Claus? (New York: Macmillan, 1904);
The Old Town (New York: Macmillan, 1909);
A Modern St. George (New York: Charity Organization Society, 1911);
Neighbors; Life Stories of the Other Half (New York: Macmillan, 1914);
Hero Tales of the Far North (New York: Macmillan, 1919);
Christmas Stories (New York: Macmillan, 1923).

Jacob Riis was not one of America's best-known newspapermen, but unlike most of them he claims a relatively prominent place in the country's social history. He was a leader in the reform movement that began to take clear shape in America in the last quarter of the nineteenth century, and more than any other he is identified with the move to relieve the slum conditions oppressing the hapless immigrants in New York City. But his efforts at reform were founded on his years of covering the slums as a police reporter for two of the country's greatest newspapers, and his journalistic career deserves more attention in the standard press histories. In addition, his pioneering efforts in photojournalism have only recently come into any significant recognition, and it may turn out to be his pictures, rather than his newspaper writings or even his books, which do the most to establish his ultimate place in communications history.

Jacob August Riis was born in the conservative

old town of Ribe, Denmark, the third of fourteen children of Niels Edward and Caroline Lundholm Riis. His father was a teacher in a Latin school, but the elder Riis often wrote for a local newspaper for extra income to help feed his large family. He wanted Jacob to pursue some kind of literary career, but to his disappointment the boy apprenticed himself to a carpenter. Riis did well in school, however, and proved particularly adept at reading English, probably because he was so attracted to the works of Charles Dickens; he also read James Fenimore Cooper.

Perhaps influenced by Dickens's tales of London squalor, Riis became concerned at an early age about conditions in his own town. As he later recalled in his autobiography, *The Making of An American* (1901), his playmates called him "Jacob the delver" because of his constant warfare with the rats nesting in the open-gutter sewer which ran underneath his house. Then, when he "could hardly have been over twelve or thirteen," he turned his attention to Rag Hall, the town's only tenement. Given one mark as a Christmas Eve present, he took it immediately to Rag Hall to share it with the poorest family there, on the condition that they should clean things up—especially the children. The bewildered recipients first checked with Mrs. Riis to see whether the gift was legitimate and then, apparently with her help, did some whitewashing and got the children "cleaned up for a season."

The youth fell in love with Elizabeth Nielsen, the daughter of a leading citizen of Ribe, and when her family rejected him as a serious suitor he precipitously set sail for America in 1870. Impetuosity and hotheadedness were lifelong traits, and in his early days in the United States they got him into some needless predicaments. When he had only $25 dollars to his name, he bought a horse for $19 dollars. Realizing that he did not know how to ride, he then had to sell the animal at a loss. Nationalistic feelings also got him into some scrapes: the French and Danes were at war with the Germans, and the Prussians took his measure more than once when the fiery youth made loud and indiscreet remarks in their presence.

Riis was also incredibly naive. His first day in America he spent half his money on a large revolver, which he wore prominently. To him, this was the country of *The Deerslayer* and of Algonquins and highwaymen. Among his early efforts to find work was a visit to the office of the *Buffalo Express*, where he applied to the editor for a reporting job. "He looked me over, a lad fresh from the shipyard, with horny hands and a rough coat, and asked,

Elizabeth Nielsen, whose mother gave Riis this picture before he left for America in 1870. Elizabeth and Riis were married six years later when he returned to Denmark.

'Who are you?' 'A carpenter,' I said. The man turned upon his heel with a loud, rasping laugh and shut the door in my face."

Riis had a difficult time his first few years in the promised land. Out of work in New York, he walked to Philadelphia and got some temporary help from a Danish family he knew there. He tried Pittsburgh and upstate New York. He had some moderate success as a salesman, because he did have energy, drive, and initiative. But often he would be cheated out of his commission or his wages. He also spent one day as a coal miner, three days on a cucumber farm, and six weeks in a brickyard.

He kept coming back to New York City, seeming to recognize somehow that his career was hidden there among the restless masses. He slept in the lodging houses then kept by the New York police for vagrants, and he never forgot seeing his dog's brains dashed against a wall by an unsympathetic sergeant. He spent some time among the hoboes but never felt that he was one of them. It was a difficult environment for a religious romantic in the fairy-tale tradition of Hans Christian Andersen, but Riis soon came to see the people of New York as divided into fairly clear types: the shiftless tramps, for whom he had little sympathy; the corrupt politicians, ridden with self-interest and in league with greedy landlords; a few reformers, whom he tended to see as idealists like himself; and that half of the population which worked hard just to stay alive and could all become respectable citizens of mainstream America if only they were given a chance.

Riis began to sense his own mission. In his autobiography he wrote of these days when he was one of the hungry poor he was to describe so fully in later years: "Things enough happened to take down my self-esteem a good many pegs. It was about this time I made up my mind to go into the newspaper business. It seemed to me that a reporter's was the highest and noblest of all callings; no one could sift wrong from right as he, and punish the wrong. In that I was right. I have not changed my opinion on that point one whit, and I am sure I never shall. The power of fact is the mightiest lever of this or of any day. The reporter has his hand upon it, and it is his grievous fault if he does not use it well."

In 1873, he saw a want ad for a city editor for a weekly newspaper in Long Island City. His naiveté let him see nothing unusual in a publisher's acquiring a city editor by means of a classified ad. His job, he said later, was "to fill the local column and attend to the affairs of Hunter's Point and Blissville generally, politics excluded. The editor attended to that. In twenty-four hours I was hard at work writing up

my then most ill-favored bailiwick. It is none too fine yet, but in those days, when every nuisance crowded out of New York found refuge there, it stunk to heaven." He worked hard for two weeks, giving Hunter's Point what he later called "a thorough raking over," then finally realized that the owner was in debt to everyone else in town, and that the new city editor would be far down on the waiting list for any pay. Next he found a job on Newspaper Row, working long hours for the New York News Association, an office selling news reports to morning and evening dailies. He got to know the city well and was soon contacted by politicians looking for someone to fill their new organ, the *South Brooklyn News*. Riis started on 20 May 1874 at $15 a week, which was raised to $25 a fortnight later when he was named editor. When the elections were over and the politicians no longer needed their sheet, they let him buy it in December for $650. Riis had saved $75 working for the news association (working fifteen-hour days, he had no time to spend it), and the sellers accepted his note for the rest. He was thereafter a one-man newspaper, writing every word in the four-page sheet. Within less than a year he had paid off the debt.

At about this time another event brought Riis's sentimental idealism to the fore. He was deeply affected by a Methodist revival meeting, and "with the heat of the convert, I decided on the spot to

A New York Police Department lodging house, of the sort where Riis slept during his early days in America

throw up my editorial work and take to preaching. But Brother Simmons would not hear of it. 'No, no, Jacob,' he said; 'not that. We have preachers enough. What the world needs is consecrated pens.' Then and there I consecrated mine."

Having established himself in a more prestigious profession, Riis wrote to the sweetheart of his youth and received encouragement: the young lady still had not married. He sold his paper back to the politicians and went back to Denmark, married her on 5 March 1876, and brought her to America; the couple eventually had four sons and two daughters, but one son died in infancy. Returning to New York, he worked for his old paper but could not stomach the editorial control exercised by its politician owners. He used his "consecrated pen" to sell ads for Brooklyn merchants, to be shown in nearby towns in connection with a magic lantern show. Next he sold ads for a city directory for Elmira. But apparently he was trying regularly to get on at one of the big papers, and he finally got a chance at the *Tribune*. After a winter of hard work as a general assignment reporter, he was assigned in 1878 to the police beat. *Tribune* police reporters operated from an office across the street from police headquarters on Mulberry Street. This locale was to be the focal point of Riis's career.

From here Riis operated in four areas of endeavor: he got his share of "beats" on the other police reporters; he began work earnestly on a number of reforms; he provided precedent for other police reporters of an idealistic bent; and he did his pioneer work in photojournalism.

It mattered little to Riis that he, still called "the Dutchman" because of his accent, was not readily accepted into the camaraderie of the Mulberry Street reporters. He was accustomed to that, and he did not let it deter him from getting for the *Tribune* its share of exclusives. He developed valuable contacts, both official and otherwise, and in general delivered the news as quickly as anyone. In short, he performed as a professional.

But Riis the idealist was not content to chronicle the daily murder, mayhem, and depravity and let it go at that. He let his sympathy for the poor show through in his news reports, and when his peers criticized him for that, he looked for other outlets. An editor at *Scribner's* magazine expressed interest, and an article appeared in the December 1889 issue which was to be the basis for his best-known book, *How the Other Half Lives* (1890). But he did not always wait for the mass media to work their effects. He often took information directly to the Health Board or to a housing commission, using statistics, pictures, and forceful argument to prod the officials into taking action. When he investigated the exploitation of children in the tenement factories, he got a statistical table from a friend at the Health Department showing how to tell age by the development of teeth and went into the factories and pried open little girls' mouths. He was the prototype activist reformer.

Not many of those who worked with Riis could embrace his sanguine and energetic idealism; police reporters were a skeptical lot. One, though, was there who would carry the work on through a later generation: Lincoln Steffens, working for the *Post*, shared the Mulberry Street beat with Riis, who in November 1890 joined the *Evening Sun*. Other writers were reporting in New York also—David Graham Phillips and Stephen Crane among them —but Steffens particularly acknowledged the Riis influence. Steffens called Riis a reformer who "worked through despair to set the wrong right" and "not only got the news, he cared about the news."

Because he cared and wanted to apply pressure the politicians could not ignore, Riis turned to photography. He had learned the power of pictures to communicate when he had used the magic lantern in his 1877 advertising scheme. One day in late 1887 or early 1888 he read of the use of flash powder to take night pictures, and within weeks he was taking camera equipment into unlit tenement quarters or up foul alleyways at night, shooting pictures to portray the unsavory living conditions of the poor. At first the powder had to be fired with a gun, and considerable excitement occurred in more than one dark alley when the explosion went off. Later Riis substituted a frying pan, less sinister-looking but actually more dangerous. Twice he set fires, and once he blinded himself for an hour and surely would have lost his eyesight had he not been wearing glasses.

Riis put the pictures to work without delay. "I recall a midnight expedition to the Mulberry Bend with the sanitary police that had turned up a couple of characteristic cases of overcrowding. In one instance two rooms that should at most have held four or five sleepers were found to contain fifteen, a week-old baby among them. Most of them were lodgers and slept there for 'five cents a spot.' There was no pretence of beds. When the report was submitted to the Health Board the next day, it did not make much of an impression—these things rarely do, put in mere words—until my negatives, still dripping from the darkroom, came to reinforce them. From them there was no appeal. It was not

Riis's photograph of lodgers sleeping in an overcrowded room for "five cents a spot"

Riis's photograph of an Italian immigrant living beneath the manure heaps along the East River (Jacob Riis Collection, Museum of the City of New York)

the only instance of the kind by a good many. Neither the landlord's protest nor the tenant's plea 'went' in face of the camera's evidence, and I was satisfied."

Had technology been ready for Riis's pictures to be published in the *Tribune* or the *Sun*, the impact would have been much greater; but halftone engraving for newspapers was still about a decade away. Some of the pictures were used in Riis books and magazine articles, but the best the *Evening Sun* could do was to copy the photos by hand, carving as much detail as possible into the woodcuts. Riis was reporting with a camera, but he was reporting directly to his official audience much of the time, unable to use the mass media as they existed at that period. Nevertheless, the impact of the pictures is powerful even today, and the Riis Collection of photographs is one of the most vivid historical holdings of the Museum of the City of New York.

Riis covered the police beat for the *Sun* until 1899. By then, his books and his news stories and pictures had established his reputation, and he was much in demand for public appearances. His prestige got a large boost from the champion of boosters, Theodore Roosevelt, who called him "New York's most useful citizen." Roosevelt, then police commissioner, had sought out Riis when the magazine article "How the Other Half Lives" came out and asked, "How can I help?" He sought Riis's advice later as governor, then as president. When the United States seemed about to acquire a portion of the Virgin Islands from Denmark in 1902, Roosevelt apparently asked Riis to consider becoming governor. Correspondence shows Riis's

reluctance to accept such an appointment so far from his active arena, but he never had to make the final decision; Denmark did not finally approve the sale until 1917.

Friendship with the president, plus national exposure gained through his books, magazine articles, and lectures, brought Riis's career to new heights, but the adversities of age began to overtake him. He was afflicted with heart disease from 1904, and in 1905 his childhood idol and bride of twenty-nine years died of pneumonia. Two years later he married Mary Phillips, a St. Louis society girl half his age, who had been impressed by his lectures and had become his secretary. She provided much care and encouragement as his heart trouble increasingly interrupted his lecture tours, for which he was receiving up to $150 per lecture. After stumping for Roosevelt just before the 1912 election, he had to return to a Battle Creek, Michigan, sanatorium for rest. He set out again, returned to Battle Creek, toured once again, then collapsed in New Orleans and went back to Battle Creek for the last time. In May 1914 came an urgent message to his family; he felt spent and wanted to come home. He barely survived the trip, and he died a few fitful days later. Educator Endicott Peabody presided over the funeral services, and Theodore Roosevelt said it was "as if I had lost my own brother." In his autobiography Riis had written, "I have been very happy. No man ever had so good a time."

A fitting monument to Riis was Mulberry Bend Park, built in 1895 on the site of the worst of New York's slum areas, one which Riis especially

Mulberry Bend Park, created on the site of New York City's worst slum

wanted to see abolished. Carrying his name, starting in 1888, was the Riis Neighborhood Settlement House, and a large park at Rockaway, New York, was named for Riis after his death.

Few journalists have seen as many tangible results which can be traced to their writings. Riis found sewage being dumped into the city's water supply, and New York was pressured to buy the Croton Watershed. He attacked the police lodging house and lived to see it abolished. He scathed the landlords and saw most of the rear tenements—the worst—torn down. He exposed the fire hazards of basement bakeshops, and most of them were eliminated. Concerned about lack of facilities for children's play, he secured school playgrounds, got

classrooms opened to boys' and girls' clubs, and helped establish a truant school.

So many results may overrepresent Riis's contribution. Historian Louis Filler sees it as a narrow one: "Riis, unprofound and unsophisticated, was the typical successful reformer of that time, thoroughly of New York, with no understanding of the nation as a whole and no conception of national policy. The West was still the Far West to him; Populism was not so much a political credo as a violent aberration of Western ignorance; for him social maturity lay in the direction of New York civilization. He had no respect for the 'yellow' press, no understanding of such individuals as Henry George, whom he considered beneath discussion. On the other hand, he could not help seeing that despite the best efforts of conservative reformers, social inequalities continued to produce unrest and to rouse the sections of the country against one another. Something, Riis concluded, had to be done."

Riis's prose, simple and direct, lacked depth. His pictures were outstanding but could not be printed in his own newspaper. His biases showed often in his reporting, especially whenever he mentioned his hero, Theodore Roosevelt.

But Riis was a man of action. He may not have been a great journalist, but he saw what a journalist, from his platform and in that time, could do. Riis was a doer, and his beloved New York City is certainly much the better for it.

The Jacob A. Riis Neighborhood Settlement House on Henry Street, New York City

Bibliography:

Lewis Fried and John Fierst, *Jacob A. Riis: A Reference Guide* (Boston: Hall, 1977).

Biographies:

Louise Ware, *Jacob A. Riis; Police Reporter, Reformer, Useful Citizen* (New York: Appleton-Century, 1938);

Alexander Alland, *Jacob A. Riis: Photographer and Citizen* (Millerton, N.Y.: Aperture, 1974);

James B. Lane, *Jacob A. Riis and the American City* (Port Washington, N.Y.: Kennikat Press, 1974);

Edith Patterson Meyer, *"Not Charity but Justice"; The Story of Jacob A. Riis* (New York: Vanguard, 1974).

References:

Louis Filler, *The Muckrakers*, new ed. (University Park: Pennsylvania State University Press, 1968), pp. 45-48, 50, 54, 92, 269;

Justin Kaplan, *Lincoln Steffens* (New York: Simon &

Schuster, 1974), pp. 49, 59-60, 122, 295;
Charles A. Madison, preface to *How the Other Half Lives*, by Riis (New York: Dover, 1971), pp. v-viii;
Arthur M. Schlesinger, *The Rise of the City, 1878-1898* (New York: Macmillan, 1933), pp. 110, 194;

Larzer Ziff, *The American 1890s* (New York: Viking, 1966), pp. 152-155, 161, 164.

Papers:
Jacob A. Riis's papers are collected at the Library of Congress; the Jacob A. Riis Photographic Collection is held by the Museum of the City of New York.

Carl Schurz
(2 March 1829-14 May 1906)

John M. Butler
Louisiana State University

MAJOR POSITIONS HELD: Washington correspondent, *New York Tribune* (1865-1866); editor, *Detroit Post* (1866); editor and part owner, *St. Louis Westliche Post* (1867-1906); editor, *New York Evening Post* (1881-1883).

SELECTED BOOKS: *An Address Delivered before the Archaean Society of Beloit College, at Its Anniversary July 13, 1858* (Beloit, Wis.: Hale, 1858);
Douglas and Popular Sovereignty. Speech of Carl Schurz, of Wisconsin. In Hampden Hall, Springfield, Mass., January 4, 1860 (Washington, D.C.: Buell & Blanchard, 1860);
The Great Issue of American Politics. Speech of Carl Schurz, of Wisconsin, at Verandah Hall, St. Louis, Missouri, August 1, 1860 (Washington, D.C.: Republican Party Congressional Committee, 1860);
Judge Douglas–The Bill of Indictment; Speech Delivered at the Cooper Institute, New York, Sept. 13, 1860 (New York: New York Tribune, 1860);
The Life of Slavery, or the Life of the Nation? Speech of Hon. Carl Schurz, at the Mass Meeting, Cooper Institute, New York, March 6, 1862 (New York: Putnam's, 1862);
"For the Great Empire of Liberty, Forward!" Speech of Maj.-Gen. Carl Schurz, of Wisconsin, Delivered at Concert Hall, Philadelphia, on Friday Evening, September 16, 1864 (New York: Gray & Green, 1864);
Speeches of Carl Schurz, Collected and Revised by the Author (Philadelphia: Lippincott, 1865);
Political Disabilities. Speech of Hon. Carl Schurz, of Missouri, Delivered in the Senate of the United States, December 15, 1870 (Washington, D.C.:

Rives & Bailey, 1870);
Annexation of San Domingo. Speech of Hon. Carl Schurz, of Missouri, Delivered in the Senate of the United States, January 11, 1871 (Washington, D.C.: Rives & Bailey, 1871);
Civil Service Reform. Speech of Hon. Carl Schurz, of Missouri, Delivered in the Senate of the United States, January 27, 1871 (Washington, D.C.: Rives & Bailey, 1871);
Usurpation of the War Powers. Speech of Hon. Carl Schurz, of Missouri, Delivered in the United States Senate, March 28 and 29, 1871 (Washington, D.C.: Congressional Globe Office, 1871);
General Amnesty. Speech of Hon. Carl Schurz, of Missouri, Delivered in the Senate of the United States, January 30, 1872 (Washington, D.C.: Rives & Bailey, 1872);
Sales of Arms to French Agents, and How They are Officially Justified. Speech of Hon. Carl Schurz, of Missouri, Delivered in the Senate of the United States, May 31, 1872 (Washington, D.C.: Rives & Bailey, 1872);
Eulogy on Charles Sumner (Boston: Lee & Shepard / New York: Lee, Shepard & Dillingham, 1874);
Currency–National Banks. Speech of Hon. Carl Schurz, of Missouri, in the United States Senate, February 27, 1874 (Washington, D.C.: Government Printing Office, 1874);
Military Interference in Louisiana. Speech of Hon. Carl Schurz, of Missouri, in the Senate of the United States, January 11, 1875 (Washington, D.C.: Government Printing Office, 1875);
To Business Men; Address by Hon. Carl Schurz, before the Union Club, of New York, Saturday Evening, October 21, 1876 (New York: Republican Na-

Carl Schurz

tional Committee, 1876);

The Currency Question. Speech of Hon. Carl Schurz, at Cincinnati, Ohio, September 28, 1878 (Washington, D.C.: Adams, 1878);

Honest Money and Labor: An Address Delivered in Boston, October 23, 1878, by the Hon. Carl Schurz (New York: Putnam's, 1879);

General James A. Garfield, Republican Candidate for President. Who He Is, and Why You Should Vote for Him (New York: Gildersleeve, 1880);

The New South (New York: American News Company, 1885);

The Life of Henry Clay (Boston & New York: Houghton, Mifflin, 1887);

The Need of a Rational Forest Policy in the United States. Address Delivered before the American Forestry Association and the Pennsylvania Forestry Association at Horticultural Hall, Philadelphia, October 15th, 1889, by Hon. Carl Schurz (Philadelphia: Spangler & Davis, 1889);

Abraham Lincoln: An Essay (Boston & New York:

Houghton, Mifflin, 1891; London: Putnam's, 1891);

Civil-Service Reform and Democracy; an Address Delivered at the Annual Meeting of the National Civil-Service Reform League, April 25, 1893, by the President, Hon. Carl Schurz (New York: National Civil-Service Reform League, 1893);

The Necessity and Progress of Civil Service Reform. An Address Delivered at the Annual Meeting of the National Civil-Service Reform League, December 12, 1894, by the President, Hon. Carl Schurz (New York: National Civil-Service Reform League, 1894);

Congress and the Spoils System. An Address Delivered at the Annual Meeting of the National Civil-Service Reform League, December 12, 1895, by the President, Hon. Carl Schurz (New York: National Civil-Service Reform League, 1895);

Encouragements and Warnings. An Address Delivered at the Annual Meeting of the National Civil-Service Reform League, December 10, 1896. By the President, Hon. Carl Schurz (New York: National Civil-Service Reform League, 1896);

The Democracy of the Merit System. An Address Delivered at the Annual Meeting of the National Civil-Service Reform League at Cincinnati, Ohio, December 16, 1897, by the President, Hon. Carl Schurz (New York: National Civil-Service Reform League, 1897);

American Imperialism; the Convocation Address Delivered on the Occasion of the Twenty-Seventh Convocation of the University of Chicago, January 4, 1899 (Boston: Estes, 1899);

The Policy of Imperialism: Address by Hon. Carl Schurz at the Anti-Imperialist Conference in Chicago, October 17, 1899 (Chicago: American Anti-Imperialist League, 1899);

Renewed Struggles; an Address Delivered at the Annual Meeting of the National Civil-Service Reform League at Indianapolis, Ind., December 14, 1899, by the President, Hon. Carl Schurz (New York: National Civil-Service Reform League, 1899);

For the Republic of Washington and Lincoln: An Address Delivered at the Philadelphia Conference, February 22, 1900 (Chicago: American Anti-Imperialist League, 1900);

For American Principles and American Honor: An Address by Hon. Carl Schurz, Delivered in Cooper Union, New York, May 24, 1900 (New York: Anti-Imperialist League of New York, 1900);

Can the South Solve the Negro Problem? (New York: American Missionary Association, 1903);

Some Object Lessons; an Address Delivered at the Annual Meeting of the National Civil-Service Reform

League at Baltimore, Md., December 10, 1903 (New York: National Civil-Service Reform League, 1904);

To the Independent Voter: An Open Letter (New York: Parker Independent Clubs, 1904);

The Reminiscences of Carl Schurz, 3 volumes (New York: McClure, 1907-1908; London: Murray, 1909);

Speeches, Correspondence and Political Papers of Carl Schurz, selected and edited by Frederic Bancroft, 6 volumes (New York: Putnam's, 1913);

American Leadership for Peace and Arbitration (Boston: World Peace Foundation, 1914);

Charles Sumner: An Essay, edited by Arthur Reed Hogue (Urbana: University of Illinois Press, 1951);

Germany and America: Essays on Problems of International Relations and Immigration, edited by Hans L. Trefousse (New York: Brooklyn College Press, 1980).

Carl Schurz traveled to America in his early twenties with ideas of liberalism and democracy which he could not find in his homeland of Germany. His intention upon arriving in America was to earn a living as a lecturer, but his political and journalistic endeavors wound up giving him a prominent place in American history. Schurz used his first years in America as a learning experience and spent the time getting acquainted with the culture and language. His study of history provided Schurz with information and topics for his early lectures; his love for history continued throughout his life, as is evident by his three published books (other than collections of his speeches), which are all biographies of political figures—including himself. His editorials, speeches, and political essays were published in many newspapers across the continent as well as in the ones he edited.

Schurz was born 2 March 1829 in Liblar, a small village on the Rhine. His father, Christian Schurz, was an orphan peasant and a self-made man who became a village schoolmaster and then went into business. His mother, Marianne Jüssen, came from a respectable peasant family.

At an early age Schurz was influenced by his maternal grandfather, Heribert Jüssen, the chief land cultivator in Liblar. It was customary in Germany for parents to take in their married children and their families, and this is how Schurz came to live with his grandfather, who was the most powerful, prestigious, and financially independent of the villagers. Schurz watched his grandfather intently as he worked with and disciplined the peasants; but

rather than yearn for the power which his grandfather possessed, Schurz would later fight for the freedom of the lower classes.

Schurz attended the elementary school in Liblar where his father was schoolmaster, and he received excellent grades. While still in elementary school, he began walking to Brull, four miles away, twice a week to take piano lessons from the church organist; a year later, he began taking Latin lessons from a priest.

There was not a Protestant in Liblar, and like virtually everybody in the neighborhood, Schurz was brought up in the Roman Catholic faith. But some liberalizing influences of his boyhood prevented him from blind credulity. The farm errand man, called "Master George," taught him to be skeptical of miracles and dared to criticize the sermons of the parish priest. His uncle Ferdinand, a disciple of Voltaire, indulged in scoffing jests on religious subjects. When the boy heard the priest declare that all except Catholics were doomed to everlasting hell fire, he wondered about his father's friend Aaron, a Jew, and moved toward tolerance. Also, the priest took the wrong side in a dispute about the new schoolteacher, who was alleged to have seduced one of his pupils. Schurz's mother, in spite of her constant admonitions to the boy to say his prayers, was most indignant and called the priest an evil man. The incident did not strengthen Schurz's trust in the clergy.

At the age of ten he was sent to the Jesuit gymnasium in Cologne to begin studies which would prepare him for the university. He remained at Cologne from 1839 until 1846, during which time his parents moved to Bonn. In 1847, at the age of sixteen, he became a candidate for his doctorate at the University of Bonn.

Much like his grandfather physically, Schurz was broad-shouldered, lean, and measured well over six feet when he entered the university. Schurz inherited from his grandfather not only his looks but also a love for history. As a child he had often sat for hours listening to his grandfather's tales of the Napoleonic Wars, so it came as no surprise when he showed a keen interest in history while at the university; his other favorite subjects were literature and languages. At the same time that his interests in these subjects were growing, his interest in institutionalized religion was declining. Although Schurz remained a religious man until his death, he realized that much was wrong with organized religions of the time, due largely to their intolerance of other faiths.

It was at the university that Schurz met

Gottfried Kinkel, a lecturer on art history and instructor in public speaking with political ideas. When Kinkel was appointed editor in August 1848 of the *Bonner Zeitung*, he made Schurz his journalistic aide. Thus, at the age of seventeen, Schurz was able to put his skillful writing and gentle sarcasm to work in the service of his political ideals.

Through his association with Kinkel, Schurz quickly became a student leader. His writings were no longer dominated by history and literature but began to deal with the liberal political movement to unify Germany. During Kinkel's absence in Berlin from March to May 1849, Schurz contributed many editorials to the *Neue Bonner Zeitung*, a successor to the *Bonner Zeitung*. He suggested changes in the form and content of the paper. Thus, an excellent student and lover of history was introduced to journalism not as a reporter but as a political revolutionist. Schurz left the university in 1849 before completing his doctorate.

In May 1850, Schurz was sought out by revolutionists, for whom he provided democratic propaganda for a unified Germany. His aid to revolutionary groups soon expanded from mere writing to actual fighting for the cause. While engaged in battle he wrote such articles as "Last Days in Rastatt," which was published in a Bonn newspaper one month after the surrender of the revolutionists. Schurz and Kinkel were captured at Rastatt before the surrender; Schurz managed to escape and later helped Kinkel to do so. The story of Schurz's and Kinkel's daring escapes gained international recognition for Schurz as a revolutionist.

Schurz's parents wanted him to ask for amnesty in order to return to Germany, but he refused. Schurz and Kinkel sailed to Edinburgh, Scotland, on 28 November 1850. Upon Schurz's arrival in Britain his name was already synonymous with the democratic cause.

From England Schurz wrote articles for revolutionary presses in Germany and other European countries. He lived in England with Kinkel for the next two years, except for short visits to Switzerland and France. He went to Paris in December 1850 but in 1851 was expelled from France as a dangerous foreigner. During this period he won the friendship

Schurz (right) with Gottfried Kinkel in London in 1852, after their escapes from a German prison
(American Embassy, Bonn-Bad Godesberg)

of Giuseppe Mazzini, Louis Kossuth, and other leaders of the democratic movement in Europe.

By 1852 it had become obvious that the democratic revolutions in Europe had failed. Schurz decided to seek his political and financial fortunes in the United States. First, however, on 6 July 1852, Schurz married eighteen-year-old Margarethe Meyer of Hamburg in London. Her father was a prosperous manufacturer who held liberal political ideas like those of his son-in-law. Margarethe had come to England to help teach kindergarten with her sister when she met Schurz; she later achieved some fame of her own by opening the first kindergarten in America at Watertown, Wisconsin, in 1856. A week after his marriage, Schurz was stricken with scarlet fever. He regained his health in a month, and he and Margarethe sailed to America on 17 September 1852.

Upon their arrival in New York, Schurz was a mere twenty-four years old but was internationally known. He planned to support his wife and himself by lecturing, but he did very little lecturing or writ-

Margarethe Meyer Schurz, whom Schurz married shortly before leaving England for the United States (Watertown Historical Society)

ing during his first years in America. He spent three years traveling the eastern and western portions of the country and set about acquiring a mastery of the English language and learning all he could about the government and laws of the United States. It has been suggested that the Schurzes were sustained by Margarethe's dowry during this period when Schurz was traveling and studying life in America. At this time he had not made a decision to become a citizen of the country. They settled first in Philadelphia and bought a house in September 1853, in time for Schurz's family's arrival from Germany and the birth of the couple's daughter, Agathe.

Schurz's career as a lecturer in America started slowly. He began by presenting lectures on French history and politics during 1789-1851. In 1853, he updated a manuscript on French history and political life and sent it to Germany to be published; when it still had not been published by 1858, he asked for it to be returned. This book and his first book—written at the age of eighteen and titled "Richard the Wanderer"—remain unpublished. During his first three years in America he also wrote numerous essays which were sent to England but never published.

Because of this infrequency of his lecturing and his failure to publish any articles, it has been speculated that Schurz may have been employed by German or other revolutionists to raise funds for their cause in America. There is a good possibility that Schurz was involved in such activities, since he was still in contact with Kinkel in England.

In 1855, Schurz's uncle Jacob Jüssen, who was living in Watertown, Wisconsin, forty miles west of Milwaukee, invited Schurz and his family to visit; they decided to make Watertown their permanent home. Shortly after their arrival in Watertown in March both of Schurz's sisters were married.

Schurz bought some real estate and saw that the family was comfortably established. In April, he took his wife and child to Europe to benefit Mrs. Schurz's health. During a short visit in London, he renewed acquaintance with Louis Kossuth, finding him old and depressed. The Kinkels were busy pursuing their interests, the professor lecturing on art history and Mrs. Kinkel teaching music.

Schurz returned home alone to check on the building of his family home in Watertown and purchased a farm. His intention was to sell off some of the farmland for town lots so as to cover the cost of his farm purchase. Confident in his future prosperity, Schurz sailed again for Europe in the autumn of 1855, meeting his wife on 17 December in London and accompanying her in early February

Schurz's home in Watertown, Wisconsin (Watertown Historical Society)

1856 to Montreux, Switzerland, where they spent several months. They returned to the United States in June 1856.

In Watertown Schurz secured an appointment as notary public, and with a partner, C. T. Palme, he undertook to carry on business as a land agent. He was elected alderman for the fifth ward, as a Republican, as well as supervisor for the fifth and sixth wards; and he was for a brief period commissioner of public improvement.

Schurz was approached by the Democratic party but preferred the young Republican party, feeling that the Democrats' principles were opposed to his ideals. He disliked slavery with all the ardor and enthusiasm he had given the revolution of 1849 in Germany. He campaigned for Frémont and became a champion of causes for German immigrants and other minorities.

In 1858, he was nominated for state treasurer but declined to accept any position lower than that of lieutenant governor. He had his will and was nominated for lieutenant governor on the first formal ballot, securing 145 votes against 22 for D. D. Cameron. At the time of his nomination, Schurz had not been naturalized as an American citizen, although his final papers would come through before his term of office would start. His forceful support of antislavery forces brought him instant attention nationally, but he was defeated in

the general election by 107 votes.

In 1859, his journalistic career resumed when he briefly edited the *Watertown Anzeiger*. He also started a Republican German newspaper in Watertown, the *Deutsch Volkszeitung*. It was during this time that Schurz wrote his famous essays and lectures entitled "True American," "American in Public Opinion Abroad," and "Douglas and Popular Sovereignty."

Schurz took his political defeats hard, but he remained a staunch Republican. The Republican platform at that time stood for popular sovereignty, prohibition of slavery from the territories, protective tariffs as a support to free labor, enactment of the homestead law, and freedom of citizens from political discrimination. Schurz was elected chairman of the Wisconsin delegation to the Chicago Republican convention in May 1860. Schurz and his fellow delegates were pledged to Senator William H. Seward of New York, but Abraham Lincoln won the presidential nomination on the third ballot. One of the committee which notified Lincoln of his nomination, Schurz spoke for him in Wisconsin, Illinois, Indiana, Ohio, Pennsylvania, and New York with great effectiveness among both natives and foreign-born. His greatest forensic effort—he considered it the greatest success of his oratorical career—was his speech in Cooper Union, New York City, 13 September 1860, which was devoted to a merciless critique of Stephen A. Douglas and was marked by sarcasm, humor, and clear exposition. It lasted three hours and was received with great enthusiasm.

Lincoln and Schurz remained warm friends after the election, and Lincoln appointed Schurz ambassador to Spain. After arriving in Madrid in 1861, Schurz, like other American representatives in Europe, devoted himself to advancing and safeguarding the Union cause abroad and gave all his leisure time to studying military campaigns and tactics—a hobby ever since his brief military experience in Germany. Finding, however, that the Northern cause was greatly weakened by the failure of the government to become clearly antislavery and receiving no encouragement from Secretary of State Seward, Schurz returned to the United States in January 1862 to discuss his views with Lincoln. Lincoln received him kindly but persisted in his policy of awaiting a more favorable public opinion at home. Schurz then sought to create public support for immediate emancipation, and to that end he delivered an address—approved beforehand by Lincoln—at Cooper Union in March 1862, which coincided with the president's request to Congress for authority to cooperate with any state which might adopt gradual emancipation.

Shortly after Schurz's return to the country, Lincoln made him a brigadier general and placed him in charge of a division. Schurz took his military duties seriously and soon won the respect of his officers and men. At the second battle of Bull Run, 30 August 1862, the new brigadier of two months' service and his division won high praise in one of the bloodiest and bitterest defeats of the Army of the Potomac, whose final withdrawal they covered. In March 1863 Schurz was promoted to major general, the highest rank in the army at that time. It was the misfortune of his division and the Eleventh Corps, of which it was a part, to bear the brunt of Stonewall Jackson's sudden attack at Chancellorsville on 1 May. Badly placed by Gen. O. O. Howard, the corps commander—despite repeated protests and warnings by Schurz—the division broke and retired in disorder before the Confederate onslaught but finally rallied to aid in preventing a complete disaster. For this the Eleventh Corps, and especially its German regiments, was violently abused and charged with cowardice in the press of the entire country. Again, after Howard put Schurz in command of the Eleventh Corps at Gettysburg, Schurz's troops took the brunt of the attack upon the right wing. Once more there were unwarranted charges

Schurz as a general in the Union army (Library of Congress)

that the Germans had failed to stand their ground. In both instances, General Howard had given the commands.

Schurz was later transferred with the corps to the western campaign, where he became involved in a controversy with Gen. Joseph Hooker. A court inquiry subsequently found that Schurz's conduct had been entirely correct and proper. He was later appointed to command a corps of instruction at Nashville. The end of the war found him chief of staff to Maj. Gen. Henry W. Slocum in Sherman's army. Schurz won the regard of Sherman, Winfield S. Hancock, and many others who ranked among the best of the Northern generals. He resigned immediately after Lee's surrender.

After the war, he toured the South to study the problems and issues of Reconstruction at President Johnson's request. His lengthy report on his travels from July to September 1866 has historical value to this day because of its detailed analysis of the situation, its clarity of purpose, and its vision. However, since Schurz wrote that the slaves should be granted freedom to vote as a condition of the readmission of the Confederate states, his report was not welcomed by Johnson, who neither acknowledged its receipt nor allowed it to be published until Congress demanded its publication.

In 1865 Schurz was named Washington correspondent of the *New York Tribune*, but early in 1866 he moved to Detroit to edit the new *Detroit Post* of Senator Zachariah Chandler. He continued to lecture and was published in the *Atlantic* at this time. The *Post* was not a success, however, and Schurz moved to St. Louis, Missouri, which had a large German population, and became half owner of the *Westliche Post* in early 1867. It is safe to assume he influenced thousands of German readers, native and foreign-born, through his newspaper writings and speeches during this turbulent period. Schurz retained his interest in the paper for the rest of his life.

In March 1868, at the age of thirty-nine, Schurz was elected United States senator from Missouri; he was the first man born in Germany to attain that honor. Schurz served only one term as senator, however, for during the administration of U. S. Grant, Congress was dominated by Democrats, and in 1874 he lost his seat. Years before the policy it outlined was adopted, Schurz introduced a bill to create a permanent civil service merit system.

Schurz was also a distinguished linguist, amazing his fellow senators on one occasion by translating at sight lengthy passages on a technical subject into four different languages. It has been said that "he was the only statesman of his generation who could make an eloquent speech either in English or German without revealing which was his native tongue."

Horace Greeley won the support of Schurz and the Liberal Republican party in 1872 but lost the election. In 1876, to the dismay and anger of many of his Liberal Republican associates, Schurz supported Rutherford B. Hayes, being assured that the latter was sound on the money question, would restore the South, and would promote civil service reform; Hayes and Schurz had developed a strong friendship when they both served as senators.

President Hayes appointed Schurz secretary of the interior in 1876; Schurz served in the position until 1881. His tenure is remembered because of his enlightened treatment of the Indians (though his policies were much misunderstood at the time), his installing of a merit promotion system, his preservation of the public domain, and the beginning of Schurz's development of national parks.

In 1881, Schurz moved to New York City to become editor in chief of the *Evening Post*, in which journalist and financier Henry Villard had just bought a controlling interest. Schurz was one of a triumvirate of editors, the other two being E. L. Godkin of the *Nation* (which was also purchased by Villard and made the weekend edition of the *Evening Post*) and Horace White. The paper became an effective advocate of liberal causes such as civil service reform and tariff revision under the three editors, with Schurz specializing in editorials on politics and foreign policy. Strains developed, however, between Schurz and Godkin and finally led to an open break between the two men. As a result, Schurz left the paper in 1883.

In May 1885 Schurz's thirty-three-page pamphlet *The New South*, an account of the findings from his tour of the South after the Civil War, was published. He also began writing a book; it would be the first of his books to be published, and it showed his great skill in dealing with history. *The Life of Henry Clay* (1887) proved to be an immediate success; Schurz received congratulatory letters from Congress and from ex-president Hayes. Four years later, his biographical sketch of Lincoln was published.

He once wrote that foreign-born citizens were "more jealously patriotic Americans than many natives are," since they watch the progress of the Republic "with triumphant joy at every success of our democratic institutions and with the keenest sensitiveness to every failure, having the standing of this country before the world constantly in mind." This describes his own attitude toward his adopted country.

In Schurz's later years he was less politically active than in his younger days. Upon his return from a trip to Europe he favored Grover Cleveland in the 1892 presidential election. However, problems with his health caused Schurz to refrain from political speaking engagements at that time.

Schurz accepted the editorship of *Harper's Weekly* after the death of the former editor in August 1892 and held the position until 1898, when he refused to support the drift toward war with Spain and the annexation of the Philippines. Schurz was elected president of the National Civil-Service Reform League at the end of 1892.

Schurz exercised his political support for William Jennings Bryan, a longtime adversary, in 1900. Schurz had opposed Bryan on the free-silver issue in 1886, but Bryan was the opponent of imperialism. Schurz felt strongly about this issue and, therefore, voted for Bryan, even though he thought Bryan would not be the best choice for president. Schurz received a great deal of criticism for his

Schurz in one of the last photographs taken of him, at his summer home above Bolton Landing, Lake George, New York (American Embassy, Bonn-Bad Godesberg)

decision and felt it necessary to resign from the presidency of the National Civil-Service Reform League. He would have one more election to regain the esteem of his admirers before his death.

In November 1901, Schurz wrote to the civil service reformer Edward M. Shepard, "The political life of a public man of character and ability is never ended so long as he is true to his best self, and willing to serve the country, and has something to say worth listening to." Shepard was one of Schurz's luncheon companions in New York; yet Schurz supported his opponent, Seth Low, in the 1901 campaign for mayor of New York. At a gathering in Cooper Union under the auspices of the German-American Reform League, Schurz, reverting to German, delivered a stinging indictment of "King" Richard Croker, the Tammany leader who was backing Shepard's candidacy: "No doubt he has extraordinary abilities in his own way," said Schurz. "There never was a successful robber chief who did not have extraordinary abilities of his trade." After Shepard's defeat, Croker retired to Ireland.

Schurz's last public speaking appearance was in June 1905 at the University of Wisconsin; thus Schurz ended his lecturing and political career in the state where it had begun. After fighting throat problems, he died of pneumonia at his home on Ninety-first Street in New York City in May 1906. His wife had died in 1876; at the time of his death three of his five children were living. None of them was to bear Schurz a namesake to continue the family line. Schurz's autobiography, *The Reminiscences of Carl Schurz* (1907-1908), covers the first forty years of his life and has been called one of the great books of the early twentieth century.

A historian has written, "We are inclined to idealize that which we love—a state of mind very unfavorable to sober, critical judgment." When writing biographies of Lincoln and Clay, two men for whom he had great esteem, Schurz certainly realized the problem journalists must overcome in their writing. The tendency to enhance the great deeds and abilities of those being written about, while deemphasizing their mistakes and weaknesses, must be continually guarded against. Schurz, as a journalist, strove to write unbiased biographies of these two political figures despite his friendship for and admiration of them.

In his biographies, editorials, and other writings, Schurz showed great insight and a penetrating study of his sources, which yielded a true interpretation of both the strengths and weaknesses of his subjects.

Joseph Schafer wrote in his biography of Schurz, "I doubt whether Schurz could have played the great part that he did in public affairs had not his nature also held the greatness of his simplicity. He could not have done in the field or in the forum or in his many messages to the people, what he did had he not been the Schurz who loved the God that the abundance of nature revealed to him."

Letters:

Intimate Letters of Carl Schurz, 1841-1869, translated and edited by Joseph Schafer (Madison: State Historical Society of Wisconsin, 1929).

Biographies:

C. V. Easum, *The Americanization of Carl Schurz* (Chicago: University of Chicago Press, 1929);

Joseph Schafer, *Carl Schurz, Militant Liberal* (Evansville, Wis.: Center Press, 1930);

C. M. Fuess, *Carl Schurz, Reformer* (New York: Dodd, Mead, 1932);

Marjorie O'Brien, *Carl Schurz: Patriot Illustrated*

(Madison: State Historical Society of Wisconsin, 1960);

Clara Little Tutt, *Carl Schurz, Patriot* (Madison: State Historical Society of Wisconsin, 1960);

Hans L. Trefousse, *Carl Schurz, a Biography* (Knoxville: University of Tennessee Press, 1982).

References:

T. A. Dodge, *The Campaign of Chancellorsville* (Boston: Osgood, 1881);

Allan Nevins, *The Evening Post: A Century of Journalism* (New York: Boni & Liveright, 1922);

E. D. Ross, *The Liberal Republican Movement in Missouri, 1865-1871* (New York: Holt, 1926);

I. M. Stewart, *The National Civil Service Reform League* (Austin: University of Texas Press, 1929).

Papers:

There are Schurz papers at the Library of Congress, the Boston Public Library, the State Historical Society of Missouri, the New York Public Library, the Watertown (Wisconsin) Historical Society, and the Wisconsin Historical Society.

Harvey W. Scott

Lauren Kessler
University of Oregon

BIRTH: Tazewell County, Illinois, 1 February 1838, to John Tucker and Ann Roelofson Scott.

EDUCATION: B.A., Pacific University, Forest Grove, Oregon, 1863.

MARRIAGE: 31 October 1865 to Elizabeth A. Nicklin, died; children: Kenneth N. and John H. 28 June 1876 to Margaret McChesney; children: Leslie M., Ambrose B., Judith M.

MAJOR POSITIONS HELD: Editor, *Portland Oregonian* (1865-1872, 1877-1910); director, Associated Press (1900-1910).

DEATH: Baltimore, Maryland, 7 August 1910.

BOOKS: *History of Portland, Oregon* (Syracuse, N.Y.: D. Mason, 1890);

Religion, Theology and Morals, compiled by Leslie M. Scott, 2 volumes (Cambridge, Md.: Riverside Press, 1917);

History of the Oregon Country, compiled by Leslie M. Scott, 6 volumes (Cambridge, Md.: Riverside Press, 1924);

Shakespeare, compiled by Leslie M. Scott (Cambridge, Md.: Riverside Press, 1928).

Harvey W. Scott—patrician journalist, "schoolmaster" of the Oregon press, Shakespeare-quoting editor of the *Portland Oregonian*—was more than the editor of the state's largest and most influential newspaper. He was, for forty-five years, a

Harvey W. Scott

major leader of political thought in Oregon and a leading spokesman for the region. He and his newspaper were credited by friends and foes alike with almost singlehandedly transforming Oregon from a Democratic into a Republican state. His forceful editorials had an influence beyond the thousands of *Oregonian* readers they reached: small-town editors of Republican newspapers statewide looked to the *Oregonian* for guidance on political issues of the day, modeled their thinking after Scott's, and often reprinted his editorials verbatim or commented on them at length. Under Scott, the *Oregonian*'s editorial voice became nationally recognized.

For more than four decades, Scott was the intellectual leader of Oregon journalism. He assumed editorship of the *Oregonian* nineteen years after the *Oregon City Spectator* became the first United States newspaper west of the Rocky Mountains. His career ran from Reconstruction days through the free-silver struggles and the era of national expansion to within four years of the start of World War I. Like Charles A. Dana of the *New York Sun*, Edwin Lawrence Godkin of the *New York Evening Post*, and Henry Watterson of the *Louisville Courier-Journal*, Scott was both a journalistic leader

and a symbol of a transitional era.

Born on an Illinois farm near Peoria, Scott was one of nine children of John Tucker and Anne Roelofson Scott. Although they were frontier farmers, the Scotts exposed their children to reading and writing. The family subscribed to several periodicals, among them Horace Greeley's *New York Tribune*, and the Scotts encouraged their children to keep diaries; perhaps this is why three of the Scott children grew up to be prominent journalists. Harvey was the most renowned, but his older sister, Abigail Scott Duniway, achieved fame both as the leader of the Oregon woman suffrage movement and as publisher / editor of her own woman suffrage weekly newspaper. Catharine Scott Coburn, a younger sister, was associate editor of the *Oregonian* from 1888 to 1913.

When Harvey Scott was fourteen, the entire family crossed the plains by ox team, arriving in Oregon City on 2 October 1852. Along the tortuous Oregon Trail, Scott's mother and one of his brothers died. The family lived for a year and a half in the Willamette Valley of Oregon, where Scott helped his father clear a farm site. When he was not clearing, planting, or harvesting, Scott attended a log schoolhouse in Amity.

In the spring of 1854 the family moved to the woods of the Puget Sound area in Washington, where Scott again helped his father clear a farm site. At seventeen, he enlisted in the Washington Territory Volunteers and spent eight months during 1855-1856 helping the home guard troops subdue Indians in the Yakima War. In late 1856 he returned to the Willamette Valley, where he lived with relatives, worked hard as a laborer, and saved money for his education.

In December he enrolled at the Tualatin Academy, Pacific University's preparatory school, and studied elementary subjects until the spring of 1857, when he exhausted his savings. He left school and worked as a woodcutter, but during the winter of 1858-1859 he attended Oregon City Academy. The following autumn the twenty-one-year-old Scott finally qualified for admission to Pacific University. During his four years of study, he supported himself by woodcutting, team driving, and school teaching. In 1863, he graduated from Pacific University with the first B.A. degree earned in the Pacific Northwest. Scott was the only member of his graduating class.

He continued teaching school for a while, then worked for several months in the Idaho mines, and finally moved to Portland to study law in the office of Judge E. D. Shattuck. While he prepared for the bar exams, he worked for $15 a week as Portland's first city librarian. It was Judge Shattuck who was responsible for Scott's entrance into the world of journalism. Henry Lewis Pittock, the *Oregonian's* owner and editor since the mid-1850s, was in the habit of soliciting editorials from outside sources. He asked Judge Shattuck for an editorial, and the judge, being too busy, suggested Harvey Scott. Scott's first regular contribution to the *Oregonian*, an editorial on Lincoln's assassination, appeared 17 April 1865. In it, the twenty-seven-year-old law student-librarian showed both his verbal strength and his youthful immoderation: "Upon this fiendish spirit of murder which has been sedulously propagated and inflamed by the disloyal men and disloyal press of the North, there must be meted out the fullest retribution. Thousands and thousands have fallen as sacrifices to the truculent spirit of revenge and hate by which this conflict was begun; but of all these martyrs, the blood of none calls so loudly for vengeance, as that of the murdered Abraham Lincoln. . . . Let all who mourn the death of noble Abraham Lincoln resolve that the fell spirit which caused it shall be eradicated utterly, even if the whole race of traitors and assassins, must, for

that purpose, be destroyed."

Scott was admitted to the Oregon Bar that September, and in October he married Elizabeth Nicklin, a young woman he had met while he was a student at Pacific University. But he never practiced law. In May of that year, Pittock hired him as editor of the *Oregonian*. Except for a five-year stint (1872-1877) as collector of customs in Portland—unlike his position at the struggling *Oregonian*, the customs job paid well and was considered a political plum—Scott held the editorship from 1865 until his death forty-five years later.

As editor of the *Oregonian*, Scott believed that a newspaper's "independence depended on [its] excellence as a newspaper, as an expert, efficient purveyor of each day's occurrences." In the thirteenth year of his editorship, he wrote that "a great journal is a universal newsgatherer, a universal truthteller." Yet Scott himself was not a newsman. He began his newspaper career on the editorial page and there his interests and his energies remained. "Events, unless they were related to economic or moral fundamentals, had no fascination for him, and little hold upon his attention," wrote Alfred Holman, one of Scott's protégés. Scott had "a sovereign con-

Newsroom of the Oregonian *in 1894. Scott did not spend much time here, preferring to concentrate on writing his "educational" editorials* (Portland Oregonian).

tempt" for the "trivialities" of the newsroom, according to Holman, his close associate for forty years. The editor apparently considered it an unpleasant duty to oversee the news content of the *Oregonian*. He knew news columns were essential to the paper, but, wrote Holman, "if there had been a way to get it done without demands on his personal attention, he would . . . have felt a distinct sense of relief." Although he wrote of the responsibility of a newspaper to gather news and report on daily intelligence, Scott clearly regarded the news function of his paper as subordinate to his department, criticism and opinion.

As to the critical function of the newspaper, Scott was equally clear. Journalism was "that branch of literature to which is entrusted the education of the popular mind." The newspaper was "an educational agency" or a "department of education"; the editor was a "public teacher." He compared the *Oregonian* to the church as a moral influence and to the college as an educational institution.

Scott saw himself as a schoolmaster. The tens of thousands of *Oregonian* readers were his daily students. His job was to contribute to the cultural education of his pioneer readers by freely instructing them in morals, philosophy, theology, literature, and history. One historian suggested that Scott's quick transformation from an "itinerant farm hand and logger" into a powerful public leader, via education and voracious reading, convinced him that it was his responsibility to "share his bounty" with his yet-to-be-transformed frontier audience. He considered it his duty to "refine" the frontier, and even his archrival of the early twentieth century, the upstart *Oregon Journal*, admitted that Oregonians "drank deeply of Mr. Scott's intelligence." He was, said his friend and admirer Holman, "the man who sat at the fountain of community intelligence."

Scott not only wanted to impart culture to rough-and-tumble readers, he wanted to educate them politically. Throughout his long career, the editor remained convinced that he had the right answers, that his opinions were the only valid ones. His detractors called him imperious, and even his staunchest ally admitted that Scott "became something of an autocrat." Holman repeats this conversation between Scott and a man who came to discuss a financial issue with him: "Well, Mr. Scott, I have as good a right to my opinion as you have to yours," [the visitor said]. "You have not," said Mr. Scott . . . ."You speak from the standpoint of mere presumption and emotion, without knowledge, without judgment. You speak after the manner of the

foolish. I speak from the basis of painstaking and laborious study. You have no right to an opinion on this subject. . . ."

Scott's arrogance apparently entered into his relationships with his fellow journalists as well. When an editor of a lesser newspaper let it be known that he thought he was Scott's equal, Scott replied: "Tell him . . . that when he shall have borne the burden and carried such honors as are attached to the leadership of journalism in this country for forty years, I will be disposed to concede him a certain equality of privilege."

Scott dealt with some of his colleagues at the *Oregonian* in a similar fashion. He sometimes allowed his editorial associates to publish opinions with which he did not agree, convinced that "soon thereafter [he] could bring the paper round with one of his own thunderbolts." It apparently never occurred to him that the *Oregonian* could be committed in its policies by editorial expressions other than his own. In fact, even after associates had dealt with a question in the editorial columns, Scott wrote about it as if it were the first time the issue was being discussed. As Holman said: "He felt himself to be the *Oregonian*; and he never could consent that the paper stood committed to anything unless he himself, by his own pen, had written it out."

What was it in Harvey Scott's character that allowed him, even at an early age, to be unshakably convinced of both the rightness and importance of his own opinions? One early historian admiringly likened him to Lincoln, a poor farmboy who had a "thirst for education" and an "indomitable will." Like Lincoln, Scott was a "devoted and untiring student" and an "indefatigable worker." One of his sons, Leslie M. Scott, believed the elder Scott's character was formed by "his youthful environment." From his pioneer heritage on the western frontier, he derived his "vigor of utterance and personality," wrote his son. "From this same experience he found his democratic sympathies . . . gained breadth of view, which he extended by reading . . . and acquired the disciplines of self-dependence and individual responsibility which mark all his work. He was a self-made man, had made his way as a youth, unaided, and gained rudiments of education through his own energies." It was the rigors of the West, concluded his son, that made Scott the man he was.

Both his close associate Alfred Holman and a later historian attribute Scott's resolute confidence in his own abilities to his voracious reading. He was a scholar, wrote Holman, and scholarship and philosophy gave him broad vision. Scott apparently had one of the finest libraries in Portland, if not the state, and, as his son remarked, "his library was his place of recreation; to companionship of his books he devoted a large part of his daily life." In reply to an inquiry about his reading habits, Scott said, "I read in the morning in bed as soon as it is light enough; then I read before breakfast and after breakfast; then after I get to the office, before lunch and a while after lunch, and of course, before dinner. Then I read a while before I start to my office for the evening, and after I have read my proofs and trudged home, before I go to bed and after I am in bed." But reading was no mere private pleasure to Scott. After dinner, he frequently treated his family and guests to two-hour discourses on Shakespeare, Milton, and Homer. In his newspaper, he inserted commentaries on Dante and Cervantes. "These commentaries," said his son, "so remote from centers of scholarship, were objects of surprise and admiration the country over." He impressed his *Oregonian* colleagues by quoting from memory Shakespearean plays, Websterian orations, and varying English translations of Homeric poems. He was, according to one recent historian, an "authentic frontiersman who became an authentic intellectual." Scott's early pioneer experiences forged in him a rugged individualism which translated into a host of political beliefs he expounded for more than four decades. His newly acquired erudition impelled him to take on the mantle of public education in cultural matters. To understand and appreciate the importance of Scott's career as an editor is to understand his self-appointed role as cultural and political educator. Not only did he care little for the news function of the *Oregonian*, he rarely involved himself in the business end of his newspaper. Scott was, pure and simple, a writer of editorials. Through this work, he became the preeminent molder of opinion for two generations of Oregonians.

When Harvey Scott began bringing culture and learning to his few thousand *Oregonian* readers in the mid-1860s, Portland was closer to a raw frontier town than a city. Transportation throughout the state—horseback, stagecoach, and riverboat—was arduous and time-consuming. What little intellectual thought Portlanders were exposed to was indigenous. Scott's "lectures" in the *Oregonian*'s editorial columns—complex, philosophical, studded with classical and Biblical references—must indeed have impressed his readers. One turn-of-the-century Oregon historian remarked that Scott had a "superstructure of culture and erudition that in breadth and strength has no superior, if it has an equal, on the Northwest coast."

One of Scott's favorite subjects was theology. In fact, he wrote so prolifically on this topic throughout his career that his son had no trouble filling two large volumes with the elder Scott's editorials, essays, and public addresses on the subject of *Religion, Theology and Morals* (1917). Scott expounded on the changing consciousness of the infinite, the unity of nature, the common history of religions, the mutual dependence of science and religion, and "rational Christianity." In the pages of the *Oregonian*, he discussed predestination, original sin, miracles, the trinity, and resurrection. He commented on the Bible—critically, historically, as a work of literature, and book by book. Scott considered much religious dogma outworn formula and firmly believed that science and religion could enhance one another.

But the keynote of Scott's theological writings was his constant reference to the permanent substance of religion as distinguished from its transitory forms. Looking at the history of religions, he saw that dogmas, creeds, and symbols change, but the underlying attitude they express remains the same. In an 1895 Thanksgiving Day address before the Portland First Baptist Church, Scott stated this belief succinctly: "The religious nature of man continually struggles for expression and its manner of expression changes from age to age. Yet we call each formulated, transitory expression a creed, as if it were to be permanent, and often contend for that creed as if it were the absolute truth; but it passes into something else in the next ages. Yet the religious feeling is the permanent force in the nature of man." Scott believed this permanent religious feeling should manifest itself in the everyday side of religion: correct living and conduct guided by both the Golden Rule and individual responsibility. Perhaps because he did not attack any particular religion—although he was philosophically critical of Roman Catholicism—Portland clergymen apparently held him in high regard. He was asked by various Methodist ministers to deliver addresses from their pulpits; Baptists, Congregationalists, and Christian Scientists all extended invitations. Scott's son reported that Portland's Jewish leaders "found satisfaction in his writings" and that Scott had good relations with the Unitarians. But not all religious leaders were happy with his theological dissertations. The Methodist bishop of Oregon complained in a letter to Scott that his articles were "cutting the ground from under the feet" of his church. The editor responded in a private letter:

> The *Oregonian* assails no religion or religious belief. It does not, however, deem itself forbidden to inquire into the concepts of religion or theological systems.... The *Oregonian*, under my hand, has dealt with these subjects ... not to the dissatisfaction of the great multitude of its readers.
>
> Your assumption that it is not the proper province of a newspaper to touch a subject which clergymen—or some of them—claim as their exclusive field, I cannot admit; more especially since, as a newspaperman, in active touch with the public mind ... I have found no feature of the *Oregonian*'s work more sought or approved than in the field from which you would bar it....

When Scott was not expounding on theological matters, he turned his attention to history. The editorial columns of the *Oregonian* were filled with Scott's efforts at regional history, from brief paragraphs to essays of nearly 5,000 words. Ranging from factual narrative to critical analysis to broad philosophical generalization, the articles often began with a reference to a news item—a piece of legislation, the death of a famous Northwesterner—that suggested to Scott the need to educate his readers about the past. As "schoolmaster" of the *Oregonian*, Scott had several reasons to include history in his editorial curriculum. "Judicious teaching of history," he said, "widens the horizon of the growing mind." One local historian wrote that Scott's "true vocation" was to make Pacific Northwest history a "living reality" to his readers. But Scott's attention to history, like his concentration on theology, was, at root, ethical: he believed the study and knowledge of regional history to be of moral worth to his readers. To a group of Oregon teachers, the editor said, "The study of our own history is chiefly valuable for its moral significance and influence.... It stirs up to activity the forces and agencies that build up character, that indicate duty, that prompt to action. These are the forces we want." Although Scott promoted Northwest history through lectures, scholarly treatises, and encouragement of expositions, the editorial page of the *Oregonian* was his primary platform.

To Scott, history was not narrowly defined. As one recent historian notes, the editor anticipated the present concept of cultural history when he envisioned the past "in broad panorama, as the total of the interrelationships among all man's interests,

actions, arts, and ideas within each age." He used his knowledge of world history to comment on local history. In one 1899 editorial, he invoked the Danes, Saxons, and Normans when discussing the instinct that brought thousands across the continent on the Oregon Trail.

Scott's interpretation of Northwest history was, of course, affected by his own assumptions and biases. He was, above all, a conservative who looked askance at innovations in society and government. He was a firm believer in individualism and was sympathetic to the social Darwinism advanced by Herbert Spencer. He believed in the ultimate goodness of work, calling it "the most moral thing in the world." As historian Lee Nash has pointed out, Scott developed his own tailored-to-Oregon "frontier thesis": Scott believed that those who successfully traversed the Oregon Trail were a special breed; "their unique character had evolved through three successive generations of frontier life, reached its highest and most purely American stage in Oregon, and was undiluted by any low, gold-grubbing element, as in California."

Scott was, in fact, one of the state's greatest boosters. "Our Pacific seaboard," he said in a 1905 address,

> is to be the seat of empire equal to that on the Atlantic. Men yet living, men not yet old, have seen the Oregon country develop from its smallest beginnings to its present greatness. And its present greatness is the promise of its future.
>
> All the multiplied resources of nature, through which great commonwealths are built up, are here in abundance. Hitherto the development has been slow; but now ... it will proceed with constantly accelerated rapidity.

Scott was usually subtler when extolling the virtues of his state and region; his *Oregonian* editorials were first and foremost historical lessons. But in addition to learning history, his readers, he hoped, would develop pride in their own past and grasp what for Scott was the ultimate historical lesson: hard work leads to success. In these editorials, Scott described the geographical, topographical, and climatic features of the region; reviewed the contributions of the early explorers and discoverers; sketched the navigational history of the area; told and retold the story of Oregon statehood; and detailed the lives and hardships of the state's early pioneers. Scott's faithful son, Leslie, compiled more than 10,000 of his father's writings and speeches on history in the six-volume *History of the Oregon Country* (1924), published fourteen years after Scott's death.

Scott's reputation as a regional historian led, from the late 1880s, to repeated invitations to speak and write on the subject. For a New York publisher specializing in local history, Scott edited and helped write a 650-page history of Portland (1890). He was the major contributor from the Northwest to the *National Cyclopaedia of American Biography*. He delivered speeches at banquets, fraternal functions, opening ceremonies, anniversary celebrations, and expositions. In the *Oregonian*, he continued to encourage the reading of regional history and often gave editorial attention to local historians and their writings. Nash, writing on "the editor as historian," concluded: "Few men anywhere at any time have been as free and powerful as the great American personal editors of the last century, of whom Scott was one of the last survivors. He was perfectly situated to indulge all his varied interests in an editorial page that was an extension of himself."

Scott's prodigious energies were not limited to cultural instruction. The *Oregonian*'s editorial page served as a forum for and extension of his political beliefs as well. Above all else, Scott was an ardent, unceasingly supportive Republican. In 1904 he wrote: "During fifty years the Democratic party has stood for nothing that the country has desired or could deem useful to it. If anything of constructive policy has come out of the Democratic party . . . one would like to be told what it is." It goes without saying that the *Oregonian*, under Scott's editorship, unfailingly endorsed state and federal Republican political candidates. So powerful was Scott's voice, so complete was the *Oregonian*'s journalistic dominance of the state—at least until 1902, when the *Oregon Journal* became the paper's only serious competitor in a half-century of publishing—that Scott was credited with converting the state from a Democratic into a Republican stronghold. In 1903, the editor of one of the state's Democratic papers wrote, with a mixture of admiration and anger: "It is a fact so patent as to be beyond cavil, that to the work of Mr. Scott and his *Oregonian* is due the fact that within twenty-five years, Oregon had been transformed from a Democratic into a sure Republican state. . . . If ever there was a condition in which a party organization from sheer gratitude was indebted to an individual, it is manifestly, signally and unquestionably true in the case of Mr. Scott."

Scott was an avid Hamiltonian—"The glory of Hamilton is the greatness of America," he wrote in 1880—who found only one thing to admire about

Jeffersonian politics: expansionism. As a pioneer and a Pacific Northwest booster, Scott naturally believed the acquisition of the Louisiana Territory was "the most important of all facts in our history because it created the conditions necessary to our national expansion and consolidation." But his expansionist ideas extended far beyond the Pacific coast. Even before the war with Spain, Scott informed his readers that expansion was the rule of national life. "We shall go on expanding our limits," he wrote in 1893, "so long as the vital impulse of our nationality is not exhausted. When we lose the impulse to expand, it will be time for some other people to take the primacy of the Western Hemisphere out of our failing hands."

When the war with Spain delivered the Philippines to the United States, Scott registered his wholehearted approval: "Men and ideas now leap oceans . . . and the notion that American ideas cannot pass beyond this continent is a strange shortsightedness, reserved, fortunately . . . to a small portion of the people." To Scott, trans-Pacific expansionism was "a new era of our national history" and "a new epoch in the history of the world"; acquisitions in the Pacific were a natural extension of the spirit that had pushed America's boundaries to the Pacific coast. Expansion would stimulate further progress, banish from domestic politics fallacies which he believed would otherwise be generated from isolationism, and promote world leadership by America. When the Democratic party called annexation of the Philippines "imperialism" and "militarism," Scott waved the bloody shirt. The Democrats, said Scott, were being hypocrites: how could a party that for generations enslaved the Southern Negroes object to American rule over the Filipinos? Further, the editor believed that the Filipinos would, under United States control, have more political and personal freedom than they had ever had.

Like many of the political thinkers of his time, Scott believed in the supremacy of the white race. His paternalistic attitude toward the Philippines is one example of this; his attitude toward Chinese immigrants is another. From 1880 to 1890, a crusade raged against the Chinese in northern California and the Pacific Northwest. Under an 1868 treaty, Chinese immigrants were allowed free entry into the country. In 1880, a new treaty gave the United States the right to regulate immigration. Two years later, Congress forbade the admission of Chinese laborers to the United States for ten years—a rule later changed into permanent exclusion. Meanwhile, on the West Coast, anti-Chinese sentiment ran high. Mobs attacked Chinese laborers in San Francisco, Tacoma, and Seattle. Portland had somewhat fewer and less violent disturbances, a fact that some local historians attributed to Harvey Scott's even-tempered—although anti-Chinese—editorials. When, in 1905, the Portland Chamber of Commerce recommended admitting a limited number of Chinese annually, Scott responded with an editorial barrage. Throughout that summer, he warned his readers of the "unconquerable antagonism" between the races, saying that a "race war" would be the result of Chinese immigration.

Considering his dogged adherence to individualism, it is not surprising that Scott and his newspaper were virulent opponents of both the organization of labor and the passage of protective legislation for workers. He believed the "collectivism" of organized labor would submerge the energetic, thrifty members of society. Labor activists were merely interested in shortening the workday, said Scott, and "the young man who is to get on in the world needs to work the most days and most hours he can—not the fewest." When workers complained of low wages or poor working conditions, Scott, time and time again, invoked his own pioneer experiences: "You who talk of hardships or of oppressive conditions and of the grinding forces of life are absurd. If all the things you and your kind complain of as oppressive and burdensome were massed together, they would not equal one-tenth part of the obstacles that had to be met in the settlement and organization of this country, and about which we never thought to complain."

This theme of frontier self-reliance runs through many of Scott's anti-labor-organization editorials. Turn-of-the-century Portland, with its lumber mills and manufacturing plants, was a different world from the one the young Harvey Scott had encountered in the 1850s; but Scott, like many of his contemporaries, was blinded to the difference this might make for workers. There were "bountiful opportunities in Oregon . . . no man need suffer poverty," wrote Scott. Voluntary hard labor was the answer to all ills, because "government can do little to help its people or provide them work." To an editor who said he would like to see what Scott would do if he were out of money, out of work, and out of friends, Scott replied in an 1894 editorial: "[I] was in exactly that position in Portland over forty years ago. But [I] didn't stand around and whine, nor look for resources in political agitation or bogus money nor join Coxey's army. [I] struck out for the country, dug a farmer's potatoes, milked the cows, and built fences for [my] food and slept in a shed."

Scott did not approve of the soup kitchens set up to feed out-of-work Portlanders in the 1890s, and his paper consistently railed against such issues of organized labor as industrial safety codes and the Fellow Servant Law, a form of what would later be called workmen's compensation. Such legislation would hurt worker initiative, Scott believed.

Scott's tenacious belief in the power of self-help and his abhorrence of protective legislation can be seen in another of his—and the *Oregonian*'s—political stands: antiprohibition. Scott was a firm believer in sobriety, and he was nothing if not a moralist, yet he resisted prohibition. It was the individual's responsibility to remain sober and thereby to remain ever-industrious, Scott believed. As one of Portland's biggest boosters, he was also concerned with the economic repercussions of prohibition. In arguing against the drys' campaign in 1904, Scott wrote that "it didn't make good sense to resist the growth of the activities of a city, though so many of the things that one or another dislike follow in its train."

But the editorial campaign that won Scott the most recognition, both locally and nationally, was his three-decade battle for "sound money." He began the fight early in his editorship when, in 1866, a plan was put forth to repay the United States' Civil War debt in depreciated greenbacks. Scott's attitude was characteristic: money is to be gained from the industrious work of the individual, not from government printing presses. The policy of repudiation of the national debt by payment in depreciated money instead of full-value gold was the first major financial issue the young editor tackled in his columns. He insisted that the government should pay its obligations in full gold. When the advocates of repudiation were defeated in 1868-1869, Scott was overjoyed.

His next battle for the gold standard was not so easily won. It started in 1877 when free-silver advocates in the West first began to mount their campaign. Oregon, like other western states, had its share of Populists, and even some of the state's leading Republican politicians were flirting with free silver. Scott fought what he called "the silver heresy" in editorial after editorial, through a period of panic and depression and even when the *Oregonian* itself was heavily in debt. "A debased and unstable silver currency will take the place of gold as fast as silver can be coined," he wrote in an 1877 editorial. "All the talk about a double standard is the merest moonshine." Free silver, wrote Scott, was economically unsound and fundamentally dishonest. As the national economy worsened, more and

Front page of the Portland Oregonian *in the year Scott returned to the paper from his job as a customs collector*

more Oregonians turned to Populism. Some of the state's Republican newspapers wavered in their support of the gold standard, but Harvey Scott's *Oregonian* remained steadfast. Scott was accused of "sitting in his isolated tower and paying no attention to what the state felt," but he dismissed his critics with characteristic arrogance: "Somebody asks if there can't be 'an honest difference of opinion' about the gold standard. There can be no honest difference of opinion where one of the parties knows nothing about what he is talking about. There may be honest ignorance. But it is entitled to no opinion." He admitted to "a certain dogmatism" in discussing the silver question, but he defended himself by saying that "there is no other method than dogmatism in dealing with fixed and unchangeable principles." To Scott, the silver "craze" was the single greatest menace to the United States during his lifetime. He fought it with all the journalistic weapons in his arsenal, and he won.

In 1896, Washington, Idaho, Montana, Nevada, and Utah all went solidly for silver, and California gave William Jennings Bryan one of its nine electoral votes. In the West, only Oregon voted solidly against the silver policy. On the Pacific coast, Scott's *Oregonian*, among the leading dailies, stood alone in its advocacy of the gold standard. "The result of the 1896 election was in the nature of a personal victory for Mr. Scott," wrote the author of one turn-of-the-century Oregon history book; Alfred Holman said that "it was universally admitted that Republicans . . . carried the gold standard issue in Oregon through the efforts of Mr. Scott." All who have written about Harvey Scott concur. Although the exact nature and extent of his influence will probably never be known, it is inarguable that Scott's *Oregonian* was a powerful, strident—and, in the end, victorious—voice in the fight against free silver.

Scott did not win all the editorial battles he waged. In the early 1900s, he and the *Oregonian* were on the losing side of two major state issues: the initiative and referendum and the direct primary. Scott was unalterably opposed to the initiative and referendum system. He objected most strenuously to the initiative, the method by which citizens, by petition, could put an issue on the state ballot. He felt it was designed for occasional and emergency use, but would "open the way to innovators, faddists and agitators, who took the opportunity to inflict their notions upon legislation at every election." He saw the initiative as a "menace to political peace and security" which would supplant representative government—"the best known method of demo-

cratic cohesion and the safest means of protection for property." In 1904, Oregon instituted the initiative and referendum.

Scott was, according to his son, "the boldest critic" of the direct primary. He believed—and was later proven to be right—that the direct primary would be harmful to the Republican party in Oregon. He felt it would destroy the "representative and cohesive forces of government" and would cause a "loss of leadership of the strongest men." He feared factionalism and the elimination of purposeful party effort. This "reversion to pure democracy" would destroy representative government, Scott thought. Although he used all the power of the *Oregonian* to fight the legislation, Oregon instituted direct primaries in 1905.

Scott lost these battles because his views were out of tune with what the majority of Oregonians wanted, but there may have been another reason as well. In the early 1900s, the *Oregonian* had, for the first time in its history, a serious journalistic rival. The *Oregon Journal* of 1902, running in the red with a circulation of barely 4,000, must not have looked like much of a threat to the 25,000-circulation *Oregonian*. But by 1906, the *Journal* boasted a circulation in excess of 25,000 and was rivaling the *Oregonian* for advertising linage. More important, the *Journal* was a staunchly Democratic paper that battled furiously for everything Scott and his *Oregonian* were against.

The *Journal* was edited, and later owned, by C. S. "Sam" Jackson, a tall, spare Virginian who had edited and managed the *Pendleton East Oregonian* for twenty-one years. From Pendleton, Jackson battled for labor legislation, flirted with Populism by supporting Henry George's single tax, and backed Populist James B. Weaver for president in 1892. When Jackson took over the two-month-old *Journal*, he vowed to continued the fight for "the poor, the weak and depressed . . . and against the strong, the entrenched in power, the privileged and the plutocratic." To Jackson, the latter included Harvey Scott and his *Oregonian*.

Jackson began the fight immediately, dubbing the powerful morning *Oregonian* "The Morning Tombstone" and writing, in the first issue under his editorship: "The *Oregonian*'s well-known prejudices against everything not in strict subservience to itself and its own ideas are patent to most people, and reduce its weight proportionately." A few years later, commenting on editorial stands taken by the *Oregonian*, Jackson wrote: "The *Oregonian* is experiencing some difficulty in keeping up with public sentiment. It has been so long a clog in the wheel of progress, it has so often and so bitterly opposed manifestly needed reforms. . . ."

Harvey Scott had finally met his match. Scott, who had seen Oregon vote solidly Republican under his political tutelage, now saw George Chamberlain, a Democrat backed by Jackson's *Journal*, win the 1902 gubernatorial election. Together Chamberlain and the *Journal* battled successfully for a number of Democratic causes, including the direct primary and initiative and referendum.

The *Oregonian* and the *Journal* were on opposite sides of another major political issue in Oregon, one that had particular significance for Scott—the battle for the enfranchisement of women. Scott's older sister, Abigail Scott Duniway, was a thirty-six-year-old mother of six and sole support of her family when she began what was undoubtedly the most tenaciously fought crusade for woman suffrage in the West. Six times (1884, 1900, 1906, 1908, 1910, 1912) Oregon suffragists, under the persistent direction of Duniway, succeeded in placing an equal suffrage amendment to the state constitution before the voters. For the better part of four decades, Duniway, traveling by horseback, stagecoach, riverboat, and the few miles of railroad then in existence, visited the towns of Oregon, delivering speeches and organizing suffrage clubs. From 1871 to 1887 she published, edited, and wrote almost all the copy for her Portland-based prosuffrage weekly, the *New Northwest*. Among the leaders of the state's journalistic community, she had one faithful supporter: Sam Jackson. Through forty of the forty-two years she devoted her energies to the suffrage movement, she had one powerful, vociferous, and unflagging opponent: her brother, Harvey Scott.

Scott used the power of the *Oregonian* against woman suffrage in two ways: he either ignored the question entirely, offering his readers no discussion of the issue, or he mounted a full-scale editorial barrage against it. Historians of the Oregon suffrage movement consider the *Oregonian*'s implicit or explicit antisuffrage stand through five of the six campaigns a major factor in the defeat of the amendment. Duniway herself called her brother "the staunchest enemy" of woman suffrage in the state. One family friend remarked in a private letter that "the rivalry or feud or whatever it was between Mr. Scott and Mrs. Duniway . . . was more or less a skeleton in the family closet."

Scott apparently objected to woman suffrage because he thought women were fiscally irresponsible. If allowed to vote, women would allocate state and federal funds for various reform programs, Scott feared, and to him self-help, not government

Abigail Scott Duniway, Scott's sister, who fought him for forty years over the woman suffrage issue

aid, was the answer to all ills. He also wrote that woman suffrage was a matter of political and social expediency, not basic human rights. It is likely that his strong opposition to enfranchisement was also a personal matter: Abigail Scott Duniway could be as stubborn, arrogant, and stolid as her brother. She was also a writer of powerful editorials and the publisher of her own newspaper.

Prior to the 1884 vote on the suffrage amendment, the *Oregonian* barely mentioned the issue in either its editorial or news columns. But during the 1900 campaign, Scott wrote full-column antisuffrage editorials for more than a week prior to election day. Commenting on the defeat of the amendment and her brother's opposition in a letter to a friend, Duniway wrote: "We cannot hope to fully overcome the few hundred antis, the 7,000 slum vote of Portland and Harvey Scott. . . . He cannot throttle liberty. But he has added 10 years more of hard, irksome toil to my own advancing age. . . . When one's foe is of one's household, the humiliation is even harder to bear." In a letter to her brother, Duniway wrote: "The most charitable construction the many loyal women of your acquaintance can put upon your conduct toward the many brave women of your household, every one of whom is a suffragist, is that the cheap male sycophants . . . have flattered you until you are insane on the sex question." Later in the letter, she said that she pitied her brother and that she thought he needed a mental rest.

Scott's opposition remained steadfast, but in the 1906, 1908, and 1910 elections, suffragists finally had a powerful Portland ally, Sam Jackson's *Oregon Journal*. The *Journal* not only gave strong editorial support to the amendment, it opened its pages to a full discussion of the issue, publishing scores of letters to the editor (unlike the *Oregonian*) and covering in depth the activities of the state suffrage organization prior to the three elections. It was not until the election of 1912, two years after Harvey Scott's death, that the *Oregonian* lent its support to the equal suffrage amendment. The amendment carried that year.

In the editorial columns of the *Oregonian*, Scott continued both his political battles and his moral instruction until his death. Throughout his career, he had little to do with the daily operation of his paper. He hired men who knew their business and gave them full responsibility to run their own departments. The paper was considered to be a well-edited daily full of facts and bereft of sensationalism; its reporters were thought of as "gentlemen"; its coverage of national and international events was praised.

Scott devoted his life to the *Oregonian*. Aside from reading and his family, he had few outside interests. His first wife died soon after the birth of their second son. In 1876 he married Margaret McChesney, a Pennsylvania farmer's daughter whom he met on one of his trips to the East Coast. They had three children.

Scott had both admirers and detractors, but he had few intimate friends. Late in life, he began to reap the benefits of his years as political and moral spokesman for the state. He was encouraged to run for the United States Senate. He was asked by President Taft to accept the Mexican ambassadorship. He began to visit New York for the annual Associated Press meetings, and there he met and apparently enjoyed the conversation of Whitelaw Reid, Henry Watterson, Melville E. Stone, and Victor F. Lawson. He occupied several positions of honor: president of the Oregon Historical Society (1898-1901), president of the Lewis and Clark Exposition (1903-1904), and director of the Associated Press (1900-1910).

When he died at age seventy-two during surgery at Johns Hopkins University hospital for a stomach ailment, he was the undisputed leader of Oregon journalism. "His voice has been the most potent ever raised within [Oregon's] boundaries," said the *Salt Lake Telegram*. The *Providence* (Rhode Island) *Journal* wrote: "By sheer force of his personality and his powerful pen he made himself the leading figure of the Pacific Coast." "Mr. Scott was an editor who put his personality into the journal which he directed and made it a force to be reckoned with. . . ," wrote the *New York Tribune*. "To newspaper readers of Oregon, Washington, and northern California," said the *Detroit News* upon Scott's death, "[he] was what Greeley and Dana were to Easterners a generation ago."

Scott himself was well aware of his position of influence. As one of his *Oregonian* colleagues wrote: "Mr. Scott often remarked, when efforts were made to stimulate in him the spirit of political ambition, that he would not 'step down' from the editorship of the *Oregonian* into the United States Senate. And this was no boast; for the editorship of the *Oregonian*, as carried out by Mr. Scott, was truly a higher place, a place of wider responsibilities and of larger powers than any official place possibly attainable by a man geographically placed as Mr. Scott was."

References:

Eric W. Allen, "Oregon Journalism in 1887," *Oregon Historical Quarterly*, 38 (September 1937): 251-264;

Joseph Gaston, *The Centennial History of Oregon, 1811-1912* (Chicago: S. J. Clarke, 1912);

Alfred Holman, "Harvey Scott, Editor," *Oregon Historical Quarterly*, 14 (June 1913): 87-133;

John B. Horner, *Oregon History and Early Literature* (Portland, Oreg.: J. K. Gill, 1919);

Otho Clarke Leiter, "Scott and the Oregonian," *Journalism Quarterly*, 5 (January 1929): 1-10;

Lee M. Nash, "Scott of the Oregonian: The Editor as Historian," *Oregon Historical Quarterly*, 70 (September 1969): 197-232;

Robert C. Notson, *Making the Day Begin: A Story of the Oregonian* (Portland, Oreg.: Oregonian Publishing Co., 1976);

Portrait and Bibliographic Record of the Willamette Valley, Oregon (Chicago: Chapman, 1903);

George S. Turnbull, *History of Oregon Newspapers* (Portland, Oreg.: Binfords & Mort, 1939);

Turnbull, "Schoolmaster of the Oregon Press," *Journalism Quarterly*, 15 (December 1938): 359-369.

Henry Villard

(10 April 1835-12 November 1900)

Jo Anne Smith
University of Florida

MAJOR POSITIONS HELD: Editor, *Racine Volks-blatt* (1856); correspondent, *New York Staats-Zeitung* (1858-1859), *Cincinnati Commercial* (1859-1860), Associated Press (1860-1861); war correspondent, *New York Herald* (1861-1862), *New York Tribune* (1862-1865); publisher, *New York Evening Post* and *Nation* (1881-1900).

BOOKS: *The Past and Present of the Pike's Peak Gold Regions* (St. Louis: Sutherland & McEvoy, 1860);
Memoirs of Henry Villard, Journalist and Financier, 1835-1900, 2 volumes (New York: Houghton Mifflin, 1904; London: Constable, 1904);
Lincoln on the Eve of '61: A Journalist's Story, edited by Harold G. and Oswald Garrison Villard (New York: Knopf, 1941);
The Early History of Transportation in Oregon, edited by Oswald Garrison Villard (Eugene: University of Oregon Press, 1944).

Henry Villard gained fame—or fortunes—in three careers: war correspondent, railroad financier, and newspaper publisher. Villard arrived in the United States as a penniless German-speaking immigrant of eighteen. Disdainful of life in "little Germanies," Villard was determined to learn a new tongue and a new way of life. Rapid assimilation brought him within a few years to a post as a highly paid Washington reporter well known to the president. By the time he reached middle age, Villard had become a millionaire business leader on the strengths of shrewdness, resourcefulness, and a remarkable talent for getting close to persons of influence.

Villard first achieved journalistic notice for his reporting of the Lincoln-Douglas debates. Shortly thereafter, a series of "scoops" from the battlefields of the Civil War established him as one of the best and best known of some 500 "specials" who reported the war for Northern newspapers. After the war his mercurial interests shifted to finance, and he became an agent representing the American interests of German bondholders. In that role, he amassed a fortune, eventually becoming president of both railroad and electric companies. He chose to invest part of his railroading wealth in his old field of journalism, buying controlling interests in the *New York Evening Post* and the *Nation*. He selected outstanding editors who shared his concepts of "quality journalism," then allowed them autonomy in creating respected journals.

Born in Speyer, Bavaria, 10 April 1835 as Ferdinand Heinrich Gustav Hilgard, he was the son of well-to-do parents, Gustav Leonhard Hilgard, a judge, and Katharina Antonia Elisabeth Pfeiffer Hilgard. Father and son, though not without affection for one another, definitely marched to two different drumbeats. Heinrich found his two young uncles' republicanism and participation in an 1848 revolutionary movement far more exciting than his stern father's loyalist role as a presiding judge. The boy's education led to continual clashes. Whereas the father favored a technical or military training or the reading of law, the son yearned for the study of "arts and letters." Years of discord became a rift when Heinrich, without his father's knowledge, switched from the technical training at the Polytechnicum in Munich to the study of poetry at the university there. When his father then had him transferred from Munich to the University of Würzburg and committed him to the study of law, Heinrich borrowed money from relatives and immigrated to New York. Fearing his father might have him returned to Germany and conscripted for military service, he changed his name to Henry Villard. At eighteen, broke and knowing no English, he began life in a new land.

Villard's stay in New York was brief. Drifting westward in search of work, he resorted at last to asking for help from relatives who earlier had immigrated to Belleville, Illinois, in quest of life as "free men." Villard worked in Illinois in the office of a recorder of deeds. Though tedious, the job forced him to learn English; it also spurred second thoughts about a career in law. Financed in part by money from his hopeful and forgiving parents, this second venture into the study of law proved no more successful than the first. Soon bored, Villard sought other outlets. He penned some unflattering letters about the "German philistinism" of the people of the area that were published in the *Belleville Zeitung*. His ungrateful attitude outraged his relatives and friends. Though he regretted hurting them, Villard later was to recall that the attention he received "rather flattered my vanity."

The heady satisfactions of being a published writer did not, however, propel Villard instantly into journalism. Craving "success" but unsure of how to find it, he began responding to a variety of seductive advertisements. He failed at persuading other young Germans of the great "free soil" opportunities in Kansas. He wound up $5 in debt after weeks of pursuing "handsome commissions" as an encyclopedia salesman. He tried schoolteaching, but disliked having to rotate as a boarder among the "sadly ignorant" families of his pupils; he kept his hand in at free-lancing but found the work "hard and discouraging owing to the uncertainty of the pay." His first newspaper job, as editor of the weekly *Volksblatt* in Racine, Wisconsin, produced similar uncertainties. Subscribers paid in farm produce or not at all, and the paper soon failed.

From Wisconsin Villard sent articles about state politics and the state's large German element to the German-language *New York Neue Zeit*, which paid him $5 for each story. In 1858, another German-language paper, the *New York Staats-Zeitung*, hired him to solicit new subscriptions and collect on old ones in Ohio. He was not, he confessed to the home office, a "successful canvasser." But he was alert and enterprising. Reminding the New York office of mid-America's growing excitement over the upcoming debates between Abraham Lincoln and Stephen A. Douglas, Villard proposed that he travel back to Illinois and cover that story for the *Staats-Zeitung*.

For Villard, now twenty-three, it was his first major news assignment. The significance of the debates was widely recognized, and many newspapers had sent reporters more skilled and more experienced than Villard to cover them. Villard was not above showing his "admiration" for these newsmen by lifting from them, especially from Robert H. Hitt of the *Chicago Press*, who was proficient at shorthand, a skill then coming into vogue among reporters. Villard learned from others in the press corps and became close friends with one of them, Horace White. The campaign trail they shared was seldom comfortable: reporters were sometimes barred from meeting rooms, often missed meals, and slept in hotel armchairs or rooms shared with a half-dozen others.

While thus experiencing some of the hard realities of on-the-spot reporting, Villard fast was sharpening one of his keenest facilities as a reporter, the ability to make contacts and inspire confidences. Both Lincoln and Douglas made themselves easily available to reporters who traveled with them, but Villard showed himself to be unusually adept at eliciting candid and reflective responses. One long conversation with Lincoln took place as the two squatted in a boxcar at a railroad flag station on a rainy evening. To pass the time, they fell into an exchange of childhood experiences, religious beliefs, family backgrounds, and ambitions. Lincoln confided to Villard misgivings about running for the Senate—fears that he lacked qualifications for the office. He then wryly remarked that his wife, Mary, on the contrary, envisioned him not just as senator but as president, too. With that, he clutched his knees in spasmodic laughter, snorting, "Just think of such a sucker as me as President!"

In early reports, Villard judged Lincoln harshly. Dispatches to New York and Philadelphia characterized Lincoln's views as fanatical, his arguments as lame and ambiguous, his manner as uncouth. The lanky candidate not only was "indescribably gawky" and "altogether uncomely," Villard wrote, but lacked the "depth, thoroughness . . . and sharp logical thinking" that Douglas so "eminently" displayed. Gradually, his view began to change, and he believed that though Lincoln was the "loser in appearance," he was making the stronger points. Villard's retrospective view, prepared years later for his memoirs, was kinder still. There, he pronounced Lincoln "a thoroughly earnest and truthful man inspired by sound conviction." He admitted that his appreciation of Lincoln's finer qualities had been blunted initially by personal dislike for Lincoln's crudity and endless supply of smutty stories.

Debate coverage for the *Staats-Zeitung* paved the way toward the transition Villard had been yearning to make, to the English-language press. The *Cincinnati Commercial* hired him in 1859 to go to Colorado to cover the Pike's Peak gold rush. There he met and traveled with Horace Greeley of the *New York Tribune*, later to be one of his employers. As was Greeley, Villard was infected with "go west!" enthusiasm. He put much time and research into preparation of a book about the area (1860); and he joined Greeley and Albert D. Richardson of the *Boston Journal* in a joint statement praising the prospects for mineral wealth in Colorado. Though the report was ridiculed by another of Villard's future employers, James Gordon Bennett of the *New York Herald*, the three men's assessment of the Colorado mine fields proved essentially correct.

The reputation he had won in reporting the Lincoln-Douglas debates brought Villard his next assignment as well: the Associated Press asked him to return to Illinois, where Lincoln, now president-elect, was ending his stay in Springfield. Villard spent several days in Springfield watching Lincoln receive streams of visitors, many seeking political favors. Again, he was struck by Lincoln's "nastiness" and social awkwardness on the one hand and by his "deep earnestness and contemplative nature" on the other. It is to Villard that history owes the most authentic account of Lincoln's farewell address at Springfield. After the train pulled out, Villard asked Lincoln to write on a pad his best recollection of the words he just had spoken. The precious manuscript, carried by Villard for months, was lost some time during his travels as a war correspondent.

Scarcely two years removed from his days as a rural subscription collector, Villard now enjoyed the status of a reporter with the "ear" of the man soon to be president. From Washington, Villard wrote to a number of newspapers offering to send dispatches from the capital. He thus became, by his own account, one of the "pioneers" of syndicated Washington coverage. He boasted that his income during that period reached $3,000 and that even Lincoln's cabinet members earned only twice that amount.

One of the papers that elected to buy Villard's syndicated reports was Bennett's *Herald*. It was an uneasy association for Villard: he liked neither the *Herald*'s style nor its editorial urgings for "conciliation and compromise" with secessionists. Just when Villard was considering severing ties with the *Herald*, Bennett summoned him to New York. There, Villard found he liked Bennett, "a man of a hard, cold, utterly selfish nature," even less than he liked Bennett's journalism. In a request Villard felt was motivated by sheer opportunism, Bennett asked Villard to serve as his personal emissary to the president.

Fort Sumter had fallen the day before and a restive crowd had marched to the *Herald*, which on the eve of the firing on the fort had called Lincoln a "pliant instrument" of a "destructive sectional party." Threatening to "get old man Bennett" and burn the building down, the crowd demanded to see the *Herald* fly the Stars and Stripes. Bennett had sent an office boy running to a bunting shop to buy the requisite banner. Other employees stored rifles in the editors' offices. Under the heat of this aroused public opinion, Bennett now wanted Villard to carry two messages to Lincoln. One was that the *Herald*, boasting the nation's largest newspaper circulation, would support "suppression of the Rebellion by force of arms." The other was that his son's yacht was available for use by the revenue service and that Bennett, Jr., himself was "available" for a commission in that service.

Returning to Washington with Bennett's messages, Villard found the city ghostly quiet, cut off from telegraph and mail service as though it "had been suddenly removed to an island in mid-ocean in a state of entire isolation." The president, eager for news, listened absorbedly to Villard's account of the threats on the *Herald* office and of Bennett's offers.

Villard subsequently turned down a captain's commission offered by Lincoln in favor of serving as a war correspondent. He negotiated with travelers on the "underground railroad" to bring news from Southern newspapers. Accounts he compiled from the South became a valued *Herald* feature. Probably his biggest story for the *Herald* came from the field in the early days of the war when, on 21 July 1861, he witnessed the first battle of Bull Run. Many Northern reporters had come to the Manassas area anticipating an overwhelming Union victory, very probably a war-ending one. When the first Union advances succeeded, some left the scene to wire home news of the great victory. Therefore when the *Herald* received Villard's grim account—an account he was able to file only after an eighteen-hour journey to a telegraph center—managing editor Frederic Hudson cautiously toned down the story. Even so, the *Herald* was first to report that the successful advances had been followed by a Union retreat that dissolved into "panic among our troops," resulting finally in "a regular stampede."

On the scene at most of the crucial battles in the first two years of the war, Villard had a penchant for getting to both news and newsmakers. Even Sherman, with his well-known antipathy toward war correspondents, not only allowed Villard at his headquarters but sought his companionship. Villard traveled with the armies of Generals Grant, McClellan, Burnside, and Hooker, talking to most of those men at length. On "breathers" in Washington, he held long and frequent discussions with cabinet members and with the president himself.

History has confirmed many of Villard's assessments of both the men and the battles. Phillip Knightley, whose study of the Northern "specials" concluded that the majority were "ignorant, dishonest and unethical" men whose stories frequently were inaccurate or even invented, called Villard "one of the better American correspondents." Not only was he more accurate than most but he was "an outspoken correspondent, not afraid of telling even Lincoln what he felt was wrong with his army."

Villard's second major scoop of the war was his account of the battle of Fredericksburg in 1862. By then he had left the *Herald* to write for Greeley's *Tribune*. As described by Frank Luther Mott, Villard's "beat" came only after an exhausting struggle. General Burnside had interdicted telegraphic communications regarding the battle, and Villard had to "ride for miles through almost impassable roads," outwitting "one of the ablest war correspondents for a rival paper," tricking a freighter captain into providing him passage, and finally putting his story aboard a train. His report of Burnside's "murderous blunder" and of the "great, general defeat" for the Army of the Potomac, the first to be received, again was toned down by a cautious editor awaiting confirmation from other sources.

As the first correspondent to return from Fredericksburg, Villard found himself much in demand. Lincoln promptly summoned him for a half-hour quizzing about his "gloomy" account of Union losses in the Confederate trap on the heights above the south bank of the Rappahannock. Bold enough to offer the president his opinion, Villard politely suggested that Lincoln order Burnside to withdraw so that Confederate troops would not be able to launch a potentially disastrous night bayonet attack. Military men and members of Congress also sought Villard's comments, and he later felt that his "earnest denunciations" had much to do with instigating a congressional investigation of events at Fredericksburg.

Villard was the only reporter to accompany the fleet on its April 1863 offensive on the harbor at Charleston. Seeming always to find a better way and a higher official, Villard boarded the flagship *New Ironsides* at the invitation of Admiral Samuel Du Pont while ten of his rivals went aboard the steamer *Nantasket* under army command. At the end of the attack on the harbor, the *Nantasket* stayed at sea for two days. Villard, meanwhile, was blithely sailing north on the admiral's dispatch boat en route to filing another scoop. The report, published in a *Tribune* extra, won congratulations from Greeley, a $100 bonus, and two weeks' leave. On his time off, Villard traveled to Boston and there he met his future wife, Helen Frances (Fanny) Garrison, daughter of famed abolitionist editor William Lloyd Garrison and, like her father, a pacifist supporter of "universal disarmament." Meeting Fanny, a woman of active intellect and resolute beliefs as well as physical beauty and a sweet temperament, was the happiest event of what became a trying year for Villard.

In June 1863, on the move with the army, Villard fell ill with fever and was taken to a military hospital at Murfreesboro. That fall he covered General Hooker's advance across the Tennessee River into Lookout Valley and the taking of fog-shrouded Lookout Mountain. But the November campaign in Tennessee brought back his illness, and he was forced to return to Washington. While there, he again was sought as an emissary to the president, this time by Secretary of the Treasury Salmon Chase. Knowing Lincoln would be seeking reelection, Chase, who had sought the 1860 GOP nomination, had let party leaders know he again was available and now wished to send a conciliatory letter to the president.

Villard used his layoff in Washington productively, joining with his old friend Horace White of the *Chicago Tribune* and with Adams S. Hill of the *New York Tribune* to organize a six-newspaper news agency. As the agency's representative, he was with Grant's army in the spring of 1864 and was first to reach Washington with news of the battles in the Wilderness. As was true of the overwhelming majority of war correspondents (historians estimate fewer than ten covered the entire conflict), Villard did not "make it" through the war. During the siege of Petersburg he was called home to Germany, arriving just prior to his sister's death. In March 1865, when he again sailed for the United States, he expected to return to the battlefields. Instead, he was greeted on arrival by news doubly shocking to him—first, that Lee had surrendered and second, that Lincoln had been assassinated.

With the war's end came the close of the most significant phase of Villard's career in journalism. He had often outshone opposition reporters both in the enterprise of his reporting and the accuracy of his reports; he regarded some of those competitors with contempt, pronouncing them "more fit to drive cattle than to write for newspapers." He had served as companion, listener, go-between, and adviser to many of the great military and political figures of his time, outspoken but conscientious in the counsel he gave. Even so, in retrospect he questioned the worth of what he and other reporters had accomplished. He criticized the "indifference of the press-men to military interests in publishing army news" and concluded that "the harm certain to be done by war correspondents far outweighs any good they can possibly do."

After his marriage in 1866 to Fanny Garrison, Villard sailed with his bride for Europe, where he conducted an interview with John Stuart Mill and reported such stories as an eruption of Mount Vesuvius and the end of the war between Prussia and Austria. Though he continued for several years to contribute stories to newspapers, his career began to shift in 1868 when he became deeply involved in civil service reforms and began actively studying the financial structures of banks and railroads.

This interest, first sparked while he was recuperating from his wartime illnesses, was pursued in greater depth during a more protracted period of recovery from an apoplectic stroke. It was during that illness in 1873, while Villard was recuperating in Germany, that German bondholders approached Villard and asked him to represent their railroad interests, part of a significant postwar influx of European investment monies. Villard's old fascination with the West reasserted itself in a search for Western railroad investments. As he built a new career in business, Fanny bore him four children, three sons and a daughter; one of the sons, Oswald

Garrison Villard, followed his father and grandfather into journalism. Within a short time, Villard's investments began to pay off handsomely. He became president of several large companies, including the Northern Pacific Railroad and the Edison General Electric Company (forerunner of General Electric) and made millions. In 1881, Villard chose to invest some of his great wealth in newspapers.

In returning to journalism, Villard sought publications that emulated his own journalistic seriousness. By buying into the *New York Evening Post* and the *Nation*, he was gaining control of publications known more for their dignity and "high class" following than for their mass appeal. The *Nation* became the weekly edition of the *Post*. Villard retained as its editor the impeccably literate, if self-righteous, E. L. Godkin, and as its literary editor, Villard's brother-in-law, Wendell Phillips Garrison, who had the courage to tell Villard his own prose was often difficult and pompous. To help run the *Post*, Villard brought in two other outstanding editors, both old acquaintances, Horace White and Carl Schurz; he named Schurz editor in chief.

Godkin, White, and Schurz were Villard's contemporaries and had much in common with him. The shy White, a friend from the days of the debates and a partner in the Washington news agency, shared Villard's keen interest in finance; he had written a banking text that was in standard use in American colleges, and he held rigidly to scholastic standards. Schurz had stumped for Lincoln during the Illinois debates; had commanded troops in Frémont's army during the war; had been a United States senator, a minister to Spain and secretary of the interior; and was a skilled speaker with an orator's ear for precise and colorful language. Godkin, who had reported war news and shared Villard's disdain for much of the "Bohemian Brigade" that covered the armies, insisted on a high moral tone and had won a following among the nation's intelligentsia. The three editors, though regarded as one of the strongest editorial combinations of their time, quarreled and split up within a couple of years. Schurz resigned; Godkin then became editor in chief, with White as his assistant. The three remained friends despite editorial and philosophical differences; Schurz continued to be sought out for counsel even after his resignation, and White eventually succeeded Godkin as editor in chief.

The newspaper venture was one of the last of his business activities to bring Villard any satisfaction. In 1884 he had to resign the presidency of the Northern Pacific, construction of which had ended in a huge deficit. He spent two years in Germany recovering from a nervous breakdown before returning to the United States to attempt to effect the financial recovery of his railroad properties. By 1890, his business interests had fallen into disarray for a second time. A frank monopolist, Villard worked for repeal of the Sherman Antitrust Act and campaigned for the election of Grover Cleveland in 1892. He also called an 1892 conference to discuss the possibility of electrically powered railroads, and he bought Milwaukee's street railway lines in order to convert them from animal power to electricity. But in 1895, failing health and disillusionment combined to drive Villard into retirement: he was growing deaf, and he felt embittered by his own business losses and by the "ingratitude" of investors for whom he had made great fortunes but who dropped him when times turned bad.

Villard's main project during his retirement years was the preparation of his *Memoirs* (1904). He revisited sites of a number of the battles he had covered as a war correspondent and obtained from government departments the official reports of those battles. He spent many hours sifting and comparing data. He was able to complete before his death a first-person account of his life from the time of his immigration to New York up to the Tennessee campaign of 1863. Other materials were prepared from his papers and edited later, appearing in the *Memoirs* as a third-person account. Villard died 12 November 1900 at Dobbs Ferry, New York.

Upon Villard's death, his son Oswald, an editorial writer on the *Post*, inherited his newspapers. Unlike his father, who as publisher had divorced himself from editorial control, Oswald Garrison Villard assumed editorial leadership. (Godkin had retired the previous year, and White served as editor in chief from 1900 to 1903.) Fanny Villard, following her husband's death, had a public career of her own as a woman suffragist, advisor to the NAACP, and head of the Diet Kitchen Association, a milk program for New York children.

Clearly, Henry Villard's main journalistic distinction came as a reporter. He was alert to the news, facile as an interviewer, and both courageous and resourceful in pursuit of a story. His work during the war has been cited by students of war correspondence as some of the best that was produced, especially among the Northern "specials." His more lasting contributions probably lay in his role as trusted go-between among prominent figures, in his faithful preservation of their words, and in his firsthand observations of their appearance and character. The significance of his later role as a

publisher came perhaps more in what he did not contribute than in what he did: after handpicking great editors, he exercised the seldom paralleled policy of staying out of editorial affairs and binding his board of directors to do the same—thus creating a rare climate in which experienced editors were free to pursue energetic, influential journalism unencumbered by publisher influence.

As Col. Robert S. Macfarlane observed in an address to the Newcomen Society in 1954, "Money for its own sake did not interest him. A certain 'constructiveness' characterized his ventures. When he built railroads, he saw beyond the profits to new growth and new development of the territory they served. When he successfully pioneered in electricity, he saw the benefits of a new and efficient source of power. His establishment of editorial independence of the *New York Evening Post* and the *Nation* was more than a minor contribution to journalistic integrity."

Other:
American Social Science Association Handbook for Immigrants to the United States, edited by Villard (New York: Hurd & Houghton, 1871).

Periodical Publications:
"Karl Otto von Bismarck-Schonhausen," *North American Review*, 108 (January 1869): 165-221;
"Historical Sketch of Social Science," *Journal of Social Science*, 1 (June 1869): 1-7;
"People's Banks of Germany," *Journal of Social Science*, 1 (June 1869): 127-136;
"German Tariff Policy Past and Present," *Yale Review*, 1 (May 1892): 10-20.

Biography:
Oswald Garrison Villard, *Henry Villard: A True Fairy Tale* (New York: Holt, 1931).

References:
Dietrich G. Buss, *Henry Villard* (New York: Arno Press, 1978);
James Blaine Hedges, *Henry Villard and the Railways of the Northwest* (New Haven: Yale University Press, 1930);
Phillip Knightley, *The First Casualty* (New York: Harcourt Brace Jovanovich, 1975);
Robert S. Macfarlane, *Henry Villard and the Northern Pacific* (New York: The Newcomen Society in North America, 1954);
Frank Luther Mott, *American Journalism*, third edition (New York: Macmillan, 1962);

Tom Reilly, "Lincoln-Douglas Debates of 1858 Forced New Role on the Press," *Journalism Quarterly* (Winter 1979): 734-743;

Carl Sandburg, *Abraham Lincoln: The War Years,* volume 1 (New York: Harcourt, Brace, 1939);

Don Carlos Seitz, *The James Gordon Bennetts* (New York: Beekman, 1974);

Louis L. Snyder and Richard B. Morris, eds., *A Treasury of Great Reporting*, second edition (New York: Simon & Schuster, 1962).

Papers:
Henry Villard's papers are in the Harvard University libraries.

Ida B. Wells-Barnett
(16 July 1862-25 March 1931)

Nora Hall
University of Minnesota

MAJOR POSITIONS HELD: Editor, *Memphis Free Speech* (1889-1892); columnist, *New York Age* (1892-1893); foreign correspondent, *Chicago Inter Ocean* (1894); editor, *Chicago Conservator* (1895-1897).

BOOKS: *The Reason Why the Colored American Is Not in the World's Columbian Exposition*, by Wells and Frederick Douglass, I. Garland Penn, and Ferdinand L. Barnett (Chicago: Ida B. Wells, 1893);

Southern Horrors. Lynch Law in All Its Phases (Chicago: Donohue & Henneberry, 1892);

A Red Record. Tabulated Statistics and Alleged Causes of Lynchings in the United States, 1892-1893-1894 (Chicago: Donohue & Henneberry, 1895);

Mob Rule in New Orleans (N.p., 1900);

Crusade for Justice: The Autobiography of Ida B. Wells, edited by Alfreda M. Duster (Chicago: University of Chicago Press, 1970).

Ida B. Wells-Barnett was an investigative journalist whose factual reporting and scholarly analysis of lynchings provided the genesis for what later became a prominent movement in the United States. As editor of the weekly *Memphis Free Speech*, Wells aroused such anger among Tennessee residents that her newspaper office and presses were destroyed by hoodlums. During her lifetime her work appeared in more than twenty-five different publications, and in 1895 she took her consciousness-raising style of journalism to Chicago's first black weekly, the *Conservator*, when she became its editor. At the *Conservator* Wells-Barnett again lashed out at societal injustices. She was determined

Ida B. Wells-Barnett (University of Chicago Library)

to do all she could to create better living conditions for black Americans.

Had Wells-Barnett written for leading muckraking magazines between 1902 and 1912 she would most assuredly have ranked among the best of the muckrakers. That her name is not included along with the militants and sensationalists of the era is purely a matter of timing, because her reportorial style was just as zealous as theirs. At a time when black oppression was commonplace in America and most blacks were afraid to speak out, Wells-Barnett used her pen to expose injustices toward her race.

Although she was often angered by the issues she brought before the public, she bore no hatred toward the white race. Wells-Barnett believed in equality, an idealistic notion not uncommon for a black woman who grew up during Reconstruction. Ida Baker Wells was born to slave parents 16 July 1862 in Holly Springs, Mississippi; the Emancipation Proclamation went into effect approximately six months later. The Reconstruction period brought Mississippians a new form of government allowing black participation; that change had a substantial impact upon Wells's philosophy of equality. Seeing black Mississippians in various political positions led her to believe that blacks would never have to experience discrimination. Reconstruction also meant blacks could receive a public education, a right previously denied them. Thus in 1866, when a representative of the Freedman's Aid Society arrived in Holly Springs to establish black educational facilities at Shaw University, four-year-old Ida Wells was one of the first to register. Shaw University became Rust College in 1870 under the sponsorship of the Mississippi Conference of the Methodist Church. In its early days, the institution provided instruction in elementary through collegiate level courses. Wells discontinued her formal education after completing high school.

Her journalistic style has often been described as courageous, determined, impassioned, and aggressive. It was these same characteristics that combined to support her in 1878, when her parents and two brothers died during a yellow fever epidemic, leaving sixteen-year-old Wells to care for a family of five. It was then that she utilized skills acquired through her education at Rust College. Wells obtained a teaching position in Holly Springs, which paid $25 a month, and cared for her siblings for two years, until two aunts assumed responsibility for the children. This freed her to pursue her career, but she continued to provide financial support for her family.

Wells's journalistic career began after her move to Memphis, Tennessee, in 1880. In Memphis, she again went to work as a teacher and taught for nine years; she was considered a competent and conscientious teacher but later admitted that she had never liked the profession. She never earned a

Ida Wells at age eighteen, about the time she moved to Memphis (University of Chicago Library)

college degree, but during her years of teaching she attended summer classes at Fisk University in Nashville. It was through articles written for the student newspaper at Fisk that her interest in journalism was first aroused. Later, in her autobiography, she would describe the profession as her "only love."

Shortly after arriving in Memphis, Wells became the editor of the *Evening Star*, a literary publication containing news, literary notes, critiques of lyceum productions, a gossip column, and a poetry section. Her work with the *Evening Star* led to a position as editor of the *Living Way*, a weekly black Baptist newspaper. Her articles for these publications were signed "Iola."

Wells already had a specific rationale guiding her journalism career at the time she wrote for the *Living Way* and the *Evening Star*. In 1880, at age eighteen, she knew that something had to be done for illiterate blacks: "I had already found out in the country that the people needed guidance in everyday life and that the leaders, the preachers, were not giving them this help." After becoming editor of the *Living Way* at twenty-five, her purpose as a journalist was clearly defined: "I had an instinctive feeling that the people who had little or no school training should have something coming into their homes weekly which dealt with their problems in a simple, helpful way. So in weekly letters to the *Living Way*, I wrote in a plain, common-sense way on the things which concerned our people." Wells's journalistic style had not yet reached its fruition—that would come later when she was editor of the *Free Speech*—but she certainly knew why she had chosen the field.

Wells's journalistic career began in earnest in 1887 with an article for the *Living Way* which described her lawsuit three years earlier against the Chesapeake, Ohio and Southwestern Railroad. Wells had taken a seat in the ladies' car because she had purchased a first-class ticket; ignoring her explanation, a conductor asked her to move to the smoking car, where blacks were seated. Wells refused to cooperate; when the conductor attempted to force her into the smoking car, she got off the train. Later she sued the railroad company. Her case attracted national attention because train coaches were required by law to be separate yet equal. Wells contended that the smoking car was inferior, but court records state that both cars contained "equal accommodations." Wells won the case in lower court and was awarded $500; but the railroad appealed to the Tennessee Supreme Court. Wells lost and was required to pay court costs of $200. She was the first Southern black to sue in a state court subsequent to the United States Supreme Court ruling in 1883 declaring the 1875 Civil Rights Act unconstitutional.

After her story on the case was picked up by several other newspapers, black editors throughout the nation asked her to submit articles and offered her paid positions on their staffs. She began submitting articles but turned down the job offers because she did not believe she could earn enough from full-time newspaper work. She continued her career as a teacher because "there seemed nothing else to do for a living except menial work, and I could not have made a living at that."

By 1889 the newspaperwoman had achieved national recognition as a writer and philosopher. Her articles for the *Living Way* were reprinted in numerous black publications throughout the country. This notoriety prompted the Rev. F. Nightingale and J. L. Fleming, owners of the *Free Speech*, to ask Wells to join the paper's staff as a writer. She refused to join the staff except as part owner and editor; the men yielded to her demands, and Wells purchased a one-third ownership through savings from her teaching duties. She

planned to continue teaching school since the *Free Speech*, a small weekly newspaper with a meager circulation of four thousand, provided very little income, but an editorial written by Wells condemning the Memphis Board of Education for poor conditions in black schools caused her dismissal from her teaching position in 1891.

In her effort to expose the ills of society, Wells criticized blacks as well as whites: her article on the school board, for example, had censured the behavior of Memphis's black schoolteachers. "I also spoke of the poor teachers given us, whose mental and moral character was not of the best," Wells wrote. Wells's militant style began with this article and continued throughout her career. The *Free Speech* editor also criticized Isaiah Montgomery, the only black member of the 1890 Mississippi Constitutional Convention, for voting for the Understanding Clause. The clause, which became a state law in 1890, made it virtually impossible for blacks to vote.

The *Free Speech* office was located at Nightingale's Baptist church until a disagreement occurred among the three owners. As a result, Nightingale withdrew from the newspaper, and the office was relocated on Hernando Street near Beale in 1891. The same year, Wells began soliciting subscriptions throughout Tennessee and Mississippi. The *Free Speech* grew in popularity; by 1892 it was solvent, and Wells was able to earn enough money through her work as editor and co-owner to support herself.

In March 1892, three black Memphis businessmen were lynched after opening a grocery store in an area previously monopolized by a white merchant. The *Free Speech* editor had written powerful editorials about crime and corruption before; however, those that she ran in her newspaper after the lynchings of Thomas Moss, Calvin McDowell, and Henry Stewart were even more forceful and launched her eight-year campaign against lynch law in the United States. Wells's muckraking style can be clearly discerned in this excerpt: "The city of Memphis has demonstrated that neither character nor standing avails the Negro if he dares to protect himself against the white man or become his rival. . . . The white mob could help itself to ammunition without pay, but the order was rigidly enforced against the selling of guns to Negroes. There is therefore only one thing left that we can do; save our money and leave a town which will neither protect our lives and property, nor give us a fair trial in the courts, but takes us out and murders us in cold blood when accused by white persons."

Editorials in the *Free Speech* continued to encourage blacks to leave Memphis, and Wells traveled to Kansas City and Oklahoma to investigate opportunities for blacks so that she could inform her readers. An article in the *Free Speech* of 21 May 1892 created an uproar, and a *Memphis Daily Commercial* editorial writer responded by encouraging Memphis residents not to tolerate such criticism from a "black scoundrel." Wells's article stated in part, "Eight Negroes lynched since last issue of the '*Free Speech*' . . . three for killing a white man, and five on the same old racket—the new alarm about raping white women. The same programme of hanging, then shooting bullets into the lifeless bodies was carried out to the letter. Nobody in this section of the country believes the old thread bare lie that Negro men rape white women. If Southern white men are not careful, they will over-reach themselves and public sentiment will have a reaction; a conclusion will then be reached which will be very damaging to the moral reputation of their women." Fleming and Wells had already made plans to move the newspaper to another state, but a mob destroyed the *Free Speech* office on 27 May. Wells was out of town at the time of the turmoil, and Fleming was told to leave Memphis. A note was left at the site of the office warning that anyone attempting to publish the paper again would be killed.

Following this incident, Wells acquired a gun for protection and moved to New York as employee and part owner of the weekly *New York Age*. Its editor, T. Thomas Fortune, was widely known at the turn of the century for his professionalism. In exchange for her subscription list from the *Free Speech*, Wells acquired a one-fourth interest in the *Age* and brought her conscientious style of journalism to her new position. She was always careful to check facts before printing information and to avoid accusations of dishonesty. She also used white sources for her articles; for lynching statistics, Wells depended on figures published in the *Chicago Tribune*. Ida B. Wells remained at the *Age*, writing two columns each week, until April 1893. She dedicated herself to educating Northerners to the horrors of lynchings, for she believed they would be moved to action only when the evils were well exposed; but her efforts went largely unnoticed. She wrote a pamphlet, *Southern Horrors. Lynch Law In All Its Phases*, which was published by the *New York Age* in 1892 and sold for fifteen cents. Ten thousand copies of *The Reason Why the Colored American Is Not in the World's Columbian Exposition* were distributed during the World's Fair at Chicago in 1893; the preface was printed in English, German, and French. Wells had written the book with newspaper

editor / abolitionist Frederick Douglass, newspaper publisher I. Garland Penn, and attorney / newspaper editor Ferdinand L. Barnett as a protest: black Americans were not allowed to participate in World's Fair activities, and these journalists wanted visitors from other countries to understand institutional racism. Additionally, shortly after moving to New York, Wells began a public-speaking campaign in another unsuccessful effort to move Northerners to action.

When an invitation came in February 1893 from Isabelle Fyvie Mayo, a Scottish author, asking Wells to come to Great Britain to lecture on lynching, the newspaperwoman gladly accepted. She had already concluded that "I had been in the North, hoping to spread the truth and get moral support for my demand that those accused of crimes be given a fair trial and punished by law instead of by mob . . . and the press was dumb. I refer . . . to the white press, since it was the medium through which I hoped to reach the white people of the country, who alone could mold public sentiment." During her first lecture campaign in Britain, which lasted two months, she was well received and extensively quoted in such journals as the Peterhead *Sentinel*, Buchan *Journal*, and *Edinburgh*.

The year following her British tour Wells became well known in women's club circles. A black women's club in Chicago established itself as the Ida B. Wells Club, and in late 1893 Wells moved to that city and began writing for the weekly *Chicago Conservator*. However, she obtained wider recognition as a correspondent for the *Chicago Inter Ocean* in 1894. The *Inter Ocean*, under the editorship of William Penn Nixon, was known for its crusades in the public interest and was an attractive employment opportunity for newspaper people. (The *Inter Ocean* was published from 1872 until 1914, when it merged with the *Record Herald*, which later became the *Herald Examiner*.) At thirty-two, Wells was the first black American hired by the *Inter Ocean*.

The Society for the Recognition of the Brotherhood of Man, an antilynching society which had been formed during her last tour, asked Wells to return to England for another speaking tour in 1894. She agreed and traveled to England in February; the tour lasted six months. Her column in the *Inter Ocean*, "Ida B. Wells Abroad," was quoted from in a number of prominent American newspapers.

Wells's *Inter Ocean* letters offer a polished, terse style that is not present in her earlier writing, but her correspondence is as poignant as ever. It is the kind of writing the muckrakers directed at the social conscience of the nation, arousing it to righteous indignation. Reporting on a speech in Liverpool, Wells wrote: "Ever since the suppression of my newspaper, the *Free Speech*, . . . I had made unsuccessful attempts to be heard in the journals and on the platforms of the American people against lynching, which was fast becoming a national evil. . . . The members of this society [Society for the Recognition of the Brotherhood of Man] . . . felt it to be their duty to express in the strongest terms denunciation of the burning alive of human beings and the lawless wholesale hangings of the same. The leading newspapers of the United Kingdom gave excellent reports of the meetings, and many of them ringing and outspoken editorials against this state of affairs. . . ."

It is not possible to measure precisely the impact of Wells's antilynching crusades. Researcher Floyd Crawford has concluded that Wells accomplished very little despite her fame and widespread support, but statistics in two of Wells's pamphlets, *A Red Record* (1895) and *Mob Rule in New Orleans* (1900), indicate otherwise. Wells's lynching statistics from 1892 to 1899 show a marked decline

in the number of blacks lynched in the United States: in 1893, 200 blacks are reported lynched; by 1896 the figure is 131. The figures for 1897 show an increase to 156, but by 1899 the number of black people reported murdered was 107.

Ida B. Wells's journalistic career declined after her second tour of Great Britain. Although she bought the *Chicago Conservator* from Ferdinand L. Barnett in 1895, she never again achieved the kind of recognition she had earned in her earlier years. Barnett was a successful Chicago attorney and political activist, and Wells's marriage to him on 27 June 1895 brought her into the political arena. At the age of thirty-five she sold the *Conservator* and resigned her post as president of the Ida B. Wells Club. According to Wells-Barnett, "I was thoroughly convinced by this time that the duties of a wife and mother were a profession in themselves and it was hopeless to expect to carry on public work." By 1904 Wells-Barnett had given birth to four children of her own and raised Barnett's two children from a previous marriage. But in 1909, when her youngest child was just five, she traveled

Wells-Barnett with her husband, Ferdinand L. Barnett (seated, second from left), and their children and grandchildren, in 1917

to Cairo, Illinois, to investigate the lynching of "Frog" James. Her thorough investigation prevented a sheriff's reinstatement by showing that he had known the lynching was to occur and had not tried to prevent it. Her account of this investigation appeared in the *Chicago Defender*, a black daily newspaper, on 1 January 1910. Race riots in East St. Louis, Illinois, in 1918 and Little Rock, Arkansas, in 1922 were also covered by Wells-Barnett for the *Defender*. In Arkansas, Wells-Barnett posed as the cousin of the wife of a convict in order to get into the prison. She interviewed the prisoner but was unable to take notes; her story was written from memory.

Aside from these journalistic endeavors, Wells-Barnett spent most of her time in the political arena after 1897. The number of articles she published on lynchings and riots during this period were modest compared to her early work. In 1910 she established the Negro Fellowship League, an organization of young men concerned about racial discrimination. She became interested in women's rights and established the Alpha Suffrage Club in 1913; she was named chairwoman of the Chicago Equal Rights League in 1915. Wells-Barnett was also active in the National American Woman Suffrage Association. She met with presidents William McKinley and Woodrow Wilson to voice complaints about discrimination against blacks. She was an independent candidate for Illinois state senator in 1930, finishing third in the race.

At age sixty-six, Wells-Barnett began to write her autobiography, *Crusade for Justice*. In the preface she states, "It is . . . for the young people who have so little of our race's history recorded that I am . . . writing about myself." Wells-Barnett died 25 March 1931 of uremic poisoning. Her husband was still living at her death; he died in 1936. The last sentence of Wells-Barnett's autobiography was never completed. It was published in 1970 as she left it.

The journalistic career of Ida B. Wells-Barnett spanned some forty-seven years, during which time she displayed enormous courage, unflinching dedication, and a dogmatic nature that left her a lone crusader in most of her battles. Her muckraking style ushered in a new form of black journalism and paved the way for the passage of civil rights legislation for blacks.

Periodical Publications:
"Afro-Americans and Africa," *AME Church Review*, 9 (July 1892): 40-44;
"Lynch Law in America," *Arena*, 23 (January 1900): 15-24;
"Lynching An Excuse for It," *Independent*, 53 (May 1901): 1133-1136;
"Booker T. Washington & His Critics," *World Today*, 6 (April 1904): 518;
"How Enfranchisement Stops Lynchings," *Original Rights Magazine*, 2 (June 1910): 42-53;
"Our Country's Lynching Record," *Survey*, 29 (February 1913): 573-574.

References:
Bettina Aptheker, "Mary Church Terrell and Ida B. Wells: A Comparative Rhetorical / Historical Analysis 1890-1920," M.A. thesis, San Jose State University, 1976;
Aptheker, "The Suppression of the Free Speech," *San Jose Studies*, 3 (November 1977): 34-40;
Floyd W. Crawford, "Ida B. Wells: Her Anti-Lynching Crusades in Britain and Repercussions from Them in the United States," research paper, Department of Social Science, Norfolk Division, Virginia State College, 1958;
T. Thomas Fortune, "Ida B. Wells, A.M.," *Women of Distinction*, edited by Lawsen A. Scruggs (Raleigh, N.C.: Fortune, 1893);
Mary B. Hutton, "The Rhetoric of Ida B. Wells: The Genesis of the Anti-Lynch Movement," Ph.D. dissertation, University of Indiana, 1975;
Dorothy Sterling, *Black Foremothers* (New York: Feminist Press, 1979);
Mildred Thompson, "Ida B. Wells-Barnett: An Exploratory Study Of An American Black Woman, 1893-1930," Ph.D. dissertation, George Washington University, 1979;
David M. Tucker, "Ida B. Wells and Memphis Lynching," *Phylon*, 32 (Summer 1971): 112-122;
Eunice Rivers Walker, "Ida B. Wells-Barnett: Her Contribution to the Field of Social Welfare," M.S.W. thesis, Loyola University, 1941;
Roland Wolseley, "Ida B. Wells-Barnett: Princess of the Black Press," *Encore*, 5 (April 1976): 2.

Papers:
Ida B. Wells-Barnett's papers are held in the Department of Special Collections, University of Chicago Library. In addition, the Frederick Douglass papers in the Library of Congress, Manuscript Division, contain some of Wells-Barnett's correspondence; the Eve Merriam papers in the Kerlan Collection in the Children's Literature Research Collections at the University of Minnesota Libraries contain the manuscript for *Independent Voices*, a

book of poetry including works by Ida B. Wells-Barnett; and the Edith T. Ross Collection in the University of Illinois at Chicago Circle Library

Manuscript Collection contains the first issue of "The Alpha Suffrage Record," a newsletter for a club founded by Ida B. Wells-Barnett.

Horace White

(10 August 1834-16 September 1916)

Mark Lipper
Shippensburg University

MAJOR POSITIONS HELD: Editor in chief, *Chicago Tribune* (1865-1874), *New York Evening Post* (1900-1903).

BOOKS: *The Silver Question: An Essay on the Proposed Remonetization of Silver in the U.S.* (New York: Scribner, Armstrong, 1876);

Third Term Politics (New York: Independent Republican Association, 1880);

The Silver Coinage Question, A Review of Senator Beck's Speech (New York: Evening Post Publishing Co., 1886);

Surplus and the Tariff (Boston: Massachusetts Tariff Reform League, 1888);

An Elastic Currency, "George Smith's Money" in the Early Northwest (New York: Evening Post Publishing Co., 1893);

The Gold Standard: How It Came into the World and Why It Will Stay (New York: Evening Post Publishing Co., 1893);

Coin's Financial Fool: A Reply to Coin's Financial School (New York: Ogilvie, 1895);

Money and Banking Illustrated by American History (Boston & London: Ginn, 1895);

The Monetary Issue in the United States: Pamphlet No. 19 in the Gold Standard Defence Association Series (London, 1896);

Abraham Lincoln in 1854 (Springfield: Illinois State Historical Society, 1908);

Plans for Monetary Reform (New York, 1912);

The Life of Lyman Trumbull (Boston: Houghton Mifflin, 1913);

The Lincoln and Douglas Debates (Chicago: University of Chicago Press, 1914).

Horace White

Horace White was one of the leading American journalists of his time and one of the last of the group of great New York editors that included Charles A. Dana and Whitelaw Reid. While he managed to keep a low profile, his influence was felt and respected by many of the personalities of his day. He knew John Brown and other militant Free-Soilers and helped his friend Abraham Lincoln achieve the highest political office in the land. Always a crusader, he not only reported but also participated in some of the major events of his time, such as the Liberal Republican movement in the East in the 1870s. He was an authority on finance and economics, and his editorials in the *New York Evening Post* for over twenty years were regarded as the most influential essays on finance in the country. An editorial in the *New York Times* mourning his death observed that White "had exerted a strong influence upon the education of the public mind and the development of an understanding of the necessity of sound government finance." The editorial concluded that "as a newspaper editor, as a speaker, as a writer of books and pamphlets, Horace White was conspicuously instrumental in securing our financial salvation."

White was born in Colebrook, New Hampshire, on 10 August 1834. Shortly after his birth, his father, Horace White, a twenty-six-year-old Dartmouth physician, became an agent of the New England Emigration Company, which outfitted wagon trains for travel westward. In the winter of 1836, Dr. White moved to the Midwest prairies with a wagon train to provide medical services to the settlers. Two years later his wife, Eliza, and two sons joined him, and they lived in the first log cabin on the site of Beloit, Wisconsin. By 1839 Beloit had become a thriving village of 200 people.

When Horace White was nine years old, his father died. In 1845 his mother married Samuel Hinman, a widower who was recognized as a stern puritan and a pillar in the Presbyterian churches of Wisconsin. White's father had been a founder of the city of Beloit; his stepfather was a founder of Beloit College. Named a trustee in 1845, he supervised construction of the first college building in 1848.

In that year, the antislavery movement was sweeping across Wisconsin, and White was caught up in the excitement of the time. He and his schoolmates joined parades, carrying banners and shouting, "Free soil, free speech, free labor, and free men." Later, White recalled that this explosion of antislavery sentiment inspired him to become a journalist so that he could continue the fight.

In 1849, at the age of fifteen, White entered the third class of Beloit College, where the aptitude for economics that would be the hallmark of his career was sharpened. A course for seniors called "Moral Philosophy" was actually a course on political economy; it was taught by the college president, Aaron L. Chapin. Chapin was a friend and disciple of the Reverend Francis Wayland, a pioneer in American economic theory, and he used Wayland's *Elements of Political Economy* (1837) as his text.

White graduated with honors from Beloit in 1853 and went to work for the *Chicago Evening Journal* in 1854. Most of his early reporting was of the commercial activity of the city; this experience was a valuable apprenticeship for his later career. In October he was given a more exciting assignment: he was sent to Springfield to cover the political doings of the State Fair week. It was there that he began his long friendship with a young politician by the name of Abraham Lincoln. White heard Lincoln denounce the Kansas-Nebraska Bill before the legislature; so impressed was White that he told his *Journal* readers: "Lincoln is a mammoth. He has this day delivered a speech, the greatest ever listened to in the state of Illinois, unless [he] himself had made a greater. . . . the speech of Mr. Lincoln has rarely been equalled in the annals of American eloquence." Recalling the experience years later, White wrote: "I have never heard anything since, whether by Mr. Lincoln, or by anybody, that I would put on a higher plane of oratory. All the strings that play upon the human heart and understanding were touched with masterly skill and force, while beyond and above all skill was the overwhelming conviction pressed upon the audience that the speaker himself was charged with an irresistible and inspiring duty to his fellow men. This conscientious impulse drove his arguments through the heads of his hearers down into their bosoms, where they made everlasting lodgment. . . ."

White's skill as a writer is evident in his description of Lincoln at that first meeting with him: "Although I heard him many times afterward, I shall longest remember him as I then saw the tall, angular form with the long angular arms, at times bent nearly double with excitement, like a large flail animating two smaller ones, the mobile face wet with perspiration which he discharged in drops as he threw his head this way and that like a projectile, not a graceful figure, yet not an ungraceful one. After listening to him a few minutes when he had got well warmed with his subject, nobody would mind whether he was graceful or not. All thought of grace or form would be lost in the exceeding attractiveness of what he was saying."

White was promoted to city editor in that first year with the *Journal*. In 1855 he also was made Chicago agent of the Associated Press, but he served in that capacity for only a short time.

Moved by stories of atrocities in "bleeding Kansas," White accepted a position as assistant secretary of the National Kansas Commission. He was responsible for receiving and forwarding money, arms, ammunition, and supplies to the Free State pioneers, including John Brown and two of his sons. He also supplied provisions to new settlers who passed through Iowa and Nebraska on their way to Kansas.

White himself went to Kansas in 1857, intending to settle there and become a leader of the antislavery forces. When he returned to Chicago to make his final arrangements, however, Dr. C. H. Ray, the editor of the ten-year-old *Chicago Tribune*, persuaded White to join his staff. White was put on salary and assigned to cover the Lincoln-Douglas debates in 1858. This was one of the most important assignments of White's career. He learned to know politicians throughout the state, gaining a foothold in the Republican party; and he won the respect of his paper with the stories he filed on the debates. He also developed close friendships with Lincoln and with Henry Villard, who was covering the debates for the *New York Staats-Zeitung*. Also in 1858 he married Martha Root of New Haven, Connecticut.

White was put in charge of the reporting staff and continued to write editorials for the *Tribune*. When the opportunity arose, he bought shares in the Tribune Company and became more influential. With the outbreak of the Civil War, White joined the "Bohemian Brigade"—the corps of newspapermen who reported the war for Northern papers. Instead of being assigned to the war zones, however, White was sent to Washington to cover sessions of Congress. He and his wife moved to the capital and, to help cover his expenses, he accepted the position of clerk of the Senate Committee on Military Affairs, which also provided him with information on how the war was being conducted. The *Tribune* cautioned its readers that its young Washington correspondent was "no trimmer or compromiser, but one who believes that to go straight forward in the path of duty is always politic; that right is ever expedient."

Early in 1863, White stopped writing for the *Tribune* because of a power shift at the paper: White's friend Dr. Ray had sold his interest, enabling Joseph Medill to take control. Probably anticipating that Medill would terminate his position, White took a clerical job in the War Department, where he soon became a favorite employee of Secretary Stanton.

But White missed being a journalist. His friend Henry Villard, who had established a reputation as one of the best war correspondents, decided to spend the winter in Washington after surviving a fever in November 1863. Also in Washington was another well-known war correspondent, Adams S. Hill, who had also given up field work with the army and had been put in charge of the *New York Tribune*'s Washington bureau. (Later Hill would serve for more than thirty years as professor of rhetoric at Harvard University.)

White's biographer says that both Villard and Hill had resigned from the *Tribune* at this time in a dispute with Horace Greeley.

The three men realized that because of the war, there was a great demand for news. They also were aware of the long-standing quarrel between the Western Associated Press and the New York Associated Press over the latter's monopolistic control of the wire service, so they started the Independent News Room Service in Washington. It was the first news agency to compete with the Associated Press. Even though the New York Associated Press had exclusive contracts with the nation's major telegraph companies, the three friends were resourceful enough to supply dispatches and features to several Western and a few Eastern papers, and they earned a lucrative living from their new business. In his memoirs, Villard wrote that the new undertaking "was bitterly attacked by the Associated Press for disturbing its monopoly."

The news service was dissolved at the end of the war, and Horace White returned to Chicago early in 1865. On 14 April he bought John Locke Scripps's share of the Tribune Company; the next issue of the *Tribune* after that transaction carried the news of President Lincoln's assassination. The newspaper was prosperous but suffered some inner turmoil. Finally, White and Alfred Cowles, who together held a majority interest, were able to depose Medill from control and persuade Dr. Ray to return as editor.

The Radical victory in the postwar election of 1866 brought national attention to the *Chicago Tribune*, which became known as the oracle of triumphant Radicalism in the old Northwest, and to its thirty-two-year-old editor in chief, Horace White. White's *Tribune* stood with other great American newspapers, such as Greeley's *New York Tribune*, Samuel Bowles's *Springfield Republican*, Murat Halstead's *Cincinnati Commercial*, and William Cullen Bryant's *New York Evening Post*, in asserting its independence of the Republican party in the disillusionment that followed shortly after General Grant's election to the presidency in 1868.

Politics was not White's only interest: he had become a student of classical economics, and it was not unusual for him to reprint in the *Tribune* selections from the works of European theoreticians. Frédéric Bastiat, the French free trader, was his favorite; in 1869 White edited a new translation of Bastiat's *Sophisms of Protection*. White also exchanged letters with English sympathizers such as John Stuart Mill and John Bright and ran some of their letters in the *Tribune*. To promote free trade, he worked with the Cobden Club of London and supported the Free Trade League in the United States that had been inspired by the British. He was convinced that laissez-faire remedies were needed to cure the nation's economic ailments.

In 1871, White and his newspaper were having some economic problems of their own. By 1869, the *Tribune* had outgrown its old quarters, so White and Cowles had invested $250,000 in the construction of a four-story "fire proof" stone building in the heart of Chicago. When the great Chicago fire swept through the city on 9 October 1871, for a while the *Tribune* building "stood on a lone isle in an ocean of fire," but soon it, too, was caught up in the flames and destroyed. Because the building had been designed to be fireproof, White and Cowles had not taken out insurance on it; White personally lost more than $100,000.

The *Tribune* did not reappear until two days after the fire. Printed in an oily machine shop on the city's west side, it contained the awesome news of the fire on a rough single sheet. White's editorial told the readers to "Cheer Up," and it pledged that "Chicago Shall Rise Again." The editorial ended: "We do not belittle the calamity that has befallen us. The world has probably never seen the like of it—certainly not since Moscow burned. But the forces of nature, no less than the forces of reason, require that the exchanges of a great region should be conducted here. Ten, twenty years may be required to reconstruct our fair city, but the capital to rebuild it fire proof will be forthcoming. The losses we have suffered must be borne; but the place, the time, and the men are here, to commence at the bottom and work up again; not at the bottom neither, for we have credit in every land, and the experience of one upbuilding of Chicago to help us. Let us all cheer up, save what is yet left, and we shall come out right. The Christian world is coming to our relief. The worst is already over. In a few days more, all the dangers will be past, and we can resume the battle of life with Christian faith and Western grit. Let us all cheer up!"

The *Chicago Tribune* had influenced the nominations of both of Illinois's favorite sons, Lincoln and Grant, at Republican conventions. But, disillusioned with the Grant administration, White joined other journalists in promoting the Liberal Republican movement. It was unusual for journalists to play such a dominant role in political organization, but the professional politicians were shying away from involvement. White was among the leaders at a Free Trade League conference in New York City on 22 November 1870, the purpose

of which was to discuss revenue and tariff reform. It was here that the Liberal Republican movement in the East began to take shape. Other editors who participated were Bryant of the *New York Evening Post*, E. L. Godkin of the *Nation*, Carl Schurz of the *St. Louis Westliche Post*, and Samuel Bowles of the *Springfield Republican*.

By the spring of 1871, Schurz was calling for the formation of a new party. Bryant and Godkin did not support his plan, but the other editors did. The Liberal Republicans of Missouri called for a mass convention at Cincinnati on 2 May 1872; more than 10,000 persons attended. Schurz was elected permanent chairman, and White headed the platform committee. Illinois's favorite son, Lyman Trumbull, and Charles Francis Adams, a favorite of the Northeast, were the main contestants for the presidential nomination; but by a strange turn of affairs, Horace Greeley emerged as the nominee on the sixth ballot, much to the disappointment of many of the leaders of the convention. In a letter he wrote from Cincinnati, which was printed on page one of the *Tribune*, White admitted that the entire convention was stunned by the Greeley nomination. While the political leaders were not for Greeley, White said, he did have convention strength among the delegates, and "the opinion of the best judges this evening is that he will be a popular candidate and the ticket will sweep the country." The judges were wrong: not only was Greeley defeated but White's political effectiveness and that of his newspaper were being questioned.

Other problems burdened White in 1873. His wife died while visiting in Würzburg, Germany, and the depression that year was taking its toll on the circulation and advertising revenues of the *Tribune*. Cowles offered to sell the controlling interest in the paper to Medill. At first Medill replied that "the damage had already been done, the usefulness and influence of the paper greatly impaired," but later he changed his mind. On 9 November 1874, White retired, and Medill once again was in control of the paper. Godkin wrote in the 5 November 1874 issue of the *Nation*: "Mr. White's management of the paper raised it to the highest rank of journalism, in the best sense of the term." Others felt he had caused the paper to lose many of its friends and much of its prestige.

Retired at the age of forty, wealthy and looking forward to a life of leisure, White turned down several offers in editing and publishing. He remarried in 1875; he and his second wife, Amelia Jane McDougell, moved from Chicago to New York City, where White was reunited with his friend Henry

Villard. Early in the 1870s, Villard had gained the confidence of German investors in American railways, and his financial successes with the Kansas Pacific Railroad and the Oregon Railway and Navigation Company had made him a wealthy man in a few years. White invested heavily in railroad bonds under Villard's supervision, and when Villard became president of the Oregon Railway and Navigation Company, he appointed White its treasurer. After six years in finance, however, White was ready to return to his first love—journalism. His friend's desire suited Villard, too.

In his history of the *New York Evening Post*, Allan Nevins writes that Villard's "interest in his original profession and a wish to devote his money to some large public end, led him . . . to conceive the plan of buying a metropolitan paper and giving it the ablest editors procurable." Instructed by Villard to negotiate for the purchase of a newspaper, White learned that the *Evening Post* was for sale. Three years after Bryant's death in 1878, it was still a prosperous and popular journal. Using about three quarters of a million dollars from Villard and about $100,000 of his own, White purchased outright control of the *Post* in 1881. Aware that people would accuse him of using the great newspaper to promote his own financial interests, Villard created a trust to protect the editorial department from all interference. On 23 May 1881, the board of trustees appointed as editor in chief Carl Schurz, who was stepping down as secretary of the interior in the Hayes cabinet. On 25 May it was announced that *Nation* editor E. L. Godkin would be Schurz's associate editor. On 1 July it was announced that the *Nation* would be issued as the weekly edition of the *New York Evening Post*, and "its contents will in the main have already appeared in the *Evening Post*." White, who wrote editorials for both publications and was busy with coverage of Wall Street, occasionally substituted for Schurz and Godkin. Nevins calls this "the ablest triumvirate ever enlisted by an American daily," with Schurz good on politics, Godkin having "an unrivaled pen for general social and political topics," and White "perhaps the best writer available on the tariff, railways, the silver question and banking."

In his editorials, White championed laissez-faire economics in the rapidly changing industrial society. He expressed alarm over the free silver uprising in 1890 and later cited the Sherman Silver Purchase Act passed that year as the main cause of the panic of 1893. When the ratio of gold and silver became the main political issue of the day, his editorials lashed out at every fanatic from the fiat money

enthusiasts to the silver advocates, exposing their deceptions, misstatements, and fallacies. These editorials were published in pamphlets that reached opinion leaders across the nation and filtered down to the public by a variety of channels.

Anticolonial but not isolationist, he criticized Seward's acquisition of Alaska, opposed Grant's attempt to annex Santo Domingo, and applauded Cleveland's halting of efforts to acquire Hawaii. While other newspaper voices around him were caught up in "jingoism," White spoke out against intervention in the Spanish-American War, arguing that American involvement in Cuba would destroy the prosperity that was becoming more evident in the wake of the panic of 1893. No matter how heated the controversy, White was rigid in upholding the literary and scholarly traditions of the *Evening Post*, and his editorial page was one of the most distinguished in American journalism.

Constant feuding between Schurz and Godkin led Schurz to resign from the paper after two years. Godkin then served as editor for a trial period of two years; when this ended in 1885, he and White served as dual editors—Godkin dealing with political and social areas of coverage and White in charge of financial and economic coverage. This was a difficult time for White: his second wife died unexpectedly in June 1885, leaving him fully responsible for the upbringing of their three daughters. Godkin retired in 1899, and White agreed to serve as editor in chief for only a short time, starting 1 January 1900.

White's editorials were given much of the credit for the Republican passage of the Currency Act in 1900 that legalized the gold standard. At the 100th anniversary banquet of the *Evening Post* a year later, Wall Street banker Joseph C. Hendrix spoke for the financial world when he said that "we recognize and appreciate the service to this country of the luminous editorial writer in all of the fight for the preservation and final adoption, and the perfect maintainance [*sic*] of the gold standard in this country—Mr. Horace White."

After his retirement on 31 January 1903, when he was succeeded by Rollo Ogden, White wrote a biography of Lyman Trumbull (1913) and edited various financial textbooks. His own book *Money and Banking Illustrated by American History* (1895) was used as a standard textbook in high schools and colleges until about 1935. In 1908, New York Governor Charles Evans Hughes appointed White chairman of a commission to investigate speculation in securities and commodities. While the commission recommended no action by the legislature, it instructed the stock exchange to show restraint and reform itself.

White died on 16 September 1916. In a note to one of White's three daughters, President Woodrow Wilson wrote: "May I extend to you my heartfelt sympathy on the death of your honored father? It is a loss which the whole country must feel because he was everywhere known for his fine public spirit and for his willingness to render disinterested public service. His career was one of moral as well as of intellectual distinction."

At a time of deep depression in his life, when he learned of the death of his first wife, Horace White had reached into his Calvinistic background to assure himself that there is a purpose in life. He wrote: "To dispel ignorance, mental and moral, our own and others, is the highest labor we can put our hands to."

Other:

Frédéric Bastiat, *Sophisms of Protection*, translated from the French by White (New York: Putnam's, 1869);

Luigi Cossa, *Taxation: Its Principles and Methods*, translated from the Italian with introduction, notes, and a compilation of the state tax systems of New York and Pennsylvania by White (New York: Putnam's, 1888);

Appianus of Alexandria, *Roman History*, translated from the Greek by White, 2 volumes (New York: Macmillan, 1899).

Biography:

Joseph Logsdon, *Horace White, Nineteenth Century Liberal* (Westport, Conn.: Greenwood, 1971).

References:

William H. Herndon and Jesse W. Weik, *Abraham Lincoln: The True Story of a Great Life*, 2 volumes (New York: Appleton, 1896);

Philip Kinsley, *The Chicago Tribune: Its First Hundred Years*, volume 2 (Chicago: Tribune Company, 1945);

Allan Nevins, *The Evening Post: A Century of Journalism* (New York: Russell & Russell, 1968);

"Two Eminent New Yorkers," *New York Times*, 18 September 1916, p. 12;

Henry Villard, *Memoirs of Henry Villard–Journalist and Financier* (Boston: Houghton Mifflin, 1904).

Papers:

White's papers are contained in the Horace White Collection, Beloit College; the Horace White Committee Papers, New York Historical Society; the Horace White Family Papers, Illinois State Historical Society; and the Horace White Miscellaneous Papers, New York Public Library.

Benjamin Wood

(13 October 1820-21 February 1900)

Carol Sue Humphrey
University of North Carolina

MAJOR POSITION HELD: Editor, *New York Daily News* (1860-1900).

BOOKS: *Fort Lafayette; or, Love and Secession* (New York: Carleton, 1862);

Speech of Benjamin Wood, of New York, on the State of the Union, in the House of Representatives, May 16th, 1862 (New York: Van Evrie, Horton, 1862);

Peace. Speech of Benjamin Wood, of New York, in the House of Representatives, February 27th, 1863 (Washington, 1863).

For forty years Benjamin Wood edited the widest-circulating daily in the United States, the *New York Daily News*. Wood and the *Daily News* were virtually synonymous: the paper, which was struggling when Wood acquired it, began its meteoric rise seven years after he purchased it and prospered until shortly before his death in 1900. Without Wood the paper was not the same, and publication ceased forever only six years after he died. During the Civil War Wood actively participated in national politics as a member of the United States House of Representatives, and through his paper he became a leading national spokesman for the Peace Democrats, or "copperheads," as they were popularly called. After the war, Wood's political activity lessened with each passing year, but he continued to

direct the *Daily News* until the week before his death.

Wood's family was of Quaker and Welsh descent, with the first Wood arriving in America in 1616. Wood's father, Benjamin, was a reasonably successful dry goods merchant in Philadelphia until the panic of 1816-1817. In 1819, he suffered a nervous breakdown, probably as a result of the failure of his business. The doctor recommended rest and a change of scenery, and the Wood family went on a tour of the South; Benjamin Wood, Jr., was born on 13 October 1820 in Shelbyville, Kentucky. Following a short visit to Cuba, the Woods settled in New York City in 1821.

Wood had a very limited education in the public schools of New York. As a young man, he shipped out as a sailor on a merchant vessel and made several voyages to the West Indies and along the Central American coast. He later became a moss gatherer in Louisiana and had traveled through nearly every state in the Union before he finally returned to New York City to start a business career. He entered the shipping industry and soon accumulated quite a fortune. Wood also profited from a series of lotteries chartered by Southern states, which he owned in partnership with several

other residents of New York, including his older brother Fernando.

During this period, Wood married for the first time. Very little is known about this marriage. His first wife died in 1849, leaving two sons; the older of these, Benjamin, became a doctor, while the other died sometime prior to his father's death in 1900.

During the 1850s, Benjamin and Fernando Wood began a partnership in political ventures. Fernando became increasingly influential in New York City Democratic circles: he organized Mozart Hall as a rival political machine to Tammany Hall, the group which generally controlled the city, and was elected three times mayor of New York. In all of these efforts, Benjamin was an able and active assistant. Both were accused of taking advantage of their influential positions in city politics: in terms later used to bring down Boss Tweed, the brothers were accused of accepting bribes for city contracts and profiting from excessive charges made for supplies delivered to the city. None of these accusations was ever proven, but the rumors haunted the Woods for many years.

Whatever the true nature of his political activities with his brother, Benjamin Wood learned a great deal about politics, and both Woods soon became potent factors in the Democratic party in both the state and city of New York. Fernando Wood had aspirations for national office and sought ways to improve his chances of success; in early 1860, he bought the *New York Daily News* to advance his possible candidacy for vice-president. The *Daily News* had been established in 1855 as a morning paper by W. Drake Parsons to serve as an organ of Tammany Hall. As one of the penny papers, the *Daily News* had made some headway among the poor. Fernando Wood installed Benjamin Wood as the new editor of the *Daily News*, thereby launching him on a successful newspaper career. In 1860, Benjamin Wood served as the chairman of the Democratic Editors, and he soon became an eloquent spokesman for views popular among the city's poorer residents. In May 1860, he bought out his brother's interest in the paper and began to carve out a more independent political position.

As tensions increased between the North and South in 1860, Wood used the editorial pages of the *Daily News* to support the South. He was in favor of the extension of slavery and praised the Southern way of life. He opposed Negro suffrage (an issue in the New York elections of 1860) and supported the rights of slaveholders to carry their slaves anywhere they wished, including the territories. Wood denied that the Declaration of Independence included

Negroes in the statement "all men are created equal...," and he urged his countrymen not to tamper with a "higher law" of nature which separated the races. Wood asserted that "the negro race under the Southern system of labor is happier than it could be in any other relation"; furthermore, slavery served the function of civilizing and Christianizing the Negroes. Wood accepted the argument that "the increase of the race and the longevity of individuals attest that slavery is the best possible condition of the negro" and characterized slavery as "true philanthropy." He concluded that the Negro race would die out if freed and exposed to competition with white men.

Not surprisingly, Wood expressed great concern over the ever-growing threat of war over the slavery issue and demanded total acquiescence to all Southern demands. Because slavery was a state institution, the federal government had no right to interfere or dictate policy concerning it, he said. He also maintained that the Washington government had no power to force the Southern states to remain in the Union; if their just grievances were not redressed, they should be allowed to leave in peace. As war became ever more likely, Wood increased his efforts to stave off the conflict by convincing his readers of the destruction and ruin that would come if fighting actually commenced. When Mayor Fernando Wood suggested in January 1861 that New York City secede with the South, Ben Wood praised the plan as the best solution if war actually came. Even as late as 14 April 1861—two days after the firing on Fort Sumter—Wood refused to concede that war was necessary and assured his readers that there would be peace within a week because the New York merchants would not support the war effort. He concluded that "the wealthy will not supply means to depreciate the rest of their property by prolonging this unnatural war."

Wood's predictions failed to materialize; the war came, and it did not end in a week. Many people became caught up in the war fervor which surfaced during the early months of the fighting, including brother Fernando, who began to support the war after the attack on Fort Sumter. On 17 April 1861, an angry crowd threatened to riot if the *Daily News* staff failed to display the Stars and Stripes in a conspicuous position on the front of its offices. Wood, however, refused to surrender, declaring that he "respect[ed] the American Flag too much to permit it to be hoisted at the demand of a mob." Wood would not allow himself to give in to threats. An editorial in the *Daily News* declared that "you shall put no muzzle in our mouths, and lay no injunction upon the language we see fit to use in this gigantic national fratricide, while there is left a free people to appeal to, or a righteous cause to maintain." In the months that followed, he continually attacked the Union cause and expressed distrust of official statements issued from Washington. He lamented "the emptiness and folly of this war against brethren" and the foolishness of fighting a war that could not be won. As a result of Wood's antiwar stance, the New York City aldermen voted on 16 May 1861 to discontinue the *Daily News* as the official paper of the city. The next day, Wood printed a statement claiming sole responsibility for all opinions expressed in the columns of his paper. In June, Wood came out publicly for peace, with or without the Union.

Because of Wood's hostility toward the war effort, his paper was included in a federal grand jury presentment of 16 August 1861. The jury accused five New York City newspapers of actions "calculated to aid and comfort the enemy" and requested the court's guidance concerning possible indictments. No official charges were ever issued, but on 22 August, the postmaster general ordered that these papers be denied the use of the mails. Wood attempted to continue publication through the use of railway express to deliver the paper to other cities, but shipments were seized in Philadelphia and Connecticut. Wood suspended publication of the *Daily News* in September 1861, but resumed it eighteen months later.

During the months in which his paper was suspended Wood wrote a novel, *Fort Lafayette; or, Love and Secession* (1862), which attacked the war and urged a cessation in the fighting. The story revolves around four main characters, two Southerners and two Northerners. Oriana and Beverly Weems, a sister and brother from the South, are convinced that the South must stand and fight for liberty and justice, not slavery. Harold Hare, a Northerner, declares that the nation cannot be divided and welcomes the war to stop Southern treason. Arthur Wayne from Vermont is Wood's spokesman for moderation: he respects both sections and sees justice in both positions; therefore, in his eyes, there is no reason or excuse for a war. In the course of the novel, Wood presents the views and motives of others involved in the conflict. Businessmen, abolitionists, and secessionists are all represented, but it is clear that Wood favors the Peace Democrats' stance which called for an end to the war. The novel ends with Oriana, Beverly, and Harold acknowledging the futility and horrors of war, while Arthur dies a martyr in a Union prison.

Wood clearly hoped that his novel would help convince people to end the war, but the book received little attention at the time.

In March 1861, Wood began serving the first of two terms (1861-1865) in the United States House of Representatives. He worked to end the fighting as quickly as possible and opposed almost every measure which was designed to further the war effort. In July 1861, he proposed a resolution calling for a convention of state delegates to meet in Louisville, Kentucky, for the purpose of peace. Wood opposed federal aid to states for the gradual abolition of slavery and felt that federal troops should be used to capture and return fugitive slaves. While serving as a congressman, Wood made only two major speeches, both of which expressed fears for the survival of the nation in any form worth saving and called for peace before it was too late. Wood urged the need for a halt to the war at any price and never ceased in his efforts to end what he saw as a hopeless and foolish conflict.

As a result of his continual struggle against the continuation of the war, the Judiciary Committee of the House of Representatives investigated him for allegedly passing on important information to the enemy. The committee never reported on its findings, and Wood was never able to settle the matter. Wood revived the *Daily News* in May 1863; early in 1865, the War Department concluded that the personal columns of the paper had been used by Confederate spies to communicate with each other in code, and Wood was ordered to cease publishing the columns or face arrest and court martial. Wood unhappily complied. These two accusations, coupled with Wood's known Southern leanings, branded him as a traitor in the eyes of many people, who could not understand how he escaped punishment for his efforts against the Union cause. The *New York Herald* castigated Wood as "a blackguard who aided the cause of the rebellion and disunion, and the cause of sedition and insurrection in the North."

Although Wood's actions against the war effort produced a great deal of public condemnation, they also helped propel him to the forefront of the peace movement. He became a leading national spokesman for the Peace Democrats, charging that the war had been brought about by fanatics and urging that all true Democrats refuse to participate. He urged the public to realize that "among the popular delusions which the bitter experience of this long protracted and disastrous fratricidal struggle has as yet failed entirely to dispel, is the belief that the superior resources of the North will ultimately crush the rebellion underfoot and compel the unwilling return of the seceded states to the Union. . . ." Wood concluded that "the practical fact is that the Union has become a thing of the past."

In 1863, he strongly criticized the federal conscription act, particularly the clause which allowed a man to buy a substitute or pay a $300 exemption fee. Wood described the war as a poor man's fight which would further enrich the wealthy and free the slaves, resulting in a larger labor pool and depressed wages. He also accused the Republicans of using conscription to decrease the number of Democratic voters. He concluded that "if the conscription act be enforced the signs already suggest that it must be done at the point of the bayonet." Wood's tirade against the draft act went on for days, right up to the time for it to take effect. The first names were drawn in New York City on 11 July 1863. On 13 July, the drawing was halted by an antidraft mob which rioted for three days. Wood cannot be directly blamed for the riots, but his anti-conscription editorials no doubt contributed to the state of mind among New York City's laboring class which led to violence and bloodshed. However, during the riot, Wood is credited with preventing the destruction of the *New York Times* office by standing in the doorway with a revolver in hand, urging the rioters to respect private property: "You know that I and *The Daily News* have been with you for the maintenance of your rights, but it is not our right to destroy the property of our fellow-citizens." Accusations of treason and plotting with the Confederacy showered upon Wood following the riot, but a thorough investigation failed to produce any evidence connecting Wood with a Confederate plot to spark insurrection at the time of the riots.

Even if Wood was not part of a plot to produce the draft riots, his name and that of his paper appeared in connection with other questionable actions in support of the South. Wood regularly printed stories from Southern newspapers in the *Daily News*, and he accepted propaganda handouts from the Confederate government. Even more damaging, Wood hired Phineas C. Wright as an editor for the *Daily News* in January 1864. Wright was the original leader of the Order of American Knights, a quasi-military secret society which plotted uprisings against the United States government in support of the Southern cause. Wright desired to use the *Daily News* to further his subversive plots, but the insurrection efforts failed, and he was arrested in May 1865. Wood was an astute man, and it seems highly unlikely that he was ignorant of Wright's plans and activities; how he managed to avoid being prosecuted as a coconspirator in Wright's plot has never been revealed. Wood continued to deny that the South could be beaten right up to Lee's surrender at Appomattox Court House.

Accompanying Wood's statements against the war were personal attacks on Abraham Lincoln. Wood described the president as "devoid either of commanding talent or vigorous statesmanship" and belonging "to that secondary class which reflects merely the thoughts of abler men." Wood criticized all of Lincoln's policies and, following the suspension of the writ of habeas corpus, accused Lincoln of making himself a dictator. During the 1864 presidential campaign, Wood concluded that "no influence except compulsion can induce any respectable proportion of the people to cast their votes for that compound of cunning, heartlessness, and folly that they now execrate in the person of their Chief Magistrate."

While Wood clearly did not support Lincoln for reelection in 1864, neither did he support the Democratic candidate. The Democrats had nominated Gen. George B. McClellan on a peace platform which Wood hailed as a "great triumph for the peace party"; but McClellan repudiated the peace plank, leaving the Peace Democrats with few options. Most, including Fernando Wood, put party

Fernando Wood, Benjamin Wood's brother and partner in business and politics. As mayor of New York, Fernando Wood wanted the city to secede with the South.

loyalty first and supported McClellan; Benjamin Wood, however, refused to back down on the peace plank and tried to foster a movement for a second convention to name a new candidate. Unsuccessful in getting another nominee, Wood threatened that thousands of Peace Democrats would stay away from the polls if McClellan failed to support a move for an immediate end to the war. Wood's pleas had little impact, but McClellan lost the election anyway. Wood also decided not to run for reelection to Congress, perhaps because he felt he could not win. He had failed to see the hopelessness of the peace movement, and, as a result, he lost touch with many of his supporters.

Lincoln's assassination changed Wood's attitude toward him somewhat. After the president's death, Wood expressed "deep abhorrence" over Lincoln's demise and declared that, while Lincoln was not "the President of our choice," he had shown "greatness of soul" in his final efforts to heal the wounds of war. Wood and the *Daily News* staff were able to rise above politics for a short time in dealing with Lincoln's untimely death. Following the assassination, Wood encouraged efforts to form a coalition of Democrats and supporters of Andrew Johnson. Wood had first looked on Johnson as a public embarrassment, but he soon began to hope that Johnson would return to the Democratic party. To Wood, it seemed abundantly clear that only the Democrats could maintain the status quo as Johnson apparently wished to do. Wood began to assure the Democratic rank and file that President Johnson really was their natural leader, while urging Johnson to return to his rightful place in the Democratic party. In one editorial, Wood told Johnson that "your nature is Democratic; the people know that it is so; obey the instincts of your nature and the people will trust you and support you." However, it soon became clear that Johnson would not return to the Democratic party, and thereafter Wood gave little space to the president and his ensuing problems with Congress.

The end of the war in 1865 found Wood's political career at its lowest point, but he still maintained a certain degree of behind-the-scenes political power. Much of his postwar support came from Irish tenement dwellers, who were helping to make his paper the most popular daily in the United States. In 1866, Irish votes elected Wood to the New York state senate as an independent candidate; they would later elect him to serve once more in Congress (1881-1883). But Wood was never able to regain the political power which he had wielded during the Civil War.

After the war, Wood continued on occasion to use the *Daily News* to express his opinions on national issues. He maintained his anti-Negro stance, still upholding slavery as a beneficial system which had advanced the Negro race as close to true civilization as it had ever been, and he attacked the 1866 Civil Rights Bill as "creating artificial equality and threatening miscegenation."

Wood's political activity declined even further after Grant's election in 1868. He had few dealings with Boss William M. Tweed. Wood became part of an anti-Tweed coalition in 1869, but it was formed for the purpose of replacing Tweed with another boss rather than actually reforming the city's government. Following Tweed's downfall, Wood's attention turned primarily to running his newspaper. Except for his 1881-1883 term in Congress and service as a presidential elector in 1884, Wood did not directly participate in politics at any level.

Wood's departure from the political arena produced many benefits for the *Daily News*. His increased involvement in the newspaper business sparked several innovations that heralded later important developments. One of the early commercial groups which provided a precedent for the modern newspaper chain included Wood as a partner. The group started the *Charleston* (South Carolina) *Daily News* in 1865, but Wood withdrew from the partnership in 1867. Wood's *Daily News* set another precedent by publishing an isolated comic strip as early as 1884, twelve years before the Yellow Kid began appearing in the *New York World*. Some of Wood's best innovations, however, came in the development of the foreign-language press. In 1870, he established the one-cent *New-Yorker Tages-Nachrichten*, a German language version of the *Daily News*; the Sunday edition, *Sonntags-Nachrichten*, first appeared in 1872. Both of these papers competed well against the immigrant-owned press and served to Americanize newspaper offerings in German, a change which helped speed up the assimilation process.

Although Wood's innovations in various aspects of newspaper work were impressive, he and his paper are most remembered for the large circulation which the *Daily News* had in the latter half of the nineteenth century. At the end of the Civil War, the paper was in dire financial straits which called for drastic measures. On 27 April 1867, the *Daily News* became New York City's only one-cent daily, published in the evening in order to sell better among laborers on their way home from work. By 1868, Wood could boast that the *Daily News* had the largest circulation (80,000) of any daily in the

United States. He had developed his paper into a sheet which stressed city news and was popular with tenement dwellers. Described by journalism historians as a "sensation-monger" which was "cheap in content as well as in price," the *Daily News* became known as the "hod-carriers' favorite." One important reason for its success, according to a contemporary trade journal, was "that it never went over the heads of its readers." Wood tailored the *Daily News* to appeal to the thousands of semiliterate laborers in New York City by presenting the news in capsule form. The *Daily News* became known for its reports of the lottery and policy drawings and increasingly sold well among men and women who barely eked out a living but could always spare a penny for a paper. Throughout the 1870s and 1880s, the *Daily News* sold between 100,000 and 175,000 copies daily and was hailed as "the Wonder of Modern Journalism." The success of Wood's *Daily News* among the immigrants and workers of New York City provided a blueprint for later papers to follow: sensationalize and simplify stories in order to appeal more to the laboring people.

Because most of the paper's readers were workers, the *Daily News* enthusiastically supported the labor movement and gained a preeminent position as a prolabor paper. As early as 1865, the *Tribune* described Wood's paper as "a greater stickler for the rights of labor—for good wages, reasonable hours, considerate treatment and all that." The *Daily News* continued to hold its labor readership throughout the latter half of the nineteenth century. As a writer observed in a journalism trade publication in 1897, "Laboring men have grown to look upon the *Daily News* as distinctly their paper. They find in it the latest news of direct interest and importance to them."

There was one big change in the *Daily News* after 1867 which helped increase its appeal to workers: the disappearance of most political commentary from the editorial page. Because of lack of interest among the paper's readers, Wood no longer wrote very many political editorials; those which did appear were copied from the *Sunday News*. The *Daily News* continued to prosper until the Pulitzer-Hearst duel adversely affected its circulation. After Wood's death, the paper was sold to Frank A. Munsey. Munsey's attempted improvements drove away readers, and the *Daily News* perished in 1906.

Very little is known about Wood's personal life after 1865. At some point during the years immediately after the Civil War, he remarried; his second wife was Ida E. W. Mayfield of Louisiana, and their only child was a daughter, Emma. Wood prospered during the late 1860s and 1870s because his paper prospered, but he gambled a great deal and was twice in serious financial difficulty. In 1879, he filed for bankruptcy and sold forty-three percent of the *Daily News* stock to Colonel William J. Brown, who remained Wood's partner and business manager of the paper for twenty-one years. In 1898, Wood sold his interest in the *Daily News* to his wife, but he continued to serve as editor in chief until the week before his death on 21 February 1900.

Even more surprising is the lack of information on Wood's paper. Everyone concedes that it had the largest circulation in the United States for most of the years between 1867 and 1890, but very little else has been written. The *New York Daily News* has generally been ignored, partly because its files for 1870 to 1900 are practically nonexistent and, more importantly, because it had little impact among the people who counted. Wood designed the paper to appeal to the tenement dwellers, and "many residents of the city [did] not see a copy of it from one year's end to the other." Frank Luther Mott ably summed up the *Daily News* as "that phenomenal but now forgotten paper of the tenement districts."

A similar epitaph could be applied to Benjamin Wood. Much of his work and accomplishments have been overlooked. Wood is now remembered only as a copperhead editor who may have been guilty of treason; the rest of his career has been obscured and obliterated by his activities during the Civil War. Many of those activities were of a questionable nature, but Wood was a very capable and effective journalist whose efforts to provide news for New York's laborers opened up a new market of newspaper readers. According to *Printer's Ink*, he saw "the possibilities of one-cent journalism at a time when its potentialities were far from apparent. . . ;" and his "influence over the workingmen of New York will probably never be equalled by any newspaper editor." Today the phenomenal circulation record of the *New York Daily News* stands as firm evidence of the contributions Benjamin Wood made in popularizing newspapers among the general populace.

References:

"Death of Benjamin Wood," *New York Times*, 22 February 1900, p. 7;

The Fourth Estate (7 October 1897, 22 December 1906);

The Journalist (21 August 1886);

David F. Long, "The New York News, 1855-1906: Spokesman for the Underprivileged," Ph.D. dissertation, Columbia University, 1950;

Frank Luther Mott, "Facetious News Writing, 1833-1883," *Mississippi Valley Historical Review*, 29 (June 1942): 35-54;

Jerome Mushkat, "Ben Wood's 'Fort Lafayette': A Source for Studying the Peace Democrats," *Civil War History*, 21 (June 1975): 160-171;

Samuel Augustus Pleasants, *Fernando Wood of New York* (New York: Columbia University Press, 1948);

Printer's Ink (7 March 1900).

Papers:
Benjamin Wood's papers are contained in the Office of Surrogate's Records, New York County.

Checklist for Further Reading

Anderson, Arlow William. *The Immigrant Takes His Stand: The Norwegian-American Press and Public Affairs, 1847-1872*. Northfield, Minn.: Norwegian-American Historical Association, 1953.

Bartow, Edith Merwin. *News and These United States*. New York: Funk & Wagnalls, 1952.

Baumgartner, Apollinaris W. *Catholic Journalism: A Study of Its Development in the United States, 1789-1930*. New York: Columbia University Press, 1931.

Beasley, Maurine. *The First Women Washington Correspondents*. Washington, D.C.: GW Washington Studies, No. 4, 1976.

Beasley and Sheila Silver. *Women in Media: A Documentary Source Book*. Washington, D.C.: Women's Institute for Freedom of the Press, 1977.

Becker, Stephen. *Comic Art in America*. New York: Simon & Schuster, 1959.

Bent, Silas. *Newspaper Crusaders: A Neglected Story*. New York: Whittlesey House, McGraw-Hill, 1939.

Bleyer, Willard Grosvenor. *Main Currents in the History of American Journalism*. Boston: Houghton Mifflin, 1927.

Blum, Eleanor. *Basic Books in the Mass Media*. Urbana: University of Illinois Press, 1972.

Brigham, Clarence S. *History and Biography of American Newspapers, 1690-1820*. Worcester, Mass.: American Antiquarian Society, 1947.

Brigham. *Journals and Journeymen: A Contribution to the History of Early American Newspapers*. Philadelphia: University of Pennsylvania Press, 1950.

Brown, Charles H. *The Correspondents' War*. New York: Scribners, 1967.

Brown. "Press Censorship in the Spanish-American War." *Journalism Quarterly*, 42 (Autumn 1965): 581-590.

Bullock, Penelope L. *The Afro-American Periodical Press, 1839-1909*. Baton Rouge: Louisiana State University Press, 1981.

Cater, Douglass. *The Fourth Branch of Government*. Boston: Houghton Mifflin, 1959.

Chafee, Zechariah, Jr. *Free Speech in the United States*. Cambridge, Mass.: Harvard University Press, 1941.

Commander, Lydia K. "The Significance of Yellow Journalism." *Arena*, 34 (August 1905): 150.

Conlin, Joseph R., ed. *The American Radical Press 1880-1960*, two volumes. Westport, Conn.: Greenwood Press, 1974.

Couperie, Pierre and Maurice C. Horn. *A History of the Comic Strip*. New York: Crown, 1968.

Cross, Harold L. *The People's Right to Know*. New York: Columbia University Press, 1953.

Dann, Martin E., ed. *The Black Press: 1827-1890*. New York: Putnam's, 1971.

Dennis, Everette E. and Melvin Dennis. "100 Years of Political Cartooning." *Journalism History*, 1 (Spring 1974).

Detweiler, Frederick G. *The Negro Press in the United States*. Chicago: University of Chicago Press, 1922.

Donald, Robert. "Sunday Newspapers in the United States." *Universal Review*, 8 (September 1890): 79.

Drewry, John E. *More Post Biographies*. Athens: University of Georgia Press, 1947.

Drewry. *Saturday Evening Post. Post Biographies of Famous Journalists*. Athens: University of Georgia Press, 1942.

Ellis, L. Ethan. *Newsprint: Producers, Publishers, Political Pressures*. New Brunswick, N.J.: Rutgers University Press, 1960.

Emery, Edwin. *History of the American Newspaper Publishers Association.* Minneapolis: University of Georgia Press, 1942.

Emery and Michael Emery. *The Press and America,* fourth edition. Englewood Cliffs, N.J.: Prentice-Hall, 1978.

Emery, Edwin and Henry Ladd Smith. *The Press and America.* New York: Prentice-Hall, 1954.

Emery, Michael C., et al. *America's Front Page News, 1690-1970.* Garden City: Doubleday, 1970.

Ernst, Morris. *The First Freedom.* New York: Macmillan, 1946.

Farrar, Ronald T. and John D. Stevens, eds. *Mass Media and the National Experience.* New York: Harper & Row, 1971.

Filler, Louis. *Crusaders for American Liberalism.* New York: Harcourt Brace Jovanovich, 1939.

Ford, Edwin H. and Edwin Emery, eds. *Highlights in the History of the American Press: A Book of Readings.* Minneapolis: University of Minnesota Press, 1954.

Gordon, George N. *The Communications Revolution: A History of Mass Media in the United States.* New York: Hastings House, 1977.

Gramling, Oliver. *AP: The Story of News.* New York: Holt, Rinehart & Winston, 1940.

Gregory, Winifred. *American Newspapers, 1821-1936: A Union List of Files Available in the United States and Canada.* New York: Wilson, 1936.

Harrison, John M. and Harry H. Stein, eds. *Muckraking—Past, Present and Future.* University Park: Pennsylvania State University Press, 1973.

Hausman, Linda Weiner. "Criticism of the Press in U.S. Periodicals, 1900-1939: An Annotated Bibliography." *Journalism Monographs,* 4 (August 1967).

Hess, Stephen and Milton Kaplan. *The Ungentlemanly Art: A History of American Political Cartoons.* New York: Macmillan, 1968.

Hohenberg, John. *Foreign Correspondence: The Great Reporters and Their Times.* New York: Columbia University Press, 1964.

Hudson, Frederic. *Journalism in the United States.* New York: Harper & Row, 1873.

Hughes, Helen M. *News and the Human Interest Story.* Chicago: University of Chicago Press, 1940.

Irwin, Will. *The American Newspaper,* edited by Clifford F. Weigle and David G. Clark. Ames: Iowa State University Press, 1969.

Jakes, John. *Great Women Reporters.* New York: Putnam's, 1969.

Jones, Robert W. *Journalism in the United States.* New York: Dutton, 1947.

Karolevitz, Robert F. *Newspapering in the Old West.* Seattle: Superior, 1965.

Katz, William A. "The Western Printer and His Publications, 1850-90." *Journalism Quarterly,* 44 (Winter 1967): 708-714.

Knight, Oliver A. *Following the Indian Wars: The Story of the Newspaper Correspondents among the Indian Campaigners, 1866-1891.* Norman: University of Oklahoma Press, 1960.

Knightley, Phillip. *The First Casualty.* New York: Harcourt Brace Jovanovich, 1975.

Kobre, Sidney. *Development of American Journalism.* Dubuque, Iowa: Wm. C. Brown, 1969.

Kobre. *The Yellow Press and Gilded Age Journalism.* Tallahassee: Florida State University Press, 1964.

Lee, Alfred McClung. *The Daily Newspaper in America.* New York: Macmillan, 1937.

Lee, James Melvin. *History of American Journalism.* Boston: Houghton Mifflin, 1917.

Liston, Robert A. *The Right to Know: Censorship in America.* New York: Franklin Watts, 1973.

Lyle, Jack, ed. *The Black American and the Press.* Los Angeles: Ward Ritchie, 1968.

Lyon, Peter. *The Wild, Wild West.* New York: Funk & Wagnalls, 1969.

Marbut, Frederick B. *News from the Capital: The Story of Washington Reporting.* Carbondale: Southern Illinois University Press, 1971.

Marty, Martin E., John G. Deedy, Jr., and David W. Silverman. *The Religious Press in America.* New York: Holt, Rinehart & Winston, 1963.

Marzolf, Marion. *Up from the Footnote: A History of Women Journalists.* New York: Hastings House, 1977.

Mathews, Joseph J. *Reporting the Wars.* Minneapolis: University of Minnesota Press, 1957.

McMurtrie, Douglas C. *A History of Printing in the United States.* New York: R. R. Bowker, 1936.

Moran, James. *Printing Presses: History and Development from the Fifteenth Century to Modern Times.* Berkeley: University of California Press, 1973.

Morris, Joe Alex. *Deadline Every Minute: The Story of the United Press.* Garden City, N.Y.: Doubleday, 1957.

Mott, Frank Luther. *American Journalism 1690-1960*, third edition. New York: Macmillan, 1960.

Mott and Ralph D. Casey, eds. *Interpretations of Journalism.* New York: Appleton-Century-Crofts, 1937.

Murrell, William. *A History of American Graphic Humor, 1865-1938.* New York: Macmillan, 1938.

Myers, John. *Print in a Wild Land.* Garden City, N.Y.: Doubleday, 1967.

Nelson, Harold L. "The Political Reform Press: A Case Study." *Journalism Quarterly*, 29 (Summer 1955): 294-302.

Nelson, ed. *Freedom of the Press from Hamilton to the Warren Court.* Indianapolis: Bobbs-Merrill, 1967.

Nelson and Dwight L. Teeter, Jr. *Law of Mass Communications: Freedom and Control of Print and Broadcast Media*, fourth edition. Mineola, N.Y.: Foundation Press, 1982.

Nevins, Allan. "American Journalism and Its Historical Treatment." *Journalism Quarterly*, 36 (Fall 1959): 411-422.

Nevins. *American Press Opinion, Washington to Coolidge.* Boston: Heath, 1928.

Nevins and George Weitenkampf. *A Century of Political Cartoons.* New York: Scribners, 1944.

North, S. N. D. *History and Present Condition of the Newspapers and Periodical Press of the United States.* Washington, 1884.

Ogilvie, William Edward. *Pioneer Agricultural Journalists: Brief Biographical Sketches of Some of the Early Editors in the Field of Agricultural Journalism.* Chicago: Arthur G. Leonard, 1927.

Park, Robert E. *The Immigrant Press and Its Control.* New York & London: Harper, 1922.

Park, "The National History of the Newspaper," in *The City*, by Park, Ernest W. Burgess, and Roderick D. McKenzie. Chicago: University of Chicago Press, 1925, pp. 80-98.

Payne, George H. *History of Journalism in the United States.* New York: Appleton-Century-Crofts, 1920.

Penn, I. Garland. *The Afro-American Press and Its Editors.* Springfield, Mass.: Wiley, 1891.

Pickett, Calder M. *Voices of the Past: Key Documents in the History of American Journalism.* Columbus, Ohio: Grid, 1977.

Pollard, James E. *The Presidents and the Press.* New York: Macmillan, 1947.

Presbrey, Frank. *The History and Development of Advertising.* New York: Doubleday, 1929.

Price, Warren C. *The Literature of Journalism: An Annotated Bibliography.* Minneapolis: University of Minnesota Press, 1959.

Price and Calder M. Pickett. *An Annotated Journalism Bibliography 1958-1968.* Minneapolis: University of Minnesota Press, 1970.

Rosewater, Victor. *History of Cooperative News-Gathering in the United States.* New York: Appleton-Century-Crofts, 1930.

Ross, Ishbel. *Ladies of the Press: The Story of Women in Journalism by an Insider.* New York & London: Harper, 1936.

Salmon, Lucy B. *The Newspaper and Authority.* New York: Oxford University Press, 1923.

Schuneman, R. Smith. "Art or Photography: A Question for Newspaper Editors of the 1890s." *Journalism Quarterly*, 42 (Winter 1965): 43-52.

Seldes, George. *Lords of the Press.* New York: Messner, 1938.

Snyder, Louis L. ed. *Masterpieces of War Reporting.* New York: Messner, 1962.

Snyder and Richard B. Morris, eds. *A Treasury of Great Reporting.* New York: Simon & Schuster, 1962.

Stein, M. L. *Under Fire: The Story of American War Correspondents.* New York: Messner, 1968.

Stevens, John D. and Hazel Dicken-Garcia. *Communication History.* Beverly Hills, Cal.: Sage, 1980.

Stewart, Kenneth and John W. Tebbel. *Makers of Modern Journalism.* Englewood Cliffs, N.J.: Prentice-Hall, 1952.

Stratton, Porter A. *The Territorial Press of New Mexico 1834-1912.* Albuquerque: University of New Mexico Press, 1969.

Taft, William H. *Newspapers as Tools for Historians.* Columbia, Mo.: Lucas, 1970.

Tebbel, John W. *The Compact History of the American Newspaper.* New York: Hawthorn, 1963.

Tebbel, *The Media in America.* New York: Crowell, 1974.

Thomas, Isaiah. *The History of Printing in America.* Albany, N.Y.: Joel Munsell, 1874.

Villard, Oswald Garrison. *The Disappearing Daily.* New York: Knopf, 1944.

Villard. *Some Newspapers and Newspaper-Men.* New York: Knopf, 1923.

Watson, Elmo Scott. *A History of Newspaper Syndicates in the United States, 1865-1935.* Chicago: Publishers' Auxiliary, 1936.

Waugh, Coulton. *The Comics.* New York: Macmillan, 1947.

Weeks, Lyman H. *A History of Paper-Manufacturing in the United States, 1690-1916.* New York: Lockwood Trade Journal Co., 1916.

Whisenhunt, Donald W. "The Frontier Newspaper: A Guide to Society and Culture." *Journalism Quarterly*, 45 (Winter 1968): 726-728.

White, David M. *From Dogpatch to Slobbovia.* Boston: Beacon Press, 1964.

White, *Pop Culture in America.* Chicago: Quadrangle Books, 1970.

White, Z. L. "Western Journalism." *Harper's*, 77 (October 1888): 678.

Wilkerson, Marcus M. *Public Opinion and the Spanish-American War.* Baton Rouge: Louisiana State University Press, 1932.

Wisan, Joseph E. *The Cuban Crisis as Reflected in the New York Press.* New York: Columbia University Press, 1934.

Wittke, Carl. *The German-Language Press in America.* Lexington: University of Kentucky Press, 1957.

Wolseley, Roland E. *The Black Press, U.S.A.* Ames: Iowa State University Press, 1971.

Wood, James Playsted. *The Story of Advertising.* New York: Roland Press, 1958.

Contributors

Maurine H. Beasley ....*University of Maryland*
Margaret A. Blanchard...*University of North Carolina*
John M. Butler...*Louisiana State University*
Barbara Creswell..*University of Alabama*
Philip B. Dematteis ....*Columbia, South Carolina*
Hazel Dicken-Garcia..*University of Minnesota*
Wallace B. Eberhard ....*University of Georgia*
George Everett ....*University of Tennessee*
Charles A. Fair...*Virginia Commonwealth University*
M. Kathleen Fair...*Virginia Commonwealth University*
Nora Hall..*University of Minnesota*
John M. Harrison..*Pennsylvania State University*
Thomas H. Heuterman...*Washington State University*
Carol Sue Humphrey ....*University of North Carolina*
Ernest C. Hynds...*University of Georgia*
Terry Hynes ....*California State University, Fullerton*
M. A. Kautsch...*University of Kansas*
Lauren Kessler ....*University of Oregon*
C. Richard King...*Stephenville, Texas*
Leonard W. Lanfranco ....*University of South Carolina*
Mark Lipper..*Shippensburg University*
Steven D. Lyons ....*Louisiana State University*
Ronald S. Marmarelli...*Central Michigan University*
Joseph P. McKerns...*Southern Illinois University*
Ellen M. Mrja ....*Mankato State University*
Shirley M. Mundt ....*Louisiana State University*
Whitney R. Mundt...*Louisiana State University*
Charles C. Russell ....*University of South Carolina*
Charles C. Self ....*University of Alabama*
Jo Anne Smith ....*University of Florida*
Rosemarian V. Staudacher...*Marquette University*
Jacqueline Steck ....*Temple University*
Harry W. Stonecipher...*Southern Illinois University*
James Glen Stovall...*University of Alabama*
William H. Taft ....*University of Missouri–Columbia*
William J. Thorn ....*Marquette University*

Cumulative Index

Dictionary of Literary Biography, Volumes 1-23
Dictionary of Literary Biography Yearbook, 1980, 1981, 1982
Dictionary of Literary Biography Documentary Series, Volumes 1-4

Cumulative Index

DLB before number: *Dictionary of Literary Biography*, Volumes 1-23
Y before number: *Dictionary of Literary Biography Yearbook*, 1980, 1981, 1982
DS before number: *Dictionary of Literary Biography Documentary Series*, Volumes 1-4

367

G

Gernsback, Hugo 1884-1967......................DLB8

Gerrold, David 1944- DLB8

Geston, Mark S. 1946- DLB8

Gibson, Wilfrid 1878-1962 ....DLB19

Gibson, William 1914- DLB7

Gillespie, A. Lincoln, Jr. 1895-1950
....DLB4

Gilliam, Florence DLB4

Gilliatt, Penelope 1932- DLB14

Gillott, Jacky 1939-1980 ....DLB14

Gilman, Caroline H. 1794-1888
....DLB3

Gilroy, Frank D. 1925- DLB7

Ginsberg, Allen 1926- DLB5, 16

Giovanni, Nikki 1943- DLB5

Gipson, Lawrence Henry 1880-1971 ....DLB17

Gissing, George 1857-1903......................DLB18

Glanville, Brian 1931-........................DLB15

Glasgow, Ellen 1873-1945 ....DLB9, 12

Glaspell, Susan 1882-1948......................DLB7, 9

Glass, Montague 1877-1934 ....DLB11

Gluck, Louise 1943- DLB5

Godwin, Gail 1937- DLB6

Godwin, Parke 1816-1904 ....DLB3

Gogarty, Oliver St. John 1878-1957 .....DLB15, 19

Gold, Herbert 1924- DLB2; Y81

Gold, Michael 1893-1967......................DLB9

Goldberg, Dick 1947- DLB7

Golding, William 1911-........................DLB15

Goodrich, Samuel Griswold 1793-1860
....DLB1

Goodwin, Stephen 1943- Y82

Gordon, Caroline 1895-1981
....DLB4, 9; Y81

Gordon, Giles 1940- DLB14

Gordon, Mary 1949- DLB6; Y81

Gordone, Charles 1925- DLB7

Goyen, William 1915- DLB2

Grady, Henry W. 1850-1889......................DLB23

Graham, W. S. 1918- DLB20

Gramatky, Hardie 1907- DLB22

Grau, Shirley Ann 1929- DLB2

Graves, Robert 1895- DLB20

Gray, Asa 1810-1888 ....DLB1

Gray, Simon 1936- DLB13

Grayson, William J. 1788-1863
....DLB3

Greeley, Horace 1811-1872......................DLB3

Green, Henry 1905-1973......................DLB15

Green, Julien 1900- DLB4

Green, Paul 1894-1981......................DLB7, 9; Y81

Greene, Asa 1789-1838 ....DLB11

Greene, Graham 1904- DLB13, 15

Greenough, Horatio 1805-1852
....DLB1

Greenwood, Walter 1903-1974
....DLB10

Greer, Ben 1948- DLB6

Gruelle, Johnny 1880-1938 ....DLB22

Persse, Isabella Augusta,
 Lady Gregory 1852-1932......................DLB10

Grey, Zane 1872-1939 ....DLB9

Griffiths, Trevor 1935- DLB13

Griswold, Rufus 1815-1857......................DLB3

Gross, Milt 1895-1953......................DLB11

Grubb, Davis 1919-1980......................DLB6

Guare, John 1938- DLB7

Guest, Barbara 1920- DLB5

Guiterman, Arthur 1871-1943......................DLB11

Gunn, James E. 1923- DLB8

Gunn, Neil M. 1891-1973......................DLB15

Guthrie, A. B., Jr. 1901- DLB6

Guthrie, Ramon 1896-1973......................DLB4

Gwynne, Erskine 1898-1948......................DLB4

M

N